Contents

BPP
LEARNING MEDIA

How our Study Text can help you pass

Streamlined studying	<ul><li>We show you the best ways to study efficiently</li><li>Our Text has been designed to ensure you can easily and quickly navigate through it</li><li>The different features in our Text emphasise important knowledge and techniques</li></ul>
Exam expertise	<ul><li>**Studying P1** on page xv introduces the key themes of the syllabus and summarises how to pass</li><li>We highlight throughout our Text how topics may be tested and what you'll have to do in the exam</li><li>We help you see the complete picture of the syllabus, so that you can answer questions that range across the whole syllabus</li><li>Our Text covers the syllabus content – no more, no less</li></ul>
Regular review	<ul><li>We frequently summarise the key knowledge you need</li><li>We test what you've learnt by providing questions and quizzes throughout our Text</li></ul>

Our other products

BPP Learning Media also offers these products for the Objective Test exams and the integrated case study (ICS) exams:

i-Pass	Providing computer-based testing in a variety of formats, ideal for self-assessment
Exam Practice Kit	Providing helpful guidance on how to pass the objective test and more question practice
Passcards	Summarising what you should know in visual, easy to remember, form
ICS Workbook	Providing help with exam skills and question practice for the integrated case study exam

You can purchase these products by visiting www.bpp.com/cimamaterials

Online Learning with BPP

BPP's online learning study modes provide flexibility and convenience, allowing you to study effectively, at a pace that suits you, where and when you choose.

Online Classroom Live	Through live interactive online sessions it provides you with the traditional structure and support of classroom learning, but with the convenience of attending classes wherever you are
Online Classroom	Through pre-recorded online lectures it provides you with the classroom experience via the web with the tutor guidance & support you'd expect from a face to face classroom

You can find out more by visiting www.bpp.com/cima

BPP LEARNING MEDIA

CIMA

OPERATIONAL

PAPER P1

MANAGEMENT ACCOUNTING

STUDY TEXT

Our text is designed to help you study **effectively** and **efficiently**.

In this edition we:

- **Highlight** the **most important elements** in the syllabus and the **key skills** you will need

- **Signpost** how each chapter links to the syllabus and the learning outcomes

- Use **overview and summary diagrams** to develop understanding of interrelations between topics

- **Provide** lots of **exam alerts** explaining how what you're learning may be tested

- **Include examples** and **questions** to help you apply what you've learnt

- **Emphasise key points** in **section summaries**

- **Test your knowledge** of what you've studied in **quick quizzes**

- **Examine your understanding** in our **practice question bank**

SUITABLE FOR EXAMS IN 2017

PUBLISHED NOVEMBER 2016

BPP LEARNING MEDIA

Third edition 2015

ISBN 9781 5097 0686 0
e-ISBN 9781 5097 0730 0

British Library Cataloguing-in-Publication Data
A catalogue record for this book
is available from the British Library

Published by

BPP Learning Media Ltd
BPP House, Aldine Place
London W12 8AA

www.bpp.com/learningmedia

Printed in the United Kingdom by

Wheatons Exeter Ltd
Hennock Road
Marsh Barton
Exeter
EX2 8RP

Your learning materials, published by BPP
Learning Media Ltd, are printed on paper obtained
from traceable sustainable sources.

We are grateful to the Chartered Institute of
Management Accountants for permission to
reproduce past examination questions. The
suggested solutions in the exam answer bank have
been prepared by BPP Learning Media Ltd.

Features in our Study Text

Chapter Overview Diagrams illustrate the connections between the topic areas you are about to cover

 Section Introductions explain how the section fits into the chapter

 Key Terms are the core vocabulary you need to learn

KEY TERM

 Key Points are points that you have to know, ideas or calculations that will be the foundations of your answers

KEY POINT

 Exam Alerts show you how subjects are likely to be tested

 Exam Skills are the key skills you will need to demonstrate in the exam, linked to question requirements

 Formulae To Learn are formulae you must remember in the exam

LEARN

 Exam Formulae are formulae you will be given in the exam

EXAM

 Examples show how theory is put into practice

 Questions give you the practice you need to test your understanding of what you've learnt

 Case Studies link what you've learnt with the real-world business environment

CASE STUDY

 Links show how the syllabus overlaps with other parts of the qualification, including Knowledge Brought Forward that you need to remember from previous exams

 Website References link to material that will enhance your understanding of what you're studying

 Further Reading will give you a wider perspective on the subjects you're covering

 Section Summary Diagrams allow you to review each section

Streamlined studying

What you should do	In order to
Read the Chapter and Section Introductions and look at the Chapter Overview Diagram	See why topics need to be studied and map your way through the chapter
Go quickly through the explanations	Gain the depth of knowledge and understanding that you'll need
Highlight the Key Points, Key Terms and Formulae To Learn	Make sure you know the basics that you can't do without in the exam
Focus on the Exam Skills and Exam Alerts	Know how you'll be tested and what you'll have to do
Work through the Examples and Case Studies	See how what you've learnt applies in practice
Prepare Answers to the Questions	See if you can apply what you've learnt in practice
Review the Chapter Summary Diagrams	Remind you of, and reinforce, what you've learnt
Answer the Quick Quiz	Find out if there are any gaps in your knowledge
Answer the Question(s) in the Practice Question Bank	Practise what you've learnt in depth

Should I take notes?

Brief notes may help you remember what you're learning. You should use the notes format that's most helpful to you (lists, diagrams, mindmaps).

Further help

BPP Learning Media's *Learning to Learn Accountancy* provides lots more helpful guidance on studying. It is designed to be used both at the outset of your CIMA studies and throughout the process of learning accountancy. It can help you **focus your studies on the subject and exam**, enabling you to **acquire knowledge, practise and revise efficiently and effectively**.

Syllabus and learning outcomes

Paper P.1 Management accounting

The syllabus comprises:

Topic and Study Weighting

		%
A	Cost accounting systems	30
B	Budgeting	25
C	Short-term decision making	30
D	Dealing with risk and uncertainty	15

Learning outcomes On completion of their studies, student should be able to:		
Lead	**Component**	**Indicative syllabus content**
A Cost accounting systems (30%)		
1 Discuss costing methods and their results.	(a) Apply marginal (or variable) throughput and absorption accounting methods in respect of profit reporting and inventory valuation	• Marginal (or variable) throughput and absorption accounting systems of profit reporting and inventory valuation including the reconciliation budget and actual profit using absorption and/or marginal costing principles.
	(b) Compare and contrast activity-based costing with traditional marginal and absorption costing methods	• Product and service costing using activity-based costing system. • The advantages and disadvantages of activity-based costing compared with traditional costing systems.
	(c) Apply standard costing methods including the reconciliation of budgeted and actual profit margins, distinguishing between planning and operational variances	• Manufacturing standards for material, labour, variable overhead and fixed overhead • Standards and variances in service industries, public services (e.g. health and law enforcement), and the professions (e.g. labour mix variances in consultancies). • Price/rate and usage/efficiency variances for materials, labour and variable overhead. • Subdivision of total usage/efficiency variances into mix and yield variances. • *Note: The calculation of mix variances on both individual and average valuation bases is required.* • Fixed overhead expenditure and volume variances. • Subdivision of the fixed overhead volume variance into capacity and efficiency variances. • Sales price and sales volume variances (calculation of the latter on a unit basis related to revenue, gross profit and contribution). • Sales mix and sales quantity variances. Application of these variances to all sectors including professional services and retail. • Planning and operational variances. • Variance analysis in an activity-based costing system.

Learning outcomes On completion of their studies, student should be able to:		
Lead	**Component**	**Indicative syllabus content**
	(d) Interpret material, labour, variable overhead, fixed overhead and sales variances	• Interpretation of variances. • The interrelationship between variances.
	(e) Explain the advantages and disadvantages of standard costing in various sectors and its appropriateness in the contemporary business environment	• Criticisms of standard costing including its use in the contemporary business environment.
	(f) Explain the impact of JIT manufacturing methods on cost accounting methods.	• The impact of JIT production on cost accounting and performance measurement systems.
2 Discuss the role of quality costing.	(a) Discuss the role of quality costing as part of a total quality management (TQM) system.	• The preparation of cost of quality reports including the classification of quality costs into prevention costs, appraisal costs, internal failure costs and external failure costs. • The use of quality costing as part of a TQM system.
3 Explain the role of environmental costing	(a) Explain the role of environmental costing as part of an environmental management system.	• The classification of environmental costs using the quality costing framework. • Linking environmental costs to activities and outputs and their implication for decision making. • The difficulties in measuring environmental costs and their impact on the external environment. • The contribution of environmental costing to improved environmental and financial performance.
B Budgeting (25%)		
1 Explain the purposes of forecasts, plans and budgets.	(a) Explain the purposes of budgets, including planning, communication, coordination, motivation, authorisation, control and evaluation, and how these may conflict.	• The role of forecasts and plans in resource allocation, performance evaluation and control. • The purposes of budgets, the budgeting process and conflicts that can arise.
2 Prepare forecasts of financial results.	(a) Calculate projected product/service volumes, revenue and costs employing appropriate forecasting techniques and taking account of cost structures.	• Time series analysis including moving totals and averages, treatment of seasonality, trend analysis using regression analysis and the application of these techniques in forecasting product and service volumes.

Learning outcomes On completion of their studies, student should be able to:		
Lead	**Component**	**Indicative syllabus content**
3. Discuss budgets based on forecasts.	(a) Prepare a budget for any account in the master budget, based on projections/forecasts and managerial targets	• The budget setting process, limiting factors, the interaction between component budgets and the master budget.
	(b) Discuss alternative approaches to budgeting.	• Alternative approaches to budget creation, including incremental approaches, zero-based budgeting and activity-based budgets.
4. Discuss the principles that underlie the use of budgets for control.	(a) Discuss the concept of the budget as a control system and the use of responsibility accounting and its importance in the construction of functional budgets that support the overall master budget.	• The use of budgets in planning and control e.g. rolling budgets and flexed budgets. • The concepts of feedback and feed-forward control. • Responsibility accounting and the link to controllable and uncontrollable costs.
5. Analyse performance using budgets, recognising alternative approaches and sensitivity to variable factors.	(a) Analyse the consequences of 'what if' scenarios.	• 'What if' analysis based on alternate projections of volumes, prices and cost structures. • The evaluation of out-turn performance using variances based on 'fixed' and 'flexed' budgets.
C Short-term decision (30%)		
1 Explain concepts of cost and revenue relevant to pricing and product decisions.	(a) Explain the principles of decision making, including the identification and use of relevant cash flows and qualitative factors	• Relevant cash flows and their use in short-term decision making. • Consideration of the strategic implications of short-term decisions.
	(b) Explain the conflicts between cost accounting for profit reporting and inventory valuation, and information required for decision making	• Relevant costs and revenues in decision making and their relation to accounting concepts.
	(c) Explain the issues that arise in pricing decisions and the conflict between 'marginal cost' principles, and the need for full recovery of all costs incurred.	• Marginal and full cost recovery as bases for pricing decisions in the short and long-term.
2. Analyse short-term pricing and product decisions.	(a) Apply relevant cost analysis to various types of short-term decisions	• The application of relevant cost analysis to short-term decisions, including special selling price decisions, make or buy decisions, discontinuation decisions and further processing decisions.

BPP
LEARNING MEDIA

Learning outcomes On completion of their studies, student should be able to:		
Lead	**Component**	**Indicative syllabus content**
	(b) Apply break-even analysis in multiple product contexts	• Multi-product break-even analysis, including break-even and profit/volume charts, contribution/sales ratio, margin of safety etc.
	(c) Analyse product mix decisions, including circumstances where linear programming methods are needed to identify 'optimal' solutions	• Simple product mix analysis in situations where there are limitations on product/service demand and one other production constraint. • Linear programming for situations involving multiple constraints. • Solution by graphical methods and simultaneous equations of two variable problems, and the meaning of 'optimal' solutions.
	(d) Explain why joint costs must be allocated to final products for financial reporting purposes but why this is unhelpful when decisions concerning process and product viability have to be taken.	• The allocation of joint costs and decisions concerning process and product viability based on relevant costs and revenues.
D Dealing with risk and uncertainty (15%)		
1. Analyse information to assess risk and its impact on short-term decisions.	(a) Discuss the nature of risk and uncertainty and the attitudes to risk by decision makers	• The nature of risk and uncertainty. • The effect of risk attitudes of individuals on decisions.
	(b) Analyse risk using sensitivity analysis, expected values, standard deviations and probability tables	• Sensitivity analysis in decision modelling and the use of 'what if' analysis to identify variables that might have significant impacts on project outcomes. • Assignment of probabilities to key variables in decision models. • Analysis of probability distributions of project outcomes. • Standard deviations. • Expected value tables and the value of perfect and imperfect information. • Decision trees for multi-stage decision problems.
	(c) Apply decision models to deal with uncertainty in decision making.	• Maximin, maximax and minimax regret criteria. • Payoff tables.

Studying P1

1 What's P1 about

1.1 Cost accounting systems

There are **different ways** of carrying out costing. These include traditional management accounting techniques and new alternatives which may be more appropriate for the modern business environment. The various costing **methods impact** upon the business's **inventory valuation** and **profitability**.

1.2 Short-term decision making

This section focuses on **short-term decision making** and the issues that must be considered in this process. Some of the areas covered will be revision but it is important to be familiar with the impact that **costs and constraints on production and sales** have on decisions.

We cover **relevant costs, short-term decisions and limiting factor analysis**. The focus is on both the calculations and also **discussion** of issues such as why certain costs are included in the decision-making process. Decision-making when there is more than one constraint is the done with **linear programming**. There is strong emphasis on **interpretation and analysis**.

1.3 Forecasting and budgeting

A budget is a plan of what the organisation is aiming to achieve and what it has set as a target. There are several different techniques used to produce a budget but they are all produced to **ensure** that **objectives are achieved**. It is important that results are measured regularly and compared to budget so that management can try to take **corrective action** if areas of the business are not performing well.

1.4 Standard costing

A standard cost is the planned unit of cost of a product or service. Without this, producing a budget would be very difficult. **Standard costing and variance analysis** act as a **control mechanism** by establishing standards and highlighting activities that do not conform to plan.

1.5 Dealing with uncertainty in analysis

This part of the syllabus looks at techniques for **measuring risk and evaluating uncertainty**. These techniques include expected values, sensitivity analysis and decision trees. You need to be familiar with the techniques and their application across a variety of decision making tools such as relevant cash flows, and CVP analysis.

2 What's required

2.1 Explanation

As well as testing your knowledge and understanding in the ICS, you are asked to demonstrate the skill of explaining key ideas, techniques or approaches. Explaining means providing simple definitions and covering the reasons **why** these approaches have been developed. You'll gain higher marks if your explanations are clearly focused on the question and you can supplement your explanations with examples. You could try using the PEA approach. Point, Explain, Apply. Make your point in a sentence. Explain that point in another sentence by answering the reader's 'so what?' or 'why?'. Then apply it to the scenario so that your point relates to the organisation or specific situation in the question.

BPP
LEARNING MEDIA

2.2 Interpretation and recommendation

You will probably have to interpret the results of calculations in the ICS. You must understand that interpretation isn't just saying figures have increased or decreased. It means explaining **why** figures have changed and also the consequences of the changes. You will also have to provide recommendations.

3 How to pass

3.1 Study the whole syllabus

You need to be comfortable with **all areas of the syllabus**, as questions in the objective test exam will cover all syllabus areas. **Wider reading** will help you understand the main risks businesses face, which will be particularly useful in the integrated case study exam.

3.2 Lots of question practice

You can **develop application skills** by attempting questions in the Practise Question Bank. While these might not be in the format that you will experience in your exam, doing the questions will enable you to answer the exam questions.

However, you should practice OT exam standard questions, which you will find in the BPP Exam Practice Kit.

4 Brought forward knowledge

The examiner may test knowledge or techniques you've learnt at lower levels. CIMA C01 *Fundamentals of Management Accounting* and C03 *Fundamentals of Business Maths* are particularly important for this paper.

5 The Integrated Case Study and links with E1 and F1

The integrated case study exam is based on the expectation that students are developing a pool of knowledge. When faced with a problem students can appropriately apply their knowledge from any syllabus. Students will avoid a historical problem of partitioning their knowledge and accessing, for example, their knowledge of IFRS only when faced with a set of financial statements.

- **Enterprise operational decisions** will **impact** upon financial and performance objectives, the financial reports, working capital, and the risks the organisation faces.

- **Financial and performance decisions** will likewise have an impact on enterprise operational decisions.

- At the same time **enterprise operations** will be **constrained** by the finance available and the level of risks the organisation is prepared to bear.

- **Financial operational decisions** will **impact** upon the **risks** the organisation bears and perhaps impose limitations on the plans the organisation can implement.

- **Costing techniques**, particularly in relation to manufacturing, environmental costing and costs of quality, will have an impact on the **choices available** for enterprise operational decisions.

6 What the examiner means

The table below has been prepared by CIMA to help you interpret the syllabus and learning outcomes and the meaning of questions.

You will see that there are 5 levels of Learning objective, ranging from Knowledge to Evaluation, reflecting the level of skill you will be expected to demonstrate. CIMA Certificate subjects only use levels 1 to 3, but in CIMA's Professional qualification the entire hierarchy will be used.

At the start of each chapter in your Study Text is a topic list relating the coverage in the chapter to the level of skill you may be called on to demonstrate in the exam.

Learning objectives	Verbs used	Definition
1 Knowledge What are you expected to know	• List • State • Define	• Make a list of • Express, fully or clearly, the details of/facts of • Give the exact meaning of
2 Comprehension What you are expected to understand	• Describe • Distinguish • Explain • Identify • Illustrate	• Communicate the key features of • Highlight the differences between • Make clear or intelligible/state the meaning or purpose of • Recognise, establish or select after consideration • Use an example to describe or explain something
3 Application How you are expected to apply your knowledge	• Apply • Calculate/ compute • Demonstrate • Prepare • Reconcile • Solve • Tabulate	• Put to practical use • Ascertain or reckon mathematically • Prove with certainty or to exhibit by practical means • Make or get ready for use • Make or prove consistent/compatible • Find an answer to • Arrange in a table
4 Analysis How you are expected to analyse the detail of what you have learned	• Analyse • Categorise • Compare and contrast • Construct • Discuss • Interpret • Prioritise • Produce	• Examine in detail the structure of • Place into a defined class or division • Show the similarities and/or differences between • Build up or compile • Examine in detail by argument • Translate into intelligible or familiar terms • Place in order of priority or sequence for action • Create or bring into existence
5 Evaluation How you are expected to use your learning to evaluate, make decisions or recommendations	• Advise • Evaluate • Recommend	• Counsel, inform or notify • Appraise or assess the value of • Propose a course of action

Competency Framework

CIMA has developed a competency framework detailing the skills, abilities and competencies that finance professionals need. The CIMA syllabus has been developed to match the competency mix as it develops over the three levels of the professional qualification. The importance of the various competencies at the operational level is shown below.

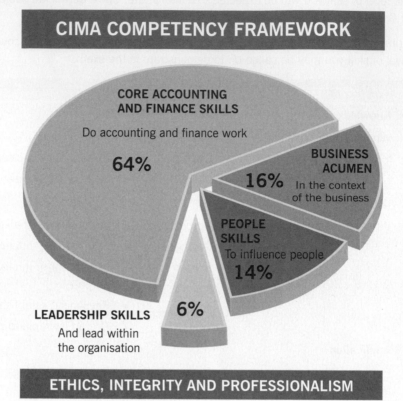

CIMA COMPETENCY FRAMEWORK

CORE ACCOUNTING AND FINANCE SKILLS

Do accounting and finance work

64%

BUSINESS ACUMEN
16% In the context of the business

PEOPLE SKILLS
To influence people
14%

LEADERSHIP SKILLS
And lead within the organisation
6%

ETHICS, INTEGRITY AND PROFESSIONALISM

Assessment

The CIMA assessment is a two-tier structure with objective tests for each subject and an integrated case study at each level.

Objective test

The objective tests are computer based and can be taken on demand. The student exam preparation on the CIMA website (www.cimaglobal.com) has additional information and tools to help you become familiar with the test style. Make sure you check back regularly as more information may be added.

Integrated case study

Candidates must pass or receive exemptions from the three objective tests at each level, before attempting the integrated case study exam for that level.

The integrated case studies are available four times a year.

The integrated case study exams will combine the knowledge and learning from all the pillars. They will be set in the context of a preseen fictional organisation based on a real industry.

COST ACCOUNTING SYSTEMS

Part A

MODERN BUSINESS CONCEPTS

In recent years there have been **significant changes in the business environment** in which both manufacturing and service organisations operate.

We look at these **changes** in some detail in **Section 1**.

Organisations have therefore adopted new **management approaches** (**Sections 4 and 5**), changed their **manufacturing systems** (**Sections 3 and 6**) and invested in **new technology (Section 2)**. It is these changes that we will be looking at in this chapter.

These changes do mean that **traditional management accounting methods may no longer be appropriate** and in the chapters that follow, we look at **alternative systems of management accounting** that have been developed and that are claimed to be more suitable for the modern business environment.

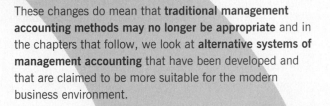

1

Topic list	Learning outcomes	Syllabus references	Ability required
1 The changing business environment	A1(f)	A1(f)(i)	Comprehension
2 Advanced manufacturing technology	A1(f)	A1(f)(i)	Comprehension
3 Just-in-time (JIT) systems	A1(f)	A1(f)(i)	Comprehension
4 Total quality management (TQM)	A2(a)	A2(a)(i)	Comprehension
5 Costs of quality and cost of quality reports	A2(a)	A2(a)(ii)	Comprehension
6 World class manufacturing (WCM)	A2(a)	A2(a)(ii)	Comprehension

Chapter Overview

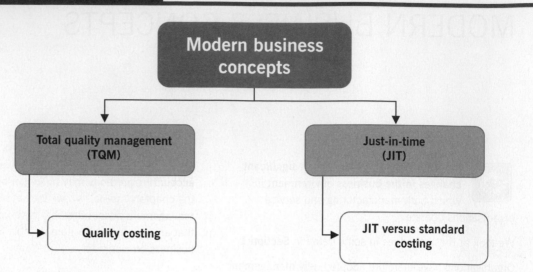

Knowledge brought forward from earlier studies

Standard costing and variance analysis

- **Standard costing** is a 'control technique that reports variances by comparing actual costs to pre-set standards so facilitating action through management by exception'.   *(CIMA Official Terminology)*

- A **variance** is 'the difference between a planned, budgeted, or standard cost and the actual cost incurred. The same comparisons may be made for revenues'.   *(CIMA Official Terminology)*

- **Variance analysis** is defined as the 'evaluation of performance by means of variances, whose timely reporting should maximise the opportunity for managerial action'.

    (CIMA Official Terminology)

1   The changing business environment

Introduction

Before the 1970s, **barriers of communication** and **geographical distance** limited the extent to which overseas organisations could compete in domestic markets. Cost increases could often be passed on to customers and so there were **few efforts to maximise efficiency and improve management practices**, or to reduce costs. **During the 1970s**, however, **overseas competitors** gained access to domestic markets by **establishing global networks for acquiring raw materials and distributing high-quality, low-priced goods**. To succeed, organisations had to compete against the best companies in the world.

1.1 The changing competitive environment for service organisations

Prior to the 1980s, many service organisations (such as the utilities, financial services and airlines industries) were either **government-owned monopolies** or were **protected by a highly regulated, non-competitive environment**. **Improvements in quality and efficiency** of operations or levels of profitability were not expected, and cost increases were often covered by increasing service prices. Cost systems to measure costs and profitability of individual services were not deemed necessary.

The competitive environment for service organisations changed radically in the **1980s**, however, following **privatisation** of government-owned monopolies and **deregulation**. The resulting intense competition and increasing product range has led to the **requirement for cost management and management accounting information systems** which allow service organisations to assess the costs and profitability of services, customers and markets.

1.2 Changing product life cycles

Today's **competitive environment**, along with high levels of **technological innovation** and **increasingly discriminating and sophisticated customer demands**, constantly **threaten a product's life cycle**. Diverse product ranges and demand for ever better products means that product life cycles have dramatically reduced.

PRODUCT LIFE CYCLE is the 'period which begins with the initial product specification and ends with the withdrawal from the market of both the product and its support. It is characterised by defined stages including research, development, introduction, maturity, decline and abandonment'.

KEY TERM

    (CIMA Official Terminology)

Organisations can no longer rely on years of high demand for products and so, to compete effectively, they need to continually **redesign their products** and to **shorten the time it takes to get them to the marketplace**.

In many organisations today, up to 90% of a product's life cycle cost is determined by decisions made early within the cycle, at the design stage. Management accounting systems that monitor spending and commitment to spend during the early stages of a product's life cycle are therefore becoming increasingly important.

1.3 Changing customer requirements

Successful organisations in today's competitive environment make **customer satisfaction** their **priority** and concentrate on the following **key success factors**.

Key success factor	Detail
Cost efficiency	Not wasting money
Quality	Focusing on total quality management (TQM), covered in Section 4
Time	Providing a speedier response to customer requests, ensuring 100% on-time delivery and reducing the time taken to develop and bring new products to market
Innovation	Developing a steady stream of innovative new products and having the flexibility to respond to customer requirements

They are also taking on board **new management approaches**.

Approach	Detail
Continuous improvement	A facet of TQM being a continuous search to reduce costs, eliminate waste and improve the quality and performance of activities that increase customer satisfaction or value
Employee empowerment	Providing employees with the information to enable them to make continuous improvements without authorisation from superiors
Total value-chain analysis	Ensuring that all the factors that add value to an organisation's products – the value chain of research and development, design, production, marketing, distribution and customer service – are co-ordinated within the overall organisational framework

1.4 Changing manufacturing systems

Traditionally, manufacturing industries have fallen into a few broad groups according to the **nature of the production process** and **materials flow**.

Type of production	Description
Jobbing industries	Industries in which **items are produced individually**, often for a specific customer order, as a 'job'. Such a business requires versatile equipment and highly skilled workers to give it the flexibility to turn its hand to a variety of jobs. The jobbing factory is typically laid out on a **functional** basis with, say, a milling department, a cutting department, finishing, assembly and so on.
Batch processing	Involves the manufacture of **standard goods in batches**. 'Batch production is often carried out using **functional** layouts but with a greater number of more **specialised machines**. With a functional layout batches move by different and complex routes through various specialised departments travelling over much of the factory floor before they are completed.' (Drury, *Management and Cost Accounting*)

Type of production	Description
Mass or flow production	Involves the **continuous production of standard items** from a sequence of continuous or repetitive operations. This sort of production often uses a **product-based** layout whereby product A moves from a milling machine to a cutting machine to a paint-spraying machine, and product B moves from a sawing machine to a milling machine to an oven and then to finishing and so on. The point is that there is no separate 'milling department' or 'assembly department' to which all products must be sent to await their turn on the machines: each product has its own dedicated machine.

In recent years, however, a new type of manufacturing system known as **group technology** (or **repetitive manufacturing**) has emerged. The system involves a **flexible or cellular arrangement of machines** that **manufacture groups of products having similar manufacturing requirements**. By grouping together facilities required to produce similar products, some of the **benefits associated with flow production systems** (lower throughput times, easier scheduling, reduced set-up times and reduced work in progress) are possible to achieve. Moreover, the increase in **customer demand for product diversity can be satisfied** by such a manufacturing system.

1.4.1 Dedicated cell layout

The modern development in this sphere is to merge the flexibility of the functional layout with the speed and productivity of the product layout. **Cellular** manufacturing involves a **U-shaped flow** along which are arranged a number of different machines that are used to make products with similar machining requirements.

The machines are operated by workers who are **multi-skilled** (can operate each machine within the cell rather than being limited to one operation such as 'lathe-operator', 'grinder', or whatever) and are able to perform routine preventative maintenance on the cell machines. The aim is to facilitate **just-in-time** production (see Section 3) and obtain the associated improvements in **quality** and reductions in **costs**.

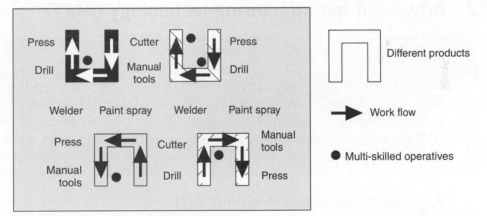

1.5 Cost reduction and value analysis

In today's environment, businesses are under pressure to offer an increased choice of quality products at a cost traditionally associated with mass production.

Cost reduction is a planned and positive approach to reducing expenditure. Cost reduction measures should be planned programmes to reduce costs rather than crash programmes to cut spending levels.

Value analysis is an example of a cost reduction technique. It is a planned, scientific approach to cost reduction which reviews the material composition of a product and the product's design so that modifications and improvements can be made that do not reduce the value of the product to the customer or user.

1.5.1 Waste

Part of cost reduction may look at elimination of waste. Waste, in this context, results from activities that do not add value. Examples of activities that do not add value include continuing production when there is no demand resulting in the build up of unnecessary inventory, or waiting time, or unnecessary movement of materials or staff. These are all waste activities because they are unnecessary actions.

Exam alert

In an ICS question on the modern manufacturing environment, consider:

- The global environment
- Cost control/reduction
- Focus on customer requirements
- Flexibility
- Shorter product life cycles
- Focus on quality

Section summary

Changes to the **competitive environment**, **product life cycles** and **customer requirements** have had a significant impact on the modern business environment.

Different approaches for **organising a manufacturing process** include **jobbing industries**, **batch processing** and **mass production**.

To compete effectively, organisations need to **continually redesign their products** and to **shorten the time it takes to get them to the marketplace**. **Manufacturing processes** must therefore be **sufficiently flexible** both to accommodate new product design rapidly and to satisfy the demand for greater product diversity.

---

2   Advanced manufacturing technology (AMT)

Introduction

Advanced manufacturing technology (AMT) is a general expression encompassing computer-aided design (CAD), computer-aided manufacturing (CAM), flexible manufacturing systems (FMS) and a wide array of innovative computer equipment. World-class manufacturers such as Toyota and BMW will probably use AMT. You don't need to know the details of AMT but you do need to realise that it has had a huge impact on manufacturing businesses. For example, labour costs are now vastly reduced.

2.1 Computer-aided design (CAD)

Computer-aided design (CAD) allows new products to be designed (and old ones modified) on a computer screen.

(a)   The effects of **changing product specifications** (for example to test stress and find weaknesses or to optimise usage of materials) can be explored.

(b)   **Designs can be assessed in terms of cost and simplicity**. A simple design is likely to produce a more reliable product and a simple product is easier to manufacture, thereby reducing the possibility of production errors. Quality and cost reduction can therefore be incorporated into a product at the design stage.

(c)   **Databases can be used** to match part requirements of the new design with existing product parts, thereby allowing a reduction in product parts required and a minimisation of inventories.

2.2 Computer-aided manufacturing (CAM)

Computer-aided manufacturing (CAM) refers to the control of the physical production process by computers.

Feature	Detail
Robots	Typically comprise computer controlled arms and attachments that can perform tasks like welding, bolting parts together and moving them about.
Computer numerically controlled (CNC) machines	Programmable machine tools for punching holes, cutting and so on. Manufacturing configurations and set-up instructions are stored on computer programs and so can be changed almost immediately via a keyboard. Flexibility and a reduction in set-up times are thus major advantages of CAM. Moreover, computers can repeat the same operation in an identical manner time and time again, without tiring or error, unlike human operators, with obvious advantages for both quality control and production control.
Automated guided vehicles (AGV)	Used for materials handling, often in place of the traditional conveyor belt approach.

The **ultimate aim** of CAM is a **set-up time of zero**. Although this may not be achievable (in the near future at least), CAM has provided, and still is providing, the **possibility** of economic **production in smaller and smaller batch sizes** with the result that the production schedule is becoming more and more driven by customer requirements.

2.3 Flexible manufacturing systems (FMS)

KEY TERM

A FLEXIBLE MANUFACTURING SYSTEM (FMS) is an 'Integrated, computer-controlled production system which is capable of producing any of a range of parts, and of switching quickly and economically between them'.   *(CIMA Official Terminology)*

A flexible manufacturing system (FMS) is a **highly automated manufacturing system**, which is computer controlled and capable of producing a broad 'family' of parts in a flexible manner. **It is characterised by small batch production, the ability to change quickly from one job to another and very fast response times**, so that output can be produced quickly in response to specific orders that come in.

The sophistication of FMSs varies from one system to another, but **features** can include the following:

- A **JIT system** (discussed later in this chapter)

- Full **computer-integrated manufacturing (CIM)** (the integration of many or all of the elements of AMT into one coherent system) or perhaps just **islands of automation (IAs)** (a series of automated sub-systems within the factory)

- **Computerised materials handling systems (MHS)**

- **Automated storage and retrieval systems (ASRS)** for raw materials and parts

2.4 Electronic data interchange (EDI)

It is not simply within the manufacturing functions of an organisation that technology has made an impact. Electronic data interchange (EDI) facilitates communication between an organisation and its customers and suppliers by the electronic transfer of information.

Section summary

Advanced manufacturing technology (AMT) is a general expression encompassing **computer-aided design (CAD)**, **computer-aided manufacturing (CAM)**, **flexible manufacturing systems (FMS)** and a wide array of innovative computer equipment.

3 Just-in-time (JIT) systems

Introduction

'Traditional' responses to the problems of improving manufacturing capacity and reducing unit costs of production might be described as follows:

- Longer production runs
- Economic batch quantities
- Reduced time on preventive maintenance, to keep production flowing
- Fewer products in the product range
- More overtime

In general terms, longer production runs and large batch sizes should mean less disruption, better capacity utilisation and lower unit costs.

Just-in-time systems challenge such 'traditional' views of manufacture.

KEY TERMS

JUST-IN-TIME (JIT) is a 'system whose objective is to produce or to procure products or components as they are required by a customer or for use, rather than for stock. A JIT system is a **pull** system, which responds to demand, in contrast to a **push** system, in which stocks act as buffers between the different elements of the system, such as purchasing, production and sales.'

JUST-IN-TIME PRODUCTION is a 'production system which is driven by demand for finished products whereby each component on a production line is produced only when needed for the next stage.'

JUST-IN-TIME PURCHASING is a 'purchasing system in which material purchases are contracted so that the receipt and usage of material, to the maximum extent possible, coincide.'   *(CIMA Official Terminology)*

Although described as a technique in the *Official Terminology*, JIT is more of a **philosophy or approach to management** since it encompasses a **commitment to continuous improvement** and the **search for excellence** in the design and operation of the production management system.

JIT has the following **essential elements**.

Element	Detail
JIT purchasing	Parts and raw materials should be purchased as near as possible to the time they are needed, using small frequent deliveries against bulk contracts.
Close relationship with suppliers	In a JIT environment, the responsibility for the quality of goods lies with the supplier. A long-term commitment between supplier and customer should therefore be established. The supplier is guaranteed a demand for products because of being the sole supplier and the supplier can plan to meet the customer's production schedules. If an organisation has confidence that suppliers will deliver material of 100% quality, on time, so that there will be no rejects, returns and hence no consequent production delays, usage of materials can be matched with delivery of materials and inventories can be kept at near zero levels. Suppliers are also chosen because of their close proximity to an organisation's plant.

Element	Detail
Uniform loading	All parts of the productive process should be operated at a speed that matches the rate at which the final product is demanded by the customer. Production runs will therefore be shorter, and there will be smaller inventories of finished goods because output is being matched more closely to demand (and so storage costs will be reduced).
Set-up time reduction	Machinery set-ups are non value added activities (see below) that should be reduced or even eliminated.
Machine cells	Machines or workers should be grouped by product or component instead of by the type of work performed. The non value added activity of materials' movement between operations is therefore minimised by eliminating space between work stations. Products can flow from machine to machine without having to wait for the next stage of processing or returning to stores. Lead times and work in progress are thus reduced.
Quality	Production management should seek to eliminate scrap and defective units during production, and to avoid the need for reworking of units, since this stops the flow of production and leads to late deliveries to customers. Product quality and production quality are important 'drivers' in a JIT system.
Pull system (Kanban)	A **Kanban**, or signal, is used to ensure that products/components are only produced when needed by the next process. Nothing is produced in anticipation of need, to then remain in inventory, consuming resources.
Preventative maintenance	Production systems must be reliable and prompt, without unforeseen delays and breakdowns. Machinery must be kept fully maintained, and so preventative maintenance is an important aspect of production.
Employee involvement	Workers within each machine cell should be trained to operate each machine within that cell and to be able to perform routine preventative maintenance on the cell machines (ie to be multi-skilled and flexible).

Question 1.1

JIT system

Learning outcome A1(f)

A company is considering changing to a JIT system. Which of the following changes in their working practices are likely to be necessary?

I	More frequent revision of inventory control levels and of the economic order quantity
II	Increase in the number of raw material suppliers in order to guarantee supply
III	Selection of suppliers close to the company's manufacturing facility
IV	Increased focus on the accurate forecasting of customer demand
V	Increased quality control activity

A	I and II
B	III, IV and V
C	II, III, IV and V
D	All of them

3.1 Value-added

JIT aims to eliminate all **non value added costs**. Value is only added while a product is actually being processed. Whilst it is being inspected for quality, moving from one part of the factory to another, waiting for further processing and held in store, value is not being added. Non value added activities (or **diversionary** activities) should therefore be eliminated.

KEY TERM

'A VALUE-ADDED cost is incurred for an activity that cannot be eliminated without the customer's perceiving a deterioration in the performance, function, or other quality of a product. The cost of a picture tube in a television set is value-added.

The costs of those activities that can be eliminated without the customer's perceiving deterioration in the performance, function, or other quality of a product are non-value-added. The costs of handling the materials of a television set through successive stages of an assembly line may be non-value-added. Improvements in plant layout that reduce handling costs may be achieved without affecting the performance, function, or other quality of the television set.'

(Horngren)

Question 1.2	Value-added activity

Learning outcome A1(f)

Which of the following is a value-added activity?

A Setting up a machine so that it drills holes of a certain size
B Repairing faulty production work
C Painting a car, if the organisation manufactures cars
D Storing materials

CASE STUDY

The following extract from an article in the *Financial Times* illustrates how 'just-in-time' some manufacturing processes can be. The emphasis is BPP's.

'Just-in-time manufacturing is down to a fine art at Nissan Motor Manufacturing (UK). **Stockholding of some components is just ten minutes** – and the holding of all parts bought in Europe is less than a day.

Nissan has moved beyond just-in-time to **synchronous supply** for some components, which means manufacturers deliver these components directly to the production line minutes before they are needed.

These manufacturers do not even receive an order to make a component until the car for which it is intended has started along the final assembly line. Seat manufacturer Ikeda Hoover, for example, has about 45 minutes to build seats to specification and deliver them to the assembly line a mile away. It delivers 12 sets of seats every 20 minutes and they are mounted in the right order on an overhead conveyor ready for fitting to the right car.

Nissan has **close relationships with this dozen or so suppliers** and deals exclusively with them in their component areas. It involves them and even their own suppliers in discussions about future needs and other issues. These companies have generally established their own manufacturing units close to the Nissan plant.

Other parts from further afield are collected from manufacturers by Nissan several times at fixed times. This is more efficient than having each supplier making individual haulage arrangements.'

3.2 Problems associated with JIT

JIT should not be seen as a panacea for all the endemic problems associated with Western manufacturing. It might not even be appropriate in all circumstances.

(a) It is **not** always **easy** to **predict** patterns of **demand**.

(b) JIT makes the organisation far more vulnerable to **disruptions** in the supply chain.

(c) JIT, originated by Toyota, was designed at a time when all of Toyota's manufacturing was done within a 50 km **radius** of its headquarters. Wide geographical spread, however, makes this difficult.

JIT and supply chains

The flight ban that affected much of Europe after the volcanic eruption in Iceland in April 2010 threatened to force worldwide car production to grind to a halt, as manufacturers were unable to source key electronic components.

The flight disruption highlighted the car industry's dependence on complex, worldwide supply chains that need multiple modes of transport to deliver goods and components just in time, to where they are needed.

Among the carmakers, BMW and Nissan said they planned to suspend some production because of disruption to supplies. Audi said it might have to cancel shifts because of missing parts.

Although all three mainly use suppliers based near their factories and use road and sea for most deliveries, they depend on air freight for a small number of high-value electronic components. Nissan UK, for example, said it might have to halt production of its Cube, Murano SUV and Rogue crossover models because it lacked supplies of a critical sensor made in Ireland.

Some commentators have questioned whether this disruption will make companies re-examine their arrangements for sourcing goods. Companies have become more vulnerable to disruption since moving to just-in-time production methods, where hardly any inventory of products is held.

> Adapted from: Wright, R and Reed, J (21 April 2010) *Pressure grows on supply chains*. [Online]
> *Financial Times*, www.ft.com

Ukraine crisis ratchets up the risk to corporate supply chains

The risk of disruption to corporate supply chains is running at near-record levels despite signs of improvement this year, according to an index created by the global trade body for purchasing managers.

Just as it appeared that dangers for businesses were starting to recede, the crisis in Ukraine came along to heighten political risk, said the Chartered Institute of Purchasing and Supply (CIPS).

The body, which represents 100,000 purchasing and supply management professionals in 150 countries, warned that businesses must 'recognise the risks to their supply chains and make the appropriate provisions before it is too late'. It urged companies to identify weaknesses among suppliers, saying exposure to the world's riskiest regions may lie three or even four tiers down.

Supply chain risk has been a source of concern since the financial crisis, especially as pressure to keep costs low means that multinational manufacturers often operate complex networks of component supplies on a **just-in-time** basis. The risk of doing business in crisis-hit economies, political instability in countries from Egypt to Bangladesh and events such as the 2011 Japanese earthquake, which damaged the Fukushima nuclear power plant, have heightened awareness of dangers.

The index was compiled jointly with Dun & Bradstreet, the data research specialist, which analysed 132 countries, weighted by exports. It assessed risk using factors such as economic prospects, trade barriers, regulation, ease of transferring money, infrastructure quality, civil disorder and the danger of expropriation. It found that global operational risk improved slightly in this year's first quarter because of economic recovery in the US, Germany and the UK. But turmoil in Ukraine and Western Europe's dependence on Russian gas have raised concern about political dangers.

Andrew Williamson, leader of economic analysis at Dun & Bradstreet, said he was still hopeful of a slight overall improvement this year as long as the situation in Eastern Europe did not worsen.

He said Ukraine and Russia were already so risky that it was difficult to downgrade the company's assessment of them further without classifying them as failed states. 'We see lots of political risk bubbling up, not just in Ukraine. There are elections going on in emerging markets such as India and Indonesia', Mr Williamson added.

David Noble, Group Chief Executive of the CIPS, said: 'The resurgence in the global economy depends very much upon the reliability of global supply chains. With political instability across the developing world, it is vital that businesses and economies recognise the risks to their supply chains and make the appropriate provisions before it is too late'.

The CIPS said the index would help managers to prepare contingency plans and identify factors that might affect the financial stability of suppliers.

Mr Williamson said that with hindsight, the 1990s, up to the Asian financial crisis, were a golden period.

The inaugural index has highlighted the disparity of risk among developing countries often grouped together such as the BRICs (Brazil, Russia, India and China). While China and India had historically stayed at a medium risk level, Russia had consistently posed a high risk to businesses and economies that rely on its exports.

Adapted from: Groom, B (5 May 2014) *Risk to corporate supply chains at near-record level*.
[Online] *Financial Times*, www.ft.com

| Question 1.3 | JIT |

Learning outcome A1(f)

Batch sizes within a JIT manufacturing environment may well be smaller than those associated with traditional manufacturing systems.

What costs might be associated with this feature of JIT?

1   Increased set-up costs

2   Opportunity cost of lost production capacity as machinery and the workforce reorganise for a different product

3   Additional materials handling costs

4   Increased administrative costs

A   None of the above
B   1, 2, 3 and 4
C   1 only
D   2 and 3 only

3.3 Modern versus traditional inventory control systems

There is no reason for the newer approaches to supersede the old entirely. A restaurant, for example, might find it preferable to use the traditional economic order quantity approach for staple non-perishable food items, but adopt JIT for perishable and 'exotic' items. In a hospital a stock-out could, quite literally, be fatal, and JIT would be quite unsuitable.

3.4 Standard costing and JIT

Some commentators have argued that **traditional variance analysis is unhelpful and potentially misleading** in the modern organisation, and can make managers focus their attention on the wrong issues. Here are just two examples:

(a)   **Efficiency variance**. Traditional variance analysis emphasises that adverse efficiency variances should be avoided, which means that managers should try to prevent idle time and keep up production. In an environment where the focus is on improving continuously, JIT should be used. In these circumstances, manufacturing to eliminate idle time could result in the production of unwanted products that must be held in store and might eventually be scrapped. Efficiency variances could focus management attention on the wrong problems.

(b)   **Materials price variance**. In a JIT environment, the key issues in materials purchasing are supplier reliability, materials quality, and delivery in small order quantities. Purchasing managers should not be shopping around every month looking for the cheapest price. Many JIT systems depend on long-term contractual links with suppliers, which means that material price variances are not relevant for management control purposes.

Section summary

JIT aims for zero inventory and perfect quality, and operates by demand-pull. It consists of **JIT purchasing** and **JIT production**, and results in lower investment requirements, space savings, greater customer satisfaction and increased flexibility.

4   Total quality management (TQM)

Introduction

Quality means 'the **degree of excellence of a thing**' – how well made it is, or how well performed if it is a service, how well it serves its purpose, and how it measures up against its rivals. These criteria imply two things:

*   That quality is something that requires care on the part of the provider
*   That **quality** is largely subjective – it is in the eye of the beholder, the **customer**

4.1 The management of quality

The **management** of quality is the process of:

(a)   Establishing **standards of quality** for a product or service

(b)   Establishing **procedures or production methods** that ought to ensure that these required standards of quality are met in a suitably high proportion of cases

(c)   **Monitoring** actual quality

(d)   Taking **control action** when actual quality falls below standard

Take the postal service as an example. The postal service might establish a standard that 90% of first class letters will be delivered on the day after they are posted, and 99% will be delivered within two days of posting.

(a)   Procedures would have to be established for ensuring that these standards could be met (attending to such matters as frequency of collections, automated letter sorting, frequency of deliveries and number of staff employed).

(b)   Actual performance could be monitored, perhaps by taking samples from time to time of letters that are posted and delivered.

(c)   If the quality standard is not being achieved, management should take control action (employ more postal workers or advertise the use of postcodes again).

Quality management becomes **total (total quality management (TQM)) when it is applied to everything a business does**.

KEY TERM

TOTAL QUALITY MANAGEMENT (TQM) is an 'integrated and comprehensive system of planning and controlling all business functions so that products or services are produced which meet or exceed customer expectations. TQM is a philosophy of business behaviour, embracing principles such as employee involvement, continuous improvement at all levels and customer focus, as well as being a

collection of related techniques aimed at improving quality such as full documentation of activities, clear goal setting and performance measurement from the customer perspective'. *(CIMA Official Terminology)*

 Exam skills

As you learn the mechanics of these new management approaches, try not to view each one in isolation. For example, the assessment may require you to give reasons why the adoption of TQM is important in a JIT environment.

4.2 Get it right, first time

One of the basic principles of TQM is that the **cost of preventing mistakes is less than the cost of correcting them** once they occur. The aim should therefore be **to get things right first time**. Every mistake, delay and misunderstanding directly costs an organisation money through **wasted time and effort**, including time taken in pacifying customers. The **lost potential for future sales because of poor customer service must also be taken into account**.

4.3 Continuous improvement

A second basic principle of TQM is dissatisfaction with the status quo: the belief that it is **always possible to improve** and so the aim should be to '**get it more right next time**'.

4.4 Quality assurance procedures

Because TQM embraces every activity of a business, quality assurance procedures **cannot be confined to the production process** but must also cover the work of sales, distribution and administration departments, the efforts of external suppliers, and the reaction of external customers.

Area	Procedure
Quality assurance of goods inwards	Suppliers' quality assurance schemes are being used increasingly. This is where the supplier guarantees the quality of goods supplied.
Inspection of output	The aim of carrying out inspection samples is to satisfy management that quality control in production is being maintained.
Monitoring customer reaction	Customer complaints should be monitored. Some companies survey customers on a regular basis.
Employees and quality	To ensure that employees have a positive attitude towards quality: • Responsibility for quality checking could be given to the worker themselves • Inter-group competition to meet and beat quality standards could be introduced

Problems can therefore be overcome by **changing people's attitudes** rather than teaching them new tricks. The key issue is to instil **understanding of, and commitment to, working practices that lead to quality**.

4.5 Empowerment and quality circles

Workers themselves are frequently the best source of information about how (or how not) to improve quality. **Empowerment** therefore has two key aspects:

(a)   Allowing workers to have the **freedom to decide how to do** the necessary work, using the skills they possess and acquiring new skills as necessary to be an effective team member

(b)   Making workers **responsible** for achieving production targets and for quality control

A **quality circle** is a group of employees who volunteer to attend regular meetings to discuss work-related quality problems and to suggest possible solutions.

4.6 Design for quality

A TQM environment aims to get it right first time, and this means that **quality, not faults, must be designed into the organisation's products and operations from the outset**.

Quality control happens at various stages in the process of designing a product or service.

(a) At the **product design stage**, quality control means trying to design a product or service so that its specifications provide a suitable balance between price and quality (of sales and delivery, as well as manufacture) that will make the product or service competitive.

(b) **Production engineering** is the **process of designing the methods for making a product** (or service) **to the design specification**. It sets out to make production methods as efficient as possible, and to avoid the manufacture of sub-standard items.

(c) **Information systems** should be designed to get the required information to the right person at the right time; **distribution systems** should be designed to get the right item to the right person at the right time; and so on.

4.6.1 Business process re-engineering

KEY TERM

BUSINESS PROCESS RE-ENGINEERING is the 'selection of areas of business activity in which repeatable and repeated sets of activities are undertaken; and the development of improved understanding of how they operate and of the scope for radical redesign with a view to creating and delivering better customer value'.
(CIMA Official Terminology)

As businesses, their market and the wider environment develop and change, it is appropriate to reconsider the way they do things from time to time. Business process re-engineering is an approach based on challenging basic assumptions about business methods and even the objectives they are designed to achieve.

Business process re-engineering involves making fundamental changes in the way an organisation functions. For example, processes which were developed during a paper-intensive processing environment may no longer be suitable for an environment which is now underpinned by IT.

4.7 Quality control and inspection

A distinction should be made between **quality control** and **inspection**.

(a) **Quality control** involves setting controls for the process of manufacture or service delivery. It is aimed at **preventing the manufacture of defective items** or the provision of defective services.

(b) **Inspection** is a technique of **identifying when defective items are being produced at an unacceptable level**. Inspection is usually carried out at three main points:

(i) Receiving inspection – for raw materials and purchased components
(ii) Floor or process inspection for work in progress (WIP)
(iii) Final inspection or testing for finished goods

4.8 Standard costing and TQM

Standard costing concentrates on **quantity** and ignores other factors contributing to an organisation's effectiveness. In a **total quality** environment, however, quantity is not an issue, **quality** is. Effectiveness in such an environment therefore centres on high-quality output (produced as a result of high-quality input); the cost of failing to achieve the required level of effectiveness is not measured in variances, but in terms of the **internal and external failure costs** which would not be identified by traditional standard costing analysis.

Standard costing might measure, say, **labour efficiency** in terms of individual tasks and the level of **output**. In a **total quality environment**, labour is most likely to be viewed as a number of **multi-task teams** who are responsible for completion of a part of the production process. The effectiveness of such a team is more appropriately measured in terms of **reworking** required, **returns** from customers, **defects** identified in subsequent stages of production and so on.

In a **TQM** environment, there are likely to be **minimal rate variances** if the workforce are paid a guaranteed weekly wage. Fixed price contracts, with suppliers guaranteeing levels of quality, are often a feature, especially if a JIT system is also in place, and so there are likely to be **few, if any, material price and usage variances**.

So **can standard costing and TQM exist together?** Or do we need to **SCRAP** standard costing in a TQM environment?

Standard costing vs TQM	
Scrap	Standard costs often incorporate a planned level of scrap in material standards. This is at odds with the TQM aim of 'zero defects' and there is no motivation to 'get it right first time'.
Continual changes	Continual improvements should alter quantities of inputs, prices and so on, whereas standard costing is best used in a stable, standardised, repetitive environment.
Responsibility	Standard costing systems make individual managers responsible for the variances relating to their part of the organisation's activities. A TQM programme, on the other hand, aims to make all personnel aware of, and responsible for, the importance of supplying the customer with a quality product.
Attainable standards	Attainable standards, which make some allowance for wastage and inefficiencies, are commonly set. The use of such standards conflicts with the elimination of waste which is a vital ingredient of a TQM programme.
Predetermined standards	Predetermined standards conflict with the TQM philosophy of continual improvement.

4.9 Problems implementing TQM in an organisation

(a) It can be demotivating because 'perfection' is hard to achieve.
(b) It relies heavily on the quality of suppliers.
(c) Change management can be difficult, depending on the culture of the business.

We will return briefly to product quality in Chapter 12a, when we look at how standard costing can help improve product quality.

Section summary

In the context of **total quality management**, 'quality' means getting it right first time, and improving continuously.

5 Costs of quality and cost of quality reports

Introduction

Cost of quality reports highlight the total cost to an organisation of producing products or services that do not conform with quality requirements. Four categories of cost should be reported: prevention costs, appraisal costs, internal failure costs and external failure costs.

5.1 Costs of quality

When we talk about quality-related costs, you should remember that a concern for **good quality saves money**; it is **poor quality that costs money**.

KEY TERMS

The COST OF QUALITY is the 'Difference between the actual cost of producing, selling and supporting, products or services and the equivalent costs if there were no failures during production or usage'.

The cost of quality can be analysed into:

COST OF CONFORMANCE. 'Costs of achieving specified quality standards.'

- COST OF PREVENTION. 'Costs incurred prior to or during production in order to prevent substandard or defective products or services from being produced.'

- COST OF APPRAISAL. 'Costs incurred in order to ensure that outputs produced meet required quality standards.'
  (CIMA Official Terminology)

COST OF NON-CONFORMANCE. 'The cost of failure to deliver the required standard of quality'.

- COST OF INTERNAL FAILURE. 'Costs arising from inadequate quality which are identified before the transfer of ownership from supplier to purchaser.'

- COST OF EXTERNAL FAILURE. 'Costs arising from inadequate quality discovered after the transfer of ownership from supplier to purchaser.'
  (CIMA Official Terminology)

Quality-related cost	Example
Prevention costs	Quality engineering
	Design/development of quality control/inspection equipment
	Maintenance of quality control/inspection equipment
	Administration of quality control
	Training in quality control
Appraisal costs	Acceptance testing
	Inspection of goods inwards
	Inspection costs of in-house processing
	Performance testing
Internal failure costs	Failure analysis
	Re-inspection costs
	Losses from failure of purchased items
	Losses due to lower selling prices for sub-quality goods
	Costs of reviewing product specifications after failures

Quality-related cost	Example
External failure costs	Administration of customer complaints section
	Costs of customer service section
	Product liability costs
	Cost of repairing products returned from customers
	Cost of replacing items due to sub-standard products/marketing errors

The **cost of conformance** is a **discretionary** cost that is incurred with the intention of **eliminating the costs of internal and external failure**. The **cost of non-conformance**, on the other hand, can **only be reduced by increasing the cost of conformance**. The **optimal investment in conformance costs** is when **total costs of quality reach a minimum** (which may be below 100% quality conformance). This is illustrated in the following diagram.

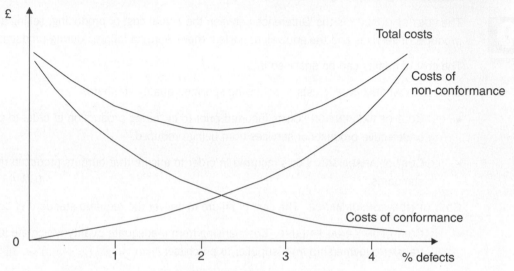

To achieve **0% defects, costs of conformance must be high**. As a **greater proportion of defects are accepted**, however, these costs can be **reduced**. At a level of **0% defects, costs of non-conformance** should be **nil** but these will **increase** as the **accepted level of defects rises**. There should therefore be an **acceptable level of defects** at which the **total costs of quality are at a minimum**.

5.2 Cost of quality reports

Shown below is a typical cost of quality report. **Some figures** in the report, such as the contribution forgone due to sales lost because of poor quality, may have to be **estimated**, but it is better to include an estimate rather than omit the category from the report.

The report has the following **uses**:

(a) By expressing each cost category as a percentage of sales revenue, **comparisons** can be made with previous periods, divisions within the group or other organisations, thereby highlighting problem areas. A comparison of the proportion of external failure costs to sales revenue with the figures for other organisations, for example, can provide some idea of the level of customer satisfaction.

(b) It can be used to make senior management aware of **how much is being spent** on quality-related costs.

(c) It can provide an indication of **how total quality costs could be reduced by a more sensible division of costs between the four categories**. For example, an increase in spending on prevention costs should reduce the costs of internal and external failure, and hence reduce total spending.

COST OF QUALITY REPORT
YEAR ENDING 31 DECEMBER 20X0

	$'000	$'000	Cost as % of annual turnover ($10m)
Prevention costs			
Design of quality control equipment	80		
Quality control training	80		
		160	1.6
Appraisal costs			
Inspection of goods inwards	90		
Inspection of WIP	100		
		190	1.9
Internal failure costs			
Scrap	150		
Rework	200		
		350	3.5
External failure costs			
Returns	500		
Contribution forgone on lost sales	400		
Handling customer complaints	100		
		1,000	10.0
		1,700	17.0

Although cost of quality reports provide a useful summary of the costs, effort and progress of quality, **non-financial quality measures** may be more appropriate for **lower levels of management**. Here are some examples of such measures:

- Number of customer complaints
- Number of warranty claims
- Number of defective units delivered to customers as a percentage of total units delivered

Section summary

Quality costs can be analysed into **prevention, appraisal, internal failure and external failure** costs and should be detailed in a **cost of quality report**.

6 World class manufacturing (WCM)

Introduction

World class manufacturing (WCM) is a term which was coined in the mid-1980s to **describe the fundamental changes taking place in manufacturing companies** we have been examining. WCM is a very broad term.

KEY TERM

'WORLD CLASS MANUFACTURING (WCM) describes the manufacture of high-quality products reaching customers quickly (or the delivery of a prompt and quality service) at a low cost to provide high performance and customer satisfaction.'

Peter J Clarke ('The old and the new in management accounting',
Management Accounting, June 1995)

The *Official Terminology*'s definition of WORLD CLASS MANUFACTURING is a 'Position of international manufacturing excellence, achieved by developing a culture based on factors such as continuous improvement, problem prevention, zero defect tolerance, customer-driven JIT-based production and total quality management'.

In essence, however, WCM can be taken to have four key elements.

Key element	Description
A new approach to product quality	Instead of a policy of trying to detect defects or poor quality in production as and when they occur, WCM sets out to identify the root causes of poor quality, eliminate them, and achieve zero defects, that is 100% quality, thereby incorporating the principles of TQM.
Just-in-time manufacturing	See Section 3.
Managing people	WCM aims to utilise the skills and abilities of the workforce to the full. Employees are given training in a variety of skills, so that they can switch from one task to another. They are also given more responsibility for production scheduling and quality. A team approach is encouraged, with strong trust between management and workers.
Flexible approach to customer requirements	The WCM policy is to develop close relationships with customers in order to know what their requirements are, supply them on time, with short delivery lead times and change the product mix quickly and develop new products or modify existing products as customer needs change.

A WCM manufacturer will have a clear **manufacturing strategy** aimed at issues such as quality and reliability, short lead times (the time from start to finish of production), flexibility and customer satisfaction. But to compete, the world class manufacturer must appreciate that it is **not just in manufacturing that he must excel**. A **clear understanding** of the relationship between all of the factors which add value to an organisation's products (the **value chain**) is vital.

6.1 The value chain

The value chain is made up of the following:

- Research and development
- Design
- Production
- Marketing

- Distribution
- Customer service
- Customers

It **starts externally** with suppliers, links them to the internal functions of R&D, design, production, marketing, distribution and customer service, and **ends externally** with suppliers.

To improve quality, reduce costs and increase innovation, the manufacturer must ensure that the **functions within the value chain are co-ordinated** within the overall organisational framework.

Section summary

World class manufacturing (WCM) aims for high quality, fast production, and the flexibility to respond to customer needs.

Chapter Summary

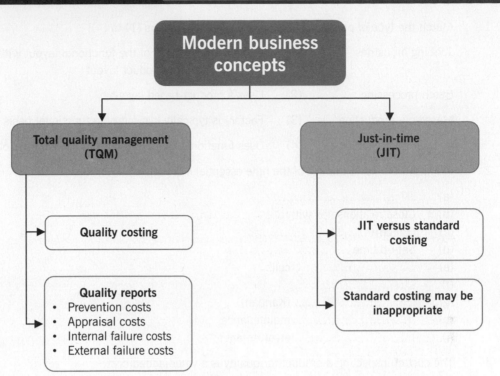

Quick Quiz

1   Match the type of production with one of the descriptions (1) to (4).

Jobbing industries   (1)   Merges the flexibility of the functional layout with the speed and productivity of the product layout

Batch processing   (2)   Uses a product-based layout

Mass/flow production   (3)   Factory is typically laid out on a functional basis

Cellular manufacturing   (4)   Uses functional layout but with a high number of specialised machines

2   Fill in the blanks in this list of the nine essential elements of JIT.

(a)   JIT ....
(b)   Close relationships with ....
(c)   Uniform ....
(d)   Set-up time ....
(e)   .... cells
(f)   ....
(g)   .... (Kanban)
(h)   .... maintenance
(i)   .... involvement

3   The cost of inspecting a product for quality is a value-added cost.

True   ☐

False   ☐

4   Which of the following is/are correct?

(a)   Cost of conformance = cost of prevention + cost of internal failure
(b)   Cost of conformance = cost of internal failure + cost of external failure
(c)   Cost of non-conformance = cost of internal failure + cost of external failure
(d)   Cost of conformance = cost of appraisal + cost of prevention
(e)   Cost of non-conformance = cost of prevention + cost of appraisal
(f)   Cost of non-conformance = cost of appraisal + cost of external failure

5   Match the cost to the correct cost category.

Costs

(a)   Administration of quality control
(b)   Product liability costs
(c)   Acceptance testing
(d)   Losses due to lower selling prices for sub-quality goods

Cost categories

- Prevention costs   - Internal failure costs
- Appraisal costs   - External failure costs

6   Proponents of synchronous manufacturing are also supporters of JIT.

True   ☐

False   ☐

7   Choose the correct words from those highlighted.

     Quality control/inspection is aimed at preventing the manufacture of defective items.

8   Which of the following is not a feature of JIT?

     A   Pull system
     C   Employee involvement
     B   Zero inventory
     D   Increased lead times

Answers to Quick Quiz

1 Jobbing industries   – description (3)
   Batch processing   – description (4)
   Mass/flow production   – description (2)
   Cellular manufacturing   – description (1)

2 (a) JIT purchasing
   (b) Close relationships with suppliers
   (c) Uniform loading
   (d) Set-up time reduction
   (e) Machine cells
   (f) Quality
   (g) Pull system (Kanban)
   (h) Preventative maintenance
   (i) Employee involvement

3 False

4 (c) and (d) are correct.

5 (a) Prevention costs
   (b) External failure costs
   (c) Appraisal costs
   (d) Internal failure costs

6 False. They regard JIT as unfocused.

7 Quality control

8 D. JIT features machine cells that help products flow from machine to machine without having to wait for the next stage of processing or returning to store. Lead times and WIP are therefore reduced.

Answers to Questions

1.1 JIT system

The correct answer is B.

Revision of inventory controls levels would not be necessary because the control level system would be abandoned completely. Parts and raw materials would be purchased in small frequent deliveries against bulk contracts. Therefore, statement I is not correct.

II is not correct because the number of suppliers would be reduced in a JIT environment. There may be a long-term commitment to a single supplier.

III is correct. Suppliers may be chosen because of their close proximity so that they can respond quickly to changes in the company's demands.

IV is correct. Accurate forecasting of demand reduces the need for inventories.

V is correct. Production management will aim to eliminate the occurrence of rejects and defective materials, since these situations stop the flow of production.

1.2 Value-added activity

The correct answer is C.

The other activities are non value adding activities.

1.3 JIT

The correct answer is B.

Now try these questions from the Practice Question Bank	Number	Level
	Q1.1 – Q1.5	Practice

ENVIRONMENTAL COSTING

 Environmental issues are becoming increasingly important in the business world. Firms have become responsible for the environmental impacts of their operations and therefore they are now more aware of problems such as carbon emissions.

The growth of environmental legislation and regulations has also affected business operations and reporting.

In Section 1 we look at why environmental costs are important to the management accountant. Then in Section 2 we look at the external environmental impacts of business activity and ways to save energy and costs. Section 3 looks at the different types of internal environmental costs, and Section 4 looks at environmental costing and environmental management systems. Section 5 looks at how activity based costing (ABC) can be adapted for use within environmental costing.

Topic list	Learning outcomes	Syllabus references	Ability required
1 The importance of environmental costs	A3(a)	A3(a)(iv)	Application
2 Environmental footprints	A3(a)	A3(a)	Application
3 Types of cost	A3(a)	A3(a)(i)	Application
4 Environmental cost accounting	A3(a)	A3(a)	Application
5 Environmental costing using activity based costing (ABC)	A3(a)	A3(a)(ii)	Application

Chapter Overview

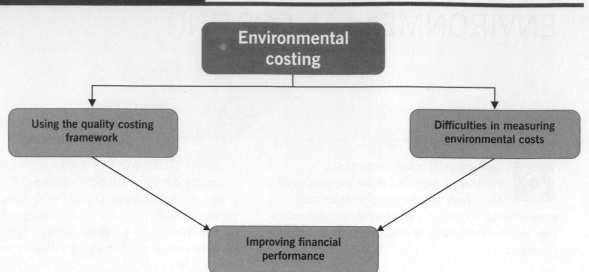

1 The importance of environmental costs

Introduction

Awareness of environmental costs is a relatively recent development. Business activities in general were formerly regarded as problems for the environmental movement, but the two are now increasingly complementary. Environmental costs, like any other costs, need to be considered with regard to planning, control and decision making. The main difference between environmental costs and other costs is that they may be more difficult to identify and to quantify. For example, businesses may suffer a loss of reputation if problems arise.

1.1 Why are environmental costs important to the management accountant?

There are, of course, ethical reasons why environmental costs are important to the management accountant. For example, using energy generates carbon dioxide emissions, and these contribute to climate change and threaten the future of our planet. Management accountants, however, should also consider environmental costs for the following reasons:

(a) Identifying environmental costs associated with individual products, services or processes helps with correct product or service **pricing**. **Correct pricing** helps to **increase profitability**.

(b) Poor environmental behaviour can result in **fines**, increased liability to **environmental taxes** and **damage** to the business's **reputation**.

(c) Recording environmental costs is important, as some may require **regulatory compliance**. Most Western countries now have laws to cover land-use planning, smoke emissions, water pollution and destruction of animals and natural habitats.

(d) Saving energy generally leads to cost savings.

Environmental accounting is a subset of social accounting. Social accounting is a method of reporting whereby a business analyses the impact it has on society and the environment. Environmental accounting involves preparation, presentation and communication of information about a business's interaction with the natural environment. It is a legal requirement in some countries such as Denmark and Australia.

1.2 Significance of environmental effects

Is there a problem and how serious is it?

CASE STUDY

India could be burnt by global warming, by Victor Mallet

Anyone sceptical about the effects of global warming should listen to those who work in the Himalayas. Asia's great mountain range is already affected by climate change and scientists say it will experience yet more dramatic impacts in the future – with possibly grave consequences.

'Throughout our field trips, we've seen that strange things have started to happen', Rajarshi Chakraborty, a biologist working for WWF, the conservation charity, told a literary mountain festival near Mussoorie in northern India late last November.

After enthusing about the discovery of more than 350 species of plants and animals in the eastern Himalayas in the two decades up to 2008, Mr Chakraborty expressed dismay about the retreat of glaciers and surprise that rhododendrons had begun flowering in February instead of April.

He is not alone. Love Raj Singh Dharmshaktu, an Indian mountaineer who has scaled Mount Everest four times, says apple harvests at his home in the highlands of Uttarakhand have been diminished by the decrease in cold weather and snowfall in winter and by extreme weather at other times of the year.

'The temperature has definitely increased. I've seen the glaciers recede very fast', he says. 'The flow of streams and waterfalls has really gone down. A long time ago, people used to fish, but now they [the rivers] are all dried up.'

Indians – because they are so numerous and because climate change is predicted to be particularly drastic in the heavily populated regions of north and central India to the south of the Himalayas – are likely to be among the worst affected victims of global climate change.

According to a report published recently by senior UK and Indian government scientists, temperatures in India will rise sharply within decades, just as the country overtakes China to become the world's most populous nation. Monsoon rains, furthermore, are expected to become more intense and more variable.

The scientists' conclusions show that average temperatures in north India are projected to rise by 2.9–5°C by about 2080 – an extraordinary change in one lifetime – if greenhouse gases continue to be emitted globally in large quantities.

Source: Mallet, V (1 February 2013) *India could be burnt by global warming*. [Online] *Financial Times*. www.FT.com

Section summary

There is increasing awareness about businesses' relationship with the natural environment. Businesses may suffer **significant costs** and a **loss of reputation** if problems arise.

2 Environmental footprints

Introduction

Much business activity takes place at some cost to the environment. This type of cost is sometimes referred to as the environmental footprint. This section looks at these costs and how they can be minimised in the business environment. Reducing the environmental footprint can save business costs and increase profits.

KEY TERM

ENVIRONMENTAL FOOTPRINT is the impact that a business's activities have on the environment, including its resource environment and pollution emissions.

2.1 Key external environmental impacts

At an individual firm or business level, environmental impact can be measured in terms of environmental costs in various areas. Much business activity takes place at some cost to the environment. A 1998 International Federation of Accountants (IFAC) report identified several examples of impacts on the environment:

- Depletion of natural resources
- Noise and aesthetic impacts
- Residual air and water emissions
- Long-term waste disposal (exacerbated by excessive product packaging)
- Uncompensated health effects
- Change in the local quality of life (through, for example, the impact of tourism)

2.2 Carbon

The first world summit on the environment was convened in Stockholm in 1972, at which time world leaders declared the intention of having regular assessments of **global environmental issues**. In 1987, the Intergovernmental Panel on Climate Change was formed by the United Nations Environmental Programme (UNEP) together with the World Meteorological Organisation (WMO).

In 1992, the UN general assembly proposed a treaty, now known as the United Nations Framework Convention on Climate Change (UNFCCC), which was subsequently accepted and signed by more than 150 nations represented at the second summit that was held in 1992 in Rio de Janeiro.

Countries ratifying the convention agreed:

(a)   To develop programmes to slow climate change
(b)   To share technology and co-operate to reduce greenhouse gas emissions
(c)   To develop a greenhouse gas inventory listing national sources and carbon sinks

At the summit, it was also agreed that the responsibility falls on the **developed nations** to lead the fight against **climate change**, as they are largely responsible for the current concentrations of **greenhouse gases (GHG)** in the atmosphere. The original target for emission reductions that was generally accepted in 1992 was that the developed nations should, at a minimum, seek to return to 1990 levels of emissions by the year 2000. Additionally, developed nations should provide financial and technological aid and assistance to the developing nations to produce inventories and work towards more **efficient energy use**.

In December 1997 the countries that met in Rio in 1992 reconvened in Kyoto to develop a set of legally binding agreements on the reduction of greenhouse gas emissions. The objective of the **Kyoto Protocol** is to **reduce greenhouse gas** concentrations in the atmosphere to a level that would prevent dangerous man-made impacts on the climate system.

The Kyoto Protocol was adopted for use in December 1997, and came into force in February 2005. By September 2011, 191 member states had ratified the Protocol, although the US has so far refused to do so. During the period 2008–2012 industrialised countries had to reduce their GHG emissions by on average 5% below their 1990 levels. For EU-15 the reduction target was 8%.

In December 2012, in Doha, Qatar, the 'Doha Amendment to the Kyoto Protocol' was adopted. The commitment period relating to this is 2013 to 2020, and includes a revised list of GHG to be reported on.

2.2.1 The EU gas emissions allowance scheme

As part of their policy towards implementation of the Kyoto Protocol, the EU **set a cap on the total amount of CO_2** emissions to be produced in the EU as a whole. The cap will be reduced annually by 37 million tonnes.

2.2.2 The EU Emissions Trading Scheme

The European Union Emissions Trading Scheme (ETS) commenced on 1 January 2005, creating the world's first multi-country emissions trading system and the largest scheme ever implemented. The EU ETS runs in phases: 2005–2007 (Phase I), 2008–2012 (Phase II, coinciding with the first commitment period of the Kyoto Protocol) and 2013–2020 (Phase III).

The **EU allowance** given to a company **represents their target** or 'cap' for a compliance period. If at the end of the period their total **emissions** during the period are **below their cap** then they have **allowances to sell**; if not, they must **purchase allowances** from companies that have exceeded their emissions reductions targets.

Emissions trading is using a **market-based mechanism** for **environment protection**. The rationale behind emission trading is to ensure that the required **overall emission** reductions take place where the cost of the reduction is lowest, thus lowering the overall costs of combating climate change. It does not impose a particular type of technology or set rigid limitations on how much can be emitted.

This approach also provides an **incentive** for economies to **reduce their greenhouse gas emissions**, because doing so has an **economic benefit** through the **sale of carbon credits** to countries who have failed to reach their targets. (The market for buying and selling carbon credits has become known as the **carbon market**.)

2.3 Energy

Businesses can **reduce** the amount of **energy** they use, which **reduces carbon emissions**, saves money and **increases profits**.

Energy consumption can be reduced in the following ways:

Vehicles	These should be regularly maintained, as inefficiencies increase energy use and therefore increase costs.
Energy bills	Monitoring and understanding energy bills can help businesses to work out how to save costs.
Heating	Increasing the temperature by one degree can increase costs by 8%, so it is important to think twice before increasing the thermostat. Space should be left around radiators to maximise their efficiency and therefore reduce costs. Rooms that are not being used should not be heated. All heating equipment should be maintained to ensure maximum efficiency.
Lighting	Lights should be switched off in rooms and corridors that are not being used. Lighting systems should be maintained to ensure maximum efficiency and therefore reduce costs.
Windows	When heating or air conditioning is on, windows should be kept shut to save energy. Windows should also be kept clean, as this increases the natural daylight reducing the need for lights.
Other equipment	Photocopiers and printers, for example, produce heat. These should not be kept near cooling systems, as more energy will be needed to counteract the heat from the photocopiers. Equipment should be turned off when it is not in use.

2.4 Water usage

Water usage links closely to energy usage because saving water saves energy. Businesses should try to save water wherever they can and this will save costs. Obvious ways of reducing water wastage include fixing dripping taps and dealing quickly with burst water pipes. Other savings can be made depending on the industry of the business, and significant cost savings can be made by commissioning a water audit.

CASE STUDY

A water cost reduction specialist surveyed HM Prison Service Parkhurst on the Isle of Wight. They detected unaccounted water losses, which were found to be leaks and wastage. The leakage detection and repair cost less than £8,000 and the savings amounted to £42,888 per annum.

H2O Building Services: www.h2obuildingservices.co.uk

Section summary

Business activity has an impact on the environment, known as the environmental footprint. Saving energy reduces carbon emissions (and therefore the footprint) and saves costs.

3   Types of cost

Introduction

The IFAC's 1998 report also listed a large number of costs that the business might suffer internally.

3.1 Direct or indirect environmental costs

- Waste management
- Remediation costs or expenses
- Compliance costs
- Environmental certification and labelling
- Environmentally driven research and development
- Legal costs and fines
- Permit fees
- Record keeping and reporting
- Environmental training

3.2 Contingent or intangible environmental costs

- Uncertain future remediation or compensation costs
- Risk posed by future regulatory changes
- Sustainability of raw material inputs
- Product quality
- Employee health and safety
- Public/customer perception

3.3 Environmental cost classification and quality

We discussed the costs of quality in Chapter 1, and they can be applied to environmental costs as well. Hansen and Mendoza (1999) draw attention to the fact that many **environmental costs arise because of poor quality controls**. They suggest that an **environmental cost report** should be **produced regularly** in the **format** of a **cost of quality report** (see Chapter 1, Section 4.2).

Environmental costs can be **classified** in the **same way** as **quality cost** classifications. To aid comparison with future periods, they should also be expressed as a percentage of turnover in the same way that quality costs are.

(a)   Environmental **prevention costs** are the costs required to eliminate environmental impacts before they occur. For example, forming environmental policies, performing site and feasibility studies, staff training.

(b)   Environmental **appraisal costs** are the costs involved with establishing whether activities are complying with environmental standards and policies. For example, developing performance measures, monitoring, testing and inspection costs, site survey costs.

(c)   Environmental **internal failure** costs are the costs of activities that must be undertaken when contaminants and waste have been created by a business but not released into the environment. Examples include maintaining pollution equipment and recycling scrap.

(d)   Environmental **external failure** costs are the costs that arise when a business releases harmful waste into the environment. A business can harm its reputation by doing this. Examples include cleaning up oil spills or decontaminating land.

Exam alert

The classification of environmental costs using the quality costing framework is specifically mentioned on the P1 syllabus. Make sure that you know these four classifications.

Clearly, failing to take sufficient account of environmental effects can have a significant impact on the business's accounts as well as the outside world.

Section summary

A business may suffer direct and indirect environmental costs such as legal costs and fines. It may also suffer contingent or intangible environmental costs such as employee health and safety. Environmental costs can be classified into:

- Environmental prevention costs
- Environmental detection costs
- Environmental internal failure costs
- Environmental external failure costs

4 Environmental cost accounting

Introduction

Businesses need to monitor and manage the impact of environmental issues. This means keeping up to date with emerging environmental issues and changes in industry best practice.

4.1 What is environmental cost accounting?

In CIMA's book *Environmental Cost Accounting: An introduction and practical guide* by Rupert Howe, environmental accounting is defined as the following:

'The generation analysis and use of monetarised environmentally-related information in order to improve corporate environmental and economic performance.'

Rupert Howe suggests that **businesses should pay for external environmental costs** that contribute to environmental problems such as climate change. This would change the prices of goods and services and their profitability. The profits reported in the financial accounts will not be **environmentally sustainable** unless the external environmental costs are included.

According to Rupert Howe, sustainable profits are:

'... profits (or loss) that would remain at the end of an accounting period after provision has been made, or expenditure incurred, to restore or avoid the most significant external environmental impacts resulting from the company's activities and operations.'

4.2 How to estimate sustainable profits

Environmental costing is a relatively new concept but several leading companies are using a consistent methodology.

 Set boundaries. The environmental costs must be controllable in some way, otherwise there is nothing that the business can do to reduce the effects.

 Establish targets. The Royal Commission on Environmental Pollution produced a report in June 2000, which suggested reducing carbon dioxide emissions by 60% by 2050. Marks & Spencer aimed to be 'carbon neutral' by 2012. (It achieved this in its UK and Irish operations.)

 Identify impacts. Every business will be different but many will produce emissions associated with energy used in the office, company cars and distribution.

STEP 4   **Valuation**. This is what the business needs to spend to avoid the impacts of environmental damage or to restore damage done, using real or market prices.

4.2.1 Valuation

Valuation is now becoming slightly easier. For example, energy emissions can be avoided by using electricity generated from **renewable energy sources such as wind or solar power**. The valuation would be any premium that would be payable for switching to renewable sources.

Another way of valuing carbon dioxide emissions is to use the price charged by an emissions **offsetting** company such as Climate Care. Climate Care can reduce the carbon emissions in the air on the business's behalf, thereby offsetting the effect of the carbon emissions.

4.3 Environmental management systems

4.3.1 ISO 14000

ISO 14000 was first published in 1996 and based on earlier quality management standards. It provides a general framework on which a number of specific standards have been based (the ISO family of standards). ISO 14001 prescribes that an environmental management system must comprise:

- An **environmental policy statement**
- An assessment of environmental aspects and legal and voluntary obligations
- A management system
- Internal audits and reports to senior management
- A public declaration that ISO 14001 is being complied with

Critics of ISO 14000 claim that its emphasis on management systems rather than performance is misplaced, and that it does not include rigorous verification and disclosure requirements.

Question 2.1	Environmental cost control systems

Learning outcome A3(a)

How do the main elements of control systems for environmental management systems differ from control systems in other areas?

4.4 Input/output analysis

Input/output analysis operates on the principle that what comes in must go out. Process flow charts can help to trace inputs and outputs, in particular waste. They effectively demonstrate the details of the processes so that the relevant information can be allocated to the main activities.

Input/output analysis may involve some fairly complex modelling, but at a simple level, it measures the input to a production process or system, and the output from the system. Any difference between the amount input and the amount output is 'residual', which is called 'waste'.

Input and output quantities are measured first, and these can then be given a cost.

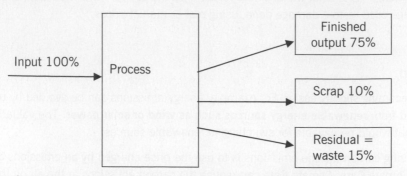

As shown in the diagram above, the input is regarded as 100% and split across the outputs which are **sold and stored goods** and **residual** (regarded as waste).

By accounting for process outputs in this way both in physical quantities and in monetary terms, businesses are forced to focus on environmental costs.

Section summary

Environmental cost accounting initially involves establishing the impacts of business activity on the environment. The impacts must then be valued on the basis of what it would cost to avoid them or to restore any damage. These costs are deducted from the main annual report to obtain an environmentally sustainable profit figure.

5 Environmental costing using activity based costing (ABC)

Introduction

The problem with traditional management accounting systems is that they fail to analyse environmental costs. Costs such as water, energy and waste become hidden within production overheads. One possible solution is to incorporate environmental costing into the activity based system.

5.1 The difficulties in measuring environmental costs

Some businesses do not separate their environmental costs from overheads at all. They do not realise that there may be benefits such as cost reduction and cost control that would be possible if the environmental costs were identified.

In many costing systems, environmental costs are hidden within general overheads and not allocated to specific cost objects. This makes it very difficult to see what activities are causing the costs to occur. There may be environmental costs being allocated to all products but which relate to one product only.

5.2 Cost drivers

Using an activity based system, **environmental costs** become **cost drivers**. To decide on the environmental cost drivers, the production processes involved in making a product or providing a service need to be carefully analysed. The **levels** of environmental **hazards** and **costs** need to be **established**. This may mean installing **tracking systems** to track environmental waste.

5.3 Life cycle costing

Environmental costs should be considered right **from** the **design stage** of a new product right up to the **end of life costs** such as decommissioning and removal. This is particularly important in some countries where businesses are held responsible for costs associated with the end of the life of the product. The consideration of future disposal or remediation costs at the design stage may influence the design of the product itself, saving on future costs.

The consideration of all the costs throughout the product's life is known as the **life cycle costing approach**.

5.3.1 Benefits of the life cycle approach

- Costs become more visible
- Potential future costs (such as disposal costs) may be prevented or reduced before they occur

5.4 Allocation of environmental costs

When allocating environmental costs, it is important to consider the following:

- Volume of emissions or waste
- How toxic the emissions or waste are
- The relative costs of treating different types of emissions

Section summary

Using an activity based system, environmental costs become cost drivers.

Chapter Summary

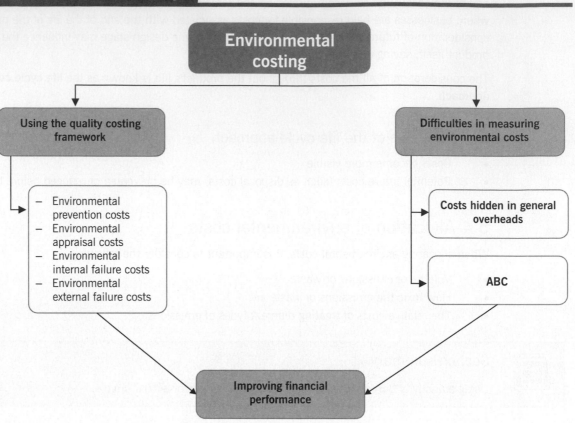

Quick Quiz

1   Fill in the blank.

    .... is the impact that a business's activities have on the environment, including its resource environment and pollution emissions.

2   What are the main elements of an environmental management system per ISO 14001?

3   Which of the following is an example of an environmental external failure cost?

    A   Maintaining pollution equipment
    B   Decontaminating land
    C   Recycling scrap
    D   Record keeping

4   What are the four steps that can be used to estimate sustainable profits?

5   Identify four reasons why environmental costs are important to management accountants.

Answers to Quick Quiz

1   Environmental footprint

2
- An environmental policy
- An assessment of environmental aspects, and legal and voluntary obligations
- A management system
- Internal audits and reports to senior management
- A public declaration that ISO 14001 is being complied with

3   B   Decontaminating land

4   Step 1   Set boundaries
       Step 2   Establish targets
       Step 3   Identify impacts
       Step 4   Valuation

5   (a)   Environmental costing can help to produce more accurate product or service pricing, leading to increased profitability.

       (b)   Poor environmental behaviour can result in fines and damage to reputation.

       (c)   Recording environmental costs is important, as some may require regulatory compliance.

       (d)   Saving energy generally leads to cost savings.

Answers to Questions

2.1 Environmental cost control systems

As we have seen in this section, they do not. Environmental management systems are a good illustration of how control systems work in practice.

Now try the questions from the Practice Question Bank	Number	Level
	Q2.1 – Q2.4	Practice

ABSORPTION COSTING AND ACTIVITY BASED COSTING

 In this chapter and the next one, we look at various costing systems. The main principles underlying absorption costing should be familiar to you from your earlier studies but we will briefly recap. We will then look at a system that has been developed to suit modern practices: **activity based costing**.

Basically, activity based costing (ABC) is the **modern alternative to traditional absorption costing**.

Objective test questions could ask you to **calculate activity based costs**, and we show you how to do this in **Section 4**. Or you could get a **discursive question** on the topic in the integrated case study (ICS), the material for which you will find in the remaining sections of this chapter.

Note that activity based costing is also on the CIMA P2 syllabus.

Topic list	Learning outcomes	Syllabus references	Ability required
1 Cost behaviour patterns and levels of activity	Revision	n/a	Comprehension
2 Determining the fixed and variable elements of semi-variable costs	Revision	n/a	Comprehension
3 The principles of absorption costing	A1(a)	A1(a)(i)	Analysis
4 The reasons for the development of ABC	A1(b)	A1(b)(i)(ii)	Analysis
5 Outline of an ABC system	A1(b)	A1(b)(i)	Analysis
6 Absorption costing versus ABC	A1(b)	A1(b)(i)	Analysis
7 Introducing an ABC system	A1(b)	A1(b)(i)	Analysis
8 Merits and criticisms of ABC	A1(b)	A1(b)(ii)	Analysis

Chapter Overview

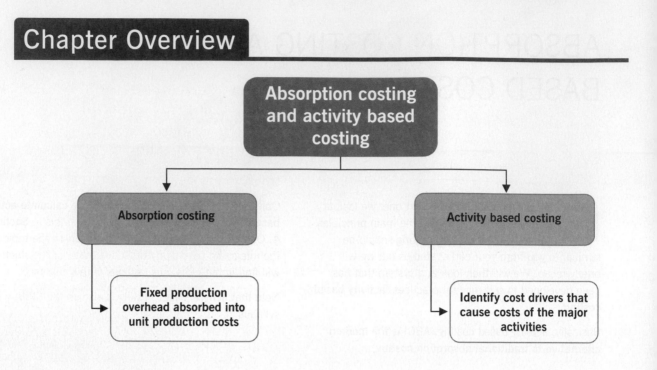

Absorption costing and activity based costing

- Absorption costing
  - Fixed production overhead absorbed into unit production costs

- Activity based costing
  - Identify cost drivers that cause costs of the major activities

Knowledge brought forward from earlier studies

Terminology

- **Absorption costing**. 'Assigns direct costs, **and** all or part of overhead to cost units using one or more overhead absorption rates'.

- The first step in absorption costing is **allocation**. Allocation is the process by which whole cost items are charged direct to a cost unit or cost centre.

- The second step in absorption costing is overhead **apportionment**. This involves apportioning general overheads to cost centres and then reapportioning the costs of service cost centres to production departments.

- The third step in absorption costing is overhead **absorption**. An absorption rate is calculated for each production department.

1 Cost behaviour patterns and levels of activity

Introduction

Cost behaviour describes how costs vary depending on the level of activity undertaken.

1.1 Levels of activity

The level of activity refers to the amount of work done, or the number of events that have occurred. Measures of the level of activity include:

- The volume of production in a period
- The number of items sold
- The value of items sold

- The number of invoices issued
- The number of units of electricity consumed
- The number of purchase orders placed

1.2 Basic principles of cost behaviour and cost behaviour patterns

The basic principle of cost behaviour is that as the level of activity rises, costs will usually rise. The question is to determine, for each item of cost, the relationship between costs and the level of activity.

The level of activity will generally be taken to be the volume of production/output.

1.3 Fixed costs

A **fixed cost** tends to be unaffected by changes in the volume of output. Fixed costs are a **period charge**, relating to a time period; as the period increases, so too will the fixed costs. Examples of fixed costs include the salary of the managing director and factory rent.

1.4 Stepped fixed cost

Consider the depreciation of a machine which may be fixed if production remains below 1,000 units per month. If production exceeds 1,000 units, a second machine may be required, and the cost of depreciation (on two machines) would go up a step. This type of cost is a step cost or a stepped fixed cost.

Examples of step costs may include rent, as accommodation requirements increase with higher output levels, or pay of employees as higher output may require more employees.

1.5 Variable costs

A **variable cost** is a cost which tends to vary directly with the volume of output. The variable cost **per unit** is the same amount for each unit produced whereas **total** variable cost increases as volume of output increases.

Examples of variable costs may be the cost of raw materials (where there is no discount for bulk purchasing since bulk purchase discounts reduce the unit cost of purchases), sales commission or direct labour costs. The latter are usually classed as a variable cost even though basic wages are often fixed.

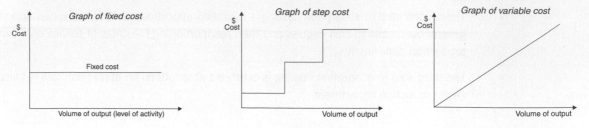

1.6 Non-linear variable costs

Although variable costs are usually assumed to be linear, there are situations where these are **curvilinear**.

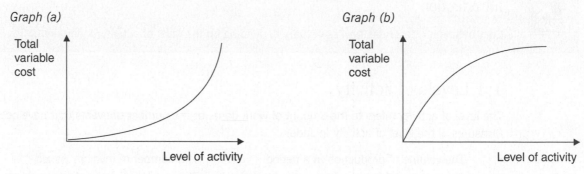

Graph (a) becomes steeper as levels of activity increase. Each additional unit of activity is adding more to total variable cost than the previous unit. Graph (b) becomes less steep as levels of activity increase. Each additional unit is adding less to total variable cost than the previous unit.

1.7 Semi-variable costs (or semi-fixed costs or mixed or hybrid costs)

Semi-variable/semi-fixed/hybrid or **mixed costs** are costs which are part-fixed and part-variable and which are thus partly affected by a change in the level of activity.

Examples of semi-variable costs may be electricity and gas bills, where there is a basic charge plus a charge per unit of consumption. A sales representative's salary is another example where a basic monthly amount is supplemented by commission on the value of sales made.

The behaviour of a semi-variable cost can be presented graphically as follows:

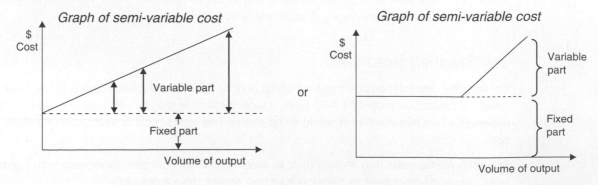

1.8 Cost behaviour and total and unit costs

If the variable cost of producing a unit is $5 per unit then it will remain at that cost per unit no matter how many units are produced. However, if the business's fixed costs are $5,000 then the fixed cost **per unit** will **decrease** the **more** units are **produced**. One unit will have fixed costs of $5,000 per unit, but if 2,500 are produced the fixed cost per unit will be $2. If 5,000 are produced the fixed cost per unit will be only $1. Thus as the level of activity increases the total costs **per unit** (fixed cost plus variable cost) will decrease.

In sketch graph form this may be illustrated as follows:

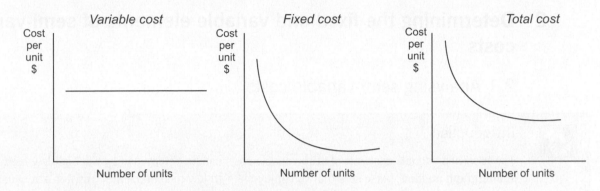

1.9 Assumptions about cost behaviour

It is often possible to assume that, within the normal or relevant range of output, costs are either fixed, variable or semi-variable. Predictions of costs for activity levels which are **outside the relevant range** are unreliable. The other problem is that we usually use data which relates to the past. This may not be representative of what will happen in the future. Managers need to bear this in mind when making decisions.

Question 3.1

Activity levels

Select the correct words in the following sentence:

The basic principle of cost behaviour is that as the level of activity rises, costs will usually (a) **rise/fall/stay the same**. In general, as activity levels rise, the variable cost per unit will (b) **rise/fall/stay the same**, the fixed cost per unit will (c) **rise/fall/stay the same** and the total cost per unit will (d) **rise/fall/stay the same**.

Question 3.2

Cost behaviour graphs

Show, by means of a sketch, a separate graph of cost behaviour patterns for each of the listed items of expense. In each case the vertical axis should relate to total cost. Label each horizontal axis clearly.

(a)   Electricity bill: a standing charge for each period plus a charge for each unit of electricity consumed

(b)   Supervisory labour

(c)   Production bonus, which is payable when output in a period exceeds 10,000 units. The bonus amounts in total to $20,000 plus $50 per unit for additional output above 10,000 units

(d)   Sales commission, which amounts to 2% of sales turnover

(e)   Machine rental costs of a single item of equipment. The rental agreement is that $10 should be paid for every machine hour worked each month, subject to a maximum monthly charge of $480

Section summary

Costs which are not affected by the level of activity are **fixed costs** or **period costs**.

A **step cost** is a cost which is fixed in nature but only within certain levels of activity.

Variable costs increase or decrease with the level of activity.

Semi-variable/semi-fixed or **mixed costs** are costs which are part-fixed and part-variable and which are thus partly affected by a change in the level of activity.

---

2 Determining the fixed and variable elements of semi-variable costs

2.1 Analysing semi-variable costs

Introduction

The fixed and variable elements of semi-variable costs can be determined by the **high-low method** or the **scattergraph method**. Make sure that you study the high-low method carefully as it is a very useful technique.

The high-low method and the scattergraph method only give an estimate, and can therefore give differing results from each other. Although you would not actually be required to draw a scattergraph, you may perhaps be required to answer an objective test question about how the technique works, or its advantages and limitations.

2.2 High-low method

(a)   Records of costs in previous periods are reviewed and the two periods with the **highest** and **lowest** volumes of activity selected.

(b)   The difference between the total cost of these two periods will be the **variable cost** of the difference in activity levels (since the same fixed cost is included in each total cost).

(c)   The variable cost per unit may be calculated from this (difference in total costs ÷ difference in activity levels), and the **fixed cost** may then be determined by substitution.

Example: the high-low method

The costs of operating the maintenance department of a computer manufacturer, Bread and Butter Ltd, for the last four months have been as follows:

Month	Cost $	Production volume Units
1	110,000	7,000
2	115,000	8,000
3	111,000	7,700
4	97,000	6,000

Required

Calculate the costs that should be expected in month 5 when output is expected to be 7,500 units. Ignore inflation.

Solution

(a)

	Units		$
High output	8,000	total cost	115,000
Low output	6,000	total cost	97,000
Variable cost of	2,000		18,000

Variable cost per unit $18,000/2,000 = $9

(b)   Substituting in either the high or low volume cost:

	High		Low
	$		$
Total cost	115,000		97,000
Variable costs (8,000 × $9)	72,000	(6,000 × $9)	54,000
Fixed costs	43,000		43,000

(c)   Estimated maintenance costs when output is 7,500 units:

	$
Fixed costs	43,000
Variable costs (7,500 × $9)	67,500
Total costs	110,500

Question 3.3	High-low method

The valuation department of a large firm of surveyors wishes to develop a method of predicting its total costs in a period. The following past costs have been recorded at two activity levels.

	Number of valuations (V)	Total cost (TC)
Period 1	420	82,200
Period 2	515	90,275

Formulate the total cost model for a period.

2.3 Scattergraph method

A scattergraph of costs in previous periods can be prepared (with cost on the vertical axis and volume of output on the horizontal axis). A **line of best fit**, which is a line drawn **by judgement** to pass through the middle of the points, thereby having as many points above the line as below it, can then be drawn and the fixed and variable costs determined.

A scattergraph of the cost and volume data in the example in Paragraph 2.2 is shown below.

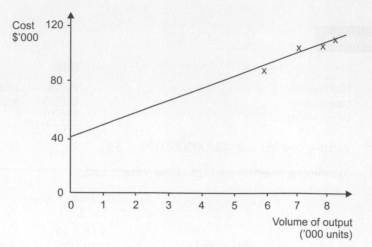

The point where the line cuts the vertical axis (approximately $40,000) is the fixed cost (the cost if there is no output). If we take the value of one of the plotted points which lies close to the line and deduct the fixed cost from the total cost, we can calculate the variable cost per unit.

Total cost for 8,000 units = $115,000
Variable cost for 8,000 units = $(115,000 – 40,000) = $75,000
Variable cost per unit = $75,000/8,000 = $9.375

Section summary

The high-low method or the scattergraph method can be used to determine the fixed and variable elements of semi-variable costs.

---

3 The principles of absorption costing

Introduction

With absorption costing, fixed production costs are absorbed into product unit costs using a predetermined overhead absorption rate, based on the normal level of production for the period.

If the actual production is different from the normal level, or actual expenditure on fixed production costs is different from that budgeted, there may be an under or over absorption of fixed production costs for the period. This amount is written off against the absorption costing profit for the period.

The principles of absorption costing are as follows:

(a)   Fixed production costs are an integral part of the production cost of an item and so should be absorbed into product costs.

(b)   Inventories are valued at their full production cost including absorbed fixed production costs.

Remember that total cost = production costs (direct and indirect costs) + non-production costs (for example, selling and distribution costs). When we use absorption costing to determine the cost per unit, we focus on the production costs only.

The first step in absorption costing is allocation. Allocation is the process by which whole cost items are charged direct to a cost unit or cost centre.

The second step is overhead apportionment. This involves apportioning general overheads to cost centres and then reapportioning the costs of service cost centres to production departments.

Having allocated and/or apportioned all overheads, the next stage in absorption costing is to add them to, or absorb them into, the cost of production.

Exam alert

Over/under absorption could easily be the subject of an objective test question. Make sure you haven't forgotten how to calculate this, as it's easy marks.

Over/under absorption = (budgeted overhead rate per unit × actual units) – actual overhead incurred

Example: absorption costing

Water and Sons makes a product, the Splash, which has a variable production cost of $6 per unit and a sales price of $10 per unit. At the beginning of September 20X0, there were no opening inventories, and production during the month was 20,000 units. Fixed costs for the month were $30,000 for production and $15,000 for administration, sales and distribution. There were no variable marketing costs.

Assume that the normal level of activity is 15,000 Splashes per month and that budgeted fixed production costs were $30,000 for the month.

Required

Prepare profit statements for September, using absorption costing, if sales were as follows:

(a)   10,000 Splashes
(b)   15,000 Splashes
(c)   20,000 Splashes

Solution

The fixed production cost per unit, based on the normal level of activity, is $30,000/15,000 = $2 per unit.

The full production cost per unit = $6 + $2 = $8 per unit.

With production of 20,000 Splashes, the fixed overhead will be over-absorbed.

	$
Fixed production costs absorbed (20,000 units × $2)	40,000
Fixed production costs incurred	30,000
Over-absorbed fixed production cost	10,000

	10,000 Splashes		15,000 Splashes		20,000 Splashes	
	$	$	$	$	$	$
Sales		100,000		150,000		200,000
Opening inventory	0		0		0	
Full production costs	160,000		160,000		160,000	
	160,000		160,000		160,000	
Less closing inventory (at full production cost)	80,000		40,000		0	
Full production of sales	80,000		120,000		160,000	
Adjustment for over-absorbed overhead	10,000		10,000		10,000	
Full production costs		70,000		110,000		150,000
Gross profit		30,000		40,000		50,000
Administration, sales and distribution costs		15,000		15,000		15,000
Net profit		15,000		25,000		35,000

Section summary

With absorption costing, fixed production costs are absorbed into product unit costs using a predetermined overhead absorption rate, based on the normal level of production for the period. Inventories are valued at their full production cost including absorbed fixed production costs.

4 The reasons for the development of ABC

Introduction

The traditional cost accumulation system of **absorption costing** was developed in a time when most organisations produced only a **narrow range of products** and when **overhead costs were only a very small fraction of total costs**. Direct labour and direct material costs accounted for the largest proportion of the costs. Errors made in attributing overheads to products were not too significant.

Nowadays, however, with the advent of **advanced manufacturing technology (AMT)**, **overheads** are likely to be far **more important** and in fact direct labour may account for as little as five per cent of a product's cost. It therefore now appears difficult to justify the use of direct labour or direct material as the basis for absorbing overheads or to believe that errors made in attributing overheads will not be significant.

Many resources are used in **non volume related support activities** (which have increased due to AMT) such as setting up, production scheduling, inspection and data processing. These support activities assist the efficient manufacture of a wide range of products (necessary if businesses are to compete effectively) and are **not, in general, affected by changes in production volume**. They tend to **vary in the long term according to the range and complexity** of the products manufactured rather than the volume of output.

The wider the range and the more complex the products, the more support services will be required. Consider, for example, factory X which produces 10,000 units of one product, the Alpha, and factory Y which produces 1,000 units each of 10 slightly different versions of the Alpha. Support activity costs in factory Y are likely to be a lot higher than in factory X but the factories produce an identical number of units. For example, factory X will only need to set up once, whereas factory Y will have to set up the production run at least ten times for the ten different products. Factory Y will therefore incur more set-up costs for the same volume of production.

Section summary

Traditional costing systems, which assume that all products consume all resources in proportion to their production volumes, tend to **allocate too great a proportion of overheads to high volume products** (which cause relatively little diversity and hence use fewer support services) and **too small a proportion of overheads to low volume products** (which cause greater diversity and therefore use more support services). **Activity based costing (ABC) attempts to overcome this problem**.

5 Outline of an ABC system

Introduction

The **major ideas** behind activity based costing are as follows:

(a) **Activities cause costs**. Activities include ordering, materials handling, machining, assembly, production scheduling and despatching.

(b) Producing products creates demand for the activities.

(c) Costs are assigned to a product on the basis of the product's consumption of the activities.

5.1 The definition of ABC

KEY TERM

ACTIVITY BASED COSTING (ABC) is an 'Approach to the costing and monitoring of activities which involves tracing resource consumption and costing final outputs. Resources are assigned to activities and activities to cost objects based on consumption estimates. The latter utilise cost drivers to attach activity costs to outputs'.   (*CIMA Official Terminology*)

5.2 The operation of an ABC system

An ABC system operates as follows:

Identify an organisation's major activities.

STEP 2

Identify the **factors that determine the size of the costs of an activity/cause the costs of an activity**. These are known as **cost drivers**.

KEY TERM

A COST DRIVER is a 'Factor influencing the level of cost. Often used in the context of ABC to denote the factor which links activity resource consumption to product outputs, for example the number of purchase orders would be a cost driver for procurement cost'.   (*CIMA Official Terminology*)

There are three types of cost driver:

(a) Transaction drivers. When the cost of an activity is affected by the number of times a specific exercise is undertaken. For example, number of set-ups, where each set-up takes the same time and resource amount.

(b) Duration drivers. When the cost of an activity is affected by the length of time it takes to perform the action. For example, set-up hours.

(c) Intensity (also called direct charging) drivers. Used when the duration driver doesn't provide accurate results. Instead, there is a charge each time an activity is performed. For example, if different products have more complicated set-ups, then the cost of the more complicated set-up is charged directly to the product.

Look at the following examples:

Costs	Possible cost driver
Ordering costs	Number of orders
Materials handling costs	Number of production runs
Production scheduling costs	Number of production runs
Despatching costs	Number of despatches

For those **costs that vary with production levels in the short term**, ABC uses **volume-related cost drivers** such as labour or machine hours. The cost of oil used as a lubricant on the machines would therefore be added to products on the basis of the number of machine hours, since oil would have to be used for each hour the machine ran.

 Collect the costs associated with each cost driver into what are known as cost pools.

 A COST POOL is 'Grouping of costs relating to a particular activity in an activity-based costing system'.

KEY TERM

(*CIMA Official Terminology*)

STEP 4 Charge the costs of each cost pool to products on the basis of their usage of the activity (measured by the number of the activity's cost drivers a product generates) using a cost driver rate (total costs in cost pool/number of cost drivers).

Question 3.4
Cost drivers

Learning outcome A1(b)

Which of the following definitions best describes a cost driver?

A　　Any activity that causes an increase in costs
B　　A collection of costs associated with a particular activity
C　　A cost that varies with production levels
D　　Any factor that causes a change in the cost of an activity

---

5.3 Transactions analysis

When using ABC, for costs that vary with production levels in the short term, the cost driver will be volume related (labour or machine hours). Overheads that vary with some other activity (and not volume of production) should be traced to products using transaction-based cost drivers such as production runs or number of orders received. One way of classifying these transactions is **logistical, balancing, quality** and **change**.

ABC recognises that factors other than volume can explain the level of overhead. Miller and Vollman ('The Hidden Factory', *Harvard Business Review*, 1985) provided a useful system for analysing the different types of transactions that cause overheads to be incurred.

Types of transaction	Detail
Logistical transactions	Those activities concerned with organising the flow of resources throughout the manufacturing process.
Balancing transactions	Those activities that ensure that demand for and supply of resources are matched.
Quality transactions	Those activities that relate to ensuring that production is at the required level of quality.
Change transactions	Those activities associated with ensuring that customers' requirements (delivery date, changed design and so on) are met.

Note that the primary driver of these transactions is not usually production volume. For example, the level of change transactions might be determined by the number of customers and the number of different product types, rather than by production volume.

Such an analysis provides a better understanding of long-term cost behaviour and allows for the costs associated with particular transactions to be assigned to only those products causing the transactions.

Section summary

An alternative to the traditional method of accounting for costs – absorption costing – is **activity based costing (ABC)**. ABC involves the identification of the factors (**cost drivers**) that cause the costs of an organisation's major activities. Support overheads are charged to products on the basis of their usage of an activity.

Transactions that cause overheads to be incurred can be classified as logical, balancing, quality and change transactions.

6 Absorption costing versus ABC

Introduction

Although ABC has obvious merits, a number of criticisms have been raised.

The following example illustrates the point that traditional cost accounting techniques result in a misleading and inequitable division of costs between low-volume and high-volume products, and that ABC can provide a more meaningful allocation of costs.

Example: activity based costing

Suppose that Cooplan manufactures four products, W, X, Y and Z. Output and cost data for the period just ended are as follows.

	Output units	Number of production runs in the period	Material cost per unit $	Direct labour hours per unit	Machine hours per unit
W	10	2	20	1	1
X	10	2	80	3	3
Y	100	5	20	1	1
Z	100	5	80	3	3
		14			

Direct labour cost per hour $5

	$
Overhead costs	
Short run variable costs	3,080
Set-up costs	10,920
Expediting and scheduling costs	9,100
Materials handling costs	7,700
	30,800

Required

Prepare unit costs for each product using conventional costing and ABC.

Solution

Using a **conventional absorption costing approach** and an absorption rate for overheads based on either direct labour hours or machine hours, the product costs would be as follows:

	W $	X $	Y $	Z $	Total $
Direct material	200	800	2,000	8,000	
Direct labour	50	150	500	1,500	
Overheads*	700	2,100	7,000	21,000	
	950	3,050	9,500	30,500	44,000
Units produced	10	10	100	100	
Cost per unit	$95	$305	$95	$305	

*$30,800 ÷ 440 hours = $70 per direct labour or machine hour.

Using **activity based costing** and assuming that the number of production runs is the cost driver for set-up costs, expediting and scheduling costs and materials handling costs and that machine hours are the cost driver for short-run variable costs, unit costs would be as follows:

	W $	X $	Y $	Z $	Total $
Direct material	200	800	2,000	8,000	
Direct labour	50	150	500	1,500	
Short-run variable overheads (W1)	70	210	700	2,100	
Set-up costs (W2)	1,560	1,560	3,900	3,900	
Expediting, scheduling costs (W3)	1,300	1,300	3,250	3,250	
Materials handling costs (W4)	1,100	1,100	2,750	2,750	
	4,280	5,120	13,100	21,500	44,000
Units produced	10	10	100	100	
Cost per unit	$428	$512	$131	$215	

Workings

1	$3,080 ÷ 440 machine hours =	$7 per machine hour
2	$10,920 ÷ 14 production runs =	$780 per run
3	$9,100 ÷ 14 production runs =	$650 per run
4	$7,700 ÷ 14 production runs =	$550 per run

Summary

Product	Conventional costing unit cost $	ABC unit cost $	Difference per unit $	Difference in total $
W	95	428	+333	+3,330
X	305	512	+207	+2,070
Y	95	131	+36	+3,600
Z	305	215	−90	−9,000

The figures suggest that the **traditional volume-based absorption costing system is flawed**.

(a)   It under-allocates overhead costs to low-volume products (here, W and X) and over-allocates overheads to higher-volume products (here, Z in particular).

(b)   It under-allocates overhead costs to smaller-sized products (here, W and Y with just one hour of work needed per unit) and over-allocates overheads to larger products (here, X and particularly Z).

6.1 ABC versus traditional costing methods

Both traditional absorption costing and ABC systems adopt the two-stage allocation process.

6.1.1 Allocation of overheads

ABC establishes **separate cost pools for support activities** such as despatching. As the costs of these activities are assigned directly to products through cost driver rates, **reapportionment of service department costs is avoided**.

6.1.2 Absorption of overheads

The principal difference between the two systems is the way in which overheads are absorbed into products.

(a) **Absorption costing** most commonly uses two **absorption bases** (labour hours and/or machine hours) to charge overheads to products.

(b) **ABC** uses **many cost drivers** as absorption bases (number of orders, number of despatches and so on).

Absorption rates under **ABC** should therefore be **more closely linked to the causes of overhead costs**.

6.2 Cost drivers

The **principal idea** of ABC is to **focus attention on what causes costs to increase**, ie the **cost drivers**.

(a) Those **costs that do vary with production volume**, such as power costs, should be traced to products using production **volume-related cost drivers** as appropriate, such as direct labour hours or direct machine hours. Such costs tend to be **short-term variable overheads** such as power costs.

Overheads that do not **vary** with output but **with some other activity** should be traced to products using **transaction-based cost drivers**, such as number of production runs and number of orders received. Such costs tend to be **long-term variable overheads** (overheads that traditional accounting would classify as fixed).

(b) Traditional costing systems allow overheads to be related to products in rather more arbitrary ways producing, it is claimed, less accurate product costs.

Question 3.5	ABC versus traditional costing

Learning outcome A1(b)

A company manufactures two products, L and M, using the same equipment and similar processes. An extract of the production data for these products in one period is shown below.

	L	*M*
Quantity produced (units)	5,000	7,000
Direct labour hours per unit	1	2
Machine hours per unit	3	1
Set-ups in the period	10	40
Orders handled in the period	15	60

	$
Overhead costs	
Relating to machine activity	220,000
Relating to production run set-ups	20,000
Relating to handling of orders	45,000
	285,000

Required

Calculate the production overheads to be absorbed by one unit of each of the products using the following costing methods:

(a) A traditional absorption costing approach using a direct labour hour rate to absorb overheads
(b) An activity based costing approach, using suitable cost drivers to trace overheads to products

Section summary

Although ABC has obvious merits, a number of criticisms have been raised.

7 Introducing an ABC system

7.1 When should ABC be introduced?

Introduction

ABC should only be introduced if the **additional information** it provides will **result in action that will increase** the organisation's overall **profitability**. This is most likely to **occur** in situations such as the following, when the **ABC analysis differs significantly from the traditional absorption costing analysis**.

- Production overheads are high in relation to direct costs, especially direct labour.
- Overhead resource consumption is not just driven by production volume.
- There is wide variety in the product range.
- The overhead resource input varies significantly across the product range.

7.2 Analysis of activities

ABC attempts to **relate the incidence of costs to the level of activities undertaken**. A **hierarchy of activities** has been suggested.

KEY TERM

The HIERARCHY OF ACTIVITIES is a 'Classification of activities by level of organisation, for example unit, batch, product sustaining and facility sustaining'.　　　　　*(CIMA Official Terminology)*

Type of activities	Costs are dependent on ...	Examples
Unit/product level	Volume of production	Machine power
Batch level	Number of batches	Set-up costs
Product sustaining	Existence of a product group/line	Product management
Facility sustaining	Organisation simply being in business	Rent and rates

KEY TERMS

CIMA Official Terminology provides definitions for two of these classifications.

PRODUCT-SUSTAINING ACTIVITIES are 'Activities undertaken to develop or sustain a product (or service). Product sustaining costs are linked to the number of products or services not to the number of units produced'.

FACILITY-SUSTAINING ACTIVITIES are 'Activities undertaken to support the organisation as a whole, and which cannot be logically linked to individual units of output'.

The difference between a unit product cost determined using traditional absorption costing and one determined using ABC will depend on the proportion of overhead cost that falls into each of the categories above.

(a)   If most overheads are related to unit level and facility level activities, the costs will be similar.

(b)   If the overheads tend to be associated with batch or product level activities, they will be significantly different.

Consider the following example.

Example: batch-level activities

XYZ produces a number of products including product D and product E, and produces 500 units of each of products D and E every period at a rate of 10 of each every hour. The overhead cost is $500,000 and a total of 40,000 direct labour hours are worked on all products. A traditional overhead absorption rate would be $12.50 per direct labour hour and the overhead cost per product would be $1.25.

Production of D requires 5 production runs per period, while production of E requires 20. An investigation has revealed that the overhead costs relate mainly to 'batch-level' activities associated with setting up machinery and handling materials for production runs.

There are 1,000 production runs per period and so overheads could be attributed to XYZ's products at a rate of $500 per run.

•   Overhead cost per D = ($500 × 5 runs)/500 = $5
•   Overhead cost per E = ($500 × 20 runs)/500 = $20

These overhead costs are activity based and recognise that overhead costs are incurred due to batch level activities. The fact that E has to be made in frequent small batches, perhaps because it is perishable, means that it uses more resources than D. This is recognised by the ABC overhead costs, not the traditional absorption costing overhead costs.

KEY POINT

As we noted in Chapter 1, in the **modern manufacturing environment**, production often takes place in short, discontinuous production runs and a high proportion of product costs are incurred at the design stage. An increasing proportion of **overhead costs** are therefore **incurred at batch or product level**.

Such an analysis of costs gives management an **indication of the decision level at which costs can be influenced**. For example, a decision to reduce production costs will not simply depend on making a general reduction in output volumes: production may need to be organised to reduce **batch** volumes; a **process** may need to be modified or eliminated; **product lines** may need to be merged or cut out; **facility** capacity may need to be altered.

7.3 ABC in service and retail organisations

ABC was **first introduced in manufacturing organisations** but it can equally well be used in **other types of organisation**. For example, the management of the Post Office in the US uses ABC. They analysed the activities associated with cash processing as follows:

Activities	Examples	Possible cost driver
Unit level	Accept cash	Number of transactions
	Processing of cash by bank	Number of transactions
Batch level	'Close out' and supervisor review of clerk	Number of 'close outs'
	Deposits	Number of deposits
	Review and transfer of funds	Number of accounts

LEARNING MEDIA

Activities	Examples	Possible cost driver
Product level	Maintenance charges for bank accounts	Number of accounts
	Reconciling bank accounts	Number of accounts

Question 3.6

ABC and retail organisations

Learning outcome A1(b)

List five activities that might be identified in a retail organisation and state one possible cost driver for each of the activities you have identified.

Section summary

ABC should only be introduced if the additional information it provides will result in action that will increase the organisation's overall profitability.

ABC identifies four levels of activities: product level, batch level, product sustaining level and facility sustaining level.

8 Merits and criticisms of ABC

Introduction

ABC has a range of uses and has many advantages over more traditional costing methods. However, the system does have its critics and it is not used as a panacea for all costing problems.

8.1 Merits of ABC

As you will have discovered when you attempted the question above, there is nothing difficult about ABC. Once the necessary information has been obtained, it is similar to traditional absorption costing. This simplicity is part of its appeal. Further merits of ABC are as follows:

(a) The **complexity of manufacturing has increased**, with wider product ranges, shorter product life cycles and more complex production processes. **ABC recognises this complexity with its multiple cost drivers**.

(b) In a more competitive environment, companies must be able to assess product profitability realistically. **ABC facilitates a good understanding of what drives overhead costs**.

(c) In modern manufacturing systems, overhead functions include a lot of non factory floor activities such as product design, quality control, production planning and customer services. **ABC is concerned with all overhead costs** and so it takes management accounting beyond its 'traditional' factory floor boundaries.

(d) By controlling the incidence of the cost driver, the level of the **cost** can be **controlled**.

(e) The costs of activities not included in the costs of the products an organisation makes or the services it provides can be considered to be **not contributing to the value of the product/service**. The following questions can then be asked:

   (i)   What is the purpose of this activity?
   (ii) How does the organisation benefit from this activity?
   (iii) Could the number of staff involved in the activity be reduced?

(f)   ABC can help with **cost management**. For example, suppose there is a fall in the number of orders placed by a purchasing department. This fall would not impact on the amount of overhead absorbed in a traditional absorption costing system as the cost of ordering would be part of the general overhead absorption rate (assuming no direct link between the overhead absorption basis of, say, direct labour hours, and the number of orders placed). The reduction in the workload of the purchasing department might therefore go unnoticed and the same level of resources would continue to be provided, despite the drop in number of orders. In an ABC system, however, this drop would be immediately apparent because the cost driver rate would be applied to fewer orders.

(g)   Many costs are driven by customers (delivery costs, discounts, after-sales service and so on), but traditional absorption costing systems do not account for this. Organisations may be trading with certain customers at a loss but may not realise it because costs are not analysed in a way that reveals the true situation. ABC can be **used in conjunction with customer profitability analysis (CPA)** to determine more accurately the profit earned by servicing particular customers.

KEY TERM

CUSTOMER PROFITABILITY ANALYSIS (CPA) is 'Analysis of the revenue streams and service costs associated with specific customers or customer groups'.   *(CIMA Official Terminology)*

(h)   Many **service businesses** have characteristics similar to those required for the successful application of ABC:

    (i)   A highly **competitive** market

    (ii)   **Diversity** of products, processes and customers

    (iii)   **Significant overhead costs** not easily assigned to individual 'products'

    (iv)   Demands placed on overhead resources by individual 'products' and customers, which are not proportional to volume

If ABC were to be used in a hotel, for example, attempts could be made to identify the activities required to support each guest by category and the cost drivers of these activities. The cost of a one-night stay midweek by a businessman could then be distinguished from the cost of a one-night stay by a teenager at the weekend. Such information could prove invaluable for **CPA**.

8.2 Criticisms of ABC

It has been suggested by critics that **activity based costing has some serious flaws**.

(a)   Some measure of (arbitrary) cost apportionment may still be required at the cost pooling stage for items like rent, rates and building depreciation.

(b)   Can a single cost driver explain the cost behaviour of all items in its associated pool?

(c)   On the other hand, the number of cost pools and cost drivers cannot be excessive, otherwise an ABC system would be too complex and too expensive.

(d)   Unless costs are caused by an activity that is measurable in quantitative terms and which can be related to production output, cost drivers will not be usable. What drives the cost of the annual external audit, for example?

(e)   ABC is sometimes introduced because it is fashionable, not because it will be used by management to provide meaningful product costs or extra information. If management is not going to use ABC information, an absorption costing system may be simpler to operate.

(f)   The costs of ABC may outweigh the benefits.

8.3 Other uses of ABC

The information provided by analysing activities can support the management functions of planning, control and decision making, provided it is used carefully and with full appreciation of its implications.

8.3.1 Planning

Before an ABC system can be implemented, management must analyse the organisation's activities, determine the extent of their occurrence and establish the relationships between activities, products/services and their cost.

The **information database** produced from such an exercise can then be **used as a basis for forward planning and budgeting**. For example, once an organisation has set its budgeted production level, the database can be used to determine the number of times that activities will need to be carried out, thereby establishing necessary departmental staffing and machine levels. Financial budgets can then be drawn up by multiplying the budgeted activity levels by cost per activity.

This activity based approach may not produce the final budget figures but it can **provide the basis for different possible planning scenarios**.

8.3.2 Control

The information database also provides an **insight into the way in which costs are structured and incurred in service and support departments**. Traditionally, it has been difficult to control the costs of such departments because of the lack of relationship between departmental output levels and departmental cost. With ABC, however, it is possible to **control or manage the costs by managing the activities that underlie them** by monitoring a number of key performance measures.

8.3.3 Decision making

Many of ABC's supporters claim that it can assist with decision making in a number of ways:

- Provides accurate and reliable cost information
- Establishes a long-run product cost
- Provides data that can be used to evaluate different ways of delivering business

It is therefore particularly suited to the following types of decision:

- Pricing
- Promoting or discontinuing products or parts of the business
- Redesigning products and developing new products or new ways to do business

Note, however, that an ABC cost is **not a true cost**; it is **simply a long-run average cost** because some costs such as depreciation are still arbitrarily allocated to products. An ABC cost is therefore **not a relevant cost** for all decisions. For example, even if a **product/service ceases** altogether, **some costs** allocated to that product/service using an activity based approach (such as building occupancy costs or depreciation) would **not disappear** just because the product/service had disappeared. Management would need to bear this in mind when making product deletion decisions.

8.4 Activity based management (ABM)

Although the terms are sometimes used interchangeably, ABM is a broader concept than ABC, being likely to incorporate ABC and activity based budgeting (ABB), which will be covered in a later chapter.

KEY TERMS

ACTIVITY BASED MANAGEMENT (ABM)

OPTIMAL ABM. 'Actions, based on activity driver analysis, that increase efficiency, lower costs and/or improve asset utilisation.'

STRATEGIC ABM. 'Actions, based on activity based cost analysis, that claim to change the demand for activities so as to improve profitability.'   (*CIMA Official Terminology*)

Section summary

ABC has a range of uses and has many advantages over more traditional costing methods. However, the system does have its critics and it is not used as a panacea for all costing problems.

Chapter Summary

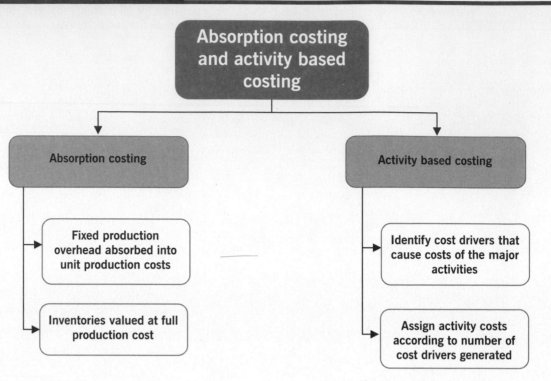

Quick Quiz

1   The costs of operating the canteen at 'Eat a lot Company' for the past three months are as follows.

Month	Cost $	Employees
1	72,500	1,250
2	75,000	1,300
3	68,750	1,175

Variable cost (per employee per month) = *50*

Fixed cost per month = *10,000*

2   Choose the correct words from those highlighted.

Traditional costing systems tend to allocate **too great/too small** a proportion of overheads to high volume products and **too great/too small** a proportion of overheads to low volume products.

3   Fill in the blanks.

The major ideas behind ABC are as follows:

(a)   Activities cause .... *costs*
(b)   Producing products creates demand for the .... *activities*
(c)   Costs are assigned to a product on the basis of the product's consumption of the .... *activity*

4   Match the most appropriate cost driver to each cost.

Costs		Cost driver	
(a)	Set-up costs	Number of machine hours	*b)*
(b)	Short-run variable costs	Number of production runs	*a)*
(c)	Materials handling and despatch	Number of orders executed	*c)*

5   ABC recognises the complexity of modern manufacturing by the use of multiple cost pools.

True   [•]

False   [ ]

6   The use of direct labour hours or direct machine hours to trace costs to products occurs with the use of absorption costing but not with the use of ABC.

True   [ ]

False   [•]

7   ABC is not a system that is suitable for use by service organisations.

True   [ ]

False   [•]

8   Activity based management is a system of management that uses activity based cost information to achieve which three of the following?

• Improve asset utilisation
• Reduce costs
Customer profitability analysis
• Simplify pricing decisions

Answers to Quick Quiz

1. Variable cost = $50 per employee per month

    Fixed costs = $10,000 per month

	Activity No employees	Cost $
High	1,300	75,000
Low	1,175	68,750
	125	6,250

    Variable cost per employee = $6,250/125 = $50

    For 1,175 employees, total cost = $68,750

    Total cost   = variable cost + fixed cost
    $68,750   = (1,175 × $50) + fixed cost

    ∴ Fixed cost   = $68,750 − $58,750
    = $10,000

2. Too great
    Too small

3. (a) Costs
    (b) Activities
    (c) Activities

4. (a) Number of production runs
    (b) Number of machine hours
    (c) Number of orders executed

5. False. Complexity is recognised by the use of multiple cost drivers.

6. False. The use of volume-related cost drivers should be used for costs that do vary with production volume.

7. False. It is highly suitable.

8. ABM is used to achieve customer profitability analysis, improve asset utilisation and reduce costs. Pricing decisions are not aims of an ABC system.

Answers to Questions

3.1 Activity levels

(a) Rise
(b) Stay the same
(c) Fall
(d) Fall

3.2 Cost behaviour graphs

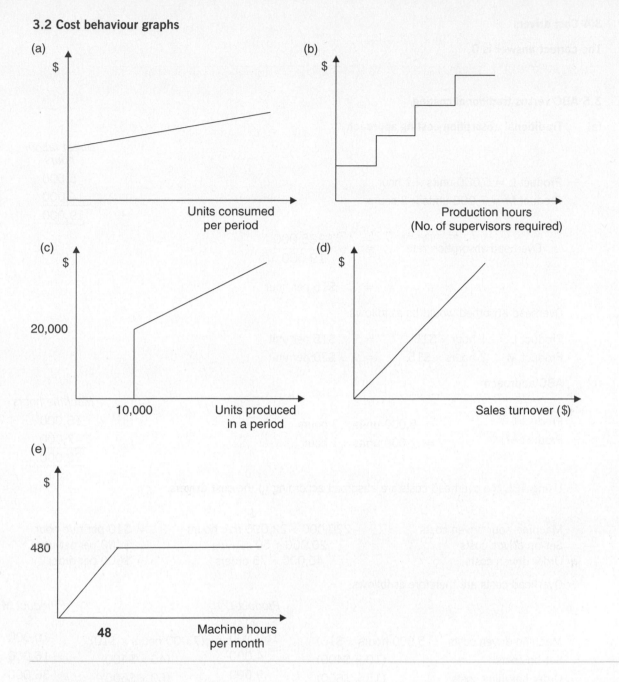

(a)

$

Units consumed
per period

(b)

$

Production hours
(No. of supervisors required)

(c)

$

20,000

10,000   Units produced
in a period

(d)

$

Sales turnover ($)

(e)

$

480

48   Machine hours
per month

3.3 High-low method

Although we only have two activity levels in this question we can still apply the high-low method.

	Valuations (V)	Total cost $
Period 2	515	90,275
Period 1	420	82,200
Change due to variable cost	95	8,075

∴ Variable cost per valuation = $8,075/95 = $85.

Period 2: fixed cost = $90,275 – (515 × $85) = $46,500

The variable cost of $85 per valuation must be added to the fixed cost.

Therefore Total Costs (TC) = Fixed costs + Variable costs = $46,500 + $85V

3.4 Cost drivers

The correct answer is D.

3.5 ABC versus traditional costing

(a)   **Traditional absorption costing approach**

		Direct labour hours
Product L = 5,000 units × 1 hour		5,000
Product M = 7,000 units × 2 hours		14,000
		19,000

$$\therefore \text{ Overhead absorption rate} \quad = \quad \frac{\$285,000}{19,000}$$

$$= \quad \$15 \text{ per hour}$$

Overhead absorbed would be as follows:

Product L	1 hour × $15	=	$15 per unit
Product M	2 hours × $15	=	$30 per unit

(b)   **ABC approach**

		Machine hours
Product L	= 5,000 units × 3 hours	15,000
Product M	= 7,000 units × 1 hour	7,000
		22,000

Using ABC the overhead costs are absorbed according to the **cost drivers**.

	$	
Machine-hour driven costs	220,000 ÷ 22,000 m/c hours	= $10 per m/c hour
Set-up driven costs	20,000 ÷ 50 set-ups	= $400 per set-up
Order driven costs	45,000 ÷ 75 orders	= $600 per order

Overhead costs are therefore as follows:

		Product L $		Product M $
Machine-driven costs	(15,000 hours × $10)	150,000	(7,000 hours × $10)	70,000
Set-up costs	(10 × $400)	4,000	(40 × $400)	16,000
Order handling costs	(15 × $600)	9,000	(60 × $600)	36,000
		163,000		122,000
Units produced		5,000		7,000
Overhead cost per unit		$32.60		$17.43

These figures suggest that product M absorbs an unrealistic amount of overhead using a direct labour hour basis. Overhead absorption should be based on the activities that drive the costs, in this case machine hours, the number of production run set-ups and the number of orders handled for each product.

3.6 ABC and retail organisations

Activities	Possible cost driver
Procure goods	Number of orders
Receive goods	Number of orders or pallets
Store goods	Volume of goods
Pick goods	Number of packs
Handle returnables/recyclables	Volume of goods

Now try these questions from the Practice Question Bank

Number	Level
Q3.1 – Q3.5	Practice

MARGINAL COSTING AND THROUGHPUT ACCOUNTING

 You should already be able to apply a system of **marginal costing** and understand how it differs from **absorption costing**.

Whereas absorption costing recognises fixed costs (usually fixed production costs) as part of the cost of a unit of output and hence as **product costs**, marginal costing treats all fixed costs as **period costs**.

The emphasis in your *Performance Operations* syllabus is on comparisons between systems. You need to be able to compare absorption costing and marginal costing methods and their effect on reported profit and inventory valuation, and on their application in different learning environments. You also need to be able to compare ABC (from the previous chapter) with marginal and absorption costing methods. Cost-based approaches to pricing are covered in **Sections 5 and 6**.

We also look at throughput accounting.

The theory of constraints (TOC) provides the basis for the development of throughput accounting (TA) (Sections 7 and 8). As a production system (TOC) and an accounting and performance monitoring system (TA), they are ideally suited to the modern manufacturing environment in which production is an immediate response to customer demand. The aim is to maximise the net return on sales. They can also be used in service industries where bottleneck processes can be identified and alleviated.

Topic list	Learning outcomes	Syllabus references	Ability required
1 The principles of marginal costing	A1(a)	A1(a)(i)	Analysis
2 The effect of marginal costing and absorption costing on reported profit and inventory valuation	A1(a)	A1(a)(i)	Analysis
3 Marginal costing and absorption costing compared	A1(a)	A1(a)(i)	Analysis
4 Marginal costing versus ABC	A1(b)	A1(b)(i)	Analysis
5 Full cost-plus pricing	C1(c)	C1(c)(i)	Analysis
6 Marginal cost-plus (mark-up) pricing	C1(c)	C1(c)(i)	Analysis
7 The theory of constraints (TOC)	A1(a)	A1(a)(i)	Analysis
8 Throughput accounting	A1(a)	A1(a)(i)	Analysis

Chapter Overview

```
                    ┌─────────────────────┐
                    │   Marginal and      │
                    │ throughput costing  │
                    └─────────────────────┘
                       │                │
            ┌──────────┘                └──────────┐
            ▼                                       ▼
    ┌───────────────┐                      ┌─────────────────────┐
    │Marginal costing│                      │Throughput accounting│
    └───────────────┘                      └─────────────────────┘
            │                                       │
            ▼                                       ▼
    ┌───────────────┐                      ┌─────────────────────┐
    │Highlights      │                     │Theory of constraints│
    │contribution    │                     └─────────────────────┘
    │= sales value   │
    │less variable   │
    │costs           │
    └───────────────┘
            │
            ▼
    ┌───────────────┐
    │Impact on       │
    │pricing         │
    └───────────────┘
```

Knowledge brought forward from earlier studies

Terminology

- **Marginal cost** is 'Part of the cost of one unit of product or service that would be avoided if the unit were not produced, or that would increase if one extra unit were produced'.

- **Contribution** is 'Sales value less variable cost of sales'.   (*CIMA Official Terminology*)

- **Marginal costing** is an alternative method of costing to absorption costing. In marginal costing, only variable costs are charged as a cost of sale and a contribution is calculated which is sales revenue minus the variable cost of sales. Closing inventories of work in progress or finished goods are valued at marginal (variable) production cost. Fixed costs are treated as a period cost, and are charged in full to the statement of profit or loss in the accounting period in which they are incurred.

1 The principles of marginal costing

Introduction

The marginal costing philosophy is that profit measurement should be based on an analysis of total contribution; that is, sales value less the variable cost of sales.

Supporters of marginal costing argue that the valuation of closing inventories should be at variable production cost (direct materials, direct labour, direct expenses (if any) and variable production overhead) because these are the only costs properly attributable to the product.

The principles of marginal costing (also known as variable costing) are as follows:

(a)   Period fixed costs are the same for any volume of sales and production (provided that the level of activity is within the 'relevant range'). Therefore, by selling an extra item of product or service the following will happen:

    (i)   Revenue will increase by the sales value of the item sold
    (ii)   Costs will increase by the variable cost per unit
    (iii)   Profit will increase by the amount of contribution earned from the extra item

(b)   Similarly, if the volume of sales falls by one item, the profit will fall by the amount of contribution earned from the item.

(c)   Since fixed costs relate to a period of time, and do not change with increases or decreases in sales volume, it is misleading to charge units of sale with a share of fixed costs. Absorption costing is therefore misleading, and it is more appropriate to deduct fixed costs from total contribution for the period to derive a profit figure.

(d)   When a unit of product is made, the extra costs incurred in its manufacture are the **variable production costs**. Fixed costs are unaffected, and no extra fixed costs are incurred when output is increased.

Before reviewing marginal costing principles any further, it will be helpful to remind yourself of the basics by looking at a numerical example.

Example: marginal costing

Water and Sons makes a product, the Splash, which has a variable production cost of $6 per unit and a sales price of $10 per unit. At the beginning of September 20X0, there were no opening inventories and production during the month was 20,000 units. Fixed costs for the month were $30,000 for production and $15,000 for administration, sales and distribution. There were no variable marketing costs.

Required

Calculate the contribution and profit for September, using marginal costing principles, if sales were as follows:

(a)   10,000 Splashes
(b)   15,000 Splashes
(c)   20,000 Splashes

Solution

The first stage in the profit calculation must be to identify the variable costs, and then the contribution. Fixed costs are deducted from the total contribution to derive the profit. All closing inventories are valued at marginal production cost ($6 per unit). Production during the month in all 3 cases is 20,000 units.

	10,000 Splashes		15,000 Splashes		20,000 Splashes	
	$	$	$	$	$	$
Sales (at $10)		100,000		150,000		200,000
Opening inventory	0		0		0	
Variable production cost	120,000		120,000		120,000	
	120,000		120,000		120,000	
Less value of closing inventory (at marginal cost)	60,000		30,000		0	
Variable cost of sales		60,000		90,000		120,000
Contribution		40,000		60,000		80,000
Less fixed costs		45,000		45,000		45,000
Profit/(loss)		(5,000)		15,000		35,000
Profit/(loss) per unit		(0.50)		1		1.75
Contribution per unit		4		4		4

The conclusions that may be drawn from this example are as follows:

(a)   The **profit per unit varies** at differing levels of sales, because the average fixed overhead cost per unit changes with the volume of output and sales.

(b)   The **contribution per unit is constant** at all levels of output and sales. Total contribution, which is the contribution per unit multiplied by the number of units sold, increases in direct proportion to the volume of sales.

(c)   Since the **contribution per unit does not change**, the most effective way of calculating the expected profit at any level of output and sales would be as follows:

(i)   Calculate the total contribution
(ii)   Deduct fixed costs as a period charge in order to find the profit

(d)   In our example, the expected profit from the sale of 17,000 Splashes would be as follows:

	$
Total contribution (17,000 × $4)	68,000
Less fixed costs	45,000
Profit	23,000

Section summary

The marginal costing philosophy is that profit measurement should be based on an analysis of total contribution; that is, sales value less the variable cost of sales.

2 The effect of marginal costing and absorption costing on reported profit and inventory valuation

Introduction

Note that if there are changes in inventories during a period, marginal and absorption costing will report different profit figures.

The results of the last example can be compared with the results for absorption costing that we calculated in the previous chapter.

	Sales volume (Splashes)		
	10,000	15,000	20,000
Marginal costing profit/(loss)	$(5,000)	$15,000	$35,000
Absorption costing profit	$15,000	$25,000	$35,000
Increase in inventory units	10,000	5,000	0

In this example, the inventory levels increased with the two lower sales volume figures and the reported **profit figure** was **higher with absorption costing** than with marginal costing.

This is because some of the fixed production **overhead** incurred during the period will be **carried forward in closing inventory** (which reduces cost of sales) to be set against sales revenue in the following period instead of being written off in full against profit in the period concerned.

If inventory levels decrease, absorption costing will report the lower profit.

This is because as well as the fixed overhead incurred, fixed production overhead that had been brought forward in opening inventory is released and is included in cost of sales.

In our example, the two reported profit figures were the same when sales volume was 20,000 Splashes, ie when production and sales volumes were equal and there was no change in inventory.

It is important to appreciate that the **differences** in reported **profits** occur only in the **short run**, ie in reporting the profit of individual accounting periods.

This is because in the long run, total costs will be the same by either method of accounting. Short-term differences are the result of changes in the level of inventory.

2.1 Calculating the difference in reported profit

The difference in the profit reported by the two systems therefore results from the fixed production overhead that is carried forward in inventory in an absorption costing system.

In our example, the profit figures can be reconciled as follows:

		Sales volume (Splashes)		
		10,000		15,000
		$		$
Marginal costing profit/(loss)		(5,000)		15,000
Increase in inventory units @ $2 per unit	(10,000 × $2)	20,000	(5,000 × $2)	10,000
Absorption costing profit		15,000		25,000

In both cases, the absorption costing profit was higher because the inventory level increased and fixed production overhead was carried forward to next month in the absorption costing valuation.

Exam alert

The calculation of the difference between reported profits and inventory valuation in the two costing systems is a subject that lends itself well to objective testing questions. The integrated case study (ICS) could ask for an explanation of the difference between absorption costing profit and marginal costing profit.

Question 4.1	Marginal versus absorption costing – effect on profit

Learning outcome A1(a)

The overhead absorption rate for product X is $10 per machine hour. Each unit of product X requires five machine hours. Opening inventory of product X on 1 January 20X9 was 150 units and closing inventory on 31 December 20X9 was 100 units. What is the difference in profit between results reported using absorption costing and results reported using marginal costing?

A   The absorption costing profit would be $2,500 less.
B   The absorption costing profit would be $2,500 greater.
C   The absorption costing profit would be $5,000 less.
D   The absorption costing profit would be $5,000 greater.

Section summary

If there are changes in inventories during a period, marginal costing and absorption costing systems will report different profit figures.

If inventory levels increase, absorption costing will report a higher profit than marginal costing.

If inventory levels decrease, absorption costing will report the lower profit.

If the opening and closing inventory volumes and values are the same, marginal costing and absorption costing will report the same profit figure.

In the long run, the total reported profit will be the same whether marginal or absorption costing is used.

The difference in reported profit is equal to the change in inventory volume multiplied by the fixed production overhead rate per unit.

3 Marginal costing and absorption costing compared

Introduction

There are arguments in favour of each costing method.

3.1 Arguments in favour of absorption costing

(a)   Fixed production costs are incurred in order to make output. It is therefore **'fair'** to charge all output with a **share** of these costs.

(b)   Closing inventory values include a share of fixed production overhead, and therefore **follow** the **requirements** of the international accounting standard on **inventory valuation (IAS 2)**.

(c)   Absorption costing is consistent with the **accruals concept** as a proportion of the costs of production are carried forward to be matched against future sales.

(d)   A problem with calculating the contribution of various products made by an enterprise is that it may **not be clear** whether the **contribution earned** by each product is **enough to cover fixed costs**, whereas by charging fixed overhead to a product it is possible to ascertain whether it is profitable or not. This is particularly important where fixed production overheads are a large proportion of total production costs. Not absorbing production would mean that a large portion of expenditure is not accounted for in unit costs.

3.2 Arguments in favour of marginal costing

(a)   It is **simple** to operate.

(b)   There are **no apportionments**, which are frequently done on an arbitrary basis, of fixed costs. Many costs, such as the marketing director's salary, are indivisible by nature.

(c)   Fixed costs will be the **same regardless of the volume of output**, because they are period costs. It makes sense, therefore, to charge them in full as a cost to the period.

(d)   The cost to produce an extra unit is the variable production cost. It is **realistic** to **value closing inventory** items at this directly attributable cost.

(e)   **Under or over absorption** of overheads is **avoided**.

(f)   Marginal costing provides the **best information for decision making**.

(g)   Fixed costs (such as depreciation, rent and salaries) relate to a period of time and should be charged against the **revenues of the period** in which they are incurred.

(h)   **Absorption costing** may **encourage over-production** since reported profits can be increased by increasing inventory levels.

Exam alert

Make sure you are completely happy with the pros and cons and calculations for each method.

Example: absorption costing encouraging over-production

To demonstrate the last argument in favour of marginal costing, consider an organisation that produces a product that sells for $60 per unit.

Variable production costs are $35 per unit and the fixed production costs of $30,000 per period are absorbed on the basis of the normal capacity of 5,000 units per period.

Fixed administration, selling and distribution overheads are $19,000 per period. There was no opening inventory for the latest period.

Required

Calculate the profit reported for sales of 5,000 units last period for production volumes of 5,000 units, 6,000 units and 7,000 units, using:

(a)   Absorption costing
(b)   Marginal costing

Solution

Absorption costing

Fixed production cost per unit = $30,000/5,000 = $6 per unit

Full production cost per unit = $35 + $6 = $41 per unit

	Production					
	5,000 units		6,000 units		7,000 units	
	$'000	$'000	$'000	$'000	$'000	$'000
Sales (5,000 units × $60)		300		300		300
Production cost @ $41 per unit	205		246		287	
Less closing inventory	–		41		82	
	205		205		205	
Less over-absorbed fixed production cost	–		6		12	
Total production cost of sales		205		199		193
Gross profit		95		101		107
Administration costs		19		19		19
Net profit		76		82		88

Marginal costing

	Production					
	5,000 units		6,000 units		7,000 units	
	$'000	$'000	$'000	$'000	$'000	$'000
Sales		300		300		300
Variable cost of production @ $35/unit	175		210		245	
Less closing inventory	–		35		70	
Variable production cost of sales		175		175		175
Contribution		125		125		125
Fixed production costs		30		30		30
Administration costs		19		19		19
Net profit		76		76		76

This example demonstrates an important point when considering the impact on profit reporting of marginal and absorption costing methods.

For a given level of sales, marginal costing will report the same level of profit whatever the level of production. In contrast, absorption costing will report higher levels of profit for the same level of sales, if production levels are higher.

Question 4.2   Shortcomings of absorption costing

Learning outcome A1(a)

A criticism of the use of absorption costing for the internal reporting of profit is that, if a manager's reward is based on the profit for the period, the manager will be encouraged to increase production even if the resulting output cannot be sold. Explain why absorption costing can have this effect.

3.3 Marginal costing – concluding remarks

In spite of the arguments in favour of marginal costing as a decision-making tool, **absorption costing** is **widely used** for general accounting purposes and inventory valuation. Fixed production costs should ultimately be charged to cost units in a fair and meaningful way. A central **problem** in cost accounting is to identify the **best method** of attributing these costs.

Section summary

For a given level of sales, marginal costing will report the same level of profit whatever the level of production. In contrast, absorption costing will report higher levels of profit for the same level of sales, if production levels are higher.

4 Marginal costing versus ABC

Introduction

Some commentators argue that only marginal costing provides suitable information for decision making but this is not true. Marginal costing provides a crude method of differentiating between different types of cost behaviour by splitting costs into their variable and fixed elements. However, such an analysis can be used only for **short-term decisions** and usually even these have longer-term implications that ought to be considered.

The problem with marginal costing is that it analyses cost behaviour patterns according to the volume of production. However, although certain costs may be fixed in relation to the volume of production, they **may in fact be variable in relation to some other cost driver**. A failure to allocate such costs to individual products could result in incorrect decisions concerning the future management of the products.

The advantage of ABC is that **it spreads costs across products according to a number of different bases**. For example, an ABC analysis may show that one particular activity that is carried out primarily for one or two products is expensive. A correct allocation of the costs of this activity may reveal that these particular products are not profitable. If these costs are fixed in relation to the volume of production, then they would be treated as **period costs** in a marginal costing system and **written off against the marginal costing contribution for the period**.

The marginal costing system would therefore make no attempt to allocate these 'fixed' costs to individual products and a false impression would be given of the long-run average cost of the products.

Thus, marginal costing may provide incorrect decision-making information, **particularly in a situation where 'fixed' costs are vary large compared with 'variable' costs**.

Exam skills

Note that the syllabus specifically mentions ABC compared with traditional methods and its relative advantages and disadvantages. Make sure that you understand the differences between the costing methods and the pros and cons.

Section summary

The main criticism of marginal costing decision-making information is that marginal costing **analyses cost behaviour patterns according to the volume of production**. However, although certain costs may be fixed in relation to the volume of production, they may in fact be **variable in relation to some other cost driver**.

5 Full cost-plus pricing

Introduction

In the next two sections we focus on cost-based approaches to pricing. In this section we concentrate on full cost-plus pricing which adds a percentage onto the full cost of the product to arrive at the selling price.

KEY TERM

FULL COST-PLUS PRICING is a method of determining the sales price by calculating the full cost of the product and adding a percentage mark-up for profit.

BPP
LEARNING MEDIA

5.1 Setting full cost-plus prices

The 'full cost' may be a fully absorbed production cost only, or it may include some absorbed administration, selling and distribution overhead.

A business might have an idea of the percentage profit margin it would like to earn, and so might **decide on an average profit mark-up** as a general guideline for pricing decisions. This would be particularly **useful for** businesses that carry out a large amount of **contract work or jobbing work**, for which individual job or contract prices must be quoted regularly to prospective customers. However, the percentage profit **mark-up does not have to be rigid and fixed**, but can be varied to suit the circumstances. In particular, the percentage mark-up can be varied to suit demand conditions in the market.

Question 4.3	Cost-plus pricing

Learning outcome A1(a)

A product's full cost is $4.75 and it is sold at full cost plus 70%. A competitor has just launched a similar product selling for $7.99.

Required

Fill in the gap in the sentence below.

The cost-plus percentage will need to be reduced by...... %.

Example: Full cost-plus pricing

Markup has begun to produce a new product, product X, for which the following cost estimates have been made.

	$
Direct materials	27
Direct labour: 4 hours at $5 per hour	20
Variable production overheads: machining, ½ hr at $6 per hour	3
	50

Production fixed overheads are budgeted at $300,000 per month and, because of the shortage of available machining capacity, the company will be restricted to 10,000 hours of machine time per month. The absorption rate will be a direct labour rate, however, and budgeted direct labour hours are 25,000 per month. It is estimated that the company could obtain a minimum contribution of $10 per machine hour on producing items other than product X.

The direct cost estimates are not certain as to material usage rates and direct labour productivity, and it is recognised that the estimates of direct materials and direct labour costs may be subject to an error of ± 15%. Machine time estimates are similarly subject to an error of ± 10%.

The company wishes to make a profit of 20% on full production cost from product X.

Required

Ascertain the full cost-plus based price.

Solution

Even for a relatively 'simple' cost-plus pricing estimate, some problems can arise, and certain assumptions must be made and stated. In this example, we can identify two problems:

(a)   Should the opportunity cost of machine time be included in cost or not?
(b)   What allowance, if any, should be made for the possible errors in cost estimates?

Different assumptions could be made.

(a) **Exclude machine time opportunity costs: ignore possible costing errors**

	$
Direct materials	27.00
Direct labour (4 hours)	20.00
Variable production overheads	3.00
	48.00
Fixed production overheads (at $\frac{\$300,000}{25,000}$ = $12 per direct labour hour)	
Full production cost	98.00
Profit mark-up (20%)	19.60
Selling price per unit of product X	117.60

(b) **Include machine time opportunity costs: ignore possible costing errors**

	$
Full production cost as in (a)	98.00
Opportunity cost of machine time: contribution forgone (½ hr × $10)	5.00
Adjusted full cost	103.00
Profit mark-up (20%)	20.60
Selling price per unit of product X	123.60

(c) **Exclude machine time opportunity costs but make full allowance for possible underestimates of cost**

	$	$
Direct materials	27.00	
Direct labour	20.00	
	47.00	
Possible error (15%)	7.05	
		54.05
Variable production overheads	3.00	
Possible error (10%)	0.30	
		3.30
Fixed production overheads (4 hours × $12)	48.00	
Possible error (labour time) (15%)	7.20	
		55.20
Potential full production cost		112.55
Profit mark-up (20%)		22.51
Selling price per unit of product X		135.06

(d) **Include machine time opportunity costs and make a full allowance for possible underestimates of cost**

	$
Potential full production cost as in (c)	112.55
Opportunity cost of machine time:	
potential contribution forgone (½ hour × $10 × 110%)	5.50
Adjusted potential full cost	118.05
Profit mark-up (20%)	23.61
Selling price per unit of product X	141.66

Using different assumptions, we could arrive at any of four different unit prices in the range $117.60 to $141.66.

5.2 Problems with and advantages of full cost-plus pricing

There are several serious **problems** with relying on a full cost approach to pricing.

(a) It **fails to recognise** that since demand may be determining price, **there will be a profit-maximising combination of price and demand**.

(b) There may be a need to **adjust prices to market and demand conditions**.

(c)   **Budgeted output volume** needs to be established. Output volume is a key factor in the overhead absorption rate.

(d)   A **suitable basis for overhead absorption** must be selected, especially where a business produces more than one product.

However, it is a **quick, simple and cheap** method of pricing which can be delegated to junior managers (which is particularly important with jobbing work where many prices must be decided and quoted each day) and, since the size of the profit margin can be varied, a decision based on a price in excess of full cost should ensure that a company working at normal capacity will **cover all of its fixed costs and make a profit**.

Section summary

In **full cost-plus pricing** the sales price is determined by calculating the full cost of the product and then adding a percentage mark-up for profit. The most important criticism of full cost-plus pricing is that it fails to recognise that since sales demand may be determined by the sales price, there will be a profit-maximising combination of price and demand.

6 Marginal cost-plus (mark-up) pricing

Introduction

This section follows on from Section 5 by looking at marginal cost-plus pricing. Whereas a full cost-plus approach to pricing draws attention to net profit and the net profit margin, a marginal (variable) cost-plus approach to pricing **draws attention to gross profit** and the **gross profit margin**, or **contribution**.

KEY TERM

MARGINAL COST-PLUS PRICING/MARK-UP PRICING is a method of determining the sales price by adding a profit margin onto either marginal cost of production or marginal cost of sales.

Question 4.4	Marginal cost pricing

Learning outcome A1(a)

A product has the following costs:

	$
Direct materials	5
Direct labour	3
Variable overheads	7

Fixed overheads are $10,000 per month. Budgeted sales per month are 400 units to allow the product to break even.

Required

Fill in the blank in the sentence below.

The mark-up which needs to be added to **marginal** cost to allow the product to break even is ...... %.

6.1 The advantages and disadvantages of a marginal cost-plus approach to pricing

The main advantages are as follows:

(a)   It is a **simple and easy** method to use.

(b)   The **mark-up percentage can be varied**, and so mark-up pricing can be adjusted to reflect demand conditions.

(c)   It **draws management attention to contribution**, and the effects of higher or lower sales volumes on profit. In this way, it helps to create a better awareness of the concepts and implications of marginal costing and cost-volume-profit analysis. For example, if a product costs $10 per unit and a mark-up of 150% is added to reach a price of $25 per unit, management should be clearly aware that every additional $1 of sales revenue would add 60 pence to contribution and profit.

(d)   In practice, mark-up pricing is used in businesses **where there is a readily identifiable basic variable cost**. Retail industries are the most obvious example, and it is quite common for the prices of goods in shops to be fixed by adding a mark-up (20% or 33.3%, say) to the purchase cost.

There are, of course, drawbacks to marginal cost-plus pricing.

(a)   Although the **size** of the mark-up can be varied in accordance with demand conditions, it **does not ensure that sufficient attention is paid to demand conditions, competitors' prices and profit maximisation**.

(b)   It **ignores fixed overheads** in the pricing decision, but the sales price must be sufficiently high to ensure that a profit is made after covering fixed costs.

Section summary

Marginal cost-plus pricing involves adding a profit margin to the marginal cost of production/sales. A marginal costing approach is more likely to help with identifying a profit-maximising price.

7 The theory of constraints (TOC)

Introduction

Theory of constraints is a set of concepts developed in the US that aim to identify the binding constraints in a production system and that strive for evenness of production flow so that the organisation works as effectively as possible. No inventories should be held, except prior to the binding constraint.

The key financial concept of TOC is to **turn materials into sales as quickly as possible**, thereby maximising throughput and the net cash generated from sales. This is to be achieved by striving for **balance in production processes**, and so **evenness of production flow** is an important aim.

KEY TERMS

THEORY OF CONSTRAINTS (TOC) is a 'Procedure based on identifying bottlenecks (constraints), maximising their use, subordinating other facilities to the demand of the bottleneck facilities, alleviating bottlenecks and re-evaluating the whole system'.

A CONSTRAINT (or BOTTLENECK RESOURCE) is an 'Activity, resource or policy that limits the ability to achieve an objective'.

(CIMA Official Terminology)

7.1 Managing constraints

One process will inevitably act as a bottleneck (or limiting factor) and constraint throughput. This is known as a **binding constraint** in TOC terminology.

In order to manage constraints effectively, **Goldratt** has proposed a **five-step process** of ongoing improvement. The process is operated as a **continuous loop**.

 Identify the **binding constraint**/bottleneck.

 Exploit

The highest possible output must be achieved from the binding constraint. This output must never be delayed and as such a buffer inventory should be held immediately before the constraint.

 Subordinate

Operations prior to the binding constraint should operate at the same speed as it, so that work in progress (WIP) does not build up.

 Elevate the system bottleneck. Steps should be taken to increase resources or improve its efficiency.

Return to Step 1

The removal of one bottleneck will create another elsewhere in the system.

KEY TERMS

THROUGHPUT CONTRIBUTION = **sales revenue – direct material cost**

CONVERSION COST (in TOC) = **all operating costs except direct material cost** (ie all costs except totally variable costs)

INVESTMENT COST = **inventory, equipment, building costs and so on**

7.2 Throughput contribution

The aim of TOC is to maximise throughput contribution while keeping conversion and investment costs to a minimum. If a strategy for increasing throughput contribution is being considered, it will therefore only be accepted if conversion and investment costs increase by a lower amount than contribution.

KEY POINT

It is important to realise that TOC is not an accounting system but a production system.

Section summary

Theory of constraints is a set of concepts developed in the US that aim to identify the binding constraints in a production system and that strive for evenness of production flow so that the organisation works as effectively as possible. No inventories should be held, except prior to the binding constraint.

Goldratt's five steps for dealing with a bottleneck activity are:

Step 1: Identify   Step 4: Elevate
Step 2: Exploit   Step 5: Return to Step 1
Step 3: Subordinate

8 Throughput accounting

Introduction

Throughput accounting is the accounting system developed in the UK, based on the theory of constraints and just-in-time (JIT) systems. It measures the throughput contribution per factory hour. It is very similar to marginal costing but can be used to make longer-term decisions about production equipment/capacity.

The concept of throughput accounting has been developed from TOC as an **alternative system of cost and management accounting in a JIT environment**.

KEY TERM

'THROUGHPUT ACCOUNTING (TA) is an approach to accounting which is largely in sympathy with the JIT philosophy. In essence, TA assumes that a manager has a given set of resources available. These comprise existing buildings, capital equipment and labour force. Using these resources, purchased materials and parts must be processed to generate sales revenue. Given this scenario the most appropriate financial objective to set for doing this is the maximisation of throughput (Goldratt and Cox, 1984) which is defined as: sales revenue **less** direct material cost.'

(Tanaka, Yoshikawa, Innes and Mitchell, *Contemporary Cost Management*)

The *CIMA Official Terminology*'s definition of THROUGHPUT ACCOUNTING (TA) is 'Variable cost accounting presentation based on the definition of throughput (sales minus material and component costs)'.

TA is different from all other management accounting systems because of what it **emphasises**:

- First, **throughput**
- Secondly, inventory minimisation
- Thirdly, cost control

TA is based on three concepts.

8.1 Concept 1

In the short run, most costs in the factory (with the exception of materials costs) are fixed. Because TA differentiates between fixed and variable costs, it is often compared with marginal costing and **some people argue that there is no difference between marginal costing and throughput accounting**. For this reason, TA is sometimes referred to as super variable costing and indeed there are some similarities in the assumptions underlying the two methods. However, on marginal costing, direct labour costs are usually assumed to be variable costs. Years ago this assumption was true, but employees are not usually paid piece rate today and they are not laid off for part of the year when there is no work, and so labour cost is not truly variable. If this is accepted, the two techniques are identical in some respects, but **marginal costing is generally thought of as being purely a short-term decision-making technique** while **TA, or at least TOC, was conceived with the aim of changing manufacturing strategy to achieve evenness of flow. It is therefore much more than a short-term decision technique.**

Because **TA combines all conversion costs** together and does not attempt to examine them in detail, it is particularly **suited to use with activity based costing (ABC)**, which examines the behaviour of these costs and assumes them to be variable in the long run. ABC was examined in detail in the previous chapter.

8.2 Concept 2

In a JIT environment, all inventory is a 'bad thing' and the **ideal inventory level is zero**. Products should not be made unless there is a customer waiting for them. This means **unavoidable idle capacity must be accepted in some operations**, but not for the operation that is the bottleneck of the moment. There is one exception to the zero inventory policy, being that a buffer inventory should be held prior to the bottleneck process.

8.3 Concept 3

Profitability is determined by the rate at which 'money comes in at the door' (that is, sales are made) and, in a JIT environment, this depends on how quickly goods can be produced to satisfy customer orders. Since the goal of a profit-orientated organisation is to make money, inventory must be sold for that goal to be achieved.

The buffer inventory and any other work in progress or finished goods inventory should be **valued at material cost only** until the output is eventually sold, so that **no value will be added and no profit earned until the sale takes place**. Producing output just to add to work in progress or finished goods inventory creates no profit, and so should not be encouraged.

| Question 4.5 | Throughput accounting vs conventional cost accounting |

Learning outcome A1(a)

Throughput accounting versus conventional cost accounting

How are the concepts of throughput accounting a direct contrast to the fundamental principles of conventional cost accounting?

Exam skills

Be prepared for a question asking you to compare and contrast marginal and throughput accounting.

8.4 Bottleneck resources

The aim of **modern manufacturing** approaches is to match production resources with the demand for them. This implies that there are **no constraints, termed bottleneck resources** in TA, within an organisation. The throughput philosophy entails the **identification** and **elimination** of these bottleneck resources. Where they **cannot be eliminated, production must be limited to the capacity of the bottleneck resource in order to avoid the build-up of work in progress**. If a rearrangement of existing resources or buying-in resources does not alleviate the bottleneck, investment in new equipment may be necessary. However, the **elimination of one bottleneck is likely to lead to the creation of another** at a previously satisfactory location. The **management of bottlenecks** therefore becomes a **primary concern** of the manager seeking to increase throughput.

(a) There is nothing to be gained by measuring and encouraging the efficiency of machines that do not govern the overall flow of work.

(b) Likewise, there is little point in measuring the efficiency of production staff working on non-bottleneck processes.

(c) Bonuses paid to encourage faster working on non-bottleneck processes are wasted and could lead to increased storage costs and more faulty goods.

Other factors that might limit throughput other than a lack of production resources (bottlenecks)

(a) The existence of a non-competitive selling price

(b) The need to deliver on time to particular customers, which may disrupt normal production flow

(c) The lack of product quality and reliability, which may cause large amounts of rework or an unnecessary increase in production volume

(d) Unreliable material suppliers, which will lead to poor-quality products that require rework

8.5 Identifying the bottleneck resource

It may not always be obvious which is the bottleneck resource, and a process of trial and error for a few periods can be an expensive and inefficient way of attempting to identify it.

If the resource constraint is machine capacity, it is possible to identify the constrained machine through the calculation of **machine utilisation rates**.

Example: machine utilisation rates

A company produces three products using three different machines. The following data is available for the latest period.

	Product L Hours per unit	Product M Hours per unit	Product N Hours per unit
Machine hours required:			
Mixing machine	2	5	3
Cutting machine	3	4	2
Finishing machine	1	2	2
Sales demand	2,700 units	1,200 units	2,500 units

Maximum capacity is as follows:

	Hours available
Mixing machine	22,000
Cutting machine	15,400
Finishing machine	7,300

Required

(a) Calculate the machine utilisation rate for each machine.
(b) Identify which of the machines is the bottleneck resource.

Solution

(a) Number of machine hours required to fulfil sales demand

	Product L Hours	Product M Hours	Product N Hours	Total Hours
Mixing machine	5,400	6,000	7,500	18,900
Cutting machine	8,100	4,800	5,000	17,000
Finishing machine	2,700	2,400	5,000	10,100

$$\text{Machine utilisation rate} = \frac{\text{machine hours required to meet sales demand}}{\text{machine hours available}}$$

	Mixing machine	Cutting machine	Finishing machine
Machine utilisation rate	$\dfrac{18,900}{22,000}$	$\dfrac{17,900}{15,400}$	$\dfrac{10,100}{7,300}$
	= 85.9%	= 116.2%	= 138.3%

(b) Capacity on the finishing machine is the bottleneck resource. The machine utilisation rate is higher than 100% and it is the largest of the 3 rates.

8.6 Throughput measures

8.6.1 Return per time period

In a throughput accounting environment, the overall **focus of attention** is the **rate at which the organisation can generate profits**. To monitor this, the return on the throughput through the bottleneck resource is monitored using:

$$\text{Return per time period} = \frac{\text{sales revenue} - \text{material costs}}{\text{time period}}$$

This measure shows the **value added** by an organisation during a particular time period. Time plays a crucial role in the measure, so **managers** are strongly **encouraged to remove bottlenecks that might cause production delays**.

8.6.2 Return per time period on bottleneck resource

In throughput accounting, the limiting factor is the bottleneck. The return per time period measure can be adapted and used for **ranking products to optimise production** in the **short term**.

$$\text{Product return per minute} = \frac{\text{sales price} - \text{material costs}}{\text{minutes on key/bottleneck resource}}$$

Ranking products on the basis of throughput contribution per minute (or hour) on the bottleneck resource is **similar in concept to maximising contribution per unit of limiting factor**. Such product rankings are for **short-term production scheduling only**. In throughput accounting, bottlenecks should be eliminated and so rankings may change quickly. Customer demand can, of course, cause the bottleneck to change at short notice too.

Rankings by TA product return and by contribution per unit of limiting factor may be different. Which one leads to profit maximisation? The correct approach depends on the variability or otherwise of labour and variable overheads, which in turn depends on the time horizon of the decision. Both are short-term profit maximisation techniques and given that labour is nowadays likely to be fixed in the short term, it could be argued that TA provides the more correct solution. An analysis of variable overheads would be needed to determine their variability.

KEY POINT

Bear in mind that the huge majority of organisations cannot produce and market products based on short-term profit considerations alone. Strategic-level issues such as market developments, product developments and the stage reached in the product life cycle must also be taken into account.

8.6.3 TA ratio

Products can also be ranked according to the **throughput accounting ratio (TA ratio)**.

$$\text{TA ratio} = \frac{\text{throughput contribution or value added per time period}}{\text{conversion cost per time period}}$$

$$= \frac{(\text{sales} - \text{material costs}) \text{ per time period}}{(\text{labour} + \text{overhead}) \text{ per time period}}$$

This measure has the **advantage** of **including the costs involved in running the factory. The higher the ratio, the more profitable the company**.

A profitable product should have a ratio greater than one. If a product's ratio is less than one, the organisation is losing money every time that product is produced.

Here's an example. Note the figures are in $ per hour.

	Product A $ per hour	Product B $ per hour
Sales price	100	150
Material cost	(40)	(50)
Throughput	60	100
Conversion cost	(50)	(50)
Profit	10	50
TA ratio	$\frac{60}{50} = 1.2$	$\frac{100}{50} = 2.0$

Profit will be maximised by manufacturing as much of product B as possible.

Question 4.6 Product return per factory hour and TA ratio

Learning outcome A1(a)

Each unit of product B requires 4 machine hours. Machine time is the bottleneck resource, there being 650 machine hours available per week.

B is sold for $120 per unit and has a direct material cost of $35 per unit. Total factory costs are $13,000 per week.

Required

Calculate the return per factory hour and the TA ratio for product B.

KEY POINT

> If conversion cost cannot be directly allocated to products (because it is not a unit-level manufacturing cost), the TA ratio cannot be calculated and products have to be ranked in terms of throughput contribution per hour or minute of bottleneck resource.

8.6.4 Effectiveness measures and cost control

Traditional efficiency measures such as standard costing variances and labour ratios are **unsuitable** in a TA environment because traditional efficiency should not be encouraged (as the **labour force should not produce just for inventory**).

Effectiveness is a **more important** issue. The **current effectiveness ratio** compares current levels of effectiveness with the standard.

$$\text{Current effectiveness ratio} = \frac{\text{standard minutes of throughput achieved}}{\text{minutes available}}$$

Question 4.7 Variances and throughput accounting

Learning outcome A1(a)

Briefly explain whether or not an adverse labour rate variance caused by overtime worked at the bottleneck is a good or bad thing in a throughput accounting environment.

8.7 Is it good or bad?

TA is seen by some as **too short term**, as all costs other than direct material are regarded as fixed. This is not true. But it does **concentrate on direct material costs** and does nothing for the control of other costs.

These characteristics make throughput accounting a **good complement for ABC**, as ABC focuses on labour and overhead costs. We covered ABC in detail in the previous chapter.

TA attempts to maximise throughput whereas traditional systems attempt to maximise profit. By attempting to maximise throughput, an organisation could be producing in excess of the profit-maximising output.

8.8 Where TA helps direct attention

- Bottlenecks
- Key elements in making profits
- Inventory reduction

- Reducing the response time to customer demand
- Evenness of production flow
- Overall effectiveness and efficiency

Example: throughput accounting

Corrie produces three products, X, Y and Z. The capacity of Corrie's plant is restricted by process alpha. Process alpha is expected to be operational for 8 hours per day and can produce 1,200 units of X per hour, 1,500 units of Y per hour, and 600 units of Z per hour.

Selling prices and material costs for each product are as follows.

Product	Selling price $ per unit	Material cost $ per unit	Throughput contribution $ per unit
X	150	70	80
Y	120	40	80
Z	300	100	200

Conversion costs are $720,000 per day.

Required

(a) Calculate the profit per day if daily output achieved is 6,000 units of X, 4,500 units of Y and 1,200 units of Z.

(b) Determine the efficiency of the bottleneck process, given the output in (a).

(c) Calculate the TA ratio for each product.

(d) In the absence of demand restrictions for the three products, advise Corrie's management on the optimal production plan.

Solution

(a)   Profit per day   =   throughput contribution – conversion cost
                         =   [($80 × 6,000) + ($80 × 4,500) + ($200 × 1,200)] – $720,000
                         = $360,000

(b)

Product	Minutes in alpha per unit	Minutes in alpha per day
X	60/1,200 = 0.05	6,000 × 0.05 = 300
Y	60/1,500 = 0.04	4,500 × 0.04 = 180
Z	60/600 = 0.10	1,200 × 0.10 = 120
		600

Total hours = 600 minutes ÷ 60 = 10 hours

Hours available = 8, hours produced = 10, ∴efficiency = 125%

(c)   TA ratio = throughput contribution per factory hour/conversion cost per factory hour

Conversion cost per factory hour = $720,000/8 = $90,000

Product	Throughput contribution per factory hour	Cost per factory hour	TA ratio
X	$80 × (60 ÷ 0.05 mins) = $96,000	$90,000	1.07
Y	$80 × (60 ÷ 0.04 mins) = $120,000	$90,000	1.33
Z	$200 × (60 ÷ 0.10 mins) = $120,000	$90,000	1.33

(d)   An attempt should be made to remove the restriction on output caused by process alpha's capacity. This will probably result in another bottleneck emerging elsewhere. The extra capacity required to remove the restriction could be obtained by working overtime, making process improvements or product specification changes. Until the volume of throughput can be increased, output should be concentrated on products Y and Z (greatest TA ratios), unless there are good marketing reasons for continuing the current production mix.

Question 4.8   Binding constraints and TA ratio

Learning outcome A1(a)

A company's binding constraint is the capacity of machine M. The throughput accounting (TA) ratio for product P on machine M is 1.4.

Explain how the TA ratio is calculated and state **four** actions that management could consider to improve the TA ratio for product P.

8.9 Throughput accounting in service and retail industries

Sales staff have always preferred to use a marginal costing approach so that they can use their discretion on discounts, and **retail organisations** have traditionally thought in terms of sales revenue less the bought-in price of goods. The throughput accounting approach is therefore **nothing new** to them.

Throughput accounting can be used very effectively in **support departments and service industries** to **highlight and remove bottlenecks**. For example, if there is a delay in processing a potential customer's application, business can be lost or the potential customer may decide not to proceed. Sometimes credit rating checks are too detailed, slowing the whole procedure unnecessarily and delaying acceptance from, say, 24 hours to 8 days.

A similar problem could occur in hospitals where work that could be done by nurses has to be carried out by doctors. Not only does this increase the cost of the work but it may well cause a bottleneck by tying up a doctor's time unnecessarily.

Question 4.9   Product costing versus TA

Learning outcome A1(a)

Here are some statements about traditional product costing. Provide the equivalent statements about throughput accounting.

Statement 1: Inventory is valued in the financial statements at full production cost.
Statement 2: Labour, material and variable overheads are treated as variable costs.
Statement 3: A process is deemed efficient if labour and machine time are fully utilised.
Statement 4: Value is added when a unit of product is produced.

Section summary

Throughput accounting is the accounting system developed in the UK, based on the theory of constraints and JIT. It measures the throughput contribution per factory hour. It is very similar to marginal costing but can be used to make longer-term decisions about production equipment/capacity.

Chapter Summary

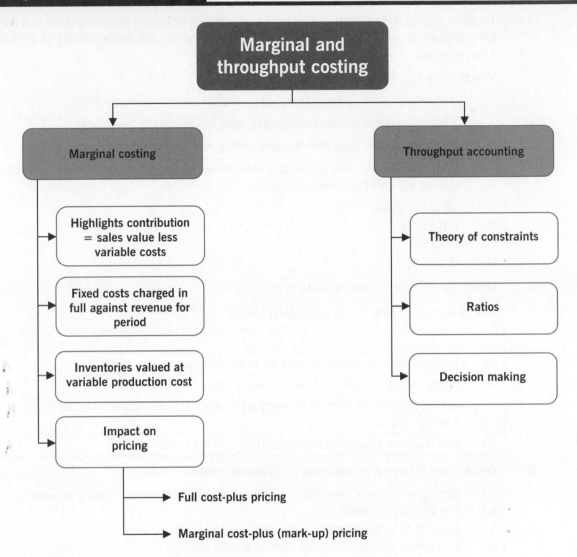

Quick Quiz

1   Marginal costing and absorption costing are different techniques for assessing profit in a period. If there are changes in inventory during a period, marginal costing and absorption costing give different results for profit obtained.

Which of the following statements are true?

I   If inventory levels increase, marginal costing will report the higher profit.

II   If inventory levels decrease, marginal costing will report the lower profit.

III   If inventory levels decrease, marginal costing will report the higher profit.

IV   If the opening and closing inventory volumes are the same, marginal costing and absorption costing will give the same profit figure.

A   All of the above

B   I, II and IV

C   I and IV

· D   III and IV

2   Identify which of the following relate to either:

A = absorption costing   M = marginal costing

		A or M
(a)	Closing inventories valued at marginal production cost	M
(b)	Closing inventories valued at full production cost	A
(c)	Cost of sales include some fixed overhead incurred in previous period in opening inventory values	M
(d)	Fixed costs are charged in full against profit for the period	A

3   Which of the following are arguments in favour of marginal costing?

(a)   Closing inventory is valued in accordance with international accounting standards.

· (b)   It is simple to operate.

. (c)   There is no under or over absorption of overheads.

· (d)   Fixed costs are the same regardless of activity levels.

. (e)   The information from this costing method may be used for decision making.

4   When opening inventories were 8,500 litres and closing inventories were 6,750 litres, a firm had a profit of $62,100 using marginal costing.

Assuming that the fixed overhead absorption rate was $3 per litre, what would be the profit using absorption costing?

5   When sales fluctuate but production is constant, absorption costing smoothes out fluctuations in profit.

True ☐

False ☑

6   HMF Co produces a single product. The budgeted fixed production overheads for the period are $500,000. The budgeted output for the period is 2,500 units. Opening stock at the start of the period consisted of 900 units and closing stock at the end of the period consisted of 300 units. If absorption costing principles were applied, the profit for the period compared to the marginal costing profit would be:

A $125,000 higher

B $125,000 lower

C $120,000 higher

· D $120,000 lower

7   Fill in the blanks in the statements below, using the words in the box. Some words may be used twice.

(a)   The theory of constraints is an approach to production management that aims to maximise
(1)............. less (2)........ and (3)........... It focuses on factors such as (4)._constraints_. which
act as (5)....*bottle*........

(b)   Throughput contribution = (6)............. minus (7) ....

(c)   TA ratio = (8) .... per factory hour ÷ (9) .... per factory hour

> • variable overhead costs
> • bottlenecks
> • material costs
> • sales revenue
> • throughput contribution
> • constraints
> • conversion cost

8   CH Ltd operates a throughput accounting system. Product B sells for $27.99, has a material cost of
$7.52 and a conversion cost of $1.91. The product spends 27 minutes on the bottleneck resource. What
is the return per factory hour for product B?

A $45.49   C $26.08
B $20.47   D $57.96

9   Throughput accounting policy is to hold zero inventories throughout all operations.

True   ☐

False   ☐ .

Answers to Quick Quiz

1   D   If inventory levels increase, then absorption costing reports the higher profit. If inventory levels do not move, then they will report the same profit figure.

2

		A or M
(a)	Closing inventories valued at marginal production cost	M
(b)	Closing inventories valued at full production cost	A
(c)	Cost of sales include some fixed overhead incurred in previous period in opening inventory values	A
(d)	Fixed costs are charged in full against profit for the period	M

3   (b), (c), (d) and (e)

4   Difference in profit = $(8,500 - 6,750) \times \$3 = \$5,250$

Since inventory levels reduced, the absorption costing profit will be lower than the marginal costing profit.

Absorption costing profit = $\$62,100 - \$5,250 = \$56,850$

5   True. Absorption costing carries fixed production overheads forward in inventory values to be matched against sales as they arise.

6   D.   Units
    Opening stock   900
    Closing stock   300

    Decrease   600 $\times \left(\dfrac{\$500,000}{2,500} \right) = 120,000$ lower

7   1   sales revenue
    2   material costs
    3   variable overhead costs
    4   bottlenecks
    5   constraints
    6   sales revenue
    7   material costs
    8   throughput contribution
    9   conversion cost

8   A.   Return per hour = (sales – material cost) per hour on bottleneck resource

    $\therefore$ Return per 27 minutes = $\$(27.99 - 7.52) = \$20.47$

    $\therefore$ Return per hour = $\$20.47 \times \dfrac{60}{27} = \$45.49$

9   False. A buffer inventory should be held prior to the bottleneck process.

Answers to Questions

4.1 Marginal versus absorption costing – effect on profit

A

Difference in profit = **change** in inventory levels × fixed overhead absorption per unit = (150 – 100) × $10 × 5 = $2,500 **lower** profit, because inventory levels **decreased**. The correct answer is therefore option A.

The key is the change in the volume of inventory. Inventory levels have **decreased** therefore absorption costing will report a **lower** profit. This eliminates options B and D.

Option C is incorrect because it is based on the closing inventory only (100 units × $10 × 5 hours).

4.2 Shortcomings of absorption costing

If a manager's reward is based on the profit for the period, then the manager will be encouraged to take actions that will increase the reported profit in the short term.

With absorption costing, all production costs are absorbed into product unit costs. Any inventory remaining at the end of the period would include absorbed fixed production costs. The higher production for the period, the greater the amount of fixed production cost that will be carried forward in inventory to be charged against the revenues of future periods. Furthermore, the higher the production level for the period, the lower the full unit cost of production will be because the same amount of fixed production cost will be shared out over a higher number of units.

Thus, the higher the production for the period, the higher the reported profit for the period will be, for a given level of sales, when an absorption costing system is used.

4.3 Cost-plus pricing

The correct answer is that the cost-plus percentage will need to be reduced by 2%.

Profits = $(7.99 – 4.75) = $3.24

Mark-up = ($3.24/$4.75) × 100% = 68%

∴% needs to be reduced by (70 – 68)% = 2%

4.4 Marginal cost pricing

The correct answer is $166^2/_3\%$.

Breakeven point is when total contribution equals fixed costs.

At breakeven point, $10,000 = 400 (price – $15)

∴ $25 = price – $15
∴ $40 = price
∴ Mark-up = ((40 – 15) /15) × 100% = $166^2/_3\%$

4.5 Throughput accounting vs conventional cost accounting

Conventional cost accounting	Throughput accounting
Inventory is an asset.	Inventory is **not** an asset. It is a result of unsynchronised manufacturing and is a barrier to making profit.
Costs can be classified either as direct or indirect.	Such classifications are no longer useful.
Product profitability can be determined by deducting a product cost from selling price.	Profitability is determined by the rate at which money is earned.
Profit is a function of costs.	Profit is a function of throughput as well as costs.

4.6 Product return per factory hour and TA ratio

Return per factory hour = $(120 − 35)/4 = $21.25
TA ratio = $21.25/$20* = 1.0625
*Cost per factory hour = $13,000/650 = $20

4.7 Variances and throughput accounting

In a **traditional** management accounting environment, **adverse** variances would be considered **bad** because they **reduce accounting profit** below the standard expected for the activity achieved.

In a **throughput** accounting environment, the **focus is on maximising throughput contribution** while keeping conversion and investment costs to the minimum level possible.

Therefore, in a throughput environment, the increased cost of overtime working would be a good thing and would increase reported profits providing the extra labour cost incurred was less than the throughput contribution added.

4.8 Binding constraints and TA ratio

The throughput accounting (TA) ratio is calculated as follows:

$$\text{TA ratio} = \frac{\text{throughput per time period}}{\text{conversion cost per time period}} = \frac{(\text{sales} - \text{material costs})\,\text{per time period}}{\text{conversion cost per time period}}$$

Actions that could be considered to improve the TA ratio are as follows:

1   Increase the selling price of product P. This will increase the throughput per time period.

2   Reduce the material cost per unit of product P. This will also increase the throughput per time period.

3   Reduce the total expenditure on conversion costs. This would reduce the conversion cost per time period.

4   Change the working practices on machine M to increase the number of hours of capacity available. This should be achieved without extra conversion cost being incurred, perhaps by altering the method of setting up the machine, to improve productivity. This action would reduce the conversion cost per time period.

4.9 Product costing versus TA

1   Inventory is valued at material cost only (ie variable cost).
2   Only direct material is treated as a variable cost.
3   Effectiveness is measured in terms of schedule adherence and meeting delivery dates.
4   Value is added when an item is sold.

Now try these questions from the Practice Question Bank

Number	Level
Q4.1 – Q4.9	Practice

SHORT-TERM DECISION MAKING

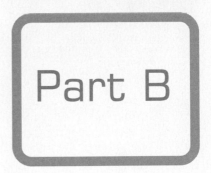

Part B

LIMITING FACTOR ANALYSIS

You have **already encountered limiting factor analysis** in your earlier studies and so we have included at the beginning of this chapter a reminder of the key concepts and basic techniques involved in this approach to allocating resources. Work through the examples and do the questions in **Section 1** to ensure that you are perfectly happy with the basics.

You need to build on this knowledge, however, and deal with situations in which organisations have 'restricted **freedom of action**'. This type of problem is covered in **Section 2**.

In **Section 3** we will be considering the approach to take if an organisation has to buy in some of its products because it **cannot make sufficient quantities in-house** to meet demand.

Shadow prices are covered in **Section 4**. Some students find it quite difficult to get their head around the concept, so go over the material a number of times if necessary until you really understand it.

We end the chapter by looking at the issues to bear in mind when **using limiting factor analysis**.

Limiting factor analysis can only be used if there is **one** limiting factor. If there are **two or more limiting factors**, a technique known as linear programming must be applied. This is covered in **Chapter 9**.

Topic list	Learning outcomes	Syllabus references	Ability required
1 Limiting factors	C2(c)	C2(c)(i)	Analysis
2 Limiting factor analysis and restricted freedom of action	C2(c)	C2(c)(i)	Analysis
3 Make or buy decisions and scarce resources	C2(c)	C2(c)(i)	Analysis
4 Limiting factors and shadow prices	C2(c)	C2(c)(i)	Analysis
5 Using limiting factor analysis	C2(c)	C2(c)(i)	Analysis

Chapter Overview

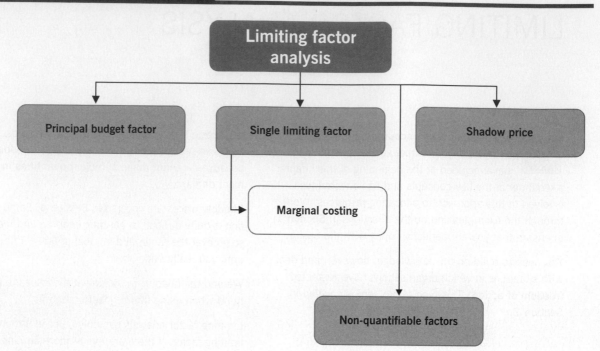

1 Limiting factors

Introduction

All companies are limited in their capacity, either for producing goods or providing services. There is always one resource that is most restrictive (the limiting factor). This section looks at examples of how to deal with limiting factors when making production decisions.

KEY TERM

A LIMITING FACTOR is any factor that is in scarce supply and that stops the organisation from expanding its activities further, that is, it limits the organisation's activities. *(CIMA Official Terminology)*

Knowledge brought forward from earlier studies

Limiting factor analysis

- An organisation might be faced with just one limiting factor (other than maximum sales demand) but there might also be several scarce resources, with two or more of them putting an effective limit on the level of activity that can be achieved.

- Examples of limiting factors include sales demand and production constraints.

  - Labour. The limit may be in terms of either total quantity or particular skills.

  - Materials. There may be insufficient available materials to produce enough units to satisfy sales demand.

  - Manufacturing capacity. There may not be sufficient machine capacity for the production required to meet sales demand.

- It is assumed in limiting factor analysis that management would make a product mix decision or service mix decision based on the option that would maximise profit, and that profit is maximised when contribution is maximised (given no change in fixed cost expenditure incurred). **In other words, marginal costing ideas are applied.**

  - Contribution will be maximised by earning the biggest possible contribution per unit of limiting factor. For example, if grade A labour is the limiting factor, contribution will be maximised by earning the biggest contribution per hour of grade A labour worked.

  - The limiting factor decision therefore involves the determination of the contribution earned per unit of limiting factor by each different product.

  - If the sales demand is limited, the profit-maximising decision will be to produce the top-ranked product(s) up to the sales demand limit.

- In limiting factor decisions, we generally assume that fixed costs are the same whatever product or service mix is selected, so that the only relevant costs are variable costs.

- When there is just one limiting factor, the technique for establishing the contribution-maximising product mix or service mix is to rank the products or services in order of contribution-earning ability per unit of limiting factor.

KEY POINTS

If resources are limiting factors, **contribution** will be **maximised** by earning the biggest possible contribution per unit of limiting factor.

Where there is just one limiting factor, the technique for establishing the contribution-maximising product or service mix is to rank the products or services in order of contribution-earning ability per unit of limiting factor.

Example: limiting factor decision

Sausage makes two products, the Mash and the Sauce. Unit variable costs are as follows:

	Mash $	Sauce $
Direct materials	1	3
Direct labour ($3 per hour)	6	3
Variable overhead	1	1
	8	7

The sales price per unit is $14 per Mash and $11 per Sauce. During July the available direct labour is limited to 8,000 hours. Sales demand in July is expected to be as follows:

Mash	3,000 units
Sauce	5,000 units

Required

Determine the production budget that will maximise profit, assuming that fixed costs per month are $20,000 and that there is no opening inventory of finished goods or work in progress.

Solution

Confirm that the limiting factor is something other than sales demand.

	Mash	Sauce	Total
Labour hours per unit	2 hours	1 hour	
Sales demand	3,000 units	5,000 units	
Labour hours needed	6,000 hours	5,000 hours	11,000 hours
Labour hours available			8,000 hours
Shortfall			3,000 hours

Labour is the limiting factor on production.

Identify the contribution earned by each product per unit of scarce resource; that is, per labour hour worked.

	Mash $	Sauce $
Sales price	14	11
Variable cost	8	7
Unit contribution	6	4
Labour hours per unit	2 hours	1 hour
Contribution per labour hour (= per unit of limiting factor)	$3	$4

Although Mashes have a higher unit contribution than Sauces, two Sauces can be made in the time it takes to make one Mash. Because labour is in short supply, it is more profitable to make Sauces than Mashes.

Determine the budgeted production and sales. Sufficient Sauces will be made to meet the full sales demand, and the remaining labour hours available will then be used to make Mashes.

(a)

Product	Demand	Hours required	Hours available	Priority for manufacture
Sauces	5,000	5,000	5,000	1st
Mashes	3,000	6,000	3,000	2nd
			(bal)	
		11,000	8,000	

(b)

Product	Units	Hours needed	Contribution per unit $	Total $
Sauces	5,000	5,000	4	20,000
Mashes (balance)	1,500	3,000	6	9,000
		8,000		29,000
Less fixed costs				20,000
Profit				9,000

Conclusion

(a) Unit contribution is **not** the correct way to decide priorities.

(b) Labour hours are the scarce resource, therefore **contribution per labour hour** is the correct way to decide priorities.

(c) The Sauce earns $4 contribution per labour hour, and the Mash earns $3 contribution per labour hour. Sauces therefore make more profitable use of the scarce resource, and should be manufactured first.

1.1 Two potentially limiting factors

You may be asked to deal with situations where two limiting factors are potentially limiting (and there are also product/service demand limitations). The approach in these situations is to find out which factor (if any) prevents the business from fulfilling maximum demand.

KEY POINT

> Where there is a **maximum potential sales demand** for an organisation's products or services, they should still be ranked in order of contribution-earning ability per unit of the limiting factor. The contribution-maximising decision, however, will be to produce the top-ranked products (or to provide the top-ranked services) up to the sales demand limit.

Example: two potentially limiting factors

Lucky manufactures and sells three products, X, Y and Z, for which budgeted sales demand, unit selling prices and unit variable costs are as follows:

	X		Y		Z	
Budgeted sales demand	550 units		500 units		400 units	
	$	$	$	$	$	$
Unit sales price		16		18		14
Variable costs: materials	8		6		2	
labour	4		6		9	
		12		12		11
Unit contribution		4		6		3

The organisation has existing inventory of 250 units of X and 200 units of Z, which it is quite willing to use up to meet sales demand. All three products use the same direct materials and the same type of direct labour. In the next year, the available supply of materials will be restricted to $4,800 (at cost) and the available supply of labour to $6,600 (at cost).

Required

Determine what product mix and sales mix would maximise the organisation's profits in the next year.

Solution

There **appear to be two scarce resources**, direct materials and direct labour. This is not certain, however, and because there is a limited sales demand as well, either of the following might apply:

- There is **no limiting factor at all**, except sales demand.
- There is **only one scarce resource** that prevents the full potential sales demand being achieved.

 Establish which of the resources, if any, is scarce.

	X Units	Y Units	Z Units
Budgeted sales	550	500	400
Inventory in hand	250	0	200
Minimum production to meet demand	300	500	200

	Minimum production to meet sales demand Units	Required materials at cost $	Required labour at cost $
X	300	2,400	1,200
Y	500	3,000	3,000
Z	200	400	1,800
Total required		5,800	6,000
Total available		4,800	6,600
(Shortfall)/surplus		(1,000)	600

Materials are a limiting factor, but labour is not.

 Rank X, Y and Z in order of contribution earned per $1 of direct materials consumed.

	X $	Y $	Z $
Unit contribution	4	6	3
Cost of materials	8	6	2
Contribution per $1 materials	$0.50	$1.00	$1.50
Ranking	3rd	2nd	1st

 Determine a production plan. Z should be manufactured up to the limit where units produced plus units held in inventory will meet sales demand, then Y second and X third, until all the available materials are used up.

Ranking	Product	Sales demand less units held Units	Production quantity Units		Materials cost $
1st	Z	200	200	(× $2)	400
2nd	Y	500	500	(× $6)	3,000
3rd	X	300	175	(× $8)	*1,400
		Total available			4,800

*Balancing amount using up total available.

Draw up a budget. The profit-maximising budget is as follows.

	X Units	Y Units	Z Units
Opening inventory	250	0	200
Add production	175	500	200
Sales	425	500	400

	X $	Y $	Z $	Total $
Revenue	6,800	9,000	5,600	21,400
Variable costs	5,100	6,000	4,400	15,500
Contribution	1,700	3,000	1,200	5,900

Exam alert

A question could ask you to calculate the optimum production plan for a business and the contribution that would result from adopting the plan.

Section summary

A **scarce resource** is a resource of which there is a limited supply. Once a scarce resource affects the ability of an organisation to earn profits, a scarce resource becomes known as a limiting factor.

If resources are limiting factors, **contribution** will be **maximised** by earning the biggest possible contribution per unit of limiting factor.

Where there is just one limiting factor, the technique for establishing the contribution-maximising product or service mix is to rank the products or services in order of contribution-earning ability per unit of limiting factor.

Where there is a **maximum potential sales demand** for an organisation's products or services, they should still be ranked in order of contribution-earning ability per unit of the limiting factor. The contribution-maximising decision, however, will be to produce the top-ranked products (or to provide the top-ranked services) up to the sales demand limit.

2 Limiting factor analysis and restricted freedom of action

Introduction

Companies are not always able to produce the profit-maximising mix of products or services due to certain restrictions on production or sales. This section focuses on such situations and how to arrive at the optimal solution.

2.1 Restrictions on freedom of action

In certain circumstances, an organisation faced with a limiting factor on production and sales **might not be able to produce the profit-maximising product mix** because the mix and/or volume of products that can be produced and sold is also restricted by a factor other than a scarce resource.

(a)   A contract to **supply a certain number of products** to a customer

(b)   Production/sales of a minimum quantity of one or more products to **provide a complete product range and/or to maintain customer goodwill**

(c)   Maintenance of a **certain market share** of one or more products

In each of these cases, the organisation might have to **produce more of a particular product or products than the level established by ranking** according to contribution per unit of limiting factor.

KEY POINT

Where companies are restricted in their freedom of what to produce, the optimum production plan must take minimum production requirements into account first. The remainder of the limiting factor can then be allocated in the normal way according to contribution per unit of that factor.

Example: restricted freedom of action

Harvey is currently preparing its budget for the year ending 30 September 20X2. The company manufactures and sells three products, Beta, Delta and Gamma.

The unit selling price and cost structure of each product is budgeted as follows:

	Beta	Delta	Gamma
	$	$	$
Selling price	100	124	32
Variable costs:			
Labour	24	48	6
Materials	26	7	8
Overhead	10	5	6
	60	60	20

Direct labour rate is budgeted at $6 per hour, and fixed costs at $1,300,000 per annum. The company has a maximum production capacity of 228,000 direct labour hours.

A meeting of the board of directors has been convened to discuss the budget and to resolve the problem as to the quantity of each product which should be made and sold. The sales director presented the results of a recent market survey, which reveals that market demand for the company's products will be as follows:

Product	Units
Beta	24,000
Delta	12,000
Gamma	60,000

The production director proposes that, since Gamma only contributes $12 per unit, the product should no longer be produced, and the surplus capacity transferred to produce additional quantities of Beta and Delta. The sales director does not agree with the proposal. Gamma is considered necessary to complement the product range and to maintain customer goodwill. If Gamma is not offered, the sales director believes that sales of Beta and Delta will be seriously affected. After further discussion, the board decided that a minimum of 10,000 units of each product should be produced. The remaining production capacity would then be allocated so as to achieve the maximum profit possible.

Required

Prepare a budget statement that clearly shows the maximum profit that could be achieved in the year ending 30 September 20X2.

Solution

 STEP 1

Ascertain whether **labour hours are a scarce resource**.

	Units demanded	Labour hours per unit	Total labour hours
Beta	24,000	4 ($24/$6)	96,000
Delta	12,000	8 ($48/$6)	96,000
Gamma	60,000	1 ($6/$6)	60,000
			252,000

 STEP 2

Rank the products.

Since only 228,000 hours are available, we need to establish which product earns the greatest contribution per labour hour.

	Beta	Delta	Gamma
Contribution ($)	40	64	12
Labour hours	4	8	1
Contribution per labour hour ($)	10	8	12
Ranking	2nd	3rd	1st

STEP 3

Determine a production plan.

The optimum production plan must take into account the requirement that 10,000 units of each product are produced, and then allocate the remaining hours according to the above ranking.

		Hours
Beta	10,000 units × 4 hours	40,000
Delta	10,000 units × 8 hours	80,000
Gamma	10,000 units × 1 hour	10,000
		130,000
Gamma	50,000 units × 1 hour (full demand)	50,000
Beta	12,000 units × 4 hours (balance)	48,000
		228,000

 STEP 4

Draw up a budget.

BUDGET STATEMENT

	$
Contribution	
Beta (22,000 units × $40)	880,000
Delta (10,000 units × $64)	640,000
Gamma (60,000 units × $12)	720,000
	2,240,000
Fixed costs	1,300,000
Profit	940,000

Learning outcome C2(c)

JJ makes two products, the K and the L. The K sells for $50 per unit, the L for $70 per unit. The variable cost per unit of the K is $35, and of the L it is $40. Each unit of K uses 2 kg of raw material. Each unit of L uses 3 kg of material.

In the forthcoming period, the availability of raw material is limited to 2,000 kg. JJ is contracted to supply 500 units of K. Maximum demand for the L is 250 units. Demand for the K is unlimited.

What is the profit-maximising product mix?

Section summary

Where companies are restricted in their freedom of what to produce, the optimum production plan must take minimum production requirements into account first. The remainder of the limiting factor can then be allocated in the normal way according to contribution per unit of that factor.

3   Make or buy decisions and scarce resources

Introduction

This section extends the decision-making process by introducing scarce resources and the issue of restricted freedom of choice.

3.1 Combining internal and external production

An organisation might **want to do more things than it has the resources for**, and so its alternatives would be as follows.

(a)   Make the best use of the available resources and ignore the opportunities to buy help from outside

(b)   Combine internal resources with buying externally so as to do more and increase profitability

Buying help from outside is justifiable if it **adds to profits**. A further decision is then required on how to split the work between **internal** and **external** effort. What parts of the work should be given to suppliers or subcontractors so as to maximise profitability?

KEY POINT

In a situation where a company must **sub-contract work to make up a shortfall in its own in-house capabilities**, its total costs will be minimised if those units bought have the lowest extra variable cost of buying per unit of scarce resource saved by buying.

Example: make or buy decision with scarce resources

MM manufactures three components, S, A and T, using the same machines for each. The budget for the next year calls for the production and assembly of 4,000 of each component. The variable production cost per unit of the final product is as follows:

BPP
LEARNING MEDIA

	Machine hours	Variable cost
		$
1 unit of S	3	20
1 unit of A	2	36
1 unit of T	4	24
Assembly		20
		100

Only 24,000 hours of machine time will be available during the year, and a subcontractor has quoted the following unit prices for supplying components: S $29; A $40; T $34.

Required

Advise MM.

Solution

The organisation's budget calls for 36,000 hours of machine time, if all the components are to be produced in-house. Only 24,000 hours are available, and so there is a shortfall of 12,000 hours of machine time, which is therefore a limiting factor. The shortage can be overcome by subcontracting the equivalent of 12,000 machine hours' output to the subcontractor.

The assembly costs are not relevant costs because they are unaffected by the decision.

The decision rule is to **minimise the extra variable costs of sub-contracting per unit of scarce resource saved** (that is, per machine hour saved).

	S	A	T
	$	$	$
Variable cost of making	20	36	24
Variable cost of buying	29	40	34
Extra variable cost of buying	9	4	10
Machine hours saved by buying	3 hours	2 hours	4 hours
Extra variable cost of buying per hour saved	$3	$2	$2.50

This analysis shows that it is **cheaper to buy A than to buy T** and it is **most expensive to buy S**. The **priority for making** the components in-house will be in the **reverse order**: S, then T, then A. There are enough machine hours to make all 4,000 units of S (12,000 hours) and to produce 3,000 units of T (another 12,000 hours). 12,000 hours' production of T and A must be sub-contracted.

The cost-minimising, and so profit-maximising, make and buy schedule is as follows:

Component	Machine hours used/saved	Number of units	Unit variable cost	Total variable cost
			$	$
Make: S	12,000	4,000	20	80,000
T	12,000	3,000	24	72,000
	24,000			152,000
Buy: T	4,000	1,000	34	34,000
A	8,000	4,000	40	160,000
	12,000			346,000

Total variable cost of components, excluding assembly costs

Question 5.2

Make or buy and limiting factors

Learning outcome C2(c)

TW manufactures two products, the D and the E, using the same material for each. Annual demand for the D is 9,000 units, while demand for the E is 12,000 units. The variable production cost per unit of the D is $10, that of the E $15. The D requires 3.5 kg of raw material per unit; the E requires 8 kg of raw material per unit. Supply of raw material will be limited to 87,500 kg during the year.

A subcontractor has quoted prices of $17 per unit for the D and $25 per unit for the E to supply the product. How many of each product should TW manufacture in order to maximise profits?

Required

Fill in the blanks in the sentence below.

TW should manufacture .... units of D and .... units of E to maximise profits.

Section summary

In a situation where a company must **subcontract work to make up a shortfall in its own in-house capabilities**, its total costs will be minimised if those units bought have the lowest extra variable cost of buying per unit of scarce resource saved by buying.

4 Limiting factors and shadow prices

Introduction

You will meet shadow prices when you cover linear programming in Chapter 9. However, they are relevant wherever there are scarce resources. This section deals with the concept of shadow prices and their relevance to short-term decision making.

4.1 Shadow prices and opportunity costs

A SHADOW PRICE is 'An increase in value which would be created by having available one additional unit of a limiting resource at the original cost'.

(*CIMA Official Terminology*)

KEY TERM

Whenever there are limiting factors, there will be **opportunity costs**. As you know, these are the **benefits forgone by using a limiting factor in one way instead of in the next most profitable way**.

For example, suppose that an organisation provides two services, X and Y, which earn a contribution of $24 and $18 per unit respectively. Service X requires 4 labour hours, and service Y requires 2 hours. Only 5,000 labour hours are available, and potential demand is for 1,000 of each of X and Y.

Labour hours would be a limiting factor, and with X earning $6 per hour and Y earning $9 per hour, the profit-maximising decision would be as follows:

	Services	Hours	Contribution $
Y	1,000	2,000	18,000
X (balance)	750	3,000	18,000
		5,000	36,000

Priority is given to Y because the **opportunity cost** of providing Y instead of more of X is $6 per hour (X's contribution per labour hour) and, since Y earns $9 per hour, the incremental benefit of providing Y instead of X would be $3 per hour.

If extra labour hours could be made available, more X (up to 1,000) would be provided, and an extra contribution of $6 per hour could be earned. Similarly, if fewer labour hours were available, the decision would be to provide fewer X and to keep provision of Y at 1,000, and so the loss of labour hours would cost the organisation $6 per hour in lost contribution. This $6 per hour, the **marginal contribution-earning potential of the limiting factor at the profit-maximising output level**, is referred to as the **shadow price** (or **dual price**) of the limiting factor.

Note that the shadow price only applies while the extra unit of resource can be obtained at its normal variable cost. The shadow price also indicates the amount by which contribution could fall if an organisation is deprived of one unit of the resource.

The shadow price of a resource is its **internal opportunity cost**. This is the marginal contribution towards fixed costs and profit that can be earned for each unit of the limiting factor that is available. Knowledge of the shadow price of a resource will help managers to decide how much it is worth paying to acquire another unit of the resource.

Section summary

The **shadow price** or **dual price** of a limiting factor is the increase in value that would be created by having one additional unit of the limiting factor at the original cost.

5 Using limiting factor analysis

Introduction

Limiting factor analysis provides us with a profit-maximising product mix, within the assumptions made. It is important to remember, however, that other considerations, so far not fully considered in our examples, might entirely alter the decision reached. These issues are considered here.

Exam alert

Don't ignore this wordy section – you must be able to discuss pertinent non-quantifiable issues.

5.1 Non-quantifiable factors

The following table gives examples of non-quantifiable factors that may have an effect on the final decision reached.

Factor	Examples
Demand	Will the decision reached (perhaps to make and sell just one product rather than two) have a harmful effect on customer loyalty and sales demand? For example, a manufacturer of knives and forks could not expect to cease production of knives without affecting sales demand for the forks.

Factor	Examples
Long-term effects	Is the decision going to affect the long-term as well as the short-term plans of the organisation? If a particular product is not produced, or produced at a level below sales demand, is it likely that competitors will take over vacated markets? Labour skilled in the manufacture of the product may be lost and a decision to reopen or expand production of the product in the future may not be possible.
Labour	If labour is a limiting factor, is it because the skills required are difficult to obtain, perhaps because the organisation is using very old-fashioned production methods, or is the organisation a high-tech newcomer in a low-tech area? Or perhaps the conditions of work are so unappealing that people simply do not want to work for the organisation.
Other limiting factors	The same sort of questions should be asked whatever the limiting factor. If machine hours are in short supply, is this because more machines are needed, or newer, more reliable and efficient machines? If materials are in short supply, what are competitors doing? Have they found an equivalent or better substitute? Is it time to redesign the product?

5.2 Assumptions in limiting factor analysis

When you are dealing with short-term decision-making questions, certain assumptions have to be made. If any of the assumptions are not valid, then the profit-maximising decision might be different. These assumptions are as follows:

(a) **Fixed costs will be the same** regardless of the decision that is taken, and so the profit-maximising and contribution-maximising output level will be the same.

This will not necessarily be true, since some fixed costs might be directly attributable to a product or service. A decision to reduce or cease altogether activity on a product or service might therefore result in some fixed cost savings, which would have to be taken into account.

(b) **The unit variable cost is constant**, regardless of the output quantity of a product or service. This implies the following:

(i) The price of resources will be unchanged regardless of quantity; for example, there will be no bulk purchase discount of raw materials.

(ii) Efficiency and productivity levels will be unchanged; regardless of output quantity the direct labour productivity, the machine time per unit, and the materials consumption per unit will remain the same.

(c) **The estimates of sales demand** for each product, and the **resources required** to make each product, **are known with certainty**.

In the example in Section 1.1, there were estimates of the budgeted sales demand for each of three products, and these estimates were used to establish the profit-maximising product mix. Suppose the estimates were wrong? The product mix finally chosen would then either mean that some sales demand of the most profitable item would be unsatisfied, or that production would exceed sales demand, leaving some inventory unsold. Clearly, once a profit-maximising output decision is reached, management will have to keep their decision under continual review, and adjust their decision as appropriate in the light of actual results.

(d) **Units of output are divisible**, and a profit-maximising solution might include fractions of units as the optimum output level.

Where fractional answers are not realistic, some rounding of the figures will be necessary.

Exam skills

An objective test question (OTQ) might present you with a situation in which there is a limiting factor, without specifically stating that this is so, and you will have the task of recognising what the situation is. You may be given a hint with the wording of the question.

(a)   'It is possible that the main raw material used in manufacturing the products will be difficult to obtain in the next year.'

(b)   'The company employs a fixed number of employees who work a maximum overtime of 8 hours on top of the basic 36 hour week. The company has also agreed that no more staff will be recruited next year.'

In (a) there is a hint that raw materials might be a limiting factor. In (b), perhaps less obviously, a maximum limit is placed on the available labour hours, and so the possibility should occur to you that perhaps labour is a limiting factor.

If you suspect the existence of a limiting factor, some quick computations should confirm your suspicions.

(a)   Calculate the amount of the scarce resource (material quantities, labour hours, machine hours and so on) needed to meet the potential sales demand.

(b)   Calculate the amount of the scarce resource available (for example, number of employees multiplied by maximum working hours per employee).

(c)   Compare the two figures. Obviously, if the resources needed exceed the resources available, there is a limiting factor on output and sales.

Section summary

Non-quantifiable factors, such as effect on customer goodwill, ability to restart production and reasons for a resource being a limiting factor, should also be borne in mind in product mix decisions.

Various **assumptions** are made in limiting factor analysis:

- Fixed costs remain the same regardless of the decision taken.
- Unit variable cost is constant regardless of the decision taken.
- Estimates of sales demand and resources required are known with certainty.
- Units of output are divisible.

Chapter Summary

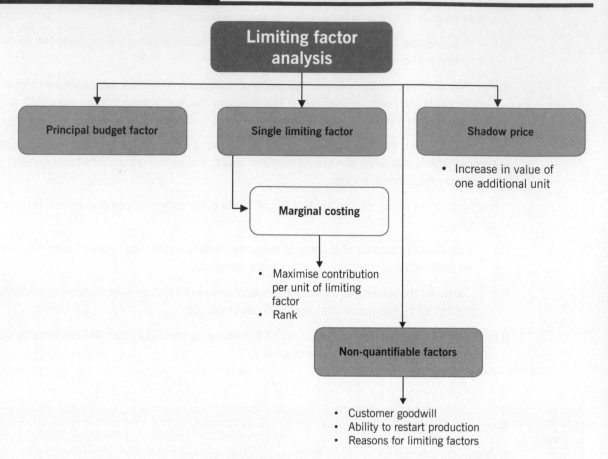

Quick Quiz

1   Choose the correct word from those highlighted.

When there is just one limiting factor, the product with the **biggest/smallest** contribution-earning ability per unit of limiting factor should be produced first.

2   Which of the following is not an example of a limiting factor?

A   Sales demand
B   Materials
C   Machine time
•   D   Profit

3   Marginal costing ideas are applied in limiting factor analysis.

True   [•]

False   [ ]

4   Put the following in the correct order of approach to adopt when dealing with limiting factor analysis and limited freedom of action.

3   (a)   Allocate resource according to ranking
2   (b)   Rank the products
1   (c)   Take into account minimum production requirements

5   Choose the correct words from those highlighted.

If an organisation has to subcontract work to make up a shortfall in its own in-house capabilities, its total costs will be minimised if those units bought have the **highest/lowest** extra **variable cost/resource requirement** of buying per **unit of scarce resource/$** saved.

6   Fill in the blanks.

The shadow price of a scarce resource indicates the amount by which contribution would ....*decrease*.......... if an organisation were deprived of one unit of the resource. The shadow price only applies while the extra unit of resource can be obtained at its ...*opportunity*............... cost.

7   Use the words listed below to fill in the blanks in the following statements about the assumptions in limiting factor analysis.

Missing words: units of output; sales demand and resources required per unit; unit variable cost; fixed costs.

(a)   .........*F.C*................ will be the same regardless of the decision taken.

(b)   The ..*unit V.C*.............. is constant, regardless of the output quantity.

(c)   The estimates of ....*sales demand*....................... are known with certainty.

(d)   ...*Units of output*...... are divisible.

8 The following details relate to three services offered by DSF.

	V $ per service	A $ per service	L $ per service
Selling price of service	120	170	176
Direct labour	20	30	20
Variable overhead	40	56	80
Fixed overhead	20	32	40
	80	118	140
Profit	40	52	36

All three services use the same direct labour, but in different quantities.

In a period when the labour used on these services is in short supply, which of the following four options shows the most and least profitable use of the labour?

	Most profitable	*Least profitable*
A	L	V
B	L	A
C	V	A
D	A	L

Answers to Quick Quiz

1   Biggest

2   D.   Limiting factors are resources or demand.

3   True

4   (b), (c), (a)

5   Lowest
Variable cost
Unit of scarce resource

6   Fall
Normal variable

7   (a)   Fixed costs
(b)   Unit variable cost
(c)   Sales demand and resources required per unit
(d)   Units of output

8   B

	V $	A $	L $
Selling price per service	120	170	176
Variable cost per service	60	86	100
Contribution per service	60	84	76
Labour cost per service	20	30	20
Contribution per $ of labour	3	2.80	3.80
Ranking	2	3	1

BPP
LEARNING MEDIA

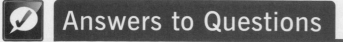
Answers to Questions

5.1 Restricted freedom of action

	K	L
Contribution per unit	$15	$30
Contribution per unit of limiting factor	$15/2 = $7.50	$30/3 = $10
Ranking	2	1

Production plan	Raw material used kg
Contracted supply of K (500 × 2 kg)	1,000
Meet demand for L (250 × 3 kg)	750
Remainder of resource for K (125 × 2 kg)	250
	2,000

The profit-maximising mix is 625K and 250L.

5.2 Make or buy and limiting factors

The correct answer is: TW should manufacture 9,000 units of D and 7,000 units of E.

	D $ per unit	E $ per unit
Variable cost of making	10	15
Variable cost of buying	17	25
Extra variable cost of buying	7	10
Raw material saved by buying	3.5 kg	8 kg
Extra variable cost of buying per kg saved	$2	$1.25
Priority for internal manufacture	1	2

Production plan	Material used kg
∴ Make D (9,000 × 3.5 kg)	31,500
E (7,000 × 8 kg)	56,000
	87,500

The remaining 5,000 units of E should be purchased from the contractor.

Now try these questions from the Practice Question Bank	Number	Level
	Q5.1 – Q5.9	Practice

RELEVANT COSTS

The chapter begins with an **introduction** to decision making (**Sections 1 and 2**) and provides some general information about the decision-making process.

In **Sections 3 to 5** of this chapter you will learn how to identify the **relevant costs and revenues** in decisions, so that management time is not wasted in considering irrelevant information. You will also learn about the **assumptions** underlying the relevant costing approach to decision making (**Section 6**) and about the importance of considering the **non-quantifiable factors** in every decision (in **Section 8**). These are topics that you looked at in your Certificate level studies, so they won't be completely new to you.

This chapter links closely with **Chapter 8**, which deals with the actual decision-making process.

Topic list	Learning outcomes	Syllabus references	Ability required
1 Decisions	C1(a)	C1(a)(i)	Analysis
2 Information for decision making	C1(a)	C1(a)(i)	Analysis
3 Relevant costs and revenues	C1(a)	C1(a)(i)	Analysis
4 Non-relevant costs and revenues	C1(a)	C1(a)(i)	Analysis
5 Some rules for identifying relevant costs	C1(a)	C1(a)(i)	Analysis
6 The assumptions in relevant costing	C1(a)	C1(a)(i), (ii)	Analysis
7 Relation to accounting concepts	C1(b)	C1(b)(i)	Analysis
8 Non-quantifiable factors in decision making	C1(a)	C1(a)(ii)	Analysis

Chapter Overview

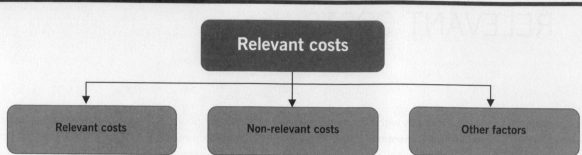

1   Decisions

Introduction

This section looks briefly at the different types of decisions you will encounter in your P1 studies.

1.1 Accept or reject decisions

These decisions are taken on the **merits of a particular opportunity** under consideration, **without the need to compare** that opportunity to other available opportunities. For example, a project with a positive return should be accepted and one with a negative return should be rejected.

If a decision is taken to go ahead with a particular course of action (the '**accept**' option), the organisation will **still be free to consider and take on any other opportunities** presented.

1.2 Ranking decisions

These decisions involve a **choice between one or more competing opportunities**, and so the different opportunities have to be **compared**. They tend to arise for one of two reasons:

(a)   Because there are not enough resources to pursue all the available opportunities.

(b)   The opportunities offer different means to the same or similar ends. In a decision whether a new regional office should be located in city A or city B, for example, both opportunities are different means towards the same end of the choice of an office location.

In this chapter, and the ones that follow, we will be looking at how to make these types of decision.

Section summary

Most decisions can be categorised as one of two types – **accept or reject** decisions or **ranking** decisions.

2   Information for decision making

Introduction

Information required for decision making differs considerably from that used for profit reporting and inventory valuation. This section examines the differences in the provision of different types of information.

2.1 Cost accounting versus information for decision making

Information derived from **cost accounting data** accumulation systems is **totally misleading** for **decision-making purposes**. Absorption costing is used for profit reporting and inventory valuation purposes but, as it does not separate fixed and variable costs, it does not provide relevant information for decision making.

KEY POINT

For one-off decisions or decisions affecting the use of marginal spare capacity, absorption costing information about unit profits is irrelevant and misleading. On the other hand, since total contribution must be sufficient to cover the fixed costs of the business, marginal costing would be unsuitable as a basis for establishing long-term sales prices for all output.

2.2 Marginal costing for decision making

As mentioned above, absorption costing is not useful for decision making, as it produces misleading information. **Marginal costing** is used for decision-making purposes, as it splits costs clearly into fixed and variable elements. This distinction is important, as fixed costs are not relevant for short-term decision making.

Typically, in the short run, fixed costs remain unchanged, which means that the **marginal cost, revenue and contribution** of each decision option are **relevant**.

When marginal costing is used for short-term decision making, the best option is always the one that **maximises contribution**.

Even if fixed costs do change, the division of costs into their fixed and variable components is still needed to allow you to identify contribution.

2.2.1 Costs that vary with activity levels

A large proportion of **short-term decisions require information** about how **costs and revenues vary with activity** so that the alternative options of each decision can be evaluated. Here are some examples:

(a)   At what level should budgeted output be set?
(b)   Should component X be manufactured internally or purchased from a supplier?
(c)   Should a one-off special order be accepted?

For each of these decisions, **management require estimates of costs at different levels of activity of the alternative courses of action**. An organisation might decide to accept a one-off order without understanding that the extra work will mean taking on new staff. Fulfilling the order at the agreed price might therefore result in an overall loss for the organisation.

For short-term decision making, **costs** should therefore be **divided** into:

(a)   **Purely variable costs**, such as direct materials, which can be easily attributed to products, services, customers and so on.

(b)   **Variable costs** that are **fixed in the short term** and which **cannot be directly attributed to cost objects**, **but** which are **avoidable** if the product is not produced, the service not provided and so on.

(c)   **Fixed costs**, which become **variable in the longer term**, **or if activity levels change significantly**. They are **not relevant to short-term decision making** based on marginal costing principles, as they do not change in the short term.

By classifying costs in this way, it is then **possible to predict total costs** at different levels of output.

Section summary

There is a **conflict** between cost accounting for **profit reporting** and **inventory valuation** and the convenient availability of information for **decision making**.

The division of **costs** into their **variable and fixed components** is **useful** in the context of **short-term decision making**.

3   Relevant costs and revenues

Introduction

Section 2 highlighted the need to use marginal costing for short-term decision-making purposes. This section focuses on how to identify relevant costs and revenues. Make sure you understand how to identify such costs before moving on to the next section, as this is a key part of the syllabus.

3.1 Relevant costs

The costs that should be used for **decision making** are often referred to as **relevant costs**.

KEY TERM

RELEVANT COSTS are 'Costs appropriate to a specific management decision. These are represented by future cash flows whose magnitude will vary depending upon the outcome of the management decision made'. *(CIMA Official Terminology)*

(a) **Future costs**

    (i)   A cost that has been incurred in the past is totally irrelevant to any decision that is being made 'now'. Such costs are **past costs** or **sunk costs**.

    (ii)   **Committed** costs are those that result from legally binding contracts. These are also not relevant (even if they have not yet been paid), as they cannot be avoided.

(b) Relevant costs are **cash flows**. This means that costs or charges such as the following, which do not reflect additional cash spending, should be ignored for the purpose of decision making.

    (i)   **Depreciation** (does not involve the movement of cash)
    (ii)   **Notional rent or interest** (a fixed overhead that does not change in the short term)
    (iii)   **All overheads absorbed**

(c) Relevant costs are **incremental costs**.

KEY TERM

INCREMENTAL or DIFFERENTIAL COSTS are 'The difference in total cost between alternatives; calculated to assist decision-making'. *(CIMA Official Terminology)*

For example, suppose a company decides to accept a contract from a customer. An existing supervisor currently earning $1,000 per month is given an extra $100 per month for taking on the extra responsibility associated with this contract. The **incremental** cost is the **additional** salary paid to the supervisor ($100) – the original salary of $1,000 was being paid anyway.

3.2 Avoidable costs and opportunity costs

Other potential relevant costs include **avoidable costs** and **opportunity costs**.

Avoidable costs (as the name suggests) are costs that could be **avoided** if an activity or sector of a business is discontinued. These costs are usually associated with shutdown or divestment decisions.

KEY TERM

AVOIDABLE COSTS are defined as 'The specific costs of an activity or sector of a business which would be avoided if that activity or sector did not exist'. *(CIMA Official Terminology)*

Opportunity cost is the **benefit sacrificed** by choosing one opportunity rather than the next best alternative. You will often encounter opportunity costs when there are several possible uses for a scarce resource.

For example, if a material is in short supply, it may be transferred from the production of one product to that of another product. The opportunity cost is the **contribution lost** from ceasing production of the original product.

KEY TERM

OPPORTUNITY COSTS are 'The value of a benefit sacrificed when one course of action is chosen, in preference to an alternative. The opportunity cost is represented by the forgone potential benefit from the best rejected course of action'. *(CIMA Official Terminology)*

| Question 6.1 | Relevant costs |

Learning outcome C1(a)

An information technology consultancy firm has been asked to do an urgent job by a client, for which a price of $2,500 has been offered. The job would require the following:

(a)   30 hours' work from one member of staff, who is paid on an hourly basis, at a rate of $20 per hour, but who would normally be employed on work for clients where the charge-out rate is $45 per hour. No other member of staff is able to do the member of staff in question's work.

(b)   The use of 5 hours of mainframe computer time, which the firm normally charges out to external users at a rate of $50 per hour. Mainframe computer time is currently used 24 hours a day, 7 days a week.

(c)   Supplies and incidental expenses of $200.

Required

Fill in the blank in the sentence below.

The relevant cost or opportunity cost of the job is $........

3.3 Relevant revenues

Relevant revenues are also **future, incremental cash flows**.

(a)   (i)   Revenue **received in the past** is totally **irrelevant** to any decision that is being made now.

        (ii)   Revenue that has **not yet been received but will be received regardless of the decision made** is **not relevant**.

(b)   Relevant revenues are **cash flows**. The book profit on the sale of a non-current asset is therefore not relevant to a decision on whether or not to sell that asset, whereas the cash received for the asset is.

(c)   Relevant revenues are **incremental revenues**. If project A earns revenue of $1,000 and project B earns revenue of $2,500, the relevant revenue in a decision about whether to choose project B instead of project A is $(2,500 – 1,000) = $1,500.

3.4 Minimum price quotations for special orders

The total relevant cost of an order represents the minimum price that the company should charge for an order if it wishes to make neither a profit nor a loss.

Section summary

Relevant costs are **future, incremental cash flows**.

4   Non-relevant costs and revenues

Introduction

Just as important as being able to identify relevant costs is the ability to identify non-relevant costs. This section focuses on the types of costs that are irrelevant to short-term decision making.

4.1 Sunk costs

KEY TERM

A SUNK COST is 'Cost that has been irreversibly incurred or committed and cannot therefore be considered relevant to a decision. Sunk costs may also be deemed **irrecoverable** costs'.

(*CIMA Official Terminology*)

An example of a sunk cost could be **development costs already incurred**. Suppose that a company has spent $250,000 in developing a new service for customers, but the marketing department's most recent findings are that the service might not gain customer acceptance and could be a commercial failure. The decision whether or not to abandon the development of the new service would have to be taken, but the $250,000 spent so far should be ignored by the decision makers because it is a sunk cost.

4.2 Committed costs

A committed cost is a **future cash outflow** that will be **incurred anyway, whatever decision is taken now** about alternative opportunities. Committed costs may exist because of contracts already entered into by the organisation, which it cannot now avoid.

4.3 Notional costs

KEY TERM

NOTIONAL COST is 'A cost used in product evaluation, decision-making and performance measurement to reflect the use of resources which have no "**actual** (observable) cost"'. (*CIMA Official Terminology*)

Examples of notional costs in cost accounting systems include the following:

(a) **Notional rent**, such as that charged to a subsidiary, cost centre or profit centre of an organisation for the use of accommodation that the organisation owns

(b) **Notional interest charges on capital employed**, sometimes made against a profit centre or cost centre

4.4 Historical costs

Although historical costs are irrelevant for decision making, historical cost data will **often** provide the **best available basis for predicting future costs**.

4.5 Non-relevant variable costs

There might be occasions when a variable cost is in fact a sunk cost. For example, suppose that a company holds some units of raw material. They have been paid for already, and originally cost $2,000. They are now obsolete and are no longer used in regular production, and they have no scrap value. However, they could be used in a special job that the company is trying to decide whether to undertake. The special job is a 'one-off' customer order, and would use up all the materials currently held.

In deciding whether the job should be undertaken, the relevant cost of the materials to the special job is nil. Their **original cost** of $2,000 is a **sunk cost**, and should be ignored in the decision.

However, if the materials did have a **scrap value** of, say, $300, then their relevant cost to the job would be the **opportunity cost** of being unable to sell them for scrap, ie $300.

4.6 Attributable fixed costs

Exam alert

There might be occasions when a fixed cost is a relevant cost, and you must be aware of the distinction between 'specific' and 'directly attributable' fixed costs, and general overheads.

(a) **Directly attributable fixed costs** are those costs that, although fixed within a relevant range of activity level, are relevant to a decision for either of the following reasons.

    (i) They would increase if certain extra activities were undertaken. For example, it may be necessary to employ an extra supervisor if a particular order is accepted. The extra salary would be an attributable fixed cost.

    (ii) They would decrease or be eliminated entirely if a decision were taken either to reduce the scale of operations or shut down entirely.

(b) **General fixed overheads** are those fixed overheads that will be **unaffected** by decisions to increase or decrease the scale of operations. An apportioned share of head office charges is an example of general fixed overheads for a local office or department. General fixed overheads are not relevant in decision making.

Exam alert

Fixed costs are assumed to be irrelevant in decision making (unless given an indication to the contrary). In activity based costing (ABC), however, the crucial assumption is that many so-called 'fixed' costs are actually variable with business complexity given a long enough period of time.

Section summary

Non-relevant costs include **sunk costs**, **committed costs**, **notional costs** and **historical costs**.

Unless you are given an indication to the contrary, you should assume that **variable costs** will be **relevant** costs and that **fixed costs** are **irrelevant** to a decision.

5 Some rules for identifying relevant costs

Introduction

In order to be able to make correct decisions, you must be able to identify the costs that are relevant to that decision. This section covers the general rules that you should follow when trying to identify relevant costs for decision making.

5.1 The relevant cost of materials

If the materials have no resale value and no other possible use, then the relevant cost of using them for the opportunity under consideration would be nil. The following diagram will be useful to help you identify the relevant cost of materials.

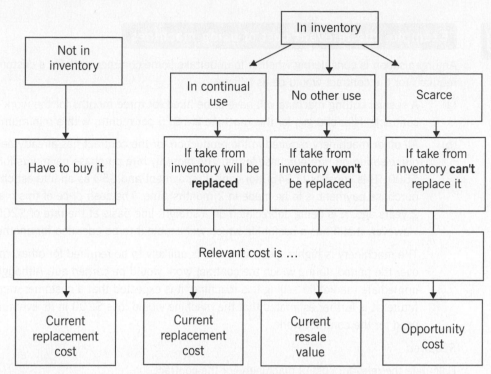

You should test your knowledge of the relevant cost of materials by attempting the following question.

Question 6.2   Relevant cost of materials

Learning outcome C1(a)

DLN has been approached by a customer who would like a special job to be done for him, and who is willing to pay $22,000 for it. The job would require the following materials.

Material	Total units required	Units already held	Book value of units held $/unit	Realisable value $/unit	Replacement cost $/unit
A	1,000	0	–	–	6.00
B	1,000	600	2.00	2.50	5.00
C	1,000	700	3.00	2.50	4.00
D	200	200	4.00	6.00	9.00

Material B is used regularly by DLN and, if units of B are required for this job, they would need to be replaced to meet other production demand.

Materials C and D are held as the result of previous overbuying, and they have a restricted use. No other use could be found for material C, but the units of material D could be used in another job as substitute for 300 units of material E, which currently costs $5 per unit (and of which the company holds no units at the moment).

Required

Fill in the blank in the sentence below.

The relevant cost of material for deciding whether or not to accept the contract is $ ....

5.2 The relevant cost of using machines

The relevant cost of using machines depends on whether the machines can be used for **another purpose** (which will create an opportunity cost) or if they have to be **acquired specifically** for the job in question.

Example: the relevant cost of using machines

An organisation is considering whether to undertake some contract work for a customer. The machinery required for the contract would be as follows:

(a)   A special cutting machine will have to be hired for three months for the work (the length of the contract). Hire charges for this machine are $75 per month, with a minimum hire charge of $300.

(b)   All other machinery required in the production for the contract has already been purchased by the organisation on hire purchase terms. The monthly hire purchase payments for this machinery are $500. This consists of $450 for capital repayment and $50 as an interest charge. The last hire purchase payment is to be made in 2 months' time. The cash price of this machinery was $9,000 2 years ago. It is being depreciated on a straight-line basis at the rate of $200 per month. However, it still has a useful life which will enable it to be operated for another 36 months.

The machinery is highly specialised and is unlikely to be required for other, more profitable jobs over the period during which the contract work would be carried out. Although there is no immediate market for selling this machine, it is expected that a customer might be found in the future. It is further estimated that the machine would lose $200 in its eventual sale value if it is used for the contract work.

Required

Calculate the relevant cost of machinery for the contract.

Solution

(a)   The cutting machine will incur an incremental cost of $300, the minimum hire charge.

(b)   The historical cost of the other machinery is irrelevant as a past cost; depreciation is irrelevant as a non-cash cost; and future hire purchase repayments are irrelevant because they are committed costs. The only relevant cost is the loss of resale value of the machinery, estimated at $200 through use. This user cost will not arise until the machinery is eventually resold and the $200 should be discounted to allow for the time value of money. However, discounting is ignored here.

(c)   Summary of relevant costs

	$
Incremental hire costs	300
User cost of other machinery	200
	500

Question 6.3   Relevant cost of using machines

Learning outcome C1(a)

A machine that originally cost $12,000 has an estimated life of 10 years and is depreciated at the rate of $1,200 a year. It has been unused for some time, however, as expected production orders did not materialise.

A special order has now been received, which would require the use of the machine for two months.

The current net realisable value of the machine is $8,000. If it is used for the job, its value is expected to fall to $7,500. The net book value of the machine is $8,400.

Routine maintenance of the machine currently costs $40 a month. With use, the cost of maintenance and repairs would increase to $60 a month for the months that the machine is being used.

Ignore the time value of money.

What is the relevant cost of using the machine for the order?

5.3 The relevant cost of labour and variable overheads

The relevant cost of **labour** and **variable overheads** will depend on whether labour is working at **full capacity**.

If labour is working at full capacity, it will have to be taken away from another activity in order to work on the new project. This will create an **opportunity cost** that must be accounted for during the decision-making process.

The diagram below can be used to determine the relevant cost of labour and variable overheads.

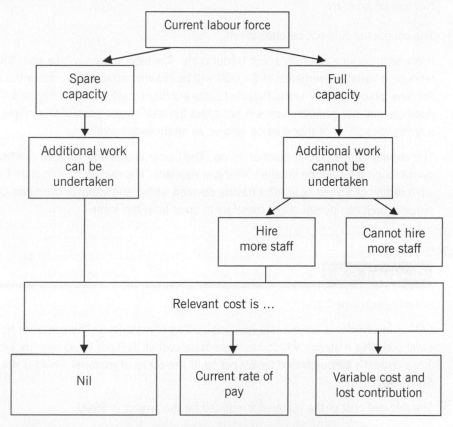

Example: relevant costs of labour and variable overheads

A company has been offered $21,000 by a prospective customer to make some purpose-built equipment. The extra costs of the machine would be $3,000 for materials. There would also be a requirement for 2,000 labour hours. Labour wages are $4 per hour, variable overhead is $2 per hour and fixed overhead is absorbed at the rate of $4 per hour.

Labour, however, is in limited supply, and if the job is accepted workers would have to be diverted from other work, which is expected to earn a contribution of $5 per hour towards fixed overheads and profit.

Required

Assess whether the contract should be undertaken.

Solution

The relevant costs of the scarce resource, labour, are the sum of the following:

*   The variable costs of the labour and associated variable overheads
*   The contribution forgone from not being able to put it to its alternative use

Fixed costs are ignored because there is no incremental fixed cost expenditure.

	$
Materials	3,000
Labour (2,000 hours at $4 per hour)	8,000
Variable overhead (2,000 hours at $2 per hour)	4,000
	15,000
Opportunity cost:	
Contribution forgone from other work (2,000 hours × $5 per hour)	10,000
Total costs	25,000
Revenue	21,000
Net loss on contract	(4,000)

The contract should not be undertaken.

It is worth thinking carefully about labour costs. The labour force will be paid $8,000 for 2,000 hours' work, and variable overheads of $4,000 will be incurred no matter whether the workers are employed on the new job or on other work. Relevant costs are future cash flows arising as a direct consequence of a decision, and the decision here will not affect the total wages paid. If this money is going to be spent anyway, should it not therefore be ignored as an irrelevant cost?

The answer to this crucial question is 'no'. The labour wages and variable overheads are relevant costs even though they will be incurred whatever happens. The reason for this is that the other work earns a contribution of $5 per hour **after having covered** labour and variable overhead costs. Work on the purpose-built equipment ought therefore to do at least the same.

Question 6.4

More relevant costing

Learning outcome C1(a)

LAM is involved in a project that requires 100 kg of material J. The company holds 50 kg of material J. It purchased this material, which has a standard cost of $10 per kg, 6 months ago for $12 per kg. Material J can currently be purchased for $9 per kg. If the 50 kg of material J held is not used, it could be sold for $8 per kg.

The relevant cost of the material J required for the project is $900.

True　☐

False　☐

Section summary

The **relevant cost of raw materials** is generally their current replacement cost unless the materials have already been purchased and will not be replaced, in which case the relevant cost of using them is the higher of their current resale value and the value they would obtain if they were put to an alternative use.

Using **machinery** will involve some **incremental costs**:

- Repair costs arising from use
- Hire charges
- Any fall in resale value of owned assets that results from their use

Depreciation is **not** a relevant cost.

The relevant cost of **labour** and **variable overheads** will depend on whether labour is working at **full capacity**.

6 The assumptions in relevant costing

Introduction

Relevant costs are future costs. Whenever anyone tries to predict what will happen in the future, the predictions are often incorrect. Cost accountants have to make the best forecasts of relevant income and costs that they can, and at the same time recognise the assumptions on which their estimates are based. This section covers the variety of assumptions that may be made – you must be aware of these.

(a) **Cost behaviour patterns are known**; if a department closes down, for example, the attributable fixed cost savings would be known.

This is not necessarily so, and it is always important to question assumptions of this nature. For example, if you are told in an examination question that a factory intends to increase production by 50%, and you are invited to assume in your number work that fixed costs and unit variable costs would be unaffected, it is important to challenge this assumption as a footnote to any report you might write in the integrated case study (ICS), making the following points.

(i) Is it clear that the factory could handle such a large increase in output?

(ii) If so, fixed costs would probably change dramatically, and there might also be a shift in unit variable costs.

(b) **The amount of fixed costs, unit variable costs, sales price and sales demand are known with certainty**. However, it is possible to apply risk and uncertainty analysis to decisions and so recognise that what will happen in the future is not certain.

(c) **The objective of decision making in the short run is to maximise 'satisfaction'**, which is often regarded as 'short-term profit'. However, there are many qualitative factors or financial considerations, other than those of profit, which may influence a final decision. You should point these out in your ICS answers if appropriate.

(d) **The information on which a decision is based is complete and reliable**. This is obviously unrealistic, and decision makers must be made aware of any inadequacies of the information that they are using for their decisions.

Section summary

There are a number of **assumptions** typically made in relevant costing.

7 Relation to accounting concepts

Introduction

Relevant revenues and costs are used for decision-making purposes rather than for reporting to external parties. This means that accounting concepts are not necessarily consistent with information for decision making.

Accounting concept	Relevance to relevant costs and decision making
Accruals	The accruals concept seeks to report transactions in the period to which they relate. However, relevant costs and revenues are calculated on a cash basis rather than an accruals basis and do not include such items as depreciation and allocated fixed costs. Decision making focuses on future costs – past costs are never relevant.
Reliability	Relevant costs and revenues are in the future; they can never be 100% reliable.
Relevance	By their very nature, relevant costs and revenues should always be relevant to the decision being made. However, detailed knowledge of the decision is necessary in order to determine what is relevant and what is not.
Completeness	Relevant costs and revenues should be complete for the decision being made but will not include any items that do not affect that decision.
Comparability	If companies are trying to make a choice between alternatives, the potential outcomes of these alternatives must be comparable – that is, all relevant costs and revenues relating to each alternative must be included. Sunk costs, non-cash costs and costs that are not affected by the decision must always be excluded.
Going concern	While future projects will only be considered if the business is still trading, not all decisions are based on the assumption that the company will continue in profitable business for the foreseeable future – for example, shutdown decisions. In addition, it should be noted that if all projects are undertaken on a relevant cost basis and are priced using the minimum price, the projects will not make enough money to cover the fixed costs of the business.

Section summary

Accounting concepts for financial reporting purposes only have **limited relevance** to decision making. Such concepts include accruals, reliability, relevance, completeness, comparability and going concern.

8 Non-quantifiable factors in decision making

Introduction

Of equal importance to quantifiable factors in decision making are the non-quantifiable factors. This section looks at examples of such factors and also offers advice on how you might treat such factors in an exam situation.

Non-quantifiable factors in decision making are factors that might influence the eventual decisions but that have not been quantified in terms of relevant costs or benefits. They may stem from **two sources**.

(a) Non-financial objectives.

(b) Factors that might be quantifiable in **money terms**, but which have not been quantified, perhaps because there is **insufficient information to make reliable estimates**. Such factors tend to focus on the **long-term implications** of decisions.

Exam alert

Decision-making questions in the ICS may ask you to detail 'other factors that should be considered' other than the figure work for the decision. However, even if the question does not invite you to do so, it is a good idea to get into the habit of adding a few notes concerning 'other factors'.

8.1 Examples of non-quantifiable factors

Non-quantifiable factors in decision making will vary with the circumstances and nature of the opportunity being considered. Here are some examples.

Factors	Details
Availability of cash	An opportunity may be profitable, but there must be sufficient cash to finance any purchases of equipment and build-up of working capital.
Inflation	The effect of inflation on the prices of various items may need to be considered, especially where a fixed price contract is involved in the decision: if the income from an opportunity is fixed by contract, but the costs might increase with inflation, the contract's profitability would be overstated unless inflation is taken into account.
Employees	Any decision involving the shutdown of a plant, creation of a new work shift, or changes in work procedures or location will require acceptance by employees, and ought to consider employee welfare.
Customers	Decisions about new products or product closures, the quality of output or after-sales service will inevitably affect customer loyalty and customer demand. It is also important to remember that a decision involving one product may have repercussions on customer attitudes towards a range of products.
Competitors	In a competitive market, some decisions may stimulate a response from rival companies. For example, the decision to reduce selling prices in order to raise demand may not be successful if all competitors take similar action.
Timing factors	There might be a choice in deciding when to take up an opportunity. The choice would not be 'accept or reject'; there would be three choices: • Accept an opportunity now • Do not accept the opportunity now, but wait before doing so • Reject the opportunity
Suppliers	Some decisions will affect suppliers, whose long-term goodwill may be damaged by a decision to close a product line temporarily. Decisions to change the specifications for purchased components, or change inventory policies so as to create patchy, uneven demand might also put a strain on suppliers. In some cases, where a company is the supplier's main customer, a decision to reduce demand or delay payments for goods received might drive the supplier out of business.
Feasibility	A proposal may look good in financial terms, but technical experts or departmental managers may have some reservations about their ability to carry it out.

Factors	Details
Flexibility and internal control	Decisions to subcontract work or to enter into a long-term contract have the disadvantages of inflexibility and lack of controllability. Where requirements may be changeable, it would be preferable to build flexibility into the organisation of operations.
Unquantified opportunity costs	Even where no opportunity costs are specified, it is probable that other opportunities would be available for using the resources to earn profit. It may be useful to qualify a recommendation by stating that a given project would appear to be viable on the assumption that there are no other more profitable opportunities available.
Political pressures	Some large companies may suffer political pressures applied by the Government to influence their investment or disinvestment decisions.
Legal constraints	A decision might occasionally be rejected because of doubts about the legality of the proposed action.

Question 6.5

Using relevant costs

Learning outcome C1(a)

An organisation in the civil engineering industry with headquarters located 22 miles from London undertakes contracts anywhere in the UK.

The organisation has had its tender for a job in North-East England accepted at $288,000, and work is due to begin in March 20X3. However, the organisation has also been asked to undertake a contract on the south coast of England. The price offered for this contract is $352,000. Both of the contracts cannot be taken simultaneously because of constraints on staff site management personnel and on plant available. An escape clause enables the organisation to withdraw from the contract in the North-East, provided notice is given before the end of November and an agreed penalty of $28,000 is paid.

The following estimates have been submitted by the organisation's quantity surveyor.

COST ESTIMATES

		North-East $	South coast $
Materials:	Held at original cost, Material X	21,600	
	Held at original cost, Material Y		24,800
	Firm orders placed at original cost, Material X	30,400	
	Not yet ordered – current cost, Material X	60,000	
	Not yet ordered – current cost, Material Z		71,200
Labour – hired locally		86,000	110,000
Site management		34,000	34,000
Staff accommodation and travel for site management		6,800	5,600
Plant on site – depreciation		9,600	12,800
Interest on capital, 8%		5,120	6,400
Total local contract costs		253,520	264,800
Headquarters costs allocated at rate of 5% on total contract costs		12,676	13,240
		266,196	278,040
Contract price		288,000	352,000
Estimated profit		21,804	73,960

Notes

1   X, Y and Z are three building materials. Material X is not in common use and would not realise much money if re-sold; however, it could be used on other contracts but only as a substitute for another material currently quoted at 10% less than the original cost of X. The price of Y, a material in common use, has doubled since it was purchased; its net realisable value if re-sold would be its

new price less 15% to cover disposal costs. Alternatively, it could be kept for use on other contracts in the following financial year.

2   With the construction industry not yet recovered from a recent recession, the organisation is confident that manual labour, both skilled and unskilled, could be hired locally on a subcontracting basis to meet the needs of each of the contracts.

3   The plant that would be needed for the south coast contract has been owned for some years and $12,800 is the year's depreciation on a straight-line basis. If the North-East contract is undertaken, less plant will be required but the surplus plant will be hired out for the period of the contract at a rental of $6,000.

4   It is the organisation's policy to charge all contracts with notional interest at 8% on the estimated working capital involved in contracts. Progress payments would be receivable from the contractee.

5   Salaries and general costs of operating the small headquarters amount to about $108,000 each year. There are usually 10 contracts being supervised at the same time.

6   Each of the two contracts is expected to last from March 20X3 to February 20X4 which, coincidentally, is the company's financial year.

7   Site management is treated as a fixed cost.

Required

As the management accountant to the organisation, do the following.

(a)   Present comparative statements to show the net benefit to the organisation of undertaking the more advantageous of the two contracts.

(b)   Explain the reasoning behind the inclusion in (or omission from) your comparative financial statements of each item given in the cost estimates and the notes relating thereto.

Section summary

Non-quantifiable factors should **always be considered** alongside the quantitative data in a decision.

Chapter Summary

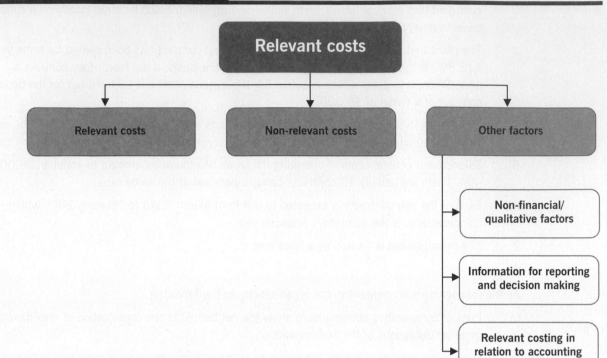

Quick Quiz

1   Tick the correct box for each of these types of cost.

	Relevant cost	*Non-relevant cost*
Incremental cost	☑	☐
Sunk cost	☐	☑
Committed cost	☐	☑

2   An attributable fixed cost is never a relevant cost.

True   ☐

False   ☑

3   The total relevant cost of a scarce resource is equal to the sum of the variable cost of the scarce resource and:

- A   The price that the resource would sell for in the open market
- B   The fixed cost absorbed by a unit of the scarce resource
- C   The contribution forgone from the next best opportunity for using the scarce resource
- D   The price that would have to be paid to replace the scarce resource

4   Which of the following is not an assumption typically made in relevant costing?

- A   Cost behaviour patterns are known.

- B   The amount of fixed costs, unit variable costs, sales prices and sales demand are known with certainty.

- C   The objective of decision making in the short run is to maximise satisfaction.

- D   There is no scarcity of resources.

5   What are the six steps in the decision-making process?

STEP ① ....

STEP ② ....

STEP ③ ....

STEP ④ ....

STEP ⑤ ....

STEP ⑥ ....

6   We detailed 12 non-quantifiable factors in decision making. List 10 of them.

7   Choose the correct words from those highlighted.

Opportunity cost is the **value/cost** of a **benefit/cost** which is **sacrificed/purchased** when one course of action is chosen, in preference to an alternative. The opportunity cost is represented by the forgone **potential/expected/net realisable value** benefit from the **best/worst** rejected course of action.

Answers to Quick Quiz

1   Relevant; non-relevant; non-relevant

2   False. It is relevant to a decision because it is a fixed cost that would be affected by the decision being taken.

3   C.   It is a common mistake to forget to include the opportunity cost.

4   D.   This is **not** an assumption in relevant costing.

5

    Identify objectives

    Search for alternative courses of action

    Collect data about the alternative courses of action

    Select the appropriate course of action

STEP 5   Implement the decision

STEP 6   Compare actual and planned outcomes, and take any necessary corrective action if the planned results have not been achieved

6   Here are all 12.

• The availability of cash	• Competitors	• Flexibility and internal control
• Inflation	• Timing factors	• Unquantified opportunity costs
• Employees	• Suppliers	• Political pressures
• Customers	• Feasibility	• Legal constraints

7   Opportunity cost is the **value** of a benefit which is **sacrificed** when one course of action is chosen, in preference to an alternative. The opportunity cost is represented by the forgone **potential** benefit from the **best** rejected course of action.

Answers to Questions

6.1 Relevant costs

The correct answer is $1,800.

The relevant cost or opportunity cost of the job would be calculated as follows.

	$
Labour (30 hours × $45)	1,350
Computer time opportunity cost (5 hours × $50)	250
Supplies and expenses	200
	1,800

6.2 Relevant cost of materials

The correct answer is $15,450.

(a) **Material A** is not yet owned. It would have to be bought in full at the replacement cost of $6 per unit. Total = $6,000.

(b) **Material B** is used regularly by the company. There is existing inventory (600 units) but if these are used on the contract under review, a further 600 units would be bought to replace them. Relevant costs are therefore 1,000 units at the replacement cost of $5 per unit. Total = $5,000.

(c) 1,000 units of **material C** are needed and 700 are already held. If used for the contract, a further 300 units must be bought at $4 each. The existing inventory of 700 will not be replaced. If they are used for the contract, they could not be sold at $2.50 each. The realisable value of these 700 units is an opportunity cost of sales revenue forgone. Total = (300 × $4) + (700 × $2.50) = $2,950.

(d) The required units of **material D** are already held and will not be replaced. There is an opportunity cost of using material D in the contract because there are alternative opportunities either to sell the existing inventory for $6 per unit ($1,200 in total) or to avoid other purchases (of material E), which would cost 300 × $5 = $1,500. Since the substitution for material E is more beneficial, $1,500 is the opportunity cost.

Total relevant cost is therefore $15,450.

6.3 Relevant cost of using machines

	$
Loss in net realisable value of the machine through using it on the order $(8,000 – 7,500)	500
Costs in excess of existing routine maintenance costs $(120 – 80)	40
Total marginal user cost	540

6.4 More relevant costing

The correct answer is $850 and so the statement is false.

	$
Material already held, relevant cost = 50 kg × $8 =	400
Material to be purchased, relevant cost = 50 kg × $9 =	450
	850

$900 is incorrect because the material held should be valued at its realisable value of $8.

6.5 Using relevant costs

One way of determining which is the more advantageous of the two contracts is to calculate the net cost or benefit of cancelling the North-East contract in favour of the work on the south coast. However, we are asked to present comparative statements, and so our approach will be to prepare statements of the relevant costs of each contract.

Did you read note 3 properly? Rent receivable is **not** an expense. Make sure that the explanations you give in part (b) do not differ from the treatment of items in part (a).

(a)   **Statements of the relevant costs of each contract**

	Note	North-East $	South coast $
Material X held ($21,600 × 90%)	1	19,440	
Material Y held ($24,800 × 2)	2		49,600
Material X on order ($30,400 × 90%)	1	27,360	
Material X not yet ordered	3	60,000	
Material Z not yet ordered	3		71,200
Labour	4	86,000	110,000
Site management	5	–	–
Staff accommodation and travel	6	6,800	5,600
Plant for North-East contract	7	(6,000)	
Plant for south coast contract	8	–	–
Interest on capital	9	–	–
Headquarters' costs	10	–	–
Penalty payment	11		28,000
Total relevant costs		193,600	264,400
Contract price		288,000	352,000
Net benefit		94,400	87,600

The **North-East** contract is therefore the **more advantageous**, with a net benefit to the organisation of $94,400.

(b)   The **reasoning** behind the treatment of each cost item is given in the following notes.

Notes

1   The relevant cost of the material X held and on order is the **opportunity cost** of the saving that is forgone by not using X as a substitute material.

2   Ignoring the time value of money and the cost of storing the material, it would not be worth selling material Y and then repurchasing it next year. In fact, the cost of borrowing is 8%, which is much less than the 15% cost of disposing of the material. The relevant cost of using material Y is the **replacement cost** that would have to be paid to obtain more material for next year's contracts.

3   Since this material has not yet been ordered, the **current cost** is the relevant cost of a decision to proceed with each contract.

4   The labour costs are the **incremental costs** that would have to be incurred if the contract goes ahead. They are therefore relevant costs of both contracts.

5   The statement that site management is treated as a fixed cost is assumed to mean that it is a **committed cost** that will be incurred irrespective of the decision concerning these contracts.

6   It is assumed that these are **incremental costs** that will only be incurred if the contracts go ahead.

7   If the North-East contract is undertaken, the **rental value received** will be $6,000. The **depreciation cost is not relevant** (see note 8).

8   It is assumed that the depreciation cost is an accounting book entry and that the **value of the plant will not be affected** by using it on either contract.

9   Although there would probably be some incremental **working capital financing costs** as a result of the contracts, we have **no way of knowing** how much they would be. They would be somewhat reduced by the effect of the progress payments received from the contractee.

10 It is assumed that the total amount of headquarters' costs **would not be affected** by the decision to undertake either contract. This is therefore not a relevant cost.

11 The penalty payment is a relevant cost of cancelling the North-East contract in order to proceed with the south coast contract.

Now try the questions from the Practice Question Bank

Number	Level
Q6.1 – Q6.5	Practice

MULTI-PRODUCT
BREAKEVEN ANALYSIS

You will have already encountered breakeven (or cost-volume-profit – CVP) analysis in your earlier studies, so you should not be surprised by the terminology or basic techniques that you meet in this chapter. But in case your memory needs refreshing, we have included a brief reminder of the material you covered at the beginning of the chapter, and a question on simple breakeven analysis. You could still be asked to carry out straightforward breakeven analysis in the exam, so make sure that you are perfectly happy with the basic stuff before moving on to the higher-level material.

You should remember that one of the **major assumptions** underpinning breakeven analysis is that it can **only be applied to one product or to a constant (fixed proportions) mix of products**. So far you will only have studied single product breakeven analysis but, as most organisations produce and sell a range of products, we are going to look at what is known as multi-product breakeven analysis. We will see how to perform the various calculations you covered at Certificate level but for multiple products, as well as how to draw breakeven and profit/volume (P/V) charts.

Topic list	Learning outcomes	Syllabus references	Ability required
1 Drawing a basic breakeven chart	C2(b)	C2(b)(i)	Analysis
2 Breakeven analysis in a multi-product environment	C2(b)	C2(b)(i)	Analysis
3 Breakeven point for multiple products	C2(b)	C2(b)(i)	Analysis
4 Contribution to sales (C/S) ratio for multiple products	C2(b)	C2(b)(i)	Analysis
5 Sales/product mix decisions	C2(b)	C2(b)(i)	Analysis
6 Target profits for multiple products	C2(b)	C2(b)(i)	Analysis
7 Margin of safety for multiple products	C2(b)	C2(b)(i)	Analysis
8 Multi-product breakeven charts	C2(b)	C2(b)(i)	Analysis
9 Further aspects of breakeven analysis	C2(b)	C2(b)(i)	Analysis

Chapter Overview

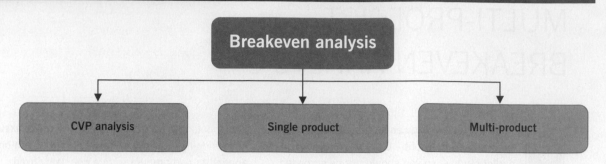

Introduction: knowledge brought forward

KEY TERM

BREAKEVEN ANALYSIS or COST-VOLUME-PROFIT ANALYSIS (CVP) is 'The study of the effects on future profit of changes in fixed cost, variable cost, sales price, quantity and mix'.   (*CIMA Official Terminology*)

CVP analysis is an example of 'what if?' analysis. 'WHAT-IF?' ANALYSIS involves changing the values of the forecast variables to see the effect on the forecast outcome. We will come back to what-if? analysis later when we cover budgeting.

Breakeven analysis

- Contribution per unit   = unit selling price – unit variable costs

- Profit   = (sales volume × contribution per unit) – fixed costs

- Breakeven point   = activity level at which there is neither profit nor loss

$$= \frac{\text{total fixed costs}}{\text{contribution per unit}} = \frac{\text{contribution required to break even}}{\text{contribution per unit}}$$

- Contribution/sales (C/S) ratio   = profit/volume (P/V) ratio = (contribution/sales) × 100%

- Sales revenue at breakeven point   = fixed costs ÷ C/S ratio

- Margin of safety (in units)   = budgeted sales units – breakeven sales units

- Margin of safety (as %) $= \dfrac{\text{budgeted sales} - \text{breakeven sales}}{\text{budgeted sales}} \times 100\%$

- Sales volume to achieve a target profit $= \dfrac{\text{fixed cost} + \text{target profit}}{\text{contribution per unit}}$

- Assumptions

    - Can only apply to one product or constant mix
    - Fixed costs same in total and unit variable costs same at all levels of output
    - Sales prices constant at all levels of activity
    - Production = sales

Breakeven, contribution and P/V charts

- Breakeven chart

- Contribution (contribution breakeven) chart

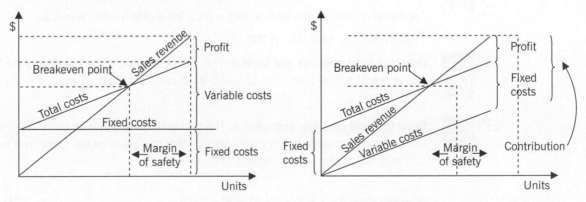

• Profit/volume (P/V) chart

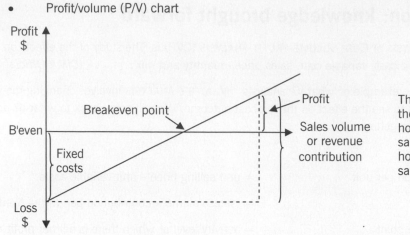

The gradient of the straight line is the contribution per unit (if the horizontal axis is measured in sales units) or the C/S ratio (if the horizontal axis is measured in sales value).

---

1 Drawing a basic breakeven chart

Introduction

You probably won't be asked to prepare a breakeven chart but you may be asked to interpret one. Follow the six steps outlined below to help with your understanding of them.

We will use the following product details to demonstrate how to draw a breakeven chart.

Selling price $60 per unit
Variable cost $40 per unit
Fixed costs $25,000 per month
Forecast sales   1,800 units per month

STEP 1 **Draw the axes and label them**. Your graph should fill as much of the page as possible; this will make it clearer and easier to read.

The furthest point on the vertical axis will be the monthly sales revenue.

1,800 units × $60 = $108,000

STEP 2 **Draw the fixed cost line and label it**. This will be a straight line parallel to the horizontal axis at the $25,000 level. The $25,000 fixed costs are incurred even with zero activity.

STEP 3 **Draw the total cost line and label it**. The best way to do this is to calculate the total costs for the maximum sales level (1,800 units). Mark this point on the graph and join it to the cost incurred at zero activity; that is, $25,000.

	$
Variable costs for 1,800 units (1,800 × $40)	72,000
Fixed costs	25,000
Total cost for 1,800 units	97,000

STEP 4 **Draw the revenue line and label it**. Once again, start by plotting the revenue at the maximum activity level. 1,800 units × $60 = $108,000. This point can be joined to the origin, since at zero activity there will be no sales revenue.

STEP 5 **Mark any required information on the chart and read off solutions as required.** Check that your chart is accurate by reading off the measures that we have already covered in this chapter: the breakeven point, the margin of safety, the profit for sales of 1,800 units.

 STEP 6 **Check the accuracy of your readings using arithmetic.** If you have time, it is good examination technique to check your answer and make adjustments for any errors in your chart.

The completed graph is shown below.

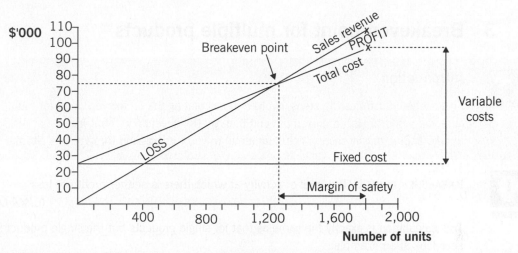

 Section summary

You can prepare a **breakeven chart** by plotting sales revenue against total cost. The breakeven point will be where the sales revenue line and total cost line intersect.

2 Breakeven analysis in a multi-product environment

 Introduction

This section introduces the important syllabus area of multi-product breakeven analysis. It focuses on one of the major assumptions that is made when calculating multi-product breakeven solutions. Make sure you understand the impact of this assumption.

KEY POINT

To perform breakeven analysis in a multi-product organisation, a **constant product sales mix** must be assumed, or all products must have the **same C/S ratio**.

2.1 A major assumption

Organisations typically produce and sell a variety of products and services. To perform breakeven analysis in a multi-product organisation, however, a constant product sales mix must be assumed. In other words, we have to assume that whenever x units of product A are sold, y units of product B and z units of product C are also sold.

Such an assumption allows us to calculate a weighted average contribution per mix, the weighting being on the basis of the quantities of each product in the constant mix. This means that the unit contribution of the product that makes up the largest proportion of the mix has the greatest impact on the average contribution per mix.

The only situation when the mix of products does not affect the analysis is when all of the products have the same ratio of contribution to sales (C/S ratio).

Section summary

To perform breakeven analysis in a multi-product organisation, a **constant product sales mix** must be **assumed**, or all products must have the **same C/S ratio**.

3 Breakeven point for multiple products

Introduction

This section illustrates the steps involved in calculating the breakeven point for multiple products. Make sure you work through the example and then try the question without looking at the solution. Your understanding of this section is fundamental to your progression through this chapter.

KEY TERM

BREAKEVEN POINT is 'The level of activity at which there is neither profit nor loss'.

(CIMA Official Terminology)

This calculation is exactly the same as that for single products but the single product is the standard mix. Let's look at an example.

Example: breakeven point for multiple products

Suppose that PL produces and sells two products. The M sells for $7 per unit and has a total variable cost of $2.94 per unit, while the N sells for $15 per unit and has a total variable cost of $4.50 per unit. The marketing department has estimated that for every five units of M sold, one unit of N will be sold. The organisation's fixed costs total $36,000.

Solution

We calculate the breakeven point as follows:

 STEP **1** Calculate **contribution per unit**

	M $ per unit	N $ per unit
Selling price	7.00	15.00
Variable cost	2.94	4.50
Contribution	4.06	10.50

 STEP **2** Calculate **contribution per mix**

= ($4.06 × 5) + ($10.50 × 1) = $30.80

STEP **3** Calculate the **breakeven point** in terms of the number of mixes

= fixed costs/contribution per mix = $36,000/$30.80

= 1,169 mixes (rounded)

 STEP **4** Calculate the **breakeven point** in terms of the **number of units of the products**

= (1,169 × 5) 5,845 units of M and (1,169 × 1) 1,169 units of N (rounded)

STEP **5**   Calculate the **breakeven point** in terms of **revenue**

= (5,845 × $7) + (1,169 × $15)

= $40,915 of M and $17,535 of N = $58,450 in total

It is important to note that the breakeven point is not $58,450 of revenue, whatever the mix of products. The breakeven point is $58,450 provided that the sales mix remains 5:1. Likewise, the breakeven point is not at a production/sales level of (5,845 + 1,169) 7,014 units. Rather, it is when 5,845 units of M and 1,169 units of N are sold, assuming a sales mix of 5:1.

Question 7.1	Breakeven point for multiple products

Learning outcome C2(b)

Alpha manufactures and sells three products, the Beta, the Gamma and the Delta. Relevant information is as follows:

	Beta	Gamma	Delta
	$ per unit	$ per unit	$ per unit
Selling price	135.00	165.00	220.00
Variable cost	73.50	58.90	146.20

Total fixed costs are $950,000.

An analysis of past trading patterns indicates that the products are sold in the ratio 3:4:5.

Required

Fill in the blanks in the sentence below.

Alpha's breakeven point in terms of revenue of the three products is .... of Beta, ... of Gamma and .... of Delta, making .... in total.

 Section summary

The **breakeven point (in number of mixes)** for a standard mix of products is calculated as fixed costs/contribution per mix.

4 Contribution to sales (C/S) ratio for multiple products

 Introduction

This section illustrates how to calculate the C/S ratio for multiple products. Remember from your previous studies that the C/S ratio can be used to calculate the breakeven point in terms of sales revenue. This is still the case for multiple products.

 LEARN   The **breakeven point in terms of sales revenue** can be calculated as fixed costs/average C/S ratio.

4.1 Calculating the ratio

An alternative way of **calculating the breakeven point** is to use the **average C/S ratio** for the standard mix.

As you should already know, the C/S ratio is sometimes called the **profit/volume ratio** or **P/V ratio**.

We can calculate the breakeven point of PL (see Section 3) as follows:

STEP ① Calculate **revenue per mix**

STEP ② Calculate **contribution per mix**

= $30.80 (see Section 3)

STEP ③ Calculate **average C/S ratio**

= ($30.80/$50.00) × 100% = 61.6%

STEP ④ Calculate **breakeven point** (total)

= fixed costs ÷ C/S ratio

= $36,000/0.616 = $58,442 (rounded)

STEP ⑤ Calculate **revenue ratio of mix**

= 35:15, or 7:3

STEP ⑥ Calculate **breakeven sales**

M = $58,442 × 7/10 = $40,909 rounded

Question 7.2　　　　　　　　　　　　　　　　　　　　　C/S ratio for multiple products

Learning outcome C2(b)

Calculate the breakeven sales revenue of products Beta, Gamma and Delta (see Question 7.1 above) using the approach shown in Section 3.

Alternatively, you might be provided with the individual C/S ratios of a number of products. For example, if an organisation sells two products (A and B) in the **ratio 2:5** and if the C/S ratio of A is **10%** whereas that of B is 50%, the average C/S ratio is calculated as follows:

$$\text{Average C/S ratio} = \frac{(2 \times 10\%) + (5 \times 50\%)}{2 + 5} = 38.6\%$$

Question 7.3　　　　　　　　　　　　　　　　　　　　　　　　　Average C/S ratio

Learning outcome C2(b)

TIM produces and sells two products, the MK and the KL. The organisation expects to sell one MK for every two KLs and have monthly sales revenue of $150,000. The MK has a C/S ratio of 20% whereas the KL has a C/S ratio of 40%. Budgeted monthly fixed costs are $30,000.

What is the budgeted breakeven sales revenue?

The C/S ratio is a measure of how much contribution is earned from each $1 of sales of the standard mix. The **C/S ratio of 33.33%** in the question above means that for every $1 of sales of the standard mix of products, a contribution of 33.33c is earned. To **earn a total contribution of, say, $20,000, sales revenue from the standard mix** must therefore be:

$$\frac{\$1}{33.33c} \times \$20,000 = \$60,006$$

Question 7.4	Using the C/S ratio

Learning outcome C2(b)

Refer back to the information in the paragraph following Question 7.2. Suppose the organisation in question has fixed costs of $100,000, and wishes to earn total contribution of $200,000.

What level of revenue must be achieved?

4.2 Points to bear in mind

KEY POINT

Any change in the proportions of products in the mix will change the contribution per mix and the average C/S ratio and hence the breakeven point.

(a) If the mix shifts towards products with lower contribution margins, the breakeven point (in units) will increase and profits will fall unless there is a corresponding increase in total revenue.

(b) A shift towards products with higher contribution margins without a corresponding decrease in revenues will cause an increase in profits and a lower breakeven point.

(c) If sales are at the specified level but not in the specified mix, there will be either a profit or a loss depending on whether the mix shifts towards products with higher or lower contribution margins.

Section summary

The **breakeven point in terms of sales revenue** can be calculated as fixed costs/average C/S ratio.

Any change in the **proportions of products** in the mix will change the **contribution per mix** and the **average C/S ratio** and hence the breakeven point.

5 Sales/product mix decisions

Introduction

In this section we focus on how to use the methodology above for making sales or product mix decisions. This is an important section, so make sure you work through the examples carefully before trying any questions on your own.

KEY POINT

If an organisation sells a number of products, the total C/S ratio is the sum of the individual weighted (by market share) C/S ratios.

Example: sales mix decisions

JM makes and sells two products, the J and the M. The budgeted selling price of the J is $60 and that of the M, $72. Variable costs associated with producing and selling the J are $30 and, with the M, $60. Annual fixed production and selling costs of JM are $3,369,600.

JM has two production/sales options. The J and the M can be sold either in the ratio two Js to three Ms or in the ratio one J to two Ms.

Required

Determine the optimal mix of products J and M.

Solution

We can decide on the optimal mix by looking at breakeven points. We need to begin by determining contribution per unit.

	J	M
	$ per unit	$ per unit
Selling price	60	72
Variable cost	30	60
Contribution	30	12

Mix 1

Contribution per 5 units sold = ($30 × 2) + ($12 × 3) = $96

$$\text{Breakeven point} = \frac{\$3,369,600}{\$96} = 35,100 \text{ sets of 5 units}$$

	J		M	
Breakeven point:				
in units	(35,100 × 2)	70,200	(35,100 × 3)	105,300
in $	(70,200 × $60)	$4,212,000	(105,300 × $72)	$7,581,600

'Total' breakeven point = $11,793,600

Mix 2

Contribution per 3 units sold = ($30 × 1) + ($12 × 2) = $54

$$\text{Breakeven point} = \frac{\$3,369,600}{\$54} = 62,400 \text{ sets of 3 units}$$

	J		M	
Breakeven point:				
in units	(62,400 × 1)	62,400	(62,400 × 2)	124,800
in $	(62,400 × $60)	$3,744,000	(124,800 × $72)	$8,985,600

'Total' breakeven point = $12,729,600

Ignoring commercial considerations, mix 1 is preferable to mix 2. This is because it results in a lower level of sales to break even (because of the higher average contribution per unit sold). The average contribution for mix 1 is $19.20 ($96 ÷ 5). In mix 2 it is $18 ($54 ÷ 3). Mix 1 contains a higher proportion (40% as opposed to 33.33%) of the more profitable product.

The following question looks at the **effect on the overall C/S ratio of changing a product/sales mix**.

Example: changing the product mix

AL sells three products – Exe, Why and Zed – in equal quantities and at the same selling price per unit. The C/S ratio for the Exe is 50%, that of the Why is 60% and the total C/S ratio is 55%. Suppose the product mix is changed to Exe 20%, Why 50% and Zed 30%.

Required

Calculate the revised C/S ratio.

Solution

Original proportions

	Exe	Why	Zed	Total
C/S ratio	0.5	0.6	0.549(W2)	
Market share	× 1/3	× 1/3	× 1/3	
	0.167	0.200	0.183(W1)	0.55

Workings

1   The total C/S ratio is the sum of the weighted C/S ratios and so this figure is calculated as 0.55 – 0.167 – 0.2 = 0.183.

2   This figure is then calculated as 0.183 ÷ $^1/_3$ = 0.549.

Revised proportions

	Exe	Why	Zed	Total
C/S ratio (as above)	0.5	0.6	0.549	
Market share	× 0.2	× 0.5	× 0.3	
	0.1	0.3	0.1647	0.5647

The total C/S ratio will increase because of the inclusion in the mix of proportionately more of Why, which has the highest C/S ratio.

Question 7.5

Sales mix decision

Learning outcome C2(b)

LL currently sells three products, U, C and Y, at the same selling price per unit.

Current product mix	U – 25%	C – 35%	Y – 40%
Current P/V ratio	Total – 43.5%	C – 45%	Y – 35%
LL decides to change the product mix to	U – 30%	C – 40%	Y – 30%

What is the revised total contribution/total sales ratio?

Section summary

If an organisation sells a number of products, the **total C/S ratio is the sum of the individual weighted (by market share) C/S ratios**.

6 Target profits for multiple products

Introduction

You should already be familiar with the problem of target profits for single products in a CVP context in Certificate Paper CO1. This section expands the concept to multiple products, illustrating the calculations in several examples.

6.1 A reminder of the formula for target profits

At **breakeven point** there is no profit – that is:

Contribution = fixed costs

Suppose an organisation wishes to achieve a certain level of profit during a period. To achieve this profit, contribution must cover fixed costs and leave the required profit:

So **total contribution required = fixed costs + required profit**

Once we know the total contribution required, we can calculate the sales revenue of each product needed to achieve a target profit. The method is similar to the method used to calculate the breakeven point.

LEARN

The number of mixes of products required to be sold to achieve a **target profit** is calculated as (fixed costs + required profit)/contribution per mix.

Example: target profits for multiple products

An organisation makes and sells three products, F, G and H. The products are sold in the proportions F:G:H = 2:1:3. The organisation's fixed costs are $80,000 per month and details of the products are as follows.

Product	Selling price $ per unit	Variable cost $ per unit
F	22	16
G	15	12
H	19	13

The organisation wishes to earn a profit of $52,000 next month. Calculate the required sales value of each product in order to achieve this target profit.

Solution

STEP 1 — Calculate **contribution per unit**

	F $ per unit	G $ per unit	H $ per unit
Selling price	22	15	19
Variable cost	16	12	13
Contribution	6	3	6

STEP 2 — Calculate **contribution per mix**

= ($6 × 2) + ($3 × 1) + ($6 × 3) = $33

Calculate the **required number of mixes**

= (Fixed costs + required profit)/contribution per mix

= ($80,000 + $52,000)/$33

= 4,000 mixes

Calculate the required sales in terms of the number of units of the products and sales revenue of each product.

Product	Units	Selling price $ per unit	Sales revenue required $
F	4,000 × 2 8,000	22	176,000
G	4,000 × 1 4,000	15	60,000
H	4,000 × 3 12,000	19	228,000
Total			464,000

The sales revenue of $464,000 will generate a profit of $52,000 if the products are sold in the mix 2:1:3.

Alternatively, the C/S ratio could be used to determine the required sales revenue for a profit of $52,000. The method is again similar to that demonstrated earlier when calculating the breakeven point.

Example: using the C/S ratio to determine the required sales

We'll use the data from the example above.

Calculate revenue per mix

= (2 × $22) + (1 × $15) + (3 × $19)

= $116

Calculate contribution per mix

= $33 (from Solution in Section 6.1)

Calculate average C/S ratio

= ($33/$116) × 100%

= 28.45%

Calculate required total revenue

= required contribution ÷ C/S ratio

= ($80,000 + $52,000) ÷ 0.2845

= $463,972

Calculate revenue ratio of mix

= (2 × $22):(1 × $15):(3 × $19)

= 44:15:57

Calculate required sales

Required sales of F = 44/116 × $463,972 = $175,989
Required sales of G = 15/116 × $463,972 = $59,996
Required sales of H = 57/116 × $463,972 = $227,986

Which, allowing for roundings, is the same answer as calculated in the first example.

Section summary

The number of mixes of products required to be sold to achieve a **target profit** is calculated as (fixed costs + required profit)/contribution per mix.

7 Margin of safety for multiple products

Introduction

It should not surprise you to learn that the calculation of the margin of safety for multiple products is exactly the same as for single products, but the single product is the standard mix. The easiest way to see how it's done is to look at an example, which we do in this section.

KEY POINT

The **margin of safety** for a multi-product organisation is equal to the budgeted sales in the standard mix less the breakeven sales in the standard mix. It may be expressed as a percentage of the budgeted sales.

Example: margin of safety for multiple products

BA produces and sells two products. The W sells for $8 per unit and has a total variable cost of $3.80 per unit, while the R sells for $14 per unit and has a total variable cost of $4.20. For every 5 units of W sold, 6 units of R are sold. BA's fixed costs are $43,890 per period.

Budgeted sales revenue for next period is $74,400, in the standard mix.

Required

Calculate the margin of safety in terms of sales revenue and also as a percentage of budgeted sales revenue.

Solution

To calculate the margin of safety, we must first determine the **breakeven point**.

STEP 1 Calculate **contribution per unit**

	W $ per unit	R $ per unit
Selling price	8.00	14.00
Variable cost	3.80	4.20
Contribution	4.20	9.80

STEP 2 Calculate **contribution per mix**

= ($4.20 × 5) + ($9.80 × 6) = $79.80

STEP 3 Calculate the **breakeven point** in terms of the **number of mixes**

= fixed costs/contribution per mix = $43,890/$79.80
= 550 mixes

STEP 4 Calculate the **breakeven point** in terms of the **number of units of the products**

= (550 × 5) 2,750 units of W and (550 × 6) 3,300 units of R

STEP 5 Calculate the **breakeven point** in terms of **revenue**

= (2,750 × $8) + (3,300 × $14)

= $22,000 of W and $46,200 of R = $68,200 in total

 STEP 6 Calculate the **margin of safety**

= budgeted sales − breakeven sales

= $74,400 − $68,200

= $6,200 sales in total, in the standard mix

Or, as a percentage

= ($74,400 − $68,200)/$74,400 × 100%

= 8.3% of budgeted sales

 ### Section summary

The **margin of safety** for a multi-product organisation is equal to the budgeted sales in the standard mix less the breakeven sales in the standard mix. It may be expressed as a percentage of the budgeted sales.

8 Multi-product breakeven charts

 ### Introduction

As well as being able to carry out CVP calculations you may be asked to produce a breakeven chart in a multiple product situation. This section focuses on the procedure involved in producing multi-product breakeven charts and profit/volume (P/V) charts.

8.1 Breakeven charts

KEY TERM

A BREAKEVEN CHART is 'A chart which indicates approximate profit or loss at different levels of sales volume within a limited range'. (*CIMA Official Terminology*)

A very serious limitation of breakeven charts is that they can show the costs, revenues, profits and margins of safety for a single product only, or at best for a **single 'sales mix' of products**.

KEY POINT

Breakeven charts for multiple products can be drawn if a constant product sales mix is assumed.

For example, suppose that FA sells 3 products, X, Y and Z, which have variable unit costs of $3, $4 and $5 respectively. The sales price of X is $8, the price of Y is $6 and the price of Z is $6. Fixed costs per annum are $10,000.

A breakeven chart cannot be drawn, because we do not know the proportions of X, Y and Z in the sales mix.

Exam alert

If you are not sure about this point, you should try to draw a breakeven chart with the information given. It should not be possible.

However, there are a number of ways in which we can overcome this problem.

8.1.1 Approach 1 – output in $ sales and a constant product mix

Assume that budgeted sales are 2,000 units of X, 4,000 units of Y and 3,000 units of Z. A breakeven chart would make the assumption that output and sales of X, Y and Z are in the proportions 2,000:4,000:3,000 at all levels of activity; in other words, that the sales mix is 'fixed' in these proportions.

We begin by carrying out some calculations.

Budgeted costs		Costs $		Revenue $
Variable costs of X	(2,000 × $3)	6,000	X (2,000 × $8)	16,000
Variable costs of Y	(4,000 × $4)	16,000	Y (4,000 × $6)	24,000
Variable costs of Z	(3,000 × $5)	15,000	Z (3,000 × $6)	18,000
Total variable costs		37,000	Budgeted revenue	58,000
Fixed costs		10,000		
Total budgeted costs		47,000		

The **breakeven chart** can now be drawn.

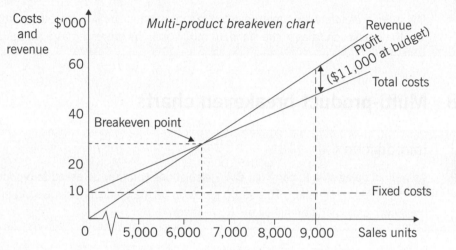

The **breakeven point** is approximately $27,500 of sales revenue. This may either be **read from the chart or computed mathematically**.

(a)   The budgeted C/S ratio for all three products together is contribution/sales = $(58,000 – 37,000)/$58,000 = 36.21%.

(b)   The required contribution to break even is $10,000, the amount of fixed costs. The breakeven point is $10,000/36.21% = $27,500 (approx) in sales revenue.

The margin of safety is approximately $(58,000 – 27,500) = $30,500.

8.1.2 Approach 2 – products in sequence

The products could be plotted in a particular sequence (say, X first, then Y, then Z).

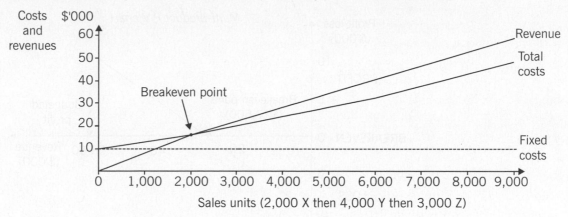

In this case, the breakeven point occurs at 2,000 units of sales (2,000 units of product X). The margin of safety is roughly 4,000 units of Y and 3,000 units of Z.

At 2,000 units of X, revenue is $16,000 and variable costs are $6,000, fixed costs are $10,000. This is the breakeven point, so all further planned production is the margin of safety.

8.1.3 Approach 3: output in terms of % of forecast sales and a constant product mix

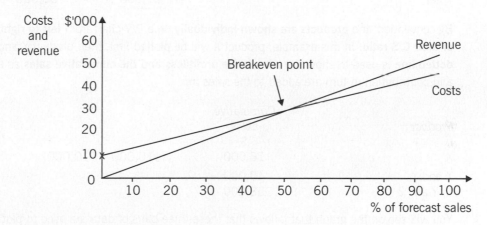

The breakeven point can be read from the graph as approximately 48% of forecast sales ($30,000 of revenue).

Alternatively, with contribution of $(58,000 – 37,000) = $21,000, 1% of forecast sales is associated with $21,000/100 = $210 contribution.

Breakeven point (%) = fixed costs/contribution per 1%

$$= \$10,000/\$210 = 47.62\%$$

∴ Margin of safety = (100 – 47.62) = 52.38%

Exam alert

The general point of setting out these three approaches is to demonstrate that output can be viewed in several different ways.

8.2 Multi-product P/V charts

The same information could be shown on a **P/V chart**, as follows:

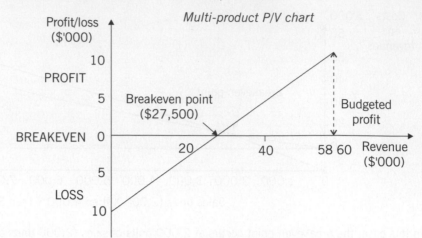

An **addition** to the chart would **show further information about the contribution earned by each product individually**, so that their performance and profitability can be compared.

	Contribution $	Sales $	C/S ratio %
Product X	10,000	16,000	62.50
Product Y	8,000	24,000	33.33
Product Z	3,000	18,000	16.67
Total	21,000	58,000	36.21

By convention, the **products are shown individually** on a P/V chart from **left to right**, in **order of the size of their C/S ratio**. In this example, product X will be plotted first, then product Y and finally product Z. A **dotted line** is used to show the **cumulative profit/loss and the cumulative sales** as each product's sales and contribution in turn are added to the sales mix.

Product	Cumulative sales $		Cumulative profit $
X	16,000	($10,000 – $10,000)	–
X and Y	40,000		8,000
X, Y and Z	58,000		11,000

You will see on the graph that follows that these three pairs of data are used to plot the dotted line, to indicate the contribution from each product. The **solid line** that joins the two ends of this dotted line **indicates the average profit** that will be earned from sales of the three products in this mix.

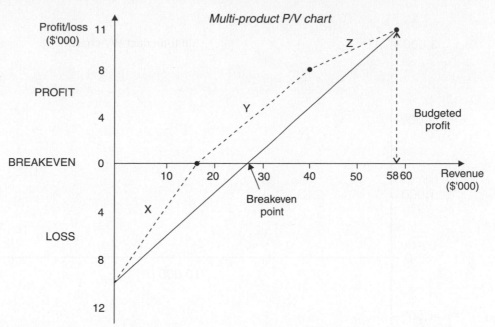

Multi-product P/V chart

The diagram **highlights** the following points:

(a)   Since X is the most profitable in terms of C/S ratio, it might be worth considering an increase in the sales of X, even if there is a consequent fall in the sales of Z.

(b)   Alternatively, the pricing structure of the products should be reviewed and a decision made as to whether the price of product Z should be raised so as to increase its C/S ratio (although an increase is likely to result in some fall in sales volume).

The **multi-product P/V chart** therefore helps to **identify** the following:

(a)   The overall company breakeven point

(b)   Which products should be expanded in output and which, if any, should be discontinued

(c)   What effect changes in selling price and sales volume will have on the company's breakeven point and profit

Question 7.6   Multi-product P/V chart

Learning outcome C2(b)

A company sells three products, X, Y and Z. Cost and sales data for one period are as follows:

	X	Y	Z
Sales volume	2,000 units	2,000 units	5,000 units
Sales price per unit	$3	$4	$2
Variable cost per unit	$2.25	$3.50	$1.25
Total fixed costs	$3,250		

Required

Construct a multi-product P/V chart based on the above information on the axes below.

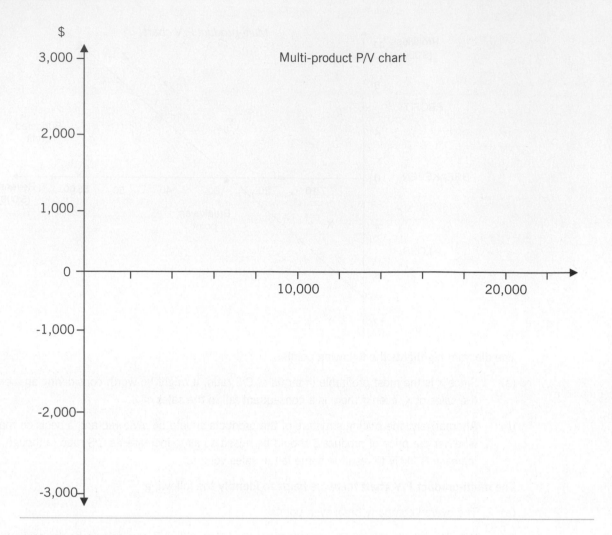

$ Multi-product P/V chart

Question 7.7

Breakeven point and sales value constraints

Learning outcome C2(b)

Sutton produces four products. Relevant data is shown below for period 2.

	Product M	Product A	Product R	Product P
C/S ratio	5%	10%	15%	20%
Maximum sales value	$200,000	$120,000	$200,000	$180,000
Minimum sales value	$50,000	$50,000	$20,000	$10,000

The fixed costs for period 2 are budgeted at $60,000.

Required

Fill in the blank in the sentence below.

The lowest breakeven sales value, subject to meeting the minimum sales value constraints, is $.............

Section summary

Breakeven charts for multiple products can be drawn if a constant product sales mix is assumed.

The **P/V chart** can show information about each product individually.

9 Further aspects of breakeven analysis

Introduction

As well as being able to carry out CVP calculations, you may be asked to criticise the CVP approach to short-term decision making. This does not only mean giving the limitations of CVP but also means being aware of the advantages.

9.1 Limitations and advantages

9.1.1 Limitations

(a) It is **assumed** that **fixed costs** are the **same in total** and **variable costs** are the **same per unit at all levels of output**. This assumption is a great **simplification**.

   (i) Fixed costs will change if output falls or increases substantially (most fixed costs are step costs).

   (ii) The variable cost per unit will decrease where economies of scale are made at higher output volumes, but the variable cost per unit will also eventually rise when diseconomies of scale begin to appear at even higher volumes of output (for example, the extra cost of labour in overtime working).

   The **assumption** is only **correct within** a normal range or **relevant range of output**. It is generally assumed that both the budgeted output and the breakeven point lie within this relevant range.

(b) It is **assumed** that **sales prices** will be **constant** at **all levels of activity**. This may not be true, especially at higher volumes of output, where the price may have to be reduced to win the extra sales.

(c) **Production** and **sales** are **assumed** to be the **same**, so that the consequences of any increase in inventory levels or of 'de-stocking' are ignored.

(d) **Uncertainty** in the estimates of fixed costs and unit variable costs is often **ignored**.

9.1.2 Advantages

(a) **Graphical representation** of cost and revenue data (breakeven charts) can be **more easily understood by non-financial managers**.

(b) A breakeven model enables **profit or loss at any level of activity** within the range for which the model is valid to be **determined**, and the C/S ratio can indicate the **relative profitability of different products**.

(c) Highlighting the breakeven point and the margin of safety gives managers some **indication** of the level of **risk** involved.

9.2 The accountant's and economist's models of breakeven analysis and the relevant range

The economist's model of breakeven analysis differs from the accountant's model we have been using for the following reasons:

(a) The economist's model assumes that **variable** (marginal) **cost per unit changes with the level of output**. It will decrease initially but will start to rise when the factory starts operating at a level beyond its efficient capacity.

(b) **Selling price per unit is not assumed to be constant** in the economist's model. The economist's philosophy is that in order to sell more, a business will have to reduce its price.

The economist's model will therefore look like this:

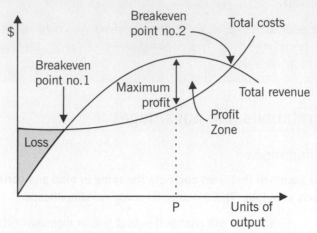

The shape of the total costs and total revenue lines means that there are **two breakeven points**. At the second, decreasing total revenue equals increasing total costs. The first is similar to the single breakeven point shown on an accountant's breakeven chart.

The accountant's breakeven chart is not intended to provide an accurate representation of total costs and total revenue behaviour in all ranges of output but rather to represent behaviour over the **relevant range**.

KEY TERM

RELEVANT RANGE. 'Activity levels within which assumptions about cost behaviour in breakeven analysis remain valid.'
(CIMA Official Terminology)

Within the **relevant range**, the **economist's and accountant's charts are not too different**. The two types of chart are superimposed below.

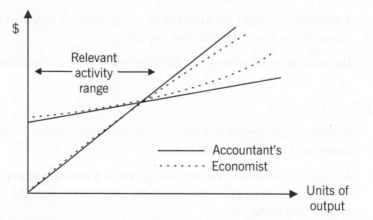

Fixed costs are also **assumed** to be **constant at all levels of output**, so that if there is no output at all, there will be a loss equal to the amount of fixed costs. It might be tempting to assume that this is true, but it could be a seriously **misleading assumption** because many **'fixed cost' items are step costs** in nature over a wide range of activity. **Fixed cost** estimates should therefore only **apply within the relevant range** of activity.

Section summary

The usefulness of CVP analysis is restricted by its **unrealistic assumptions**, such as constant sales price at all levels of activity. However, CVP has the advantage of being more **easily understood** by non-financial managers due to its graphical depiction of cost and revenue data.

The economist's model of breakeven analysis differs from the accountant's model due to its assumption that **selling price** and **variable cost per unit do not remain constant** as sales and production volumes increase.

However, the accountant's model and economist's model tend to be similar in the short run over the **relevant range**.

Chapter Overview

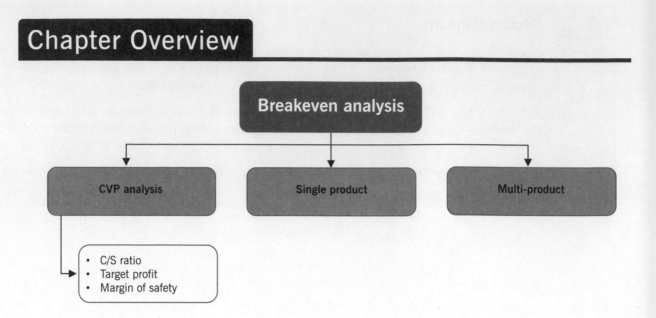

Quick Quiz

1 Fill in the blanks.

$$\text{Breakeven point} = \frac{\text{contrib per mix (to break even)}}{\text{Contribution per mix}} = \frac{\text{F.C (total)}}{\text{Contribution per mix}}$$

2 C/S ratio = P/V ratio × 100.

True ☐

False ☑

3 Fill in the blanks.

$$\text{Margin of safety (as \%)} = \left(\frac{\text{budgeted sales} - \text{breakeven sales}}{\text{budgeted sales}} \right) \times 100\%$$

4 Mark the following on the breakeven chart below.

- Profit
- Sales revenue
- Total costs
- Margin of safety

- Variable costs
- Fixed costs
- Breakeven point

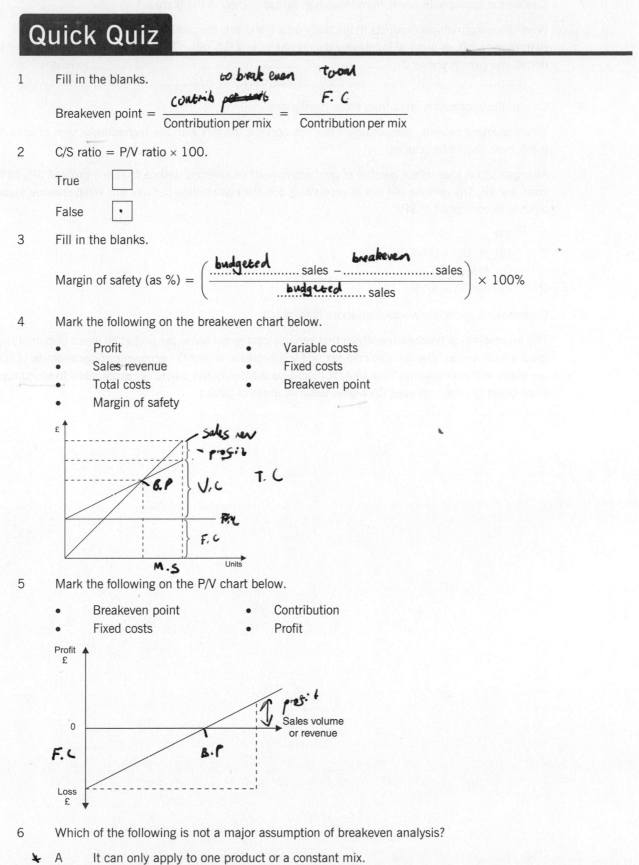

5 Mark the following on the P/V chart below.

- Breakeven point
- Fixed costs

- Contribution
- Profit

6 Which of the following is not a major assumption of breakeven analysis?

A It can only apply to one product or a constant mix.

B Fixed costs are the same in total and unit variable costs are the same at all levels of output.

C Sales prices vary in line with levels of activity.

D Production level is equal to sales level.

7   Choose the appropriate words from those highlighted and fill in the blanks.

When showing multiple products individually on a P/V chart, the products are shown from **left to right/right to left**, in order of **increasing/decreasing** size of C/S ratio. The line joining the two ends of the dotted line (which shows ....) indicates ....

8   Choose the appropriate word from those highlighted.

When choosing between two possible sales mix options, the mix with the **higher/lower** level of sales to break even should be selected.

9   An organisation that sells a number of products in fixed proportions wishes to earn a profit of $P. Its fixed costs are $F. The revenue per mix of products is $R, the contribution per mix $C. What revenue must it achieve to earn profit of $P?

     A $R
     B   ($F + $P) ÷ ($C/$R)
     C $F + $P
     D   ($F + $P) ÷ $R/$C

10   Choose the appropriate words from those highlighted.

The assumption in breakeven analysis that variable cost is the same per unit at all levels of output is a great simplification. The variable cost per unit will decrease where (1) **economies/diseconomies** of scale are made at higher volumes of output, but will also eventually rise where (2) **economies/diseconomies** of scale begin to appear at even (3) **higher/lower** volumes of output.

Answers to Quick Quiz

1 Breakeven point = $\dfrac{\text{Total fixed costs}}{\text{Contribution per unit}}$ = $\dfrac{\text{Contribution required to break even}}{\text{Contribution per unit}}$

2 False. The C/S ratio is another name for the P/V ratio.

3 Margin of safety (as %) = $\left(\dfrac{\text{Budgeted sales} - \text{breakeven sales}}{\text{Budgeted sales}} \right) \times 100\%$

4

5

6 C. Sales prices **are constant** at all levels of activity.

7 When showing multiple products individually on a P/V chart, the products are shown from **left to right**, in order of **decreasing** size of C/S ratio. The line joining the two ends of the dotted line (which shows **the cumulative profit/loss and the cumulative sales**) indicates **the average profit which will be earned from sales of the products in the mix**.

8 Lower

9 B. This is required contribution ÷ C/S ratio.

10 (1) Economies
   (2) Diseconomies
   (3) Higher

Answers to Questions

7.1 Breakeven point for multiple products

The correct answer is **$393,660 of Beta, $641,520 of Gamma and $1,069,200 of Delta,** making **$2,104,380 in total.**

 Calculate **contribution per unit**

	Beta $ per unit	Gamma $ per unit	Delta $ per unit
Selling price	135.00	165.00	220.00
Variable cost	73.50	58.90	146.20

 Calculate **contribution per mix**

= ($61.50 × 3) + ($106.10 × 4) + ($73.80 × 5)

= $977.90

Calculate the **breakeven point** in terms of the **number of mixes**

= fixed costs/contribution per mix

= $950,000/$977.90 = 972 mixes (rounded up)

 Calculate the **breakeven point** in terms of the **number of units of the products**

= (972 × 3) 2,916 units of Beta, (972 × 4) 3,888 units of Gamma and (972 × 5) 4,860 units of Delta (rounded)

 Calculate the **breakeven point** in terms of **revenue**

= (2,916 × $135) + (3,888 × $165) + (4,860 × $220)

= $393,660 of Beta, $641,520 of Gamma and $1,069,200 of Delta = $2,104,380 in total

---

7.2 C/S ratio for multiple products

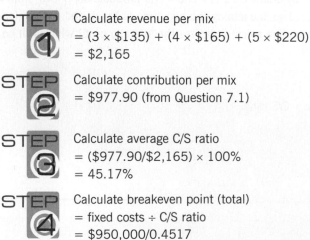

Calculate revenue per mix
= (3 × $135) + (4 × $165) + (5 × $220)
= $2,165

Calculate contribution per mix
= $977.90 (from Question 7.1)

Calculate average C/S ratio
= ($977.90/$2,165) × 100%
= 45.17%

Calculate breakeven point (total)
= fixed costs ÷ C/S ratio
= $950,000/0.4517
= $2,103,166 (rounded)

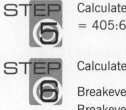

STEP 5 Calculate revenue ratio of mix
= 405:660:1,100, or 81:132:220

STEP 6 Calculate breakeven sales

Breakeven sales of Beta   = 81/433 × $2,103,166 = $393,433
Breakeven sales of Gamma = 132/433 × $2,103,166 = $641,150
Breakeven sales of Delta = 220/433 × $2,103,166 = $1,068,583

7.3 Average C/S ratio

Average C/S ratio = $\dfrac{(20\% \times 1) + (40\% \times 2)}{3}$ = 33.33%

Sales revenue at the breakeven point = $\dfrac{\text{fixed costs}}{\text{C/S ratio}}$ = $\dfrac{\$30,000}{0.333}$ = $90,000

7.4 Using the C/S ratio

Sales revenue must be $\dfrac{\$1}{38.6c}$ × $200,000 = $518,135

7.5 Sales mix decision

The revised C/S ratio is 45%.

	U	C	Y	Total
P/V ratio	0.55*	0.45	0.35	
Market share	× 0.25	× 0.35	× 0.40	
	0.1375	0.1575	0.140	0.435

*0.1375/0.25

With revised proportions:

	U	C	Y	Total
P/V ratio	0.55	0.45	0.35	
Market share	× 0.30	× 0.40	× 0.30	
	0.165	0.18	0.105	0.45

7.6 Multi-product P/V chart

	X	Y	Z	Total
Contribution per unit	$0.75	$0.50	$0.75	$
Budgeted contribution (total)	$1,500	$1,000	$3,750	6,250
Fixed costs				3,250
Budgeted profit				3,000

Product		Cumulative sales $		Cumulative profit $
Z		10,000	($3,750 – $3,250)	500
Z and X		16,000		2,000
Z, X and Y		24,000		3,000

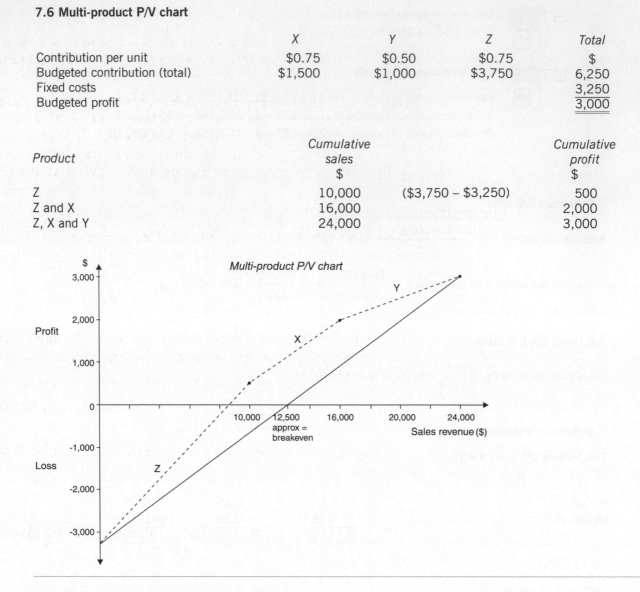

Multi-product P/V chart

7.7 Breakeven point and sales value constraints

The correct answer is $390,000

Breakeven point occurs when contribution = fixed costs.

∴ Minimum breakeven point occurs when contribution is $60,000.

Contribution achieved from minimum sales value

			$
M	5% × $50,000		2,500
A	10% × $50,000		5,000
R	15% × $20,000		3,000
P	20% × $10,000		2,000
			12,500

Product P has the highest C/S ratio and so should be produced first (as it earns more contribution per $ of revenue than the others).

Contribution from sales of P between minimum and maximum points = $170,000 × 20% = $34,000.

∴ Required contribution from Product R (which has the next highest C/S ratio)

$$= \$(60,000 - 12,500 - 34,000)$$
$$= \$13,500$$

Revenue from Product R of $13,500/0.15 = $90,000 will produce $13,500 of contribution.

∴ Lowest breakeven sales

> = $130,000 (minimum sales) + $170,000 (from P) + $90,000 (from R)
> = $390,000

Now try the questions from the Practice Question Bank

Number	Level
Q7.1 – Q7.7	Practice

SHORT-TERM DECISION MAKING

 In this chapter we will be continuing our study of relevant cash flows and short-term decision making.

Sections 1 to 4 cover a **range of short-term decision-making scenarios**. Regardless of the scenario you encounter in an assessment question, remember that the key to short-term decision making is identifying and accounting for the **relevant** cash flows (that were covered in Chapter 6).

Section 5 covers **joint cost allocation**, a topic that was originally covered at Certificate level (Paper C01).

Topic list	Learning outcomes	Syllabus references	Ability required
1 Make or buy decisions	C2(a)	C2(a)(i)	Analysis
2 Either/or problems	C2(a)	C2(a)(i)	Analysis
3 Shutdown problems	C2(a)	C2(a)(i)	Analysis
4 Choosing between options	C2(a)	C2(a)(i)	Analysis
5 Allocation of joint costs	C2(d)	C2(d)(i)	Comprehension

Chapter Overview

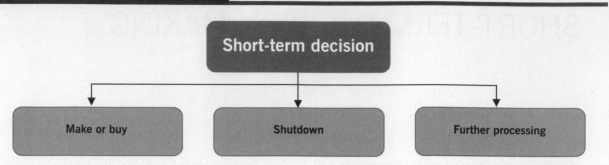

1 Make or buy decisions

Introduction

Make or buy decisions are quite common in companies as they try to decide whether it would be more profitable to outsource production to an external organisation. This section looks at the procedures involved in reaching the correct decision.

1.1 Factors to consider in make or buy decisions

While it is often tempting to outsource responsibility for a product to an external party, there are various factors that must be considered before the best decision for the company can be made.

The most important factor to remember is that the decision **should not be based solely on cost considerations**. Management should weigh up the non-financial benefits of internal production against those of outsourcing.

The **'make' option** should give management **more direct control** over the work, but the **'buy' option** often has the benefit that the external organisation has a **specialist skill and expertise** in the work. Other issues to consider are:

(a)   How can **spare capacity** freed up by subcontracting be used **most profitably**?

(b)   Could the decision to use an outside supplier cause an **industrial dispute**?

(c)   Would the subcontractor be **reliable** with delivery times and product quality?

(d)   Does the company wish to be **flexible** and maintain **better control** over operations by making everything itself?

1.2 Reaching the correct decision

Where there are **no scarce resources** and the company has **freedom of choice**, the relevant costs of a make or buy decision are the **differential costs** between the make and buy options.

The variable cost of producing the goods in-house is likely to be less than the cost of buying in. However, the company must also consider the **savings in directly attributable fixed costs** that will arise from using an outside supplier.

The following example illustrates the process.

Example: make or buy

An organisation makes four components, W, X, Y and Z, for which costs in the forthcoming year are expected to be as follows:

	W	X	Y	Z
Production (units)	1,000	2,000	4,000	3,000
Unit marginal costs	$	$	$	$
Direct materials	4	5	2	4
Direct labour	8	9	4	6
Variable production overheads	2	3	1	2
	14	17	7	12

Directly attributable fixed costs per annum and committed fixed costs are as follows:

	$
Incurred as a direct consequence of making W	1,000
Incurred as a direct consequence of making X	5,000
Incurred as a direct consequence of making Y	6,000
Incurred as a direct consequence of making Z	8,000
Other fixed costs (committed)	30,000
	50,000

A subcontractor can supply units of W, X, Y and Z for $12, $21, $10 and $14 respectively.

Required

Decide whether the organisation should make or buy the components, and state any other issues that may be considered before the final decision is reached.

Solution

(a) The relevant costs are the differential costs between making and buying, and they consist of differences in unit variable costs plus differences in directly attributable fixed costs. Subcontracting will result in some fixed cost savings.

	W $	X $	Y $	Z $
Unit variable cost of making	14	17	7	12
Unit variable cost of buying	12	21	10	14
	(2)	4	3	2
Annual requirements (units)	1,000	2,000	4,000	3,000
Extra variable cost of buying (per annum)	(2,000)	8,000	12,000	6,000
Fixed costs saved by buying	1,000	5,000	6,000	8,000
Extra total cost of buying	(3,000)	3,000	6,000	(2,000)

(b) The company would save $3,000 pa by subcontracting component W (where the purchase cost would be less than the marginal cost per unit to make internally) and would save $2,000 pa by subcontracting component Z (because of the saving in fixed costs of $8,000).

(c) Important **further considerations** would be as follows:

(i) If components W and Z are subcontracted, the company will have spare capacity. How should that **spare capacity be profitably used**? Are there **hidden benefits** to be obtained from subcontracting? Would the company's workforce resent the loss of work to an outside subcontractor, and might such a decision cause an **industrial dispute**?

(ii) Would the subcontractor be **reliable with delivery times**, and would they supply components of the same **quality** as those manufactured internally?

(iii) Does the company wish to be **flexible** and **maintain better control** over operations by making everything itself?

(iv) Are the **estimates** of fixed cost savings **reliable**? In the case of product W, buying is clearly cheaper than making in-house. In the case of product Z, the decision to buy rather than make would only be financially beneficial if the fixed cost savings of $8,000 could really be 'delivered' by management.

Section summary

If an organisation has the freedom of choice about whether to **make internally or buy externally and has no scarce resources** that put a restriction on what it can do itself, the relevant costs for the decision will be the differential costs between the two options.

2 Either/or problems

Introduction

This section contains a detailed example of how to tackle the more complicated type of relevant cost question – the either/or decision. You will notice that proper layout makes the task much easier and it also increases your chances of gaining marks!

Example: do now or do later?

MM currently carries out Process B, the output from which can be sold for $20 per unit and has variable unit costs of $7.50 per unit. Process B has directly attributable fixed operating costs of $40,000 per annum. MM also carries out Process C by using equipment that has running costs of $25,000 per annum. The equipment could be sold **now** for $50,000 (but this would incur dismantling costs of $7,500) or in one year's time for $45,000 with dismantling costs of $8,750.

Process B could be adapted so that it incorporated Process C.

(a) The existing Process B machinery would have to be removed, either now at a dismantling cost of $12,500 and with the sale of the machinery for $100,000, or in one year's time for $75,000 with dismantling costs of $13,750.

(b) Alternative Process B machinery would have to be leased. This would cost $10,000 per annum and have annual fixed running costs of $30,000.

The existing Process B machinery originally cost $250,000 when bought 5 years ago. It is being depreciated at 10% per annum.

Required

Prepare an analysis on an incremental opportunity cost basis to decide on financial grounds whether to adopt Process B immediately or to delay it for one year. **Ignore the time value of money**.

Solution

	Adapt now $	Adapt in one year $	Net (savings) /costs $
Savings			
Sale of Process C equipment	(50,000)	(45,000)	(5,000)
Sale of Process B machinery	(100,000)	(75,000)	(25,000)
Costs			
Fixed operating costs	0	40,000	(40,000)
Removal of Process B machinery	12,500	13,750	(1,250)
Process C – running costs	0	25,000	(25,000)
Process C – dismantling costs	7,500	8,750	(1,250)
Leased Process B equipment running costs	30,000	0	30,000
Leasing costs	10,000	0	10,000
Net (savings) less costs			(57,500)

Conclusion. Adapting now will bring savings of $57,500 more than adapting in one year.

There are lessons to be learned here about extracting information from complex Paper 2 questions. Note the following points:

(a)   You should do **savings and costs separately** and put **one type in brackets** (it doesn't matter which way round you do this, as long as you are consistent within the question: we have put savings in brackets in keeping with the accounting convention that they are credits). This is important because it is easy to get the signs wrong when you come to work out the differences.

(b)   Subtract column 2 from column 1 taking **care with the minus signs**. For instance:

$$-50,000 - (-45,000) = -5,000$$

(c)   Adapting now means that the fixed operating costs of $40,000 will not be incurred so a **nought** goes in the 'now' column. Adapting in one year means that fixed operating costs of $40,000 will have to be paid for another year. The net benefit of adapting now is therefore a saving of $40,000.

(d)   There are some **red herrings** in the information given. Unit selling prices and costs are not relevant, since they do not change, whenever Process B is adapted. Original cost and depreciation are not relevant because they are not future cash flows.

Section summary

The best approach to a complex **either/or problem** is to draw up a three-column table with columns for the first option (say, adapt now) and the second (say, adapt later), and a third column for the differences between the options (Column 1 minus Column 2).

3 Shutdown problems

Introduction

Another decision that a company may have to take is whether to discontinue an operation. This could mean the closure of a production line, factory, division or other activity. This section focuses on the costs and other factors that must be considered before this important decision can be made. As with previous sections, note how the information in the solution is presented.

3.1 Types of shutdown decisions

Decisions to be made in shutdown or discontinuance problems include the following:

- Whether or not to close down a product line, department or other activity
- If the decision is to shut down, whether the closure should be permanent or temporary
- If there is a choice about the timing of the closure, when it should take place

Read our four-step guide method in Section 3.2 below when you come to work through these decisions.

3.2 Financial considerations

The basic method is to use short-run relevant costs to calculate contributions and profits or losses.

1   Calculate what is earned by the process at present (perhaps in comparison with others).

2   Calculate what will be the financial consequences of closing down (selling machines, redundancy costs etc).

3   Compare the results and act accordingly.

4   Bear in mind that some fixed costs may no longer be incurred if the decision is to shut down and they are therefore relevant to the decision.

Bear these in mind as you read through the example below.

Example: adding or deleting products

An organisation manufactures three products, Pawns, Rooks and Bishops. The present net annual income from these is below.

	Pawns $	Rooks $	Bishops $	Total $
Sales	50,000	40,000	60,000	150,000
Variable costs	30,000	25,000	35,000	90,000
Contribution	20,000	15,000	25,000	60,000
Fixed costs	17,000	18,000	20,000	55,000
Profit/loss	3,000	(3,000)	5,000	5,000

The organisation is concerned about its poor profit performance, and is considering whether or not to cease selling Rooks. It is felt that selling prices cannot be raised or reduced without adversely affecting net income. $5,000 of the fixed costs of Rooks are direct fixed costs that would be saved if production ceased. All other fixed costs, it is considered, would remain the same.

Solution

By stopping production of Rooks, the consequences would be a $10,000 fall in profits.

	$
Loss of contribution	(15,000)
Savings in fixed costs	5,000
Incremental loss	(10,000)

Suppose, however, it were possible to use the resources realised by stopping production of Rooks and switch to producing a new item, Crowners, which would sell for $50,000 and incur variable costs of $30,000 and extra direct fixed costs of $6,000. A new decision is now required, as follows.

	Rooks $	Crowners $
Sales	40,000	50,000
Less variable costs	25,000	30,000
	15,000	20,000
Less direct fixed costs	5,000	6,000
Contribution to shared fixed costs and profit	10,000	14,000

It would be more profitable to shut down production of Rooks and switch resources to making Crowners, in order to boost profits by $4,000 to $9,000.

3.3 Non-quantifiable considerations

As usual, the decision is not merely a matter of choosing the best financial option.

(a)   A product may be retained if it is providing a contribution, albeit a small one. Retaining a wide range of **low volume/low contribution products** would add to the **complexity** and hence costs of manufacture, however, but very little to overall profit. Low volume/low contribution products should therefore be examined on a regular basis.

(b)   The **effect on demand for other products** if a particular product is no longer produced should be taken into account.

(c)   The extent to which demand for **other products** (existing or new) can expand to **use** the **capacity** vacated by the product being deleted is an issue.

(d)   The **pricing policy** should be considered. Is the product a **loss leader?** Is the product in the introductory stage of its **life cycle** and consequently priced low to help it to become accepted and hence maximise its long-term market share?

Question 8.1
Deleting products

Learning outcome C2(a)

A company's product range includes product F, on which the following data (relating to a year's production) are available.

	$
Revenue	200,000
Materials cost	157,000
Machine power cost	14,000
Overheads: Type A	28,000
Type B	56,000

Type A overheads would be avoided if production of product F ceased, but type B overheads would not be. Both types of overheads are absorbed in direct proportion to machine power cost, and that cost is a purely variable cost.

Production of product F should be discontinued.

True ☐

False ☐

3.4 Relative profitability

The relative profitability of products can be judged by **calculation** of their contribution to sales **(C/S) ratios**. Suppose an organisation produces three products, A, B and C, and that production capacity is limited. If product A has a C/S ratio of 22%, product B a C/S ratio of 27% and product C a C/S ratio of 25%, given unlimited demand for the three products, the organisation should concentrate on producing product B.

Example: shutdown decisions

You may consider by now that you understand the basic principles of selecting relevant cash flows for decision making and it may therefore be useful at this stage to test your understanding with a more advanced example. Attempt your own solution before reading on.

Ayeco, with a head office in Ayetown, has three manufacturing units. One is in Beetown, the second in Ceetown and the third in Deetown. The company manufactures and sells an air conditioner under the brand name of Ayecool at a price of $200. It is unable to utilise fully its manufacturing capacity.

Summarised statements of profit or loss for the year are shown below.

	Beetown $'000	Ceetown $'000	Deetown $'000	Total $'000
Costs				
Direct materials	200	800	400	1,400
Direct wages	200	900	350	1,450
Production overhead: variable	50	300	150	500
fixed	200	600	300	1,100
Subtotal	650	2,600	1,200	4,450
Selling overhead: variable	25	200	100	325
fixed	75	250	150	475
Administration overhead	100	450	200	750
Subtotal	850	3,500	1,650	6,000
Head office costs	50	200	100	350
Total	900	3,700	1,750	6,350
Profit	100	300	250	650
Sales	1,000	4,000	2,000	7,000

The management of the company has to decide whether or not to renew the lease of the property at Beetown, which expires next year. The company has been offered an extension to the lease at an additional cost of $50,000 per annum. This situation concerning the lease has been known for some time, so the accountant has collected relevant information to aid the decision. It is estimated that the cost of closing down Beetown would be offset by the surplus obtained by the sale of plant, machinery and inventories.

If Ayeco does not renew the lease of the Beetown property, it has two alternatives.

(a)   Accept an offer from Zeeco, a competitor, to take over the manufacture and sales in the Beetown area and pay to Ayeco a commission of $3 for each unit sold.

(b)   Transfer the output at present made in Beetown to either Ceetown or Deetown. Each of these units has sufficient plant capacity to undertake the Beetown output but additional costs in supervision, salaries, storage and maintenance would be incurred. These additional costs are estimated as amounting yearly to $250,000 at Ceetown and to $200,000 at Deetown.

If the Beetown sales are transferred to either Ceetown or Deetown, it is estimated that additional transport costs would be incurred in delivering to customers in the region of Beetown, and that these would amount to $15 per unit and $20 per unit respectively.

Required

Present a statement to the board of directors of Ayeco to show the estimated annual profit that would arise from the following alternative courses of action.

(a)   Continuing production at all three sites
(b)   Closing down production at Beetown and accepting the offer from Zeeco
(c)   Transferring Beetown sales to Ceetown
(d)   Transferring Beetown sales to Deetown

Comment on your statement, indicating any problems that may arise from the various decisions that the board may decide to take.

Solution

The main difficulty in answering this question is to decide what happens to fixed cost expenditure if the Beetown factory is closed, and what would be the variable costs of production and sales at Ceetown or Deetown if work was transferred from Beetown.

Fixed costs

It should be assumed that the direct fixed costs of the Beetown factory will be saved when shutdown occurs. These costs will include rent, depreciation of machinery, salaries of administrative staff and so on, and it is therefore probably correct to assume that savings on shutdown will include all fixed costs charged to Beetown with the exception of the apportioned head office costs.

Variable cost of production

The variable cost of production at Ceetown or Deetown is more tricky, because the variable cost/sales ratio and the contribution/sales ratio differs at each factory.

	Beetown %	Ceetown %	Deetown %
Direct materials/sales	20.0	20.0	20.0
Direct wages/sales	20.0	22.5	17.5
Variable production overhead/sales	5.0	7.5	7.5
Variable selling overhead/sales	2.5	5.0	5.0
Total variable costs/sales	47.5	55.0	50.0
Contribution/sales	52.5	45.0	50.0

Labour appears to be less efficient at Ceetown and more efficient at Deetown, but variable overheads are more costly at both Ceetown and Deetown than at Beetown. It is probably reasonably accurate to assume that the variable cost/sales ratio of work transferred from Beetown will change to the ratio that is current at the factory to which the work is transferred. Transport costs would then be added as an additional cost item.

Statement of estimated annual profit

Option 1 Continuing production at all three sites

	$
Profit before rent increase on lease	650,000
Increase in annual cost of lease	50,000
Revised estimate of annual profit	600,000

Option 2 Accepting the offer from Zeeco

	$	$
Current estimate of total profit		650,000
Less revenue lost from closing Beetown	(1,000,000)	
Direct costs saved at Beetown	850,000	
	(150,000)	
Commission from Zeeco* (5,000 × $3)	15,000	
Net loss from closure		(135,000)
Revised estimate of total profit		515,000

*   Number of units = $1,000,000 ÷ $200 per unit = 5,000 units.

Option 3 Transfer work to Ceetown

	$	$	$
Current estimate of total profit			650,000
Direct costs saved by closing Beetown		850,000	
Extra costs at Ceetown			
Variable costs (55% of $1,000,000)	(550,000)		
Extra costs of supervision etc	(250,000)		
Extra costs of transport (5,000 units × $15)	(75,000)		
		(875,000)	
Net extra costs of transfer			(25,000)
Revised estimate of total profit			625,000

Option 4 Transfer work to Deetown

	$	$	$
Current estimate of total profit			650,000
Direct costs saved by closing Beetown		850,000	
Extra costs at Deetown			
Variable costs (50% of $1,000,000)	(500,000)		
Extra costs of supervision etc	(200,000)		
Extra costs of transport (5,000 units × $20)	(100,000)		
		(800,000)	
Net savings from transfer			50,000
Revised estimate of total profit			700,000

Conclusion. The preferred option should be to transfer production from Beetown to Deetown, since profits would rise to $700,000, and would be $75,000 higher than profits obtainable from the next most profitable option (option 3).

Comments on the example

The example above illustrates how accounting information for decision making can often be presented in a concise form, without the need to reproduce a complete table of revenues, costs and profits for each option. You should study the presentation of the figures above, and note how they show only the relevant costs or benefits arising as a direct consequence of each decision option.

The eventual management decision may not be to transfer to Deetown, because other **non-quantifiable factors** might influence the final decision.

(a)   Concern for employees at Beetown and the wish to avoid redundancies

(b)   Problems in recruiting additional staff at Deetown

(c)   The possibility that the extra workload at Deetown might reduce labour efficiency there, making costs of production higher than those estimated in the statement

(d)   Difficulties in assembling and organising a transport fleet might persuade management to reject options 3 and 4

3.5 When to close

As well as being able to deal with 'whether to close' situations, you may be required to handle 'when to close' situations. This is similar to the 'do now or do later' example above.

Example: when to close

Daisy currently publishes, prints and distributes a range of catalogues and instruction manuals. The management have now decided to discontinue printing and distribution, and concentrate solely on publishing. Stem will print and distribute the range of catalogues and instruction manuals on behalf of Daisy, commencing either at 30 June 20X0 or at 30 November 20X0. Stem will receive $65,000 per month for a contract that will commence on either 30 June 20X0 or 30 November 20X0.

The results of Daisy for a typical month are as follows.

	Publishing $'000	Printing $'000	Distribution $'000
Salaries and wages	28.0	18.0	4.0
Materials and supplies	5.5	31.0	1.1
Occupancy costs	7.0	8.5	1.2
Depreciation	0.8	4.2	0.7

Other information has been gathered relating to the possible closure proposals.

(a) Two specialist staff from printing will be retained at their present salary of $1,500 each per month in order to fulfil a link function with Stem. One further staff member will be transferred to publishing to fill a staff vacancy through staff turnover, anticipated in July. This staff member will be paid at their present salary of $1,400 per month, which is $100 more than that of the staff member who is expected to leave. On closure, all other printing and distribution staff will be made redundant and paid an average of two months' redundancy pay.

(b) The printing department has a supply of materials (already paid for), which cost $18,000 and which will be sold to Stem for $10,000 if closure takes place on 30 June 20X0. Otherwise the material will be used as part of the July 20X0 printing requirements. The distribution department has a contract to purchase pallets at a cost of $500 per month for July and August 20X0. A cancellation clause allows for non-delivery of the pallets for July and August for a one-off payment of $300. Non-delivery for August only will require a payment of $100. If the pallets are taken from the supplier, Stem has agreed to purchase them at a price of $380 for each month's supply that is available. Pallet costs are included in the distribution materials and supplies cost stated for a typical month.

(c) Company expenditure on apportioned occupancy costs to printing and distribution will be reduced by 15% per month if printing and distribution departments are closed. At present, 30% of printing and 25% of distribution occupancy costs are directly attributable costs that are avoidable on closure, while the remainder are apportioned costs.

(d) Closure of the printing and distribution departments will make it possible to sublet part of the building for a monthly fee of $2,500 when space is available.

(e) Printing plant and machinery has an estimated net book value of $48,000 at 30 June 20X0. It is anticipated that it will be sold at a loss of $21,000 on 30 June 20X0. If sold on 30 November 20X0, the prospective buyer will pay $25,000.

(f) The net book value of distribution vehicles at 30 June 20X0 is estimated as $80,000. They could be sold to the original supplier at $48,000 on 30 June 20X0. The original supplier would purchase the vehicles on 30 November 20X0 for a price of $44,000.

Required

Using the above information, prepare a summary to show whether Daisy should close the printing and distribution departments on financial grounds on 30 June 20X0 or on 30 November 20X0. Explanatory notes and calculations should be shown.

Solution

		Handover 30.06.X0 $	Handover 30.11.X0 $	Net savings/ (costs) of 30.06.X0 handover $
Relevant inflows				
Inventory (W2)		10,000		10,000
Pallet sale (W3)		380		380
Rent	(5 × $2,500)	12,500		12,500
Non-current asset sales				
Printing		27,000	25,000	2,000
Distribution		48,000	44,000	4,000
Total inflows		97,880	69,000	28,880
Relevant outflows				
Salaries and wages (W1)		15,500	110,000	(94,500)
Materials and supplies (W2)			142,500	(142,500)
Pallets (W3)		600		600
Occupancy costs (W4)				
Apportioned		29,112	34,250	(5,138)
Direct			14,250	(14,250)
Stem fee	(5 × $65,000)	325,000		325,000
Total outflows		370,212	301,000	69,212
Net inflow/(outflow)		(272,332)	(232,000)	(40,332)

Conclusion. The operation should be kept open until 30 November 20X0.

Workings

1   *Salaries and wages*

	Printing $	Distribution $	Total $
Costs if 30.06.X0 handover			
2 × $1,500 × 5 months	15,000	–	15,000
$100 × 5 months		500	500
			15,500
Costs if 30.11.X0 handover			
5 months usual costs	90,000	20,000	110,000

2   *Inventory*

The $18,000 cost of production is a sunk cost from previous periods. Therefore only the income is recorded. Also, the $10,000 income could be seen as one of the opportunity costs of continuing production.

			$
Therefore materials costs are:	printing	($31,000 × 5 − $18,000) =	137,000
	distribution	($1,100 × 5) =	5,500
			142,500

3   *Pallets*

The alternative flows can be estimated as follows:

Take both deliveries

		$
Payment (2 × $500) =		1,000
Resale (2 × $380) =		760
Net flow		240

Take one delivery (ie July)

	$
Payment	500
Cancellation fee (August)	100
	600
Sale to Stem	380
Net flow	220

Take no deliveries

Cancellation fee	$300

Only the July delivery should be taken.

4   *Site costs*

	Printing $	*Distribution* $	*Total* $
Total occupancy costs (5 months)	42,500	6,000	48,500
Of which directly attributable (30%/25%)	(12,750)	(1,500)	(14,250)
∴ apportioned costs	29,750	4,500	34,250
Reduction in apportioned costs (15%)	(4,463)	(675)	(5,138)
Apportioned costs after closure	25,287	3,825	29,112

3.5.1 Temporary closure

The decision whether to shut down temporarily should take into account the following factors:

(a)   The impact on the organisation's other products and the product in question
(b)   Problems of recruitment of skilled labour when production begins again
(c)   Possibility of plant obsolescence
(d)   Problems of closing down and restarting production in some industries
(e)   Expenditure on disconnection of services, start-up costs and so on

If contribution is only just covering fixed costs but improved trading conditions in the future seem likely, it may be worth continuing the business.

Exam alert

Be very careful when setting out any relevant cost evaluation. **Do not** incorporate in the same analysis both the incremental costs and revenues that would apply if the decision proceeded (such as continuing with a product) **and** the avoidable costs if it did not (deleting the product). This is an easy mistake to make. You should consider first a decision to continue with the product and then compare it with a decision to delete the product.

3.6 Idle production capacity

If an organisation does decide to shut down a factory, department, product line or other activity, it may well be faced with a decision about what to do with the resulting idle production capacity.

(a) **Marketing strategies** could be used to increase demand for existing products.

(b) **Idle plant and machinery could be moved to another department** or factory, thereby reducing expenditure on new plant and machinery and/or interest charges.

(c) **Special orders could be accepted**, providing that the contribution generated is either greater than any reduction in fixed overheads that would occur if the idle capacity was not used or greater than any increase in fixed overheads if the idle capacity were to be used.

(d) **Space could be sublet** to a third party.

Such considerations are particularly important if the closure is only temporary.

Section summary

Non-quantifiable factors in shutdown problems include the impact on employees, customers, competitors and suppliers.

4 Choosing between options

Introduction

In this section we look at an alternative choice type question, which is basically a matter of comparing relevant costs and revenues.

Example: options available

AA has three options for Machine A.

Option 1 Dispose of Machine A in one year's time for $8,750.

Option 2 Modify Machine A now at a cost of $6,250. This choice is being considered in conjunction with another decision, Decision A.

Decision A would mean that production output would increase by 25,000 units per annum except in the first year when 25% of the production enhancement would be lost due to running in. Production units sell for $20 per unit and have variable costs of $7.50 per unit.

The modification will mean that Machine A can only be sold for $5,000 in one year's time. However, it will reduce the production enhancement loss from 25% to 15%.

Option 3 Modify Machine A now at a cost of $2,500, which will mean that the company does not have to hire an alternative machine at a cost of $7,500. This modification would mean that Machine A will have a disposal cost of $625 in one year's time.

Required

Determine what the company should do with Machine A. **Ignore the time value of money.**

Solution

Summary final answer

	(Saving)/cost	Reference
Option 1	$(8,750)	W1
Option 2	$(30,000)	W2
Option 3	$(4,375)	W3

Conclusion. Option 2 is clearly the best because it gives the highest revenue.

1   **Option 1**

The revenue from **Option 1** is given in the question: $8,750.

2   **Option 2**

	$
Reduction in impact of production losses ($25,000 \times (25 - 15)\% \times \$(20 - 7.50)$)	(31,250)
Modification (given)	6,250
Sales value after one year (given)	(5,000)
Saving	(30,000)

3   **Option 3**

	$
Modification (given)	2,500
Hire costs avoided (given)	(7,500)
Disposal cost (given)	625
Saving	(4,375)

Wording

The 'double negative' wording of Option 2 may have confused you. The enhancement is 25,000 units × $12.50 contribution = $312,500. Decision A reduces this enhancement by 25% to $234,375. Use of Machine A only reduces it by 15% to $265,625 and therefore **saves** $31,250.

Section summary

Many of the decision scenarios covered in this chapter could be described as cost/benefit comparisons because you need to compare the costs and benefits associated with the decision in order to determine what action to take.

5 Allocation of joint costs

Introduction

In your earlier studies you covered the techniques of process costing, which is the costing method that applies when goods or services are produced in a sequence of continuous processes. Here we look at the methods of accounting for joint products and by-products which arise as a result of a continuous process and the various decision problems that can occur.

5.1 Joint products and by-products

KEY TERM

JOINT PRODUCTS are defined in *CIMA Official Terminology* as 'Two or more products produced by the same process and separated in processing, each having a sufficiently high saleable value to merit recognition as a main product'.

KEY POINT

Features of joint products

(a)   They are produced in the same process.
(b)   They are indistinguishable from each other until the separation point.
(c)   They each have a substantial sales value (after further processing, if necessary).
(d)   They may require further processing after the separation point.

For example, in the oil refining industry the following joint products all arise from the same process.

(a)   Diesel fuel
(b)   Petrol
(c)   Paraffin
(d)   Lubricants

KEY TERM

A BY-PRODUCT is defined in *CIMA Official Terminology* as 'Output of some value produced incidentally in manufacturing something else (main product)'.

What exactly distinguishes a joint product from a by-product?

The answer lies in management attitudes to their products, which in turn is reflected in the cost accounting system.

(a)   A **joint product** is regarded as an important saleable item, and so it should be **separately costed**. The profitability of each joint product should be assessed in the cost accounts.

(b)   A **by-product** is not important as a saleable item, and whatever revenue it earns is a 'bonus' for the organisation. It is not worth costing by-products separately, because of their relative insignificance. It is therefore equally irrelevant to consider a by-product's profitability. The only question is how to account for the 'bonus' net revenue that a by-product earns.

5.2 Problems in accounting for joint products

Costs incurred prior to this point of separation are **common or joint costs**, and these need to be allocated (apportioned) in some manner to each of the joint products. In the following sketched example, there are two different split-off points.

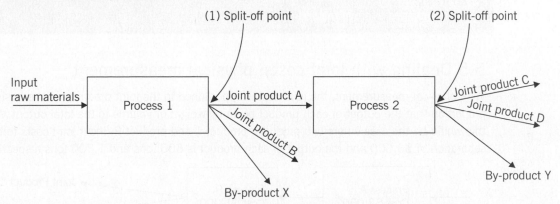

The special problems in accounting for joint products are basically of two different sorts.

(a)   How joint costs should be apportioned between products.

(b)   Whether it is more profitable to sell a joint product at one stage of processing, or to process the product further and sell it at a later stage. In the above diagram, product A has been processed further but product B has been sold at the split-off point.

We will return to the second problem later in this section. Let us for now consider the first problem.

5.3 Apportioning joint costs to joint products

The problem of costing for joint products concerns **joint costs**; that is, those common processing costs shared between the units of eventual output up to their 'split-off point'. Some method needs to be devised for sharing the joint costs between the individual joint products for the following reasons.

(a)   **To put a value to inventory held at the period end** of each joint product for **financial reporting purposes** in particular, but also for management reports. For external reporting it is necessary that inventory valuation includes an apportionment of the common costs of production, as well as any directly attributable costs of further processing.

(b)   **To record the costs and therefore the profit from each joint product**. However, this is of **limited value** because the costs and therefore profit from one joint product are influenced by the share of costs assigned to the other joint products. Management decisions would be based on the apparent relative profitability of the products that has arisen due to the arbitrary apportionment of the joint costs.

(c)   Perhaps to assist in **pricing decisions**.

5.4 Some examples of the joint costs problem

(a)   How to spread the joint costs of oil refining between the joint products made (petrol, naphtha, kerosene and so on)

(b)   How to spread the joint costs of running the telephone network between telephone calls in peak rate times and cheap rate times, or between local calls and long-distance calls

KEY POINT

Methods used to apportion joint costs to joint products

(a)   Physical measurement

(b)   Relative sales value apportionment method 1; sales value at split-off point

(c)   Relative sales value apportionment method 2; sales value of end product less further processing costs after split-off point

(d)   A weighted average method

5.5 Dealing with joint costs: physical measurement

With physical measurement, the joint cost is apportioned to the joint products on the basis of the proportion that the output of each product bears by weight or volume to the total output. An example of this would be the case where two products, product 1 and product 2, incur joint costs to the point of separation of $3,000 and the output of each product is 600 tons and 1,200 tons respectively.

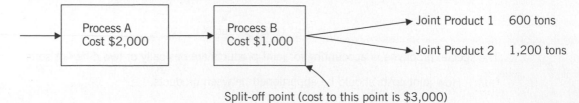

Product 1 sells for $4 per ton and product 2 for $2 per ton.

The division of the joint costs ($3,000) between product 1 and product 2 could be based on the tonnage of output.

	Product 1	Product 2	Total
Output	600 tons	1,200 tons	1,800 tons
Proportion of joint cost	$\dfrac{600}{1,800}$	$\dfrac{1,200}{1,800}$	
	$	$	$
Apportioned cost	1,000	2,000	3,000
Sales	2,400	2,400	4,800
Profit	1,400	400	1,800
Profit/sales ratio	58.3%	16.7%	37.5%

This method is unsuitable where the products separate during the processes into **different states**, for example where one product is a gas and another is a liquid. Furthermore, this method does not take into account the **relative income-earning potentials of the individual products**, with the result that one product might appear very profitable and another might appear to be incurring losses.

5.6 Dealing with joint costs: sales value at split-off point

With relative sales value apportionment of joint cost, the cost is **apportioned according to the product's ability to produce income**. This method is most widely used because the assumption that some profit margin should be attained for all products under normal marketing conditions is satisfied. The joint cost is apportioned to each product in the proportion that the sales value of that product bears to the sales value of the total output from the particular processes concerned. Using the previous example where the sales price per ton is $4 for product 1 and $2 for product 2:

(a) Joint costs of processes to split-off point $3,000
(b) Sales value of product 1 at $4 per ton $2,400
(c) Sales value of product 2 at $2 per ton $2,400

```
                                          ──────▶ Product 1 (value $2,400)
       ┌──────────────┐         ──────────
       │    JOINT      │────────
       │    COSTS      │
       │    $3,000      │────────
       └──────────────┘         ──────────
              ◀──── split-off point ──────▶ Product 2 (value $2,400)
```

	Product 1	Product 2	Total
Sales	$2,400	$2,400	$4,800
Proportion of joint cost apportioned	$\left(\dfrac{2,400}{4,800}\right)$	$\left(\dfrac{2,400}{4,800}\right)$	
Apportioned cost	1,500	1,500	3,000
Sales	2,400	2,400	4,800
Profit	900	900	1,800
Profit/sales ratio	37.5%	37.5%	37.5%

A comparison of the different gross profit margins resulting from the application of the above methods for allocating joint costs will illustrate the greater acceptability of the relative sales value apportionment method. Physical measurement gives a higher profit margin to product 1, not necessarily because product 1 is highly profitable, but because it has been given a smaller share of joint costs.

5.7 Dealing with joint costs: sales value minus further processing costs

Joint products may have no known market value at the point of separation, because they need further separate processing to make them ready for sale. The allocation of joint costs should be accomplished as follows:

(a)   Ideally, by determining a **relative sales value at the split-off point** for each product.

(b)   If a relative sales value cannot be found, a residual sales value at the split-off point can be determined.

     (i)   Take the final sales value of each joint product

     (ii)   Deduct the further processing costs for each product

This residual sales value is sometimes referred to as the **notional** or **proxy sales value** of a joint product.

Example: sales value minus further processing costs

JT has a factory where four products are originated in a common process.

During period 4, the costs of the common process were $16,000. Output was as follows.

	Units made	Units sold	Sales value per unit
Product P1	600		
Product Q1	400		
Product R	500	400	$7
Product S	600	450	$10

Products P1 and Q1 are further processed, separately, to make end products P2 and Q2.

	Units processed	Units sold	Cost of further processing	Sales value per unit
Product P1/P2	600	600	$1,000	$10 (P2)
Product Q1/Q2	400	300	$2,500	$20 (Q2)

Required

Calculate the costs of each joint product and the profit from each of them in period 4. There was no inventory at the beginning of the period.

Solution

(a)   It is helpful to begin a solution to joint product problems with a diagram of the process.

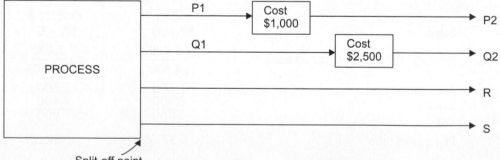

(b)   Next we calculate the notional sales values of P1 and Q1 at the split-off point.

	P2 $	Q2 $
Sales value of production	6,000	8,000
Less further processing costs	1,000	2,500
Notional sales value, P1, Q1	5,000 (P1)	5,500 (Q1)

(c)   Now we can apply sales values to apportion joint costs.

Joint product	Sales value of production $	%	Apportionment of joint costs $
P1	5,000	25	4,000
Q1	5,500	27.5	4,400
R	3,500	17.5	2,800
S	6,000	30	4,800
	20,000	100	16,000

(d)   We can now draw up the profit statement.

	P1/2 $	Q1/2 $	R $	S $	Total $
Joint costs	4,000	4,400	2,800	4,800	16,000
Further processing	1,000	2,500	–	–	3,500
Cost of production	5,000	6,900	2,800	4,800	19,500
Less inventory at period end	0	1,725	560	1,200	3,485
Cost of sales	5,000	5,175	2,240	3,600	16,015
Sales	6,000	6,000	2,800	4,500	19,300
Profit	1,000	825	560	900	3,285
Profit/sales ratio	17%	14%	20%	20%	17%

Question 8.2   Units method of splitting common costs

Learning outcome C2(d)

Refer back to the example above and fill in the blanks in the sentence below.

The profit for the period is $................ and the value of the inventory held at period end is $......... if joint costs are apportioned using the units method.

5.8 Dealing with joint costs: weighted average method

The weighted average method of joint cost apportionment is a development of the units method of apportionment. Since units of joint product may not be comparable in physical resemblance or physical weight (they may be gases, liquids or solids) units of each joint product may be multiplied by a weighting factor, and '**weighted units**' would provide a basis for apportioning the joint costs.

Example: weighted average method

MG manufactures four products which emerge from a joint processing operation. In April, the costs of production were as follows:

	$
Direct materials	24,000
Direct labour	2,000
	26,000

Production overheads are added using an absorption rate of 400% of direct labour costs. Output from the process during April was as follows.

Joint product	Output
D	600 litres
W	400 litres
F	400 kilograms
G	500 kilograms

Units of output of D, W, F and G are to be given weightings of 3, 5, 8 and 3 respectively for apportioning joint costs.

Required

Apportion the joint costs.

Solution

Total costs are $26,000 for direct costs plus $8,000 overhead. The costs would be $34,000, apportioned as follows.

Joint product	Output units	Weighting	Weighted units
D	600	3	1,800
W	400	5	2,000
F	400	8	3,200
G	500	3	1,500
			8,500

The costs are therefore apportioned at a rate of $34,000/8,500 = $4 per weighted unit.

Joint product	Apportionment of common cost $
D	7,200
W	8,000
F	12,800
G	6,000
	34,000

KEY POINT

You should be able to appreciate the **arbitrary nature of joint cost allocation**. The resulting product costs should never be used as a basis for decisions concerning process or product viability because the apparent relative profitability of the products has arisen due to the arbitrary apportionment of the joint costs.

5.9 The further processing decision

A different type of decision-making problem with joint products occurs when there is a **choice between selling part-finished output and processing it further**. This decision problem is best explained by a simple example.

Example: further processing

An organisation manufactures two joint products, A and B. The costs of common processing are $15,000 per batch, and output per batch is 100 units of A and 150 units of B. The sales value of A at split-off point is $90 per unit, and the sales value of B is $60 per unit. An opportunity exists to process product A further, at an extra cost of $2,000 per batch, to produce product C. One unit of joint product A is sufficient to make one unit of C which has a sales value of $120 per unit.

Should the organisation sell product A, or should it process A and sell product C?

Solution

The problem is resolved on the basis that product C should be sold if the sales value of C minus its further processing costs exceeds the sales value of A.

	$
Sales value of C, per batch (100 × $120)	12,000
Sales value of A, per batch (100 × $90)	9,000
Incremental revenue from further processing	3,000
Further processing cost	2,000
Benefit from further processing in order to sell C	1,000 per batch

If the further processing cost had exceeded the incremental revenue from further processing, it would have been unprofitable to make and sell C. It is worth noting that the **apportionment of joint processing costs between A and B is irrelevant to the decision**, because the total extra profit from making C will be $1,000 per batch whichever method of apportionment is used.

KEY POINT

When there is a **choice between processing part-finished output further or selling it**, the further processing is worthwhile if the further processing cost is less than the incremental revenue gained from further processing.

Exam skills

You must be able to apportion joint costs using the four methods illustrated.

Question 8.3 Joint products decision

Learning outcome C2(d)

PCC produces two joint products, Pee and Cee, from the same process. Joint processing costs of $150,000 are incurred up to split-off point, when 100,000 units of Pee and 50,000 units of Cee are produced. The selling prices at split-off point are $1.25 per unit for Pee and $2.00 per unit for Cee.

The units of Pee could be processed further to produce 60,000 units of a new chemical, Peeplus, but at an extra fixed cost of $20,000 and variable cost of 30p per unit of input. The selling price of Peeplus would be $3.25 per unit.

Required

Choose the correct words from those highlighted.

The organisation **should convert/should not convert** Pee to Peeplus.

5.10 Costing by-products

A by-product is a supplementary or secondary product (arising as the result of a process) whose **value is small relative to that of the principal product**. Nevertheless the by-product has some commercial value, and has to be accounted for.

Question 8.4	Another joint products decision

Learning outcome C2(d)

Ruffage manufactures two products, T42 and 24T. These products are made jointly in process A, and then processed further, separately, with the manufacture of T42 completed in process B and 24T in process C. Costs and revenues for September were as follows.

2,000 tonnes of material (costing $36,000) were input to process A, 500 tonnes (costing $5,000) were added in process B and 1,000 tonnes (costing $8,000) were added in process C. Labour and overhead were $24,000 in process A, $20,000 in process B and $25,000 in process C.

Output from process A was 1,000 tonnes of part-finished T42 and 1,000 tonnes of part-finished 24T. At this stage in processing the sales value of T42 is $26 per tonne and of 24T is $39 per tonne. All completed output of T42 (1,500 tonnes) was sold in the month for $66,000 and all completed output of 24T (2,000 tonnes) was sold for $66,000.

Required

(a)   Calculate the profitability of each product in the month, assuming that joint costs in process A are apportioned using the following methods:

    (i)   On a physical units basis
    (ii)   On the basis of sales value at the point of separation

(b)   Comment on what these figures suggest about the following:

    (i)   Whether either product makes losses and ought not to be manufactured

    (ii)   Whether either product should be sold partially finished as output from process A, instead of processed further in process B or C

Section summary

(a) **Features of joint products**

    (i)   They are produced in the same process.

    (ii)   They are indistinguishable from each other until the separation point.

    (iii)   They each have a substantial sales value (after further processing, if necessary).

    (iv)   They may require further processing after the separation point.

(b) A **by-product** is a product that is similarly produced at the same time and from the same common process as the 'main product' or joint products. The distinguishing feature of a by-product is its relatively low sales value in comparison to the main product. In the timber industry, for example, by-products include sawdust, small offcuts and bark.

(c) Joint products are not separately identifiable until a certain stage is reached in the processing operations. This stage is the '**split-off point**', sometimes referred to as the **separation point**.

(d) **Methods used to apportion joint costs to joint products**

    (i)   Physical measurement

    (ii)   Relative sales value apportionment method 1; sales value at split-off point

    (iii)   Relative sales value apportionment method 2; sales value of end product less further processing costs after split-off point

    (iv)   A weighted average method

(e) The usual method of **accounting for a by-product** is to deduct its net realisable value from the cost of production of the main product.

Chapter Summary

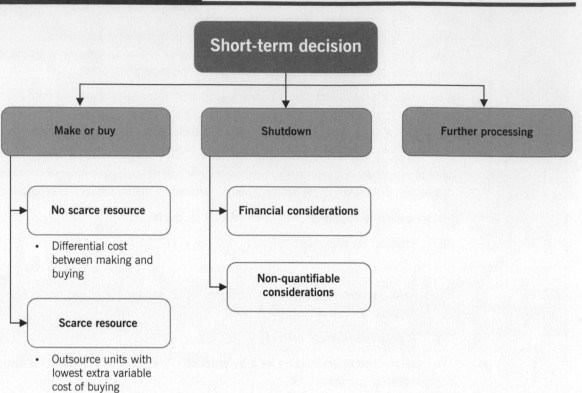

Short-term decision

Make or buy

No scarce resource

- Differential cost between making and buying

Scarce resource

- Outsource units with lowest extra variable cost of buying

Shutdown

Financial considerations

Non-quantifiable considerations

Further processing

Quick Quiz

1   Fixed costs should never be taken into account in an accept/reject decision.

     True   ☐

     False   ☑

2   What are the relevant costs in a make or buy decision?

     A   The sum of the relevant costs of the two options
   ﹅ B   The opportunity costs associated with the decision
     C   The differential costs between the two options
     D   The incremental costs of the two options

3   Choose the correct words from those highlighted.

     In a situation where a company must subcontract work to make up a shortfall in its own in-house capabilities, its total costs will be minimised if those units bought have the **lowest/highest** extra **variable/fixed** cost of **buying/making** per unit of scarce resource.

4   Fill in the blank.

     An organisation produces four products for which there is unlimited demand. Production capacity is limited. The organisation should concentrate on producing the product with the ....*highest*...... C/S ratio.

5   Sunny plc manufactures both work and leisure clothing. The company is considering whether to cease production of leisure clothing. List the **costs that are relevant** to the decision to cease production.

6   Joint cost allocations are essential for the purposes of determining relative product profitability.

     True   ☐

     False   ✗

7   When deciding, purely on financial grounds, whether or not to process a joint product further, the information required is:

     (i)   The value of the joint process costs
     (ii)   The method of apportioning the joint costs between the joint products
   ﹅ (iii)   The sales value of the joint product at the separation point
   ﹅ (iv)   The final sales value of the joint product
   ﹅ (v)   The further processing cost of the joint product

     Which of the above statements are correct?

     A   (i), (ii) and (iii) only
   ﹅ B   (iii), (iv) and (v) only
     C   (iv) and (v) only
     D   (i), (ii), (iv) and (v) only

8   Choose the correct words from those highlighted.

     A joint product should be processed further if **post-separation/pre-separation** costs are **greater than/less than** the **increase in revenue/additional fixed costs**.

Answers to Quick Quiz

1   False. Additional fixed costs incurred as a result of accepting the order must be taken into account.

2   C.   You need to know the difference in cost between the two options.

3   lowest, variable, buying

4   highest

5   Those costs that will be saved if production of leisure clothing ceases (that is, all variable costs plus any fixed costs that are specific to producing and selling leisure clothing (such as advertising))

   (a)   Any closure costs such as the cost of equipment disposal and staff redundancies

   (b)   **Opportunity costs** such as the loss of any contribution that would have been earned from the continued manufacture and sale of leisure clothing

   (c)   The **opportunity costs** of continuing to produce leisure clothing such as the potential contribution that could be earned from using the capacity released to produce work clothing (although these costs will only occur if work clothing production has capacity constraints)

   Any fixed costs, which will continue whether or not leisure clothing ceases are not relevant.

6   False

7   B.   Any costs incurred up to the point of separation are irrelevant.

8   post-separation, less than, increase in revenue

Answers to Questions

8.1 Deleting products

Production of product F should continue, and so the statement is false.

	$	$
Revenue		200,000
Less: Materials cost	157,000	
Machine power cost	14,000	
Type A overheads	28,000	
		199,000
Contribution		1,000

Production of product F should be continued, because it makes a contribution of $1,000 a year.

8.2 Units method of splitting common costs

The correct answers are $3,091 and $3,291.

Joint product	Units produced	%	Apportionment of common costs $
P1	600	28.6	4,576
Q1	400	19.0	3,040
R	500	23.8	3,808
S	600	28.6	4,576
	2,100	100.0	16,000

Profit statement

	P1/2 $	Q1/2 $	R $	S $	Total $
Joint costs of production	4,576	3,040	3,808	4,576	16,000
Further processing	1,000	2,500	–	–	3,500
Cost of production	5,576	5,540	3,808	4,576	19,500
Less closing inventory	0	1,385	762	1,144	3,291
Cost of sales	5,576	4,155	3,046	3,432	16,209
Sales	6,000	6,000	2,800	4,500	19,300
Profit/(loss)	424	1,845	(246)	1,068	3,091
Profit/sales ratio	7%	31%	–	24%	16%

8.3 Joint products decision

The correct answer is 'should convert'.

The only relevant costs/incomes are those that compare selling Pee against selling Peeplus. Every other cost is irrelevant: they will be incurred regardless of what the decision is.

	Pee			Peeplus
Selling price per unit	$1.25			$3.25
	$		$	$
Total sales	125,000			195,000
Post-separation processing costs	–	Fixed	20,000	
	–	Variable	30,000	50,000
Sales minus post-separation (further processing) costs	125,000			145,000

It is $20,000 more profitable to convert Pee into Peeplus.

8.4 Another joint products decision

(a) (i) **Units basis of apportionment**

	Product T42 $	Product 24T $	Total $
Process A costs (apportioned 1:1)	30,000	30,000	60,000
Process B costs	25,000	–	25,000
Process C costs	–	33,000	33,000
Total costs	55,000	63,000	118,000
Revenue	66,000	66,000	132,000
Profit	11,000	3,000	14,000

(ii) **Sales revenue basis of apportionment**

	Product T42 $	Product 24T $	Total $
Process A costs (apportioned 26:39)	24,000	36,000	60,000
Process B costs	25,000		25,000
Process C costs	–	33,000	33,000
Total costs	49,000	69,000	118,000
Revenue	66,000	66,000	132,000
Profit	17,000	(3,000)	14,000

(b) (i) Product 24T makes a loss when the sales revenue basis of apportionment is used, but not when the units basis of apportionment is used. The difference between statements of profit or loss is due simply to how the common costs in process A are shared between the two products.

Although product 24T **makes a loss by one method**, it would be **wrong to conclude that it should not be made at all**. If the company continues to make T42, it has got to make 24T as well, at least in process A, since the products are output jointly from a common process. And if product 24T does **make some contribution** towards covering fixed overheads, it is **worth making and selling**, if no better alternative exists.

(ii)   In this situation, there is some **choice**. Product 24T can either be sold as part-finished output from process A, for $39 per tonne, or processed further in process C. The **relevant analysis** of this decision would be:

	$
Revenue from process C output	66,000
Revenue obtainable from sale of process A output (1,000 × $39)	39,000
Extra revenue from further processing	27,000
Costs of process C	33,000
Possible loss in process C	(6,000)

Not all of the $33,000 of process C costs might be **avoidable**. If there are some fixed and unavoidable costs charged to process C, there would be a smaller loss incurred by operating process C instead of selling part-finished product 24T. It might even be profitable to run process C, for example if avoidable costs were only $25,000, say, out of the $33,000 total costs for process C.

Even so, the possibility ought to be drawn to management's attention that it **might be more profitable to close down process C and sell product 24T in its part-complete form**. Neither method of cost apportionment that we used brings out this information for management's attention, and so both methods of costing are **inadequate** in this respect.

Now try the questions from the Practice Question Bank	**Number**	**Level**
	Q8.1 – Q8.2	Practice

LINEAR PROGRAMMING: THE GRAPHICAL METHOD

In Chapter 5 we saw how to determine the profit-maximising allocation of resources when an organisation is faced with just one resource constraint.

When there is **more than one resource constraint** (limiting factor), the technique of **linear programming** can be used. This technique can be applied to problems with the following features.

(a) There is a single objective, which is to maximise or minimise the value of a certain function. The objective in commercial decision making is usually to maximise contribution and thus maximise profit.

(b) There are several constraints, typically scarce resources, that limit the value of the objective function.

There are two linear programming techniques. The graphical method is used for problems involving two products. The simplex method is used if the problem involves more than two products. You need to understand the graphical method for P1.

Section 1 provides a detailed step by step approach to graphical linear programming. Make sure that you really understand how to carry out each step before you move on to the next.

Topic list	Learning outcomes	Syllabus references	Ability required
1 The graphical method	C2(c)	C2(c)(ii)(iii)	Analysis
2 The graphical method using simultaneous equations	C2(c)	C2(c)(ii)(iii)	Analysis
3 Using linear programming	C2(c)	C2(c)(ii)(iii)	Analysis
4 Sensitivity analysis	C2(c)	C2(ii)(iii)	Analysis

Chapter Overview

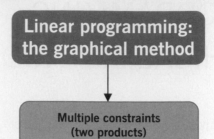

Linear programming:
the graphical method

Multiple constraints
(two products)

Introduction: knowledge brought forward

Manipulating inequalities

Inequality symbols

Equations are called inequalities when the '=' sign is replaced by one of the following.

(a)   > means 'greater than'

(b)   ≥ means 'is greater than or equal to'

(c)   < means 'is less than'

(d)   ≤ means 'is less than or equal to'

Solving inequalities

We can solve inequalities in the same way we can solve equations. For example, the inequality $7x - 2 > 0$ can be solved by getting x on its own, but the answer will be a range of values rather than a specific number.

$7x - 2 > 0$

$7x > 2$ (add 2 to both sides)

$x > \dfrac{2}{7}$ (divide both sides by 7)

Rules for manipulating inequalities

(i)   Adding or subtracting the same quantity from both sides of an inequality leaves the inequality symbol unchanged

(ii)   Multiplying or dividing both sides by a **positive** number leaves the inequality symbol unchanged

(iii)   Multiplying or dividing both sides by a **negative** number **reverses** the inequality so < changes to >

Example: Solving inequalities

Find the range of values of x satisfying $x - 5 < 2x + 7$

$x - 5 < 2x + 7$

$x < 2x + 12$ (add 5 to both sides)

$-x < 12$ (subtract 2x from both sides)

$x > -12$ (multiply both sides by –1 and so reverse the inequality)

Simultaneous equations

Simultaneous equations are two or more equations which are satisfied by the same variable values. They can be solved graphically or algebraically.

Example: Simultaneous equations

The following two linear equations both involve the unknown values x and y. There are as many equations as there are unknowns and so we can find the values of x and y.

$$y = 3x + 16$$

$$2y = x + 72$$

Solution: Graphical approach

One way of finding a solution is by a **graph**. If both equations are satisfied together, the values of x and y must be those where the straight line graphs of the two equations **intersect**.

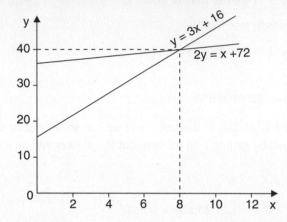

Since both equations are satisfied, the values of x and y must lie on both the lines. Since this happens only once, at the intersection of the lines, the value of x must be 8, and of y 40.

Solution: Algebraic approach

A more common method of solving simultaneous equations is by **algebra**.

(a)   Returning to the original equations, we have:

$$y = 3x + 16 \qquad (1)$$

$$2y = x + 72 \quad (2)$$

(b)   Rearranging these, we have:

y – 3x	=	16 (3)
2y – x	=	72 (4)

(c)   If we now multiply equation (4) by 3, so that the coefficient for x becomes the same as in equation (3) we get:

6y – 3x	=	216 (5)
y – 3x	=	16 (3)

(d)   Subtracting (3) from (5) we get:

$$5y = 200$$

$$y = 40$$

(e)   Substituting 40 for y in any equation, we can derive a value for x. Thus substituting in equation (4) we get:

2(40) – x	=	72
80 – 72	=	x
8	=	x

(f)   The solution is y = 40, x = 8.

1 The graphical method

Introduction

Linear programming is used when there is more than one scarce resource. This section looks at the steps involved in solving a linear programming problem using the graphical method. There are several steps in the process, so make sure you understand each step before moving on to the next one.

1.1 A definition of linear programming

Before we work through the steps involved in solving this constraints problem using the graphical approach to linear programming, it is worth reading the *CIMA Official Terminology* definition of linear programming to get a glimpse of what we will be doing.

KEY TERM

LINEAR PROGRAMMING is 'The use of a series of linear equations to construct a mathematical model. The objective is to obtain an optimal solution to a complex operational problem, which may involve the production of a number of products in an environment in which there are many constraints'.

(CIMA Official Terminology)

Linear programming can be used to maximise a quantity; for example, to maximise profit or efficiency. It can also be used to minimise a quantity; for example, to minimise costs or time.

Example: WX Ltd

The following example will be used throughout the chapter to illustrate the graphical method of linear programming.

WX Ltd manufactures two products, A and B. Both products pass through two production departments, mixing and shaping. The organisation's objective is to maximise contribution to fixed costs.

Product A is sold for $1.50 whereas product B is priced at $2.00. There is unlimited demand for product A but demand for B is limited to 13,000 units per annum. The machine hours available in each department are restricted to 2,400 per annum. Other relevant data are as follows:

Machine hours required	Mixing Hours	Shaping Hours
Product A	0.06	0.04
Product B	0.08	0.12

Variable cost per unit	$
Product A	1.30
Product B	1.70

Question 9.1

Constraints

Learning outcome C2(c)

What are the constraints in the situation facing WX Ltd?

1.2 Solving the problem using the graphical method: Steps 1–3

KEY POINT

The steps in the graphical method are as follows:

1   Define variables
2   Establish objective function
3   Establish constraints
4   Draw a graph of the constraints
5   Establish the feasible region
6   Determine the optimal product mix

Let's start solving WX's problem.

Define variables

What are the **quantities that WX can vary**? Obviously not the number of machine hours or the demand for product B. The only things that it can vary are the **number of units of each type of product produced**. It is those numbers that the company has to determine in such a way as to obtain the maximum possible profit. Our variables (which are usually products being produced) will therefore be as follows.

Let x = number of units of product A produced.
Let y = number of units of product B produced.

Establish objective function

KEY TERM

The OBJECTIVE FUNCTION is a quantified statement of the aim of a resource allocation decision.

We now need to introduce the question of contribution or profit. We know that the **contribution on each type of product** is as follows:

		$ per unit
Product A	$(1.50 – 1.30) =	0.20
Product B	$(2.00 – 1.70) =	0.30

The **objective of the company is to maximise contribution** and so the **objective function to be maximised** is as follows:

Contribution (C) = 0.2x + 0.3y

Establish constraints

KEY TERM

A CONSTRAINT is 'An activity, resource or policy that limits the ability to achieve objectives'.

(CIMA Official Terminology)

However, the **value of the objective function** (the maximum contribution achievable from producing products A and B) is **limited by the constraints** facing WX. To incorporate this into the problem, we need to **translate the constraints into inequalities involving the variables** defined in Step 1. An inequality is an equation taking the form 'greater than or equal to' or 'less than or equal to'.

(a)   Consider the **mixing department machine hours** constraint.

   (i)   **Each unit of product A** requires 0.06 hours of machine time. Producing five units therefore requires 5×0.06 hours of machine time and, more generally, **producing x units will require 0.06x hours**.

   (ii)   Likewise, producing **y units of product B will require 0.08y hours**.

   (iii)   The total machine hours needed in the mixing department to make x units of product A and y units of product B is $0.06x + 0.08y$.

   (iv)   We know that this **cannot be greater than 2,400 hours** and so we arrive at the following inequality.

   $0.06x + 0.08y \leq 2,400$

Question 9.2   Inequalities

Learning outcome C2(c)

How can the constraint facing the shaping department be written as an inequality?

_____

(b)   The final inequality is easier to obtain. The **number of units of product B produced and sold is y** but this has to be **less than or equal to 13,000**. Our inequality is therefore as follows:

   $y \leq 13,000$

(c)   We also need to add **non-negativity constraints** ($x \geq 0$, $y \geq 0$) since negative numbers of products cannot be produced. (Linear programming is simply a mathematical tool and so there is nothing in this method that guarantees that the answer will 'make sense'. An unprofitable product may produce an answer that is negative. This is mathematically correct but nonsense in operational terms. Always remember to include the non-negativity constraints. The examiner will not appreciate 'impossible' solutions.)

The **problem** has now been reduced to the following **four inequalities** and **one equation**.

Maximise contribution (C) = $0.2x + 0.3y$, subject to the following constraints:

$0.06x + 0.08y \quad \leq 2,400$

$0.04x + 0.12y \quad \leq 2,400$

$\quad\quad 0 \leq y \quad \leq 13,000$

$\quad\quad 0 \quad \leq x$

Question 9.3   Formulation of linear programming model

Learning outcome C2(c)

An organisation makes two products, X and Y. Product X has a contribution of $124 per unit and product Y $80 per unit. Both products pass through two departments for processing, and the times in minutes per unit are as follows:

	Product X	Product Y
Department 1	150	90
Department 2	100	120

Currently there is a maximum of 225 hours per week available in department 1 and 200 hours in department 2. The organisation can sell all it can produce of X but EU quotas restrict the sale of Y to a maximum of 75 units per week. The organisation, which wishes to maximise contribution, currently makes and sells 30 units of X and 75 units of Y per week.

Required

Assume x and y are the number of units of X and Y produced per week. Formulate a linear programming model of this problem, filling in the blanks in (a) and (b) below.

(a)   The objective function is to maximise weekly contribution, given by C = ...

(b)   The constraints are:

Department 1 .... EU quota ....

Department 2 .... Non-negativity ....

1.3 Steps 4 and 5: graphing the problem and establishing feasible region

A **graphical solution** is **only possible** when there are **two variables** in the problem. One variable is represented by the **x axis** of the graph and one by the **y axis**. Since non-negative values are not usually allowed, the graph shows **only zero and positive values of x and y**.

1.3.1 Graphing equations and constraints

A **linear equation with one or two variables** is shown as a **straight line on a graph**. Thus y = 6 would be shown as follows.

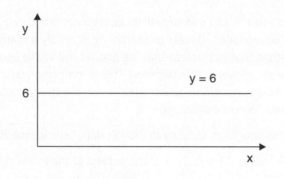

If the problem included a **constraint that y could not exceed 6**, the inequality y ≤ 6 would be represented by the **shaded area of the graph below**.

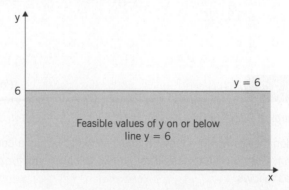

The equation 4x + 3y = 24 is also a straight line on a graph. To **draw any straight line**, we **need only to plot two points and join them up**. The easiest points to plot are the following:

*   x = 0 (in this example, if x = 0, 3y = 24, y = 8)
*   y = 0 (in this example, if y = 0, 4x = 24, x = 6)

By plotting the points (0, 8) and (6, 0) on a graph, and joining them up, we have the line for
4x + 3y = 24.

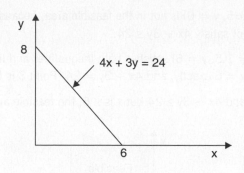

Any combination of values for x and y on the line satisfies the equation. Thus at a point where x = 3 and
y = 4, 4x + 3y = 24. Similarly, at a point where x = 4.5 and y = 2, 4x + 3y = 24.

If we had a **constraint 4x + 3y ≤ 24, any combined value of x and y within the shaded area below (on
or below the line) would satisfy the constraint**.

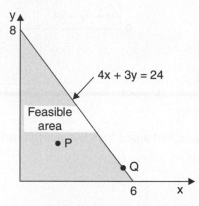

Consider point P, which has co-ordinates of (2, 2). Here 4x + 3y = 14, which is less than 24; and at
point Q where x = 5½, y = ⅔ 4x + 3y = 24. **Both P and Q lie within the feasible area** or **feasible
region. A feasible area enclosed on all sides may also be called a feasible polygon**.

1.3.2 Establishing the feasible region

KEY TERM

A FEASIBLE REGION is 'The area contained within all of the constraint lines shown on a graphical depiction
of a linear programming problem. All feasible combinations of output are contained within or located on
the boundaries of the feasible region'.   (*CIMA Official Terminology*)

When there are **several constraints**, the **feasible area** of combinations of values of x and y must be an
area **where all the inequalities are satisfied**. Thus, if **y ≤ 6 and 4x + 3y ≤ 24** the **feasible area** would be
the **shaded area** in the following graph.

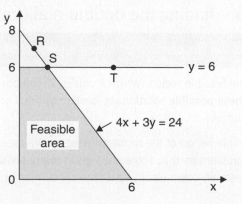

(a)   Point R (x = 0.75, y = 7) is not in the feasible area because although it satisfies the inequality 4x + 3y ≤ 24, it does not satisfy y ≤ 6.

(b)   Point T (x = 5, y = 6) is not in the feasible area, because although it satisfies the inequality y ≤ 6, it does not satisfy 4x + 3y ≤ 24.

(c)   Point S (x = 1.5, y = 6) satisfies both inequalities and lies just on the boundary of the feasible area since y = 6 exactly, and 4x + 3y = 24. Point S is thus at the intersection of the two lines.

Similarly, if y ≥ 6 and 4x + 3y ≥ 24 but x is ≤ 6, the feasible area would be the shaded area in the graph below.

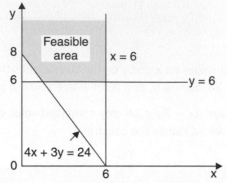

Question 9.4   Feasible region

Learning outcome C2(c)

Draw the feasible region that arises from the constraints facing WX on the graph below.

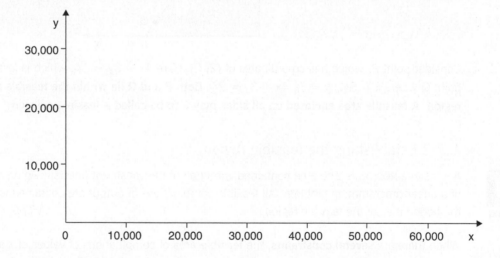

1.4 Step 6 – finding the optimum allocation of resources

KEY POINT

> The **optimal solution** can be found by 'sliding the iso-contribution (or profit) line out'.

Having found the feasible region (which includes all the possible solutions to the problem) we need to **find which of these possible solutions is 'best'** or **optimal** in the sense that it yields the maximum possible contribution.

Look at the feasible region of the problem faced by WX (see the solution to the question above). Even in such a simple problem as this, there are a **great many possible solution points within the feasible area**. Even to write them all down would be a time-consuming process and also an unnecessary one, as we shall see.

Here is the graph of WX's problem.

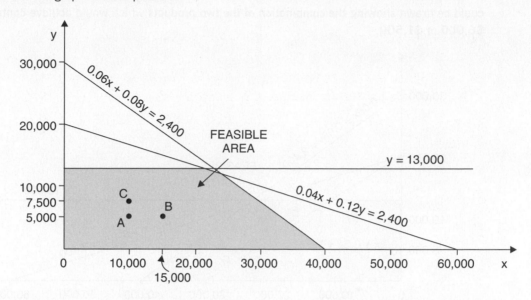

(a) Consider point A at which 10,000 units of product A and 5,000 units of product B are being manufactured. This will yield a contribution of $(10,000 \times \$0.20) + (5,000 \times \$0.30) = \$3,500$.

(b) We would clearly get more contribution at point B, where the same number of units of product B is being produced but where the number of units of product A has increased by 5,000.

(c) We would also get more contribution at point C where the number of units of product A is the same but 2,500 more units of product B are being produced.

This argument suggests that the **'best' solution** is going to be at a **point on the edge of the feasible area** rather than in the middle of it.

This still leaves us with quite a few points to look at but there is a way in which we can **narrow down still further the likely points at which the best solution will be found**. Suppose that WX wishes to earn contribution of $3,000. The company could sell the following combinations of the two products.

(a) 15,000 units of A, no B
(b) No A, 10,000 units of B
(c) A suitable mix of the two, such as 7,500 A and 5,000 B

The **possible combinations required to earn contribution of $3,000** could be **shown by the straight line $0.2x + 0.3y = 3,000$**.

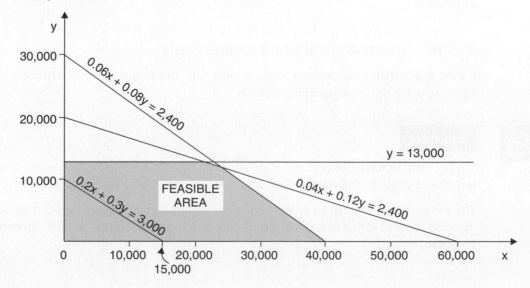

Likewise for profits of $6,000 and $1,500, lines of 0.2x + 0.3y = 6,000 and 0.2x + 0.3y = 1,500 could be drawn **showing the combination of the two products** which would **achieve contribution of $6,000 or $1,500**.

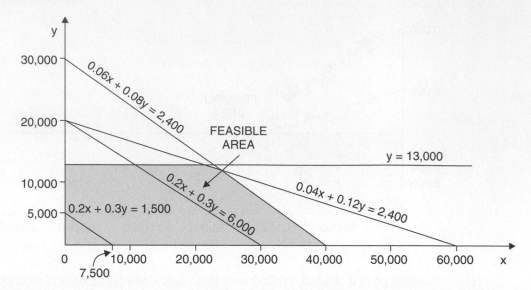

The **contribution lines are all parallel**. (They are called **iso-contribution lines**, 'iso' meaning equal.) A similar line drawn for any other total contribution would also be parallel to the three lines shown here. **Bigger contribution is shown by lines further from the origin** (0.2x + 0.3y = 6,000), smaller contribution by lines closer to the origin (0.2x + 0.3y = 1,500). As WX tries to increase possible contribution, we need to 'slide' any contribution line outwards from the origin, while always keeping it parallel to the other contribution lines.

As we do this there will come a point at which, if we were to **move the contribution line out any further, it would cease to lie in the feasible region**. Greater contribution could not be achieved, because of the constraints. In our example concerning WX this will happen, as you should test for yourself, where the contribution line just passes through the intersection of 0.06x + 0.08y = 2,400 and 0.04x + 0.12y = 2,400 (at co-ordinates (24,000, 12,000)). The point (24,000, 12,000) will therefore give us the optimal allocation of resources (to produce 24,000 units of A and 12,000 units of B).

As we mentioned at the beginning, linear programming can be used to minimise quantities, for example costs, as well as maximising quantities such as contribution. In the case of **maximising contribution** we find points on the contribution line in the feasible region **as far from the origin as possible**. In the case of **minimising costs**, we would find points on the total cost line in the feasible region **as close to the origin as possible**.

1.5 Minimum contractual requirements

If there is a particular order that a business must fulfil, this should be taken into account before formulating the linear programming problem.

Example

WX Ltd manufactures two products, A and B. Both products pass through two production departments, mixing and shaping. The organisation's objective is to maximise contribution to fixed costs.

There is unlimited demand for product A but demand for B is limited to 13,000 units per annum. The machine hours available in each department are restricted to 2,400 per annum. Other relevant data are as follows.

Machine hours required	Mixing Hours	Shaping Hours
Product A	0.06	0.04
Product B	0.08	0.12

Contribution per unit	$
Product A	0.20
Product B	0.30

WX Ltd has signed a contract to provide 6,000 units of Product A and 6,000 units of Product B to Z Ltd and does not want to let Z Ltd down. The maximum demand for Product B will still be 13,000 from other clients.

Required

Formulate the linear programming problem (Steps 1 to 3).

Solution

As before we have:

Define variables

Let x = number of units of product A produced.
Let y = number of units of product B produced.

Establish objective function

Contribution (C) = 0.2x + 0.3y

STEP 3

Establish constraints

	Available	Required for order	Remaining
Mixing machine hours	2,400	840*	1,560
Shaping machine hours	2,400	960**	1,440

* (6,000 × 0.06) + (6,000 × 0.08) = 840
**(6,000 × 0.04) + (6,000 × 0.12) = 960

$0.06x + 0.08y \leq$ 1,560 (mixing machine hours)
$0.04x + 0.12y \leq$ 1,440 (shaping machine hours)
$y \leq$ 13,000
$x, y \geq 0$

1.6 The graphical solution with a twist

Example

This example shows that it is not always necessarily easy to identify the decision variables in a problem.

DCC operates a small plant for the manufacture of two joint chemical products X and Y. The production of these chemicals requires two raw materials, A and B, which cost $5 and $8 per litre respectively. The maximum available supply per week is 2,700 litres of A and 2,000 litres of B.

The plant can operate using either of two processes, which have differing operating costs and raw materials requirements for the production of X and Y, as follows.

Process	Raw materials consumed Litres per processing hour		Output Litres per hour		Cost $ per hour
	A	B	X	Y	
1	20	10	15	20	500
2	30	20	20	10	230

The plant can run for 120 hours per week in total, but for safety reasons, process 2 cannot be operated for more than 80 hours per week.

X sells for $18 per litre, Y for $24 per litre.

Required

Formulate a linear programming model, and then solve it, to determine how the plant should be operated each week.

Solution

Define variables

You might decide that there are two decision variables in the problem, the quantity of X and the quantity of Y to make each week. If so, begin by letting these be x and y respectively.

You might also readily recognise that the aim should be to maximise the total weekly contribution, and so the objective function should be expressed in terms of maximising the total contribution from X and Y.

The contribution per litre from X and Y cannot be calculated because the operating costs are expressed in terms of processing hours.

	Process 1		Process 2	
	$ per hour	$ per hour	$ per hour	$ per hour
Costs:				
Material A		100		150
Material B		80		160
Operating cost		500		230
		680		540
Revenue:				
X (15 × $18)	270		(20 × $18) 360	
Y (20 × $24)	480		(10 × $24) 240	
		750		600
Contribution		70		60

The **decision variables** should be **processing hours in each process**, rather than litres of X and Y. If we let the processing hours per week for process 1 be P_1 and the processing hours per week for process 2 be P_2 we can now formulate an objective function, and constraints, as follows.

Establish objective function

Maximise $70P_1 + 60P_2$ (total contribution) subject to the constraints below.

Establish constraints

$20P_1 + 30P_2$	$\leq$	2,700 (material A supply)
$10P_1 + 20P_2$	$\leq$	2,000 (material B supply)
P_2	$\leq$	80 (maximum time for P_2)
$P_1 + P_2$	$\leq$	120 (total maximum time)
$P_1, P_2 \geq$	0	

Graph the problem

The graphical solution looks like this.

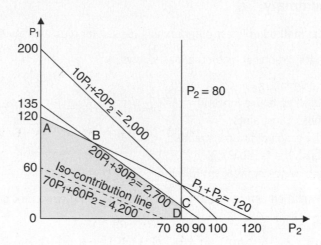

Define feasible area

The material B constraint is not critical, and the feasible area for a solution is shown as ABCD0 on the graph.

Determine optimal solution

The optimal solution, determined using the iso-contribution line $70P_1 + 60P_2 = 4,200$, is at point A, where $P_1 = 120$ and $P_2 = 0$.

Production would be (120×15) 1,800 litres of X and (120×20) 2,400 litres of Y.

Total contribution would be $(120 \times \$70) = \$8,400$ per week.

Question 9.5

Determining the optimal solution

Learning outcome C2(c)

On 20 days of every month GS makes two products, the Crete and the Corfu. Production is carried out in three departments – tanning, plunging and watering. Relevant information is as follows.

	Crete	Corfu
Contribution per unit	$75	$50
Minutes in tanning department per unit	10	12
Minutes in plunging department per unit	15	10
Minutes in watering department per unit	6	15
Maximum monthly sales (due to government quota restrictions)	3,500	4,000

	Tanning	Plunging	Watering
Number of employees	7	10	5
Hours at work per day per employee	7	6	10
Number of idle hours per day per employee	0.5	1	0.25

Due to union restrictions, employees cannot be at work for longer than the hours detailed above.

Required

Use the graphical method of linear programming to determine the optimum monthly production of Cretes and Corfus and the monthly contribution if GS's objective is to maximise contribution.

Section summary

The **graphical method** of linear programming is used for problems involving two products.

The steps in the graphical method are as follows:

1 Define variables
2 Establish objective function
3 Establish constraints
4 Draw a graph of the constraints
5 Establish the feasible region
6 Determine the optimal product mix

The **optimal solution** can be found by 'sliding the iso-contribution (or profit) line out'.

2 The graphical method using simultaneous equations

Introduction

Instead of a 'sliding the contribution line out' approach, simultaneous equations can be used to determine the optimal allocation of resources. This section also considers the impact of slack and surplus in solving linear programming problems.

Example: using simultaneous equations

An organisation manufactures plastic-covered steel fencing in two qualities: standard and heavy gauge. Both products pass through the same processes involving steel forming and plastic bonding.

The standard gauge sells at $15 a roll and the heavy gauge at $20 a roll. There is an unlimited market for the standard gauge but outlets for the heavy gauge are limited to 13,000 rolls a year. The factory operations of each process are limited to 2,400 hours a year. Other relevant data is given below.

Variable costs per roll

	Direct material	Direct wages	Direct expense
	$	$	$
Standard	5	7	1
Heavy	7	8	2

BPP
LEARNING MEDIA

Processing hours per 100 rolls

	Steel forming Hours	Plastic bonding Hours
Standard	6	4
Heavy	8	12

Required

Calculate the allocation of resources and hence the production mix that will maximise total contribution.

Solution

 Define variables

Let the number of rolls of standard gauge to be produced be x and the number of rolls of heavy gauge be y.

 Establish objective function

Standard gauge produces a contribution of $2 per roll ($15 − $(5 + 7 + 1)) and heavy gauge a contribution of $3 ($20 − $(7 + 8 + 2)).

Therefore the objective is to maximise contribution (C) = 2x + 3y subject to the constraints below.

 Establish constraints

The constraints are as follows:

$0.06x + 0.08y \leq 2{,}400$	(steel forming hours)
$0.04x + 0.12y \leq 2{,}400$	(plastic bonding hours)
$y \leq 13{,}000$	(demand for heavy gauge)
$x, y \geq 0$	(non-negativity)

Graph problem

The graph of the problem can now be drawn.

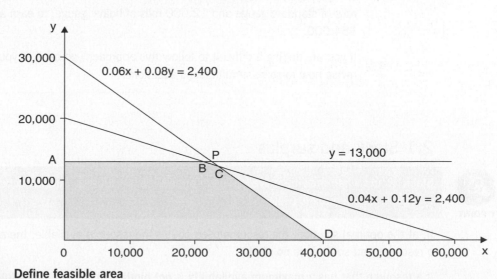

 Define feasible area

The combinations of x and y that satisfy all three constraints are represented by the area 0ABCD.

STEP 6 Determine optimal solution

Which combination will maximise contribution? Obviously, the more units of x and y, the bigger the contribution will be, and the optimal solution will be at point B, C or D. It will not be at A, since at A, y = 13,000 and x = 0, whereas at B, y = 13,000 (the same) and x is greater than zero.

Using simultaneous equations to calculate the value of x and y at each of points B, C and D, and then working out total contribution at each point from this, we can establish the contribution-maximising product mix.

Point B

y	=	13,000 (1)
0.04x + 0.12y	=	2,400 (2)
0.12y	=	1,560 (3) ((1) × 0.12)
0.04x	=	840 (4) ((2) − (3))
x	=	21,000 (5)

Total contribution = (21,000 × $2) + (13,000 × $3) = $81,000.

Point C

0.06x + 0.08y	=	2,400 (1)
0.04x + 0.12y	=	2,400 (2)
0.12x + 0.16y	=	4,800 (3) ((1) × 2)
0.12x + 0.36y	=	7,200 (4) ((2) × 3)
0.2y	=	2,400 (5) ((4) − (3))
y	=	12,000 (6)
0.06x + 960	=	2,400 (7) (substitute in (1))
x	=	24,000 (8)

Total contribution = (24,000 × $2) + (12,000 × $3) = $84,000.

Point D

Total contribution = 40,000 × $2 = $80,000.

Comparing B, C and D, we can see that contribution is maximised at C, by making 24,000 rolls of standard gauge and 12,000 rolls of heavy gauge, to earn a contribution of $84,000.

If you are finding it difficult to follow this approach, go back to your previous notes to revise how to solve simultaneous equations.

2.1 Slack and surplus

KEY POINT

Slack occurs when maximum availability of a resource is not used. **Surplus** occurs when more than a minimum requirement is used.

If, at the optimal solution, the resource used equals the resource available, there is **no spare capacity** of a resource and so there is **no slack**.

If a resource that has a **maximum availability** is **not binding** at the optimal solution, there will be **slack**.

In the example above, the optimal solution is x = 24,000, y = 12,000.

If we substitute these values into the inequalities representing the constraints, we can determine whether the constraints are binding or whether there is slack.

Steel forming hours: $(0.06 \times 24{,}000) + (0.08 \times 12{,}000) = 2{,}400$ = availability
Constraint is **binding**.

Plastic bonding hours: $(0.04 \times 24{,}000) + (0.12 \times 12{,}000) = 2{,}400$ = availability
Constraint is **binding**.

Demand: Demand of $12{,}000 \leq$ maximum demand of $13{,}000$
There is **slack**.

Note that because we had already determined the optimal solution to be at the intersection of the steel forming hours and plastic bonding hours constraints, we knew that they were binding!

If a minimum quantity of a resource must be used and, at the optimal solution, **more than that quantity is used**, there is a **surplus** on the minimum requirement.

For example, suppose in a particular scenario a minimum of 8,000 grade A labour hours had to be worked in the production of products x and y, such that (say) $3x + 2y \geq 8{,}000$. If 10,000 hours are used to produce the optimal solution, there is a surplus of 2,000 hours.

We will be looking at this form of constraint in the next section.

Section summary

Simultaneous equations can be used to solve linear programming problems rather than using the iso-contribution (profit) lines.

Slack occurs when maximum availability of a resource is not used. **Surplus** occurs when more than a minimum requirement is used.

---

3 Using linear programming

Introduction

Although linear programming is a useful technique for solving multi-variable problems, it is still subject to a number of assumptions and practical difficulties. Make sure you are familiar with these, as you may be asked to criticise the technique in the exam.

3.1 Assumptions and non-quantifiable factors

The assumptions and non-quantifiable factors highlighted in Chapter 5 in relation to **limiting factor analysis** also apply to **linear programming**, so make sure you refresh your memory. Further assumptions that are made in linear programming are:

(a)   The **total amount available of each scarce resource is known with accuracy**.

(b)   There is **no interdependence between the demand** for the different products or services, so that there is a completely free choice in the product or service mix without having to consider the consequences for demand or selling prices per unit.

In spite of these assumptions, linear programming is a useful technique in practice. Some statistical studies have been carried out suggesting that linear cost functions do apply over fairly wide ranges of output, and so the assumptions underlying linear programming may be valid.

3.2 Uses of linear programming

(a) **Budgeting**. If scarce resources are ignored when a budget is prepared, the budget is unattainable and is of little use for planning and control. When there is more than one scarce resource, linear programming can be used to identify the most profitable use of resources.

(b) **Calculation of relevant costs**. The calculation of relevant costs is essential for decision making. The **relevant cost** of a **scarce resource** is calculated as **acquisition cost of the resource plus opportunity cost**. When **more than one scarce resource** exists, the **opportunity cost** (or **shadow price**) should be established using linear programming techniques.

(c) **Selling different products**. Suppose that an organisation faced with resource constraints manufactures products X and Y, and linear programming has been used to determine the shadow prices of the scarce resources. If the organisation now wishes to manufacture and sell a modified version of product X (Z), requiring inputs of the scarce resources, the relevant costs of these scarce resources can be determined (see above) to ascertain whether the production of X and Y should be restricted in order to produce Z.

(d) **Maximum payment for additional scarce resources**. This use of shadow prices has been covered in this chapter.

(e) **Control**. Opportunity costs are also important for cost control: standard costing can be improved by incorporating opportunity costs into variance calculations. For example, adverse material usage variances can be an indication of material wastage. Such variances should be valued at the standard cost of the material plus the opportunity cost of the loss of one scarce unit of material. Such an approach highlights the true cost of the inefficient use of scarce resources and encourages managers of responsibility centres to pay special attention to the control of scarce factors of production. For organisations using an optimised production technology (OPT) strategy, this approach is particularly useful because variances arising from bottleneck operations will be reported in terms of opportunity cost rather than purchase cost.

(f) **Capital budgeting**. Linear programming can be used to determine the combination of investment proposals that should be selected if investment funds are restricted in more than one period.

3.3 Practical difficulties with using linear programming

Difficulties with applying the linear programming technique in practice include the following:

(a) It may be **difficult to identify** which **resources** are likely to be in **short supply** and **what the amount of their availability will be**.

Estimates of future availability will inevitably be prone to inaccuracy and any such inaccuracies will invalidate the profit-maximising product mix derived from the use of linear programming.

(b) Management may **not make product mix decisions that are profit maximising**. They may be more concerned to develop a production/sales plan that has the following features:

(i)   Realistic
(ii) Acceptable to the individual managers throughout the organisation
(iii) Acceptable to the rest of the workforce
(iv) Promises a 'satisfactory' profit and accounting return

In other words, management might look for a **satisfactory product mix** that achieves a satisfactory return, sales revenue and market share while at the same time plans operations and targets of achievement that employees can accept as realistic, not too demanding and unreasonable, and not too threatening to their job security.

(c) The **assumption of linearity may be totally invalid except over smaller ranges**. For example, in a profit maximisation problem, it may well be found that there are substantial changes in unit variable costs arising from increasing or decreasing returns to scale.

(d)   The linear programming model is essentially **static** and is therefore not really suitable for analysing in detail the effects of changes in the various parameters, for example over time.

(e)   In some circumstances, a practical solution derived from a linear programming model may be of **limited use** as, for example, where the variables may only take on **integer values**. A solution must then be found by a combination of rounding up and trial and error.

(f)   The **shadow price** of a scarce resource **only applies up to a certain limit**.

Section summary

Various **assumptions** are made in linear programming, including the following:

- Fixed costs remain the same regardless of the decision taken.
- Unit variable cost is constant regardless of the decision taken.
- Estimates of sales demand and resources required are known with certainty.
- Units of output are divisible.

4   Sensitivity analysis

Introduction

Sensitivity analysis is used to find out what would happen to the optimal solution if variables were **changed**. This is an essential process as variables such as the availability of material and labour and the contribution for individual products are not certain. This section focuses on how to carry out sensitivity analysis. Make sure you understand the concept of **shadow prices**.

KEY POINT

Sensitivity analysis with linear programming can be carried out in one of two ways.

(a)   By **considering the value of each limiting factor or binding resource constraint**
(b)   By **considering sale prices (or the contribution per unit)**

4.1 Limiting factor sensitivity analysis

We use the shadow price to carry out sensitivity analysis on the availability of a limiting factor.

4.1.1 Shadow prices

KEY TERM

The SHADOW PRICE or DUAL PRICE of a limiting factor is the increase in value that would be created by having one additional unit of the limiting factor at the original cost.

Question 9.6   Shadow prices 1

Learning outcomes C2(c)

Choose the correct words from those highlighted.

A shadow price is the **increase/decrease** in **contribution/revenue** created by the availability of an extra unit of a **resource/limiting resource** at **its original cost/a premium price**.

So in terms of linear programming, the shadow price is the **extra contribution or profit that may be earned by relaxing by one unit a binding resource constraint**.

BPP
LEARNING MEDIA

Suppose the availability of materials is a binding constraint. If one extra kilogram becomes available so that an alternative production mix becomes optimal, with a resulting increase over the original production mix contribution of $2, the shadow price of a kilogram of material is $2.

Note, however, that this increase in contribution of $2 per extra kilogram of material made available is calculated on the **assumption** that the **extra kilogram would cost the normal variable amount**.

Note the following points.

(a)   The shadow price therefore represents the maximum **premium** above the basic rate that an organisation should be **willing to pay for one extra unit** of a resource.

(b)   Since shadow prices indicate the effect of a one unit change in a constraint, they provide a measure of the **sensitivity** of the result.

(c)   The **shadow price** of a constraint that is **not binding** at the optimal solution is **zero**.

(d)   Shadow prices are **only valid for a small range** before the constraint becomes non-binding or different resources become critical.

Depending on the resource in question, shadow prices enable management to make **better informed decisions** about the payment of overtime premiums, bonuses, premiums on small orders of raw materials and so on.

4.1.2 Calculating shadow prices

In the earlier example of WX, the availability of time in both departments are limiting factors because both are used up fully in the optimal product mix. Let us therefore calculate the effect if **one extra hour of shaping department machine time** was made available so that 2,401 hours were available.

The **new optimal product mix would be at the intersection of the two constraint lines** $0.06x + 0.08y = 2,400$ and $0.04x + 0.12y = 2,401$.

Solution by simultaneous equations gives $x = 23,980$ and $y = 12,015$.

(You should solve the problem yourself if you are doubtful about the derivation of the solution.)

Product	Units	Contribution per unit $	Total contribution $
A	23,980	0.20	4,796.0
B	12,015	0.30	3,604.5
			8,400.5

Contribution in original problem
((24,000 × $0.20) + (12,000 × $0.30))   8,400.0
Increase in contribution from one extra hour of shaping time   0.5

The **shadow price of an hour of machining time in the shaping department is therefore $0.50**.

The **shadow price** of a limiting factor also shows **by how much contribution would fall if the availability of a limiting resource fell by one unit**. The **shadow price** (also called **dual price**) of an hour of machine time in the shaping department would again be calculated as $0.50. This is the **opportunity cost** of deciding to put an hour of shaping department time to an alternative use.

We can now make the following points:

(a)   The management of WX should be prepared to **pay up to $0.50 extra per hour** (ie $0.50 over and above the normal price) of shaping department machine time to obtain more machine hours.

(b)   This **value** of machine time **only applies as long as shaping machine time is a limiting factor**. If more and more machine hours become available, there will eventually be so much machine time that it is no longer a limiting factor.

| Question 9.7 | Shadow prices 2 |

Learning outcome C2(c)

What is the shadow price of one hour of machine time in the mixing department?

4.1.3 Ranges for limiting factors

We can calculate **how many hours will be available before machine time in the shaping department ceases to be a limiting factor**.

Look back at the third graph in Section 1.4. As more hours become available, the constraint line moves out away from the origin. It ceases to be a limiting factor when it passes through the intersection of the sales constraint and the mixing department machine time constraint which is at the point (22,667, 13,000).

So, if x = 22,667 and y = 13,000, our new constraint would be 0.04x + 0.12y = H (hours) where H = (0.04 × 22,667) + (0.12 × 13,000) = 2,466.68 hours.

The shadow price of shaping department machine time is therefore $0.50 but only up to a maximum supply of 2,466.68 hours (that is 66.68 hours more than the original 2,400 hours). Extra availability of machine time above 2,466.68 hours would not have any use, and the two limiting factors would become sales demand for product B and machine time in the mixing department.

4.2 Selling price sensitivity analysis

KEY POINT

Selling price sensitivity analysis is carried out by changing the slope of the 'iso-contribution' line.

The optimal solution in our WX example was to make 24,000 units of product A and 12,000 units of product B. Would this solution change if the **unit sales price of A increased by 10c?**

The **contribution would increase** to 0.3x + 0.3y (in place of 0.2x + 0.3y). The **iso-contribution lines would now have a steeper slope** than previously, parallel (for example) to 0.3x + 0.3y = 3,000.

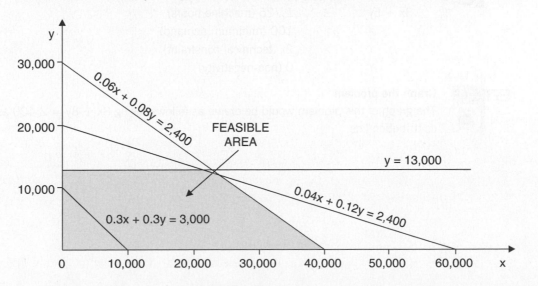

If you were to place a ruler along the iso-contribution line and move it away from the origin as usual, you would find that its **last point within the feasible region** was the point (40,000, 0).

Therefore if the sales price of A is raised by 10c, WX's contribution-maximising product mix would be to produce 40,000 units of A and none of B.

Example: sensitivity analysis

SW makes two products, X and Y, which each earn a contribution of $8 per unit. Each unit of X requires four labour hours and three machine hours. Each unit of Y requires three labour hours and five machine hours.

Total weekly capacity is 1,200 labour hours and 1,725 machine hours. There is a standing weekly order for 100 units of X which must be met. In addition, for technical reasons, it is necessary to produce at least twice as many units of Y as units of X.

Required

(a)   Determine the contribution-maximising production plan each week.

(b)   Calculate the shadow price of the following:

   (i)   Machine hours

   (ii)   Labour hours

   (iii) The minimum weekly demand for X of 100 units

Solution

Solution (a): production plan

The linear programming problem may be formulated as follows:

 STEP 1 **Define variables**

Let x = number of units of X produced and y = number of units of Y produced.

 STEP 2 **Establish objective function**

Maximise contribution (c) = 8x + 8y subject to the constraints below.

 STEP 3 **Establish constraints**

4x + 3y	≤	1,200 (labour hours)
3x + 5y	≤	1,725 (machine hours)
X	≥	100 (minimum demand)
Y	≥	2x (technical constraint)
Y	≥	0 (non-negativity)

 STEP 4 **Graph the problem**

The graph of this problem would be drawn as follows, using 8x + 8y = 2,400 as an iso-contribution line.

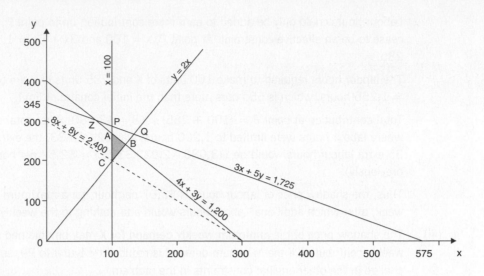

STEP 5

Establish feasible polygon

The feasible polygon is ABC. Using the slope of the iso-contribution line, we can measure that the contribution-maximising point is point A.

STEP 6

Determine optimal solution

At point A, the effective constraints are $x = 100$ and $4x + 3y = 1,200$.

∴ If $x = 100$, $(4 \times 100) + 3y = 1,200$

∴ $3y = 1,200 - 400$ and so $y = 266\frac{2}{3}$

It is important to be aware that in linear programming, the optimal solution is likely to give values to the decision variables that are in fractions of a unit. In this example, contribution will be maximised by making $266\frac{2}{3}$ units of Y.

	Contribution
	$
Make 100 units of X	800.00
$266\frac{2}{3}$ units of Y	2,133.33
Total weekly contribution	2,933.33

Solution (b): sensitivity analysis

(i)   **Machine hours** are not fully utilised in the optimal solution. 100 units of X and $266\frac{2}{3}$ units of Y need $(300 + 1,333.33) = 1,633.33$ machine hours, leaving 91.67 **machine hours unused**. Machine hours, not being an effective constraint in the optimal solution, have a **shadow price of $0**. Obtaining one extra machine hour would add nothing to the contribution.

(ii)   The shadow price of **labour hours** would be obtained by calculating the total weekly contribution if the labour hours constraint was 1,201 hours. It should be possible to see fairly easily that the **new optimal solution** would be where $x = 100$ and $4x + 3y = 1,201$. Therefore $x = 100$, $y = 267$ and total weekly contribution would be $(100 + 267) \times \$8 = \$2,936$.

Since contribution with 1,200 labour hours as the constraint was $2,933.33, the **shadow price of labour hours** is $(2,936 - 2,933.33) = \$2.67$ per hour. This is the amount by which total contribution would rise if one extra labour hour per week were made available.

Note that there is a **limitation** to the number of extra labour hours that could be used to earn extra contribution. As more and more labour hours are added, the constraint line will move further and further away from the origin. For example, if we added 800 labour hours capacity each week, the constraint $4x + 3y \leq (1,200 + 800)$ (ie $4x + 3y \leq 2,000$) would be so much further away from the origin that it would no longer be an effective constraint. Machine hours would now help to impose limitations on production, and the profit-maximising output would be at point P on the graph.

Labour hours could only be added to earn more contribution up to point P, after which they would cease to be an effective constraint. At point P, x = 100 and 3x + 5y = 1,725. Therefore y = 285.

The labour hours required to make 100 units of X and 285 units of Y are (4 × 100) + (3 × 285) = 1,255 hours, which is 55 hours more than the initial constraint limit.

Total contribution at point P = (100 + 285) × $8 = $3,080. Since total contribution at point A, where labour hours were limited to 1,200 hours, was $2,933.33, the extra contribution from the 55 extra labour hours would be $(3,080 – 2,933.33)/55 = $2.67 per hour (as calculated previously).

Thus, the shadow price of labour hours is $2.67 per hour, for a maximum of 55 extra hours per week, after which additional labour hours would add nothing to the weekly contribution.

(iii) The shadow price of the **minimum weekly demand for X** may be obtained by calculating the weekly contribution if the minimum demand is reduced by 1 unit to 99, so that x ≥ 99, given no change in the other original constraints in the problem.

The new optimal solution would occur where x = 99 and 4x + 3y = 1,200. Therefore y = 268.

Total contribution per week when x = 99 and y = 268 is (99 + 268) × $8 = $2,936. Since the contribution when x ≥ 100 was $2,933.33, the **shadow price** of the minimum demand for X is $(2,936 – 2,933.33) = **$2.67 per unit**. In other words, by reducing the minimum demand for X, the weekly contribution can be raised by $2.67 for each unit by which the minimum demand is reduced below 100 per week.

As with the constraint on labour hours, this shadow price is **only applicable up to a certain amount**. If you refer back to the graph of the problem, you should be able to see that if the minimum constraint on X is reduced beyond point Z, it will cease to be an effective constraint in the optimal solution, because at point Z the machine hours limitation will begin to apply.

Question 9.8

Ranges for shadow prices

Learning outcome C2(c)

By how many units per week can the minimum demand be reduced before the shadow price of $2.67 per unit referred to above ceases to apply?

Section summary

The **shadow price** or **dual price** of a limiting factor is the increase in value that would be created by having one additional unit of the limiting factor at the original cost.

Selling price sensitivity analysis is carried out by changing the slope of the 'iso-contribution' line.

Chapter Summary

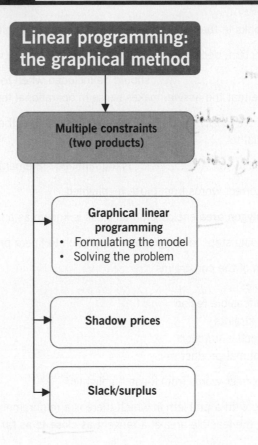

Linear programming: the graphical method

Multiple constraints (two products)

Graphical linear programming
- Formulating the model
- Solving the problem

Shadow prices

Slack/surplus

Quick Quiz

1   Fill in the blanks in the statements below with one of the following terms.

Objective function; decision variable; constraint; inequality; non-negativity constraints.

(a)   ......**Non**..................... should be included when formulating linear programming solutions to ensure that the answer makes sense in operational terms.

(b)   An .....**inequality**............. is an equation taking the form 'greater than or equal to' or 'less than or equal to'.

(c)   An ...**objective**............. is a quantified statement of the aim of a resource allocation decision.

2   Choose the correct words from those highlighted.

A feasible **polygon/area** enclosed on all sides is known as a feasible **polygon/area**.

3   Put the following steps in the graphical approach to linear programming in the correct order.

Draw a graph of the constraints
Define variables
Establish the feasible region
Establish constraints
Establish objective function
Determine optimal product mix

4   Choose the correct words from those highlighted.

When dealing with a problem in which there is a requirement to minimise costs, we look for a total cost line touching the feasible area at a tangent **as close to/as far from** the origin as possible.

5   The shadow price of a scarce resource is not the same as its dual price.

True   ☐

False   ☒

6   In what circumstances does slack arise?

A   At the optimal solution, when the resource used equals the resource available

B   At the optimal solution, when a minimum quantity of a resource must be used, and more than that quantity is used

•C   At the optimal solution, when the resource used is less than the resource available

D   At the optimal solution, when a minimum quantity of resource is used

7   Draw the feasibility polygon for the following inequalities.

$2x + 3y \leq 12$
$y \geq 2x$
$x \geq 0, y \geq 0$

8   Choose the correct words from those highlighted.

If a **maximum/minimum** quantity of a resource must be used and, at the optimal solution, **more than/less than** that quantity is used, there is a surplus on the **minimum/maximum** requirement.

Answers to Quick Quiz

1   (a)   Non-negativity constraints
     (b)   Inequality
     (c)   Objective function

2   area
     polygon

3   Define variables
     Establish objective function
     Establish constraints
     Draw a graph of the constraints
     Establish the feasible region
     Determine optimal product mix

4   as close to

5   False

6   C.   If a resource has a maximum availability and it's not binding at the optimal solution, there will be slack.

7   Start with the inequality $y \geq 2x$. The equation $y = 2x$ is a straight line, and you need to plot two points to draw it, such as (0, 0) and (2, 4).

     Since $y \geq 2x$, feasible combinations of x and y lie above this line (for example if $x = 2$, y must be 4 or more).

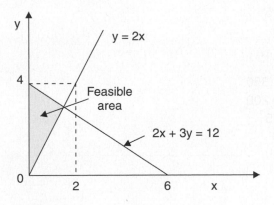

8   minimum
     more than
     minimum

Answers to Questions

9.1 Constraints

These are the constraints that will prevent WX Ltd from producing and selling as much of each product as it chooses.

The constraints are machine hours in each department and sales demand for product B. There is no restriction on the availability of labour hours. Selling price cannot be a constraint.

9.2 Inequalities

The constraint facing the shaping department can be written as follows:

$0.04x + 0.12y \leq 2,400$

The constraint has to be a 'less than equal to' inequality, because the amount of resource used $(0.04x + 0.12y)$ has to be 'less than equal to' the amount available of 2,400 hours.

9.3 Formulation of linear programming model

(a)   The objective function is to maximise weekly contribution, given by $C = 124x + 80y$.

(b)   The constraints are:

Department 1	$150x + 90y$	$\leq$	225×60 minutes
Department 2	$100x + 120y$	$\leq$	200×60 minutes
EU quota	y	$\leq$	75
Non-negativity	x, y	$\geq$	0

These constraints can be simplified to:

Department 1	$15x + 9y$	$\leq$	1,350
Department 2	$10x + 12y$	$\leq$	1,200
EU quota	y	$\leq$	75
Non-negativity	x, y	$\geq$	0

9.4 Feasible region

If $0.06x + 0.08y = 2,400$, then if $x = 0$, $y = 30,000$ and if $y = 0$, $x = 40,000$.

If $0.04x + 0.12y = 2,400$, then if $x = 0$, $y = 20,000$ and if $y = 0$, $x = 60,000$.

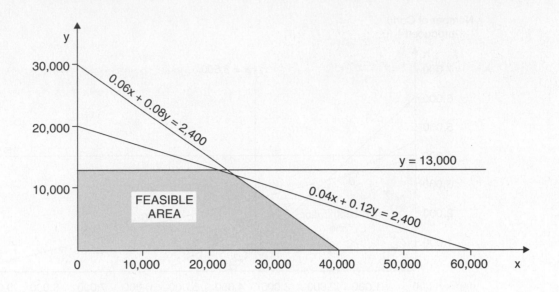

9.5 Determining the optimal solution

Calculate the number of productive hours worked in each department each month

Number of employees × number of productive hours worked each day × number of days each month.

Tanning   = $7 \times (7 - 0.5) \times 20 = 910$ hours
Plunging   = $10 \times (6 - 1) \times 20 = 1,000$ hours
Watering   = $5 \times (10 - 0.25) \times 20 = 975$ hours

Define variables

Let the number of Cretes produced each month = x and the number of Corfus produced each month = y.

Establish objective function

The contribution is $75 per Crete and $50 per Corfu. The objective function is therefore maximise C = 75x + 50y subject to the constraints below.

Establish constraints

Tanning	$x/6 + y/5 \leq 910$
Plunging	$x/4 + y/6 \leq 1,000$
Watering	$x/10 + y/4 \leq 975$
Monthly sales units	$x \leq 3,500, y \leq 4,000$
Non negativity	$x \geq 0, y \geq 0$

Graph the problem

The problem can be solved using the following graph which includes a sample contribution line 75x + 50y = 150,000.

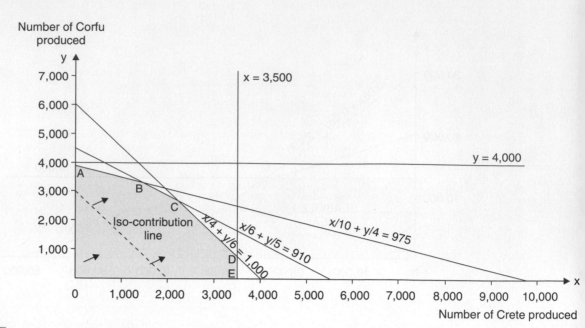

 Define the feasible area

The feasible region for a solution is OABCDE.

Determine the optimal solution

Moving the sample contribution line across the feasible region it can be seen that the optimum solution is at any point along the line $x/4 + y/6 = 1,000$ between C and D (as the sample contribution line has the same gradient as the plunging constraint). The co-ordinates of point C are (2,175, 2,737.5) while those of point D are (3,500, 750).

The contribution from any of these solutions is $((75 \times 3,500) + (50 \times 750)) = \$300,000$ (using the co-ordinates of D).

9.6 Shadow prices 1

The correct answer is: A shadow price is the **increase** in **contribution** created by the availability of an extra unit of a **limiting resource** at its **original cost**.

9.7 Shadow prices 2

If we assume that one **less** hour of machine time in the mixing department is available, the new optimal solution is at the intersection of $0.06x + 0.08y = 2,399$ and $0.04x + 0.12y = 2,400$.

Solution by simultaneous equations gives $x = 23,970$, $y = 12,010$.

Product	Units	Contribution per unit $	Total contribution $
A	23,970	0.20	4,794
B	12,010	0.30	3,603
			8,397
Contribution in original problem			8,400
Reduction in contribution			3

∴ Shadow price of one hour of machine time in the mixing department is $3.

9.8 Ranges for shadow prices

At point Z:	$4x + 3y = 1{,}200$	.... (1)
	$3x + 5y = 1{,}725$	.... (2)
Multiply (1) by 3	$12x + 9y = 3{,}600$	.... (3)
Multiply (2) by 4	$12x + 20y = 6{,}900$	.... (4)
Subtract (3) from (4)	$11y = 3{,}300$	

$$y = 300$$

Substituting in (1) $4x + 900 = 1{,}200$

$$4x = 300$$
$$x = 75$$

The shadow price of the minimum demand for X is $2.67 per unit demanded, but only up to a total reduction in the minimum demand of $(100 - 75) = 25$ units per week.

Now try the questions from the Practice Question Bank	**Number**	**Level**
	Q9.1 – Q9.5	Practice

BPP
LEARNING MEDIA

BUDGETING

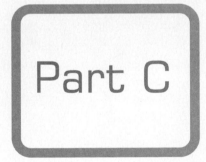

Part C

FORECASTING TECHNIQUES

In Chapter 11a, we will see how to prepare budgets but first we will look at where the figures that go into the budgets come from. To produce a budget calls for the **preparation of forecasts of costs and revenues**. Various quantitative techniques can assist with these '**number-crunching**' **aspects of budgeting**. This chapter aims to provide an understanding of those techniques. Note that the techniques will be described within their budgetary context.

We will be covering **two principal forecasting techniques** in this chapter, **regression analysis** and **time series analysis**.

Regression analysis can be applied to costs and revenues, while time series analysis is generally applied to revenue.

Multiple choice or objective test questions on forecasting techniques are **likely**. **Longer questions** could **involve both regression analysis and time series analysis**. For example, you might have to apply seasonal variations to a trend determined using regression analysis.

Much of this chapter will be **revision** from your earlier studies in business mathematics, but work through all of the material slowly and carefully to ensure that you have a thorough knowledge of quantitative forecasting techniques.

Topic list	Learning outcomes	Syllabus references	Ability required
1 Forecasting using historical data	B2(a)	B2(a)(i)	Application
2 Linear regression analysis	B2(a)	B2(a)(i)	Application
3 Scatter diagrams and correlation	B2(a)	B2(a)(i)	Application
4 Sales forecasting	B2(a)	B2(a)(i)	Application
5 Regression and forecasting	B2(a)	B2(a)(i)	Application
6 The components of time series	B2(a)	B2(a)(i)	Application
7 Finding the trend	B2(a)	B2(a)(i)	Application
8 Finding the seasonal variations	B2(a)	B2(a)(i)	Application
9 Time series analysis and forecasting	B2(a)	B2(a)(i)	Application
10 Forecasting problems	B2(a)	B2(a)(i)	Application

Chapter Overview

```
                    ┌─────────────────────────┐
                    │   Preparing forecasts   │
                    └─────────────────────────┘
                       │                    │
                       ▼                    ▼
        ┌──────────────────────┐   ┌──────────────────────┐
        │  Time series analysis │   │   Linear regression  │
        └──────────────────────┘   └──────────────────────┘
```

1 Forecasting using historical data

Introduction

Numerous techniques have been developed for using past costs as the basis for forecasting future values. These techniques range from simple arithmetic and visual methods to advanced computer-based statistical systems. With all these, there is the **presumption that the past will provide guidance to the future**.

Before using any extrapolation techniques, **past data** must therefore be critically examined to **assess their appropriateness for the intended purpose**. The following checks should be made.

(a)   The **time period** should be long enough to include any periodically paid costs but short enough to ensure that averaging of variations in the level of activity has not occurred.

(b)   The **data** should be examined to ensure that any non-activity level factors affecting costs were roughly the same in the past as those forecast for the future. Such factors might include changes in technology, changes in efficiency, changes in production methods, changes in resource costs, strikes and weather conditions. Changes to the past data are frequently necessary.

(c)   The **methods of data collection** and the accounting policies used should not introduce bias. Examples might include depreciation policies and the treatment of by-products.

(d)   Appropriate choices of **dependent** and **independent variables** must be made.

The two forecasting methods that follow (the scatter diagram method and linear regression analysis) are based on the assumption that a **linear relationship** links levels of cost and levels of activity.

Knowledge brought forward from earlier studies

Linear relationships

*   A **linear relationship** can be expressed in the form of an equation which has the general form $Y = a + bX$.

    Where Y   is the **dependent** variable, depending for its value on the value of X

            X   is the **independent** variable, whose value helps to determine the corresponding value of y

            a   is a **constant**, a fixed amount

            b   is a constant, being the **coefficient of X** (that is, the number by which the value of X should be multiplied to derive the value of Y)

*   If there is a linear relationship between total costs and level of activity, Y = total costs, X = level of activity, a = fixed cost (the cost when there is no activity level) and b = variable cost per unit.

*   The graph of a linear equation is a **straight line** and is determined by two things, the **gradient** (or slope) of the straight line and the point at which the straight line crosses the Y axis (the **intercept**).

    –   Gradient = b in the equation $Y = a + bX = (Y_2 - Y_1)/(X_2 - X_1)$ where (X_1, Y_1), (X_2, Y_2) are two points on the straight line

    –   Intercept = a in the equation $Y = a + bX$

1.1 The high-low method

An important technique that you have already covered when analysing linear cost behaviour patterns is the **high-low method**. Have a go at the following question to ensure that you remember how to use it. Some of the cost and revenue behaviour patterns are quite complicated, so you will need to prepare careful workings.

Question 10.1

Analysing cost behaviour and making projections

Learning outcome B2(a)

The manager of a nail salon is using the results of two recent periods to forecast the revenues and costs for a forthcoming period. The results for the two periods to be used as a basis for forecasting are as follows:

	Period 1		Period 2	
Activity				
Number of manicures		240		305
Number of pedicures		180		246
	£	£	£	£
Revenue		9,780		11,574.00
Materials	756		991.80	
Staff salaries	5,100		6,862.00	
Utilities	712		856.10	
Laundry	466		570.80	
Rent	430		430.00	
Other	375		375.00	
		7,839		10,085.70
Profit		1,941		1,488.30

The manager has ascertained the following information.

1   Revenue for period 4 is expected to be £6,095 for manicures and £4,125 for pedicures.

2   The variable element of all costs varies in direct proportion to the total number of manicures and pedicures.

3   All staff are paid a fixed salary, plus a bonus for each customer. The fixed element of staff salary costs increases by £1,500 per period once total activity reaches 450 manicures and pedicures because of the need to employ temporary staff.

4   The variable element of laundry costs is expected to increase by 50% in period 4.

5   Forecast activity for period 4 is as follows:

- 265 manicures
- 165 pedicures

Required

Prepare a forecast profit statement for period 4.

Section summary

(a)   A number of quantitative methods may be used by the management accountant to obtain information for inclusion in budgets.

(b)   Before using any technique based on past data, the past data must be assessed for appropriateness for the intended purpose. There is no point in using a 'sophisticated' technique with unreliable data.

2 Linear regression analysis

Introduction

You will have learned simple linear regression analysis in your earlier studies. However, as **regression analysis** is specifically mentioned in the P1 syllabus, we will start from basics in this Study Text.

Linear regression analysis, also known as the '**least squares technique**', is a **statistical method** of estimating costs using historical data from a number of previous accounting periods. The analysis is used to derive a **line of best fit that has the general form**:

Y = a + bX where

Y, the dependent variable = total cost
X, the independent variable = the level of activity
a, the intercept of the line on the Y axis = the fixed cost
b, the gradient of the line = the variable cost per unit of activity

Historical data is collected from previous periods and adjusted to a common price level to remove inflationary differences. This provides a number of readings for activity levels (X) and their associated costs (Y). Then, by substituting these readings into the formulae below for a and b, estimates of the fixed cost and variable cost per unit are provided.

EXAM

If $Y = a + bX$, $b = \dfrac{n\Sigma XY - \Sigma X \Sigma Y}{n\Sigma X^2 - (\Sigma X)^2}$ and $a = \bar{Y} - b\bar{X}$

where $\bar{X}, \bar{Y}$ are the average values of X and Y and n is the number of pairs of data for X and Y.

An example will help to illustrate this technique.

Example: least squares method

The transport department of Norwest Council operates a large fleet of vehicles. These vehicles are used by the various departments of the Council. Each month, a statement is prepared for the transport department, comparing actual results with budget. One of the items in the transport department's monthly statement is the cost of vehicle maintenance. This maintenance is carried out by the employees of the department. To facilitate control, the transport manager has asked that future statements should show vehicle maintenance costs analysed into fixed and variable costs.

Data from the six months from January to June Year 2 inclusive are given below.

Year 2	Vehicle maintenance cost £	Vehicle running hours
January	13,600	2,100
February	15,800	2,800
March	14,500	2,200
April	16,200	3,000
May	14,900	2,600
June	15,000	2,500

Required

Analyse the vehicle maintenance costs into fixed and variable costs, based on the data given, utilising the least squares method.

Solution

If Y = a + bX, where Y represents costs and X represents running hours (since costs depend on running hours) then b = (nΣXY − ΣXΣY)/(nΣX² − (ΣX)²), when n is the number of pairs of data, which is 6 in this problem.

X	Y	XY	X²
'000 hours	£'000		
2.1	13.6	28.56	4.41
2.8	15.8	44.24	7.84
2.2	14.5	31.90	4.84
3.0	16.2	48.60	9.00
2.6	14.9	38.74	6.76
2.5	15.0	37.50	6.25
15.2	90.0	229.54	39.10

Variable cost per hour, b = (6(229.54) − (15.2)(90.00))/(6(39.1) − (15.2)²)
= (1,377.24 − 1,368)/(234.6 − 231.04) = 9.24/3.56 = £2.60

Fixed costs (in £'000), a = $\overline{Y} - b\overline{X}$ = (ΣY/n) − (bΣX/n) = (90/6) − (2.6(15.2)/6) = 8.41 approx, say £8,400.

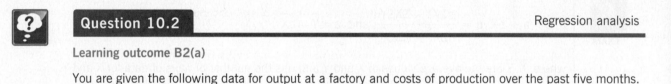

Question 10.2
Regression analysis

Learning outcome B2(a)

You are given the following data for output at a factory and costs of production over the past five months.

Month	Output '000 units	Costs £'000
	X	y
1	20	82
2	16	70
3	24	90
4	22	85
5	18	73

Required

(a) Calculate an equation to determine the expected cost level for any given output volume.
(b) Prepare a budget for total costs if output is 22,000 units.

2.1 The conditions suited to the use of linear regression analysis

The conditions that should apply if linear regression analysis is to be used to estimate costs are also limitations of the method.

(a) **A linear cost function is assumed**. This assumption can be tested by measures of reliability, such as the correlation coefficient and the coefficient of determination (which ought to be reasonably close to 1). We will be looking at these concepts later in the chapter.

(b) When calculating a line of best fit, there will be a range of values for X. In the question above, the line Y = 28 + 2.6X was predicted from data with output values ranging from X = 16 to X = 24. Depending on the degree of correlation between X and Y, we might safely use the estimated line of best fit to forecast values for Y, provided that the value of X remains within the range 16 to 24. We would be on less safe ground if we used the equation to predict a value for Y when X = 10, or

30, or any other value outside the range 16 to 24, because we would **have to assume that costs behave in the same way outside the range of x values used to establish the line in the first place**.

(c)   **It assumes that past behaviour of the data will continue into the future**.

(d)   **Only two variables are used. In reality there may be many variables that affect the dependent variable**.

KEY TERMS

INTERPOLATION means using a line of best fit to predict a value within the two extreme points of the observed range. Interpolation is generally considered to be safer than extrapolation.

EXTRAPOLATION means using a line of best fit to predict a value outside the two extreme points.

(e)   The **historical data** for cost and output should be **adjusted to a common price level** (to overcome cost differences caused by inflation) and the historical data should also be **representative of current technology, current efficiency levels and current operations** (products made).

(f)   As far as possible, **historical data should be accurately recorded** so that variable costs are properly matched against the items produced or sold, and fixed costs are properly matched against the time period to which they relate. For example, if a factory rental is £120,000 per annum, and if data is gathered monthly, these costs should be charged £10,000 to each month instead of £120,000 in full to a single month.

(g)   Management should either be **confident that conditions** that have existed in the past **will continue into the future or amend the estimates** of cost produced by the linear regression analysis to **allow for expected changes** in the future.

(h)   As with any forecasting process, the **amount of data available is very important**. Even if correlation is high, if we have fewer than about ten pairs of data, we must regard any forecast as being somewhat unreliable.

(i)   It must be assumed that the value of one variable, Y, can be predicted or estimated from the value of one other variable, X.

Question 10.3	Limitations of regression analysis

Learning outcomes B2(a)

The relationship between total operating cost and quantity produced (in a manufacturing company) is given by the linear regression model TC = 5,000 + 500Q, where TC = total operating cost (in £) per annum and Q = quantity produced per annum (kg).

Explain five reservations that you might have about relying on the above model for budgetary planning purposes.

Exam alert

In an objective test question (OTQ) you could be given a regression equation that you need to use to determine the expected or standard cost for an actual level of activity. By comparing this standard cost with an actual cost provided, you can then establish a total cost variance.

Section summary

Linear regression analysis (least squares technique) involves determining a **line of best fit**.

BPP
LEARNING MEDIA

3 Scatter diagrams and correlation

3.1 The scatter diagram method of forecasting

> **Introduction**
>
> **Scatter diagrams** can be used to estimate the fixed and variable components of costs.

By this method of cost estimation, cost and activity data are plotted on a graph. A **'line of best fit'** is then drawn. This line should be drawn through the middle of the plotted points as closely as possible so that the distance of points above the line are equal to distances below the line. Where necessary, costs should be adjusted to the same indexed price level to allow for inflation.

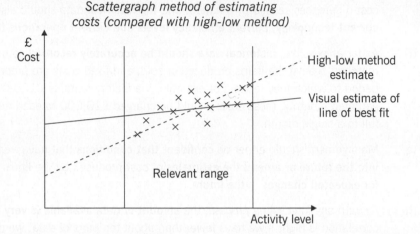

Scattergraph method of estimating costs (compared with high-low method)

The fixed cost is the intercept of the line of best fit on the vertical axis. Suppose the fixed cost is £500 and that one of the plotted points (which is very close to the line or actually on it) represents output of 100 units and total cost of £550. The variable cost of 100 units is therefore calculated as £(550 – 500) = £50 and so the variable cost per unit is £0.50. The equation of the line of best fit is therefore **approximately** Y = 500 + 0.5X.

If the company to which this data relates wanted to forecast total costs when output is 90 units, a forecast based on the equation would be 500 + (0.5 × 90) = £545. Alternatively, the **forecast could be read directly from the graph using the line of best fit**.

The disadvantage of the scatter diagram method is that the cost line is drawn by visual judgement and so is a **subjective approximation**. The subjectivity is very clear from the diagram, which demonstrates how **different** our estimates of fixed and variable costs would be if we used the **high-low method** of cost analysis.

3.2 Correlation

Correlation describes the extent to which the values of two variables are related. Two variables might be **perfectly** correlated, **partly** correlated or **uncorrelated**. The correlation may be **positive** or **negative**. The degree of correlation between two variables can be measured using the **Pearsonian coefficient of correlation, r**. The **coefficient of determination** indicates the variations in the dependent variable that can be explained by variations in the independent variable.

KEY POINT

Although your P1 syllabus does not specifically mention correlation, it does include regression analysis. The successful application of linear regression models depends on X and Y being closely linearly related. Therefore, an understanding of correlation is essential to the ability to discuss the quality or reliability of a forecast prepared using regression techniques.

KEY TERM

CORRELATION is the degree to which change in one variable is related to change in another – in other words, the interdependence between variables.

3.3 Degrees of correlation

Two variables might be **perfectly correlated**, **partly correlated**, **uncorrelated** or subject to **non-linear correlation**.

Perfect correlation

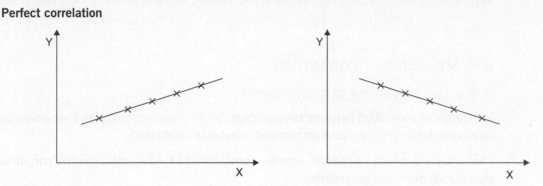

All the pairs of values lie on a straight line. An **exact linear relationship** exists between the two variables.

Partial correlation

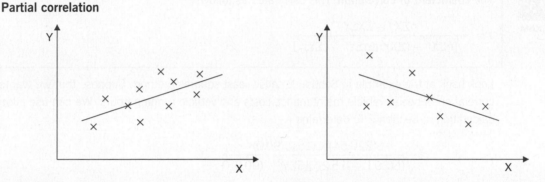

In the left-hand diagram, although there is no exact relationship, **low values of X tend to be associated with low values of Y, and high values of X with high values of Y**.

In the right-hand diagram, there is no exact relationship, but **low values of X tend to be associated with high values of Y and vice versa**.

No correlation   **Non-linear or curvilinear correlation**

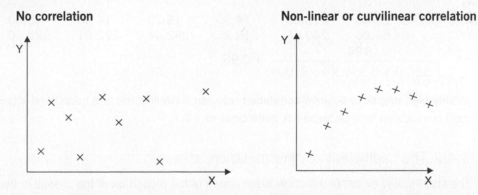

In the left-hand diagram, the values of these two variables are not correlated with each other.

In the right-hand diagram, there is a relationship between X and Y, since the points are on an obvious curve but it is not a linear relationship.

3.3.1 Positive and negative correlation

Correlation, whether perfect or partial, can be **positive** or **negative**.

POSITIVE CORRELATION is the type of correlation where low values of one variable are associated with low values of the other, and high values of one variable are associated with high values of the other.

NEGATIVE CORRELATION is the type of correlation where low values of one variable are associated with high values of the other, and high values of one variable with low values of the other.

3.4 Measures of correlation

3.4.1 The coefficient of correlation, r

The **degree of correlation between two variables** can be measured using the **Pearsonian coefficient of correlation** (also called the **product moment correlation coefficient**).

r has a value between −1 (perfect negative correlation) and +1 (perfect positive correlation). If r = 0 then the variables are uncorrelated.

The **coefficient of correlation**, r, is calculated as follows:

$$r = \frac{n\Sigma XY - \Sigma X \Sigma Y}{\sqrt{[n\Sigma X^2 - (\Sigma X)^2][n\Sigma Y^2 - (\Sigma Y)^2]}}$$

Look back at the example in Section 2 called least squares method. Suppose that we wanted to know the correlation between vehicle maintenance costs and vehicle running hours. We can use a lot of the calculation in Section 2 to determine r.

$$r = \frac{6(229.54) - (15.2)(90.0)}{\sqrt{[6(39.1) - (15.2)^2][6\Sigma Y^2 - (90.0)^2]}}$$

$$= \frac{1,377.24 - 1,368}{\sqrt{[(234.6 - 231.04)(6\Sigma Y^2 - 8,100)]}}$$

All we need to calculate is ΣY^2.

							Total
Y (£'000)	13.60	15.80	14.50	16.20	14.90	15.00	90.00
Y^2	184.96	249.64	210.25	262.44	222.01	225.00	1,354.30

$$r = \frac{9.24}{\sqrt{(3.56)(6 \times (1,354.30) - 8,100)}} = 0.96$$

A **fairly high degree of positive correlation** between X (vehicle running hours) and Y (vehicle maintenance cost) is indicated here **because r is quite close to +1**.

3.4.2 The coefficient of determination, r^2

The COEFFICIENT OF DETERMINATION is a measure of the proportion of the change in the value of one variable that can be explained by variations in the value of the other variable.

In our example, $r^2 = (0.96)^2 = 0.9216$, and so 92% of variation in the value of Y (cost) can be explained by a linear relationship with X (running hours). This leaves only 8% of variations in y to be predicted from other factors. It is therefore **likely that vehicle** running hours could be used with a high degree of confidence to predict costs during a period.

3.5 Correlation and causation

If two variables are well correlated this may be due to pure chance or there may be a reason for it. The **larger the number of pairs of data**, the **less likely it is that the correlation is due to chance**, though that possibility should never be ignored.

If there is a reason, it may not be causal. Monthly net income is well correlated with monthly credit to a person's bank account, for the logical (rather than causal) reason that for most people the one equals the other. **Even if there is a causal explanation** for a correlation, it **does not follow that variations in the value of one variable cause variations in the value of the other**. Sales of ice cream and of sunglasses are well correlated, not because of a direct causal link but because the weather influences both variables.

Having said this, it is of course possible that where two variables are correlated, there is a direct causal link to be found.

3.6 The interactions of r^2 and r with linear regression

The successful application of linear regression models depends on X and Y being closely linearly related. r measures the strength of the linear relationship between two variables but **what numerical value of r is suggestive of sufficient linearity in data to allow one to proceed with linear regression?** The lower the value of r, the less chance of forecasts made using linear regression being adequate.

If there is a perfect linear relationship between the two variables ($r = \pm1$), we can predict y from any given value of X with great confidence. If correlation is high (for example $r = 0.9$), the actual values will all be quite close to the regression line and so predictions should not be far out. If correlation is below about 0.7, predictions will only give a very rough guide to the likely value of Y.

If $r = 0.75$, say, you may feel that the linear relationship between the two variables is fairly strong. But $r^2 = 56.25\%$ indicates that only just over half of the variations in the dependent variable can be explained by a linear relationship with the independent variable. The low figure could be because a non-linear relationship is a better model for the data or because extraneous factors need to be considered. It is a **common rule of thumb that $r^2 \geq 80\%$ indicates that linear regression may be applied for the purpose of forecasting**.

Section summary

Scatter diagrams can be used to estimate the fixed and variable components of costs.

4 Sales forecasting

Introduction

The sales budget is frequently the first budget prepared, since **sales is usually the principal budget factor**, but before the sales budget can be prepared a sales forecast has to be made.

Sales forecasting is complex **and** difficult, and involves the consideration of a number of factors including the following:

- Past sales patterns
- The economic environment
- Results of market research
- Anticipated advertising during the budget period
- Competition
- Changing consumer taste

- New legislation
- Pricing policies and discounts offered
- Legislation
- Environmental factors
- Distribution and quality of sales outlets and personnel

As well as bearing in mind those factors, management can use a number of forecasting methods, often combining them to reduce the level of uncertainty.

Method	Detail
Sales personnel	They can be asked to provide estimates.
Market research	Especially relevant for new products or services.
Mathematical models	Set up so that repetitive computer simulations can be run that permit managers to review the results that would be obtained in various circumstances.
Mathematical techniques	See later in this chapter.

Section summary

Sales forecasting techniques include asking sales personnel, market research, and using mathematical models and techniques.

5 Regression and forecasting

Introduction

The same regression techniques as those considered earlier in the chapter can be used to **calculate a regression line (a trend line) for a time series**. A time series is simply a series of figures or values recorded over time (such as total annual costs for the last ten years). The determination of a trend line is particularly useful in forecasting. (We will be looking at time series and trend lines in more detail in the next section.)

The years (or days, or months) become the X variables in the regression formulae by numbering them from one upwards.

Example: regression and forecasting

Sales of product B over the 7-year period from year 1 to year 7 were as follows.

Year	Year 1	Year 2	Year 3	Year 4	Year 5	Year 6	Year 7
Sales of B ('000 units)	22	25	24	26	29	28	30

There is high correlation between time and the volume of sales.

Required

Calculate the trend line of sales, and forecast sales in year 8 and year 9.

Solution

Workings

Year	X	Y	XY	X^2
1	1	22	22	1
2	2	25	50	4
3	3	24	72	9
4	4	26	104	16
5	5	29	145	25
6	6	28	168	36
7	7	30	210	49
	$\Sigma X = \underline{\underline{28}}$	$\Sigma Y = \underline{\underline{184}}$	$\Sigma XY = \underline{\underline{771}}$	$\Sigma X^2 = \underline{\underline{140}}$

n = 7

Where Y = a + bX
    b = $((7 \times 771) - (28 \times 184))/((7 \times 140) - (28 \times 28)) = 245/196 = 1.25$
    a = $(184/7) - ((1.25 \times 28)/7) = 21.2857$, say 21.3
    Y = 21.3 + 1.25X where X = 1 in year 1, X = 2 in year 2 and so on

Using this trend line, predicted sales in year 8 (X = 8) would be $21.3 + 1.25 \times 8 = 31.3 = 31,300$ units.

Similarly, for year 9 (X = 9) predicted sales would be $21.3 + 1.25 \times 9 = 32.55 = 32,550$ units.

Section summary

When **regression analysis** is used for **forecasting sales**, the years (or days, or months) become the x variables in the regression formulae by numbering them from 1 upwards.

6   The components of time series

Introduction

A **time series** records a series of figures or values over time. A time series has four components: a **trend**, **seasonal variations**, **cyclical variations** and **random variations**.

KEY TERM

A TIME SERIES is a series of figures or values recorded over time.

Examples of time series

*   Output at a factory each day for the last month
*   Monthly sales over the last two years
*   The Retail Prices Index each month for the last ten years

A graph of a time series is called a **historigram**.

(Note the 'ri'; this is not the same as a histogram.) For example, consider the following time series.

Year	Year 0	Year 1	Year 2	Year 3	Year 4	Year 5	Year 6
Sales (£'000)	20	21	24	23	27	30	28

The historigram is as follows:

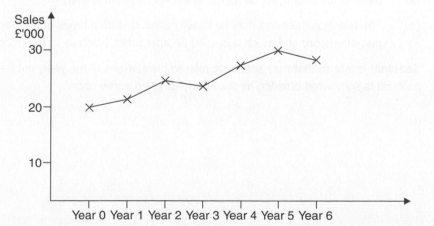

The horizontal axis is always chosen to represent time, and the vertical axis represents the values of the data recorded.

Components of a time series

- A **trend**

- **Seasonal variations** or fluctuations

- Cycles, or **cyclical variations**

- Non-recurring, **random variations**, caused by unforeseen circumstances such as a change in government, a war, technological change or a fire

6.1 The trend

KEY TERM

The TREND is the underlying long-term movement over time in values of data recorded.

In the following examples of time series, there are three types of trend.

Year	Output per labour hour Units	Cost per unit £	Number of employees
4	30	1.00	100
5	24	1.08	103
6	26	1.20	96
7	22	1.15	102
8	21	1.18	103
9	17	1.25	98
	(A)	**(B)**	**(C)**

(a) In time series **(A)** there is a **downward trend** in the output per labour hour. Output per labour hour did not fall every year, because it went up between year 5 and year 6, but the long-term movement is clearly a downward one.

(b) In time series **(B)** there is an **upward trend** in the cost per unit. Although unit costs went down in year 7 from a higher level in year 6, the basic movement over time is one of rising costs.

(c) In time series **(C)** there is **no clear movement** up or down, and the number of employees remained fairly constant. The trend is therefore a static, or level one.

6.2 Seasonal variations

KEY TERM

SEASONAL VARIATIONS are short-term fluctuations in recorded values, due to different circumstances that affect results at different times of the year, on different days of the week, at different times of day, or whatever.

Here are two examples of seasonal variations.

(a) Sales of ice cream will be higher in summer than in winter.

(b) The telephone network may be heavily used at certain times of the day (such as mid-morning and mid-afternoon) and much less used at other times (such as in the middle of the night).

Seasonal is a term that may appear to refer to the seasons of the year, but its meaning in time series analysis is somewhat broader, as the examples given above show.

> ### Example: a trend and seasonal variations
>
> The number of customers served by a company of travel agents over the past four years is shown in the following historigram.
>
>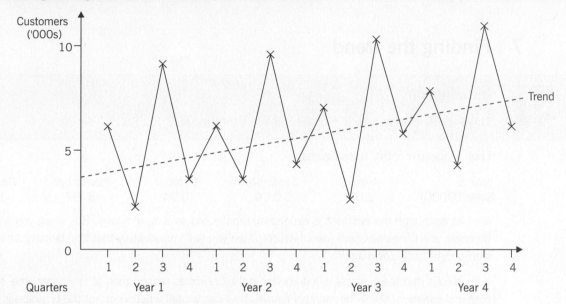
>
> In this example, there would appear to be large seasonal fluctuations in demand, but there is also a basic upward trend.

6.3 Cyclical variations

Cyclical variations are **medium-term changes in results caused by circumstances that repeat in cycles**. In business, cyclical variations are commonly associated with economic cycles, successive booms and slumps in the economy. Economic cycles may last a few years. Cyclical variations are longer term than seasonal variations.

6.4 Summarising the components

In practice, a time series could incorporate all of the four features we have been looking at and, to make reasonably accurate forecasts, the four features often have to be isolated. We can begin the process of isolating each feature by summarising the components of a time series as follows.

The **actual time series, TS = T + SV + C + R**

Where **TS**   **= the actual time series   C   = the cyclical component**
      T   **= the trend series   R   = the random component**
     SV   **= the seasonal component**

Though you should be aware of the cyclical component, it is unlikely that you will be expected to carry out any calculation connected with isolating it. The mathematical model that we will use, the **additive model**, therefore excludes any reference to C and is **TS = T + SV + R**.

The ADDITIVE MODEL expresses a time series as TS = T + SV + R.

KEY TERM

Section summary

A **time series** records a series of figures or values over time. A time series has four components: a **trend**, **seasonal variations**, **cyclical variations** and **random variations**.

7 Finding the trend

Introduction

This section looks at how to find the trend in a time series.

Look at these monthly sales figures.

Year 6	August	September	October	November	December
Sales (£'000)	0.02	0.04	0.04	3.20	14.60

It looks as though the business is expanding rapidly and so it is, in a way. But when you know that the business is a Christmas card manufacturer, then you see immediately that the January sales will no doubt slump right back down again.

It is obvious that the business will do better in the Christmas season than at any other time; that is the seasonal variation. Using the monthly figures, how can we tell whether or not the business is doing well overall – whether there is a rising sales trend over time other than the short-term rise over Christmas?

One possibility is to compare figures with the equivalent figures of a year ago. However, many things can happen over a year to make such a comparison misleading; for example, new products might now be manufactured and prices will probably have changed.

In fact, there are a number of ways of overcoming this problem of distinguishing trend from seasonal variations. One such method is called **moving averages**. This method attempts to **remove seasonal (or cyclical) variations from a time series by a process of averaging so as to leave a set of figures representing the trend**.

A **moving average** is an average of the results of a fixed number of periods. Since it is an average of several time periods, it is **related to the mid-point of the overall period**.

Example: moving averages

Year	Sales Units	Year	Sales Units
0	390	4	470
1	380	5	440
2	460	6	500
3	450		

Required

Take a moving average of the annual sales over a period of three years.

Solution

(a)   Average sales in the 3-year period year 0 – year 2 were (390 + 380 + 460)/3 = 1,230/3 = 410. This average relates to the middle year of the period, year 1.

(b)   Similarly, average sales in the 3-year period year 1 – year 3 were (380 + 460 + 450)/3 = 1,290/3 = 430. This average relates to the middle year of the period, year 2.

(c)   The average sales can also be found for the periods year 2 – year 4, year 3 – year 5 and year 4 – year 6, to give the following:

Year	Sales	*Moving total of 3 years' sales*	*Moving average of 3 years' sales (÷ 3)*
0	390		
1	380	1,230	410
2	460	1,290	430
3	450	1,380	460
4	470	1,360	453
5	440	1,410	470
6	500		

Note the following points:

(i)   The moving average series has five figures relating to years 1 to 5. The original series had seven figures for years 0 to 6.

(ii)   There is an upward trend in sales, which is more noticeable from the series of moving averages than from the original series of actual sales each year.

The above example averaged over a three-year period. Over what period should a moving average be taken? The answer to this question is that the **moving average that is most appropriate will depend on the circumstances and the nature of the time series**.

(a)   A moving average that takes an average of the results in many time periods will represent results over a longer term than a moving average of two or three periods.

(b)   On the other hand, with a moving average of results in many time periods, the last figure in the series will be out of date by several periods. In our example, the most recent average related to year 5. With a moving average of five years' results, the final figure in the series would relate to year 4.

(c)   When there is a known cycle over which seasonal variations occur, such as all the days in the week or all the seasons in the year, the most suitable moving average would be one that covers one full cycle.

7.1 Moving averages of an even number of results

In the previous example, **moving averages were taken of the results in an <u>odd</u> number of time periods, and the average then related to the mid-point of the overall period**.

If a **moving average** were taken of results in an **even number of time periods**, the basic technique would be the same, but the mid-point of the overall period would not relate to a single period. For example, suppose an average were taken of the following four results.

Spring	120	
Summer	90	
Autumn	180	average 115
Winter	70	

The average would relate to the mid-point of the period, between summer and autumn.

The trend line average figures need to relate to a particular time period; otherwise, seasonal variations cannot be calculated. To overcome this difficulty, we take a **moving average of the moving average**. An example will illustrate this technique.

Example: moving averages over an even number of periods

Calculate a moving average trend line of the following results of Linden.

Year	Quarter	Volume of sales '000 units
5	1	600
	2	840
	3	420
	4	720
6	1	640
	2	860
	3	420
	4	740

Solution

A moving average of four will be used, since the volume of sales would appear to depend on the season of the year, and each year has four quarterly results. The moving average of four does not relate to any specific period of time; therefore a second moving average of two will be calculated on the first moving averages.

Year	Quarter	Actual volume of sales '000 units (A)	Moving total of 4 quarters' sales '000 units (B)	Moving average of 4 quarters' sales '000 units (B ÷ 4)	Mid-point of 2 moving averages Trend line '000 units (C)
5	1	600			
	2	840			
	3	420	2,580	645.0	650.00
	4	720	2,620	655.0	657.50
6	1	640	2,640	660.0	660.00
	2	860	2,640	660.0	662.50
	3	420	2,660	665.0	
	4	740			

By taking a mid point (a moving average of two) of the original moving averages, we can relate the results to specific quarters (from the third quarter of year 5 to the second quarter of year 6).

Question 10.4   Trend figures

Learning outcomes B2(a)

Actual sales volumes during years 3 and 4 were as follows.

Year	Quarter	Actual sales volume '000 units
3	1	47
	2	59
	3	92
	4	140
4	1	35
	2	49
	3	89
	4	120

What trend figures can be calculated from the information above? (Choose A, B, C or D from the following.)

Year	Quarter	A	B	C	D
3	2	338	–	–	84.50
	3	326	83.000	84.50	81.50
	4	316	80.250	81.50	79.00
4	1	313	78.625	79.00	78.25
	2	293	75.750	78.25	73.25
	3	–	–	73.25	–

Section summary

Trend values can be distinguished from seasonal variations by a process of **moving averages**.

8 Finding the seasonal variations

Introduction

Once a trend has been established, we can find the seasonal variations. As we saw earlier, the additive model for time series analysis is TS = T + SV+ R. We can therefore write TS – T = SV + R. In other words, if we deduct the trend series from the actual series, we will be left with the seasonal and residual components of the time series. If we assume that the random component is relatively small, and hence negligible, the **seasonal component can be found as SV = TS – T**, the **de-trended series**.

The actual and trend sales for Linden (as calculated in the previous example) are set out below. The **difference between the actual results for any one quarter (TS) and the trend figure for that quarter (T)** will be the seasonal variation for that quarter.

Year	Quarter	Actual	Trend	Seasonal variation
5	1	600		
	2	840		
	3	420	650.00	–230.00
	4	720	657.50	62.50
6	1	640	660.00	–20.00
	2	860	662.50	197.50
	3	420		
	4	740		

Suppose that seasonal variations for the third and fourth quarters of year 6 and the first and second quarters of year 7 are –248.75, 62.50, –13.75 and 212.50 respectively. The variation between the actual result for a particular quarter and the trend line average is not the same from year to year, but an **average of these variations can be taken**.

Year	Q_1	Q_2	Q_3	Q_4
5			–230.00	62.50
6	–20.00	197.50	–248.75	62.50
7	–13.75	212.50		
Total	–33.75	410.00	–478.75	125.00
Average (÷ 2)	–16.875	205.00	–239.375	62.50

Variations around the basic trend line should cancel each other out, and add up to zero. At the moment, they do not. We therefore **spread the total of the variations** (11.25) **across the four quarters** (11.25 ÷ 4) **so that the final total of the variations sum to zero**.

	Q_1	Q_2	Q_3	Q_4	Total
Estimated quarterly variations	– 16.8750	205.0000	–239.3750	62.5000	11.250
Adjustment to reduce variations to 0	–2.8125	–2.8125	–2.8125	–2.8125	–11.250
Final estimates of quarterly variations	–19.6875	202.1875	–242.1875	59.6875	0

These might be rounded as follows Q_1: –20 Q_2: 202 Q_3:-242 Q_4: 60   Total: 0

8.1 Seasonal variations using the proportional model

The method of estimating the seasonal variations in the above example was to use the differences between the trend and actual data. This model **assumes that the components of the series are independent** of each other, so that an increasing trend does not affect the seasonal variations and make them increase as well, for example.

The alternative is to use the **proportional model** whereby each actual figure is expressed as a proportion of the trend. Sometimes this method is called the **multiplicative model**.

KEY TERM

The **PROPORTIONAL (MULTIPLICATIVE) MODEL** summarises a time series as TS = T × SV × R (or TS = T*SV*R).

The **trend component** will be the **same whichever model is used** but the values of the **seasonal and random components** will **vary according to the model being applied**.

The example in Section 7.1 can be reworked on this alternative basis. The trend is calculated in exactly the same way as before but we need a different approach for the seasonal variations. The proportional model is TS = T × SV × R and, just as we calculated SV = TS – T for the additive model (example in Section 7.1), we can calculate **SV = TS/T** for the proportional model.

Year	Quarter	Actual (TS)	Trend (T)	Seasonal percentage (TS/T)
5	1	600		
	2	840		
	3	420	650.00	0.646
	4	720	657.50	1.095
6	1	640	660.00	0.970
	2	860	662.50	1.298
	3	420		
	4	740		

Suppose that seasonal variations for the next 4 quarters are 0.628, 1.092, 0.980 and 1.309 respectively. The summary of the seasonal variations expressed in proportional terms is therefore as follows.

Year	Q_1 %	Q_2 %	Q_3 %	Q_4 %
5			0.646	1.095
6	0.970	1.298	0.628	1.092
7	0.980	1.309		
Total	1.950	2.607	1.274	2.187
Average	0.975	1.3035	0.637	1.0935

Instead of summing to zero, as **with the additive approach**, the **averages should sum (in this case) to 4.0, 1.0 for each of the 4 quarters**. They actually sum to 4.009 so 0.00225 has to be deducted from each one.

	Q_1	Q_2	Q_3	Q_4
Average	0.97500	1.30350	0.63700	1.09350
Adjustment	–0.00225	–0.00225	–0.00225	–0.00225
Final estimate	0.97275	1.30125	0.63475	1.09125
Rounded	0.97	1.30	0.64	1.09

Note that the **proportional model is better than the additive model when the trend is increasing or decreasing over time**. In such circumstances, seasonal variations are likely to be increasing or decreasing too. The additive model simply adds absolute and unchanging seasonal variations to the trend figures whereas the proportional model, by multiplying increasing or decreasing trend values by a constant seasonal variation factor, takes account of changing seasonal variations.

Section summary

Seasonal variations can be estimated using the **additive** model or the **proportional** (**multiplicative**) model.

9 Time series analysis and forecasting

Introduction

By extrapolating a trend and then adjusting for seasonal variations, forecasts of future values can be made.

Making forecasts of future values

 Find a trend line using moving averages or using linear regression analysis (see Section 5).

 Use the trend line to forecast future trend line values.

 Adjust these values by the average seasonal variation applicable to the future period, to determine the forecast for that period. With the additive model, add (or subtract for negative variations) the variation. With the multiplicative model, multiply the trend value by the variation proportion.

Extending a trend line outside the range of known data, in this case forecasting the future from a trend line based on historical data, is known as **extrapolation**.

Example: forecasting

The sales (in £'000) of swimwear by a large department store for each period of three months and trend values found using moving averages are as follows:

Quarter	Year 4		Year 5		Year 6		Year 7	
	Actual	Trend	Actual	Trend	Actual	Trend	Actual	Trend
	£'000	£'000	£'000	£'000	£'000	£'000	£'000	£'000
First			8		20	40	40	57
Second			30	30	50	45	62	
Third			60	31	80	50	92	
Fourth	24		20	35	40	54		

Using the additive model, seasonal variations have been determined as follows:

Quarter 1	Quarter 2	Quarter 3	Quarter 4
–£18,250	+£2,750	+£29,750	–£14,250

Required

Predict sales for the last quarter of year 7 and the first quarter of year 8, stating any assumptions.

Solution

We might guess that the trend line is rising steadily, by (57 – 40)/4 = 4.25 per quarter in the period first quarter year 6 to first quarter year 7 (57 being the prediction in first quarter year 7 and 40 the prediction in first quarter year 6). Since the trend may be levelling off a little, a quarterly increase of +4 in the trend will be assumed.

		Trend	Seasonal variation	Forecast
First quarter	Year 7	57		
Fourth quarter	Year 7 (+ (3 × 4))	69	–14.25	54.75
First quarter	Year 8 (+ (4 × 4))	73	–18.25	54.75

Rounding to the nearest thousand pounds, the forecast sales are £55,000 for each of the 2 quarters.

Note that you could actually plot the trend line figures on a graph, extrapolate the trend line into the future and read off forecasts from the graph using the extrapolated trend line.

If we had been using the proportional model, with an average variation for (for example) quarter 4 of 0.8, our prediction for the fourth quarter of year 7 would have been 69 × 0.8 = 55.2, say £55,000.

9.1 Advantages of time series analysis

(a)   Time series analysis can help to predict future variables and explain past variables.

(b)   A review of the trend line after each time period will allow the accuracy of the forecasts to be assessed. It is possible that forecasts using time series will become more accurate over time as more data is collected and compared to previous forecasts.

Question 10.5	Regression analysis and seasonal variations

Learning outcome B2(a)

The trend in a company's sales figures can be described by the linear regression equation Y = 780 + 4X, where X is the month number (with January year 3 as month 0) and Y is sales in thousands of pounds. The average seasonal variation for March is 106%.

The forecast sales for March year 5 (to the nearest £'000) are:

A   £890,000
B   £933,000
C   £937,000
D   £941,000

9.2 Assumptions and limitations of time series analysis

The assumptions that are made when performing time series analysis can be seen as its disadvantages.

(a)   The model is based on past data, and assumes that what has happened in the past will happen in the future.

(b)   The model assumes that a linear relationship trend exists. It is possible that a non-linear relationship may exist.

(c)   Seasonal variations are assumed to be constant or proportional to the trend line.

Section summary

Forecasts can be made by calculating a **trend line** (using moving averages or linear regression), using the trend line to forecast future trend line values, and adjusting these values by the **average seasonal variation** applicable to the future period.

10 Forecasting problems

Introduction

All forecasts are subject to error, but the likely errors vary from case to case.

- The **further into the future** the forecast is for, the **more unreliable** it is likely to be.
- The **less data** available on which to base the forecast, the **less reliable** the forecast.
- The **pattern** of trend and seasonal variations **may not continue** in the future.
- **Random variations** may upset the pattern of trend and seasonal variation.

There are a number of changes that also may make it difficult to forecast future events.

Type of change	Examples
Political and economic changes	Changes in interest rates, exchange rates or inflation can mean that future sales and costs are difficult to forecast.
Environmental changes	The opening of high-speed rail links might have a considerable impact on some companies' markets.
Technological changes	These may mean that the past is not a reliable indication of likely future events. For example, new faster machinery may make it difficult to use current output levels as the basis for forecasting future production output.
Technological advances	Advanced manufacturing technology is changing the cost structure of many firms. Direct labour costs are reducing in significance, and fixed manufacturing costs are increasing. This causes forecasting difficulties because of the resulting changes in cost behaviour patterns, breakeven points and so on.
Social changes	Alterations in taste, fashion and the social acceptability of products can cause forecasting difficulties.

Section summary

Certain changes may make it difficult to forecast future events. These include political and economic changes, environmental changes, technological changes and social changes.

Chapter Summary

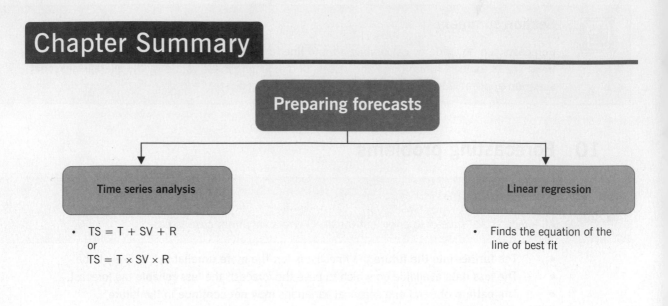

Preparing forecasts

Time series analysis

- TS = T + SV + R
  or
  TS = T × SV × R

Linear regression

- Finds the equation of the
  line of best fit

Quick Quiz

1   In the equation Y = a + bX, which is the dependent variable?

 •   A   Y   C   b
     B   a   D   X

2   Fill in the missing words.

     Extrapolation involves using a ...Line......... of best ..Fit.......... to predict a value ..between... *outside* the two extreme points of the observed range.

3   Between sales of suntan cream and sales of cold drinks, one would expect (assuming spending money to be unlimited):

   (A)   Positive, but spurious, correlation   ✗ C   Positive correlation indicating direct causation
     B   Negative, but spurious, correlation   D   Negative correlation indicating direct causation

4   Which of the following statements is/are true of the coefficient of determination?

		True	False
(a)	It is the square of the Pearsonian coefficient of correlation.	✓	
(b)	It can never quite equal 1.		✓
(c)	If it is high, this proves that variations in one variable cause variations in the other.	✓	

5   Choose the appropriate words from those highlighted.

     When using **regression analysis/analytical regression** for forecasting, the X variables are the **years (or days or months)/the level of sales (or costs)**.

6   What are the four components of a time series?

     A   Trend, seasonal variations, cyclical variations, relative variations
     B   Trend, systematic variations, cyclical variations, relative variations
     C   Trend, systematic variations, seasonal variations, random variations
   , D   Trend, seasonal variations, cyclical variations, random variations

7   The multiplicative model expresses a time series as TS = T + SV + R.

     True   ☐

     False ☑

8   A time series for weeks 1 to 12 has been analysed into a trend and seasonal variations, using the additive model. The trend value is 84 + 0.7w, where w is the week number. The actual value for week 9 is 88.7. What is the seasonal variation for week 9?

     A   90.3
   • B   −1.6
     C   1.6
     D   6.3

9 List six factors to consider when forecasting sales.

1 ....

2 ....

3 ....

4 ....

5 ....

6 ....

10 Complete the following table.

Year	Quarter	Actual volume of sales Units	Moving total of 4 quarters' sales Units	Moving average of 4 quarters' sales Units	Trend
3	1	1,350			
	2	1,210			
	3	1,080			
	4	1,250			
4	1	1,400			
	2	1,260			
	3	1,110			
	4	1,320			

11 The further into the future the forecast is for, the more reliable it is likely to be.

True ☐

False ☐

12 The time series for sales in 20X7 at Teatime Ltd is 930. The trend for 20X7 is 400 and the random component is zero. Calculate the seasonal variation (assume additive model).

Answers to Quick Quiz

1   A

2   line; fit; outside

3   A   When cold drinks sell well, so will suntan cream. Neither sales level causes the other; both are caused by the weather.

4   Statement (a) is true. The coefficient of determination is r^2.
    Statement (b) is false. r can reach 1 or –1, so r^2 can reach 1.
    Statement (c) is false. Correlation does not prove a causal link.

5   regression analysis, years (or days or months)

6   D

7   False. The multiplicative model expresses a time series as TS = T × SV × R.

8   B   For week 9, the trend value is 84 + (0.7 × 9) = 90.3. The seasonal variation is actual – trend = 88.7 – 90.3 = –1.6, indicating that the value for week 9 is below what one might expect from the trend.

9   Here are some examples.

   • Past sales patterns
   • The economic environment
   • Results of market research
   • Anticipated advertising during the budget period
   • Competition

   • New legislation
   • Environmental factors
   • Pricing policies and discounts offered
   • Distribution and quality of sales outlets and personnel

10

Year	Quarter	Actual volume of sales Units	Moving total of 4 quarters' sales Units	Moving average of 4 quarters' sales Units	Trend
3	1	1,350			
	2	1,210			
	3	1,080	4,890	1,222.5	1,228.75
	4	1,250	4,940	1,235.0	1,241.25
4	1	1,400	4,990	1,247.5	1,251.25
	2	1,260	5,020	1,255.0	1,263.75
	3	1,110	5,090	1,272.5	
	4	1,320			

11   False. It is likely to be more unreliable.

12   Time series = trend + seasonal variation + random component

   930   =   400 + SV
   SV   =   930 – 400 = 530
   SV   =   530

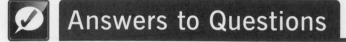

Answers to Questions

10.1 Analysing cost behaviour and making projections

Forecast profit statement for period 4

	£	£
Revenue		10,220
Materials (W1)	774	
Staff salaries (W2)	5,120	
Utilities (W3)	723	
Laundry (W4)	646	
Rent	430	
Other	375	
		8,068
Profit		2,152

Workings

1   *Material costs*

Period 1	£756/420	= £1.80 per unit
Period 2	£991.80/551	= £1.80 per unit

This is a wholly variable cost.

Forecast for period 4 = £1.80 × (265 + 165) = £774

2   *Staff salaries*

To use the high-low method it will be necessary to eliminate the effect of the step in fixed costs that occurs at the 450 total activity level.

	Units		£
High activity	551	(£6,862 – £1,500)	5,362
Low activity	420		5,100
	131		262

Variable cost per unit   = £262/131 = £2 (the staff bonus)

Substitute in low activity:

Fixed cost	= £5,100 – (420 × £2) = £4,260
Forecast for 430 total units in period 4	= £4,260 + (430 × £2) = £5,120

3   *Utilities*

	Units	£
High activity	551	856.10
Low activity	420	712.00
	131	144.10

Variable cost per unit   = £144.10/131 = £1.10

Substitute in low activity:

Fixed cost	= £712 – (420 × £1.10) = £250
Forecast for period 4	= £250 + (430 × £1.10) = £723

4   *Laundry*

	Units	£
High activity	551	570.80
Low activity	420	466.00
	131	104.80

Variable cost per unit   = £104.80/131 = £0.80

Substitute on low activity:

Fixed cost   = £466 – (420 × £0.80) = £130
Forecast for period 4   = £130 + (430 × £0.80 × 1.5) = £646

10.2 Regression analysis

(a)   *Workings*

X	Y	XY	X^2
20	82	1,640	400
16	70	1,120	256
24	90	2,160	576
22	85	1,870	484
18	73	1,314	324
$\Sigma X = 100$	$\Sigma Y = 400$	$\Sigma XY = 8,104$	$\Sigma X^2 = 2,040$

n   =   5 (there are five pairs of data for x and y values)
b   = $(n\Sigma XY - \Sigma X\Sigma Y)/(n\Sigma X^2 - (\Sigma X)^2) = ((5 \times 8,104) - (100 \times 400))/ ((5 \times 2,040) - 100^2)$
     =   (40,520 – 40,000)/(10,200 – 10,000) = 520/200 = 2.6
a   = $\overline{Y} - b\overline{X} = (400/5) - (2.6 \times (100/5)) = 28$
Y   =   28 + 2.6X

Where Y = total cost, in thousands of pounds and X = output, in thousands of units.

(b)   If the output is 22,000 units, we would expect costs to be 28 + 2.6 × 22 = 85.2 = £85,200.

10.3 Limitations of regression analysis

(a)   The reliability of the model is unknown if we do not know the correlation coefficient. A low correlation would suggest that the model may be unreliable.

(b)   The model is probably valid only over a certain range of quantity produced. Outside this range, the relationship between the two variables may be very different.

(c)   The model is based on past data, and assumes that what has happened in the past will happen in the future.

(d)   The model assumes that a linear relationship exists between the quantity produced per annum and the total operating costs per annum. It is possible that a non-linear relationship may exist.

(e)   The fixed costs of £5,000 per annum may be misleading if they include an element of allocated costs.

10.4 Trend figures

The correct answer is B.

Year	Quarter	Actual sales	Moving total of 4 quarters' sales	Moving average	Mid-point trend
		'000 units	'000 units	'000 units	'000 units
3	1	47			
	2	59			
			338	84.5	
	3	92			83.000
			326	81.5	
	4	140			80.250
			316	79.0	
4	1	35			78.625
			313	78.25	
	2	49			75.750
			293	73.25	
	3	89			
	4	120			

10.5 Regression analysis and seasonal variations

The correct answer is C.

X = 26

Forecast = $1.06 \times [780 + (4 \times 26)] = 937.04 = £937,040$ or about £937,000.

Now try these questions from the Practice Question Bank

Number	Level
Q10.1 – Q10.6	Practice

BUDGETS FOR PLANNING

 This chapter begins a new topic, **budgeting**. You may recognise much of this chapter from your earlier studies. You have already covered most of the topics in this chapter at a basic level and so we have included a couple of deemed knowledge boxes on the most straightforward areas.

The chapter begins by explaining the **reasons for operating a budgetary planning and control system** (**Section 1**), and explains some of the **key terms** associated with budgeting and reminds you of the steps in the preparation of a master budget (**Section 2**).

You should have already covered budget preparation in earlier studies (including the preparation of cash budgets) but we will look at some more complex examples in **Sections 4 and 5**.

Section 6 explains how the budgeting process does not stop once the master budget has been prepared but is a **constant task** of the management accountant.

We review a number of **alternative approaches to budgeting** in **Section 7**.

Topic list	Learning outcomes	Syllabus references	Ability required
1 Budgetary planning and control systems	B1(a)	B1(a)(ii)	Comprehension
2 The preparation of budgets	B1(a)	B1(a)(ii)	Comprehension
3 The sales budget	B3(a)	B3(a)(i)	Application
4 Production and related budgets	B3(a)	B3(a)(i)	Application
5 Cash budgets and the master budget	B3(a)	B3(a)(i)	Application
6 Monitoring procedures	B1(a)	B1(a)(ii)	Comprehension
7 Alternative approaches to budgeting	B3(b)	B3(b)(i)	Application

Chapter Overview

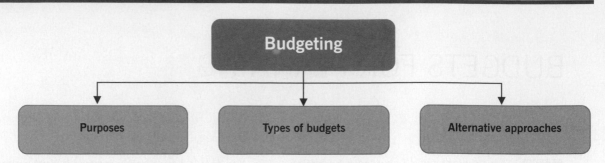

```
                    ┌─────────────────┐
                    │   Budgeting     │
                    └────────┬────────┘
          ┌──────────────────┼──────────────────┐
          ▼                  ▼                  ▼
  ┌───────────────┐  ┌───────────────┐  ┌────────────────────┐
  │   Purposes    │  │ Types of      │  │ Alternative        │
  │               │  │ budgets       │  │ approaches         │
  └───────────────┘  └───────────────┘  └────────────────────┘
```

1 Budgetary planning and control systems

Introduction

A **budget** is a quantified plan of action for a forthcoming accounting period. A **budget** is a plan of what the organisation is aiming to achieve and what it has set as a target, whereas a **forecast** is an estimate of what is likely to occur in the future.

KEY TERM

The BUDGET is the 'Quantitative expression of a plan for a defined period of time. It may include planned sales volumes and revenues; resource quantities, costs and expenses; assets, liabilities and cashflows'.

(CIMA Official Terminology)

The **objectives of budget preparation** are shown in the table below. Sometimes these objectives can **conflict with one another**. For example, **planning can conflict with motivation**. Targets set in the planning process must be **challenging but fair**, otherwise individuals will become dissatisfied. Integration may also conflict with evaluation. For example, the **goals of the organisation** as a whole may not coincide with the **personal aspirations of individual managers**. Managers may therefore build 'slack' into their expenditure estimates in order to increase the chances of receiving a bonus for achieving targets. Motivation and evaluation may also cause conflict. For example, managers might resent control information that is used in evaluation, as they may see it as part of a system of trying to find fault in their work. This is more likely when budgets are imposed on managers without their consultation.

Objective	Comment
Planning	Compelling managers to plan is probably the most important feature of a budgetary planning and control system. Planning forces management to look ahead, to set out detailed plans for achieving the targets for each department, each operation and (ideally) each manager and to anticipate problems. It thus prevents management from relying on ad hoc or uncoordinated planning which may be detrimental to the performance of the organisation. It also helps managers to foresee potential threats or opportunities, so that they may take action now to avoid or minimise the effect of the threats and to take full advantage of the opportunities.
Responsibility	Objectives are set for the organisation as a whole, and for individual departments and operations within the organisation. Quantified expressions of these objectives are then drawn up as targets to be achieved within the timescale of the budget plan. Budgetary planning and control systems require that managers of budget centres are made responsible for the achievement of budget targets for the operations under their personal control.
Integration and co-ordination	The activities of different departments or sub-units of the organisation need to be co-ordinated to ensure maximum integration of effort towards common goals. This concept of co-ordination implies, for example, that the purchasing department should base its budget on production requirements and that the production budget should in turn be based on sales expectations. Although straightforward in concept, co-ordination is remarkably difficult to achieve, and there is often 'sub-optimality' and conflict between departmental plans in the budget so that the efforts of each department are not fully integrated into a combined plan to achieve the company's best targets. Communication is important here to ensure that each person affected by the plans is aware of what they are supposed to be doing.
Motivation	The interest and commitment of employees can be retained via a system of feedback of actual results, which lets them know how well or badly they are performing. The identification of controllable reasons for departures from budget with managers responsible provides an incentive for improving future performance.

Objective	Comment
Evaluation and control	As well as providing a yardstick for control by comparison, the monitoring of actual results compared with the budget can provide a basis for evaluating the performance of the budget holder. As a result of this evaluation the manager might be rewarded, perhaps with a financial bonus or promotion. Alternatively the evaluation process might highlight the need for more investment in staff development and training.

Section summary

The **objectives** of a budgetary planning and control system are as follows:

P – Planning
R – Responsibility
I – Integration and co-ordination
M – Motivation
E – Evaluation and control

2   The preparation of budgets

Introduction

Having seen why organisations prepare budgets, we will now turn our attention to the mechanics of budget preparation. We will begin by defining and explaining a number of terms.

2.1 Planning

KEY TERM

PLANNING is described in *CIMA Official Terminology* as the 'Establishment of objectives, and the formulation, evaluation and selection of the policies, strategies, tactics and action required to achieve them. Planning comprises long-term/strategic planning, and short-term operational planning. The latter is usually for a period of up to one year'.

The overall planning process therefore covers both the long and short term.

Type of planning	Detail
Strategic/corporate/ long-range planning	Covers periods longer than one year and involves 'The formulation, evaluation and selection of strategies for the purpose of preparing a long-term plan of action to attain objectives'. (*CIMA Official Terminology*)
Budgetary/short- term tactical planning	Involves preparing detailed plans, which generally cover one year, for an organisation's functions, activities and departments. Works within the framework set by the strategic plans and converts those strategic plans into action.
Operation planning	Planning on a very short-term or day to day basis and is concerned with planning how an organisation's resources will be used. Works within the framework set by the budgetary plans and converts the budgetary plans into action.

2.1.1 The value of long-term planning

A **budgetary planning and control system** operating in **isolation** without any form of long-term planning as a framework is **unlikely to produce maximum potential benefits** for an organisation.

(a)   Without stated long-term objectives, managers do not know what they should be trying to achieve and so there are no criteria against which to assess possible courses of action.

BPP
LEARNING MEDIA

(b)   Without long-term planning, budgets may simply be based on a sales forecast. Performance can therefore only be judged in terms of previous years' results, no analysis of the organisation's potential having been carried out.

(c)   Many business decisions need to be taken on a long-term basis. For instance, new products cannot simply be introduced when sales of existing products begin to decline. Likewise, capital equipment cannot necessarily be purchased and installed in the short term if production volumes start to increase.

(d)   With long-term planning, limiting factors (other than sales) that might arise can possibly be anticipated, and avoided or overcome.

2.2 The budget period

KEY TERM

The BUDGET PERIOD is the 'Period for which a budget is prepared and used, which may then be sub-divided into control periods'.   (*CIMA Official Terminology*)

Except for capital expenditure budgets, the budget period is commonly the accounting year (sub-divided into 12 or 13 control periods).

2.3 The budget manual

KEY TERM

The BUDGET MANUAL is a collection of instructions governing the responsibilities of persons and the procedures, forms and records relating to the preparation and use of budgetary data. It is likely to contain the objectives of the budgetary process, the organisational structure, principal budget outlines, administrative details and procedural matters.

2.4 The responsibility for preparing budgets

The initial responsibility for preparing the budget will normally be with the managers (and their subordinates) who will be carrying out the budget, selling goods or services and authorising expenditure. However, the budget is normally set as part of a longer process, involving the authorisation of set targets by senior management and the negotiation process with the budget holders. Depending on the size of the organisation there may be a large number of **budget centres** and a separate **budget holder** would be responsible for setting and achieving the budget for the centre.

Examples of the functional budgets that would be prepared and **the managers responsible for their preparation** are as follows:

(a)   The **sales manager** should draft the **sales budget** and **selling overhead** cost centre budgets.

(b)   The **purchasing manager** should draft the material purchases budget.

(c)   The **production manager** should draft the **direct production** cost budgets.

(d)   Various **cost centre managers** should prepare the individual production, administration and distribution cost centre budgets for their own cost centre.

(e)   The **cost accountant** will **analyse** the budgeted overheads to determine the overhead absorption rates for the next budget period.

2.5 Budget committee

The **co-ordination** and **administration** of budgets is usually the responsibility of a **budget committee** (with the managing director as chairman).

(a)   The budget committee is assisted by a **budget officer** who is usually an accountant. Every part of the organisation should be represented on the committee, so there should be a representative from sales, production, marketing and so on.

(b) **Functions of the budget committee**

(i) **Co-ordination** of the preparation of budgets, which includes the issue of the budget manual

(ii) **Issuing of timetables** for the preparation of functional budgets

(iii) **Allocation of responsibilities** for the preparation of functional budgets

(iv) **Provision of information** to assist in the preparation of budgets

(v) **Communication of final budgets** to the appropriate managers

(vi) **Comparison** of actual results with budget and the investigation of variances

(vii) **Continuous assessment** of the budgeting and planning process, in order to improve the planning and control function

2.6 Budget preparation

Let us now look at the steps involved in the preparation of a budget. The procedures will differ from organisation to organisation, but the step by step approach described in this chapter is indicative of the steps followed by many organisations. The preparation of a budget may take weeks or months, and the budget committee may meet several times before the functional budgets are co-ordinated and the master budget is finally agreed.

KEY TERM

The *CIMA Official Terminology* defines a DEPARTMENTAL/FUNCTIONAL BUDGET as 'A budget of income and/or expenditure applicable to a particular function.

A function may refer to a department or a process. Functional budgets frequently include:

- Production cost budget (based on a forecast of production and plant utilisation)
- Marketing cost budget, sales budget
- Personnel budget
- Purchasing budget
- Research and development budget'

2.7 The principal budget factor

The first task in the budgetary process is to identify the **principal budget factor**. This is also known as the **key** budget factor or **limiting** budget factor.

KEY TERM

The PRINCIPAL BUDGET FACTOR is the factor that limits the activities of an organisation.

Likely principal budget factors

(a) The **principal budget factor** is usually **sales demand**: a company is usually restricted from making and selling more of its products because there would be no sales demand for the increased output at a price which would be acceptable/profitable to the company.

(b) Other possible factors:

(i) Machine capacity
(ii) Distribution and selling resources
(iii) The availability of key raw materials
(iv) The availability of cash

Once this factor is defined then the remainder of the budgets can be prepared. For example, if sales are the principal budget factor then the production manager can only prepare their budget after the sales budget is complete.

Management may not know what the limiting budget factor is until a draft budget has been attempted. The first draft budget will therefore usually begin with the preparation of a draft sales budget.

Knowledge brought forward from earlier studies

Steps in the preparation of a budget

 Identification of **principal/key/limiting budget factor**

 Preparation of a **sales budget**, assuming that sales is the principal budget factor (in units and in sales value for each product, based on a sales forecast)

 Preparation of a **finished goods inventory budget** (to determine the planned change in finished goods inventory levels)

 Preparation of a **production budget** (calculated as sales + closing inventory – opening inventory)

 Preparation of **budgets for production resources**

- Materials usage
- Machine usage
- Labour

 Preparation of a **raw materials inventory budget** (to determine the planned change in raw materials inventory levels)

 Preparation of a **raw materials purchases budget** (calculated as usage + inventory – opening inventory)

 Preparation of **overhead cost budgets** (such as production, administration, selling and distribution and R&D)

 Calculation of **overhead absorption rates** (if absorption costing is used)

 Preparation of a **cash budget** (and others as required, **capital expenditure** and **working capital** budgets)

Preparation of a **master budget** (budgeted statement of profit or loss and budgeted statement of financial position)

Remember that it is **unlikely** that the execution of the **above steps** will be **problem-free** as data from one budget becomes an input in the preparation of another budget. For example, the materials purchases budget will probably be used in preparing the payables budget. The payables budget will then become an input to the cash budget, and so on. The budgets must therefore be **reviewed in relation to one another**. Such a review may indicate that some budgets are out of balance with others and need modifying so that they will be compatible with other conditions, constraints and plans. The budget officer must identify such inconsistencies and bring them to the attention of the manager concerned.

Alternatively, there may have been a **change in one of the organisational policies**, such as a change in selling prices, which will need to be **incorporated into the budget**. The revision of one budget may lead to the revision of all budgets. This process must continue until all budgets are acceptable and co-ordinated with each other.

If such changes are made manually, the process can be very time consuming and costly. Computer **spreadsheets** can help immensely.

Question 11a.1   Budgets

Learning outcome B3(a)

A company that manufactures and sells a range of products, with sales potential limited by market share, is considering introducing a system of budgeting.

Required

(a)   List (in order of preparation) the functional budgets that need to be prepared.

(b)   State which budgets will comprise the master budget.

(c)   Consider how the work outlined in (a) and (b) can be co-ordinated in order for the budgeting process to be successful.

Section summary

The **budget committee** is the co-ordinating body in the preparation and administration of budgets.

The **principal budget factor** should be identified at the beginning of the budgetary process, and the budget for this is prepared before all the others.

3 The sales budget

Introduction

We have already established that, for many organisations, the principal budget factor is sales volume. The sales budget is therefore **often the primary budget** from which the majority of the other budgets are derived.

Before the sales budget can be prepared, a sales forecast has to be made. A **forecast** is an estimate of what is likely to occur in the future. A budget, in contrast, is a plan of what the organisation is aiming to achieve and what it has set as a target. We will be looking at forecasting techniques in detail in the next chapter.

On the basis of the sales forecast and the production capacity of the organisation, a sales budget will be prepared. This may be subdivided, possible subdivisions being by product, by sales area, by management responsibility and so on.

Once the sales budget has been agreed, related budgets can be prepared.

Section summary

For many organisations, the **principal budget factor** is sales volume.

4 Production and related budgets

Introduction

If the principal budget factor was production capacity, then the production budget would be the first to be prepared. To assess whether production is the principal budget factor, the **production capacity available** must be determined, taking account of a number of factors.

- **Available labour**, including idle time, overtime and standard output rates per hour

- **Availability of raw materials** including allowances for losses during production

- **Maximum machine hours available**, including expected idle time and expected output rates per machine hour

It is, however, normally sales volume that is the constraint and therefore the production budget is usually prepared after the sales budget and the finished goods inventory budget.

The production budget will show the quantities and costs for each product and product group, and will tie in with the sales and inventory budgets. This co-ordinating process is likely to show any shortfalls or excesses in capacity at various times over the budget period.

If there is likely to be a **shortfall**, then consideration should be given to how this can be avoided. Possible **options** include the following:

- Overtime working
- Subcontracting
- Machine hire
- New sources of raw materials

A significant shortfall means that production capacity is, in fact, the limiting factor.

If **capacity exceeds sales volume** for a length of time then consideration should be given to **product diversification**, a **reduction in selling price** (if demand is price elastic) and so on.

Once the production budget has been finalised, the labour, materials and machine budgets can be drawn up. These budgets will be based on budgeted activity levels, planned inventory positions and projected labour and material costs.

Example: the production budget and direct labour budget

Landy manufactures two products, A and B, and is preparing its budget for 20X3. Both products are made by the same grade of labour, grade Q. The company currently holds 800 units of A and 1,200 units of B in inventory, but 250 of these units of B have just been discovered to have deteriorated in quality, and must therefore be scrapped. Budgeted sales of A are 3,000 units and of B 4,000 units, provided that the company maintains finished goods inventories at a level equal to 3 months' sales.

Grade Q labour was originally expected to produce 1 unit of A in 2 hours and 1 unit of B in 3 hours, at an hourly rate of £2.50 per hour. In discussions with trade union negotiators, however, it has been agreed that the hourly wage rate should be raised by 50p per hour, provided that the times to produce A and B are reduced by 20%.

Required

Prepare the production budget and direct labour budget for 20X3.

Solution

The expected time to produce a unit of A will now be 80% of 2 hours = 1.6 hours, and the time for a unit of B will be 2.4 hours. The hourly wage rate will be £3, so that the direct labour cost will be £4.80

for A and £7.20 for B (thus achieving a saving for the company of 20p per unit of A produced and 30p per unit of B).

(a) **Production budget**

	Product A		Product B	
	Units	Units	Units	Units
Budgeted sales		3,000		4,000
Closing inventories ($^3/_{12}$ of 3,000)	750	($^3/_{12}$ of 4,000)	1,000	
Opening inventories (minus inventories scrapped)	800		950	
(Decrease)/increase in inventories		(50)		50
Production		2,950		4,050

(b) **Direct labour budget**

	Grade Q Hours	Cost £
2,950 units of product A	4,720	14,160
4,050 units of product B	9,720	29,160
Total	14,440	43,320

It is assumed that there will be no idle time among grade Q labour which, if it existed, would have to be paid for at the rate of £3 per hour.

4.1 The standard hour

KEY TERM

A STANDARD HOUR or standard minute is the 'Amount of work achievable at standard efficiency levels in an hour or minute'.
(*CIMA Official Terminology*)

This is a useful concept in budgeting for labour requirements. For example, budgeted **output of different products or jobs** in a period could be converted into standard hours of production, and a labour budget constructed accordingly.

Standard hours are particularly useful when management wants to monitor the production levels of a variety of dissimilar units. For example, product A may take five hours to produce and product B, seven hours. If four units of each product are produced, instead of saying that total output is eight units, we could state the production level as (4 × 5) + (4 × 7) standard hours = 48 standard hours.

Example: direct labour budget based on standard hours

Truro manufactures a single product, Q, with a single grade of labour. Its sales budget and finished goods inventory budget for period 3 are as follows.

Sales	700 units
Opening inventories, finished goods	50 units
Closing inventories, finished goods	70 units

The goods are inspected only when production work is completed, and it is budgeted that 10% of finished work will be scrapped.

The standard direct labour hour content of product Q is three hours. The budgeted productivity ratio for direct labour is only 80% (which means that labour is only working at 80% efficiency).

The company employs 18 direct operatives, who are expected to average 144 working hours each in period 3.

Required

(a) Prepare a production budget.

(b) Prepare a direct labour budget.

(c)   Comment on the problem that your direct labour budget reveals, and suggest how this problem might be overcome.

Solution

(a)   **Production budget**

	Units
Sales	700
Add closing inventory	70
	770
Less opening inventory	50
Production required of 'good' output	720

Wastage rate 10%

Total production required $720 \times \dfrac{100*}{90} = 800$ units

(*Note that the required adjustment is 100/90, not 110/100, since the waste is assumed to be 10% of total production, not 10% of good production.)

(b)   Now we can prepare the **direct labour budget**.

Standard hours per unit	3
Total standard hours required = 800 units × 3 hours	2,400 hours
Productivity ratio	80%

Actual hours required $2,400 \times \dfrac{100}{80} = 3,000$ hours

(c)   If we look at the **direct labour budget** against the information provided, we can identify the problem.

	Hours
Budgeted hours available (18 operatives × 144 hours)	2,592
Actual hours required	3,000
Shortfall in labour hours	408

The (draft) budget indicates that there will not be enough direct labour hours to meet the production requirements.

Overcoming insufficient labour hours

(i)   **Reduce the closing inventory** requirement below 70 units. This would reduce the number of production units required.

(ii)   Persuade the workforce to do some **overtime** working.

(iii) Perhaps **recruit** more direct labour if long-term prospects are for higher production volumes.

(iv)   **Improve** the **productivity** ratio, and so reduce the number of hours required to produce the output.

(v)   If possible, **reduce** the **wastage** rate below 10%.

Example: the material purchases budget

Tremor manufactures two products, S and T, which use the same raw materials, D and E. One unit of S uses 3 litres of D and 4 kilograms of E. One unit of T uses 5 litres of D and 2 kilograms of E. A litre of D is expected to cost Y3 and a kilogram of E Y7.

Budgeted sales for 20X2 are 8,000 units of S and 6,000 units of T; finished goods in inventory at 1 January 20X2 are 1,500 units of S and 300 units of T, and the company plans to hold inventories of 600 units of each product at 31 December 20X2.

Inventories of raw material are 6,000 litres of D and 2,800 kilograms of E at 1 January, and the company plans to hold 5,000 litres and 3,500 kilograms respectively at 31 December 20X2.

The warehouse and stores managers have suggested that a provision should be made for damages and deterioration of items held in store, as follows:

Product S: loss of 50 units
Product T: loss of 100 units
Material D: loss of 500 litres
Material E: loss of 200 kilograms

Required

Prepare a material purchases budget for the year 20X2.

Solution

To calculate material purchase requirements, it is first of all necessary to calculate the budgeted production volumes and material usage requirements.

	Product S		Product T	
	Units	Units	Units	Units
Sales		8,000		6,000
Provision for losses		50		100
Closing inventory	600		600	
Opening inventory	1,500		300	
(Decrease)/increase in inventory		(900)		300
Production budget		7,150		6,400

	Material D		Material E	
	Litres	Litres	Kg	Kg
Usage requirements				
To produce 7,150 units of S		21,450		28,600
To produce 6,400 units of T		32,000		12,800
Usage budget		53,450		41,400
Provision for losses		500		200
		53,950		41,600
Closing inventory	5,000		3,500	
Opening inventory	6,000		2,800	
(Decrease)/increase in inventory		(1,000)		700
Material purchases budget		52,950		42,300

	Material D	Material E	
Cost per unit	Y3 per litre	Y7 per kg	
Cost of material purchases	Y158,850	Y296,100	
Total purchases cost		Y454,950	

Question 11a.2

Learning outcome B3(a)

J purchases a basic commodity and then refines it for resale. Budgeted sales of the refined product are as follows:

	April	May	June
Sales in kg	9,000	8,000	7,000

- The basic raw material costs £3 per kg.

- Material losses are 10% of finished output.

- The target month-end raw material inventory level is 5,000 kg plus 25% of the raw material required for next month's budgeted production.

- The target month-end inventory level for finished goods is 6,000 kg plus 25% of next month's budgeted sales.

What are the budgeted raw material purchases for April?

A	8,500 kg	C	9,444.25 kg
B	9,350 kg	D	9,831.25 kg

4.2 Non-production overheads

In the modern business environment, an increasing proportion of overheads are not directly related to the volume of production, such as administration overheads and research and development costs.

4.3 Key decisions in the budgeting process for non-production overheads

It is important to decide:

(a)   Which fixed costs are committed (will be incurred no matter what) and which fixed costs will depend on management decisions.

(b)   What factors will influence the level of variable costs. Administration costs for example may be partly governed by the number of orders received.

Section summary

To assess whether production is the principal budget factor, the production capacity available must be determined.

5   Cash budgets and the master budget

Introduction

Cash budgets show the expected receipts and payments during a budget period and are a vital management planning and control tool.

KEY TERM

A CASH BUDGET is a 'Detailed budget of estimated cash inflows and outflows incorporating both revenue and capital items'.

(CIMA Official Terminology)

5.1 The usefulness of cash budgets

The cash budget is one of the most important planning tools that an organisation can use. It shows the **cash effect of all plans made within the budgetary process** and hence its preparation can lead to a **modification of budgets** if it shows that there are insufficient cash resources to finance the planned operations.

It can also give management an indication of **potential problems** that could arise, and allows them the opportunity to take action to avoid such problems. A cash budget can show **four positions**. Management will need to take appropriate action depending on the potential position.

Cash position	Appropriate management action
Short-term surplus	• Pay suppliers early to obtain discount • Attempt to increase sales by increasing receivables and inventories • Make short-term investments
Short-term deficit	• Increase payables • Reduce receivables • Arrange an overdraft
Long-term surplus	• Make long-term investments • Expand • Diversify • Replace/update non-current assets
Long-term deficit	• Raise long-term finance (such as via issue of share capital) • Consider shutdown/disinvestment opportunities

Exam alert

A cash budgeting question in an integrated case study (ICS) could ask you to recommend appropriate action for management to take, based on the cash budget. Ensure your advice takes account both of whether there is a surplus or deficit and whether the position is long or short term.

5.2 What to include in a cash budget

A cash budget is prepared to show the expected receipts of cash and payments of cash during a budget period.

Sources of cash receipts

- Cash sales
- Payments by customers for credit sales
- The sale of property, plant and equipment
- The issue of new shares or loan inventory and less formalised loans
- The receipt of interest and dividends from investments outside the business

Remember that bad debts will **never be received in cash** and doubtful debts may not be received, so you have to adjust if necessary for such items.

Although all the **receipts** above would affect a cash budget, they would **not all appear in the statement of profit or loss**.

(a)   The issue of new shares or loan inventory would appear in the statement of financial position.

(b)   The cash received from an asset affects the statement of financial position, and the profit or loss on the sale of an asset, which appears in the statement of profit or loss, is not the cash received

but the difference between cash received and the written down value of the asset at the time of sale.

Reasons for paying cash

- Purchase of inventories
- Payroll costs or other expenses
- Purchase of capital items
- Payment of interest, dividends or taxation

Not all payments are **statement of profit or loss items**. The purchase of property, plant and equipment and the payment of VAT affect the statement of financial position. Some costs in the statement of profit or loss such as profit or loss on sale of non-current assets or depreciation are not cash items but are costs derived from accounting conventions.

In addition, the **timing** of cash receipts and payments **may not coincide** with the recording of statement of profit or loss transactions. For example, a dividend might be declared in the results for year 6 and shown in the statement of profit or loss for that year, but paid in cash in year 7.

Cash budgets are most effective if they are treated as **rolling budgets**. (See the next chapter.)

Knowledge brought forward from earlier studies

Steps in the preparation of a cash budget

- Set up a proforma cash budget.

	Month 1 £	Month 2 £	Month 3 £
Cash receipts: receipts from customers	X	X	X
Loan etc	X	X	X
	X̄	X̄	X̄
Cash payments: payments to suppliers	X̄	X̄	X̄
Wages etc	X	X	X
	X̄	X̄	X̄
Opening balance	X	X	X
Net cash flow (receipts – payments)	X	X	X
Closing balance	X̄	X̄	X̄

- Enter the figures that can be entered straightaway (receipts or payments that you are told occur in a specific month).

- Sort out cash receipts from customers.

    – Establish budgeted sales month by month.

    – Establish the length of credit period taken by customers, using the following formula:

$$\text{Receivables collection period (no of days' credit)} = \frac{\text{Average (or year-end) receivables}}{\text{Total credit sales in period}} \times \text{no of days in period}$$

    – Hence determine when budgeted sales revenue will be received as cash (by considering cash receipts from customers, ignoring any provision for doubtful debts).

    – Establish when opening receivables will pay.

- Establish when any other cash income will be received.

- Sort out cash payments to suppliers.

    – Establish production quantities and materials usage quantities each month.

    – Establish materials inventory changes and hence the quantity and cost of materials purchases each month.

– Establish the length of credit period taken from suppliers, using the following formula:

$$\text{Payables payment period} \atop \text{(no of days' credit)} = \frac{\text{Average (or year-end) payables}}{\text{Total purchases on credit in period}} \times \text{no of days in period}$$

– Hence calculate when cash payments to suppliers will be made and when the amount due to opening payables will be paid.

• Establish when any other cash payments (excluding non-cash items such as depreciation) will be made.

Example: income statement and cash budget

Penny operates a retail business. Purchases are sold at cost plus $33^{1}/_{3}\%$.

(a)

	Budgeted sales in month £	Labour cost in month £	Expenses incurred in month £
January	40,000	3,000	4,000
February	60,000	3,000	6,000
March	160,000	5,000	7,000
April	120,000	4,000	7,000

(b) It is management policy to have sufficient inventory in hand at the end of each month to meet half of next month's sales demand.

(c) Suppliers for materials and expenses are paid in the month after the purchases are made/expenses incurred. Labour is paid in full by the end of each month. Labour costs and expenses are treated as period costs in the statement of profit or loss.

(d) Expenses include a monthly depreciation charge of £2,000.

(e) (i) 75% of sales are for cash.
    (ii) 25% of sales are on one month's credit.

(f) The company will buy equipment costing £18,000 for cash in February and will pay a dividend of £20,000 in March. The opening cash balance at 1 February is £1,000.

Required

(a) Prepare a cash budget for February and March.
(b) Prepare a statement of profit or loss for February and March.

Solution

(a) CASH BUDGET

	February £	March £
Receipts		
Receipts from sales	55,000 (W1)	135,000 (W2)
Payments		
Trade payables	37,500 (W3)	82,500 (W3)
Expense payables	2,000 (W4)	4,000 (W4)
Labour	3,000	5,000
Equipment purchase	18,000	–
Dividend	–	20,000
Total payments	60,500	111,500
Receipts less payments	(5,500)	23,500
Opening cash balance b/f	1,000	(4,500)*
Closing cash balance c/f	(4,500)*	19,000

Workings

1   *Receipts in February*

	£
75% of Feb sales (75% × £60,000)	45,000
25% of Jan sales (25% × £40,000)	10,000
	55,000

2   *Receipts in March*

	£
75% of Mar sales (75% × £160,000)	120,000
25% of Feb sales (25% × £60,000)	15,000
	135,000

3   *Purchases*

	January		February	
		£		£
For Jan sales	(50% of £30,000)	15,000		
For Feb sales	(50% of £45,000)	22,500	(50% of £45,000)	22,500
For Mar sales		–	(50% of £120,000)	60,000
		37,500		82,500

These purchases are paid for in February and March.

4   *Expenses*

Cash expenses in January (£4,000 – £2,000) and February (£6,000 – £2,000) are paid in February and March respectively. Depreciation is not a cash item.

(b)   STATEMENT OF PROFIT OR LOSS

	February		March	
	£	£	£	£
Sales		60,000		160,000
Cost of purchases (75%)		45,000		120,000
Gross profit		15,000		40,000
Less: labour	3,000		5,000	
expenses	6,000		7,000	
		9,000		12,000
Net profit		6,000		28,000

KEY POINT

(a)   The asterisks show that the cash balance at the end of February is carried forward as the opening cash balance for March.

(b)   The fact that profits are made in February and March **disguises** the fact that there is a **cash shortfall** at the end of February.

(c)   Steps should be taken either to ensure that an **overdraft facility** is available for the cash shortage at the end of February or to **defer certain payments** so that the overdraft is avoided.

(d)   Some payments must be made on due dates (payroll, taxation and so on) but it is possible that other payments can be delayed, depending on the requirements of the business and/or the goodwill of suppliers.

5.3 A comparison of profit and cash flows

Look at the example above. Had you noticed that the total profit of £34,000 differs from the total receipts less total payments (£18,000)? Profit and cash flows during a period need not be the same amount and, in fact, are actually more likely to be different.

(a) **Sales** and **cost of sales** are recognised in a **statement of profit or loss** as soon as they are **made/incurred**. The **cash budget** does not show figures for sales and cost of sales but is concerned with **cash actually received** from customers and **paid** to suppliers.

(b) A **statement of profit or loss** may include **accrued** amounts for rates, insurance and other expenses. In the **cash budget**, such amounts will appear in full in the **period in which they are paid**. There is no attempt to apportion payments to the period to which they relate.

(c) Similarly, a **statement of profit or loss** may show a charge for **depreciation**. This is not a cash expense and will never appear in a cash budget. The **cash budget** will show **purchase of a non-current asset** as a payment in the **period when the asset is paid for**, and may also show the proceeds on disposal of a non-current asset as a receipt of cash. No attempt is made to allocate the purchase cost over the life of the asset.

Question 11a.3	Cash budgets (receipts)

Learning outcome B3(a)

X will begin trading on 1 January 20X3. The following sales revenue is budgeted for January to March 20X3.

January	February	March
€13,000	€17,000	€10,000

Five per cent of sales will be for cash. The remainder will be credit sales. A discount of 5% will be offered on all cash sales. The payment pattern for credit sales is expected to be as follows:

Invoices paid in the month after sale	75%
Invoices paid in the second month after sale	23%
Bad debts	2%

Invoices are issued on the last day of each month.

The amount budgeted to be received from customers in March 20X3 is:

A   €15,428
B   €15,577.50
C   €15,928
D   €16,065.50

5.4 The role of the master budget

KEY TERM

The MASTER BUDGET 'Consolidates all subsidiary budgets and is normally comprised of the budgeted profit and loss account, balance sheet and cash flow statement'.   (*CIMA Official Terminology*)

It is this master budget that is **submitted** to senior managers or directors for their approval. If the master budget is **approved** as an acceptable plan for the forthcoming budget period then it acts as an **instruction and authorisation** to budget managers, to allow them to take action to achieve their budgets.

If the master budget is not approved as an acceptable plan then it will be returned to the budget committee for amendment. The **amended** master budget will then be reviewed again by senior management. Thus, budgeting is an **iterative process** and it may be necessary to perform many iterations before an acceptable, workable budget is adopted and approved.

Section summary

Cash budgets show the expected receipts and payments during a budget period and are a vital management planning and control tool.

The **master budget** is a summary of the functional (subsidiary) budgets and cash budget, and includes a budgeted statement of profit or loss and a budgeted statement of financial position.

6 Monitoring procedures

Introduction

The budgeting process does not end for the forthcoming year once the budget period has begun: budgeting should be seen as a **continuous and dynamic process**.

The budgeting process does not stop once the budgets have been agreed. **Actual results should be compared on a regular basis with the budgeted results**. The frequency with which such comparisons are made depends very much on the organisation's circumstances and the sophistication of its control systems but it should occur at least **monthly**. Management should receive a report detailing the differences and should investigate the reasons for the differences. If the **differences** are **within the control** of management, **corrective action** should be taken to bring the reasons for the difference under control and to ensure that such inefficiencies do not occur in the future.

The differences may have occurred, however, because the budget was **unrealistic** to begin with or because the actual conditions did not reflect those anticipated (or could have possibly been anticipated). This would therefore **invalidate** the remainder of the budget.

Because the original budget was unrealistic or because of changes in anticipated conditions, the budget committee may need to reappraise the organisation's future plans and may need to adjust the budget to take account of such changes. The **revised budget** then represents a revised statement of formal operating plans for the remaining portion of the budget period.

Section summary

The budgeting process does not end for the forthcoming year once the budget period has begun: budgeting should be seen as a **continuous and dynamic process**.

7 Alternative approaches to budgeting

Introduction

This section looks at incremental budgeting, zero based budgeting, programme planning and activity based budgeting.

7.1 Incremental budgeting

The **traditional approach** to budgeting is to **base next year's budget on the current year's results plus an extra amount for estimated growth or inflation next year**. This approach is known as **incremental budgeting** since it is concerned mainly with the increments in costs and revenues that will occur in the coming period.

Question 11a.4

Incremental budgeting 1

Learning outcome B3(b)

CP produces two products, X and Y. In the year ended 30 April 20X1, it produced 4,520 X and 11,750 Y and incurred costs of £1,217,200.

The costs incurred are such that 60% are variable. 70% of these variable costs vary with the number of X produced, with the remainder varying with the output of Y.

The budget for the three months to 31 October 20X1 is being prepared using an incremental approach based on the following:

- All costs will be 5% higher than the average paid in the year ended 30 April 20X1.

- Efficiency levels will be unchanged.

- Expected output:

  X   1,210 units
  Y   3,950 units

What is the budgeted cost for the output of X (to the nearest £100) for the 3 months ending 31 October 20X1?

A   £100
B   £127,800
C   £536,800
D   £134,200

Incremental budgeting is a reasonable procedure if current operations are as effective, efficient and economical as they can be. It is also appropriate for budgeting for costs such as staff salaries, which may be estimated on the basis of current salaries plus an increment for inflation and are hence administratively fairly easy to prepare.

7.1.1 The advantages and limitations of incremental budgeting

Advantages of incremental budgeting

- It is simple, cheap and relatively quick to administer.

Limitations of incremental budgeting

- It does not identify inefficient operations. Inefficiencies will continue.

- It does not help to eliminate wasteful expenditure.

- It is not suitable for changing environments, as it is based on the past and assumes that activities will continue to be the same.

- It encourages managers to spend up to the budget because if they don't, the budget is likely to be cut in the next period.

- It doesn't produce challenging performance targets or encourage managers to find ways of improving the business.

Question 11a.5

Incremental budgeting 2

Learning outcome B3(b)

Explain what is meant by incremental budgeting and discuss its suitability for budgeting for rent costs and for advertising expenditure.

In general, however, it is an **inefficient form of budgeting**, as it **encourages slack** and **wasteful spending** to creep into budgets. Past inefficiencies are perpetuated because cost levels are rarely subjected to close scrutiny.

To ensure that inefficiencies are not concealed, however, alternative approaches to budgeting have been developed. One such approach is **zero based budgeting (ZBB)**.

7.2 Zero based budgeting (ZBB)

7.2.1 The principles of ZBB

ZBB rejects the assumption inherent in incremental budgeting that this year's activities will continue at the same level or volume next year, and that next year's budget can be based on this year's costs plus an extra amount, perhaps for expansion and inflation.

KEY TERM

ZERO BASED BUDGETING is a method of budgeting that requires each cost element to be specifically justified, as though the activities to which the budget relates were being undertaken for the first time. Without approval, the budget allowance is zero.

In reality, however, managers do not have to budget from zero, but can **start from their current level of expenditure and work downwards**, asking what would happen if any particular aspect of current expenditure and current operations were removed from the budget. In this way, every aspect of the budget is examined in terms of its cost and the benefits it provides, and the selection of better alternatives is encouraged.

7.2.2 Implementing ZBB

The implementation of ZBB involves a number of steps but of greater importance is the **development of a questioning attitude** by all those involved in the budgetary process. Existing practices and expenditures must be challenged and searching questions asked.

- Does the activity need to be carried out?
- What would be the consequences if the activity were not carried out?
- Is the current level of provision adequate?
- Are there alternative ways of providing the function?
- How much should the activity cost?
- Is the expenditure worth the benefits achieved?

The three steps of ZBB

STEP 1

Define decision packages, comprehensive descriptions of specific organisational activities (decision units) which management can use to evaluate the activities and rank them in order of priority against other activities. There are two types.

(a) **Mutually exclusive packages** contain alternative methods of getting the same job done. The best option among the packages must be selected by comparing costs and benefits and the other packages are then discarded.

(b) **Incremental packages** divide one aspect of an activity into different levels of effort. The 'base' package will describe the minimum amount of work that must be done to carry out the activity and the other packages describe what additional work could be done, at what cost and for what benefits.

Evaluate and rank each activity (decision package) on the basis of its benefit to the organisation. This can be a lengthy process. Minimum work requirements (those that are essential to get a job done) will be given high priority and so too will work that meets legal obligations. In the accounting department, these would be minimum requirements to operate the payroll, payables ledger and receivables ledger systems, and to maintain and publish a satisfactory set of accounts.

Allocate resources in the budget according to the funds available and the evaluation and ranking of the competing packages.

Example: step 1

Suppose that a cost centre manager is preparing a budget for maintenance costs. He might first consider two mutually exclusive packages. Package A might be to keep a maintenance team of two men per shift for two shifts each day at a cost of £60,000 per annum, whereas package B might be to obtain a maintenance service from an outside contractor at a cost of £50,000. A cost-benefit analysis will be conducted because the quicker repairs obtainable from an in-house maintenance service might justify its extra cost. If we now suppose that package A is preferred, the budget analysis must be completed by describing the incremental variations in this chosen alternative.

(a) The **'base' package** would describe the minimum requirement for the maintenance work. This might be to pay for one man per shift for two shifts each day at a cost of £30,000.

(b) **Incremental package 1** might be to pay for two men on the early shift and one man on the late shift, at a cost of £45,000. The extra cost of £15,000 would need to be justified, for example by savings in lost production time, or by more efficient machinery.

(c) **Incremental package 2** might be the original preference, for two men on each shift at a cost of £60,000. The cost-benefit analysis would compare its advantages, if any, over incremental package 1; and so on.

Question 11a.6   ZBB

Learning outcome B3(b)

What might the base package and incremental packages for a personnel department cover?

	Base	Incremental
A	Recruitment	Training
B	Dismissal	Recruitment
C	Training	Pension administration
D	Pension administration	Recruitment

7.2.3 The advantages and limitations of ZBB

Advantages of ZBB

- It is possible to identify and **remove inefficient or obsolete operations**.
- It forces employees to **avoid wasteful expenditure**.
- It can **increase motivation**.
- It responds to changes in the business environment.
- ZBB documentation provides an in-depth appraisal of an organisation's operations.
- It **challenges the status quo**.
- In summary, ZBB should result in a **more efficient allocation of resources**.

The major **disadvantage** of ZBB is the **volume of extra paperwork** created. The assumptions about costs and benefits in each package must be continually updated and new packages developed as soon as new activities emerge. The following problems might also occur.

(a)   **Short-term benefits** might be **emphasised** to the detriment of long-term benefits.

(b)   It may give the impression **that all decisions have to be made in the budget**. Management must be able to meet unforeseen opportunities and threats at all times, however, and must not feel restricted from carrying out new ideas simply because they were not approved by a decision package, cost-benefit analysis and the ranking process.

(c)   It may be a **call for management skills** both in constructing decision packages and in the ranking process **which the organisation does not possess**. Managers may therefore have to be trained in ZBB techniques.

(d)   The organisation's information systems may not be capable of providing suitable information.

(e)   **The ranking process can be difficult**. Managers face three common problems.

     (i)   A large number of packages may have to be ranked.

     (ii)   It can be difficult to rank packages that appear to be equally vital, for legal or operational reasons.

     (iii)   It is difficult to rank activities that have qualitative rather than quantitative benefits – such as spending on staff welfare and working conditions.

In summary, perhaps the **most serious drawback to ZBB is that it requires a lot of management time and paperwork**. One way of obtaining the benefits of ZBB but of overcoming the drawbacks is to apply it selectively on a rolling basis throughout the organisation. This year finance, next year marketing, the year after personnel and so on. In this way, all activities will be thoroughly scrutinised over a period of time.

Question 11a.7	Base and incremental packages

Learning outcome B3(b)

What might the base and incremental packages cover in your department if your organisation used ZBB?

7.2.4 Using ZBB

ZBB is not particularly suitable for direct manufacturing costs, which are usually budgeted using standard costing, work study and other management planning and control techniques. ZBB is best applied to **support expenses**; that is, expenditure incurred in departments that exist to support the essential production function. These support areas include marketing, finance, quality control, personnel, data processing, sales and distribution. In many organisations, these expenses make up a large proportion of the total expenditure. These activities are less easily quantifiable by conventional methods and are more **discretionary** in nature. We return to the problem of budgeting for discretionary costs later in this section.

ZBB can also be successfully applied to **service industries** and **not-for-profit organisations** such as local and central government, educational establishments and hospitals, and in any organisation where alternative levels of provision for each activity are possible, and costs and benefits are separately identifiable.

Question 11a.8

Learning outcome B3(b)

You work for a large multinational company that manufactures weedkillers. It has been decided to introduce zero based budgeting (ZBB) in place of the more traditional incremental budgeting. The manager of the research and development department has never heard of ZBB.

Required

Write a report to the manager of the research and development department that explains how ZBB may assist in planning and controlling discretionary costs.

7.3 Programme planning and budgeting systems

A programme planning and budgeting system (PPBS) sets a budget in terms of **programmes** (groups of activities with common objectives). By focusing on objectives, the budget is therefore **orientated towards the ultimate output of the organisation**. This contrasts with the traditional approach to budgeting, which focuses on inputs (such as material and labour).

Such an approach is therefore particularly useful for **public sector** and **not-for-profit** organisations, such as government departments, schools, hospitals and charities, to ensure that expenditure is **focused** on programmes and activities that generate the most **beneficial results**.

Disadvantages of using traditional budgeting for public sector and not-for-profit organisations

(a)   Activities often span several years but the emphasis is on annual figures.

(b)   It is difficult to incorporate into a budget report planned or actual achievements (number of sufferers helped, level of education and so on), as these achievements tend to be non-financial in nature.

(c)   Costs relating to a particular objective are spread across a number of cost categories. For example, the costs relating to an objective of a police force to protect people and property from traffic hazards might be allocated to a variety of traditional cost categories – personnel, transport, administration, training and so on. It would be impossible to tell how much was spent, or authorised, to achieve that objective.

(d)   There is no evidence as to how effectively or efficiently resources are being used.

PPBS would overcome these problems, as the emphasis would be on objectives and the best use of resources to achieve effectiveness over the medium to long term.

PPBS approach

 Review long-term objectives (such as, for a police force, protect persons and property and deal with offenders).

 Set out the programmes of activities needed to achieve the objectives (such as police patrol on foot, police patrol in vehicles and so on).

 Evaluate the alternative programmes in terms of costs and benefits, and select the most appropriate programmes.

 Analyse the programmes selected, finding out (for example) what would happen to the level of achievement of objectives if resources allocated to a particular programme were reduced by, say, 10%.

7.4 Discretionary costs

KEY TERM

A DISCRETIONARY (or MANAGED or POLICY) COST is 'A cost whose amount within a time period is determined by a decision taken by the appropriate budget holder. Marketing, research and training are generally regarded as discretionary costs'.   (*CIMA Official Terminology*)

7.4.1 Budgeting for discretionary costs

It is much easier to set budgets for **engineered costs** (costs for which there is a **demonstrable relationship between the input** to a process and the **output** of that process) than for **discretionary costs** (costs for which there is **no clear relationship between the input and output of a process**, often because the **output is difficult to measure**, in terms of quantity and/or quality). It is obviously easier to budget for direct material costs (engineered cost) than for the cost of the accounts department (discretionary cost).

Budgeting for discretionary costs can be made **easier** by **converting them into engineered costs**.

*   Develop suitable output measures
*   Understand how input impacts on output

For example, by analysing the work undertaken to process an invoice for payment, an **average time** for dealing with an invoice can be established and the relationship between the number of invoices processed and the resources required to do this ascertained.

The analysis required for **activity based costing** will also add to an understanding of the relationship between the inputs and outputs of a process.

If a discretionary cost cannot be converted into an engineered cost, ZBB or PPBS will be needed.

7.4.2 Control of discretionary costs

Discretionary costs **cannot be controlled on the basis of outputs** because of the difficulty in specifying outputs in financial terms. However, in order to set minimum standards of performance, some measure of output is needed. An accounts department may be required to pay invoices within two weeks of receipt, for example.

Inputs can be **controlled**, however, if the **budget** acts as a device to ensure financial resources allocated to the activity are not exceeded.

7.5 Activity based budgeting

KEY TERM

ACTIVITY BASED BUDGETING is a 'Method of budgeting based on an activity framework and utilising cost driver data in the budget-setting and variance feedback processes'.   (*CIMA Official Terminology*)

At its **simplest**, activity based budgeting (ABB) is merely the **use of costs determined using** activity based costing (ABC) **as a basis for preparing budgets**.

A budget for an activity is therefore based on the budgeted number of the activity's cost driver × the appropriate cost driver rate. For example, if an organisation expects to place 500 orders and the rate per order is £100, the budgeted cost of the ordering activity will be 500 × £100 = £50,000.

Implementing ABC leads to the realisation that the **business as a whole** needs to be **managed** with far more reference to the behaviour of activities and cost drivers identified.

(a)   **Traditional budgeting may make managers 'responsible' for activities that are driven by factors beyond their control**: the cost of setting up new personnel records and of induction training would traditionally be the responsibility of the personnel manager, even though such costs are driven by the number of new employees required by managers other than the personnel manager.

(b)   The **budgets for costs not directly related to production** are often traditionally set using an **incremental approach** because of the difficulty of linking the activity driving the cost to production level. But this assumes that all of the cost is unaffected by any form of activity level, which is often

not the case in reality. Some of the costs of the purchasing department, for example, will be fixed (such as premises costs) but some will relate to the number of orders placed or the volume of production, say. Surely the budget for the purchasing department should take some account of the expected number of orders?

More **formally**, therefore, ABB involves **defining the activities** that underlie the financial figures in each function and using the level of activity to decide **how much resource should be allocated**, how well it is being **managed** and to explain **variances** from budget.

Claimed results of using ABB

(a) Different activity levels will provide a foundation for the base package and incremental packages of ZBB.

(b) The organisation's overall strategy and any actual or likely changes in that strategy will be taken into account because ABB attempts to manage the business as the sum of its interrelated parts.

(c) Critical success factors (an activity in which a business must perform well if it is to succeed) will be identified and key metrics devised to monitor progress towards them.

(d) The focus is on the whole of an activity, not just its separate parts, and so there is more likelihood of getting it right first time. For example, what is the use of being able to produce goods in time for their despatch date if the budget provides insufficient resources for the distribution manager who has to deliver them?

(e) Traditional accounting tends to focus on the nature of the costs being incurred (the input side) and traditional budgeting tends to mirror this. ABB emphasises the activities that are being achieved (the outputs).

7.6 Imposed style of budgeting

KEY TERM

IMPOSED/TOP-DOWN BUDGETING is a 'Budgeting process where all budget allowances are set without permitting the ultimate budget holders to have the opportunity to participate in the budgeting process'.

(*CIMA Official Terminology*)

Advantages of imposed budgeting

- Strategic plans are likely to be incorporated into planned activities.
- They enhance the co-ordination between the plans and objectives of divisions.
- They use senior management's awareness of total resource availability.
- They decrease the input from inexperienced or uninformed lower-level employees.
- They decrease the period of time taken to draw up the budgets.

Disadvantages of imposed budgeting

- Dissatisfaction, defensiveness and low morale among employees; it is hard for people to be motivated to achieve targets set by somebody else.

- The feeling of team spirit may disappear.

- The acceptance of organisational goals and objectives could be limited.

- The feeling of the budget as a punitive device could arise.

- Managers who are performing operations on a day to day basis are likely to have a better understanding of what is achievable.

- Unachievable budgets could result if consideration is not given to local operating and political environments. This applies particularly to overseas divisions.

- Lower-level management initiative may be stifled.

7.7 Participative style of budgeting

KEY TERM

PARTICIPATIVE/BOTTOM-UP BUDGETING is a 'Budgeting process where all budget holders have the opportunity to participate in setting their own budgets'.   (*CIMA Official Terminology*)

Advantages of participative budgeting

- They are based on information from employees most familiar with the department.
- Knowledge spread among several levels of management is pulled together.
- Morale and motivation is improved.
- They increase operational managers' commitment to organisational objectives.
- In general they are more realistic.
- Co-ordination between units is improved.
- Specific resource requirements are included.
- Senior managers' overview is mixed with operational level details.
- Individual managers' aspiration levels are more likely to be taken into account.

Disadvantages of participative budgets

- They consume more time.
- Changes implemented by senior management may cause dissatisfaction.
- Budgets may be unachievable if managers are not qualified to participate.
- They may cause managers to introduce budgetary slack and budget bias.
- They can support 'empire building' by subordinates.
- An earlier start to the budgeting process could be required.
- Managers may set 'easy' budgets to ensure that they are achievable.

7.7.1 Motivation

Motivation is what makes people behave in the way that they do. It comes from **individual attitudes**, or group attitudes. Individuals will be motivated by **personal desires and interests**. These may be in line with the objectives of the organisation, and some people 'live for their jobs'. Other individuals see their job as a chore, and their motivations will be unrelated to the objectives of the organisation they work for.

It is therefore vital that the goals of management and the employees harmonise with the goals of the organisation as a whole. This is known as **goal congruence**. Although obtaining goal congruence is essentially a behavioural problem, **it is possible to design and run a budgetary control system which will go some way towards ensuring that goal congruence is achieved**. Managers and employees must therefore be favourably disposed towards the budgetary control system so that it can operate efficiently.

The management accountant should therefore try to ensure that employees have positive attitudes towards **setting budgets, implementing budgets** (that is, putting the organisation's plans into practice) and feedback of results (**control information**).

Other behavioural aspects of budgeting:

- A budget amount can be seen as an amount that must be spent entirely during the year to ensure that the amount is not reduced in the next year.
- Budgets need to be set at the right level of difficulty to be motivators.

Section summary

- The principle behind **zero based budgeting** is that the budget for each cost centre should be prepared from 'scratch' or zero. Every item of expenditure must be justified to be included in the budget for the forthcoming period.

- There is a three-step approach to ZBB:
    - Define decision packages
    - Evaluate and rank packages
    - Allocate resources

- ZBB is particularly useful for budgeting for discretionary costs.

- **PPBS** is particularly useful for public sector and non profit seeking organisations.

- **Activity based budgeting** is a 'Method of budgeting based on an activity framework and utilising cost driver data in the budget-setting and variance feedback processes'.

(CIMA Official Terminology)

Chapter Summary

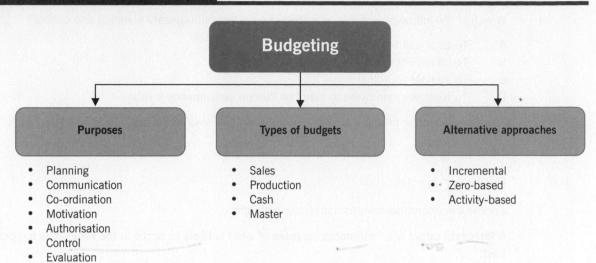

Budgeting

Purposes	Types of budgets	Alternative approaches
• Planning	• Sales	• Incremental
• Communication	• Production	• Zero-based
• Co-ordination	• Cash	• Activity-based
• Motivation	• Master	
• Authorisation		
• Control		
• Evaluation		

Quick Quiz

1   Which of the following is not an objective of a system of budgetary planning and control?

    A   To establish a system of control
    B   To co-ordinate activities
    C   To compel planning
    D   To motivate employees to maintain current performance levels

2   Sales is always the principal budget factor and so it is always the first budget to be prepared.

    True   ☐

    False   ☐

3   Choose the appropriate words from those highlighted.

    A **forecast/budget** is an **estimate/guarantee** of what is **likely to occur in the future/has happened in the past**.

    A **forecast/budget** is a **quantified plan/unquantified plan/guess** of what the organisation is aiming to **achieve/spend**.

4   Fill in the blanks.

    When preparing a production budget, the quantity to be produced is equal to sales .... opening inventory .... + ... closing inventory.

5   Which of the following should be included in a cash budget?

	Include	Do not include
Funds from the issue of share capital	•	
Revaluation of a non-current asset		•
Receipt of dividends from outside the business	•	
Depreciation of production machinery		•
Bad debts written off		•
Repayment of a bank loan	•	

6   What are the three components of the master budget?

    1   budgeted p&l
    2   balance sheet
    3   cash flow

Answers to Quick Quiz

1   D   The objective is to motivate employees to **improve** their performance.

2   False. The budget for the principal budget factor must be prepared first, but sales is not always the principal budget factor.

3   A **forecast** is an **estimate** of what is **likely to occur in the future**.

     A **budget** is a **quantified plan** of what the organisation is aiming to **achieve**.

4   When preparing a production budget, the quantity to be produced is equal to sales **minus** opening inventory **plus** closing inventory.

5

	Include	Do not include
Funds from the issue of share capital	✓	
Revaluation of a non-current asset		✓
Receipt of dividends from outside the business	✓	
Depreciation of production machinery		✓
Bad debts written off		✓
Repayment of a bank loan	✓	

6   Budgeted cash flow, budgeted statement of financial position and budgeted statement of profit or loss

Answers to Questions

11a.1 Budgets

(a)   The **sequence of budget preparation** will be roughly as follows:

   (i)   Sales budget. (The market share limits demand and so sales is the principal budget factor. All other activities will depend on this forecast.)

   (ii)   Finished goods inventory budget (in units)

   (iii)   Production budget (in units)

   (iv)   Production resources budgets (materials, machine hours, labour)

   (v)   Overhead budgets for production, administration, selling and distribution, research and development and so on

   Other budgets required will be the capital expenditure budget, the working capital budget (receivables and payables) and, very importantly, the cash budget.

(b)   The **master budget** is the summary of all the functional budgets. It often includes a summary statement of profit or loss and statement of financial position.

(c)   Procedures for preparing budgets can be contained in a **budget manual** which shows which budgets must be prepared when and by whom, what each functional budget should contain and detailed directions on how to prepare budgets including, for example, expected price increases, rates of interest and rates of depreciation.

   The formulation of budgets can be co-ordinated by a **budget committee** comprising the senior executives of the departments responsible for carrying out the budgets: sales, production, purchasing, personnel and so on.

   The budgeting process may also be assisted by the use of a **spreadsheet/computer budgeting package**.

11a.2 Material purchases budget

The correct answer is B.

	March kg	*April* kg	*May* kg
Required finished inventory:			
Base inventory	6,000	6,000	6,000
+ 25% of next month's sales	2,250	2,000	1,750
= Required inventory	8,250	8,000	7,750
Sales for month		9,000	8,000
		17,000	15,750
Less opening inventory		8,250	8,000
Required finished production		8,750	7,750
+ 10% losses = raw material required		9,625	8,525
Required material inventory:			
Base inventory	5,000.00	5,000.00	
+ 25% of material for next month's production	2,406.25	2,131.25	
= Required closing material inventory	7,406.25	7,131.25	
Production requirements		9,625.00	
		16,756.25	
Less opening inventory		7,406.25	
Required material purchases		9,350.00	

11a.3 Cash budgets (receipts)

The correct answer is A.

	Received in March €
Cash sales (5% × €10,000) × 95%	475.00
February sales (€17,000 × 95%) × 75%	12,112.50
January sales (€13,000 × 95%) × 23%	2,840.50
	15,428.00

11a.4 Incremental budgeting 1

The correct answer is D.

Proportion of actual annual costs related to X = £1,217,200 × 0.6 × 0.7 = £511,224

Proportion applicable to 3-month period = £511,224/4 = £127,806

Inflated cost = £127,806 × 1.05 = £134,196

Option A is the budgeted cost per X. If you selected option B, you forgot to inflate the cost. If you selected **option C**, you forgot to reduce the annual cost to a quarterly cost.

11a.5 Incremental budgeting 2

Incremental budgeting is a method of setting budgets whereby **the latest period's budget is used as a base for preparing the budget for the forthcoming period**. Adjustments are made for any expected changes, for example changes in staffing levels or in the level of activity.

Incremental budgeting may be appropriate for budgeting for rent because the rent cost for the forthcoming period may be **estimated on the basis of the current rent plus an increment for the annual rent increase**.

Incremental budgeting might not be appropriate for budgeting for advertising expenditure because such expenditure is not so easily quantifiable and is more discretionary in nature. Using incremental budgeting for advertising expenditure could allow **slack (unnecessary expenditure)** and wasteful spending to creep into the budget. Simply adding an increment to the current year's budget **does not force managers to question whether the current level of expenditure is necessary**. Furthermore, there will be a tendency for the relevant manager to **ensure that the current budget is spent**, in case the allowance is removed for the forthcoming year, if it is not spent this year.

11a.6 ZBB

The correct answer is A.

The base package might cover the recruitment and dismissal of staff. Incremental packages might cover training, pension administration, trade union liaison, staff welfare and so on.

11a.8 Using ZBB

REPORT

To: R&D manager
From: Management accountant   Date: 01.01.X6
Subject: Zero based budgeting

Discretionary cost is 'expenditure whose value is a matter of policy'; that is, it is not vital to the continued existence of an organisation in the way that, say, raw materials are to a manufacturing business. ZBB was developed originally to help management with the difficult task of allocating resources in precisely such areas. Research and development is a frequently cited example; others are advertising and training.

Within a research and development department, ZBB will establish priorities by ranking the projects that are planned and in progress. Project managers will be forced to consider the benefit obtainable from their work in relation to the costs involved. The result may be an overall increase in R&D expenditure, but only if it is justified.

It is worth mentioning that when R&D costs are subsequently being monitored, care is needed in interpreting variances. A favourable expenditure variance may not be a good thing: it may mean that not enough is being spent on R&D activity.

BUDGETS FOR PERFORMANCE EVALUATION

This chapter focuses on how budgets can be used for control purposes. **Budgetary control** is the comparison of actual results with budgeted results. **Variances** are calculated to identify the differences between actual and budgeted results and these differences are reported to management so that appropriate **action** can be taken.

Such an approach relies on a system of **flexible** (as opposed to fixed) budgets. We look at the difference between the two types in **Section 1**. **Flexible budgets** are vital for both **planning and control** – **Section 2** shows how they are constructed and **Section 3** looks at their use in the overall **budgetary control process**.

Section 4 examines the use of computer spreadsheets in budget construction. **Section 5** examines how **rolling budgets** encourage management to focus on future performance. **Section 6** looks at two **types of control** that can be used once budgetary control statements have been prepared.

Topic list	Learning outcomes	Syllabus references	Ability required
1 Fixed and flexible budgets	B5(a)	B5(a)(ii)	Evaluation
2 Preparing flexible budgets	B5(a)	B5(a)(ii)	Evaluation
3 Flexible budgets and budgetary control	B5(a)	B5(a)(ii)	Evaluation
4 Using spreadsheets to build business models	B5(a)	B5(a)(i)	Evaluation
5 Rolling budgets	B4(a)	B4(a)(i)	Evaluation
6 Budgeting as a control system	B4(a)	B4(a)(iii)	Comprehension
7 Feedback and feedforward control mechanisms	B4(a)	B4(a)(ii)	Comprehension

Chapter Overview

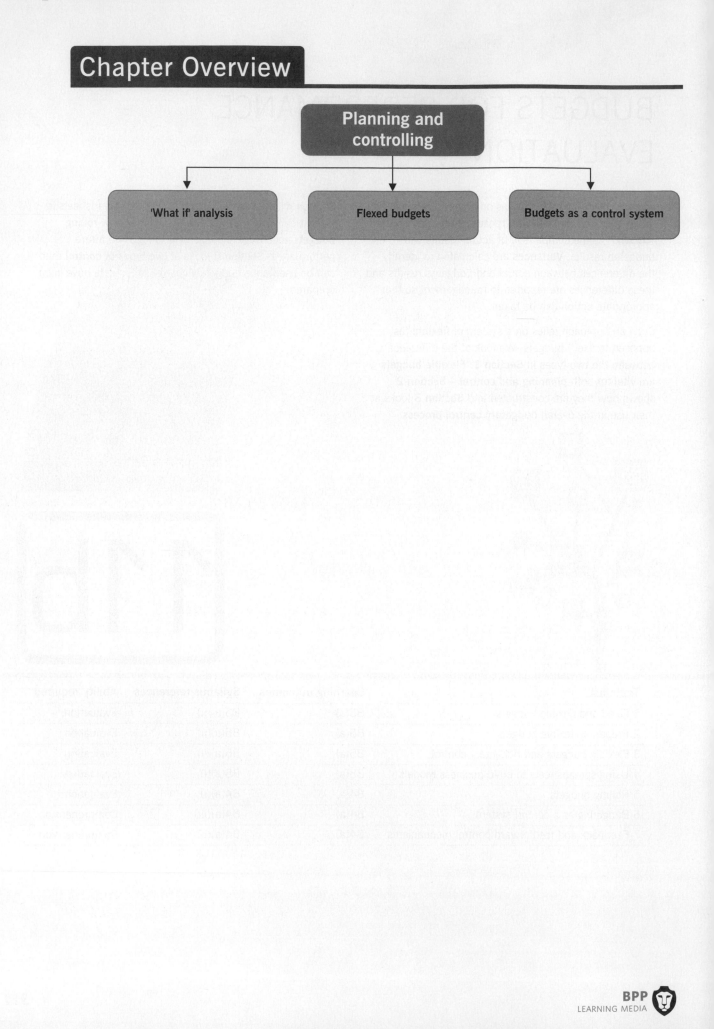

1 Fixed and flexible budgets

Introduction

This section focuses on the differences between fixed and flexible budgets. Make sure you understand what is meant by each type of budget before moving on.

1.1 Fixed budgets

The master budget prepared before the beginning of the budget period is known as the **fixed** budget. By the term 'fixed', we do not mean that the budget is kept unchanged. Revisions to a fixed master budget will be made if the situation so demands. The term 'fixed' means the following:

(a) The budget is prepared on the basis of an **estimated volume of production** and an **estimated volume of sales**, but no plans are made for the event that actual volumes of production and sales may **differ** from budgeted volumes.

(b) When **actual volumes** of production and sales during a control period (month or four weeks or quarter) are achieved, a fixed budget is **not adjusted** (in retrospect) to represent a new target for the new levels of activity.

The major purpose of a fixed budget lies in its use at the **planning** stage, when it seeks to define the broad objectives of the organisation.

KEY TERM

A FIXED BUDGET is 'A budget set prior to the control period, and not subsequently changed in response to changes in activity or costs or revenues. It may serve as a benchmark in performance evaluation'.

(CIMA Official Terminology)

Fixed budgets (in terms of a **pre-set expenditure limit**) are also useful for **controlling any fixed cost**, and **particularly non-production fixed costs** such as advertising, because such costs should be unaffected by changes in activity level (within a certain range).

1.2 Flexible budgets

KEY TERM

A FLEXIBLE BUDGET is a budget which, by recognising different cost behaviour patterns, is designed to change as volume of activity changes.

Two uses of flexible budgets

(a) **At the planning stage.** For example, suppose that a company expects to sell 10,000 units of output during the next year. A master budget (the fixed budget) would be prepared on the basis of these expected volumes. However, if the company thinks that output and sales might be as low as 8,000 units or as high as 12,000 units, it may prepare **contingency** flexible budgets, at volumes of, say, 8,000, 9,000, 11,000 and 12,000 units, and then assess the possible outcomes.

(b) **Retrospectively.** At the end of each control period, flexible budgets can be used to compare actual results achieved with what results should have been under the circumstances. Flexible budgets are an essential factor in budgetary control.

(i) Management needs to know about how good or bad actual performance has been. To provide a measure of performance, there must be a yardstick (budget/standard) against which actual performance can be measured.

(ii) Every business is dynamic, and actual volumes of output cannot be expected to conform exactly to the fixed budget. Comparing actual costs directly with the fixed budget costs is meaningless.

(iii)   For useful control information, it is necessary to compare actual results at the actual level of activity achieved against the results that should have been expected at this level of activity, which are shown by the flexible budget.

Section summary

Fixed budgets remain unchanged regardless of the level of activity; **flexible budgets** are designed to flex with the level of activity.

Flexible budgets are prepared using marginal costing and so mixed costs must be split into their fixed and variable components (possibly using the **high/low method**).

Flexible budgets should be used to show what cost and revenues should have been for the actual level of activity. Differences between the flexible budget figures and actual results are **variances**.

2 Preparing flexible budgets

Introduction

This section focuses on how to prepare flexible budgets. This is something that should be familiar from your previous studies but make sure you work through the example to reacquaint yourself with the process.

Knowledge brought forward from earlier studies

The preparation of flexible budgets

- The first step in the preparation of a flexible budget is the determination of **cost behaviour patterns**, which means deciding whether costs are fixed, variable or semi-variable.

- Fixed costs will remain constant as activity levels change.

- For non-fixed costs, divide each cost figure by the related activity level. If the cost is a **linear variable cost**, the cost per unit will remain constant. If the cost is a **semi-variable cost**, the unit rate will reduce as activity levels increase.

- Split semi-variable costs into their fixed and variable components using the **high/low method** or the **scattergraph method**.

- Calculate the **budget cost allowance** for each cost item as budget cost allowance = budgeted fixed cost* + (number of units produced/sold × variable cost per unit)**.

    *nil for totally variable cost **nil for fixed cost

KEY TERM

The BUDGET COST ALLOWANCE/FLEXIBLE BUDGET is the budgeted cost ascribed to the level of activity achieved in a budget centre in a control period. It comprises variable costs in direct proportion to volume achieved and fixed costs as a proportion of the annual budget.

Example: fixed and flexible budgets

Suppose that Gemma expects production and sales during the next year to be 90% of the company's output capacity; that is, 9,000 units of a single product. Cost estimates will be made using the high-low method and the following historical records of cost.

Units of output/sales	Cost of sales
	Yen
9,800	44,400
7,700	38,100

The company's management is not certain that the estimate of sales is correct, and has asked for flexible budgets to be prepared at output and sales levels of 8,000 and 10,000 units. The sales price per unit has been fixed at Y5.

Required

Prepare appropriate budgets.

Solution

If we assume that within the range 8,000 to 10,000 units of sales all costs are fixed, variable or mixed (in other words, there are no stepped costs, material discounts, overtime premiums, bonus payments and so on) the fixed and flexible budgets would be based on the estimate of fixed and variable cost.

		Yen
Total cost of 9,800 units	=	44,400
Total cost of 7,700 units	=	38,100
Variable cost of 2,100 units	=	6,300

The variable cost per unit is Yen 3.

		Yen
Total cost of 9,800 units	=	44,400
Variable cost of 9,800 units (9,800 × Yen 3)	=	29,400
Fixed costs (all levels of output and sales)	=	15,000

The fixed budgets and flexible budgets can now be prepared as follows:

	Flexible budget 8,000 units Yen	Fixed budget 9,000 units Yen	Flexible budget 10,000 units Yen
Sales (× Yen 5)	40,000	45,000	50,000
Variable costs (× Yen 3)	24,000	27,000	30,000
Contribution	16,000	18,000	20,000
Fixed costs	15,000	15,000	15,000
Profit	1,000	3,000	5,000

Have a go at the following question. It is more complicated than the last example because it includes inflation. You will need to recall your studies of index numbers from CIMA Certificate C03 *Fundamentals of Business Mathematics*.

Question 11b.1   High-low method

Learning outcome B5(a)

Rice and Faull Ltd has recorded the following total costs during the last five years.

Year	Output volume Units	Total cost $	Average price level index
0	65,000	145,000	100
1	80,000	179,000	112
2	90,000	209,100	123
3	60,000	201,600	144
4	75,000	248,000	160

What will be the expected costs in Year 5 when output is 85,000 units and the average price level index is 180?

2.1 The need for flexible budgets

We have seen that flexible budgets may be prepared in order to plan for variations in the level of activity above or below the level set in the fixed budget. It has been suggested, however, that since many cost items in modern industry are fixed costs, the value of flexible budgets in planning is dwindling.

(a) In many manufacturing industries, plant costs (depreciation, rent and so on) are a very large proportion of total costs, and these tend to be fixed costs.

(b) Wage costs also tend to be fixed, because employees are generally guaranteed a basic wage for a working week of an agreed number of hours.

(c) With the growth of service industries, labour (wages or fixed salaries) and overheads will account for most of the costs of a business, and direct materials will be a relatively small proportion of total costs.

Flexible budgets are nevertheless necessary and, even if they are not used at the planning stage, they must be used for variance analysis.

2.2 The budget committee

The **co-ordination** and **administration** of budgets is usually the responsibility of a **budget committee** (with the managing director as chairman).

(a) The budget committee is assisted by a **budget officer** who is usually an accountant. Every part of the organisation should be represented on the committee, so there should be a representative from sales, production, marketing and so on.

(b) **Functions of the budget committee**

    (i) **Co-ordination** of the preparation of budgets, which includes the issue of the budget manual

    (ii) **Issuing of timetables** for the preparation of functional budgets

    (iii) **Allocation of responsibilities** for the preparation of functional budgets

    (iv) **Provision of information** to assist in the preparation of budgets

    (v) **Communication of final budgets** to the appropriate managers

    (vi) **Comparison** of actual results with budgets and the investigation of variances

    (vii) **Continuous assessment** of the budgeting and planning process, in order to improve the planning and control function

Section summary

The **budget cost allowance/flexible budget** is the budgeted cost ascribed to the level of activity achieved in a budget centre in a control period. It comprises variable costs in direct proportion to volume achieved and fixed costs as a proportion of the annual budget.

3 Flexible budgets and budgetary control

Introduction

Flexible budgets are essential for control purposes. They represent the expected revenues, costs and profits for the actual units produced and sold, and are then compared to actual results to determine any differences (or variances). Variances should already be familiar to you from your earlier studies – in this section we show how flexible budgets can be used to identify potential control issues.

KEY TERM

'Budgetary control is carried out via a MASTER BUDGET devolved to responsibility centres, allowing continuous monitoring of actual results versus budget, either to secure by individual action the budget objectives or to provide a basis for budget revision.'   *(CIMA Official Terminology)*

In other words, individual managers are held responsible for investigating differences between budgeted and actual results, and are then expected to take corrective action or amend the plan in the light of actual events.

It is therefore vital to ensure that valid comparisons are being made. Consider the following example.

Example: flexible budgets and budgetary control

Penny manufactures a single product, the Darcy. Budgeted results and actual results for May are as follows:

	Budget	*Actual*	*Variance*
Production and sales of the Darcy (units)	7,500	8,200	
	$	$	$
Sales revenue	75,000	81,000	6,000 (F)
Direct materials	22,500	23,500	1,000 (A)
Direct labour	15,000	15,500	500 (A)
Production overhead	22,500	22,800	300 (A)
Administration overhead	10,000	11,000	1,000 (A)
	70,000	72,800	2,800 (A)
Profit	5,000	8,200	3,200 (F)

Note. (F) denotes a favourable variance and (A) an unfavourable or adverse variance.

In this example, the variances are meaningless for the purposes of control. All costs were higher than budgeted but the volume of output was also higher; it is to be expected that actual variable costs would be greater than those included in the fixed budget. However, it is not possible to tell how much of the increase is due to **poor cost control** and how much is due to the **increase in activity**.

Similarly, it is not possible to tell how much of the increase in sales revenue is due to the increase in activity. Some of the difference may be due to a difference between budgeted and actual selling price but we are unable to tell from the analysis above.

For control purposes, we need to know the answers to questions such as the following:

- Were actual costs higher than they should have been to produce and sell 8,200 Darcys?
- Was actual revenue satisfactory from the sale of 8,200 Darcys?

Instead of comparing actual results with a fixed budget that is based on a different level of activity to that actually achieved, the correct approach to budgetary control is to compare actual results with a budget that has been **flexed** to the actual activity level achieved.

Suppose that we have the following estimates of the behaviour of Penny's costs.

(a)   Direct materials and direct labour are variable costs.

(b)   Production overhead is a semi-variable cost, the budgeted cost for an activity level of 10,000 units being $25,000.

(c)   Administration overhead is a fixed cost.

(d)   Selling prices are constant at all levels of sales.

Solution

The **budgetary control analysis** should therefore be as follows:

	Fixed budget	Flexible budget	Actual results	Variance
Production and sales (units)	7,500	8,200	8,200	
	$	$	$	$
Sales revenue	75,000	82,000 (W1)	81,000	1,000 (A)
Direct materials	22,500	24,600 (W2)	23,500	1,100 (F)
Direct labour	15,000	16,400 (W3)	15,500	900 (F)
Production overhead	22,500	23,200 (W4)	22,800	400 (F)
Administration overhead	10,000	10,000 (W5)	11,000	1,000 (A)
	70,000	74,200	72,800	1,400 (F)
Profit	5,000	7,800	8,200	400 (F)

Workings

1   Selling price per unit = $75,000/7,500 = $10 per unit
        Flexible budget sales revenue = $10 × 8,200 = 482,000

2   Direct materials cost per unit = $22,500/7,500 = $3
        Budget cost allowance = $3 × 8,200 = $24,600

3   Direct labour cost per unit = $15,000/7,500 = $2
        Budget cost allowance = $2 × 8,200 = $16,400

4   Variable production overhead cost per unit = $(25,000 – 22,500)/(10,000 – 7,500)
        = $2,500/2,500 = $1 per unit

        ∴ Fixed production overhead cost = $22,500 – (7,500 × $1) = $15,000

        ∴ Budget cost allowance = $15,000 + (8,200 × $1) = $23,200

5   Administration overhead is a fixed cost and hence budget cost allowance = $10,000

Comment

(a)   In selling 8,200 units, the expected profit should have been not the fixed budget profit of $5,000, but the flexible budget profit of $7,800. Instead actual profit was $8,200, ie $400 more than we should have expected.

        One of the reasons for this improvement is that, given output and sales of 8,200 units, the cost of resources (material, labour etc) was $1,400 lower than expected. (A comparison of the fixed budget and the actual costs in the example in Section 3 appeared to indicate that costs were not being controlled since all of the variances were adverse.)

(b)   The sales revenue was, however, $1,000 less than expected because a lower price was charged than budgeted.

We know this because flexing the budget has eliminated the effect of changes in the volume sold, which is the only other factor that can affect sales revenue. You have probably already realised that this variance of $1,000 (A) is a **selling price variance**.

The lower selling price could have been caused by the increase in the volume sold (to sell the additional 700 units the selling price had to fall below $10 per unit). We do not know if this is the case but without flexing the budget we could not know that a different selling price to that budgeted had been charged. Our initial analysis above had appeared to indicate that sales revenue was ahead of budget.

The difference of $400 between the flexible budget profit of $7,800 at a production level of 8,200 units and the actual profit of $8,200 is due to the net effect of cost savings of $1,400 and lower than expected sales revenue (by $1,000).

The difference between the original budgeted profit of $5,000 and the actual profit of $8,200 is the total of the following:

(a) The savings in resource costs/lower than expected sales revenue (a net total of $400 as indicated by the difference between the flexible budget and the actual results).

(b) The effect of producing and selling 8,200 units instead of 7,500 units (a gain of $2,800 as indicated by the difference between the fixed budget and the flexible budget). This is the **sales volume contribution variance**.

A **full variance analysis statement** would be as follows:

	$	$
Fixed budget profit		5,000
Variances		
Sales volume	2,800 (F)	
Selling price	1,000 (A)	
Direct materials cost	1,100 (F)	
Direct labour cost	900 (F)	
Production overhead cost	400 (F)	
Administration overhead cost	1,000 (A)	
		3,200 (F)
Actual profit		8,200

If management believes that any of the variances are large enough to justify it, they will investigate the reasons for their occurrence to see whether any corrective action is necessary.

Question 11b.2   Flexible budget

Learning outcome B5(a)

Flower budgeted to sell 200 units and produced the following budget.

	$	$
Sales		71,400
Variable costs		
Labour	31,600	
Material	12,600	
		44,200
Contribution		27,200
Fixed costs		18,900
Profit		8,300

Actual sales turned out to be 230 units, which were sold for $69,000. Actual expenditure on labour was $27,000 and on material $24,000. Fixed costs totalled $10,000.

Required

Prepare a flexible budget that will be useful for management control purposes.

3.1 Flexible budgets, control and computers

The production of flexible budget control reports is an area in which computers can provide invaluable assistance to the cost accountant, calculating flexed budget figures using fixed budget and actual results data, and hence providing detailed variance analysis. For control information to be of any value it must be produced quickly: speed is one of the many advantages of computers.

3.2 Flexible budgets using activity based costing data

Instead of flexing budgets according to the number of units produced or sold, in an activity based costing environment it is possible to use **more meaningful bases for flexing the budget**. The budget cost allowance for each activity can be determined according to the number of **cost drivers**.

Suppose the budget for a production department for a given period is as follows:

	$
Wages	220,000
Materials	590,000
Equipment	20,000
Power, heat and light	11,000
	841,000

However, this budget gives little indication of the link between the level of activity in the department and the costs incurred.

Suppose the activities in the department have been identified as sawing, hammering, finishing, reworking and production reporting. The budget might therefore be restated as follows:

Activities	Cost driver	Budgeted cost per unit of cost driver $	Budgeted no of cost drivers	Budget $
Sawing	Number of units sawed	50.00	5,000	250,000
Hammering	Number of units hammered together	10.00	35,000	350,000
Finishing	Number of sq metres finished	0.50	400,000	200,000
Reworking	Number of items reworked	12.40	2,500	31,000
Production reporting	Number of reports	400.00	25	10,000
				841,000

Advantages of this approach

(a)   Costs classified as fixed in the first budget can now be seen to be variable and hence can be more readily controlled.

(b)   The implications of increases/decreases in levels of activity are immediately apparent. For example, if acceptable quality levels were raised, requiring an additional 200 units per annum to be reworked, budgeted costs would increase by 200 × $12.40 = $2,480.

A **flexible budget** would be prepared as follows:

	Actual no of cost drivers	Budgeted cost per unit of cost driver $	Flexed budget $	Actual cost $	Variance $
Sawing	6,000	50.00	300,000	297,000	3,000 (F)
Hammering	40,000	10.00	400,000	404,000	4,000 (A)
Finishing	264,400	0.50	132,200	113,200	19,000 (F)
Reworking	4,500	12.40	55,800	56,100	300 (A)
Production reporting	30	400.00	12,000	13,700	1,700 (A)
			900,000	884,000	16,000 (F)

3.3 The link between standard costing and budget flexing

The calculation of standard cost variances and the use of a flexed budget to control costs and revenues are **very similar in concept**.

For example, a direct material total variance in a standard costing system is calculated by **comparing the material cost that should have been incurred for the output achieved, with the actual cost that was incurred**.

Exactly the same process is undertaken when a budget is flexed to provide a basis for comparison with the actual cost: **the flexible budget cost allowance for material cost is the same as the cost that should have been incurred for the activity level achieved**. In the same way as for standard costing, this is then compared with the actual cost incurred in order to practise control by comparison.

However, there are differences between the two techniques.

(a)   **Standard costing variance analysis is more detailed**. The total material cost variance is analysed further to determine how much of the total variance is caused by a difference in the price paid for materials (the material price variance) and how much is caused by the usage of material being different from the standard (the material usage variance). In flexible budget comparisons only total cost variances are derived.

(b)   **For a standard costing system to operate it is necessary to determine a standard unit cost for all items of output**. All that is required to operate a flexible budgeting system is an understanding of the cost behaviour patterns and a measure of activity to use to flex the budget cost allowance for each cost element.

Section summary

Budgetary control is based around a system of **budget centres**. Each centre has its own budget which is the responsibility of the **budget holder**.

4 Using spreadsheets to build business models

Introduction

Budget construction can be very complicated, particularly if assumptions regarding costs, selling prices or sales volumes are changed several times. Spreadsheets make the process much easier. This section demonstrates how spreadsheet packages can be used to assist in the initial budget-setting process and in the construction of flexible budgets.

KEY TERM

A SPREADSHEET is 'The term commonly used to describe many of the modelling packages available for microcomputers, being loosely derived from the likeness to a "spreadsheet of paper" divided into rows and columns'.   (*CIMA Computing Terminology*)

It is a type of general purpose software package with **many business applications**, not just accounting ones. It **can be used to build a model**, in which data is presented in **cells** at the intersection of these **rows and columns**. It is up to the model builder to determine what data or information should be presented in the spreadsheet, how it should be presented and how the data should be manipulated by the spreadsheet program. The most widely used spreadsheet packages are Lotus 1-2-3 and Excel.

The idea behind a spreadsheet is that the model builder should **construct a model as follows**:

(a)   Identify what data goes into each row and column, and **insert text** (for example, column headings and row identifications).

(b) **Specify how the numerical data in the model should be derived**. Numerical data might be derived using one of the following methods:

    (i) **Insertion into the model via keyboard input**.

    (ii) **Calculation from other data in the model** by means of a formula specified within the model itself. The model builder must insert these formulae into the spreadsheet model when it is first constructed.

    (iii) **Retrieval from data on a disk file** from another computer application program or module.

4.1 The advantages of spreadsheets

The uses of spreadsheets are really only limited by your imagination, and by the number of rows and columns in the spreadsheet, but some of the more **common accounting applications** are listed below.

- Statements of financial position
- Cash flow analysis/forecasting
- General ledger
- Inventory records
- Job cost estimates
- Market share analysis and planning

- Profit projections
- Profit statements
- Project budgeting and control
- Sales projections and records
- Tax estimation

The great value of spreadsheets derives from their **simple format** of rows, columns and worksheets of data, and the ability of the data **users to have direct access themselves** to their spreadsheet model via their own PC. For example, an accountant can construct a cash flow model with a spreadsheet package on the PC on their desk: they can **create** the model, **input** the data, **manipulate** the data and **read or print the output** direct. They will also have fairly **instant access** to the model whenever it is needed, in just the time it takes to load the model into the PC. Spreadsheets therefore bring computer modelling within the everyday reach of data users.

4.2 The disadvantages of spreadsheets

Spreadsheets have disadvantages if they are not properly used.

(a) A **minor error in the design** of a model at any point can **affect the validity of data** throughout the spreadsheet. Such errors can be very difficult to trace.

(b) Even if it is properly designed in the first place, it is very **easy to corrupt** a model by accidentally changing a cell or inputting data in the wrong place.

(c) It is possible to **become overdependent on them**, so that simple one-off tasks that can be done in seconds with a pen and paper are done on a spreadsheet instead.

(d) The possibility for experimentation with data is so great that it is possible to **lose sight of the original intention** of the spreadsheet.

(e) Spreadsheets **cannot take account of qualitative factors** since they are invariably difficult to quantify. Decisions should not be made on the basis of quantitative information alone.

4.3 'What-if?' analysis

KEY TERM

'WHAT-IF?' ANALYSIS involves changing the values of the forecast variables to see the effect on the forecast outcome. The information provided helps managers to understand the sensitivity of the forecast to the value of the variables.

Once a model has been constructed, the consequences of changes or amendments to budget/plan assumptions may be tested by asking **'what if?' questions, a form of sensitivity analysis**. For example, a spreadsheet may be used to develop a cash flow model, such as that shown below.

BPP
LEARNING MEDIA

A	B	C	D
1	*Month 1*	*Month 2*	*Month 3*
2 Sales	1,000	1,200	1,440
3 Cost of sales	(650)	(780)	(936)
4 Gross profit	350	420	504
5			
6 Receipts:			
7 Current month	600	720	864
8 Previous month	–	400	480
9	–	–	–
10	600	1,120	1,344
11 Payments	(650)	(780)	(936)
12	(50)	340	408
13 Balance b/f	–	(50)	290
14 Balance c/f	(50)	290	698

Typical 'what if?' questions for sensitivity analysis

(a)   What if the cost of sales is 68% of sales revenue, not 65%?

(b)   What if payment from receivables is received 40% in the month of sale, 50% one month in arrears and 10% two months in arrears, instead of 60% in the month of sale and 40% one month in arrears?

(c)   What if sales growth is only 15% per month, instead of 20% per month?

Using the spreadsheet model, the answers to such questions can be obtained simply and quickly, using the editing facility in the program. The information obtained should **provide management with a better understanding of what the cash flow position in the future might be**, and **what factors are critical to ensuring that the cash position remains reasonable**. For example, it might be found that the cost of sales must remain less than 67% of sales value to achieve a satisfactory cash position.

Question 11b.3   Spreadsheets

Learning outcomes B5(a)

(a)   Write out the formulae that would appear in column C of the spreadsheet shown above.

(b)   Comment on the effect on the cash balances if **all** of the 'what if?' conditions listed in Paragraph 4.3 applied. Perform the calculations manually, then if you have access to a spreadsheet package, you could use it to check your answer.

(c)   Which cells in column C would have to be changed, and how, if the 'what if?' conditions applied?

(d)   How could the design of the spreadsheet model be improved to facilitate sensitivity analysis?

Section summary

Spreadsheet packages can be used to build business models to assist in forecasting and planning.

'What-if?' analysis involves changing the values of the forecast variables to see the effect on the forecast outcome. The information provided helps managers to understand the sensitivity of the forecast to the value of the variables.

5   Rolling budgets

Introduction

Rolling budgets encourage management to focus on future performance and can be particularly useful when future events cannot be forecast reliably.

KEY TERMS

A ROLLING BUDGET is defined as 'A budget continuously updated by adding a further accounting period (month or quarter) when the earliest accounting period has expired. Its use is particularly beneficial where future costs and/or activities cannot be forecast accurately'.   (*CIMA Official Terminology*)

For example, a budget may initially be prepared for January to December in Year 1. At the end of the first month, that is, at the end of January Year 1, the first month's budget is deleted. A further month is then added onto the end of the remaining budget, for January Year 2. The remaining portion of the original budget is updated in the light of current conditions.

This contrasts to a PERIODIC BUDGET, which is prepared for a set control period, for example January to December Year 1, and a different budget is prepared for the next control period, January to December Year 2.

5.1 Advantages and disadvantages of rolling budgets

(a)   **Advantages**

   (i)   Budgets are reassessed regularly by management and so should be more accurate.

   (ii)   Uncertainty is reduced. Rolling budgets focus detailed planning and control on short-term prospects where the degree of uncertainty is much smaller, especially in times of change.

   (iii) Planning and control is based on a recent, updated plan which is likely to be far more realistic than a fixed annual budget prepared months ago.

   (iv)   The budget is continuous and will always extend a number of months ahead, encouraging managers to think about the future. This is not the case with fixed periodic budgets.

   (v)   A realistic budget that takes account of recent performance and market conditions is likely to have a better motivational influence on managers.

(b)   **Disadvantages**

   (i)   Rolling budgets are time consuming and expensive as a number of budgets must be produced during the accounting period.

   (ii)   The volume of work required with each reassessment of the budget can be off-putting for managers.

   (iii) Each revised budget may require revision of standards or stock valuations, which could put additional pressure on the accounts department each time a rolling budget is prepared.

Section summary

Rolling budgets are continuously updated by adding a further accounting period (month or quarter) when the earliest accounting period has expired.

6 Budgeting as a control system

Introduction

In order to prepare a budget for an organisation as a whole, individual budgets have to be prepared for sub-sections of the organisation, such as individual departments, products or activities. This section looks at the key features of budget control systems and controllable and uncontrollable costs, and why it is so important for budgetary control to correctly separate costs into these categories.

6.1 Budget control systems: key features

KEY TERM

A BUDGET CENTRE is 'A section of an entity for which control may be exercised through budgets prepared'.

(CIMA Official Terminology)

Budgetary control is based around a system of budget centres. Each budget centre will have its own budget and a manager will be responsible for managing the budget centre and ensuring that the budget is met.

The **selection of budget centres** in an organisation is therefore a **key first step in setting up a control system**. What should the budget centres be? What income, expenditure and/or capital employment plans should each budget centre prepare? And how will measures of performance for each budget centre be made?

A well-organised system of control should have the following features.

Feature	Explanation
A hierarchy of budget centres	If the organisation is quite large, a hierarchy is needed. Subsidiary companies, departments and work sections might be budget centres. Budgets of each section would then be consolidated into a departmental budget, departmental budgets in turn would be consolidated into the subsidiary's budget, and the budgets of each subsidiary would be **combined into a master budget** for the group as a whole.
Clearly identified responsibilities for achieving budget targets	Individual managers should be made responsible for achieving the budget targets of a particular budget centre.
Responsibilities for revenues, costs and capital employed	Budget centres should be organised so that all the revenues earned by an organisation, all the costs it incurs, and all the capital it employs are made the responsibility of someone within the organisation, at an appropriate level of authority in the management hierarchy.

Budgetary control and budget centres are therefore part of the overall system of **responsibility accounting** within an organisation.

KEY TERM

RESPONSIBILITY ACCOUNTING is a system of accounting that segregates revenue and costs into areas of personal responsibility in order to monitor and assess the performance of each part of an organisation.

6.2 The controllability principle

Care must be taken to distinguish between controllable costs and uncontrollable costs in variance reporting. The **controllability principle** is that managers of responsibility centres should only be held accountable for costs over which they have **some influence**. From a **motivation** point of view this is important because it can be very demoralising for managers who feel that their performance is being judged on the basis of something over which they have no influence. It is also important from a **control**

point of view in that control reports should ensure that information on costs is reported to the manager who is able to take action to control them.

6.3 Controllable and uncontrollable costs

KEY TERM

A **CONTROLLABLE COST** is a 'Cost which can be controlled, typically by a cost, profit or investment centre manager'.   (*CIMA Official Terminology*)

Responsibility accounting attempts to associate costs, revenues, assets and liabilities with the managers most capable of controlling them. As a system of accounting, it therefore distinguishes between **controllable** and **uncontrollable** costs.

Most **variable costs** within a department are thought to be **controllable in the short term** because managers can influence the efficiency with which resources are used, even if they cannot do anything to raise or lower price levels.

A cost that is not controllable by a junior manager might be controllable by a senior manager. For example, there may be high direct labour costs in a department caused by excessive overtime working. The junior manager may feel obliged to continue with the overtime to meet production schedules, but his senior may be able to reduce costs by hiring extra full-time staff, thereby reducing the requirements for overtime.

A cost that is not controllable by a manager in one department may be controllable by a manager in another department. For example, an increase in material costs may be caused by buying at higher prices than expected (controllable by the purchasing department) or by excessive wastage (controllable by the production department) or by a faulty machine producing rejects (controllable by the maintenance department).

Some costs are **non-controllable**, such as increases in expenditure items due to inflation. Other costs are **controllable, but in the long term rather than the short term**. For example, production costs might be reduced by the introduction of new machinery and technology, but in the short term, management must attempt to do the best they can with the resources and machinery at their disposal.

6.3.1 The controllability of fixed costs

It is often assumed that all fixed costs are non-controllable in the short run. This is not so.

(a)   **Committed fixed costs** are those costs arising from the possession of plant, equipment, buildings and an administration department to **support the long-term needs of the business**. These costs (depreciation, rent, administration salaries) are largely **non-controllable in the short term** because they have been committed by longer-term decisions affecting longer-term needs. When a company decides to cut production drastically, the long-term committed fixed costs will be reduced, but only after redundancy terms have been settled and assets sold.

(b)   A **discretionary cost** is a cost whose amount, within a particular time period, is **determined by**, and can be **altered by**, the **budget holder**. **Discretionary fixed costs**, such as advertising and research and development costs, are incurred as a result of a top management decision, but could be **raised or lowered at fairly short notice** (irrespective of the actual volume of production and sales).

6.3.2 Controllability and apportioned costs

Managers should only be held accountable for costs over which they have some influence. This may seem quite straightforward in theory, but it is not always so easy in practice to distinguish controllable from uncontrollable costs. **Apportioned overhead costs provide a good example.**

Example: apportioned costs

Suppose that a manager of a production department in a manufacturing company is made responsible for the costs of their department. These costs include **directly attributable overhead items** such as the costs of indirect labour employed and indirect materials consumed in the department. The department's overhead costs also include an apportionment of costs from other cost centres, such as rent and rates for the building it shares with other departments and a share of the costs of the maintenance department.

Should the production manager be held accountable for any of these apportioned costs?

Solution

(a) Managers should not be held accountable for costs over which they have no control. In this example, apportioned rent and rates costs would not be controllable by the production department manager.

(b) Managers should be held accountable for costs over which they have some influence. In this example, it is the responsibility of the maintenance department manager to keep maintenance costs within budget. But their costs will be partly variable and partly fixed, and the variable cost element will depend on the volume of demand for their services. If the production department's staff treat their equipment badly we might expect higher repair costs, and the production department manager should therefore be made accountable for the repair costs that their department makes the maintenance department incur on its behalf.

(c) Charging the production department with some of the costs of the maintenance department prevents the production department from viewing the maintenance services as 'free services'. Over-use would be discouraged and the production manager is more likely to question the activities of the maintenance department, possibly resulting in a reduction in maintenance costs or the provision of more efficient maintenance services.

Question 11b.4

Try to discover some of your organisation's committed fixed costs and discretionary fixed costs. You will then be able to use them as examples in the exam.

Note. There is no solution to this question at the end of the chapter – this is a research question for you to try.

6.3.3 Controllability and dual responsibility

Quite often a particular cost might be the **responsibility of two or more managers**. For example, raw materials costs might be the responsibility of the purchasing manager (prices) and the production manager (usage). A **reporting system must allocate responsibility appropriately**. The purchasing manager must be responsible for any increase in raw materials prices whereas the production manager should be responsible for any increase in raw materials usage.

Exam skills

You can see that there are **no clear-cut rules** as to which costs are controllable and which are not. Each situation and cost must be reviewed separately and a decision taken according to the control value of the information and its behavioural impact.

6.4 Budgetary control reports

If the **budget holders** (managers of budget centres) are to attempt to meet budgets, they must receive regular budgetary control reports so that they can monitor the budget centre's operations and take any necessary control action.

The **amount of detail** included in reports will **vary** according to the needs of management. In general terms, there should be **sufficient detail** within the reports to **motivate the individual manager to take the most appropriate action** in all circumstances. A form of **exception reporting** can be used for **top management**, with reports just detailing significant variances.

Section summary

A **budget centre** is defined in *CIMA Official Terminology* as 'A section of an entity for which control may be exercised through budgets prepared'.

Responsibility accounting is a system of accounting that segregates revenue and costs into areas of personal responsibility in order to monitor and assess the performance of each part of an organisation.

Controllable costs are those that can be influenced by the budget holder. **Uncontrollable costs** cannot be so influenced.

7   Feedback and feedforward control mechanisms

Introduction

Following on from the key concepts of budgets as control mechanisms, we move on to how information is relayed to the budget participants.

7.1 Feedback

KEY TERM

The term 'FEEDBACK' is used to describe both the process of reporting back control information to management and the control information itself. In a business organisation, it is information produced from within the organisation (**management control reports**) with the purpose of helping management and other employees with control decisions.

(a)   **Single loop feedback**, normally expressed as feedback, is the feedback of relatively small variations between actual and plan in order that corrective action can bring performance in line with planned results. This implies that the existing plans will not change. This type of feedback is associated with budgetary control and standard costing.

(b)   **Double loop feedback**, also known as **higher level feedback**, ensures that plans, budgets, organisational structures and the control systems themselves are revised to meet changes in conditions.

(c)   Feedback will most often be **negative**: targets were missed and this was **not** what was required. It may, however, be **positive**: targets were missed, but other targets were hit that were better than those we were aiming at. Negative feedback would result in control action to get back on target. Positive feedback means that the target should be moved.

7.2 The feedback loop in the control cycle

Feedback loop in the control cycle

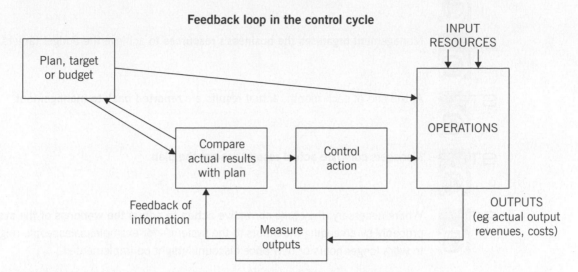

The elements in the control cycle, illustrated in the diagram, are as follows:

 Plans and targets are set for the future. These could be long-, medium- or short-term plans. Examples include budgets, profit targets and standard costs.

 Plans are put into operation. As a consequence, materials and labour are used, and other expenses are incurred.

 Actual results are recorded and analysed.

 Information about actual results is fed back to the management concerned, often in the form of accounting reports. This reported information is **feedback.**

 The feedback is used by management to compare actual results with the plan or targets (what should be or should have been achieved).

 By comparing actual and planned results, management can then do one of three things, depending on how they see the situation.

Management's potential reactions to divergences from planned performance

(a)   **They can take controlling action**. By identifying what has gone wrong, and then finding out why, corrective measures can be taken.

(b)   **They can decide to do nothing**. This could be the decision when actual results are going better than planned, or when poor results were caused by something that is unlikely to happen again in the future.

(c)   **They can alter the plan or target** if actual results are different from the plan or target, and there is nothing that management can do (or nothing, perhaps, that they want to do) to correct the situation.

It may be helpful at this stage to relate the control system to a **practical example, such as monthly sales**.

STEP ①   A **sales budget** or plan is prepared for the year.

 STEP ②   Management **organises the business's resources** to achieve the budget targets.

 STEP ③   At the end of each month, **actual results** are **reported back to management**.

 STEP ④   Managers **compare actual results against the plan**.

STEP ⑤   Where necessary, they **take corrective action to adjust the workings of the system**, probably by amending the inputs to the system – for example, salespeople might be asked to work longer hours or new price discounts might be implemented.

This monthly sales example demonstrates how variance analysis is a form of feedback control. Variances can give negative or positive feedback. An adverse cost variance would be negative feedback and a favourable sales variance may well be seen as positive feedback.

KEY POINT

Variance analysis can be seen as a form of feedback control.

7.3 Feedforward control

KEY TERM

FEEDFORWARD CONTROL is the 'Forecasting of differences between actual and planned outcomes, and the implementation of action, before the event, to avoid such differences'.   (*CIMA Official Terminology*)

Most control systems make use of a comparison between results of the current period (historical costs) and the planned results. Past events are therefore used as a means of controlling or adjusting future activity. A major criticism of this approach to control activity is that it is backward looking.

Consider, however, a **cash budget**. This is used to identify likely peaks and troughs in cash balances, and if it seems probable that, say, a higher overdraft facility will be needed later in the year, control action will be taken in advance of the actual need, to make sure that the facility will be available. This is an example of **feedforward control**; that is, control based on comparing original targets or actual results with a **forecast** of future results.

The 'information revolution', which has arisen from computer technology, management information systems theory and the growing use of quantitative techniques, has widened the scope for the use of this control technique. Forecasting models can be constructed that enable regular revised forecasts to be prepared about what is now likely to happen in view of changes in key variables (such as sales demand and wage rates).

If regular forecasts are prepared, managers will have both the current forecast and the original plan to guide their action. The original plan may or may not be achievable in view of the changing circumstances. The current forecast indicates what is expected to happen in view of these circumstances.

Examples of control comparisons

 Current forecast versus plan. What action must be taken to get back to the plan, given the differences between the current forecast and the plan? Is any control action worthwhile?

 If **control action** is **planned**, the current forecast will need to be amended to take account of the effects of the control action and a **revised forecast** prepared.

 The next comparison should then be **revised forecast versus plan** to determine whether the plan is now expected to be achieved.

 A comparison between the **original current forecast** and the **revised forecast** will show what the expected effect of the control action will be.

 At the **end of a control period**, actual results will be analysed and two comparisons may be made.

- **Actual results versus the revised forecast**. Why did differences between the two occur?

- **Actual results so far in the year versus the plan**. How close are actual results to the plan?

 At the same time, a **new current forecast** should be prepared, and the cycle of comparisons and control action may begin again.

It is in this way that costs are constantly controlled and monitored.

Another example of a system of feedforward control is target costing. This is when a business sets a target rate of return for its products or services. The results are forecast periodically and, if it looks as if the target will not be met, action is taken to bring it back in line with target.

KEY POINT

> **Target costing** can be seen as a form of feedforward control.

 ## Section summary

The term '**feedback**' is used to describe both the process of reporting back control information to management and the control information itself.

Variance analysis can be seen as a form of feedback control.

Feedforward control is based on comparing original targets or actual results with a **forecast** of future results.

Target costing can be seen as a form of feedforward control.

Chapter Summary

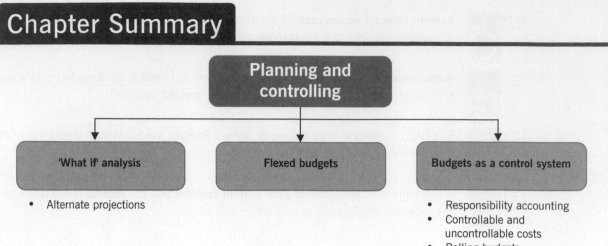

Planning and controlling

'What if' analysis

- Alternate projections

Flexed budgets

Budgets as a control system

- Responsibility accounting
- Controllable and uncontrollable costs
- Rolling budgets
- Feedback and feedforward control

Quick Quiz

1   Fill in the blanks.

A flexible budget is a budget which, by recognising ......*cost behaviour*......, is designed to
......*change*...... as the level of activity changes.

2   An extract of the costs incurred at two different activity levels is shown. Classify the costs according to
their behaviour patterns and show the budget cost allowance for an activity of 1,500 units.

		1,000 units $	2,000 units $	Type of cost	Budget cost allowance for 1,500 units $
(a)	Fuel	3,000	6,000	*V.C*	*4500*
(b)	Photocopying	9,500	11,000	*semi*	*10,250*
(c)	Heating	2,400	2,400	*Fixed*	*2400*
(d)	Direct wages	6,000	8,000	*semi*	*7000*

3   What is the controllability principle?

4   Feedforward control is based on comparing original targets or actual results with a forecast of future
results.

True   ☐

False   ☑

5   Choose the appropriate words from those highlighted.

The correct approach to budgetary control is to compare **actual/budgeted** results with a budget that has
been flexed to the **actual/budgeted** level of activity.

6   Not all fixed costs are non-controllable in the short term.

True   ☑

False   ☐

7   What is goal congruence (in terms of organisational control systems)?

- A   When the goals of management and employees harmonise with the goals of the organisation as a
whole

B   When the goals of management harmonise with the goals of employees

C   When the work-related goals of management harmonise with their personal goals

D   When an organisation's goals harmonise with those of its customers

8   For each organisation, there is an ideal solution to the conflicts caused by the operation of a budgetary
control system and it is the responsibility of the management accountant to find that solution.

True   ☐

False   ☑

Answers to Quick Quiz

1   cost behaviour patterns
     flex or change

2   (a)   Variable $4,500
     (b)   Semi-variable $10,250
     (c)   Fixed $2,400
     (d)   Semi-variable $7,000

3   The principle that managers should only be held responsible for costs that they have direct control over

4   True

5   actual
     actual

6   True.   Discretionary fixed costs can be raised or lowered at fairly short notice.

7   A.

8   False.   There are no ideal solutions. Management and the management accountant have to develop their own ways of dealing with the conflicts, taking into account the organisation, the business and the personalities involved.

Answers to Questions

11b.1 High-low method

The correct answer is $297,000.

Price levels should be adjusted to a common basis, say index level 100.

(a)

	Output	Total cost $	Cost at price level index = 100 $
High level	90,000 units	209,100 × (100/123)	= 170,000
Low level	60,000 units	201,600 × (100/144)	= 140,000
Variable cost	30,000 units		= 30,000

The variable cost is therefore $1 per unit.

(b)   Use the variable cost to determine the fixed cost.

	$
Total cost of 90,000 units (Index 100)	170,000
Variable cost of 90,000 units (× $1)	90,000
Fixed costs (Index 100)	80,000

(c)   Costs in Year 5 for 85,000 units will be as follows:

	$
Variable costs (Index 100)	85,000
Fixed costs (Index 100)	80,000
Total costs (Index 100)	165,000

At Year 5 price levels (Index 180) = $165,000 × (180/100) = $297,000.

11b.2 Flexible budget

	Budget 200 units $	Budget per unit $	Flexed budget 230 units $	Actual 230 units $	Variance $
Sales	71,400	357	82,110	69,000	13,110 (A)
Variable costs					
Labour	31,600	158	36,340	27,000	9,340 (F)
Material	12,600	63	14,490	24,000	9,510 (A)
	44,200	221	50,830	51,000	
Contribution	27,200	136	31,280	18,000	13,280 (A)
Fixed costs	18,900		18,900	10,000	8,900 (F)
Profit	8,300		12,380	8,000	4,380 (A)

11b.3 Spreadsheets

(a) C2: B2*1.2   C10: @ SUM(C7 ... C9) or = SUM (C7... C9)
     C3: C2*0.65   C11: C3
     C4: C2 + C3   C12: C10 + C11
     C7: C2*0.6   C13: B14
     C8: B2*0.4   C14: C12 + C13

Note that the figures are entered into each cell as either positive or negative and so C4, for example, is calculated by **adding** 1,200 and -780.

(b)

A	B Month 1		C Month 2		D Month 3
Sales	1,000	(+15%)	1,150	(+15%)	1,323
Cost of sales (68%)	680		782		900
Gross profit	320		368		423
Receipts					
Current month (40%)	400		460		529
Previous month (50%)	–		500		575
Two months in arrears (10%)	–		–		100
	400		960		1,204
Payments	(680)		(782)		(900)
	(280)		178		304
Balance b/f	–		(280)		(102)
Balance c/f	(280)		(102)		202

The cash position would be substantially worse if all of the 'what if?' conditions occurred simultaneously. Although the cash balance would become positive during month 3, the closing balance would be much lower. If these conditions were to apply, then management would need to make arrangements to finance a large short-term deficit during months 1 and 2.

(c) C2: B2*1.15
     C3: C2*0.68
     C7: C2*0.4
     C8: B2*0.5
     C9: Blank (but D9 would have B2*0.1)

(d) It would be much easier to conduct sensitivity analysis if the items that are variable were allocated specific cells outside the body of the cash flow table. For example, rows 15–19 could contain the following:

	A	B
15	Cost of sales/sales	0.68
16	Receipts – current month	0.40
17	– 1 month in arrears	0.50
18	– 2 months in arrears	0.10
19	Sales growth	1.15

The formulae in row C would then read as follows:

C2 B2*B19
C3 C2*B15
C7 C2*B16
C8 B2*B17
C9 A2*B18

(Note that B17, for example, is an absolute cell address whereas C2 is a relative cell address.)

Further sensitivity analysis could be conducted simply by changing the values in cells B15–B19, rather than having to rewrite each column each time a variable is changed.

At Year 5 price levels (Index 180) = \$165,000 × (180/100) = \$297,000.

Now try these questions from the Practice Question Bank

Number	Level
Q11.1 – Q11.8	Examination

VARIANCE ANALYSIS

Part D

STANDARD COSTING

In this chapter we will be looking at **standard costs** and **standard costing**.

Standard costing was covered at Certificate level, but we obviously look at the topic in more depth for your studies of this syllabus.

We begin this chapter by reviewing the **main principles of standard costing** in **Section 1**, as well as looking in some detail at the **way in which standard costs are set**

in **Section 2**. **Section 3** then looks at the special case of setting standard costs in a service environment.

Section 4 deals with why costing systems and standard costs must be **reviewed** on a regular basis. **Section 5** provides you with clarification of the **difference between budgets and standards**.

We conclude by addressing some criticisms of standard costing systems in advanced manufacturing environments.

Topic list	Learning outcomes	Syllabus references	Ability required
1 The uses of standard costing	A1(c)(e)	A1(c)(i)	Comprehension
2 Setting standards for manufacturing	A1(c)	A1(c)(i)	Comprehension
3 Setting standards in service industries	A1(c)	A1(c)(ii)	Comprehension
4 Updating standards	A1(c)	A1(c)(i)	Comprehension
5 Budgets and standards compared	A1(c)	A1(c)(i)	Comprehension
6 Criticisms of standard costing	A1(e)	A1(e)(i)	Comprehension
7 Economy, efficiency and effectiveness	A1(c)	A1(c)(ii)	Comprehension

Chapter Overview

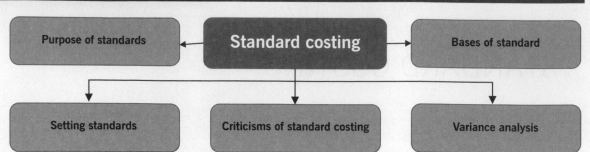

1 The uses of standard costing

Introduction

A **standard** is a **predetermined unit of cost** for inventory valuation, budgeting and control.

1.1 What is a standard cost?

KEY TERM

STANDARD COST is the 'Planned unit cost of a product, component or service'. (*CIMA Official Terminology*)

Standard costs are usually drawn up for a **unit of production** or a unit of service rendered but it is also possible to have a standard cost **per routine task completed**, or a standard cost per £1 of sale. A standard cost per unit of production may include administration, selling and distribution costs but, in many organisations, the assessment of standards is confined to **production costs only**.

1.2 What is standard costing?

KEY TERMS

STANDARD COSTING is a 'Control technique that reports **variances** by comparing actual costs to pre-set standards so facilitating action through **management by exception**'. (*CIMA Official Terminology*)

MANAGEMENT BY EXCEPTION is the 'Practice of focusing on activities which require attention and ignoring those which appear to be conforming to expectations'. (*CIMA Official Terminology*)

A standard cost, when established, is an **average expected unit cost**. Because it is only an average, actual results will **vary** to some extent above and below the average. **Variances** should only be reported where the difference between actual and standard is **significant**.

Standard costing is the **preparation of standard costs** to be used in the following circumstances.

(a) To assist in setting budgets and evaluating managerial performance

(b) To act as a **control device** by establishing standards, highlighting (via **variance analysis**) activities that do not conform to plan and thus alerting management to those areas that may be out of control and in need of corrective action

(c) To enable the principle of '**management by exception**' to be practised

(d) To **provide a prediction of future costs** to be used in decision-making situations

(e) To **value inventories and cost production** for cost accounting purposes; it is an alternative method of valuation to methods like first-in first-out (FIFO), last-in first-out (LIFO) or replacement costing

(f) To **motivate staff and management** by the provision of challenging targets

(g) To provide guidance on improvement of efficiency and minimisation of waste

Although the use of standard costs to simplify the keeping of cost accounting records should not be overlooked, we will be **concentrating** on the **control and variance analysis** aspect of standard costing.

1.3 When standard costing is used

Standard costing can be used in a variety of costing situations.

However, the **greatest benefit** from its use can be gained if there is a **degree of repetition** in the production process. It is therefore most suited to **mass production** and **repetitive assembly** work. However, a standard cost can be calculated **per task if there is a similarity of tasks**. In this way, standard costing can be used by some **service organisations**.

Section summary

Standard costs are established but the actual results will vary. These variances should only be reported where the difference between actual and standard is significant.

2 Setting standards for manufacturing

Introduction

A **standard cost card** shows full details of the standard cost of each product.

2.1 Setting standard costs

A standard cost implies that a standard or target exists for every single element that contributes to the product. Examples include the types, usage and prices of materials and parts, the grades, rates of pay and times for the labour involved, the production methods, tools and so on.

The standard cost for each part of the product is recorded on a **standard cost card**.

KEY TERM

A STANDARD COST CARD is a 'Document or digital record detailing, for each individual product, the standard inputs required for production as well as the standard selling price. Inputs are normally divided into labour, material and overhead categories, and both price and quantity information is shown for each'.

(CIMA Official Terminology)

An example of a standard cost card is given below.

STANDARD COST CARD
Product: the Splodget, No 12345

	Cost	Requirement	Y	Y
Direct materials				
A	Y2.00 per kg	6 kg	12.00	
B	Y3.00 per kg	2 kg	6.00	
	Y4.00 per litre	1 litre	4.00	
Others			2.00	
				24.00
Direct labour				
Grade I	Y4.00 per hour	3 hours	12.00	
Grade II	Y5.40 per hour	5 hours	27.00	
				39.00
Variable production overheads	Y1.00 per hour	8 hours		8.00
Fixed production overheads	Y3.00 per hour	8 hours		24.00
Standard full cost of production				95.00

Standard costs may be used in **both marginal and absorption costing systems**. The card illustrated has been prepared under an absorption costing system, with selling and administration costs excluded from the standard.

The **responsibility for setting** standard costs should be shared between **managers able to provide the necessary information** about levels of expected efficiency, prices and overhead costs. Standard costs are **usually revised once a year** (to allow for the new overheads budget, inflation in prices, and any changes in expected efficiency of materials usage or of labour). However, they may be **revised more frequently if conditions are changing rapidly**.

The standard for each type of cost (labour, material and so on) is made up of a **standard resource price** and a **standard resource usage**.

2.2 Setting standards for materials costs

Direct material prices will be estimated by the purchasing department from their existing knowledge.

- Purchase contracts already agreed
- The forecast movement of prices in the market

- Pricing discussions with regular suppliers
- The availability of bulk purchase discounts

- Quotations and estimates from potential suppliers
- Material quality required

Price inflation can cause difficulties in setting realistic standard prices. Suppose that a material costs £10 per kilogram at the moment and, during the course of the next 12 months, it is expected to go up in price by 20% to £12 per kilogram. **What standard price should be selected?**

- The **current price** of £10 per kilogram
- The **expected price** for the year, say, £11 per kilogram

Either price would be possible, but neither would be entirely satisfactory.

(a)   If the **current price** were used in the standard, the reported price variance would become **adverse** as soon as prices go up, which might be very early in the year. If prices go up gradually rather than in one big jump, it would be difficult to select an appropriate time for revising the standard.

(b)   If an **estimated mid-year price** were used, price variances should be **favourable** in the **first half** of the year and **adverse** in the **second half**, again assuming that prices go up gradually. Management could only really check that in any month, the price variance did not become excessively adverse (or favourable) and that the price variance switched from being favourable to adverse around month six or seven and not sooner.

Standard costing for materials is therefore more **difficult in times of inflation but it is still worthwhile**.

(a)   **Usage** and **efficiency** variances will still be **meaningful**.

(b)   Inflation is **measurable**: there is no reason why its effects cannot be removed from the variances reported.

(c)   Standard costs can be **revised**, as long as this is not done too frequently.

2.3 Setting standards for labour rates

Direct labour rates per hour will be set by discussion with the human resources department and by reference to the payroll and to any agreements on pay rises and/or bonuses with trade union representatives of the employees. A separate average hourly rate or weekly wage will be set for each different labour grade/type of employee (even though individual rates of pay may vary according to age and experience).

2.4 Setting standards for material usage and labour efficiency

To estimate the materials required to make each product (material usage) and also the labour hours required (labour efficiency), **technical specifications** must be prepared for each product by production experts (in either the production department or the work study department).

Material usage and labour efficiency standards are known as **performance standards**.

2.5 Types of performance standard

The setting of standards raises the problem of **how demanding** the standard should be. Should the standard represent a perfect performance or an easily attainable performance? The type of performance standard used can have behavioural implications. There are four types of standard.

Type of standard	Description
Ideal	These are based on **perfect operating conditions**: no wastage, no spoilage, no inefficiencies, no idle time and no breakdowns. Variances from ideal standards are useful for pinpointing areas where a close examination may result in large savings in order to maximise efficiency and minimise waste. However, ideal standards are likely to have an unfavourable motivational impact because reported variances will always be adverse. Employees will often feel that the goals are unattainable and not work so hard.
Attainable	These are based on the hope that a standard amount of work will be carried out efficiently, machines properly operated or materials properly used. **Some allowance is made for wastage and inefficiencies.** If well set, they provide a useful psychological incentive by giving employees a realistic, but challenging, target of efficiency. The consent and co-operation of employees involved in improving the standard are required.
Current	These are based on **current working conditions** (current wastage, current inefficiencies). The disadvantage of current standards is that they do not attempt to improve on current levels of efficiency.
Basic	These are **kept unaltered over a long period of time**, and may be out of date. They are used to show changes in efficiency or performance over a long period of time. Basic standards are perhaps the least useful and least common type of standard in use.

Ideal standards, attainable standards and current standards each have their supporters and it is by **no means clear which of them is preferable**.

Question 12a.1
Performance standards

Learning outcome A1(c)

Which of the following statements is not true?

A   Variances from ideal standards are useful for pinpointing areas where a close examination might result in large cost savings.

B   Basic standards may provide an incentive to greater efficiency even though the standard cannot be achieved.

C   Ideal standards cannot be achieved and so there will always be adverse variances. If the standards are used for budgeting, an allowance will have to be included for these 'inefficiencies'.

D   Current standards or attainable standards are a better basis for budgeting, because they represent the level of productivity that management will wish to plan for.

2.6 Setting standards for variable overheads

Standard variable overhead costs are usually charged to products using a **standard rate per labour hour**.

Where labour hours are to be used as the basis for charging variable overhead costs, the number of standard labour hours for each product will have already been determined when setting the standard labour costs.

Careful analysis of overhead costs will be necessary in order to determine which costs are variable with the selected measure of activity, and which costs are fixed. Examples of overhead costs that might vary with the number of direct labour hours worked include power costs and the cost of lubricating oils. In order to determine the standard variable overhead cost per hour, it will be necessary **to prepare forecasts of the hourly expenditure on each cost separately**. These would then be summed to derive the standard total variable production overhead cost per hour.

2.7 Setting standards for fixed overheads

In a **marginal costing** system there is **no need** to determine a **standard unit rate** for **fixed overheads**, since these are not attributed to individual units, but are treated as **period costs** and are charged directly to the statement of profit or loss.

In an **absorption costing** system the **standard overhead absorption rate** is the **same** as the **predetermined overhead absorption rate**.

The standard overhead absorption rate will depend on the total value of budgeted overheads for the forthcoming period and on the planned activity or production volume for the period.

Production volume will **depend on two factors**.

(a)   **Production capacity** (or '**volume capacity**') measured perhaps in standard hours of output.

(b)   **Efficiency of working**, by labour or machines, allowing for rest time and contingency allowances. This will depend on the type of performance standard to be used (ideal, current, attainable and so on).

Suppose that a department has a workforce of 10 employees, each of whom works a 36-hour week to make standard units, and each unit has a standard production time of 2 hours. The expected efficiency of the workforce is 125%.

(a)   **Budgeted capacity**, in direct labour hours, would be 10 × 36 = 360 production hours per week.

(b)   **Budgeted efficiency** is 125% so that the workforce should take only 1 hour of actual production time to produce 1.25 standard hours of output.

(c)   This means in our example that **budgeted output** is 360 production hours × 125% = 450 standard hours of output per week. At 2 standard hours per unit, this represents production activity or volume of 225 units of output per week.

Output, **capacity** and **efficiency** are interrelated items, and you should check your understanding of them by attempting the following question.

Question 12a.2	Linking capacity, efficiency and output

Learning outcome A1(c)

ABC carries out routine office work in a sales order processing department, and all tasks in the department have been given standard times. There are 40 clerks in the department who work on average 140 hours per month each. The efficiency ratio of the department is 110%.

Required

Calculate the budgeted output in the department.

2.7.1 Capacity levels

When standard absorption costing is used, capacity levels are needed to establish a standard absorption rate for fixed production overhead. Any one of three capacity levels might be used for budgeting.

KEY TERMS

- FULL CAPACITY is 'Output achievable if sales orders, supplies and workforce for example, were all available'.

- PRACTICAL CAPACITY is 'Full capacity less an allowance for known unavoidable volume losses'.

- BUDGETED CAPACITY is 'Standard hours planned for the budget period, taking account of, for example, budgeted sales, workforce and expected efficiency'.   (*CIMA Official Terminology*)

(a) **Full capacity** is the **theoretical** capacity, assuming continuous production without any stoppages due to factors such as machine downtime, supply shortages or labour shortages. Full capacity would be associated with **ideal standards**.

(b) **Practical capacity** acknowledges that **some stoppages are unavoidable**, such as maintenance time for machines, resetting time between jobs and some machine breakdowns. Practical capacity is below full capacity, and would be associated with **attainable standards**.

(c) **Budgeted capacity** is the capacity (labour hours, machine hours) **needed to produce the budgeted output**, and would be associated with **current standards**, which relate to current conditions but may not be representative of normal practical capacity over a longer period of time.

Idle capacity is defined as the **practical capacity** in a period **less the budgeted capacity** measured in standard hours of output. It represents unused capacity that ought to be available, but which is not needed because the budgeted volume is lower than the practicable volume that could be achieved.

2.8 Setting standards for selling price and margin or contribution

As well as standard costs, standard selling prices and standard margins or contributions can be set. The standard selling price will depend on a number of factors including the following:

- Anticipated market demand
- Competing products and competitors' actions
- Manufacturing costs
- Inflation estimates

The standard sales margin or contribution is the difference between the standard total or variable cost and the standard selling price.

Section summary

A **standard cost card** shows full details of the standard cost of each product.

The standard for each type of cost (labour, material and so on) is made up of a **standard resource price** and a **standard resource usage**.

Performance standards are used to set efficiency targets. There are four types: ideal, attainable, current and basic.

3 Setting standards in service industries

Introduction

It can be difficult to apply standard costing in a service environment because of the difficulty in establishing a measurable cost unit and the heterogeneous nature of most services.

3.1 Difficulties in applying standard costing in service environments

Standard costing was originally used in manufacturing environments and a criticism levelled at standard costing was its **apparent lack of applicability in service industries**.

The application of standard costing in service industries does have its problems.

- It can be **difficult to establish a measurable cost unit** for some services.

- In some service organisations **every cost unit will be different or heterogeneous**. For example, each haircut provided in a salon will be different.

- Since the **human influence is so great** in many services, it can be difficult to predict and control the quality of the output and the resources used in its production.

To overcome these problems and enable the application of standard costing for planning and control in service industries, it is therefore necessary to do the following:

(a) **Establish a measurable cost unit**. This is relatively easy in some service organisations. For example, in your earlier studies you will have learned about cost units for transport companies, such as a passenger-mile or a tonne-mile, or for hotels, such as a guest-night. (You might recall that these are referred to as **composite cost units**.)

(b) **Attempt to reduce the heterogeneity of services**. If every service provided to the customer is the same as the last, then it will be possible to set a standard cost for the service and use this to maximise efficiency and reduce waste.

(c) **Reduce the element of human influence**. This can be achieved by swapping machines for humans wherever possible.

3.2 McDonaldization

McDonaldization is a term coined by George Ritzer in his 1993 book *The McDonaldization of Society*. Ritzer analysed the success of the US hamburger chain, and noted that McDonald's principles of operations are now being applied to many sectors of society.

The application of McDonaldization in service industries is **assisting the use of standard costing for cost planning and control** because it overcomes the problems referred to above.

Ritzer identified four dimensions of McDonaldization.

(a) **Calculability**. The content of every McDonald's meal is identical and standardised. Every burger should contain a standard amount of meat, every bun is of the same size and all fries are of the same thickness. **The human element is eliminated as far as possible** in the actual production process in order to make the food in a standard time using standard materials. Human initiative is eliminated in actually putting together the meal at the point of sale through the issuing of standard instructions concerning the content of each type of meal ordered. Thus each meal is a **measurable** standard cost unit for which a **standard cost can be established** and the actual cost can be measured for cost control purposes.

(b) **Control**. Control over the service is achieved in particular by **reducing the human influence**, which can lead to variation in output and quality. Again, machines and technology substitute for humans. Automatic drinks dispensers that measure the exact quantity to be delivered and cash registers that require only one button to be pressed to record the sale of a complete meal are examples of improved control and the reduction of the possibility of human error in the delivery of the service.

(c) **Efficiency**. Ritzer described efficiency as 'the optimum method of getting from one point to another'. Every McDonald's business is organised to ensure maximum efficiency so that the customer can get exactly what they want as quickly as possible. This **increases customer satisfaction and also increases the company's profitability**.

(d) **Predictability**. The McDonald's service is the **same in every outlet throughout the world**, whether a meal is purchased in Shanghai or in London. Again, this helps with the standardisation of the service and the setting of standard costs throughout the organisation.

McDonaldization is an extreme form of rationalisation.

Exam alert

Be prepared to think of sensible criticisms of applying McDonaldization to a given business.

Question 12a.3	McDonaldization of services

Learning outcome A1(c)

State three service industries where McDonaldization could be applied to standardise the delivery of services.

3.3 Diagnostic related groups

The use of standard costing to plan and control costs in the **health service** has been assisted by the development of **diagnostic related groups (DRGs)** or **reference groups**.

DRGs provide a **system of classifying patients** according to their diagnosis, age and length of stay. This classification helps to determine the resources that should be used to treat and care for the patient.

The concept of DRGs was originally developed in the US in order to calculate a **standard cost for each category of patient**. There are more than 500 different possible DRG classifications and the resulting standard cost can be used for billing purposes by the healthcare insurance industry. This means that the insurance company pays the hospital a **standard rate for each DRG** and the hospital would then need to contain its costs below the payment received.

The use of DRGs **enables the principles of standard costing to be applied in the health service in order to maximise efficiency and minimise waste**.

The main criticism of the DRG approach is that it does not take account of the fact that **each patient is different**. Patients may require a different level of treatment depending on the progression of the illness, their general health and so on. A patient may require more or less than the standard treatment but the **hospital is paid a fixed rate** for the treatment of a **given DRG**. The hospital may be **reluctant to provide anything other than the standard** treatment.

Section summary

It can be difficult to apply standard costing in a service environment because of the difficulty in establishing a measurable cost unit and the heterogeneous nature of most services.

The four dimensions of McDonaldization are calculability, control, efficiency and predictability.

Diagnostic related groups (DRGs) or reference groups are used in the healthcare industry to group together patients with similar lengths of stay and resource requirements. Standard costs can be established for each DRG which can be used for cost planning and control.

4 Updating standards

Introduction

When an organisation introduces a system of standard costing, it is quite possible that the standards initially set will not be the most accurate reflection of what occurs 'on average'. **Initial standards** may need **substantial revision** in the early period of a standard costing system's life before they are really useful measures for control purposes.

4.1 The need to update standards

The evolution of standards does not stop after a couple of accounting periods. Standards must be **continuously reviewed** to ensure that they **mirror** what is **currently happening** and that they are the **most accurate 'average'**.

Out of date standards will produce **variances** that are **illogical bases** for planning, control, decision making or performance evaluation. Current operational performance cannot be compared to out of date standards.

4.2 Improvement of the standard setting process

Standard setting procedures may be refined and extended to enable more accurate standards to be set.

(a)   **Work study** methods may be established within the organisation. These enable accurate estimates of labour time to be made.

(b)   The introduction of **computerised information systems** provides more reliable standards.

With CAD/CAM (computer-aided design/computer-aided manufacture) systems the planning of manufacturing requirements can be **computerised**, with the useful spin-off that standard costs can also be constructed by computer, thus saving administrative time and expense while providing far more accurate standards.

4.3 Revision of standards

In practice, standard costs are usually revised **once a year** to allow for the new overheads budget, inflation in prices and wage rates, and any changes in expected efficiency of material usage, labour or machinery.

Some argue that standards should be revised **as soon as there is any change in the basis upon which they were set**. Clearly, for example, if a standard is based on the cost of a material that is no longer available or the use of equipment that has been replaced, it is meaningless to compare actual performance using the new material and equipment with the old standard.

Frequent changes in standards can cause **problems**.

(a)   They may become **ineffective as motivators and measures of performance**, since it may be perceived that target setters are constantly 'moving the goal posts'.

(b)   The **administrative effort** may be too time consuming (although the introduction of computer systems renders this objection less forceful).

The most **suitable approach** would therefore appear to be a policy of revising the standards **whenever changes of a permanent and reasonably long-term nature occur**, but not in response to temporary 'blips' in price or efficiency.

BPP
LEARNING MEDIA

Section summary

In general, standards should be **revised** whenever changes of a permanent or reasonably long-term nature occur.

5 Budgets and standards compared

Introduction

You will recall from your earlier studies that a **budget** is a **quantified monetary plan** for a **future period**, which **managers will try to achieve**. Its major function lies in **communicating plans** and **co-ordinating activities** within an organisation.

On the other hand, a **standard** is a **carefully predetermined quantity target** that can be **achieved in certain conditions**.

Budgets and standards are **similar** in the following ways:

(a) They both involve looking to the future and **forecasting** what is likely to happen given a certain set of circumstances.

(b) They are both **used for control purposes**. A budget aids control by setting financial targets or limits for a forthcoming period. Actual achievements or expenditures are then compared with the budgets and action is taken to correct any variances where necessary. A standard also achieves control by comparison of actual results against a predetermined target.

As well as being similar, **budgets and standards are interrelated**. For example, a standard unit production cost can act as the basis for a production cost budget. The unit cost is multiplied by the budgeted activity level to arrive at the budgeted expenditure on production costs.

There are, however, **important differences between budgets and standards**.

Budgets	Standards
Gives planned total aggregate costs for a function or cost centre	Shows the unit resource usage for a single task, for example the standard labour hours for a single unit of production
Can be prepared for all functions, even where output cannot be measured	Limited to situations where repetitive actions are performed and output can be measured
Expressed in money terms	Need not be expressed in money terms, for example a standard rate of output does not need a financial value put on it

Section summary

Budgets and standards are very similar and interrelated, but there are important differences between them.

6 Criticisms of standard costing

Introduction

Standard costing is most appropriate in a **stable, standardised** and **repetitive** environment and one of the main objectives of standard costing is to ensure that **processes conform to standards,** that they do not vary and that **variances** are **eliminated**. This may seem **restrictive** and **inhibiting** in the business environment of the early 21st century.

6.1 Standard costing in the modern business environment

Critics of standard costing have argued that traditional variance analysis has limited applicability in the modern business environment. The modern business environment is characterised by a need to respond to **customer demands** for **immediate availability of products, shortening product life cycles and higher quality standards** and continuous improvement.

6.2 Standard costing and new technology

Standard costing has **traditionally** been associated with **labour-intensive** operations, but can it be **applied to capital-intensive production too?**

(a) In an environment that includes advanced manufacturing technology (AMT), the **cost of labour** is a **small proportion** of total costs and so labour rate and efficiency variances will have little control value.

(b) **Fixed costs** represent a **significant** proportion of total costs but there is some **doubt** over the **relevance** of the information provided by **fixed overhead volume variances**.

(c) **Material usage** variances should be virtually non-existent given the accuracy afforded by machines as opposed to human operators.

(d) It is quite possible that, with AMT, **variable overheads** are **incurred** in relation to machine time rather than labour time, and standard costs should reflect this where appropriate.

In an AMT environment, **machine efficiency variances** will be of **value**, however, and standards will still be needed for costing, pricing and budgeting purposes.

Question 12a.4   Variance analysis and product quality

Learning outcome A1(e)

AB has been receiving an increasing number of customer complaints about a general weakness in the quality of its products in recent months. The company believes that its future success is dependent on product quality and it is therefore determined to improve it.

Required

Describe the contribution that variance analysis can make towards the aim of improved product quality.

6.3 Other problems with using standard costing in today's environment

(a) Variance analysis concentrates on only a **narrow range of costs**, and does not give sufficient attention to issues such as quality and customer satisfaction.

(b) Standard costing places **too much emphasis on direct labour costs**. Direct labour is only a small proportion of costs in the modern manufacturing environment and so this emphasis is not appropriate.

(c)   Many of the variances in a standard costing system focus on the control of **short-term variable costs**. In most modern manufacturing environments, the majority of costs, including direct labour costs, tend to be fixed in the short run.

(d)   The use of standard costing relies on the existence of **repetitive operations** and relatively **homogeneous** output. Nowadays many organisations are continually forced to respond to customers' changing requirements, with the result that output and operations are not so repetitive.

(e)   Standard costing systems were **developed** when the **business environment** was more **stable** and **less prone to change**. The current business environment is more dynamic and it is not possible to assume stable conditions.

(f)   Standard costing systems **assume** that **performance to standard is acceptable**. Today's business environment is more focused on continuous improvement.

(g)   Most standard costing systems produce **control statements weekly or monthly**. The modern manager needs much more prompt control information in order to function efficiently in a dynamic business environment.

This long list of criticisms of standard costing may lead you to believe that such systems have little use in today's business environment. However, standard costing systems can be adapted to remain useful.

6.4 The role in modern business of standards and variances

(a)   **Planning**. Even in an environment where the focus is on continual improvement, budgets will still need to be quantified. For example, the planned level of prevention and appraisal costs needs to be determined. Standards can be set, such as returns of a particular product should not exceed one per cent of deliveries during a budget period.

(b)   **Control**. Cost and mix changes from plan will still be relevant in many processing situations.

(c)   **Decision making**. Existing standards can be used as the starting point in the construction of a cost for a new product.

(d)   **Improvement and change**. Variance trends can be monitored over time.

Section summary

Critics argue that standard costing is most appropriate in a standard, stable and repetitive environment and therefore is of limited usefulness in the modern business environment. However, standard costing can be adapted to remain useful for cost planning and control.

7 Economy, efficiency and effectiveness

Introduction

The three Es (economy, efficiency and effectiveness) are important in any type of business but are generally associated with measuring the performance of public sector organisations.

7.1 Not-for-profit organisations (NFPOs)

Not-for-profit organisations (NFPOs) include private sector organisations such as charities, churches and much of the public sector. Commercial organisations generally have market competition and the **profit motive** to guide the process of managing resources economically, efficiently and effectively. However, NFPOs cannot by definition be judged by profitability.

7.2 How can performance be measured?

(a) **Economy**. This, fairly obviously, means spending money more frugally.

(b) **Efficiency**. This means getting out as much as possible for what goes in. It is a measure of input in relation to output. This measure links economy to effectiveness.

(c) **Effectiveness**. This means getting done, by means of economy and efficiency, what was supposed to be done. This is an output measure and measures what the organisation achieves in relation to its objectives. The key to effectiveness is to find the optimum level of expenditure to achieve a given objective. The problem is that it is difficult to measure effectiveness. For example, locking up young people for petty crime may be effective in the short term but it is expensive. It may be more 'effective' to provide youth recreational facilities to treat the cause of petty crime.

Section summary

Economy, efficiency and effectiveness are associated with measuring the performance of not-for-profit organisations.

Chapter Summary

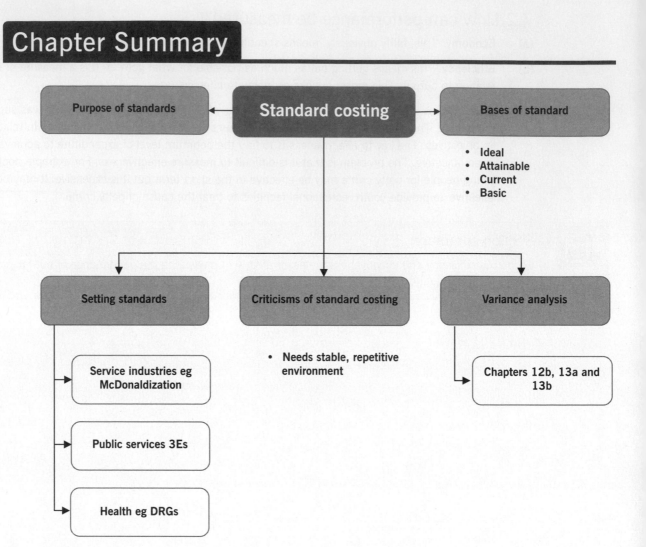

Standard costing

Purpose of standards ← Standard costing → Bases of standard
- Ideal
- Attainable
- Current
- Basic

Setting standards

Criticisms of standard costing

Variance analysis

Setting standards →
- Service industries eg McDonaldization
- Public services 3Es
- Health eg DRGs

Criticisms of standard costing
- Needs stable, repetitive environment

Variance analysis →
- Chapters 12b, 13a and 13b

Quick Quiz

1   Which one of the following statements is true?

    A   Standard costing is not well suited to mass production.

    B   Standard costing can never be used by service organisations.

    C   Standard costing is most suited to repetitive assembly work.

    D   If there is a degree of repetition in the production process, standard costing should not be used.

2   Match the types of performance standard to the correct descriptions.

Performance standards	Descriptions
(a) Ideal	(1) If well set, can provide a useful psychological incentive
(b) Attainable	(2) Do not attempt to improve on current levels of efficiency
(c) Current	(3) Least common type of standard in use
(d) Basic	(4) Likely to have an unfavourable motivational effect

3   An attainable standard is based on perfect operating conditions.

    True   ☐

    False   ☐

4   State Ritzer's four dimensions of McDonaldization.

5   Variance control reports should be produced either promptly or accurately.

    True   ☐

    False   ☐

6   Standards should be amended every time there is a change in price or efficiency.

    True   ☐

    False   ☐

7   Fill in the gaps using the following words.

standards/budgets/aggregate total/budgets/single task/standards

    (a)   Budgets are prepared for .... costs; standards are for a ....

    (b)   .... can be prepared for all functions; .... are only suitable for repetitive actions where output can be measured.

    (c)   .... are expressed in money terms; .... need not be expressed in money terms.

8   During the month of June, CTF plc produced the following items.

	Units	Standard minutes per unit
Item C	7,200	5
Item T	5,970	8
Item F	6,600	11

What was the output in standard hours?

Answers to Quick Quiz

1   C   Standard costing is most appropriate in a stable, standardised and repetitive environment.

2   (a)   4
     (b)   1
     (c)   2
     (d)   3

3   False. An ideal standard is based on perfect operating conditions.

4   Calculability, control, efficiency, predictability

5   False. They should be produced promptly **and** accurately.

6   False. It is probably best to revise standards whenever changes of a permanent or long-term nature occur.

7   (a)   aggregate total
            single task
     (b)   budgets
            standards
     (c)   budgets
            standards

8

	Units	Standard minutes per unit	Standard hours
Item C	7,200	5	600
Item T	5,970	8	796
Item F	6,600	11	1,210
			2,606

Answers to Questions

12a.1 Performance standards

The correct answer is B.

Statement B is describing ideal standards, not basic standards.

12a.2 Linking capacity, efficiency and output

Capacity	=	$40 \times 140 = 5,600$ hours per month
Efficiency	=	110%
Budgeted output	=	$5,600 \times 110\% = 6,160$ standard hours of work per month

---

12a.3 McDonaldization of services

Possible service industries where McDonaldization could be applied include the following:

- Exhaust and tyre fitting centres, where a detailed manual dictates the activities of operatives for each standard type of fitting

- Call centres, where a machine provides the caller with numbered options from which to select the desired service and the person that answers is using a standard script

- Laboratory testing of blood samples, where the procedures to be followed by laboratory technicians can be standardised

---

12a.4 Variance analysis and product quality

As variance analysis is generally expressed in terms of purely quantitative measures, such as quantity of raw materials used and price per unit of quantity, issues of **quality** would **appear** to be **excluded** from the reporting process. Quality would appear to be an excuse for spending more time, say, or buying more expensive raw materials.

Variance analysis, however, **can** be used to enhance product quality and to keep track of quality control information. This is because variance analysis measures both the **planned use** of **resources** and the **actual use** of **resources** in order to **compare** the two.

Variance analysis can be **adapted** to take account of quality issues as follows:

(a) Variance analysis reports should routinely include **measures such as defect rates**. Although zero defects will be most desirable, such a standard of performance may not be reached at first. However, there should be an expected rate of defects: if this is exceeded, then management attention is directed to the excess.

(b) The **absolute number of defects** should be measured **and their type**. If caused by certain materials and components this can shed light on, say, a favourable materials price variance which might have been caused by substandard materials being purchased more cheaply. Alternatively, if the defects are caused by shoddy assembly work this can shed light on a favourable labour efficiency variance if quality is being sacrificed for speed.

(c) It should also be possible to provide **financial measures for the cost of poor quality**. These can include direct costs such as the wages of inspection and quality control staff, the cost of time in rectifying the defects, and the cost of the materials used in rectification.

(d) Measures could be built into materials price and variance analysis, so that the **materials price variance** as currently reported includes a **factor reflecting the quality of materials purchased**.

 BPP
LEARNING MEDIA

BASIC VARIANCE ANALYSIS

 In earlier studies you will have covered the calculation of basic cost and sales variances. Because students often find variance analysis quite difficult (although, really, it isn't) we are going to **go over the basic cost variances** again in detail in **Sections 1 to 5**.

We will be **analysing sales variances in more detail** than you did in earlier studies, and will be looking at the selling price and sales volume variances in **Section 6**. **Section 7** looks at **non-production cost variances**.

This is a **key chapter** in terms of topic **examinability**. Variance calculation and interpretation lends itself well to objective testing or longer calculation-based questions.

In **Chapters 13a and 13b** we will build on your revision of the basics in this chapter and cover a number of **additional variance analysis topics**. These include splitting the material usage and labour efficiency variances into mix and yield components, and preparing statements to reconcile budgeted profit to actual profit using variances.

Topic list	Learning outcomes	Syllabus references	Ability required
1 Variances	A1(c)	A1(c)(iii)	Analysis
2 Direct material cost variances	A1(c)	A1(c)(iii)	Analysis
3 Direct labour cost variances	A1(c)	A1(c)(iii)	Analysis
4 Variable overhead variances	A1(c)	A1(c)(iii)	Analysis
5 Fixed overhead variances	A1(c)	A1(c)(v)(vi)	Analysis
6 Sales variances	A1(c)	A1(c)(vii)	Analysis
7 Non-production cost variances	A1(c)	A1(c)(iii)	Analysis

Chapter Overview

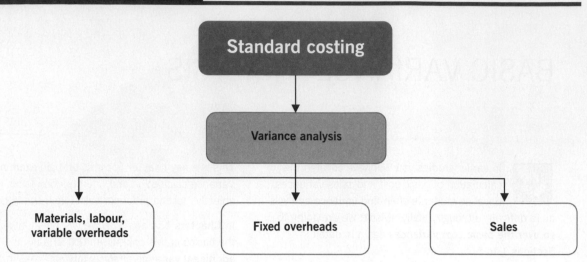

1 Variances

Introduction

The process by which the total difference between standard and actual results is analysed is known as variance analysis.

KEY TERMS

A VARIANCE is the 'Difference between planned, budgeted, or standard cost and the actual cost incurred. The same comparisons may be made for revenues'.

VARIANCE ANALYSIS is the 'Evaluation of performance by means of variances, whose timely reporting should maximise the opportunity for managerial action'. (*CIMA Official Terminology*)

When **actual results are better than expected results**, we have a **favourable** variance (F). If, on the other hand, **actual results are worse than expected results**, we have an **adverse** variance (A).

Variances can be divided into three main groups.

- Variable cost variances

    - Direct material
    - Direct labour
    - Variable production overhead

- Fixed production overhead variances

- Sales variances

Section summary

A favourable variance occurs when actual results are better than expected results. An adverse variance occurs when actual results are worse than expected results.

2 Direct material cost variances

Introduction

The direct material total variance is the difference between what the output actually cost and what it should have cost, in terms of material.

KEY TERMS

The DIRECT MATERIAL TOTAL VARIANCE is 'A measurement of the difference between the standard material cost of the output produced and the actual cost incurred'.

The DIRECT MATERIAL PRICE VARIANCE is 'The difference between the actual price paid for purchased materials and their standard cost'.

The DIRECT MATERIAL USAGE VARIANCE 'Measures efficiency in the use of material, by comparing the standard material usage for actual production with actual material used, the difference valued at standard cost'. (*CIMA Official Terminology*)

The **direct material total variance** can be **divided into two sub-variances**.

(a) **The direct material price variance**

This is the difference between what the actual amount of material purchased **should have** cost and what it **did** cost.

(b) **The direct material usage variance**

This is the difference between the standard quantity of materials that **should have been used** for the number of units **actually produced**, and the **actual quantity** of materials **used**, valued at the standard cost per unit of material. In other words, it is the difference between how much material should have been used and how much material was used, valued at standard cost.

 Example: direct material variances

Product X has a standard direct material cost as follows:

10 kilograms of material Y at £10 per kilogram = £100 per unit of X.

During period 4, 1,000 units of X were manufactured, using 11,700 kilograms of material Y which cost £98,600.

Required

Calculate the following variances.

(a) The direct material total variance
(b) The direct material price variance
(c) The direct material usage variance

Solution

(a) **The direct material total variance**

This is the difference between what 1,000 units should have cost and what they did cost.

	£
1,000 units should have cost (× £100)	100,000
but did cost	98,600
Direct material total variance	1,400 (F)

The variance is favourable because the units cost less than they should have cost.

Now we can break down the direct material total variance into its two constituent parts: the direct material price variance and the direct material usage variance.

(b) **The direct material price variance**

This is the difference between what 11,700 kg should have cost and what 11,700 kg did cost.

	£
11,700 kg of Y should have cost (× £10)	117,000
but did cost	98,600
Material Y price variance	18,400 (F)

The variance is favourable because the material cost less than it should have.

(c) **The direct material usage variance**

This is the difference between how many kilograms of Y should have been used to produce 1,000 units of X and how many kilograms were used, valued at the standard cost per kilogram.

1,000 units should have used (× 10 kg)	10,000 kg
but did use	11,700 kg
Usage variance in kg	1,700 kg (A)
× standard cost per kilogram	× £10
Usage variance in £	£17,000 (A)

The variance is adverse because more material **was used** than **should have been used**.

(d)   **Summary**

	£
Price variance	18,400 (F)
Usage variance	17,000 (A)
Total variance	1,400 (F)

2.1 Materials variances and opening and closing inventory

Suppose that a company uses raw material P in production, and that this raw material has a standard price of $3 per metre. During one month, 6,000 metres are bought for $18,600, and 5,000 metres are used in production. At the end of the month, inventory will have been increased by 1,000 metres. In variance analysis, the problem is to decide the **material price variance**. Should it be calculated on the basis of **materials purchased** (6,000 metres) or on the basis of **materials used** (5,000 metres)?

The answer to this problem depends on **how closing inventories** of the raw materials will be **valued**.

(a)   If they are valued at **standard cost** (1,000 units at $3 per unit), the price variance is calculated on material **purchases** in the period.

(b)   If they are valued at **actual cost** (FIFO) (1,000 units at $3.10 per unit), the price variance is calculated on materials **used in production** in the period.

A **full standard costing system** is usually in operation and therefore the price variance is usually calculated on **purchases** in the period. The variance on the full 6,000 metres will be written off to the costing statement of profit or loss, even though only 5,000 metres are included in the cost of production.

There are two main **advantages** in extracting the material price variance at the time of **receipt**.

(a)   If variances are extracted at the time of receipt they will be **brought to the attention of managers earlier** than if they are extracted as the material is used. If it is necessary to correct any variances, then management action can be more timely.

(b)   Since variances are extracted at the time of receipt, **all inventories will be valued at standard price**. This is administratively easier and it means that all issues from inventories can be made at standard price. If inventories are held at actual cost it is necessary to calculate a separate price variance on each batch as it is issued. Since issues are usually made in a number of small batches, this can be a time-consuming task, especially with a manual system.

Question 12b.1	Materials price variance

Learning outcome A1(c)

What is the material price variance based on the information in Paragraph 2.1?

A $3,100 (A)
B $600 (A)
C $3,100 (F)
D $600 (F)

Section summary

The direct material total variance is the sum of the direct material price variance and the direct material usage variance.

3 Direct labour cost variances

Introduction

The direct labour total variance is the difference between what the output should have cost and what it did cost, in terms of labour.

KEY TERMS

The **DIRECT LABOUR TOTAL VARIANCE** 'Indicates the difference between the standard direct labour cost of the output which has been produced and the actual direct labour cost incurred'.

The **DIRECT LABOUR RATE VARIANCE** 'Indicates the actual cost of any change from the standard labour rate of remuneration'.

The **DIRECT LABOUR EFFICIENCY VARIANCE** 'Indicates the standard labour cost of any change from the standard level of labour efficiency'.   (*CIMA Official Terminology*)

The calculation of direct labour variances is very similar to the calculation of direct material variances.

The **direct labour total variance** can be **divided into two sub-variances**.

(a)   **The direct labour rate variance**

This is similar to the direct material price variance. It is the difference between the **standard cost** and the **actual cost** for the **actual number of hours paid for**.

In other words, it is the difference between what labour **should have** cost and what it **did cost**.

(b)   **The direct labour efficiency variance**

This is similar to the direct material usage variance. It is the difference between the **hours** that **should have been worked** for the number of **units actually produced**, and the **actual** number of **hours worked**, valued at the **standard rate** per hour.

In other words, it is the difference between how many hours should have been worked and how many hours were worked, valued at the standard rate per hour.

Example: direct labour variances

The standard direct labour cost of product X is as follows:

2 hours of grade Z labour at £5 per hour = £10 per unit of product X

During period 4, 1,000 units of product X were made, and the direct labour cost of grade Z labour was £8,900 for 2,300 hours of work.

Required

Calculate the following variances.

(a)   The direct labour total variance
(b)   The direct labour rate variance
(c)   The direct labour efficiency (productivity) variance

Solution

(a) **The direct labour total variance**

This is the difference between what 1,000 units **should have cost** and what they **did** cost.

	£
1,000 units should have cost (× £10)	10,000
but did cost	8,900
Direct labour total variance	1,100 (F)

The variance is favourable because the units cost less than they should have done.

Again we can analyse this total variance into its two constituent parts.

(b) **The direct labour rate variance**

This is the difference between what 2,300 hours should have cost and what 2,300 hours did cost.

	£
2,300 hours of work should have cost (× £5 per hr)	11,500
but did cost	8,900
Direct labour rate variance	2,600 (F)

The variance is favourable because the labour cost less than it should have cost.

(c) **The direct labour efficiency variance**

1,000 units of X should have taken (× 2 hrs)	2,000 hours
but did take	2,300 hours
Efficiency variance in hours	300 hours (A)
× standard rate per hour	×£5
Efficiency variance in £	£1,500 (A)

The variance is adverse because more hours were worked than should have been worked.

(d) **Summary**

	£
Rate variance	2,600 (F)
Efficiency variance	1,500 (A)
Total variance	1,100 (F)

3.1 Idle time variance

Idle time occurs when no actual work is done but the workforce still has to be paid for the time at work. The idle time variance is (hours paid – hours worked) × standard direct labour rate per hour.

A company may operate a costing system in which **any** idle time is **recorded**. Idle time may be caused by machine breakdowns or not having work to give to employees, perhaps because of bottlenecks in production or a shortage of orders from customers. Time paid for without any work being done is unproductive and therefore inefficient. In variance analysis, **idle time is usually an adverse efficiency variance**. If, however, idle time is built into the cost budget, it could be a favourable variance.

KEY TERM

The DIRECT LABOUR IDLE TIME VARIANCE 'occurs when the hours paid exceed the hours worked and there is an extra cost caused by this idle time'. (*CIMA Official Terminology*)

When idle time is recorded separately, it is helpful to provide control information that identifies the cost of idle time separately and, in variance analysis, there will be an idle time variance **as a separate part of the**

total labour efficiency variance. The remaining **efficiency variance** will then relate only to the productivity of the labour force during the **hours spent actively working**.

Example: labour variances with idle time

Refer to the standard cost data in the previous example called direct labour variances. During period 5, 1,500 units of product X were made and the cost of grade Z labour was £17,500 for 3,080 hours. During the period, however, there was a shortage of customer orders and 100 hours were recorded as idle time.

Required

Calculate the following variances.

(a)   The direct labour total variance
(b)   The direct labour rate variance
(c)   The idle time variance
(d)   The direct labour efficiency variance

Solution

(a)   **The direct labour total variance**

	£
1,500 units of product X should have cost (× £10)	15,000
but did cost	17,500
Direct labour total variance	2,500 (A)

Actual cost is greater than standard cost. The variance is therefore adverse.

(b)   **The direct labour rate variance**

The rate variance is a comparison of what the hours paid should have cost and what they did cost.

	£
3,080 hours of grade Z labour should have cost (× £5)	15,400
but did cost	17,500
Direct labour rate variance	2,100 (A)

Actual cost is greater than standard cost. The variance is therefore adverse.

(c)   **The idle time variance**

The idle time variance is the hours of idle time, valued at the standard rate per hour.

Idle time variance = 100 hours (A) × £5 = £500 (A)

It is an **adverse** variance because it was not built into the cost budget.

(d)   **The direct labour efficiency variance**

The efficiency variance considers the hours **actively worked** (the difference between hours paid for and idle time hours). In our example, there were (3,080 – 100) = 2,980 hours when the labour force was not idle. The variance is calculated by taking the amount of output produced (1,500 units of product X) and comparing the time it should have taken to make them, with the actual time spent **actively** making them (2,980 hours). Once again, the variance in hours is valued at the standard rate per labour hour.

1,500 units of product X should take (× 2 hours)	3,000 hours
but did take (3,080 – 100)	2,980 hours
Direct labour efficiency variance in hours	20 hours (F)
× standard rate per hour	× £5
Direct labour efficiency variance in £	£100 (F)

(e)   **Summary**

	£
Direct labour rate variance	2,100 (A)
Idle time variance	500 (A)
Direct labour efficiency variance	100 (F)
Direct labour total variance	2,500 (A)

KEY POINTS

(a)   Remember that, if idle time is recorded, the actual hours used in the **efficiency variance** calculation are the **hours worked and not the hours paid for**.

(b)   If there is a budgeted level of idle time and the actual level is less than the budgeted level, the idle time variance will be favourable.

(c)   Some organisations might experience 'expected' or 'normal' idle time at less busy periods, perhaps because demand is seasonal or irregular (but they wish to maintain and pay a constant number of workers). In such circumstances, the standard labour rate may include an allowance for the cost of the expected idle time. Only the impact of unexpected/abnormal idle time would be included in the idle time variance.

Question 12b.2   Labour variances

Learning outcome A1(c)

Growler Ltd is planning to make 100,000 units per period of product AA. Each unit of AA should require 2 hours to produce, with labour being paid £11 per hour. Attainable work hours are less than clock hours, so 250,000 hours have been budgeted in the period.

Actual data for the period was:

Units produced	120,000
Direct labour cost	£3,200,000
Clock hours	280,000

Required

Calculate the following variances.

(a)   Labour rate variance
(b)   Labour efficiency variance
(c)   Idle time variance

Question 12b.3   Idle time and efficiency variances

Learning outcome A1(c)

There is seasonal demand for CH Ltd's product N. Average idle time during control period 11 is expected to be 10% of hours paid. An allowance for this idle time is included in the standard labour rate, which is €15.30 before the allowance. Standard (productive) time per unit is six labour hours.

During control period 11, 1,800 units of N were manufactured, 13,500 hours were paid for and 12,420 hours were actually worked.

What are the idle time and labour efficiency variances?

	Idle time	Labour efficiency
A	€4,590 (F)	€27,540 (A)
B	€4,590 (A)	€27,540 (F)
C	€4,131 (A)	€24,786 (A)
D	€4,131 (F)	€24,786 (F)

Section summary

The direct labour total variance is the sum of the direct labour rate variance and the direct labour efficiency variance.

The **idle time variance** is the number of hours of idle time valued at the standard rate per hour.

Idle time variance = (hours paid – hours worked) × standard direct labour rate per hour

4 Variable overhead variances

Introduction

The variable overhead total variance is the difference between what the output should have cost and what it did cost, in terms of variable overheads. You should be able to follow the same pattern for calculating the variances as you did for the material and labour variances.

Suppose that the variable production overhead cost of product X is as follows:

2 hours at £1.50 = £3 per unit

During period 6, 400 units of product X were made. The labour force worked 820 hours, of which 60 hours were recorded as idle time. The variable overhead cost was £1,230.

Calculate the following variances.

(a) The variable overhead total variance
(b) The variable overhead expenditure variance
(c) The variable overhead efficiency variance

Since this example **relates to variable production costs**, the total variance is **based on actual units of production**. (If the overhead had been a **variable selling cost**, the variance would be **based on sales volumes**.)

	£
400 units of product X should cost (× £3)	1,200
but did cost	1,230
Variable production overhead total variance	30 (A)

In many variance reporting systems, the variance analysis goes no further, and expenditure and efficiency variances are not calculated. However, the adverse variance of £30 may be explained as the **sum of two factors**.

(a) The hourly rate of spending on variable overheads was higher than it should have been; that is, there is an **expenditure variance**.

(b) The labour force worked inefficiently, and took longer to make the output than it should have done. This means that spending on variable overhead was higher than it should have been; in other words, there is an **efficiency (productivity) variance**. The variable overhead efficiency variance is exactly the same, in hours, as the direct labour efficiency variance, and occurs for the same reasons.

It is usually assumed that **variable overheads are incurred during active working hours**, but are not incurred during idle time (for example, the machines are not running, therefore power is not being consumed, and no indirect materials are being used). This means in our example that although the labour force was paid for 820 hours, they were actively working for only 760 of those hours and so variable overhead spending occurred during 760 hours.

(a) **The variable overhead expenditure variance**

This is the **difference between the amount of variable overhead that should have been incurred in the actual hours actively worked, and the actual amount of variable overhead incurred.**

	£
760 hours of variable overhead should cost (× £1.50)	1,140
but did cost	1,230
Variable overhead expenditure variance	90 (A)

(b) **The variable overhead efficiency variance**

If you already know the direct **labour efficiency variance**, the variable overhead efficiency variance is **exactly the same in hours**, but **priced at the variable overhead rate per hour**. In our example, the efficiency variance would be as follows:

400 units of product X should take (× 2 hours)	800 hours
but did take (active hours)	760 hours
Variable overhead efficiency variance in hours	40 hours (F)
× standard rate per hour	× £1.50
Variable overhead efficiency variance in £	£60 (F)

(c) **Summary**

	£
Variable overhead expenditure variance	90 (A)
Variable overhead efficiency variance	60 (F)
Variable overhead total variance	30 (A)

Exam skills

Learn the following.

Material price, labour rate or variable overhead expenditure variance		**Material usage or labour/variable overhead efficiency variance**	
Actual kg or hours should have cost	X	X units should have used/taken (kg/hours)	X
But did cost	X	But did use/take	X
	X A/F		X
		× standard rate per kg/hour	× X
			X A/F

Section summary

Variances	What they measure
Price (material) Rate (labour) Expenditure (variable overhead)	Measure the difference between what should have been paid for the actual quantity of materials/labour hours/variable overheads and what was paid.
Usage (material) Efficiency (labour and variable overhead)	Measure the difference between what the quantities of material used or hours taken should have been and what was actually used or taken. These differences are converted into monetary values by multiplying by the standard price.

5 Fixed overhead variances

Introduction

Fixed overhead variances are the same as material and labour variances, in that they **measure the difference between what the output should have cost and what it did cost**. However, there is a fundamental difference underlying their calculation.

Fixed costs do not vary with changes in output (provided output remains within the relevant range). This is a statement of fact, since it describes the way in which fixed costs behave. The **budgeted or planned level of fixed costs should therefore be the same whatever the level of output**. So if an organisation budgets fixed costs to be £5,000 for budgeted output of 100 units, the expected fixed costs if actual output is 120 units should still be £5,000.

Contrast this with standard material and labour costs, which vary according to the actual level of output (because they are variable costs).

In this sense, there is no equivalent to a usage or efficiency variance when dealing with fixed overheads.

5.1 Fixed overhead variances and marginal costing

If the **actual fixed cost differs** from the **planned fixed cost**, the only reason can be that **expenditure** was **higher or lower than planned**.

The **fixed overhead expenditure variance** is therefore the **difference between planned expenditure and actual expenditure**. This is the only fixed overhead variance that occurs if marginal costing is being used.

5.2 Fixed overhead variances and absorption costing

The calculation of fixed overhead variances is slightly more complicated when absorption costing is used.

The fixed overhead total variance in an absorption costing system may be broken down into two parts as usual.

- An **expenditure variance**

- A **volume variance**. This in turn may be split into two parts.

  - A **volume efficiency variance**
  - A **volume capacity variance**

In an absorption costing system, **fixed overhead variances** are an attempt to **explain** the **reasons for any under- or over-absorbed overhead**.

Remember that the absorption rate is calculated as budgeted fixed overhead ÷ budgeted level of activity.

Generally, the level of activity used in the overhead absorption rate will be units of production or hours of activity. More often than not, if just one product is being produced, the level of activity is in terms of units produced.

You should remember from your earlier studies that if the budgeted overhead expenditure or the budgeted activity level or both are incorrect, then we will have under- or over-absorbed overhead.

5.3 Expenditure variance

The fixed overhead **expenditure variance** measures the under or over absorption caused by the **actual overhead expenditure being different from budget**.

5.4 Volume variance

As we have already stated, the fixed overhead volume variance is made up of the following sub-variances.

- Fixed overhead efficiency variance
- Fixed overhead capacity variance

These variances arise if the denominator (ie the budgeted activity level) is incorrect.

The fixed overhead efficiency and capacity variances measure the under- or over-absorbed overhead caused by the **actual activity level** being different from the budgeted activity level used in calculating the absorption rate.

There are two reasons why the **actual activity** level may be different from the **budgeted activity level** used in calculating the absorption rate.

(a)   The workforce may have worked more or less efficiently than the standard set. This deviation is measured by the **fixed overhead efficiency variance**.

(b)   The hours worked by the workforce could have been different to the budgeted hours (regardless of the level of efficiency of the workforce) because of overtime and strikes etc. This deviation from the standard is measured by the **fixed overhead capacity variance**.

5.5 How to calculate the variances

FIXED OVERHEAD TOTAL VARIANCE is the difference between fixed overhead incurred and fixed overhead absorbed (the under- or over-absorbed fixed overhead).

FIXED OVERHEAD EXPENDITURE VARIANCE is the difference between the overhead that should have been incurred and that which was incurred. It is calculated as the difference between the budgeted fixed overhead expenditure and actual fixed overhead expenditure.

FIXED OVERHEAD VOLUME VARIANCE is a measure of the over or under absorption of fixed overhead costs caused by actual production volume differing from that budgeted. It is calculated as the difference between actual and budgeted production/volume multiplied by the standard absorption rate per **unit**.

FIXED OVERHEAD VOLUME EFFICIENCY VARIANCE is the difference between the number of hours that actual production should have taken, and the number of hours actually taken (that is, worked) multiplied by the standard absorption rate per **hour**.

FIXED OVERHEAD VOLUME CAPACITY VARIANCE is the difference between budgeted (planned) hours of work and the actual hours worked, multiplied by the standard absorption rate per **hour**.

You should now be ready to work through an example to demonstrate all of the fixed overhead variances.

Example: fixed overhead variances

Suppose that a company budgets to produce 1,000 units of product E during August. The expected time to produce a unit of E is 5 hours, and the budgeted fixed overhead is $20,000. The standard fixed overhead cost per unit of product E will therefore be 5 hours at $4 per hour (= $20 per unit). Actual fixed overhead expenditure in August turns out to be $20,450. The labour force manages to produce 1,100 units of product E in 5,400 hours of work.

Required

Calculate the following variances.

(a)   The fixed overhead total variance
(b)   The fixed overhead expenditure variance
(c)   The fixed overhead volume variance
(d)   The fixed overhead volume efficiency variance
(e)   The fixed overhead volume capacity variance

Solution

(a)   **Fixed overhead total variance**

	$
Fixed overhead incurred	20,450
Fixed overhead absorbed (1,100 units × $20 per unit)	22,000
Fixed overhead total variance (= under-/over-absorbed overhead)	1,550 (F)

The variance is favourable because more overheads were absorbed than budgeted.

(b)   **Fixed overhead expenditure variance**

	$
Budgeted fixed overhead expenditure	20,000
Actual fixed overhead expenditure	20,450
Fixed overhead expenditure variance	450 (A)

The variance is adverse because expenditure was greater than budgeted.

(c)   **Fixed overhead volume variance**

The production volume achieved was greater than expected. The fixed overhead volume variance measures the difference at the standard rate.

	$
Actual production at standard rate (1,100 × $20 per unit)	22,000
Budgeted production at standard rate (1,000 × $20 per unit)	20,000
Fixed overhead volume variance	2,000 (F)

The variance is favourable because output was greater than expected.

(i)   The labour force may have worked efficiently, and produced output at a faster rate than expected. Since overheads are absorbed at the rate of $20 per unit, more will be absorbed if units are produced more quickly. This **efficiency variance** is exactly the same in hours as the direct labour efficiency variance, but is valued in $ at the standard absorption rate for fixed overhead.

(ii)   The labour force may have worked longer hours than budgeted, and therefore produced more output, so there may be a **capacity variance**.

(d)   **Fixed overhead volume efficiency variance**

The volume efficiency variance is calculated in the same way as the labour efficiency variance.

1,100 units of product E should take (× 5 hours)	5,500 hours
but did take	5,400 hours
Fixed overhead volume efficiency variance in hours	100 hours (F)
× standard fixed overhead absorption rate per hour	× $4
Fixed overhead volume efficiency variance in $	$400 (F)

The labour force has produced 5,500 standard hours of work in 5,400 actual hours and so output is 100 standard hours (or 20 units of product E) higher than budgeted for this reason and the variance is **favourable**.

(e)   **Fixed overhead volume capacity variance**

The volume capacity variance is the difference between the budgeted hours of work and the actual active hours of work (excluding any idle time).

Budgeted hours of work	5,000 hours
Actual hours of work	5,400 hours
Fixed overhead volume capacity variance	400 hours (F)
× standard fixed overhead absorption rate per hour	× $4
Fixed overhead volume capacity variance in $	$1,600 (F)

Since the labour force worked 400 hours longer than planned, we should expect output to be 400 standard hours (or 80 units of product E) higher than budgeted and hence the variance is **favourable**.

The variances may be summarised as follows:

	$
Expenditure variance	450 (A)
Efficiency variance	400 (F)
Capacity variance	1,600 (F)
Over-absorbed overhead (total variance)	1,550 (F)

Exam skills

In general, a favourable cost variance will arise if actual results are less than expected results. Be aware, however, of the **fixed overhead volume variance** and the **fixed overhead volume capacity variance** which give rise to favourable and adverse variances in the following situations.

(a)   A favourable fixed overhead volume variance occurs when actual production is **greater than** budgeted (planned) production

(b)   An adverse fixed overhead volume variance occurs when actual production is **less than budgeted** (planned) production

(c)   A favourable fixed overhead volume capacity variance occurs when actual hours of work are **greater than** budgeted (planned) hours of work

(d)   An adverse fixed overhead volume capacity variance occurs when actual hours of work are **less than** budgeted (planned) hours of work

Question 12b.4

Fixed overhead variances

Learning outcome A1(c)

In an absorption costing system the fixed overhead total variance can be analysed into the fixed overhead expenditure variance and the fixed overhead volume variance.

Explain briefly the meaning of each of these three variances in an absorption costing system.

Question 12b.5

Variance calculations

Learning outcome A1(c)

Brian produces and sells one product only, the Blob, and the standard cost for one unit is as follows:

	£
Direct material A – 10 kilograms at £20 per kg	200
Direct wages – 5 hours at £6 per hour	30
Fixed overhead	50
Total standard cost	280

The fixed overhead included in the standard cost is based on an expected monthly output of 900 units.

During April the actual results were as follows:

Production	800 units
Material A	7,800 kg used, costing £159,900
Direct wages	4,200 hours worked for £24,150
Fixed overhead	£47,000

Required

(a) Calculate material price and usage variances.
(b) Calculate labour rate and efficiency variances.
(c) Calculate fixed overhead expenditure and volume variances.

Question 12b.6

Capacity variance

Learning outcome A1(c)

A manufacturing company operates a standard absorption costing system. Last month 25,000 production hours were budgeted and the budgeted fixed production overhead cost was $125,000. Last month the actual hours worked were 24,000 and the standard hours for actual production were 27,000.

What was the fixed production overhead capacity variance for last month?

A $5,000 adverse
B $5,000 favourable
C $10,000 adverse
D $10,000 favourable

5.6 Variance analysis and activity based costing (ABC)

The activity based costing (ABC) approach assumes that overheads are variable, based on the activity level.

Example: variances and ABC

Suppose that a company budgets to produce 1,000 units of product E during August. All overheads are associated with the number of production runs, and the expected number of production runs is 500. The budgeted fixed overhead is $20,000. Actual fixed overhead expenditure in August turns out to be $20,450, and 1,100 units of product E were produced in 540 production runs.

Required

Calculate the fixed overhead total variance and its sub-variances adopting the traditional approach and then calculate the efficiency and expenditure variances using an ABC approach.

Solution

Applying the **traditional fixed overhead cost variance analysis** gives the following results.

(a)   **Fixed overhead total variance**

	$
Fixed overhead incurred	20,450
Standard cost (1,100 units × ($20,000/1,000))	22,000
Fixed overhead total variance	1,550 (F)

(b)   **Fixed overhead expenditure variance**

	$
Budgeted fixed overhead expenditure	20,000
Actual fixed overhead expenditure	20,450
Fixed overhead expenditure variance	450 (A)

(c)   **Fixed overhead volume variance**

	$
Actual production at standard rate (1,100 × $20 per unit)	22,000
Budgeted production at standard rate (1,000 × $20 per unit)	20,000
Fixed overhead volume variance	2,000 (F)

Adopting an **ABC approach** gives the following results.

The **efficiency variance** highlights the impact of undertaking **more or fewer activities** (production runs) than budget.

	$
Number of production runs should have been (1,100 × 0.5 per unit)	550
but was	540
	10 (F)
× standard cost per run ($20,000/500)	× 40
Efficiency variance	400 (F)

The **expenditure variance** highlights the effect of **paying more or less than budget** for the **actual** number of **activities** (production runs) undertaken.

	$
540 production runs should have cost (× $40 per run)	21,600
but did cost	20,450
Expenditure variance	1,150 (F)

Section summary

The only fixed overhead variance that occurs in a marginal costing system is the fixed overhead expenditure variance.

In an absorption costing system, the fixed overhead total variance is the sum of the fixed overhead expenditure variance and the fixed overhead volume variance. The fixed production overhead volume variance can be further subdivided into an **efficiency** and a **capacity** variance.

6 Sales variances

Introduction

The **selling** (or **sales**) **price variance** is the difference between what revenue should have been for the quantity sold and the actual revenue.

6.1 Selling price or sales price variance

KEY TERM

The SALES PRICE VARIANCE is the 'Change in revenue caused by the actual selling price differing from that budgeted'. *(CIMA Official Terminology)*

Suppose that the standard selling price of product X is £15. Actual sales in Year 3 were 2,000 units at £15.30 per unit. The selling price variance is calculated as follows:

	£
Sales revenue from 2,000 units should have been (× £15)	30,000
but was (× £15.30)	30,600
Selling price variance	600 (F)

The variance is favourable because the price was higher than expected.

6.2 Sales volume variance

The sales volume variance in units is calculated as the difference between the **actual units sold** and the **budgeted quantity**. This variance in units can be valued in one of three ways.

(a) At the **standard gross profit margin per unit**. This is the **sales volume profit variance** and it measures the change in profit (in an absorption costing system) caused by the sales volume differing from budget.

(b) At the **standard contribution per unit**. This is the **sales volume contribution variance** and it measures the change in profit (in a marginal costing system) caused by the sales volume differing from budget.

(c) At the **standard revenue per unit**. This is the **sales volume revenue variance** and it measures the change in sales revenue caused by sales volume differing from that budgeted. (This is rarely used, so you should only use it if a question specifically requires it.)

Suppose that a company budgets to sell 8,000 units of product J for $12 per unit. The standard variable cost per unit is $4 and the standard full cost is $7 per unit. Actual sales were 7,700 units, at $12.50 per unit.

The sales volume variance in units is 300 units adverse (8,000 units budgeted – 7,700 units sold). The variance is **adverse** because actual sales volume was less than budgeted. The sales volume variance in units can be evaluated in the three ways described above.

(a)   Sales volume profit variance   = 300 units × standard gross profit margin per unit
                                            = 300 units × $(12 – 7)
                                            = $1,500 (A)

(b)   Sales volume contribution variance   = 300 units × standard contribution per unit
                                            = 300 units × $(12 – 4)
                                            = $2,400 (A)

(c)   Sales volume revenue variance   = 300 units × standard revenue per unit
                                            = 300 units × $12
                                            = $3,600 (A)

Note that the sales volume profit variance (in an absorption costing system) and the sales volume contribution variance (in a marginal costing system) can be derived from the sales volume revenue variance, if the profit mark-up percentage and the contribution to sales (C/S) ratio respectively are known.

In our example, the profit mark-up percentage is 41.67% ($5/$12) and the C/S ratio is 66.67% ($8/$12).

Therefore the sales volume profit variance and the sales volume contribution variance, derived from the sales volume revenue variance, are as follows:

Sales volume profit variance = $3,600 (A) × 41.67% = $1,500 (A), as above

Sales volume contribution variance = $3,600 (A) × 66.67% = $2,400 (A), as above

Question 12b.7	Sales variance

Learning outcome A1(c)

Jasper has the following budget and actual figures for Year 4.

	Budget	Actual
Sales units	600	620
Selling price per unit	€30	€29

Standard full cost of production = €28 per unit. Standard variable cost of production = €19 per unit.

Calculate the following sales variances.

(a)   Selling price variance
(b)   Sales volume profit variance
(c)   Sales volume contribution variance
(d)   Sales volume revenue variance

6.3 The significance of sales variances

The possible **interdependence** between sales price and sales volume variances should be obvious to you. A **reduction** in the sales **price** might **stimulate** bigger sales **demand**, so that an adverse sales price variance might be counterbalanced by a favourable sales volume variance. Similarly, a price rise would give a favourable price variance, but possibly at the cost of a fall in demand and an adverse sales volume variance.

It is therefore important in analysing an unfavourable sales variance that the overall consequence should be considered; that is, has there been a counterbalancing favourable variance as a direct result of the unfavourable one?

Question 12b.8	Sales variances for professional services

Learning outcome A1(c)

A management consultancy has an IT division that operates a standard absorption costing system. Details from the latest period are as follows:

Standard charge per hour of client services	£180
Standard absorption cost per hour of client service provided	£110
Budgeted hours to be charged to clients per period	780
Actual hours charged to clients during period	730
Actual amount billed to clients during period	£139,800

Calculate the following variances for the period.

(a)   The selling price variance
(b)   The sales volume profit variance

Section summary

The **selling** (or **sales**) **price variance** is the difference between what revenue should have been for the quantity sold and the actual revenue.

The sales volume variance in units is the difference between the actual units sold and the budgeted quantity. This variance in units can be valued in one of three ways: in terms of standard revenue, standard gross margin or standard contribution margin.

7   Non-production cost variances

Introduction

Non-production costs, such as administration and selling/distribution costs, must **also** be **monitored** and **controlled**.

Some selling/distribution costs may **vary with units sold**, and variances for such costs can be calculated in much the **same way as variable production overhead variances**.

Simple **expenditure variances** may be all that is required for monitoring and controlling **most non-production costs**, however, such as administration.

Section summary

Most **non-production cost variances** can be monitored and controlled using simple expenditure variances.

Chapter Summary

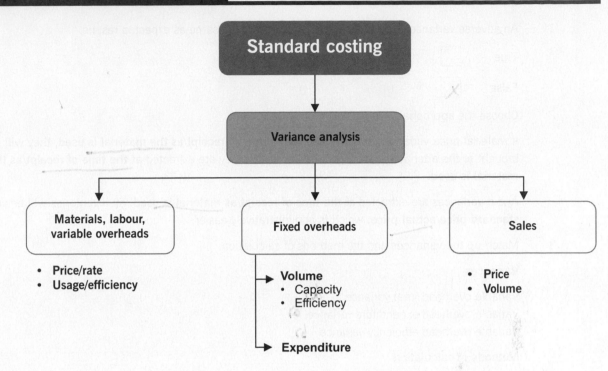

Standard costing

Variance analysis

Materials, labour, variable overheads

- Price/rate
- Usage/efficiency

Fixed overheads

- **Volume**
  - Capacity
  - Efficiency
- **Expenditure**

Sales

- Price
- Volume

Quick Quiz

1   An adverse variance occurs when actual results are the same as expected results.

      True   ☐

      False   ☒

2   Choose the appropriate words from those highlighted.

      If material price variances are extracted **at the time of receipt/as the material is used**, they will be brought to the attention of managers earlier than if they are extracted **at the time of receipt/as the material is used**.

      And if variances are extracted **at the time of receipt/as material is used**, all inventories will be valued at **standard price/actual price**, which is administratively easier.

3   Match up the variances and the methods of calculation.

      Variances

      Variable overhead total variance   d)
      Variable overhead expenditure variance   a)
      Variable overhead efficiency variance   b)

      Methods of calculation

      (a)   The difference between the amount of variable overhead that should have been incurred in the actual hours worked, and the actual amount of variable overhead incurred

      (b)   The labour efficiency variance in hours valued at the standard variable overhead rate per hour

      (c)   The difference between budgeted variable overhead expenditure and actual overhead expenditure

      (d)   The difference between what actual production should have cost in terms of variable overhead, and what it did cost

      (e)   The difference between the labour hours that should have been worked for the actual level of output, and the labour hours actually paid, valued at the standard variable overhead rate per hour

4   Which of the following statements about the fixed production overhead volume variance is true?

      A   It is the same in a standard marginal costing system as in a standard absorption costing system.
      B   It does not exist in a standard absorption costing system.
    • C   It does not exist in a standard marginal costing system.
      D   It is the difference between budgeted overhead expenditure and actual overhead expenditure.

5   Fill in the blank.

      standard gross profit margin per unit

      Sales volume profit variance = (actual sales volume – budgeted sales volume) × ....

6   Which of the following is not a suitable basis for valuing the sales volume variance?

      A   Selling price
      B   Contribution
    • C   Absorption rate
      D   Profit

7   HMF plc uses standard absorption costing. In June, the following information was recorded.

	Budget	Actual
Output and sales (units)	17,400	16,400
Selling price per unit	£25	£30
Variable cost per unit	£15	£15
Total fixed overheads	$42,500	$45,800

The sales price variance for June was:

A $87,000 favourable

• B $82,000 favourable

C $82,000 adverse

D $131,200 adverse

Answers to Quick Quiz

1   False. It occurs when actual results are worse than expected results.

2   at the time of receipt
as the material is used
at the time of receipt
standard price

3   Total variance (d)
Expenditure variance (a)
Efficiency variance (b)

4   C   This variance does not exist in a standard marginal costing system.

5   Standard profit per unit

6   C   All others are specifically mentioned in the syllabus.

7   B

	£
Sales revenue from 16,400 units should have been (× £25)	410,000
but was (× £30)	492,000
Selling price variance	82,000 (F)

Answers to Questions

12b.1 Materials price variance

The correct answer is B.

The price variance would be calculated as follows:

	$
6,000 metres of material P purchased should cost (× $3)	18,000
but did cost	18,600
Price variance	600 (A)

12b.2 Labour variances

The information means that clock hours have to be multiplied by 200,000/250,000 (80%) in order to arrive at a realistic efficiency variance.

(a)   **Labour rate variance**

	£'000
280,000 hours should have cost (× £11)	3,080
but did cost	3,200
Labour rate variance	120 (A)

(b)   **Labour efficiency variance**

120,000 units should have taken (× 2 hours)	240,000 hours
but did take (280,000 × 80%)	224,000 hours
Variance in hours	16,000 hours (F)
× standard rate per hour	× £11
Labour efficiency variance	£176,000 (F)

(c)   **Idle time variance**

280,000 × 20%   56,000 hours
                                                                    × £11
                                                                 £616,000 (A)

12b.3 Idle time and efficiency variances

The correct answer is A.

The basic standard rate per hour must be increased to allow for idle time. The revised standard hourly rate is €15.30/0.9 or €17.

Variances are now calculated at this revised rate.

Idle time should have been (10% × 13,500 hours paid)	1,350 hours
but was (13,500 – 12,420)	1,080 hours
	270 hours (F)
× standard rate per hour worked	× €17
Idle time variance	£4,590 (F)

Efficiency variance

1,800 units should have taken (× 6 hours)	10,800 hours
but did take	12,420 hours
	1,620 hours (A)
× standard rate per hour worked	× €17
Efficiency variance	€27,540 (A)

Options C and D have been evaluated at the original standard rate of €15.30.

12b.4 Fixed overhead variances

Fixed overhead total variance

The fixed overhead total variance in an absorption costing system evaluates the **amount of under- or over-absorbed** fixed production **overhead** for the period. If the overhead is **over absorbed**, then the fixed overhead total variance will be **favourable**. If the overhead is **under absorbed**, then the variance will be **adverse**.

The other two variances sum to the fixed overhead total variance and they attempt to evaluate the reason why the fixed production overhead was under or over absorbed.

Fixed overhead expenditure variance

The expenditure variance is the **under or over absorption caused by** the **expenditure** on overheads **being different from that budgeted**. The variance is calculated as the difference between the budgeted expenditure for the period and the actual expenditure. If the **actual expenditure exceeds** the **budgeted** expenditure, then this potentially leads to under absorption and the variance is **adverse**. If the actual expenditure is lower than budgeted, then over absorption could result and the variance is favourable.

Fixed overhead volume variance

The volume variance is the **under or over absorption caused by** the **volume of activity being different from that budgeted**. The variance is calculated as the difference between budgeted and actual activity, multiplied by the standard overhead absorption rate per unit of activity. If the **actual activity** is **lower than budgeted**, then this could lead to under absorption and the variance is **adverse**. If the actual activity is higher than budgeted, the potential over absorption means that the variance is favourable.

12b.5 Variance calculations

(a) **Material price variance**

	£
7,800 kg should have cost (× £20)	156,000
but did cost	159,900
Price variance	3,900 (A)

Material usage variance

800 units should have used (× 10 kg)	8,000 kg
but did use	7,800 kg
Usage variance in kg	200 kg (F)
× standard cost per kilogram	× £20
Usage variance in £	£4,000 (F)

(b) **Labour rate variance**

	£
4,200 hours should have cost (× £6)	25,200
but did cost	24,150
Rate variance	1,050 (F)

Labour efficiency variance

800 units should have taken (× 5 hours)	4,000 hours
but did take	4,200 hours
Efficiency variance in hours	200 hours (A)
× standard rate per hour	× £6
Labour efficiency variance in £	£1,200 (A)

(c) **Fixed overhead expenditure variance**

	£
Budgeted expenditure (£50 × 900)	45,000
Actual expenditure	47,000
Expenditure variance	2,000 (A)

Fixed overhead volume variance

	£
Budgeted production at standard rate (900 × £50)	45,000
Actual production at standard rate (800 × £50)	40,000
Volume variance	5,000 (A)

12b.6 Capacity variance

The correct answer is A.

Standard fixed overhead absorption rate per hour = $125,000/25,000 = $5 per hour

Fixed overhead volume capacity variance

Budgeted hours of work	25,000 hours
Actual hours of work	24,000 hours
Fixed overhead volume capacity variance	1,000 hours (A)
× standard fixed overhead absorption rate per hour	× $5
Fixed overhead volume capacity variance in $	$ 5,000 (A)

Remember that the capacity variance represents part of the over/under absorption of overheads. As the company worked fewer hours than budgeted (and the standard fixed overhead absorption rate is calculated using budgeted hours) this will result in an under absorption of overheads.

12b.7 Sales variance

(a)
	£
Sales revenue for 620 units should have been (× £30)	18,600
but was (× £29)	17,980
Selling price variance	620 (A)

(b)
Budgeted sales volume	600 units
Actual sales volume	620 units
Sales volume variance in units	20 units (F)

Sales volume profit variance = 20 units × €(30 – 28) = €40(F)

(c)   Sales volume contribution variance = 20 units × €(30 – 19) = €220(F)

(d)   Sales volume revenue variance = 20 units × €30 = €600(F)

In this question you were asked to calculate both the **sales volume profit** variance and the **sales volume contribution** variance to give you some practice. However, the two variances would **never** be found together in the **same system in a real situation**. Either a **marginal** costing system is used, in which case the sales volume **contribution** variance is calculated, or an **absorption** costing system is used, in which case a sales volume **profit** variance is calculated.

12b.8 Sales variances for professional services

(a)
	£
Sales revenue for 730 hours should have been (× £180)	131,400
but was	139,800
Selling price variance	8,400 (F)

(b)
Budgeted sales volume	780 hours
Actual sales volume	730 hours
Sales volume variance in units	50 hours
× standard profit per unit (£(180 – 110))	× £70
Sales volume profit variance	£3,500 (A)

FURTHER VARIANCE ANALYSIS

Chapter 12 should have **refreshed your memory** on the basics of standard costing and those variances which you should have covered in your earlier studies.

We begin this chapter by looking at how we can reconcile between **budgeted profit** and **actual profit**, using the range of variances we covered in Chapter 12b to draw up an **operating statement**.

Section 2 considers the impact on variance analysis of using **marginal costing**, which we covered at various points in the last chapter but will consolidate here.

Section 3 is about what we call the '**backwards approach**' to variance analysis. Basically, this means that you are provided with the variances and have to calculate standard and actual data.

The chapter then moves on to more advanced variance analysis. When a product requires **two or more materials** in its make-up the materials usage variance can be split into a **materials mix variance** and a **materials yield variance**. Likewise, labour efficiency variances can be split into a **labour mix variance** and a **labour yield variance**. Don't be put off by these new terms. The **basic principle of variance calculation** covered in the previous chapter **still applies**: an actual result is compared with an original standard result.

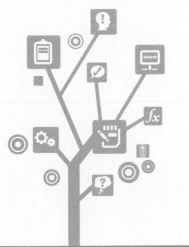

Topic list	Learning outcomes	Syllabus references	Ability required
1 Operating statements	A1(c)	A1(c)(iii)(v)	Application
2 Variances in a standard marginal costing system	A1(c)	A1(c)(iii)(v)	Analysis
3 Working backwards approach to variance analysis	A1(c)	A1(c)(iii)(v)	Analysis
4 Materials mix and yield variances	A1(c)	A1(c)(iv)	Analysis
5 Labour mix and yield variances	A1(c)	A1(c)(iv)	Analysis
6 Sales mix and quantity variances	A1(c)	A1(c)(viii)	Analysis
7 Planning and operational variances	A1(c)	A1(c)(ix)	Analysis

Chapter Overview

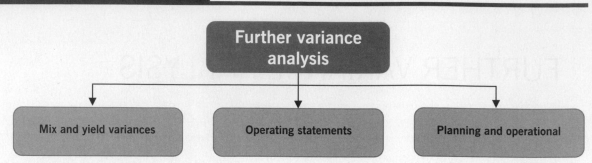

1 Operating statements

Introduction

So far, we have considered how variances are calculated without considering how they combine to **reconcile the difference between budgeted profit and actual profit** during a period. This reconciliation is usually presented as a report to senior management at the end of each control period. The report is called an **operating statement** or statement of variances.

KEY TERM

An OPERATING STATEMENT is a report for management, normally prepared on a regular basis showing actual costs and revenues, usually comparing actual with budget and showing variances.

An extensive example will now be introduced, both to revise the variance calculations from Chapter 12b and to show how to combine them into an operating statement.

Example: variances and operating statements

Sydney manufactures one product, and the entire product is sold as soon as it is produced. There are no opening or closing inventories and work in progress is negligible. The company operates a standard absorption costing system and analysis of variances is made every month. The standard cost card for the product, a boomerang, is as follows:

STANDARD COST CARD – BOOMERANG

		£
Direct materials	0.5 kg at £4 per kg	2.00
Direct wages	2 hours at £2.00 per hour	4.00
Variable overheads	2 hours at £0.30 per hour	0.60
Fixed overhead	2 hours at £3.70 per hour	7.40
Standard cost		14.00
Standard profit		6.00
Standing selling price		20.00

Selling and administration expenses are not included in the standard cost, and are deducted from profit as a period charge.

Budgeted output for the month of June Year 7 was 5,100 units. Actual results for June Year 7 were as follows:

Production of 4,850 units was sold for £95,600.
Materials consumed in production amounted to 2,300 kg at a total cost of £9,800.
Labour hours paid for amounted to 8,500 hours at a cost of £16,800.
Actual operating hours amounted to 8,000 hours.
Variable overheads amounted to £2,600.
Fixed overheads amounted to £42,300.
Selling and administration expenses amounted to £18,000.

Required

Calculate all variances and prepare an operating statement for the month ended 30 June Year 7.

Solution

(a)

	£
2,300 kg of material should cost (× £4)	9,200
but did cost	9,800
Material price variance	600 (A)

(b)

4,850 boomerangs should use (× 0.5 kg)	2,425 kg
but did use	2,300 kg
Material usage variance in kg	125 kg (F)
× standard cost per kg	× £4
Material usage variance in £	£500 (F)

(c)

	£
8,500 hours of labour should cost (× £2)	17,000
but did cost	16,800
Labour rate variance	200 (F)

(d)

4,850 boomerangs should take (× 2 hours)	9,700 hours
but did take (active hours)	8,000 hours
Labour efficiency variance in hours	1,700 hours (F)
× standard cost per hour	× £2
Labour efficiency variance in £	£3,400 (F)

(e) Idle time variance 500 hours (A) × £2   £1,000 (A)

(f)

	£
8,000 hours incurring variable o/hd expenditure should cost (× £0.30)	2,400
but did cost	2,600
Variable overhead expenditure variance	200 (A)

(g) Variable overhead efficiency variance in hours is the same as the labour efficiency variance:

1,700 hours (F) × £0.30 per hour   £510 (F)

(h)

	£
Budgeted fixed overhead (5,100 units × 2 hours × £3.70)	37,740
Actual fixed overhead	42,300
Fixed overhead expenditure variance	4,560 (A)

(i)

	£
Actual production at standard rate (4,850 units × £7.40)	35,890
Budgeted production at standard rate (5,100 units × £7.40)	37,740
Fixed overhead volume variance	1,850 (A)

(j)

Revenue from 4,850 boomerangs should be (× £20)	97,000
but was	95,600
Selling price variance	1,400 (A)

(k)   In order to reconcile the budget and actual profit, the sales volume variance in units must be valued at the standard profit per unit.

Budgeted sales volume	5,100 units
Actual sales volume	4,850 units
Sales volume variance in units	250 units (A)
× standard profit per unit	× £6
Sales volume profit variance in £	£1,500 (A)

There are several ways in which an operating statement may be presented. Perhaps the most common format is one that reconciles budgeted profit to actual profit. In this example, **sales and administration costs will be introduced at the end of the statement**, so that we shall **begin with 'budgeted profit before sales and administration costs'**.

Sales variances are reported first, and the **total of the budgeted profit and the two sales variances** results in a figure for '**actual sales minus the standard cost of sales**'. The **cost variances** are then reported, and an **actual profit** (before sales and administration costs) calculated. **Sales and administration costs** are then **deducted** to reach the **actual profit**.

SYDNEY – OPERATING STATEMENT JUNE YEAR 7

	(F) £	(A) £	£	£
Budgeted profit before sales and administration costs (5,100 × £6)				30,600
Sales volume profit variance				1,500 (A)
Budgeted profit from actual sales				29,100
Selling price variance				1,400 (A)
Actual sales minus the standard cost of sales				27,700
Cost variances				
Material price		600		
Material usage	500			
Labour rate	200			
Labour efficiency	3,400			
Labour idle time		1,000		
Variable overhead expenditure		200		
Variable overhead efficiency	510			
Fixed overhead expenditure		4,560		
Fixed overhead volume		1,850		
	4,610	8,210		3,600 (A)
Actual profit before sales and admin costs				24,100
Sales and administration costs				18,000
Actual profit, June year 7				6,100

Check	£	£
Sales		95,600
Materials	9,800	
Labour	16,800	
Variable overhead	2,600	
Fixed overhead	42,300	
Sales and administration	18,000	
		89,500
Actual profit		6,100

Section summary

An **operating statement/statement of variances** is a report, usually to senior management, at the end of a control period, reconciling budgeted profit for the period to actual profit.

2 Variances in a standard marginal costing system

Introduction

At various stages in Chapter 12b we looked at the ways in which variances in a marginal costing system differ from those in an absorption costing system. In this section we will summarise these differences and look at how an operating statement would appear in a marginal costing system.

2.1 How marginal costing variances differ from absorption costing variances

If an organisation uses **standard marginal costing** instead of standard absorption costing, there will be two differences in the way the variances are calculated.

(a) In marginal costing, fixed costs are not absorbed into product costs and so there are no fixed cost variances to explain any under or over absorption of overheads. There will, therefore, be **no fixed overhead volume variance**. There will be a fixed overhead expenditure variance which is calculated in exactly the same way as for absorption costing systems.

(b) The **sales volume variance in units** will be valued at **standard contribution margin** (sales price per unit minus variable costs of sale per unit). It will be called the **sales volume contribution variance**.

KEY TERM

The SALES VOLUME CONTRIBUTION VARIANCE is a 'Measure of the effect on contribution of not achieving the budgeted volume of sales'.   (*CIMA Official Terminology*)

Question 13a.1   Impact of costing system on variances

Learning outcome A1(c)

What is the monetary difference between absorption costing and marginal costing sales volume variances?

A   Variance in units × selling price per unit
B   Variance in units × contribution per unit
C   Variance in units × fixed overhead absorption rate per unit
D   Sales volume × fixed overhead absorption rate per unit

2.2 Preparing a marginal costing operating statement

Returning once again to the example of Sydney, the variances in a system of standard marginal costing would be as follows:

(a) There is no fixed overhead volume variance.

(b) The standard contribution per unit of boomerang is £(20 – 6.60) = £13.40 and so the sales volume contribution variance of 250 units (A) is valued at (× £13.40) = £3,350 (A).

The other variances are unchanged. However, this operating statement differs from an absorption costing operating statement in the following ways.

(a) It **begins with the budgeted contribution** (£30,600 + budgeted fixed production costs £37,740 = £68,340) or 5,100 units × £13.40 per unit.

(b) The subtotal before the analysis of cost variances is **actual sales** (£95,600) **less the standard variable cost of sales** (4,850 × £6.60) = £63,590.

(c) **Actual contribution** is highlighted in the statement.

(d) Budgeted fixed production overhead is adjusted by the fixed overhead expenditure variance to show the **actual fixed production overhead expenditure**.

Therefore a **marginal costing** operating statement might look like this.

SYDNEY – OPERATING STATEMENT JUNE YEAR 7

	£	£	£
Budgeted contribution			68,340
Sales volume contribution variance			3,350 (A)
Budgeted contribution from actual sales			64,990
Selling price variance			1,400 (A)
Actual sales minus the standard variable cost of sales			63,590
Variable cost variances	(F)	(A)	
	£	£	
Material price		600	
Material usage	500		
Labour rate	200		
Labour efficiency	3,400		
Labour idle time		1,000	
Variable overhead expenditure		200	
Variable overhead efficiency	510		
	4,610	1,800	
			2,810 (F)
Actual contribution			66,400
Budgeted fixed production overhead		37,740	
Expenditure variance		4,560 (A)	
Less: actual fixed production overhead			(42,300)
actual profit before sales and administration costs			24,100
Less sales and administration costs			(18,000)
Actual profit			6,100

Notice that the actual profit is the same as the profit calculated by standard absorption costing because there were no changes in inventory levels. Absorption costing and marginal costing do not normally produce an identical profit figure.

Question 13a.2

Operating statement

Learning outcome A1(c)

MilBri, a manufacturing firm, operates a standard marginal costing system. It makes a single product, LI, using a single raw material AN.

Standard costs relating to LI have been calculated as follows:

Standard cost schedule – LI

	Per unit
	£
Direct material, AN, 100 kg at £5 per kg	500
Direct labour, 10 hours at £8 per hour	80
Variable production overhead, 10 hours at £2 per hour	20
	600

The standard selling price of an LI is £900 and MilBri produce 1,020 units a month. Budgeted fixed production overheads are £40,000 per month.

During December, 1,000 units of LI were produced and sold. Relevant details of this production are as follows:

Direct material AN

90,000 kg costing £720,000 were bought and used.

Direct labour

8,200 hours were worked during the month and total wages were £63,000.

Variable production overhead

The actual cost for the month was £25,000.

Fixed production overhead

The actual expenditure for the month was £41,400.

Each LI was sold for £975.

Required

Calculate the following for the month of December and present the results in an operating statement that reconciles the budgeted contribution with the actual gross profit for the month.

(a)   Variable production cost variance
(b)   Direct labour cost variance, analysed into rate and efficiency variances
(c)   Direct material cost variance, analysed into price and usage variances
(d)   Variable production overhead variance, analysed into expenditure and efficiency variances
(e)   Selling price variance
(f)   Sales volume contribution variance
(g)   Fixed production overhead expenditure variance

2.3 The inventory adjustment

If **actual sales and production volumes** are **different**, there will be a **closing inventory** value in the actual profit calculation. If these inventories are **valued at actual cost** rather than standard cost, an **inventory adjustment** must be made in **the operating statement**.

Inventory adjustment =   difference between inventory at standard cost and inventory at actual cost, where inventory at actual cost = ((units in closing inventory ÷ production volume) × total of actual production costs)

This **difference** is simply **added to the bottom of the operating statement**.

	£	£
Actual profit, with inventory at standard cost		X
Inventory adjustment		
inventory at standard cost	X	
inventory at actual cost	X	
Actual profit, with inventory at actual cost		X / X

KEY POINT

An inventory adjustment is **only needed if inventory is valued at actual cost** (either marginal or total absorption) in the actual statement of profit or loss.

Section summary

In a **standard marginal costing system**, there will be no fixed overhead volume variance and the sales volume variance will be valued at standard contribution margin, not standard profit margin.

3   Working backwards approach to variance analysis

Introduction

Examination questions usually provide you with data about actual results and you have to calculate variances. One way in which your understanding of the topic can be tested, however, is to provide information about variances from which you have to 'work backwards' to determine the actual results.

Example: working backwards

The standard cost card for the trough, one of the products made by Pig, is as follows:

	£
Direct material 16 kg × £6 per kg	96
Direct labour 6 hours × £12 per hour	72
Fixed production overhead 6 hours × £14 per hour	84
	252

Pig reported the following variances in control period 13 in relation to the trough.

Direct material price: £18,840 favourable   Fixed production overhead expenditure: £14,192 adverse
Direct material usage: £480 adverse   Fixed production overhead volume: £11,592 favourable
Direct labour rate: £10,598 adverse
Direct labour efficiency: £8,478 favourable

Actual fixed production overhead cost £200,000 and direct wages, £171,320. Pig paid £5.50 for each kg of direct material. There were no opening or closing inventories of the material.

Required

Calculate the following.

(a)   Budgeted output   (d)   Average actual wage rate per hour
(b)   Actual output   (e)   Actual number of kilograms purchased and used
(c)   Actual hours worked

Solution

(a)   Let budgeted output = q

Fixed production overhead expenditure variance = budgeted overhead – actual overhead
                                      = £(84q – 200,000) = £14,192 (A)

Therefore   84q – 200,000 = –14,192
             84q = –14,192 + 200,000
              q = 185,808 ÷ 84

Therefore q = 2,212 units*

(b)

	£
Total direct wages cost	171,320
Adjust for variances:	
Labour rate	(10,598)
Labour efficiency	8,478
Standard direct wages cost	169,200

∴ Actual output = total standard cost ÷ unit standard cost
                = £169,200 ÷ £72 = 2,350 units

(c)

	£
Total direct wages cost	171,320.0
Less rate variance	(10,598.0)
Standard rate for actual hours	160,722.0
÷ standard rate per hour	÷ £12.0
Actual hours worked	13,393.5 hours

(d) Average actual wage rate per hour = actual wages/actual hours = £171,320/13,393.5 = £12.79 per hour.

(e) Number of kg purchased and used = x

	£
x kg should have cost (× £6)	6.0x
but did cost (× £5.50)	5.5x
Direct material price variance	0.5x

∴ £0.5x = £18,840

∴ x = 37,680 kg

---

*Alternative approach to find budgeted output

	£
Budgeted expenditure (budgeted output × overhead absorption per unit) £84/unit	
Actual expenditure given	200,000
Variance	14,192 (A)

∴ Budgeted expenditure = £200,000 – £14,192 = £185,808

∴ Budgeted output = $\dfrac{£185,808}{£84}$ = 2,212 units

Question 13a.3

Working backwards

Learning outcome A1(c)

The standard material content of 1 unit of product A is 10 kg of material X which should cost £10 per kilogram. In June, 5,750 units of product A were produced and there was an adverse material usage variance of £1,500.

The quantity of material X used in June was:

A   56,000 kg

B   57,350 kg

C   57,650 kg

D   59,000 kg

Section summary

Exam questions might provide you with information about variances from which you have to 'work backwards' to determine the actual results.

4 Materials mix and yield variances

Introduction

When a product requires two or more raw materials in its make-up, it is often possible to sub-analyse the materials usage variance into materials mix and materials yield variances.

Adding a greater proportion of one material (therefore a smaller proportion of a different material) might make the materials mix cheaper or more expensive.

For example, the standard mix of materials for a product might consist of the following:

	£
($^2/_3$) 2 kg of material A at £1.00 per kg	2.00
($^1/_3$) 1 kg of material B at £0.50 per kg	0.50
	2.50

It may be possible to change the mix so that one kilogram of material A is used and two kilograms of material B. The new mix would be cheaper.

	£
($^1/_3$) 1 kg of material A	1
($^2/_3$) 2 kg of material B	1
	2

By changing the proportions in the mix, the efficiency of the combined material usage may change. In our example, in making the proportions of A and B cheaper, at 1:2, the product may now require more than 3 kilograms of input for its manufacture, and the new materials requirement per unit of product might be 3.6 kilograms.

	£
($^1/_3$) 1.2 kg of material A at £1.00 per kg	1.20
($^2/_3$) 2.4 kg of material B at £0.50 per kg	1.20
	2.40

In establishing a materials usage standard, management may therefore have to **balance** the **cost** of a particular **mix** of materials **with** the **efficiency of the yield** of the mix.

Once the standard has been established, it may be possible to exercise control over the materials used in production by calculating and reviewing mix and yield variances.

KEY TERMS

'If different materials can be substituted, the [DIRECT MATERIAL] MIX VARIANCE measures the cost of any variation from the standard mix'.

The DIRECT MATERIAL YIELD VARIANCE 'Measures the effect on cost of any difference between the actual material usage and that justified by the output produced'.   (*CIMA Official Terminology*)

4.1 Calculating the variances

The mix variance for each material input is based on the following:

(a)   The change in the material's weighting within the overall mix

(b)   Whether the material's unit standard cost is greater or less than the standard weighted average cost of all material inputs

A **yield variance** is calculated as the **difference between the standard output from what was actually input**, and the **actual output**, valued at the standard cost per unit of output.

4.2 When to calculate mix and yield variances

Mix and yield variances have no meaning, and should never be calculated, unless they are a guide to control action. They are **only appropriate in the following situations**.

(a) Where **proportions of materials in a mix are changeable and controllable**. If the materials in a mix are in different units, say kilograms and litres, they are obviously completely different and so cannot be substituted for each other.

(b) Where the **usage variance of individual materials is of limited value because of the variability of the mix**, and a combined yield variance for all the materials together is more helpful for control.

It would be **totally inappropriate** to calculate a mix **variance where the materials in the 'mix' are discrete items**. A chair, for example, might consist of wood, covering material, stuffing and glue. These materials are separate components, and it would not be possible to think in terms of controlling the proportions of each material in the final product. The usage of each material must be controlled separately.

4.3 Other limitations of mix and yield variances

(a) Mix and yield variances are often interdependent and therefore one variance cannot be assessed without considering the other.

(b) Mix and yield variances do not take into account the quality of the output. For example, improving the mix by making it cheaper is likely to affect the quality of the output.

(c) Actual prices and rates may differ from the standard prices and rates used in the mix and yield variances. Therefore, mix and yield variances must be considered in conjunction with material price and labour rate variances to obtain the complete picture.

Example: materials usage, mix and yield variances

A company manufactures a chemical, Dynamite, using two compounds, Flash and Bang. The standard materials usage and cost of one unit of Dynamite are as follows:

		£
Flash	5 kg at £2 per kg	10
Bang	10 kg at £3 per kg	30
	15 kg	40

In a particular period, 80 units of Dynamite were produced from 500 kg of Flash and 730 kg of Bang.

Required

Calculate the materials usage, mix and yield variances.

Solution

(a) **Usage variance**

	Flash	*Bang*
80 units of Dynamite should have used	400 kg	800 kg
but did use	500 kg	730 kg
Usage variance in kg	100 kg (A)	70 kg (F)
× standard cost per kg	× £2	× £3
Usage variance in £	£200 (A)	£210 (F)

Total usage variance   £10 (F)

The total usage variance can be analysed into mix and yield variances.

(b)   **Mix variance**

Actual input = (500 + 730) kg = 1,230 kg

Standard mix of actual input

Flash 5/15 = 1/3 ∴ 1/3 × 1,230 kg =	410 kg
Bang 10/15 = 2/3 ∴ 2/3 × 1,230 kg =	820 kg
	1,230 kg

	'Should' mix *Actual quantity* *Standard mix*	*'Did' mix* *Actual quantity* *Actual mix*	*Difference*	*Standard* *price*	*Variance*
Flash	410 kg	500 kg	90 kg (A)	£2	£180 (A)
Bang	820 kg	730 kg	90 kg (F)	£3	£270 (F)
	1,230 kg	1,230 kg	–		£90 (F)

The **total difference** or mix variance in **kg** must **always** be **zero** as the mix variance measures the change in the relative proportions of the actual total input. The variance is calculated by comparing the expected mix of the total actual input with the actual mix of the total actual input: the difference between the two totals is zero.

The favourable total variance is due to the greater use in the mix of the cheaper material, Flash. However, this cheaper mix may have an adverse effect on the yield that is obtained from the mix, as we shall now see.

(c)   **Yield variance**

Each unit of output (Dynamite) requires	5 kg	of Flash, costing	£10
	10 kg	of Bang, costing	£30
	15 kg		£40

Actual input	
1,230 kg should have yielded (÷ 15 kg)	82 units of Dynamite
but did yield	80 units of Dynamite
Yield variance in units	2 units (A)
× standard cost per unit of output	× £40
Yield variance in £	£80 (A)

The adverse yield variance is due to the output from the input being less than standard.

The mix variance and yield variance together add up to the usage variance, which is favourable, because the adverse yield from the mix did not negate the price savings that were made by using proportionately more of the cheaper material.

KEY POINT

CIMA recommends two approaches to valuing mix variances. **Either or both may be tested**, because both methods are on your syllabus. The one above (valuing the individual mix variances in units at the **individual standard prices**) is the easier of the two and so, if given a choice, we recommend that it is the approach you use. The second approach is shown below. Don't neglect this second method because the examiner may specifically ask for it to be used in a question.

4.4 Mix variances: alternative approach

This approach uses a **weighted average price** to value the individual mix variances in units.

The standard weighted average price of the input materials is £40/15 kg = £2.67 per kg.

	'Should' mix Actual quantity Standard mix	'Did' mix Actual quantity Actual mix	Difference*	£ (W1)	Variance**
Flash	410 kg	500 kg	90 kg more	× £0.67 less	£60 (F)
Bang	820 kg	730 kg	90 kg less	× £0.33 more	£30 (F)
	1,230 kg	1,230 kg			

Workings

Flash

Difference between weighted average price and standard price	= £(2.67 – 2)
	= £0.67 less than average

Bang

Difference between weighted average price and standard price	= £(2.67 – 3)
	= £0.33 more than average

*Here we calculate a **difference in units** (more or less than standard) rather than a variance.

To determine whether a mix variance is (A) or (F) using the weighted average method see below.

	Variance
Input more than standard of a material **costing more** than average	(A)
Input more than standard of a material **costing less** than average	(F)
Input less than standard of a material **costing more** than average	(F)
Input less than standard of a material **costing less** than average	(A)

In this example:

More Flash than standard was input, and Flash **costs less** than the average price, so the variance is **favourable**.

Less Bang than standard was input, and Bang **costs more** than the average price, so the variance is **favourable**.

Question 13a.4	Mix and yield variances

Learning outcome A1(c)

The standard materials cost per unit of product D456 is as follows:

		£
Material X	3 kg at £2.00 per kg	6
Material Y	5 kg at £3.60 per kg	18
	8 kg	24

During period 2, 2,000 kg of material X costing £4,100 and 2,400 kg of material Y costing £9,600 were used to produce 500 units of D456.

Required

Calculate price, mix and yield variances.

Question 13a.5

Learning outcome A1(c)

Explain briefly the limitations of the calculation of materials mix and yield variances.

Summary

- Both methods are based on individual mix **variances in units** calculated as the **difference between actual input and the standard mix of actual input**.

- The **total mix variance in units** is **zero** using **both methods**.

- The **first method values** the individual mix variances in units at the **individual standard prices**.

- The **second method values** the individual mix variances in units at the **difference between the weighted average price and the standard price**.

- The **total mix variance** in £ is the **same** under both methods.

4.5 Deviations from standardised mix

In an exam question under an old syllabus, candidates were given the percentage deviations for standardised mix and the data used to calculate those deviations. They then had to calculate deviations for a third month and comment on the usefulness of such analysis for operational control.

The question stated that the deviations were shown in weight and were from the standard mix for the quantity input expressed as a percentage of the standardised weight for each ingredient. This sounds complicated but is actually referring to the individual mix variances in units (think about it!). And because source data for the figures shown was provided, candidates could check their understanding of the method of calculation.

Try the question below, to see whether you could have coped with the exam question.

Question 13a.6

Learning outcome A1(c)

Standard mix for one litre of product J

0.4 litres of ingredient O
0.2 litres of ingredient H
0.5 litres of ingredient N

Actual usage in control period 2

Ingredient O	420 litres
Ingredient H	180 litres
Ingredient N	550 litres
Actual output	1,000 litres

Calculate the percentage deviation from the standardised mix using the method of calculation described above.

Section summary

When two or more types of material are mixed together to produce a product, it is possible to carry out further analysis on the usage variance. The **mix variance** explains how much of the usage variance was caused by a change in the relative proportions of the materials used. The **yield variance** shows how much of the usage variance was caused by using more or less material than the standard allowance.

The purpose of a mix variance is to provide management with information to help in controlling the proportion of each item actually used. If it is not possible for managers to exercise control over the actual mix of material, then there is little to be gained by calculating mix variances.

5 Labour mix and yield variances

Introduction

If more than one type of labour is used in a product, the labour efficiency variance can be analysed further into a **labour mix (team composition) variance** and a **labour yield (team productivity or output) variance**.

KEY TERMS

'Where substitutions between the grades of labour used to operate a process are possible, the [DIRECT LABOUR] MIX VARIANCE measures the cost of any variation from the standard mix.'

The DIRECT LABOUR YIELD VARIANCE 'Measures the effect on cost of any difference between the actual labour hours worked and the hours justified by output produced'.   (*CIMA Official Terminology*)

The labour mix variance is also known as the **team composition variance**, the labour yield variance as the **labour output variance** or **team productivity variance**.

The calculations are the same as those required for materials mix and yield variances.

KEY POINT

Don't confuse labour efficiency with labour yield variances. Remember that the labour efficiency variance is the total of the labour mix and labour yield variances.

Example: labour mix variances

Two grades of labour work together in teams to produce product X. The standard composition of each team is 5 grade A employees paid at £6 per hour and 3 grade B employees paid at £4 per hour. Output is measured in standard hours and expected output is 95 standard hours for 100 hours worked in total. During the last period, 2,280 standard hours of output were produced using 1,500 hours of grade A labour (costing £9,750) and 852 hours of grade B labour (costing £2,982).

Required

Calculate all possible labour variances.

Solution

Initial working

Calculation of **standard rate per hour of output**

Labour grade

			£
A	5.00	hours × £6 =	30
B	3.00	hours × £4 =	12
	8.00	hours	42
Less 5%	0.40	hours	
	7.60	hours	

∴ Standard rate per hour of output = £42/7.6 = £5.5263 per standard hour.

Direct labour total variance

	£
2,280 standard hours of output should have cost (× £5.5263)	12,600
but did cost	12,732
Direct labour total variance	132 (A)

Direct labour rate variance

		A £		B £
Actual hours worked should have cost	(1,500 × £6)	9,000	(852 × £4)	3,408
but did cost		9,750		2,982
Direct labour rate variance		750 (A)		426 (F)
Total direct labour rate variance			£324 (A)	

Direct labour efficiency variance

		A		B
2,280 standard hours of output should take an input of	(2,280 ÷ 0.95 × ⁵/₈)	1,500 hours	(2,280 ÷ 0.95 × ³/₈)	900 hours
but did take		1,500 hours		852 hours
Efficiency variance in hours		–		48 hours (F)
× standard rate per hour		× £6		× £4
		–		£192 (F)

The **labour efficiency variance** can be analysed further into the **team composition** variance (the **labour mix** variance) and the **team productivity** variance (the **labour yield** variance).

Team composition (labour mix) variance

Again there are two approaches to valuing the variance.

Approach 1

Total actual hours = 1,500 + 852 = 2,352 hours

Standard mix of actual input

		Hours
A	5/8 × 2,352 =	1,470
B	3/8 × 2,352 =	882
		2,352

	'Should' mix Actual hours Standard mix	'Did' mix Actual hours Actual mix	Difference	× Standard price	Variance
A	1,470 hours	1,500 hours	30 hours (A)	× £6	£180 (A)
B	882 hours	852 hours	30 hours (F)	× £4	£120 (F)
	2,352 hours	2,352 hours	–		£60 (A)

Approach 2

The standard weighted rate per hour of labour is £42/8 = £5.25 per hour.

	'Should' mix Actual hours Standard mix	'Did' mix Actual hours Actual mix	Difference	£ (W1)	Variance
X	1,470 hours	1,500 hours	30 hours more	× £0.75 more	£22.50 (A)
Y	882 hours	852 hours	30 hours less	× £1.25 less	£37.50 (A)
	2,352 hours	2,352 hours	–		£60.00 (A)

Workings

	X	Y
Difference between w/av price and standard price	£(5.25 – 6) = £0.75 more	£(5.25 – 4) = £1.25 less

Team productivity (labour yield) variance

2,352 hours of work should have produced (× 0.95)	2,234.4 standard hours
but did produce	2,280.0 standard hours
Team productivity variance in hours	45.6 standard hours (F)
× standard rate per standard hour	× £5.5263
Team productivity variance in £	£252 (F)

Question 13a.7   Labour mix variances

Learning outcome A1(c)

A firm has established the following standard composition of a team of its staff performing the year-end audit of a medium-sized company.

	Standard hours to perform audit	Rate per hour $	Standard labour cost of audit $
Audit manager	30	450	13,500
Junior auditors	120	170	20,400
Audit clerks	50	50	2,500
	200		36,400

A year-end audit has just been completed for company X and the hours recorded in respect of each grade of staff are as follows.

	Actual hours to perform audit
Audit manager	27
Junior auditors	125
Audit clerks	58
	210

Required

Calculate the following labour variances for the company X audit.

(a)   The labour efficiency variance
(b)   The labour yield variance
(c)   The labour mix variance, using the weighted average valuation basis

Variance tree diagram

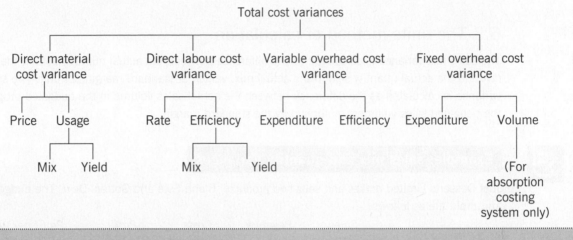

Section summary

If more than one type of labour is used in a product, the labour efficiency variance can be analysed further into a **labour mix (team composition) variance** and a **labour yield (team productivity or output) variance**.

6 Sales mix and quantity variances

Introduction

The sales volume profit variance can be analysed further into a sales mix variance and a sales quantity variance.

6.1 Sales volume variance

You learned how to calculate the sales volume variance in Chapter 12b. It measures the increase or decrease in the standard profit or contribution as a result of the sales volume being higher or lower than budgeted. It is calculated as the difference between actual sales units and budgeted sales units, multiplied by the standard profit per unit.

6.2 Sales mix and quantity variances

If a company **sells more than one product**, it is possible to analyse the overall sales volume variance into a sales mix variance and a sales quantity variance.

KEY TERMS

The SALES MIX VARIANCE occurs when the proportions of the various products sold are different from those in the budget.

The SALES QUANTITY VARIANCE shows the difference in contribution/profit because of a change in sales volume from the budgeted volume of sales.

KEY POINT

A sales mix variance and a sales quantity variance are only meaningful where management can control the proportions of the products sold.

In particular, sales mix variances are only of use if there is some kind of link between the products in question.

- Complementary products, such as pancake mix and lemon juice
- Substitute products, such as branded and 'own-label' goods
- Same products, different sizes
- Products produced within a limiting factor environment

6.3 The units method of calculation

The sales mix variance is calculated as the difference between the actual quantity sold in the standard mix and the actual quantity sold in the actual mix, valued at standard margin per unit. The sales quantity variance is calculated as the difference between the actual sales volume in the budgeted proportions and the budgeted sales volumes, multiplied by the standard margin.

Example: sales mix and quantity variances

Just Desserts Limited makes and sells two products, Bland Fete and Gotters Dew. The budgeted sales and profit are as follows:

	Sales Units	Revenue £	Costs £	Profit £	Profit per unit £
Bland Fete	400	8,000	6,000	2,000	5
Gotters Dew	300	12,000	11,100	900	3
				2,900	

Actual sales were 280 units of Bland Fete and 630 units of Gotters Dew. The company management is able to control the relative sales of each product through the allocation of sales effort, advertising and sales promotion expenses.

Required

Calculate the sales volume profit variance, the sales mix variance and the sales quantity variance.

Solution

(a)

	Bland Fete	Gotters Dew
Budgeted sales	400 units	300 units
Actual sales	280 units	630 units
Sales volume variance in units	120 units (A)	330 units (F)
× standard margin per unit	× £5	× £3
Sales volume variance in £	£600 (A)	£990 (F)
Total **sales volume variance**	£390 (F)	

The favourable sales volume variance indicates that a potential increase in profit was achieved as a result of the change in sales volume compared with budgeted volume. Now we will see how to analyse this favourable variance into its mix and quantity elements.

(b) When we look at the mix of sales in this example, it is apparent that a bigger proportion than budgeted of the less profitable Gotters Dew has been sold, therefore the **sales mix variance** will be adverse. Again, there are two methods for calculating the mix variance – the individual units method and the weighted average method.

Individual units method

(i)   Take the **actual total of sales** and **convert** this total into a **standard or budgeted mix**, on the assumption that sales should have been in the budgeted proportions or mix.

(ii) The difference between actual sales and 'standard mix' sales for each product is then converted into a variance by multiplying by the standard margin.

		Units
Total quantity sold (280 + 630)		910
Budgeted mix for actual sales:	⁴/₇ Bland Fete	520
	³/₇ Gotters Dew	390
		910

	'Should' mix *Actual quantity* *Standard mix*	'Did' mix *Actual quantity* *Actual mix*	*Difference*	× *Standard margin*	*Variance*
Bland Fete	520 units	280 units	240 (A)	× £5	£1,200 (A)
Gotters Dew	390 units	630 units	240 (F)	× £3	£720 (F)
	910 units	910 units	–		£480 (A)

The profit would have been £480 higher if the 910 units had been sold in the budgeted mix of 4:3.

Weighted average method

	'Should' mix *Actual quantity* *Standard mix*	'Did' mix *Actual quantity* *Actual mix*	*Difference*	£ *(W1)*	*Variance* £
Bland Fete	520 units	280 units	240 less	× £0.86 more	206.40 (A)
Gotters Dew	390 units	630 units	240 more	× £1.14 less	273.60 (A)
	910 units	910 units	–		480 (A)

The Bland Fete variance is adverse because it is a more profitable product and fewer units than standard were sold. The Gotters Dew variance is adverse because more units were sold than the standard mix and it is a less profitable product.

Workings

Difference between standard and average profit per unit

	Standard mix Units	*Standard profit per unit*	*Average profit per unit**	*Difference*
Bland Fete	400	£5	£4.14	£5 – £4.14 = £0.86 more
Gotters Dew	300	£3	£4.14	£3 – £4.14 = £1.14 less
	700			

*(5×400)+(300×3))/700 = £4.14

(c)   The **sales quantity variance** is calculated as follows:

	Actual sales *Standard mix*	*Standard sales* *Standard mix*	*Difference* *in units*	× *Standard profit*	*Variance*
Bland Fete	520 units	400 units	120 units (F)	× £5	£600 (F)
Gotters Dew	390 units	300 units	90 units (F)	× £3	£270 (F)
	910 units	700 units	210 units		£870 (F)

Summary

	£
Sales mix variance	480 (A)
Sales quantity variance	870 (F)
Sales volume profit variance	390 (F)

If an organisation uses **standard marginal costing** instead of standard absorption costing, then standard **contribution** rather than standard **profit margin** is used in the calculations.

Exam alert

Make sure that you learn what each variance means. Separating the volume variance into quantity and mix components shows whether it is more beneficial to maximise total sales volume or whether it is better to promote sales of the most profitable mix of products.

Exam skills

Try not to confuse the sales volume profit variance with the sales quantity profit variance.

Section summary

The sales volume profit variance can be analysed further into a sales mix variance and a sales quantity variance.

7 Planning and operational variances

Introduction

To date in your studies, we have been looking at variances that are calculated using what we will call the **conventional approach** to variance analysis, whereby an **actual cost** is **compared** with an **original standard cost**. In this section of the chapter, we will be examining **planning** and **operational variances**. They are not really alternatives to the conventional approach; they merely provide a much **more detailed analysis**.

KEY TERMS

A PLANNING VARIANCE (or REVISION VARIANCE) compares an original standard with a revised standard that should or would have been used if planners had known in advance what was going to happen.

An OPERATIONAL VARIANCE (or OPERATING VARIANCE) compares an actual result with the revised standard.

EX ANTE means original budget/standard. EX POST means revised budget/standard.

Planning and operational variances are based on the principle that variances ought to be reported by taking as the **main starting point** not the original standard, but a **standard** which can be seen, in hindsight, to be the **optimum** that should have been **achievable**.

This idea is that the monetary value of variances ought to be a realistic reflection of what the causes of the variances have cost the organisation. In other words, they should show the cash (and profit) gained or lost as a consequence of operating results being different to what should have been achieved. Variances can be valued in this way by **comparing actual results with a realistic standard or budget**. Such variances are called **operational variances**.

Planning variances arise because the **original standard and revised, more realistic standards are different** and have nothing to do with operational performance. In most cases, it is unlikely that anything could be done about planning variances: they are **not controllable by operational managers but by senior management**.

In other words, the **cause of a total variance** might be one or both of the following:

- Adverse or favourable operational performance (**operational variance**)
- Inaccurate planning, or faulty standards (**planning variance**)

KEY TERMS

CIMA Official Terminology defines an OPERATIONAL VARIANCE as 'Classification of variances in which non-standard performance is defined as being that which differs from an *ex post* standard. Operational **variances can relate to any element of the standard product specification'**.

CIMA Official Terminology defines PLANNING VARIANCES as 'Classification of variances caused by *ex ante* budget allowances being changed to an *ex post* basis. Also known as revision variances'.

7.1 Calculating total planning and operational variances

We will begin by looking at how to split a total cost variance into its planning and operational components.

Example: total cost planning and operational variances

At the beginning of 20X0, WB set a standard marginal cost for its major product of £25 (5 kg × £5) per unit. The standard cost is recalculated once each year. Actual production costs during August 20X0 were £304,000, when 8,000 units were made.

With the benefit of hindsight, the management of WB realises that a more realistic standard cost for current conditions would be £40 (4 kg × £10) per unit. The planned standard cost of £25 is unrealistically low.

Required

Calculate the planning and operational variances.

Solution

With the benefit of hindsight, the **realistic standard should have been £40**. The variance caused by favourable or adverse **operating** performance should be calculated by comparing actual results against this realistic standard.

	£
Revised standard cost for revised standard kg for actual output (£10 × 4 kg × 8,000)	320,000
Actual cost	304,000
Total **operational** variance	16,000 (F)

The variance is favourable because the actual cost was lower than would have been expected using the revised basis. (You can still think of this in terms of 'should have cost' but 'did cost' in your mind to help you decide whether it is adverse or favourable.)

The **planning** variance reveals the extent to which the original standard was at fault.

		£
Revised standard cost for revised kg for actual output	£10 × 4 kg × 8,000	320,000
Original standard cost for original kg for actual output	£5 × 5 kg × 8,000	200,000
Planning variance		120,000 (A)

It is an adverse variance because the original standard was too optimistic, overestimating the expected profits by understating the standard cost. More simply, it is adverse because the revised cost is much higher than the original cost.

	£
Planning variance	120,000 (A)
Operational variance	16,000 (F)
Total	104,000 (A)

If **traditional variance analysis** had been used, the total cost variance would have been the same, but **all the 'blame' would appear to lie on actual results** and operating inefficiencies (rather than some being due to faulty planning).

	£
Standard cost of 8,000 units (× £25)	200,000
Actual cost of 8,000 units	304,000
Total cost variance	104,000 (A)

Question 13a.8	Total planning and operational variances

Learning outcome A1(c)

Suppose a budget is prepared, which includes a raw materials cost per unit of product of £2 (2 kg of copper at £1 per kg). Due to a rise in world prices for copper during the year, the average market price of copper rose to £1.50 per kg. During the year, 1,000 units were produced at a cost of £3,250 for 2,200 kg of copper.

The planning and operational variances are:

	Operational variance	Planning variance
A	£250 (A)	£1,000 (A)
B	£250 (A)	£1,100 (A)
C	£250 (F)	£1,000 (F)
D	£250 (A)	£1,000 (F)

7.2 Operational price and usage variances

So far we have only considered planning and operational variances in total, without carrying out the usual two-way split. In Question 13a.8 above, for instance, we identified a total operational variance for materials of £250 without considering whether this operational variance could be split between a usage variance and a price variance.

This is not a problem as long as you retain your grasp of knowledge you already possess. You know that a **price** variance measures the difference between the actual amount of money paid and the amount of money that should have been paid for that quantity of materials (or whatever). Thus, in our example:

	£
Revised standard price of actual purchases (£1.50 × 2,200 kg)	3,300
Actual price of actual purchases (2,200 kg)	3,250
Operational price variance	50 (F)

The variance is favourable because the materials were purchased more cheaply than would have been expected.

Similarly, a **usage** variance measures the difference between the actual physical quantity of materials used or hours taken and the quantities that should have been used or taken for the actual volume of production. Those physical differences are then converted into money values by applying the appropriate standard cost.

In our example, we are calculating **operational variances**, so we are not interested in planning errors. This means that the **appropriate standard cost is the revised standard cost** of £1.50.

Actual output should have used		2,000 kg
but did use		2,200 kg
Operational usage variance in kg		200 kg (A)
× revised standard cost per kg		× £1.50
Operational usage variance in £		£300 (A)

The two variances of course reconcile to the total variance as previously calculated.

	£	
Operational price variance	50	(F)
Operational usage variance	(300)	(A)
Total operational variance	250	(A)

7.3 Operational variances for labour and overheads

Precisely the same argument applies to the calculation of operational variances for labour and overheads, and the examples already given should be sufficient to enable you to answer the question below.

Question 13a.9	Planning and operational variances

Learning outcome A1(c)

A new product requires 3 hours of labour per unit at a standard rate of £6 per hour. In a particular month, the budget is to produce 500 units. Actual results were as follows:

Hours worked	1,700
Production	540 units
Wages cost	£10,500

Within minutes of production starting, it was realised that the job was extremely messy and the labour force could therefore claim an extra 25p per hour in 'dirty money'.

Required

What are the planning and operational variances?

	Planning	Operational rate	Operational efficiency
A	£405 (F)	£125 (F)	£500 (A)
B	£405 (A)	£125 (F)	£500 (A)
C	£405 (F)	£300 (A)	£500 (F)
D	£405 (A)	£300 (F)	£480 (A)

7.4 Planning sub-variances

So far we have looked at the total planning variances. Now we'll look at how to calculate specific planning variances.

The labour **rate**/material **price variance** shows the effect of a change in the standard rate or price and is calculated as follows.

	£
The original standard cost for the revised standard hours/kg etc for actual output was	X
The revised standard cost for the revised standard hours/kg etc for actual output is	X
Planning labour rate/material price variance	X

The labour **efficiency**/material **usage** planning variance shows the effect of a change in the standard hours or usage of material per unit and is calculated as follows:

The original standard hours/kg etc for actual output was	X
The revised standard hours/kg etc for actual output is	X
Labour efficiency/material usage planning variance in hours/kg etc	X
× standard rate per hour/standard cost per kg etc	× £ X
Labour efficiency/material usage planning variance in £	£ X

Example: planning rate variance

Bean Ltd operates a standard absorption costing system. The following information is available for product P.

Budgeted production	3,000 units
Direct material cost: 10 kg × £2.05	£20.50 per unit

Actual results for the quarter were:

Production		3,200 units
Direct material (purchased and used): 15,000 kg	£72,000	

In retrospect, it is realised that the standard cost for material should have been £2.50 per kg during the period.

Required

Calculate the material price planning variance.

Solution

	£
Original standard cost for the revised standard hours for actual output	
(£2.05 × 10 kg × 3,200)	65,600
Revised standard cost for the revised standard hours for actual output	
(£2.50 × 10 kg × 3,200)	80,000
Material price planning variance	14,400 (A)

7.5 Two planning errors

In the example above there was only one planning error, which was the error in the standard cost. It is also possible to make a mistake with the number of standard hours. There would then be two planning errors. The following example includes two planning errors.

Example: two planning errors

A company estimates that the standard direct labour cost for a product should be £20 (4 hours × £5 per hour). Actual production of 1,000 units took 6,200 hours at a cost of £23,800. In retrospect, it is realised that the standard cost should have been 6 hours × £6 per hour = £36 per unit.

Required

Calculate the planning and operational variances.

Solution

(a) **Operational variances**

(i)

1,000 units should take (× 6 hours)	6,000 hours
but did take	6,200 hours
Efficiency variance in hours	200 hours (A)
× revised standard cost per hour	× £6 (A)
Efficiency variance in £	£1,200 (A)

(ii)

	£
Revised standard price of actual hours paid (£6 × 6,200)	37,200
Actual price of actual hours paid	23,800
Rate variance	13,400 (F)

(iii) **Check**

	£
Revised standard cost for revised std hrs (£36 × 1,000 units)	36,000
Actual costs	23,800
Total operational variance (1,200 (A) + 13,400 (F))	12,200 (F)

(b) **Planning variance**

	£
Revised standard cost for revised standard hours for actual o/put (£6 × 6 hours × 1,000)	36,000
Original standard cost for original standard hours for actual o/put (£5 × 4 hours × 1,000)	20,000
Total planning variance	16,000 (A)

Planning rate variance

	£
Original standard cost for revised standard hours for actual output (£5 × 6 hours × 1,000)	30,000
Revised standard cost for revised standard hours for actual output (£6 × 6 hours × 1,000)	36,000
Planning rate variance	6,000 (A)

Planning efficiency variance

The original standard hours for actual output were (4 hours × 1,000)	4,000
The revised standard hours for actual output are (6 hours × 1,000)	6,000
Labour efficiency planning variance in hours	2,000 (A)
× original standard rate per hour	× £5
Labour efficiency planning variance in £	10,000 (A)

Question 13a.10	Planning variances and sub-variances

Learning outcome A1(c)

The standard materials cost of a product is 3 kg × £1.50 per kg = £4.50. Actual production of 10,000 units used 28,000 kg at a cost of £50,000. In retrospect, it was realised that the standard materials cost should have been 2.5 kg per unit at a cost of £1.80 per kg (so that the **total** cost per unit was correct).

Required

Calculate the planning and operational variances in as much detail as possible.

7.6 Planning and operational sales variances

Our final calculations in this chapter deal with planning and operational sales variances.

Example: planning and operational sales variances

Dimsek budgeted to make and sell 400 units of its product, the role, in the 4-week period no 8, as follows:

	£
Budgeted sales (100 units per week)	40,000
Variable costs (400 units × £60)	24,000
Contribution	16,000
Fixed costs	10,000
Profit	6,000

At the beginning of the second week, production came to a halt because inventories of raw materials ran out, and a new supply was not received until the beginning of week 3. As a consequence, the company lost one week's production and sales. Actual results in period 8 were as follows.

	£
Sales (320 units)	32,000
Variable costs (320 units × £60)	19,200
Contribution	12,800
Fixed costs	10,000
Actual profit	2,800

In retrospect, it is decided that the optimum budget, given the loss of production facilities in the third week, would have been to sell only 300 units in the period.

Required

Calculate appropriate planning and operational variances.

Solution

The **planning** variance **compares the revised budget** with the **original budget**.

Revised sales volume, given materials shortage	300 units
Original budgeted sales volume	400 units
Planning variance in units of sales	100 units(A)
× standard contribution per unit	× £40
Planning variance in £	£4,000 (A)

Arguably, **running out of raw materials is an operational error** and so the loss of sales volume and contribution from the materials shortage is an opportunity cost that could have been avoided with better purchasing arrangements. The operational variances are variances calculated in the usual way, except that actual results are compared with the revised standard or budget. There is a sales volume contribution variance which is an **operational variance**, as follows:

Actual sales volume	320 units
Revised sales volume	300 units
Operational sales volume variance in units	20 units (F)
(possibly due to production efficiency or marketing efficiency)	
× standard contribution per unit	× £40
	£800 (F)

These variances can be used as **control information** to reconcile budgeted and actual profit.

	£	£
Operating statement, period 8		
Budgeted profit		6,000
Planning variance	4,000 (A)	
Operational variance – sales volume contribution	800 (F)	
		3,200 (A)
Actual profit in period 8		2,800

You will have noticed that in this example sales volume variances were **valued at contribution forgone**, and there were no fixed cost volume variances. This is because contribution forgone, in terms of lost revenue or extra expenditure incurred, is the nearest equivalent to **opportunity cost** that is readily available to management accountants (who assume linearity of costs and revenues within a relevant range of activity).

Question 13a.11	Sales planning and operational variances

Learning outcome A1(c)

KSO budgeted to sell 10,000 units of a new product during 20X0. The budgeted sales price was £10 per unit, and the variable cost £3 per unit.

Although actual sales in 20X0 were 10,000 units and variable costs of sales were £30,000, sales revenue was only £5 per unit. With the benefit of hindsight, it is realised that the budgeted sales price of £10 was hopelessly optimistic, and a price of £4.50 per unit would have been much more realistic.

Required

Calculate planning and operational variances.

7.7 The value of planning and operational variances

Advantages of a system of planning and operational variances

(a) The analysis highlights those variances that are **controllable** and those that are **non-controllable**.

(b) **Managers' acceptance** of the use of variances for performance measurement, and their **motivation**, is likely to increase if they know they will not be held responsible for poor planning and faulty standard setting.

(c) The **planning and standard-setting processes** should improve; standards should be more accurate, relevant and appropriate.

(d) Operational variances will provide a 'fairer' reflection of actual performance.

The limitations of planning and operational variances, which must be overcome if they are to be applied in practice

(a) It is difficult to **decide in hindsight** what the **realistic standard** should have been.

(b) It may become **too easy to justify all the variances as being due to bad planning**, so no operational variances will be highlighted.

(c) Establishing realistic revised standards and analysing the total variance into planning and operational variances can be a **time-consuming** task, even if a spreadsheet package is devised.

(d) Even though the intention is to provide more meaningful information, **managers may be resistant** to the very idea of variances and refuse to see the virtues of the approach. Careful presentation and explanation will be required until managers are used to the concepts.

Exam alert

You must be able to calculate the variances as well as being able to **explain** what they mean. Make sure that you make notes on Section 7.7 so that you can discuss the variances as well as calculating them.

7.8 Management reports involving planning and operational variances

The format of a management report that includes planning and operational variances should be tailored to the information requirements of the managers who receive it.

From the **point of view of senior management** reviewing performance as a whole, a layout that identifies **all of the planning variances together**, and then **all of the operational variances**, may be most illuminating. The difference due to planning is the responsibility of the planners, and the remainder of the difference is due to functional managers.

One possible layout is shown below.

OPERATING STATEMENT PERIOD 1

	£	£
Original budget contribution		X
Planning variances		
Material usage	X	
Material price	X	
Labour efficiency	X	
Labour idle time	X	
Labour rate	X	
Selling price	X	
		X
Revised budget contribution		X
Sales volume contribution variance		X
Revised standard contribution from sales achieved		X
Operational variances	X	
Selling price	X	
Material usage	X	
Material price	X	
Labour efficiency	X	
Labour rate	X	
Variable overhead expenditure	X	
Variable overhead efficiency	X	
		X
Actual contribution		X
Less: fixed costs budget	X	
expenditure variance	X	
		X
Actual margin		X

Section summary

A planning and operational variance attempts to **divide a total variance** (which has been calculated conventionally) into a group of **variances** which have arisen because of **inaccurate planning or faulty standards (planning variances)** and a group of **variances** which have been caused by **adverse or favourable operational performance (operational variances)**.

Chapter Summary

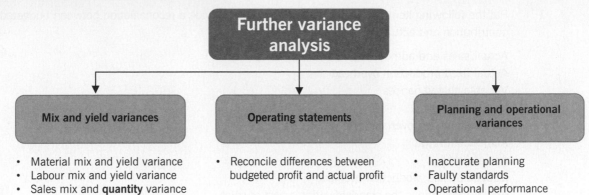

Further variance analysis

Mix and yield variances
- Material mix and yield variance
- Labour mix and yield variance
- Sales mix and **quantity** variance

Operating statements
- Reconcile differences between budgeted profit and actual profit

Planning and operational variances
- Inaccurate planning
- Faulty standards
- Operational performance

Quick Quiz

1   Put the following items in the correct order so as to provide a reconciliation between budgeted contribution and actual profit.

Actual sales and admin costs
Actual fixed production overhead
Variable cost variances
Sales variances
Fixed production overhead expenditure variance
Actual contribution
Actual profit
Budgeted fixed production overhead
Actual sales minus the standard variable cost of sales
Budgeted contribution
Actual profit before sales and admin costs

2   Which of the following statements about the materials mix variance is true?

A   It should only be calculated if the proportions in the mix are controllable.
B   In quantity, it is always the same as the usage variance.
C   In quantity, it is always zero whatever method of calculation is used.
D   It can only be calculated for a maximum of three materials in the mix.

3   Fill in the blanks. *total*   *yield*

Materials .... variance = materials mix variance + materials .... variance.

4   The labour mix variance is sometimes known as the team mix variance and the labour yield variance is sometimes known as the team yield variance.

True   ☐

False ☑

5   The material cost for an actual production level of 510 units was £32,130. There was a material price variance of £1,020 (A) and the standard price per kg was £6.10. How many kg of material were used?

Ⓐ   5,100 kg
B   5,434 kg
C   5,267 kg
D   Impossible to tell from the information provided

6   In an operational and planning approach to variance analysis, which standards are used to calculate the operational variances?

Ex ante standards   ☒

Ex post standards   ☐

7   Chocos Ltd uses a standard absorption costing system. The following information is available from the standard cost card.

Production budget	3,000 units	Actual production	3,200 units
Direct material per unit	8 kg	Direct material purchased and used 10,000 kg	£57,500
Direct material cost per kg	£5.50		

With the benefit of hindsight, the management of Chocos Ltd realises that a more realistic standard cost for current conditions would be £5.90.

Calculate the material price planning variance.

Answers to Quick Quiz

1

	£	£
Budgeted contribution		X
Sales variances		X
Actual sales minus standard variable cost of sales		X
Variable cost variances		X
Actual contribution		X
Budgeted fixed production overhead	X	
Fixed production overhead expenditure variance	X	
Actual fixed production overhead		X
Actual profit before sales and admin costs		X
Actual sales and admin costs		X
Actual profit		X

2   A   It should only be calculated if the proportions in the mix are controllable.

3   Materials usage variance = materials mix variance + materials yield variance.

4   False. They are sometimes known as the team composition variance and the team productivity variance.

5   A

Total actual material cost	£32,130
Price variance	£(1,020)
Standard price for actual usage	£31,110
÷ standard cost per kg	÷ £6.10
Actual kg used	5,100

6   *Ex post* standards

7

	£
Original standard cost for revised standard kg for actual output	
(£5.50 × 8 kg × 3,200)	140,800
Revised standard cost for revised standard kg for actual output	
(£5.90 × 8 kg × 3,200)	151,040
Material price planning variance	10,240 (A)

Answers to Questions

13a.1 Impact of costing system on variances

The correct answer is C.

13a.2 Operating statement

(a) This is simply a **'total'** variance.

	£
1,000 units should have cost (× £600)	600,000
but did cost (see working)	808,000
Variable production cost variance	208,000 (A)

(b) **Direct labour cost variances**

	£
8,200 hours should cost (× £8)	65,600
but did cost	63,000
Direct labour rate variance	2,600 (F)

1,000 units should take (× 10 hours)	10,000 hours
but did take	8,200 hours
Direct labour efficiency variance in hours	1,800 hours (F)
× standard rate per hour	× £8
Direct labour efficiency variance in £	£14,400 (F)

Summary

	£
Rate	2,600 (F)
Efficiency	14,400 (F)
Total	17,000 (F)

(c) **Direct material cost variances**

	£
90,000 kg should cost (× £5)	450,000
but did cost	720,000
Direct material price variance	270,000 (A)

1,000 units should use (× 100 kg)	100,000 kg
but did use	90,000 kg
Direct material usage variance in kg	10,000 kg (F)
× standard cost per kg	× £5
Direct material usage variance in £	£50,000 (F)

Summary

	£
Price	270,000 (A)
Usage	50,000 (F)
Total	220,000 (A)

(d)   **Variable production overhead variances**

	£
8,200 hours incurring o/hd should cost (× £2)	16,400
but did cost	25,000
Variable production overhead expenditure variance	8,600 (A)

Efficiency variance in hours (from (b))	1,800 hours (F)
× standard rate per hour	× £2
Variable production overhead efficiency variance	£3,600 (F)

Summary

	£
Expenditure	8,600 (A)
Efficiency	3,600 (F)
Total	5,000 (A)

(e)   **Selling price variance**

	£
Revenue from 1,000 units should have been (× £900)	900,000
but was (× £975)	975,000
Selling price variance	75,000 (F)

(f)   **Sales volume contribution variance**

Budgeted sales	1,020 units
Actual sales	1,000 units
Sales volume variance in units	20 units (A)
× standard contribution margin (£(900 – 600))	× £300
Sales volume contribution variance in £	£6,000 (A)

(g)   **Fixed production overhead expenditure variance**

	£
Budgeted expenditure	40,000
Actual expenditure	41,400
Fixed production overhead expenditure variance	1,400 (A)

Workings

	£
Direct material	720,000
Total wages	63,000
Variable production overhead	25,000
	808,000

MilBri – OPERATING STATEMENT FOR DECEMBER

	£	£	£
Budgeted contribution (1,020 × £(900 – 600))			306,000
Sales volume contribution variance			6,000 (A)
Budgeted contribution from actual sales			300,000
Selling price variance			75,000 (F)
Actual sales minus the standard variable cost of sales			375,000
Variable cost variances	*(F)*	*(A)*	
Material price		270,000	
Material usage	50,000		
Labour rate	2,600		
Labour efficiency	14,400		
Variable overhead expenditure		8,600	
Variable overhead efficiency	3,600		
	70,600	278,600	208,000 (A)
Actual contribution			167,000
Budgeted fixed production overhead		40,000	
Expenditure variance		1,400 (A)	
Actual fixed production overhead			41,400
Actual gross profit			125,600

Check on actual gross profit:

	£	£
Sales revenue (£975 × 1,000)		975,000
Material cost	720,000	
Labour cost	63,000	
Variable production overhead cost	25,000	
Fixed production overhead cost	41,400	
Actual gross profit	849,400	
		125,600

13a.3 Working backwards

The correct answer is C.

Let the quantity of material X used = Y

5750 units should have used (× 10 kg)	57,500 kg
but did use	Y kg
Usage variance in kg	(Y – 57,500) kg
× standard price per kg	× £10
Usage variance in £	£1,500 (A)

$\therefore \quad 10(Y - 57,500) = 1,500 \quad Y - 57,500 = 150 \quad \therefore Y = 57,650$ kg

> **Alternative approach**
>
> $\text{Usage variance in kg} = \dfrac{\text{Usage variance £}}{\text{Standard price}} = \dfrac{£1,500}{£10}(A) = 150 \text{ kg (A)}$
>
> $\therefore$ Quantity of X actually used 57,500 + 150 = 57,650 kg

13a.4 Mix and yield variances

	£
Price variances	
2,000 kg of X should cost (× £2)	4,000
but did cost	4,100
Material X price variance	100 (A)
2,400 kg of Y should cost (× £3.60)	8,640
but did cost	9,600
Material Y price variance	960 (A)

First approach for mix variances

Total quantity used (2,000 + 2,400) kg = 4,400 kg

Standard mix for actual use = $^3/_8$ × (1,650 kg) + $^5/_8$ Y (2,750 kg) = 4,400 kg

	'Should' mix Actual quantity Standard mix	'Did' mix Actual quantity Actual mix	Difference	× Standard price	Variance
X	1,650 kg	2,000 kg	350 kg (A)	× £2	£700 (A)
Y	2,750 kg	2,400 kg	350 kg (F)	× £3.60	£1,260 (F)
	4,400 kg	4,400 kg	–		£560 (F)

Alternative approach for mix variances

The alternative method will produce the same total mix variance, but a different split between the mix variance for each material.

The standard weighted average price of the input materials is £24/8 kg = £3 per kg.

	'Should' mix Actual quantity Standard mix	'Did' mix Actual quantity Actual mix	Difference	£ (W1)	Variance
X	1,650 kg	2,000 kg	350 kg more	× £1 less	£350 (F)
Y	2,750 kg	2,400 kg	350 kg less	× £0.60 more	£210 (F)
	4,400 kg	4,400 kg	–		£560 (F)

Workings

	X	Y
Difference between w/av price and standard price	£(3 – 2) = £1 less	£(3 – 3.60) = £0.60 more

Yield variance

Each unit of D456 requires	3 kg	of X, costing	£6
	5 kg	of Y, costing	£18
	8 kg		£24

4,400 kg should have yielded (÷ 8 kg)	550 units
but did yield	500 units
Yield variance in units	50 units (A)
× standard material cost per unit of output	× £24
Yield variance in £	£1,200 (A)

13a.5 Limitations of mix and yield variances

Some limitations of the calculation of material mix and yield variances are as follows:

(a)   A **change in the mix** of materials used will almost certainly have an **impact upon the yield**, but this will not be isolated from other causes of the yield variance, such as substandard materials quality.

(b)   If a **favourable mix variance can be established**, without adverse effects upon yield or output quality, the **standard mix is obsolete**.

(c)   Changes in actual unit costs of some ingredients may make a change in mix economically viable. An attempt **to optimise the price variance** may therefore result in an **adverse mix variance**.

(d)   **Changes to the proportions of the input materials** are **assumed** to have **no impact on product quality**.

13a.6 Deviations from standardised mix

Quantity input = (420 + 180 + 550) = 1,150 litres

Standard mix for the quantity input

The standardised mix for the quantity input is the calculation we carry out to determine the individual mix variances in units. You can check you have done it correctly by ensuring that the sum of the individual components equals total quantity input.

	Standardised mix for quantity input	Litres
O	1,150 × (0.4/1.1) =	418.18
H	1,150 × (0.2/1.1) =	209.09
N	1,150 × (0.5/1.1) =	522.73
		1,150.00

Deviations – absolute

These are simply the differences between the actual input and the standard input calculated above.

	Actual input Litres	Standard mix for actual input (see above) Litres	Deviation (or difference) Litres
O	420	418.18	1.82 (A)
H	180	209.09	29.09 (F)
N	550	522.73	27.27 (A)
	1,150	1,150.00	–

Deviations as a %

O	$(1.82/418.18) \times 100\% = 0.435\%$
H	$(29.09/209.09) \times 100\% = 13.913\%$
N	$(27.27/522.73) \times 100\% = 5.217\%$

13a.7 Labour mix variances

(a) **Labour efficiency variance**

	Audit manager	Junior auditors	Audit clerks	Total $
Audit should take	30 hours	120 hours	50 hours	
but did take	27 hours	125 hours	58 hours	
Efficiency variance in hours	3 hours (F)	5 hours (A)	8 hours (A)	
× standard rate per hour	× $450	× $170	× $50	
	$1,350 (F)	$850 (A)	$400 (A)	$100 (F)

(b) **Labour yield variance**

Standard weighted average labour rate per hour $= \dfrac{\$36,400}{200} = \$182$

Audit should have taken	200 hours
but did take	210 hours
Labour yield variance in hours	10 hours (A)
× standard rate per hour	× $182
Labour yield variance	$1,820 (A)

(c) **Labour mix variance**

	Should mix Actual hours Standard mix	Did mix Actual hours Actual mix	Difference	$	Variance $
Audit manager	31.5	27	4.5 less	× $268 more	1,206 (F)
Junior auditor	126.0	125	1.0 less	× $12 less	12 (A)
Audit clerks	52.5	58	5.5 more	× $132 less	726 (F)
	210.0	210	–		1,920 (F)

13a.8 Total planning and operational variances

The correct answer is A.

Operational variance

	£
Revised standard cost for revised standard kg for actual output (£1.50 × 2 kg × 1,000)	3,000
Actual cost for 1,000 units	3,250
Total operational variance	250 (A)

Planning variance

	£
Revised standard cost for revised standard kg for actual output (£1.50 × 2 kg × 1,000)	3,000
Original standard cost for original standard kg for actual output (£1 × 2 kg × 1,000)	2,000
Total planning variance	1,000 (A)

13a.9 Planning and operational variances

The correct answer is B.

Keep calm and calculate the **total** variance in the normal way to begin with. Then you will understand what it is that you have to analyse. Next, follow through the workings shown above, substituting the figures in the exercise for those in the example.

	£
Total labour variance	
540 units should have cost (× 3 hrs × £6)	9,720
but did cost	10,500
	780 (A)

	£
Planning variance	
Revised standard cost for revised standard hours for actual output (£6.25 × 3 hours × 540)	10,125
Original standard cost for original standard hours for actual output (£6 × 3 hours × 540)	9,720
	405 (A)

	£
Operational rate variance	
Revised standard cost of actual hours paid (£6.25 × 1,700)	10,625
Actual cost of actual hours paid	10,500
	125 (F)

Operational efficiency variance	
540 units should have taken (× 3 hours)	1,620 hours
but did take	1,700 hours
Operational efficiency variance in hours	80 hours (A)
× revised standard rate per hour	× £6.25
Operational efficiency variance in £	£500 (A)

13a.10 Planning variances and sub-variances

As always, calculate the **total** materials variance first, to give you a point of reference. Then follow through the workings above.

	£
Total materials variance	
10,000 units should have cost (× £4.50)	45,000
but did cost	50,000
	5,000 (A)
Operational price variance	
Revised standard price of actual purchases (£1.80 × 28,000)	50,400
Actual price of actual purchases	50,000
	400 (F)
Operational usage variance	
10,000 units should use (× 2.5 kg)	25,000 kg
but did use	28,000 kg
Variance in kg	3,000 kg (A)
× standard rate per kg	× 1.80
	£5,400
	(A)

BPP
LEARNING MEDIA

Planning variance

	£
Original standard cost for revised standard kg for actual output (£1.50 × 2.5 kg × 10,000)	37,500
Revised standard cost for revised standard kg for actual output (£1.80 × 2.5 kg × 10,000)	45,000
Planning rate variance	7,500 (A)

	£
The original standard kg for actual output (10,000 × 3 kg)	30,000
The revised standard kg for actual output (10,000 × 2.5 kg)	25,000
Efficiency planning variance in kg	5,000 (F)
× standard rate per kg	× £1.50
Planning efficient variance	7,500 (F)

Total planning variance

	£
Revised standard cost for revised standard kg for actual output (£1.80 × 2.5 kg × 10,000)	45,000
Original standard cost for original standard kg for actual output (£1.50 × 3 kg × 10,000)	45,000
Total planning variance	–

(Note that total planning variance = planning rate variance + planning efficiency variance.)

13a.11 Sales planning and operational variances

The only variances are selling price variances.

Planning (selling price) variance

	£
Original budget (10,000 × £10.00)	100,000
Revised budget (10,000 × £4.50)	45,000
Planning variance	55,000 (A)

The original variance was too optimistic and so the planning variance is an adverse variance.

Operational (selling price) variance

	£
Actual sales (10,000 × £5)	50,000
Revised sales (10,000 × £4.50)	45,000
Operational (selling price) variance	5,000 (F)

The total difference between budgeted and actual profit of £50,000 (A) is therefore analysed as follows:

	£
Operational variance (selling price)	5,000 (F)
Planning variance	55,000 (A)
	50,000 (A)

INTERPRETATION OF VARIANCES

The **calculation of variances** in itself **does little to help management**. Managers need to know whether or not a variance should be investigated, why the variance might have occurred, what it means and whether its occurrence is linked to any other reported variance. Sections 1 to 4 will explain how this is done.

In **Section 1** we will look at the issues that need to be considered before management decide **whether they need to look into the occurrence of a variance** more closely.

Section 2 looks at the **models** that can be used to determine whether or not a variance is worthy of **investigation**. You may need to think back to your *Business Maths* studies at Fundamentals level here!

Joint variances, which arise when both price and quantity of inputs differ from standards, are covered briefly in **Section 3**. Such variances are of particular relevance when allocating responsibility for the occurrence of variances.

Section 4 looks at **why variances might occur** and at the meaning of fixed overhead variances.

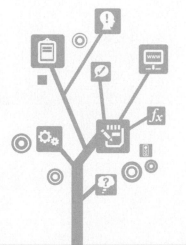

Topic list	Learning outcomes	Syllabus references	Ability required
1 To investigate or not to investigate?	A1(d)	A1(d)(i)(ii)	Analysis
2 Variance investigation models	A1(d)	A1(d)(i)(ii)	Analysis
3 Joint variances: the controllability principle	A1(d)	A1(d)(i)(ii)	Analysis
4 Interpreting variances	A1(d)	A1(d)(i)(ii)	Analysis

Chapter Overview

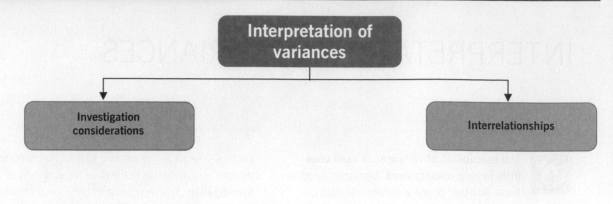

1 To investigate or not to investigate?

Introduction

Before management decide whether or not to investigate a particular variance, there are a number of factors that should be considered.

Materiality

Small variations in a single period are bound to occur and **are unlikely to be significant**. Obtaining an 'explanation' is likely to be time consuming and irritating for the manager concerned. The explanation will often be 'chance', which is not, in any case, particularly helpful. For such variations, further investigation is not worthwhile.

Controllability

Controllability must also influence the decision whether to investigate further. If there is a general worldwide price increase in the price of an important raw material, there is **nothing that can be done internally** to control the effect of this. If a central decision is made to award all employees a 10% increase in salary, staff costs in division A will increase by this amount and the variance is not controllable by division A's manager. Uncontrollable variances call for a **change in the plan**, not an investigation into the past.

Variance trend

If, say, an efficiency **variance** is £1,000 adverse in month 1, the obvious conclusion is that the process is **out of control** and that corrective action must be taken. This may be correct, but what if the same variance is £1,000 adverse every month? The **trend** indicates that the process is **in control** and the standard has been wrongly set. Suppose, though, that the same variance is consistently £1,000 adverse for each of the first 6 months of the year but that production has steadily fallen from 100 units in month 1 to 65 units by month 6. The variance trend in absolute terms is constant but, relative to the number of units produced, efficiency has got steadily worse.

Cost

The likely cost of an investigation needs to be weighed against the cost to the organisation of allowing the variance to continue in future periods.

Interrelationship of variances

Generally speaking, individual variances should not be looked at in isolation. One variance might be interrelated with another, and much of it might have occurred only because the other, interrelated, variance occurred too. When two variances are **interdependent (interrelated), one** will usually be **adverse** and the other **one favourable**. Here are some examples.

Interrelated variances	Explanation
Materials price and usage	If cheaper materials are purchased in order to obtain a favourable price variance, materials wastage might be higher and an adverse usage variance will occur. If the cheaper material is more difficult to handle, there might be an adverse labour efficiency variance too.
	If more expensive material is purchased, however, the price variance will be adverse but the usage variance might be favourable.

BPP
LEARNING MEDIA

Interrelated variances	Explanation
Labour rate and efficiency	If employees in a workforce are paid higher rates for experience and skill, using a highly skilled team might lead to an adverse rate variance and possibly a favourable efficiency variance. In contrast, a favourable rate variance might indicate a larger than expected proportion of inexperienced workers, which could result in an adverse labour efficiency variance, and perhaps poor materials handling and high rates of rejects and hence an adverse materials usage variance.
Selling price and sales volume	We looked at this in Chapter 12b.
Materials mix and yield variance (calculations of these variances were covered in the previous chapter)	If the mix is cheaper than standard, there may be a resulting lower yield, so that a favourable mix variance might be offset by an adverse yield variance.
	Alternatively, a mix that is cheaper than standard might have no effect on yield, but the end product might be of sub-standard quality. Sales volumes might then be affected, or sales prices might have to be reduced to sell off the output that customers are not willing to buy at the normal price.

Because management accountants analyse total variances into component elements, ie materials price and usage, labour rate, idle time, efficiency, and so on, they should not lose sight of the overall 'integrated' picture of events, and any interdependence between variances should be reported whenever it is suspected to have occurred.

Question 13b.1
Interdependence between variances

Learning outcome A1(d)

There is likely to be interdependence between an adverse labour rate variance and:

A   A favourable materials usage variance
B   An adverse fixed overhead expenditure variance
C   An adverse selling price variance
D   None of the above

Exam skills

'Interpretation of variances and the interrelationship between variances' are specific syllabus topics. You could be required to perform calculations in the objective test questions (OTQs) **and** to analyse and **explain** results in the integrated case study (ICS).

The **efficiency variance** reported in any control period, whether for materials or labour and overhead, will **depend on the efficiency level in the standard cost**.

The performance standard used

(a)   If an **ideal standard** is used, **variances** will always be **adverse**.

(b)   If an **attainable standard** is used, or a **current** standard, we should expect **small variances around the standard** from one period to the next, which may not necessarily be significant.

(c)   Management might set a **target** standard **above the current** standard but **below the ideal** standard of efficiency. In such a situation, there will probably be adverse efficiency variances, though not as high as if ideal standards were used. However, if there is **support from the workforce** in trying to

improve efficiency levels to the new standard, management would hope to see the **adverse efficiency variances gradually diminish** period by period, until the workforce eventually achieves 100% efficiency at the target standard level.

It is therefore necessary to make a judgement about what an adverse or favourable efficiency variance signifies, in relation to the 'toughness' of the standard set. **Trends** in efficiency variances; that is, gradual improvements or deteriorations in efficiency, should be monitored, because these might be more informative than the variance in a single control period.

1.1 Management signals from variance trend information

Variance analysis is a means of assessing performance, but it is only a method of signalling to management areas of possible weakness where control action might be necessary. It does not provide a ready-made diagnosis of faults, nor does it provide management with a ready-made indication of what action needs to be taken. It merely **highlights items for possible investigation**.

Signals that may be extracted from variance trend information

(a)   Materials price variances may be favourable for a few months, then shift to adverse variances for the next few months and so on. This could indicate that prices are **seasonal** and perhaps inventory could be built up in cheap seasons.

(b)   Regular, perhaps fairly slight, increases in adverse price variances usually indicate the workings of general **inflation**. If desired, allowance could be made for general inflation when flexing the budget.

(c)   Rapid large increases in adverse price variances may suggest a sudden **scarcity** of a resource. It may soon be necessary to seek out cheaper substitutes.

Question 13b.2	Trends in variances

Learning outcome A1(d)

A production department has experienced an improving trend in reported labour efficiency variances but a worsening trend in machine running expenses. Suggest possible reasons for these trends and comment on the management action that may be necessary.

1.1.1 Percentage variance charts

A trend in variances is often easier to appreciate when the variances are presented as percentages. These percentages become even easier to interpret and understand when presented graphically.

Example: percentage variance charts

The standard cost of a material is £15 per kg and the standard usage for 1 unit of product B is 10 kg. In the first six months of the year, actual usage and costs and associated variances have been as follows:

	Output Units	Usage Kg	Cost £	Price variances £	Usage variances £
January	30	300	4,800	300 (A)	–
February	40	425	6,800	425 (A)	375 (A)
March	35	385	6,160	385 (A)	525 (A)
April	42	465	6,975	–	675 (A)
May	38	420	6,300	–	600 (A)
June	40	435	6,525	–	525 (A)

Required

(a)   Calculate the price and usage variances in percentage terms (based on standard cost or usage).

(b)   Comment on the trend as revealed by the absolute and percentage variances.

(c)   Present a percentage variance chart of the data.

Solution

(a)

	Price variances %		Usage variances %	
January	$6^2/_3$ (A)	(300/4,500 × 100%)*	0	
February	$6^2/_3$ (A)	(425/6,375 × 100%)	6.25 (A)	(25/400 × 100%)**
March	$6^2/_3$ (A)	(385/5,775 × 100%)	10.00 (A)	(35/350 × 100%)
April	–		10.70 (A)	(45/420 × 100%)
May	–		10.50 (A)	(40/380 × 100%)
June	–		8.75 (A)	(35/400 × 100%)

*Price variance ÷ what actual usage should have cost × 100%

**(Actual usage − what should have been used) ÷ what should have been used × 100%

(b)   The absolute price variances indicate that suppliers were charging more than had been anticipated but the price charged appears to be **fluctuating**. The percentage measures show that there was a **temporary blip** of a constant amount in the first quarter of the year. Perhaps a bulk discount was not being claimed, and **corrective action** was taken in April.

There is less to choose between the two approaches for the usage variance. The process seems to have gone out of control in February but corrective action appears to be bringing it back under control. Both absolute and percentage measures show this, but the percentage measures more clearly indicate that the control action is working (compare June and April).

(c)

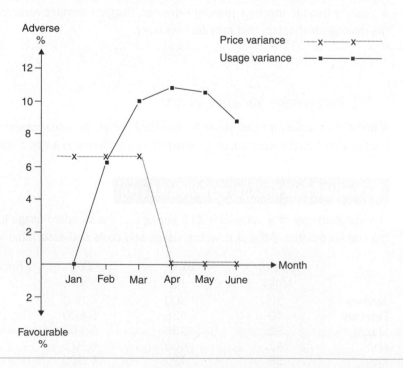

| Question 13b.3 | Percentage variance chart |

Learning outcome A1(d)

What conclusion could you reach from the following percentage variance chart?

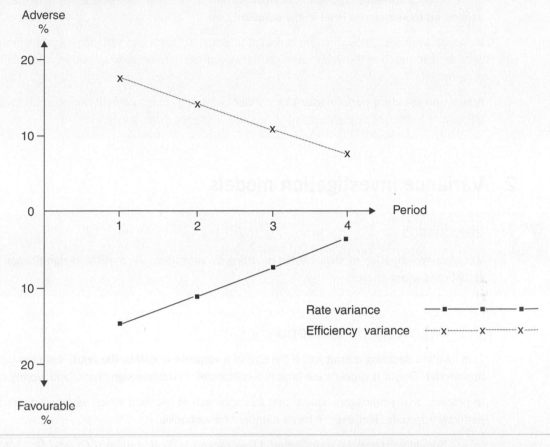

A variance may represent a small percentage of the standard value but involve significant amounts of money. Both percentages and absolute values should therefore be considered when analysing variances.

KEY POINT

1.2 Why might actual and standard performance differ?

Here are some common reasons.

Reason	Comment
Measurement errors	Scales may be misread. Pilfering or wastage may go unrecorded.
Out of date standards	Price standards may become out of date during periods of high inflation. Standards may also become out of date due to technological development.
Efficient or inefficient operations	Spoilage, idle time, better-quality material or more highly skilled labour may all affect efficiency of operations.
Random or chance fluctuations	A standard is an average figure. Individual measurements are likely to deviate from the standard.

Section summary

Before investigating variances, management should bear in mind **materiality**, **controllability**, **variance trend**, **cost**, **interrelationships** and **performance standards**.

The **efficiency variance** reported in any control period, whether for materials or labour and overhead, will **depend on the efficiency level in the standard cost**.

Individual variances should not be looked at in isolation, since one variance might be **interrelated** with another, and much of the variance might have occurred only because the other, interrelated variance occurred too.

Actual and standard performance might differ because of measurement errors, out of date standards, efficient or inefficient operations and/or random or chance fluctuations.

2 Variance investigation models

Introduction

Variance investigation models involve **reporting by exception**, the **statistical significance model** and **statistical control charts**.

2.1 Reporting by exception

This involves **deciding a limit** and if the size of a **variance is within the limit**, it should be considered **immaterial**. Only if it exceeds the limit is it considered materially significant, and worthy of investigation.

In practice, many managers believe that this approach to deciding which variances to investigate is perfectly adequate. However, it has a number of **drawbacks**.

(a)   Should variances be investigated if they exceed 10% of standard? Or 5%? Or 15%?

(b)   Should a different fixed percentage be applied to favourable and unfavourable variances?

(c)   Suppose that the fixed percentage is, say, 10% and an important category of expenditure has in the past been very closely controlled so that adverse variances have never exceeded, say, 2% of standard. Now if adverse variances suddenly shoot up to, say, **8% or 9%** of standard, there might well be **serious excess expenditures incurred that ought to be controlled** but, with the fixed percentage limit at 10%, the variances would not be 'flagged' for investigation.

(d)   **Unimportant categories** of low-cost expenditures might be loosely controlled, with variances commonly exceeding 10% in both a favourable and adverse direction. These would be regularly – and **unnecessarily** – flagged for investigation.

(e)   Where actual expenditures have **normal and expected wide fluctuations** from period to period, but the 'standard' is a fixed expenditure amount, variances will be **flagged for investigation unnecessarily often**.

(f)   There is **no attempt to consider the costs and potential benefits of investigating variances** (except insofar as the pre-set percentage is of 'material significance').

(g)   The **past history of variances in previous periods is ignored**. For example, if the pre-set percentage limit is set at 10% and an item of expenditure has regularly exceeded the standard by, say, 6% per month for a number of months in a row, in all probability there is a situation that ought to warrant control action. Using the pre-set percentage rule, however, the variance would never be flagged for investigation in spite of the cumulative adverse variances.

Some of the difficulties can be overcome by **varying the pre-set percentage from account to account** (for example, 5% for direct labour efficiency, 2% for rent and rates, 10% for sales representatives' expenditure, 15% for postage costs, 5% for direct materials price, 3% for direct materials usage and so on). On the other hand, some difficulties, if they are significant, can only be overcome with a different cost-variance investigation model.

2.2 Statistical significance model

The normal distribution and standard deviation were covered in CIMA Certificate C03 *Fundamentals of Business Mathematics*. You may need to read through your old notes if you have forgotten the concepts.

Historical data are used to **calculate** both a standard as **an expected average** and the **expected standard deviation** around this average when the process is under control. An **in-control process** (process being material usage, fixed overhead expenditure and so on) is one in which any resulting **variance is simply due to random fluctuations** around the expected outcome. An **out-of-control process**, on the other hand, is one in which **corrective action can be taken to remedy any variance**.

By assuming that variances that occur are normally distributed around this average, a **variance will be investigated if it is <u>more</u> than a distance from the expected average that the estimated normal distribution suggests is likely if the process is in control**. (Note that such a variance would be deemed significant.)

(a)   A 95% or 0.05 significance level rule would state that variances should be investigated if they exceed 1.96 standard deviations from the standard.

(b)   A 99% or 0.01 significance level rule would state that variances should be investigated if they exceed 2.58 standard deviations from the standard. This is less stringent than a 0.05 significance level rule.

(c)   For simplicity, 1.96 and 2.58 standard deviations can be rounded up to 2 and 3 standard deviations respectively.

For example, data could be collected and analysed to reveal the following pattern.

Mean weight per batch   450 kg
Standard deviation   50 kg

Assume that a 0.05 significance level rule is in use for investigating variances, and that the weights conform to a normal distribution.

Suppose that in June, one sample batch weighed 600 kg. 95% of outcomes will be within +/–1.96 standard deviations of the mean. So 95% of outcomes will be in the range 450 +/– (1.96 × 50), that is 352 kg to 548 kg. The actual weight of this batch was 600 kg, so this batch falls outside the 95% limit and the variance should be investigated.

Question 13b.4	Investigating variances

Learning outcomes A1(d)

Data has been collected and analysed, and reveals that travel costs per month are Y25,000, with a standard deviation of Y2,000. A 0.01 significance rule is in use. Actual travel expenses are Y28,750. Should the resulting variance be investigated?

The statistical significance rule has two principal **advantages** over the reporting by exception approach.

(a) **Important costs** that normally vary by only a small amount from standard will be **signalled for investigation if variances increase significantly**.

(b) Costs that **usually fluctuate by large amounts will not be signalled** for investigation unless variances are extremely large.

The main **disadvantage** of the statistical significance rule is the problem of assessing standard deviations in expenditure.

2.3 Statistical control charts

By marking variances and control limits on a control chart, **investigation** is signalled not only when a particular **variance exceeds the control limit** (since it would be non-random and worth investigating) but also when the **trend of variances shows a progressively worsening movement** in actual results (even though the variance in any single control period has not yet overstepped the control limit).

The $\bar{x}$ **control chart** is based on the principle of the statistical significance model. For each cost item, a chart is kept of monthly variances and **tolerance limits are set at 1, 2 or 3 standard deviations**.

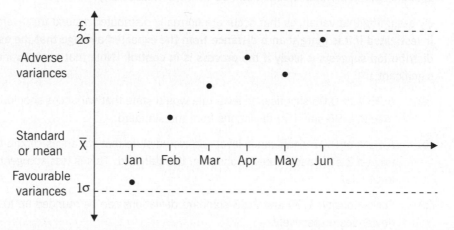

In this example, variances do not exceed the tolerance limits in any month, but the chart shows a worsening of variances over time, and so management might decide that an investigation is warranted, perhaps when it exceeds an inner warning limit.

Using a **cusum chart, the cumulative sum of variances** over a long period of time **is plotted**. If the variances are not significant, these 'sums' will simply fluctuate in a random way above and below the average to give a total or cumulative sum of zero. But if significant variances occur, the cumulative sum will start to develop a positive or negative drift, and when it exceeds a set tolerance limit the situation must be investigated.

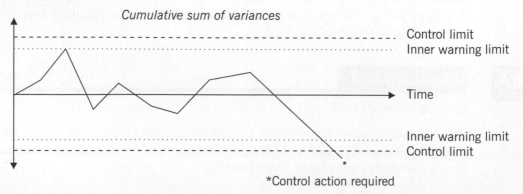

The **advantage** of the multiple period approach over the single period approach is that **trends are detectable earlier**, and control action would be introduced sooner than might have been the case if only current-period variances were investigated.

Section summary

Variance investigation models involve **reporting by exception**, the **statistical significance model** and **statistical control charts**.

3 Joint variances: the controllability principle

Introduction

A **joint** or **composite variance** should be reported to each of the managers jointly responsible for it.

Suppose that a company makes a standard product, which uses 6 kilograms of material at £2 per kilogram. If actual output during a period is 100 units, which uses 640 kilograms at a cost of £2.30 per kilogram, the variances would be calculated as follows:

	£
640 kilograms should cost (× £2)	1,280
but did cost (× £2.30)	1,472
Price variance	192 (A)
100 units should use (× 6 kg)	600 kg
but did use	640 kg
Usage variance in kg	40 kg (A)
× standard cost per kg	× £2
Usage variance in £	£80 (A)

The **usage variance** would probably be **reported to the production manager**, and the **price variance** to the **purchasing manager**. Each would be held responsible for 'controlling' their respective variance item.

This traditional method of reporting fails to show that some of the price variance could have been avoided by the production manager. If the usage of materials had not been adverse, there would have been no need to buy the extra 40 kilograms of material, and the savings would have been 40 kg × £2.30 = £92. The purchasing manager could also have avoided the variance, of course, by buying all the materials at £2 per kilogram. This means that the **excess purchase price of the excess usage of materials could have been avoided by either the purchasing manager or the production manager**.

The name sometimes given to this **adverse price of adverse usage is a joint or composite variance**.

This is an application of the **controllability principle** in variance reporting. The principle is that managers should only be held responsible for costs over which they can exercise control.

KEY TERM

A JOINT VARIANCE is 'A variance which is caused by both the prices and quantities of inputs differing from the specifications in the original standard'.

(CIMA Official Terminology)

Section summary

A **joint** or **composite variance** should be reported to each of the managers jointly responsible for it.

4 Interpreting variances

4.1 Material price variances

Introduction

An **adverse** price variance would suggest that the **managers responsible for buying decisions have paid too much for the materials**, and should be more careful in future. There are **reasons** why a large adverse or favourable price variance might occur, however, which are **outside the buying management's control**.

Reason	Comment
Inflation	This was discussed in Chapter 12a.
Seasonal variations in prices	If material prices fluctuate seasonally, the standard price might be an average price for the year as a whole, on the assumption that it is impractical to buy a whole year's supply in the cheap season and store it until needed. In such a situation, price variances should be favourable for purchases in the cheap season and adverse for purchases in the more expensive season.
Rush orders	If buying managers are asked to make an order for immediate delivery, they might have to forgo a bulk purchase discount, or pay more for the quick supply lead time. The responsibility for the resulting adverse price variance should therefore belong to whoever made the rush order necessary in the first place.

Price variances should be **reported in the period when the purchases are made**, not when the materials are issued from stores and used. This is mainly because control information about price variances ought to be made available as soon as possible after the buying decision that gave rise to the variance; that is, when the materials are bought.

4.2 Materials usage variances

A materials usage variance indicates that the quantity of materials consumed was larger or smaller than standard. It could indicate that materials **wastage** was higher or lower than it should have been or that the quantity of **rejects** was above or below standard. Wastage costs money, and should be kept to a minimum. The size of a materials usage variance, however, just like the size of a labour efficiency variance, **depends on the standard rate of usage** (or efficiency) and **whether the standard was attainable or ideal**.

In certain circumstances, it could be worthwhile carrying out further analysis into mix and yield variances. These variances were covered in the previous chapter.

4.3 Labour rate variances

It might be tempting to think that the rate variance is something that operational managers can do little about, since rates of pay will be agreed at a senior level. A rate variance might, however, be due to **unexpected overtime working** (with overtime paid at a premium rate) or **productivity bonuses** added onto basic rates. To some extent, these should be **controllable by operational managers**.

4.4 Labour efficiency variances

The labour efficiency variance indicates that the actual production time needed to do the work was longer or less than expected. **Inefficiency costs money**: after all, if it takes three hours to make a unit of product instead of two hours, the unit cost of production will be higher and the profit from selling the unit will be less.

A standard time for labour to produce an item of work will normally take into account **contingency allowances** for down time and rest periods. Whether or not there is an allowance for these factors will depend on the type of **performance standard** used (ideal, attainable and so on). In a production industry based on batch production or jobbing work, the standard time will include an allowance for setting up times and clearing up times for each batch or job finished.

An **adverse** labour efficiency variance might indicate **poor labour productivity** in a period, for which a **badly motivated** workforce or **weak supervision** might be to blame, but other causes of a variance might be as follows:

(a)   Excessively **high down times**, due to a serious machine breakdown, or a bottleneck in production which left many of the workforce idle and waiting for work

(b)   **Shorter batch runs** than expected, which increase the amount of setting-up time and cleaning-up time between batches, when no physical output is being produced

4.5 Overhead variances

Variances are supposed to provide management with **control information**. For example, an adverse material price variance of £100 tells management that the material used cost £100 more than it should have cost. But what about information provided by overhead variances? What control information can managers get from the fact that there is an adverse fixed overhead volume variance of £450? The information is not nearly as clear or understandable as that provided by labour and material variances, is it? But why is this?

4.5.1 Fixed overhead volume variance

Unlike expenditure variances or variable cost efficiency variances, the fixed overhead volume variance is **not a true reflection of the extra or lower cash spending** by an organisation as a result of the variance occurring. This is because the **variance** is **valued** in terms of **overhead absorption rates**. The estimates used in the calculation of these rates are often quite **arbitrary** but it is these absorption rates that determine the value assigned to the **overhead volume variance**.

Together with the expenditure variance, the **fixed overhead volume variance** shows the **under- or over-absorbed fixed overhead**. Under/over absorption is simply a **book balancing exercise**, however, which occurs as a result of the cost ascertainment process of absorption costing, and the level of under-/over-absorbed overhead depends on the **accuracy** of the **original estimates** used in calculating the absorption rates. The level of under/over absorption is **not control information**; it is simply a figure used to balance the books.

Perhaps the overhead volume variance would be more useful, however, if the losses or gains in output were valued in terms of **contribution** rather than in terms of absorption rates (which have arbitrary elements and were designed for quite a different purpose). The existence of a fixed overhead volume variance can therefore be important; it is only the **monetary value** given to the variance that **can be misleading** to managers.

4.5.2 Variable overhead efficiency variance

This arises because labour is either **more** or **less efficient than standard**. Variable production overheads tend to be incurred in **direct proportion** to **production hours** worked, and so if the workforce spends too much time on a job, it will incur not only more labour cost than it should, but also more variable overhead cost too.

4.5.3 Expenditure variances

The **fixed overhead expenditure variance** probably provides the **most useful** management information as the size of the variance can be said to be **controllable**.

(a) It does have its limitations, however. It is made up of a price component and a usage component. It can therefore vary if there are changes in charges (for example salary increases) or if quantities change (for example if more staff are taken on).

(b) For such variances to have any practical value as a control measure, the variances for each **cost centre** need to be calculated, and reported to the **managers responsible**. Within each overhead cost centre, the manager should be able to analyse the total variance into indirect **materials** cost variances, indirect **labour** cost variances and excess or favourable spending on other items, such as depreciation and postage.

4.6 Selling price variance

This is perhaps the variance with the **most obvious meaning**. A selling price variance indicates by how much actual selling prices of products or services have exceeded or been less than standard.

Selling price variances will be **common**. Many companies sell their products to customers at a discount, with the size of the discount depending on the size of the order or who the customer is. (For example, regular customers might be given a minimum discount on their purchases, regardless of order quantity.) The standard selling price might ignore discounts altogether, or it might have an allowance for the average expected discount. In either event, the actual sales prices and standard sales prices will usually differ.

4.7 Sales volume variance

A sales volume variance will result in **higher than expected sales revenue if it is favourable, but there will be an off-setting increase in the cost of sales**. Similarly, an adverse sales volume variance will result in lower than expected sales revenue, but there will be an offsetting reduction in the cost of sales.

The **net effect** of a sales volume variance is an **increase or reduction in profitability**, which is valued in terms of **profit margin** when a standard **absorption costing system** is in use and in terms of **contribution** margin, when a standard **marginal costing system** is in use.

4.8 Summary

Variance	Favourable	Adverse
Material price	Unforeseen discounts received Greater care in purchasing Change in material standard	Price increase Careless purchasing Change in material standard
Material usage	Material used of higher quality than standard More efficient use of material Errors in allocating material to jobs	Defective material Excessive waste or theft Stricter quality control Errors in allocating material to jobs
Labour rate	Use of workers at a rate of pay lower than standard	Wage rate increase
Idle time	Idle time was build into budget to allow for bad weather, say, but none occurred	Machine breakdown, illness or injury to worker
Labour efficiency	Output produced more quickly than expected because of worker motivation, better-quality materials etc Errors in allocating time to jobs	Lost time in excess of standard Output lower than standard set because of lack of training, sub-standard materials etc Errors in allocating time to jobs

Variance	Favourable	Adverse
Fixed overhead expenditure	Savings in costs incurred More economical use of services	Increase in cost of services used Excessive use of services Change in type of service used

Overhead expenditure variances ought to be traced to the individual cost centres where the variances occurred.

| **Fixed overhead volume** | Production or level of activity greater than budgeted | Production or level of activity less than budgeted |

Question 13b.5

Reasons for variances

Learning outcome A1(d)

M absorbs fixed production overhead at a predetermined rate based on budgeted output. Extracts from the variance analysis for April are as follows:

Fixed production overhead expenditure variance   £6,000 (F)
Fixed production overhead volume variance   £1,000 (A)

Consider the following statements concerning production in April.

Statement

1   The fixed production overhead was over absorbed by £5,000.
2   Production output was higher than budget.
3   Production overhead expenditure was £6,000 lower than budgeted.

Which of these statements is/are consistent with the reported variances?

A   Statement 1 only
B   Statements 2 and 3 only
C   Statements 1 and 3 only
D   Statements 1, 2 and 3 only

Question 13b.6

Standard costing and inflation

Learning outcome A1(d)

Jot down ideas for answering the following questions.

(a)   Explain the problems concerning control of operations that a manufacturing company can be expected to experience in using a standard costing system during periods of rapid inflation.

(b)   Suggest three methods by which the company could try to overcome the problems to which you have referred in your answer to (a) above, indicating the shortcomings of each method.

Section summary

An adverse material price variance may be partly due to inflation and therefore not wholly within the buying management's control.

Chapter Summary

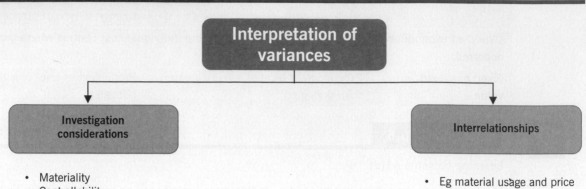

Interpretation of variances

Investigation considerations

- Materiality
- Controllability
- Variance trend
- Cost
- Interrelationships
- Performance standards

Interrelationships

- Eg material usage and price

Quick Quiz

1   Favourable variances are never worthy of investigation because they result in profit increases.

     True   ☐

     False   ☒

2   Which of the following is not a reason why actual and standard performance might differ?

     A   Measurement errors
     Ⓑ   Realistic standards
     C   Efficient or inefficient operations
     D   Random or chance fluctuations

3   Choose the correct words from those highlighted.

     A **cusum/cumus** chart plots **individual/the cumulative sum of** variances **over a period of time/on a one-off basis**.

4   The following variances were reported for period 1.

     Direct labour rate   £2,800 adverse
     Direct labour efficiency   £1,350 favourable

     Which of the following statements are consistent with these variances?

     A   Direct labour achieved levels of efficiency that were higher than standard,
          and were accordingly paid bonuses at higher rates than standard.

     B   The original standard labour rate was unrealistically low because it failed to
          take account of rapid wage inflation.

     C   The production manager elected to use more skilled labour at a higher hourly
          rate of pay than budgeted.

5   If ideal standards are used, reported efficiency variances will tend to be favourable.

     True   ☐

     False   ☒

6   The joint variance based on the excess labour rate over the standard rate and the excess number of hours worked over standard is the responsibility of the production manager.

     True   ☐ ,

     False   ☐

7   Data has been collected and reveals that labour times for a batch of product C have a mean standard labour time of 48 hours. Assume that the times conform to a normal distribution and that the standard deviation is 4 hours. The company policy is to investigate variances that fall outside the range that includes 95% of outcomes. In June, one batch took 57 hours.

     Should this be investigated?

Answers to Quick Quiz

1   False. Variances are interrelated so one favourable variance could be the cause of a more significant adverse variance. This may result in a profit decrease.

2   B   Out of date standards would cause a difference.

3   A **cusum** chart plots **the cumulative sum** of variances **over a period of time**.

4   All of the statements are consistent with the reported variances.

5   False. They will tend to be adverse.

6   True.   Although it is also the responsibility of the manager responsible for labour rates.

7   95% of the outcomes will be within +/–1.96 standard deviations of the mean. So 95% of outcomes will be in the range 48 +/– (1.96 × 4); that is, 40.16 hours to 55.84 hours. The actual number of hours was 57, so this batch falls outside the 95% limit and should be investigated.

Answers to Questions

13b.1 Interdependence between variances

The correct answer is A.

A higher paid and hence more skilled workforce could use materials most efficiently.

13b.2 Trends in variances

Gradually improving labour efficiency variances may signal that the **employees** were **inexperienced** at first and that the standard time was set based on measures taken in the early stages of production. However, the employees are now **increasing in speed as they learn the task** and the efficiency variances are improving as a result.

Alternatively, the improving trend could indicate the success of a recently introduced **productivity bonus scheme** which has not been incorporated into the standard cost.

In either case, opportunities should be sought to encourage the trend and the standard cost should be **revised** if it is to **remain useful** for control purposes.

Another reason, which may be connected with the increased machine running expense, is that employees are operating the machine at a higher speed than expected in the standard, thus **improving the rate of output** and the labour efficiency variance, but increasing the machine running expenses. Management will need to investigate the overall effect of these changes on total costs and on the product quality.

The worsening trend in machine running expenses may be the result of operating the machines at a faster speed than standard, thus **increasing the power costs**. Another possible cause is that the **equipment may be deteriorating** and will soon need repair or even replacement. Management will need to investigate whether repair or replacement of the machine is necessary.

13b.3 Percentage variance chart

These variances could be **interrelated**. As the rate has increased (reducing favourable percentage rate variance), the efficiency has tended more closer to standard levels (reducing percentage adverse efficiency variance).

Since both variances are tending towards a zero percentage it may not be necessary to undertake detailed investigation at this stage.

(Such conclusions may not have been immediately apparent from absolute figures.)

13b.4 Investigating variances

Variance

	Y
Travel costs should have been	25,000
But were	28,750
	3,750 (A)

Number of standard deviations = 3,750/2,000 = 1.875

At a 99% significance level rule, variances should be investigated if they exceed 2.58 standard deviations from the standard. Therefore this variance would not be investigated.

13b.5 Reasons for variances

The correct answer is C.

Statement 1 is correct because over-absorbed fixed overhead is represented by a favourable total overhead variance.

If the production output was higher than budget, the volume variance would be favourable. Statement 2 is incorrect.

The expenditure variance is favourable, therefore actual overhead expenditure was lower than budgeted.

Statement 3 is correct.

13b.6 Standard costing and inflation

(a) (i)   Inflation should be budgeted for in standard prices. But **how** can the rate of inflation and the timing of inflationary increases be accurately **estimated**? Who decides **how much inflationary 'allowance'** should be added to each manager's expenditure budget?

(ii)   How can actual expenditure be judged against a **realistic 'standard' price level**. Ideally, there would be an external price index (for example, one published by the Office for National Statistics) but even external price indices are not reliable guides to the prices an organisation ought to be paying.

(iii)   The existence of inflation tends to **eliminate the practical value of price variances** as a pointer to controlling spending.

(iv)   Inflation affects operations more directly. Usually, costs go up before an organisation can put up the prices of its own products to customers. Inflation therefore tends to **put pressure on a company's cash flows**.

(v)   To provide useful and accurately valued variances (accurate efficiency variances as well as reliable price variances) the **standard costs ought to be revised frequently**. This would be an administrative burden on the organisation.

(vi)   If the organisation uses standard costs for pricing or inventory valuation, frequent revisions of the standard would be necessary to keep prices ahead of costs or inventories sensibly valued.

(b) To overcome the problems, we could suggest the following:

(i) **Frequent revision** of the standard costs. **Problem** – the administrative burden.

(ii) **Incorporating estimates** of the rate of inflation and the timing of inflation into budget expenditure allowances and standard costs. **Problem** – accurate forecasting.

(iii) Constructing **internal indices** of material prices to measure what actual price levels should have been. **Problem** – the administrative burden of constructing and maintaining the index.

(iv) A **determined effort** by management to **keep costs down**, and resist unnecessary spending. Cost control can minimise the damaging effects of price inflation. **Problem** – obtaining the co-operation of all management and employees in cost control efforts.

Now try the questions from the Practice Question Bank

Number	Level
Q13.1 – Q13.12	Practice

DEALING WITH UNCERTAINTY IN ANALYSIS

RISK AND UNCERTAINTY IN DECISION MAKING

In this chapter we look at risk and uncertainty for short-term decision making.

Section 1 contains a general discussion of risk and uncertainty.

Sections 2 to 6 describe the various methods of analysing uncertainty and risk using probability. You need to understand the merits and limitations of these methods for your exam. The uncertainty about the future outcome from taking a decision can sometimes be reduced by obtaining more information first about what is likely to happen. In Section 7 we look at how to **value** that **information** to see if it is worth obtaining it.

Section 8 looks again at a topic we considered in Chapter 9 – **sensitivity analysis. Simulation models**, the topic of Section 9, can be used to deal with decision problems involving a number of uncertain variables.

Topic list	Learning outcomes	Syllabus references	Ability required
1 Risk and uncertainty in decision making	D1(a)	D1(a)(i)(ii)	Analysis
2 Probability analysis and expected values	D1(b)	D1(b)(ii)(iii)(v)	Analysis
3 Data tables	D1(b)	D1(b)	Analysis
4 The maximin, maximax and minimax regret bases for decision making	D1(c)	D1(c)(i), (ii)	Analysis
5 Using the standard deviation to measure risk	D1(b)	D1(b), (iv)	Analysis
6 Decision trees	D1(b)	D1(vi)	Application
7 The value of information	D1(b)	D1(b)(v)	Application
8 Sensitivity analysis	D1(b)	D1(b)(i)	Application
9 Simulation models	D1(b)	D1(b)(i)	Application

Chapter Overview

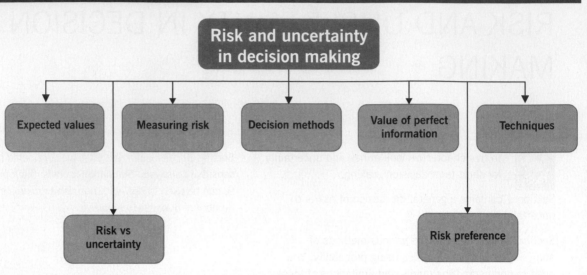

1 Risk and uncertainty in decision making

1.1 What are risk and uncertainty?

Introduction

An example of a **risky situation** is one in which we can say that there is a 70% probability that returns from a project will be in excess of $100,000 but a 30% probability that returns will be less than $100,000. If no information can be provided on the returns from the project, we are faced with an **uncertain** situation.

KEY TERMS

RISK involves situations or events that may or may not occur, but whose probability of occurrence can be calculated statistically and the frequency of their occurrence predicted from past records. Thus insurance deals with risk.

UNCERTAIN EVENTS are those whose outcome cannot be predicted with statistical confidence.

1.2 Risk and capital investment decisions

In general, **risky projects** are those that have **future cash flows**, and hence project returns, that are likely to be **variable**. The **greater the variability**, the **greater the risk**.

The problem of **risk is more acute with capital investment decisions** for the following reasons.

(a)   **Estimates** of capital expenditure might be for **several years ahead**, such as those for major construction projects. Actual costs may escalate well above budget as the work progresses.

(b)   Estimates of benefits will be for several years ahead, sometimes 10, 15 or 20 years ahead or even longer, and such long-term estimates can at best be approximations.

Exam alert

In everyday usage, the terms risk and uncertainty are not clearly distinguished. If you are asked for a definition, do not make the **mistake of believing that the latter** is a more **extreme version of the former**. It is not a question of degree, it is a question of whether or **not sufficient information is available to allow the lack of certainty to be quantified**. As a rule, however, the terms are used interchangeably.

1.3 Risk preference

KEY TERMS

A RISK SEEKER is a decision maker who is interested in the best outcomes no matter how small the chance that they may occur.

A RISK NEUTRAL decision maker is concerned with what will be the most likely outcome.

A RISK AVERSE decision maker acts on the assumption that the worst outcome might occur.

This has clear implications for managers and organisations. A **risk-seeking manager** working for an **organisation** that is characteristically **risk averse** is likely to make decisions that are **not congruent with the goals of the organisation**. There may be a role for the management accountant here, who could be instructed to present decision-making information in such a way as to ensure that the manager considers **all** of the possibilities, including the worst.

What is an acceptable amount of risk will vary from organisation to organisation. For large public companies it is largely a question of what is acceptable to the shareholders. A 'safe' investment will

CASE STUDY

BPP
LEARNING MEDIA

attract investors who are to some extent risk averse, and so the company will be obliged to follow relatively 'safe' policies. A company that is recognised as being an innovator or a 'growth' inventory in a relatively new market will attract investors who are looking for high performance, and are prepared to accept some risk in return. Such companies will be expected to make 'bolder' (more risky) decisions.

The risk of an individual strategy should also be considered in the context of the overall 'portfolio' of investment strategies adopted by the company.

(a)   If a **strategy is risky**, but its outcome is **not related to the outcome of other strategies**, then adopting that strategy will help the company to **spread its risks**.

(b)   If a **strategy is risky**, but is **inversely related** to other adopted strategies (so that if strategy A does well, other adopted strategies will do badly and vice versa) then adopting strategy A would actually **reduce the overall risk of the company's investment portfolio**.

Section summary

People may be **risk seekers**, **risk neutral** or **risk averse**.

In a **risky situation** the **probability** of the outcome can be **quantified**.

In an **uncertain situation** there is not sufficient information for the outcome to be predicted with statistical confidence.

2 Probability analysis and expected values

Introduction

Much of this section will be familiar to you from your earlier studies of CIMA Certificate C03 *Fundamentals of Business Mathematics*.

2.1 Histograms and probability distributions

2.1.1 Frequency distributions

A **frequency distribution** (or **table**) records the number of times each value of a variable occurs.

2.1.2 Histograms

A frequency distribution can be represented pictorially by means of a **histogram**. As you should remember from your earlier studies, a histogram is a chart that looks like a bar chart except that the bars are joined together. On a histogram, frequencies are represented by the area covered by the bars (not the height of the bars).

2.1.3 Probability distributions

If we convert the frequencies in the following frequency distribution table into proportions, we get a **probability distribution**.

Marks out of 10 (statistics test)	Number of students (Frequency distribution)	Proportion or probability (Probability distribution)
0	0	0.00
1	0	0.00
2	1	0.02 (1/50)
3	2	0.04
4	4	0.08
5	10	0.20
6	15	0.30
7	10	0.20
8	6	0.12
9	2	0.04
10	0	0.00
	50	1.00

KEY TERM

A PROBABILITY DISTRIBUTION is an analysis of the proportion of times each particular value occurs in a set of items.

A **graph of the probability distribution** would be the same as the graph of the frequency distribution (histogram), but with the **vertical axis marked in proportions** rather than in numbers.

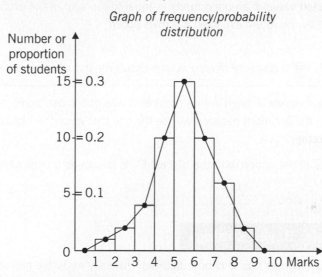

Graph of frequency/probability distribution

(a) The area under the curve in the frequency distribution represents the total number of students whose marks have been recorded, 50 people.

(b) **The area under the curve in a probability distribution is 100%, or 1** (the total of all the probabilities).

2.2 Expected values

Knowledge brought forward from earlier studies

Probability

- **Mutually exclusive outcomes** are outcomes where the occurrence of one of the outcomes excludes the possibility of any of the others happening.

- **Independent events** are events where the outcome of one event in no way affects the outcome of the other events.

- **Dependent** or **conditional** events are events where the outcome of one event depends on the outcome of the others.

- The **addition laws** for two events, A and B, are as follows:

  P(A or B) = P(A) + P(B) when A and B have mutually exclusive outcomes.
  P(A or B) = P(A) + P(B) – P(A and B) when A and B are independent events.

- The **multiplication laws** for two events, A and B, are as follows:

  P(A and B) = 0 when A and B have mutually exclusive outcomes.
  P(A and B) = P(A) P(B) when A and B are independent events.
  P(A and B) = P(A) P(B| A) = P(B) P(A| B) when A and B are dependent/conditional events.

Although the outcome of a decision may not be certain, sometimes probabilities can be assigned to the various possible outcomes from an analysis of previous experience.

Where probabilities are assigned to different outcomes, it is common to evaluate the worth of a decision as the expected value, or weighted average, of these outcomes.

KEY TERM

EXPECTED VALUE is 'The financial forecast of the outcome of a course of action multiplied by the probability of achieving that outcome. The probability is expressed as a value ranging from 0 to 1'.

(*CIMA Official Terminology*)

LEARN

> The **expected value** of an opportunity is equal to the sum of the probabilities of an outcome occurring multiplied by the return expected if it does occur:
>
> $$EV = \Sigma \, px$$
>
> Where p is the probability of an outcome occurring and x is the value (profit or cost) of that outcome.

If a decision maker is faced with a number of alternative decisions, each with a range of possible outcomes, the optimum decision will be the one that gives the highest **expected value** (EV = Σpx). This is **Bayes' strategy**.

KEY TERM

The choice of the option with the highest EV is known as BAYES' STRATEGY.

Example: Bayes' strategy

Suppose a manager has to choose between mutually exclusive options A and B, and the probability distributions of the profits of both options are as follows:

Option A		Option B	
Probability	Profit $	Probability	Profit $
0.8	5,000	0.1	(2,000)
0.2	6,000	0.2	5,000
		0.6	7,000
		0.1	8,000

The expected value (EV) of profit of each option would be measured as follows.

Probability		Option A Profit $		EV of Profit $	Probability		Option B Profit $		EV of Profit $
0.8	×	5,000	=	4,000	0.1	×	(2,000)	=	(200)
0.2	×	6,000	=	1,200	0.2	×	5,000	=	1,000
		EV	=	5,200	0.6	×	7,000	=	4,200
					0.1	×	8,000	=	800
							EV	=	5,800

In this example, since it offers a higher EV of expected profit, option B would be selected in preference to A, unless further risk analysis is carried out.

Question 14.1

Learning outcomes D1(c)

A manager has to choose between mutually exclusive options A, B, C and D and the probable outcomes of each option are as follows.

Option A		Option B		Option C		Option D	
Probability	Cost $	Probability	Cost $	Probability	Cost $	Probability	Cost $
0.1	30,000	0.5	21,000	0.29	15,000	0.03	14,000
0.1	60,000	0.5	20,000	0.54	20,000	0.30	17,000
0.1	80,000			0.17	30,000	0.35	21,000
0.7	5,500					0.32	24,000

All options will produce an income of $30,000.

Which option should be chosen?

A	Option A		C	Option C
B	Option B		D	Option D

2.2.1 Limitations of expected values (EVs)

Referring back to the example in 2.2 called Bayes' strategy, we decided on a preference for B over A on the basis of EV. Note, however, that A's worst possible outcome is a **profit** of $5,000, whereas B might incur a **loss** of $2,000 (although there is a 70% chance that profits would be $7,000 or more, which would be more than the best profits from option A).

Since the **decision must be made once only** between A and B, the EV of profit (which is merely a weighted average of all possible outcomes) has severe limitations as a decision rule by which to judge preference, as it **ignores the range of outcomes** and their **probabilities**. **Utility theory** can help overcome this problem.

EVs are more **valuable** as a guide to decision making where they refer to **outcomes that will occur many times over**.

- The probability that so many customers per day will buy a tin of peaches
- The probability that a call centre will receive so many phone calls per hour

Utility theory attaches weights to the sums of money involved depending on the person's attitude to risk.

2.3 EVs and elementary risk analysis

Where some analysis of risk is required when probabilities have been assigned to various outcomes, an elementary, but extremely useful, form of risk analysis is a form of the worst possible/most likely/best possible analysis.

Example: elementary risk analysis

Skiver has budgeted the following results for the coming year.

Sales Units	Probability	EV of sales Units
30,000	0.3	9,000
40,000	0.4	16,000
50,000	0.3	15,000
		40,000

The budgeted sales price is $10 per unit, and the expected cost of materials is as follows.

Cost per unit of output	Probability	EV
$		$
4	0.2	0.8
6	0.6	3.6
8	0.2	1.6
		6.0

Materials are the only variable cost. All other costs are fixed and are budgeted at $100,000.

The **EV of profit** is $60,000.

	$
Sales (EV 40,000 units) at $10 each	400,000
Variable costs (40,000 × $6)	240,000
Contribution	160,000
Fixed costs	100,000
Profit	60,000

The table below shows the total contribution depending on the level of sales and the material cost per unit.

Contribution table

		Sales units		
		30,000	40,000	50,000
Material cost per unit	$4 (contribution = $6)	$180,000	$240,000	$300,000
	$6 (contribution = $4)	$120,000	$160,000	$200,000
	$8 (contribution = $2)	$60,000	$80,000	$100,000

Given that fixed costs are $100,000, you can see from the table that Skiver will make a **loss** if material costs are $8 per unit **and** sales are **either** 30,000 pa **or** 40,000 pa. The chance that one **or** other of these events will occur is 14%, as calculated below.

Sales	Probability	Material cost	Probability	Joint probabilities
30,000 units	0.3	$8	0.2	0.06
40,000 units	0.4	$8	0.2	0.08
		Combined probabilities		0.14

However, there is also a chance that sales will be 50,000 units and material will cost $4, so that contribution would be $300,000 in total and profits $200,000. This is the **best possible outcome** and it has a 0.3 × 0.2 = 0.06 or 6% probability of occurring.

A **risk averse** decision maker might feel that a 14% chance of making a loss was unacceptable, whereas a **risk seeker** would be attracted by the 6% chance of making $200,000 profit. The **risk neutral** decision maker would need to consider the EV of profit of $60,000.

2.4 EVs and more complex risk analysis

As we have seen, EVs can be used to compare two or more mutually exclusive alternatives: the alternative with the most favourable EV of profit or cost would normally be preferred. However, **alternatives can also be compared** by looking at the **spread of possible outcomes**, and the **probabilities** that they will occur. The technique of drawing up **cumulative probability tables** can be helpful, as the following example shows.

Example: mutually exclusive options and cumulative probability

QRS is reviewing the price that it charges for a major product line. Over the past 3 years the product has had sales averaging 48,000 units per year at a standard selling price of $5.25. Costs have been rising steadily over the past year and the company is considering raising this price to $5.75 or $6.25. The sales manager has produced the following schedule to assist with the decision.

Price	$5.75	$6.25
Estimates of demand (units)		
Pessimistic estimate (probability 0.25)	35,000	10,000
Most likely estimate (probability 0.60)	40,000	20,000
Optimistic estimate (probability 0.15)	50,000	40,000

Currently, the unit cost is estimated at $5.00, analysed as follows:

	$
Direct material	2.50
Direct labour	1.00
Variable overhead	1.00
Fixed overhead	0.50
	5.00

The cost accountant considers that the most likely value for unit variable cost over the next year is $4.90 (probability 0.75) but that it could be as high as $5.20 (probability 0.15) and it might even be as low as $4.75 (probability 0.10). Total fixed costs are currently $24,000 pa, but it is estimated that the corresponding total for the ensuing year will be $25,000 with a probability of 0.2, $27,000 with a probability of 0.6, $30,000 with a probability of 0.2. (Demand quantities, unit costs and fixed costs can be assumed to be statistically independent.)

Required

Analyse the foregoing information in a way that you consider will assist management with the problem, give your views on the situation and advise on the new selling price. Calculate the expected level of profit that would follow from the selling price that you recommend.

Solution

In this example, there are two mutually exclusive options, a price of $5.75 and a price of $6.25. Sales demand is uncertain, but would vary with price. Unit contribution and total contribution depend on sales price and sales volume, but total fixed costs are common to both options. Clearly, it makes sense to begin looking at EVs of contribution and then to think about fixed costs and profits later.

(a)   A probability table can be set out for each alternative, and an EV calculated, as follows:

Price $5.75

Sales demand Units	Probability (a)	Variable cost per unit $	Probability (b)	Unit cont'n $	Total cont'n $'000	Joint proba-bility* (a × b)	EV of cont'n $'000
35,000	0.25	5.20	0.15	0.55	19.25	0.0375	0.722
		4.90	0.75	0.85	29.75	0.1875	5.578
		4.75	0.10	1.00	35.00	0.0250	0.875
40,000	0.60	5.20	0.15	0.55	22.00	0.0900	1.980
		4.90	0.75	0.85	34.00	0.4500	15.300
		4.75	0.10	1.00	40.00	0.0600	2.400
50,000	0.15	5.20	0.15	0.55	27.50	0.0225	0.619
		4.90	0.75	0.85	42.50	0.1125	4.781
		4.75	0.10	1.00	50.00	0.0150	0.750
						EV of contribution	33.005

The EV of contribution at a price of $5.75 is $33,005.

*Remember to check that the joint probabilities sum to 1.

Alternative approach

An alternative method of calculating the EV of contribution is as follows:

EV of contribution   =   EV of sales revenue − EV of variable costs

EV of sales revenue =   EV of sales units × selling price

                    =   ((35,000 × 0.25) + (40,000 × 0.60) + (50,000 × 0.15)) × $5.75

                    =   40,250 × $5.75 = $231,437.50

EV of variable costs =   EV of sales units × EV of unit variable costs

                    =   40,250 × (($5.20 × 0.15) + ($4.90 × 0.75) + ($4.75 × 0.10)) = 40,250 × $4.93 = $198,432.50

∴ EV of contribution = $(231,437.50 − 198,432.50) = $33,005

This method is quicker and simpler, but an extended table of probabilities will help the risk analysis when the two alternative selling prices are compared.

Price $6.25

Sales demand Units	Probability (a)	Variable cost per unit $	Probability (b)	Unit cont'n $	Total cont'n $'000	Joint proba- bility (a × b)	EV of cont'n $'000
10,000	0.25	5.20	0.15	1.05	10.50	0.0375	0.394
		4.90	0.75	1.35	13.50	0.1875	2.531
		4.75	0.10	1.50	15.00	0.0250	0.375
20,000	0.60	5.20	0.15	1.05	21.00	0.0900	1.890
		4.90	0.75	1.35	27.00	0.4500	12.150
		4.75	0.10	1.50	30.00	0.0600	1.800
40,000	0.15	5.20	0.15	1.05	42.00	0.0225	0.945
		4.90	0.75	1.35	54.00	0.1125	6.075
		4.75	0.10	1.50	60.00	0.0150	0.900
					EV of contribution		<u>27.060</u>

The EV of contribution at a price of $6.25 is $27,060.

(b)   The EV of **fixed costs** is $27,200.

Fixed costs $	Probability	EV $
25,000	0.2	5,000
27,000	0.6	16,200
30,000	0.2	6,000
		<u>27,200</u>

(c)   **Conclusion**

On the basis of EVs alone, a price of $5.75 is preferable to a price of $6.25, since it offers an EV of contribution of $33,005 and so an EV of profit of $5,805, whereas a price of $6.25 offers an EV of contribution of only $27,060 and so an EV of loss of $140.

Additional information

A comparison of cumulative probabilities would add to the information for risk analysis. The cumulative probabilities can be used to compare the **likelihood of earning a total contribution of a certain size with each selling price**.

Refer back to the two probability tables above. You should be able to read the probabilities and related total contributions straight from each table.

The table below shows that no matter whether fixed costs are $25,000, $27,000 or $30,000, the **probability of at least breaking even** is much higher with a price of $5.75 than with a price of $6.25. The only reason for favouring a price of $6.25 is that there is a better **probability of earning bigger profits** (a contribution of $50,000 or more), and so although a risk averse decision maker would choose a price of $5.75, a risk-seeking decision maker might gamble on a price of $6.25.

Probability of total contribution of at least $	Price $5.75 probability	Workings	Price $6.25 probability	Workings
15,000	1.0000		0.7750	(1 – 0.0375 – 0.1875)
20,000	0.9625	(1 – 0.0375)	0.7500	(0.775 – 0.025)
25,000	0.8725	(0.9625 – 0.09)	0.6600	etc
27,000	0.8725		0.6600	
30,000	0.6625	(0.8725 – 0.1875 – 0.0225)	0.2100	
35,000	0.2125	etc	0.1500	
40,000	0.1875		0.1500	
50,000	0.0150		0.1275	
60,000	0.0000		0.0150	

2.5 The advantages and disadvantages of point estimate probabilities

A **point estimate probability** means an estimate of the **probability of particular outcomes occurring**. In the previous example, there were point estimate probabilities for **variable costs** ($5.20 or $4.90 or $4.75) but in **reality**, the **actual** variable cost per unit **might be any amount**, from below $4.75 to above $5.20. Similarly, point estimate probabilities were given for period fixed costs ($25,000 or $27,000 or $30,000) but in reality, actual fixed costs might be any amount between about $25,000 and $30,000.

This is a disadvantage of using point estimate probabilities: they can be **unrealistic**, and can only be an **approximation** of the risk and uncertainty in estimates of costs or sales demand.

In spite of their possible disadvantages, point estimate probabilities can be very helpful for a decision maker.

(a)   They provide some estimate of risk, which is probably **better than nothing**.

(b)   **If there are enough point estimates** they are likely to be a **reasonably good approximation of** a continuous probability distribution.

(c)   Alternatively, it can be **assumed** that point estimate probabilities **represent a range** of values, so that if we had the probabilities for variable cost per unit, say, of $5.20, $4.90, and $4.75 we could assume that those actually represent probabilities for the ranges, say, $5.05 to $5.30, and $4.82 to $5.04 and $4.70 to $4.81.

Section summary

If a decision maker is faced with a number of alternative decisions, each with a range of possible outcomes, the optimum decision will be the one that gives the highest **expected value** (EV = Σpx). This is **Bayes' strategy**.

The calculation of **joint probabilities** and **cumulative probabilities** adds to the information for risk analysis.

BPP
LEARNING MEDIA

3   Data tables

Introduction

Data tables are often produced using spreadsheet packages and show the effect of changing the values of variables.

A **one-way or one-input data table shows the effect of a range of values of one variable**. For example, it might show the effect on profit of a range of selling prices. A **two-way or two-input data table shows the results of combinations of different values of two key variables**. The effect on contribution of combinations of various levels of demand and different selling prices would be shown in a two-way data table.

Any combination of variable values can therefore be changed and the **effects monitored**.

Example: a one-way data table

Suppose a company has production costs that it would expect to be in the region of $5m were it not for the effects of inflation. Economic forecasts for the inflation rate in the coming year range from 2% to 10%. Profit (before inflation is taken into account) is expected to be $475,000.

By using a spreadsheet package and with three or four clicks of the mouse, the data table below is produced. This shows the effects of different levels of inflation on production costs and profit.

		Production costs $'000	Profit $'000
	2%	5,100	375
	3%	5,150	325
Inflation rate	4%	5,200	275
	5%	5,250	225
	6%	5,300	175
	7%	5,350	125
	8%	5,400	75
	9%	5,450	25
	10%	5,500	(25)

So if inflation were to be 7%, the company could expect production costs to be in the region of $5,350,000 and profit to be about $125,000 ($(475,000 – (7% × $5m)).

Example: two-way data table

Suppose now that the company mentioned in the example above is not sure that its production costs will be $5m. They could be only $4.5m or they could be up to $5.5m.

We therefore need to examine the effects of both a range of rates of inflation and three different production costs on profit, and so we need a two-way data table as shown below.

Two-way data table showing profit for a range of rates of inflation and production costs

		Production costs		
		$4,500,000	$5,000,000	$5,500,000
		$'000	$'000	$'000
	2%	385	375	365
	3%	340	325	310
Inflation rate	4%	295	275	255
	5%	250	225	200
	6%	205	175	145
	7%	160	125	90
	8%	115	75	35
	9%	70	25	(20)
	10%	25	(25)	(75)

So if production costs were $5,500,000 and the rate of inflation was 4%, the profit should be $255,000 ($(475,000 – (4% × $5,500,000)).

3.1 Data tables and probability

If a probability distribution can be applied to either or both of the variables in a data table, a revised table can be prepared to provide improved management information.

Example: data tables and probability

Estimates of levels of demand and unit variable costs, with associated probabilities, for product B are shown below. Unit selling price is fixed at $100.

Levels of demand

Pessimistic	Probability of 0.4	10,000 units
Most likely	Probability of 0.5	12,500 units
Optimistic	Probability of 0.1	13,000 units

Unit variable costs

Optimistic	Probability of 0.3	$20
Most likely	Probability of 0.4	$30
Pessimistic	Probability of 0.3	$35

Required

Produce a two-way data table showing levels of contribution that incorporates information about both the variables and the associated probabilities.

Solution

Table of total contributions

The shaded area on this table shows the possible total contributions and the associated joint probabilities.

Demand			10,000	12,500	13,000
Probability			0.4	0.5	0.1
Unit variable cost	Probability	Unit contribution			
$20	0.3	$80	$800,000	$1,000,000	$1,040,000
			0.12	0.15	0.03
$30	0.4	$70	$700,000	$875,000	$910,000
			0.16	0.20	0.04
$35	0.3	$65	$650,000	$812,500	$845,000
			0.12	0.15	0.03

Section summary

Data tables are often produced using spreadsheet packages and show the effect of changing the values of variables.

4 The maximin, maximax and minimax regret bases for decision making

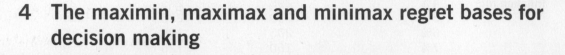

Introduction

The **assumption** made so far in this chapter has been that when there is a decision to make, and probabilities of the various outcomes have been estimated, the decision maker should **prefer the option with the highest EV of profit**.

For **once-only decisions**, this choice of option with the best EV does not necessarily make sense. It provides one rational basis for decision making, but it is not the only rational basis.

There are several other ways of making a choice, including the following:

(a) **Playing safe**, and **choosing the option with the least damaging results if events were to turn out badly**.

(b) Looking for the **best outcome**, no matter how small the chance that it might occur.

(c) Looking at the opportunity loss when we choose an option but come to regret it.

(d) **Balancing the EV of profit against the risk**, measured as the **standard deviation of variations in possible profit around the EV**. We cover this in Section 5.

The 'play it safe' basis for decision making is referred to as the **maximin basis**. This is short for '**maximise the minimum achievable profit**'. (It might also be called '**minimax**' which is short for '**minimise the maximum potential cost or loss**'.) Maximin decisions are taken by **risk averse** decision makers.

A basis for making decisions by looking for the best outcome is known as the **maximax basis**, short for '**maximise the maximum achievable profit**'. (It can also be called the **minimin cost rule** – minimise the minimum costs or losses.) Maximax decisions are taken by **risk-seeking** decision makers.

The 'opportunity loss' basis for decision making is known as **minimax regret**.

Example: maximin decision basis

Suppose that a manager is trying to decide which of three mutually exclusive projects to undertake. Each of the projects could lead to varying net profits which are classified as outcomes I, II and III. The manager has constructed the following **pay-off table or matrix** (a **conditional profit table**).

Project	Net profit if outcome turns out to be		
	I	II	III
A	$50,000	$65,000	$80,000
B	$70,000	$60,000	$75,000
C	$90,000	$80,000	$55,000
Probability	0.2	0.6	0.2

Required

Decide which project should be undertaken.

Solution

If the project with the **highest EV of profit** were chosen, this would be project C.

Outcome	Probability	Project A EV $	Project B EV $	Project C EV $
I	0.2	10,000	14,000	18,000
II	0.6	39,000	36,000	48,000
III	0.2	16,000	15,000	11,000
		65,000	65,000	77,000

However, if the **maximin criterion** were applied the assessment would be as follows:

Project selected	The worst outcome that could happen	Profit $
A	I	50,000
B	II	60,000
C	III	55,000

By **choosing B**, we are **'guaranteed' a profit of at least $60,000**, which is more than we would get from projects A or C if the worst outcome were to occur for them. (We want the maximum of the minimum achievable profits.)

The decision would therefore be to **choose project B**.

The main **weakness** of the maximin basis for decision making is that it **ignores the probabilities** that **various different outcomes might occur**, and so in this respect, it is not as good as the EV basis for decision making.

Example: maximax

Here is a payoff table showing the profits that will be achieved depending upon the action taken (D, E or F) and the circumstances prevailing (I, II or III).

		Profits Actions		
		D	E	F
	I	100	80	60
Circumstances	II	90	120	85
	III	(20)	10	85
Maximum profit		100	120	85

Action E would be chosen if the maximax rule is followed.

Criticisms of this approach would be that it ignores probabilities and that it is over-optimistic.

4.1 Minimax regret

Minimax regret considers the extent to which we might come to regret an action we had chosen.

Regret for any combination of action and circumstances	=	Payoff for **best** action in those circumstances	−	Payoff of the action **actually taken** in those circumstances

An alternative term for regret is **opportunity loss**. We may apply the rule by considering the maximum opportunity loss associated with each course of action and choosing the course that offers the smallest

maximum. If we choose an action that turns out not to be the best in the actual circumstances, we have lost an opportunity to make the extra profit we could have made by choosing the best action.

Look at the example below. Follow through the solution and make sure you understand how the maximum regret is arrived at.

Example: minimax regret

A manager is trying to decide which of three mutually exclusive projects to undertake. Each of the projects could lead to varying net costs which the manager calls outcomes I, II and III. The following payoff table or matrix has been constructed.

		Outcomes (net profit)		
		I	*II*	*III*
		(Worst)	*(Most likely)*	*(Best)*
	A	50	85	130
Project	B	70	75	140
	C	90	100	110

Which project should be undertaken?

Solution

A table of regrets can be compiled, as follows, showing the amount of profit that might be forgone for each project, depending on whether the outcome is I, II or III.

	Outcome			*Maximum*
	I	*II*	*III*	
Project A	40*	15***	10	40
Project B	20**	25	0	25
Project C	0	0	30	30

*90 – 50   **90 – 70   ***100 – 85   etc

The **maximum regret** is 40 with project A, 25 with B and 30 with C. The lowest of these three maximum regrets is 25 with B, and so project B would be selected if the minimax regret rule is used.

Section summary

The maximin basis means maximise the minimum achievable profit.

The maximax basis means maximise the maximum achievable profit.

The minimax regret basis means minimise the maximum regrets.

5 Using the standard deviation to measure risk

Introduction

Risk can be measured by the possible variations of outcomes around the expected value. One useful measure of such variations is the **standard deviation of the expected value**.

LEARN

> The standard deviation is s = $\sqrt{\Sigma p(x-\bar{x})^2}$ = $\sqrt{\text{variance}}$
>
> Where $\bar{x}$ is the EV of profit
>   x represents each possible profit
>   p represents the probability of each possible profit

The decision maker can then **weigh up the EV of each option against the risk** (the standard deviation) that is **associated with it**.

Example: measuring risk

The management of RC is considering which of two mutually exclusive projects to select. Details of each project are as follows:

	Project S			Project T	
Probability		Profit $'000	Probability		Profit $'000
0.3		150	0.2		(400)
0.3		200	0.6		300
0.4		250	0.1		400
			0.1		800

Required

Determine which project seems preferable, S or T.

Solution

On the basis of EVs alone, T is marginally preferable to S, by $15,000.

	Project S				Project T	
Probability	profit $'000	EV $'000		Probability	profit $'000	EV $'000
0.3	150	45		0.2	(400)	(80)
0.3	200	60		0.6	300	180
0.4	250	100		0.1	400	40
				0.1	800	80
	EV of profit	205			EV of profit	220

Project T is **more risky**, however, offering the prospect of a profit as high as $800,000 but also the possibility of a loss of $400,000.

One measure of this risk is the **standard deviation of the EV of profit**.

(a)   **Project S**

Probability p	Profit x $'000	$x - \bar{x}$	$p(x - \bar{x})^2$
0.3	150	−55	907.5*
0.3	200	−5	7.5
0.4	250	45	810.0
		Variance	1,725.0

*0.3 × (−55)^2

Standard deviation = $\sqrt{1,725}$ = 41.533 = $41,533

(b) **Project T**

Probability p	Profit x $'000	$x - \bar{x}$	$p(x - \bar{x})^2$
0.2	(400)	−620	76,880
0.6	300	80	3,840
0.1	400	180	3,240
0.1	800	580	33,640
		Variance	117,600

Standard deviation $= \sqrt{117,600} = 342.929 = \$342,929$

If the management are **risk averse**, they might therefore **prefer project S** because, although it has a smaller EV of profit, the possible profits are subject to less variation.

The **risk associated with project T can be compared with the risk associated with project S** if we calculate the **coefficient of variation** for each project: the **ratio of the standard deviation of each project to its EV**.

	Project S	Project T
Standard deviation	$41,533	$342,929
EV of profit	$205,000	$220,000
Coefficient of variation (standard deviation/EV of profit)	0.20	1.56

Question 14.2 — Using the standard deviation to measure risk

Learning outcome D1(c)

Fill in the blank in the sentence below.

On the basis of the information below, a 'risk averse' decision maker would choose project ....

Project A		Project B	
Estimated net cash flow $	Probability	Estimated net cash flow $	Probability
		1,000	0.2
2,000	0.3	2,000	0.2
3,000	0.4	3,000	0.2
4,000	0.3	4,000	0.2
		5,000	0.2

Question 14.3 — Standard deviation of the net present value

Learning outcome D1(c)

Frame is considering which of two mutually exclusive projects, A or B, to undertake. There is some uncertainty about the running costs with each project, and a probability distribution of the net present value (NPV) for each project has been estimated, as follows:

Project A		Project B	
NPV $'000	Probability	NPV $'000	Probability
− 20	0.15	+ 5	0.2
+ 10	0.20	+ 15	0.3
+ 20	0.35	+ 20	0.4
+ 40	0.30	+ 25	0.1

Required

Choose the correct words from those highlighted in the sentence below.

The organisation should choose **project A/project B** if management are risk averse.

Section summary

Risk can be measured by the possible variations of outcomes around the expected value. One useful measure of such variations is the **standard deviation of the expected value**.

6   Decision trees

Introduction

A probability problem such as 'what is the probability of throwing a six with one throw of a die?' is fairly straightforward and can be solved using the basic principles of probability.

More complex probability questions, although solvable using the basic principles, require a clear logical approach to ensure that all possible choices and outcomes of a decision are taken into consideration. **Decision trees** are a useful means of interpreting such probability problems.

KEY TERM

A DECISION TREE is 'A pictorial method of showing a sequence of interrelated decisions and their expected outcomes. Decision trees can incorporate both the probabilities of, and values of, expected outcomes, and are used in decision-making'.   (*CIMA Official Terminology*)

Exactly how does the use of a decision tree permit a clear and logical approach?

- All the possible **choices** that can be made are shown as **branches** on the tree.
- All the possible **outcomes** of each choice are shown as **subsidiary branches** on the tree.

6.1 Constructing a decision tree

There are two stages in preparing a decision tree.

- Drawing the tree itself to show all the choices and outcomes
- Putting in the numbers (the probabilities, outcome values and EVs)

Every **decision tree starts** from a **decision point** with the **decision options** that are currently being considered.

(a)   It helps to identify the **decision point**, and any subsequent decision points in the tree, with a symbol. Here, we shall use a **square shape**.

(b)   There should be a **line**, or **branch**, for each **option** or **alternative**.

It is conventional to draw decision trees from left to right, and so a decision tree will start as follows.

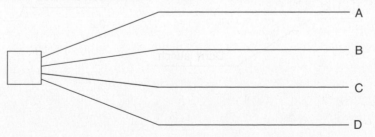

The **square** is the **decision point**, and A, B, C and D represent **four alternatives** from which a choice must be made (such as buy a new machine with cash, hire a machine, continue to use an existing machine, raise a loan to buy a machine).

If the outcome from any choice is certain, the branch of the decision tree for that alternative is complete.

If the outcome of a particular choice is uncertain, the various possible outcomes must be shown.

We show the various possible outcomes on a decision tree by inserting an **outcome point** on the **branch** of the tree. Each possible outcome is then shown as a **subsidiary branch**, coming out from the outcome point. The probability of each outcome occurring should be written onto the branch of the tree that represents that outcome.

To distinguish decision points from outcome points, **a circle will be used as the symbol for an outcome point**.

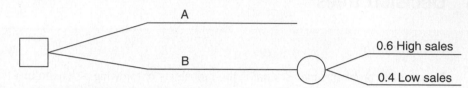

In the example above, there are two choices facing the decision maker, A and B. The outcome if A is chosen is known with certainty, but if B is chosen, there are two possible outcomes, high sales (0.6 probability) or low sales (0.4 probability).

When several outcomes are possible, it is usually simpler to show two or more stages of outcome points on the decision tree.

Example: several possible outcomes

A company can choose to launch a new product XYZ or not. If the product is launched, expected sales and expected unit costs might be as follows:

Sales		Unit costs	
Units	Probability	£	Probability
10,000	0.8	6	0.7
15,000	0.2	8	0.3

(a)   The decision tree could be drawn as follows:

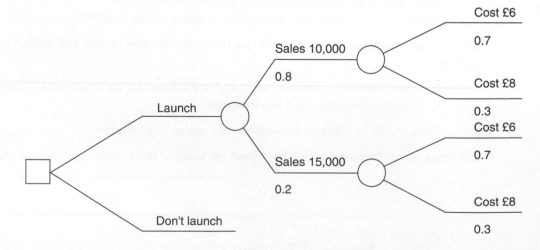

(b)   The layout shown above will usually be easier to use than the alternative way of drawing the tree, which is as follows:

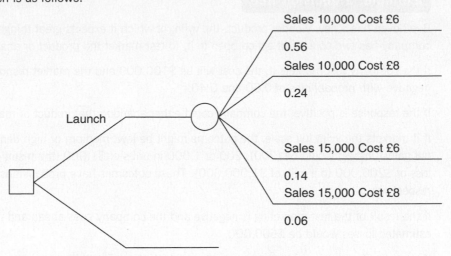

Sometimes, a **decision taken now** will lead to **other decisions to be taken in the future**. When this situation arises, the decision tree can be drawn as a **two-stage tree**, as follows:

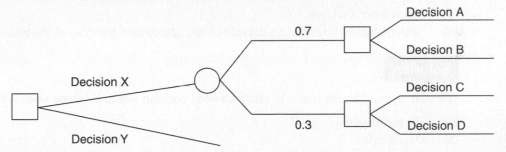

In this tree, either a choice between A and B or a choice between C and D will be made, depending on the outcome that occurs after choosing X.

The decision tree should be in **chronological order** from **left to right**. When there are two-stage decision trees, the first decision in time should be drawn on the left.

Example: a decision tree

Beethoven has a new wonder product, the vylin, of which it expects great things. At the moment, the company has two courses of action open to it, to test market the product or abandon it.

If the company test markets it, the cost will be $100,000 and the market response could be positive or negative with probabilities of 0.60 and 0.40.

If the response is positive, the company could either abandon the product or market it full scale.

If it markets the vylin full scale, the outcome might be low, medium or high demand, and the respective net gains/(losses) would be (200), 200 or 1,000 in units of $1,000 (the result could range from a net loss of $200,000 to a gain of $1,000,000). These outcomes have probabilities of 0.20, 0.50 and 0.30 respectively.

If the result of the test marketing is negative and the company goes ahead and markets the product, estimated losses would be $600,000.

If, at any point, the company abandons the product, there would be a net gain of $50,000 from the sale of scrap. All the financial values have been discounted to the present.

Required

(a)   Draw a decision tree.
(b)   Include figures for cost, loss or profit on the appropriate branches of the tree.

Solution

The starting point for the tree is to **establish what decision has to be made now**. What are the options?

(a)   To test market
(b)   To abandon

The outcome of the 'abandon' option is known with certainty. There are two possible outcomes of the option to test market, positive response and negative response.

Depending on the outcome of the test marketing, another decision will then be made, to abandon the product or to go ahead.

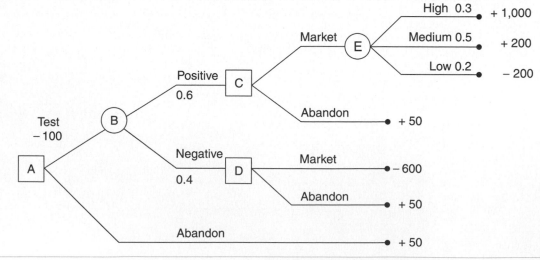

6.2 Evaluating the decision with a decision tree

Rollback analysis evaluates the EV of each decision option. You have to work from right to left and calculate EVs at each outcome point.

The EV of each decision option can be evaluated, using the decision tree to help with keeping the logic on track. The basic rules are as follows.

(a)   We start on the **right-hand side** of the tree and **work back** towards the left-hand side and the current decision under consideration. This is sometimes known as the **'rollback' technique** or **'rollback analysis'**.

(b)   Working from **right to left**, we calculate the **EV of revenue, cost, contribution or profit** at each outcome point on the tree.

In the above example, the right-hand-most outcome point is point E, and the EV is as follows:

	Profit	Probability	
	x	p	px
	$'000		$'000
High	1,000	0.3	300
Medium	200	0.5	100
Low	(200)	0.2	(40)
		EV	360

This is the EV of the decision to market the product if the test shows positive response. It may help you to write the EV on the decision tree itself, at the appropriate outcome point (point E).

(a)   **At decision point C**, the **choice** is as follows:

(i)   Market, EV = +360 (the EV at point E)
(ii)   Abandon, value = +50

The choice would be to market the product, and so the EV at decision point C is +360.

(b)   **At decision point D**, the **choice** is as follows:

(i)   Market, value = – 600
(ii)   Abandon, value = +50

The choice would be to abandon, and so the EV at decision point D is +50.

The second stage decisions have therefore been made. If the original decision is to test market, the company will market the product if the test shows positive customer response, and will abandon the product if the test results are negative.

The evaluation of the decision tree is completed as follows:

(a)   **Calculate the EV at outcome point B.**

        0.6 × 360   (EV at C)
+   0.4 × 50   (EV at D)
=   216 + 20 = 236

(b)   **Compare the options at point A**, which are as follows.

(i)   Test: EV = EV at B minus test marketing cost = 236 – 100 = 136
(ii)   Abandon: value = 50

The choice would be to test market the product, because it has a **higher EV of profit**.

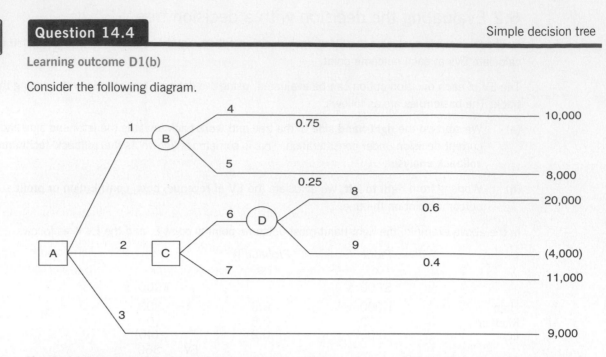

Question 14.4   Simple decision tree

Learning outcome D1(b)

Consider the following diagram.

If a decision maker wished to maximise the value of the outcome, which options should be selected?

A   Option 2 and option 7
B   Option 3
C   Option 1 and option 4
D   Option 2, option 6 and option 8

Evaluating decisions by using **decision trees has a number of limitations**.

(a)   The time value of money may not be taken into account.

(b)   Decision trees are not very suitable for use in complex situations.

(c)   The outcome with the highest EV may have the greatest risks attached to it. Managers may be reluctant to take risks that may lead to losses.

(d)   The probabilities associated with different branches of the 'tree' are likely to be estimates, and possibly unreliable or inaccurate.

Section summary

Decision trees are diagrams that illustrate the choices and possible outcomes of a decision.

Rollback analysis evaluates the EV of each decision option. You have to work from right to left and calculate EVs at each outcome point.

7 The value of information

Introduction

The **value of perfect information** is the difference between the EV of profit with perfect information and the EV of profit without perfect information. Imperfect information is better than no information at all but could be wrong in its prediction of the future.

PERFECT INFORMATION removes all doubt and uncertainty from a decision, and enables managers to make decisions with complete confidence that they have selected the optimum course of action.

KEY TERM

7.1 The value of perfect information

If we **do not have perfect information** and we must choose between two or more decision options, we would select the decision option that offers the **highest EV** of profit. This option will not be the best decision under all circumstances. There will be some probability that what was really the best option will not have been selected, given the way actual events turn out.

With **perfect information**, the **best decision option will always be selected**. The profits from the decision will depend on the future circumstances which are predicted by the information; nevertheless, the EV of profit with perfect information should be higher than the EV of profit without the information.

The **value of perfect information** is **the difference between these two EVs**.

Example: the value of perfect information

The management of Ivor Ore must choose whether to go ahead with either of two mutually exclusive projects, A and B. The expected profits are as follows:

	Profit if there is strong demand	Profit/(loss) if there is weak demand
Option A	$4,000	$(1,000)
Option B	$1,500	$500
Probability of demand	0.3	0.7

Required

(a) Ascertain what the decision would be, based on expected values, if no information about demand were available.

(b) Calculate the value of perfect information about demand.

Solution

If there were **no information** to help with the decision, the project with the higher EV of profit would be selected.

Probability	Project A		Project B	
	Profit	EV	Profit	EV
	$	$	$	$
0.3	4,000	1,200	1,500	450
0.7	(1,000)	(700)	500	350
		500		800

Project B would be selected.

This is clearly the better option if demand turns out to be weak. However, if demand were to turn out to be strong, project A would be more profitable. There is a 30% chance that this could happen.

STEP 2

Perfect information will indicate for certain whether demand will be weak or strong. If demand is forecast 'weak', project B would be selected. If demand is forecast as 'strong', project A would be selected, and perfect information would improve the profit from $1,500, which would have been earned by selecting B, to $4,000.

Forecast demand	Probability	Project chosen	Profit	EV of profit
			$	$
Weak	0.7	B	500	350
Strong	0.3	A	4,000	1,200
		EV of profit with perfect information		1,550

STEP 3

	$
EV of profit without perfect information (ie if project B is always chosen)	800
EV of profit with perfect information	1,550
Value of perfect information	750

Provided that the information does not cost more than $750 to collect, it would be worth having.

Question 14.5   Decision based on EV of profit

Learning outcome D1(b)

Watt Lovell must decide at what level to market a new product, the urk. The urk can be sold nationally, within a single sales region (where demand is likely to be relatively strong) or within a single area. The decision is complicated by uncertainty about the general strength of consumer demand for the product, and the following conditional profit table has been constructed.

		Weak	Demand Moderate	Strong
		$	$	$
Market:	nationally (A)	(4,000)	2,000	10,000
	in one region (B)	0	3,500	4,000
	in one area (C)	1,000	1,500	2,000
Probability		0.3	0.5	0.2

Option B should be selected, based on EVs of profit. **True or false?**

Question 14.6   Perfect information

Learning outcome D1(b)

Using the information in your answer to the question above ('Decision based on EV of profit'), fill in the blank in the sentence below.

The value of information about the state of demand is $.......... .

7.2 Perfect information and decision trees

When the option exists to obtain information, the decision can be shown, like any other decision, in the form of a decision tree, as follows. We will suppose, for illustration, that the cost of obtaining perfect information is $400.

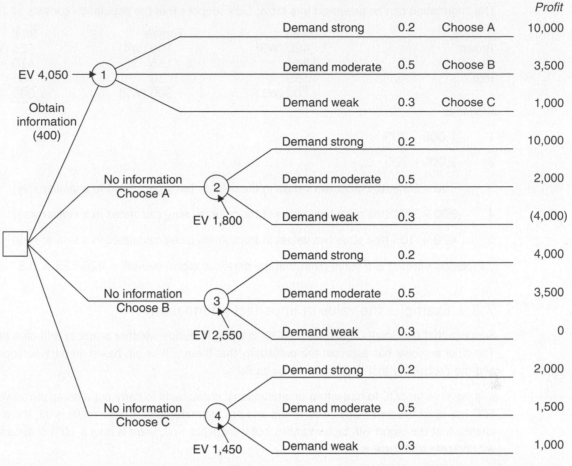

The decision would be to obtain perfect information, since the EV of profit is $4,050 – $400 = $3,650.

Exam skills

You should check carefully that you understand the logic of this decision tree and that you can identify how the EVs at outcome boxes 1, 2, 3 and 4 have been calculated.

7.3 The value of imperfect information

There is one serious drawback to the technique we have just looked at: in practice **useful information is never perfect** unless the person providing it is the sole source of the uncertainty. Market research findings or information from pilot tests and so on are likely to be reasonably accurate, but they can still be wrong: they provide imperfect information. It is possible, however, to arrive at an assessment of **how much it would be worth paying for such imperfect information, given that we have a rough indication of how right or wrong it is likely to be**.

Suppose we are considering the sex and hair colour of people in a given group or population consisting of 70% men and 30% women. We have established the probabilities of hair colourings as follows:

	Men	Women
Brown	0.60	0.35
Blonde	0.35	0.55
Red	0.05	0.10

This shows, for example, that 5% of men in such a sample have red hair. These probabilities of sex and hair colouring might be referred to as **prior probabilities**.

Posterior probabilities consider the situation in reverse or retrospect, so that we can ask the question: 'Given that a person taken at random from the population is brown-haired what is the probability that the person is male (or female)?'.

The information can be presented in a table. Let's suppose that the population consists of 1,000 people.

	Male	Female	Total
Brown	420 (W3)	105 (W4)	525 (W5)
Blonde	245	165	410
Red	35	30	65
	700 (W1)	300 (W2)	1,000

Workings

1   1,000 × 70%

2   1,000 – 700

3   700 × 60% (the other two values in the column being calculated in a similar way)

4   300 × 35% (the other two values in the column being calculated in a similar way)

5   420 + 105 (the other two values in the column being calculated in a similar way)

∴ P(person selected is a male, given that the person is brown-haired) = 420/525 = 0.8

7.3.1 Example: the value of imperfect information

Suppose that the Small Oil Company (SOC) is trying to decide whether or not to drill on a particular site. The chief engineer has assessed the probability that there will be oil, based on past experience, as 20%, and the probability that there won't be oil as 80%.

It is possible for SOC to hire a firm of international consultants to carry out a complete survey of the site. SOC has used the firm many times before and has estimated that if there really is oil, there is a 95% chance that the report will be favourable, but if there is no oil, there is only a 10% chance that the report will indicate that there is oil.

Required

Determine whether drilling should occur.

Solution

Read the information given carefully. We are given **three** sets of probabilities.

(a)   The probability that there will be oil (0.2) or there will not be (0.8). These outcomes are mutually exclusive.

(b)   The probability that, if there is oil, the report will say there is oil (0.95) or say there is no oil (0.05).

(c)   The probability that, if there is no oil, the report will say there **is** oil (0.1) or say there is no oil (0.9).

Both (b) and (c) describe conditional events, since the existence of oil or otherwise influences the chances of the survey report being correct.

SOC, meanwhile, faces a number of choices that we can show as a decision tree.

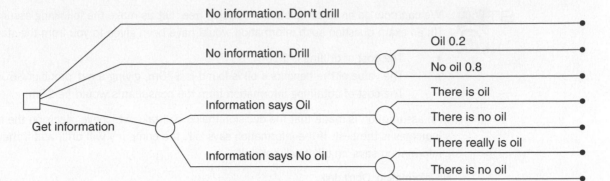

We must now calculate the probabilities of the following outcomes.

- The information will say 'oil' or 'no oil'.
- The information will be right or wrong if it says 'oil'.
- The information will be right or wrong if it says 'no oil'.

If you check the information given in the problem, you will find that these probabilities are not given.

(a)   We are told that the engineer has assessed that there is a 20% chance of oil and an 80% chance of no oil (ignoring information entirely). These are the **prior probabilities** of future possible outcomes.

(b)   The **probabilities that there will be oil or no oil once the information has been obtained are posterior probabilities**.

 We can tabulate the various probabilities as percentages.

Actual outcome

		Oil		No oil		Total	
Survey	Oil	19	(W2)	8	(W3)	27	(W4)
result:	No oil	1		72		73	
Total		20	(W1)	80		100	

Workings

1   The engineer estimates 20% probability of oil and 80% of no oil.

2   If there is oil, ie in 20 cases out of 100, the survey will say so in 95% of these cases, ie in 20 × 0.95 = 19 cases. The 1 below the 19 is obtained by subtraction.

3   In the 80 per 100 cases where there is in fact no oil, the survey will wrongly say that there is oil 10% of the time; ie 80 × 0.10 = 8 cases. The 72 below the 8 is obtained by subtraction.

4   The horizontal totals are given by addition.

 We can now provide all the probabilities needed to complete the tree.

P (survey will say there is oil)   = 27/100   = 0.27

P (survey will say there is no oil)   = 73/100   = 0.73

If survey says oil   P (there is oil)   = 19/27 = 0.704

                                     P (there is no oil)   = 8/27 = 0.296 (or 1–0.704)

If survey says no oil   P (there is oil)   = 1/73 = 0.014

                                     P (there is no oil)   = 72/73 = 0.986 (or 1–0.014)

STEP 3

We can now go on to complete the decision tree. Let us make the following assumptions. (In an exam question such information would have been given to you from the start.)

*   The cost of drilling is $10m.
*   The value of the benefits if oil is found is $70m, giving a net 'profit' of $60m.
*   The cost of obtaining information from the consultants would be $3m.

An assumption is made that the decision maker will take whichever decision the information indicates is the best. If the information says 'oil', the company will drill, and if the information says 'no oil' it will not drill.

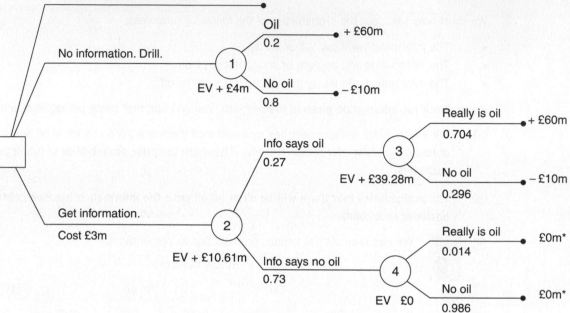

*The information is 'no oil', so the company won't drill, regardless of whether there really is oil or not.

STEP 4

We can now perform rollback analysis.

		$m
EV at point 3 =	0.704 × $60m	42.24
	0.296 × ($10m)	(2.96)
		+ 39.28

		$m
EV at point 2 =	0.27 × $39.28m	10.61
	0.73 × $0	0.00
		+ 10.61

STEP 5

There are three choices.   EV

(a)   Do not obtain information and do not drill $0

(b)   Do not obtain information and drill   +$4 million

(c)   Obtain information first, decide about drilling later ($(10.61m – 3m))

+$7.61 million

The decision should be to obtain the information from a survey first.

STEP 6

The value of the imperfect information is the difference between (b) and (c), $3.61 million.

Exam alert

If you are asked to calculate the maximum amount that should be paid for a forecast, you need to calculate 'the value of imperfect information' using the approach we have explained.

Section summary

Perfect information is guaranteed to predict the future with 100% accuracy. **Imperfect information** is better than no information at all but could be wrong in its prediction of the future.

The **value of perfect information** is the difference between the EV of profit with perfect information and the EV of profit without perfect information. **Imperfect information** is better than no information at all but could be wrong in its prediction of the future.

8 Sensitivity analysis

Introduction

We have already encountered sensitivity analysis in relation to NPV analysis. Here we look at it in more general terms.

KEY TERM

SENSITIVITY ANALYSIS is 'A modelling and risk assessment procedure in which changes are made to significant variables in order to determine the effect of these changes on the planned outcome. Particular attention is thereafter paid to variables identified as being of special significance'.

(CIMA Official Terminology)

Two useful approaches to sensitivity analysis

(a)   Estimate by how much costs and revenues would need to differ from their estimated values before the decision would change.

(b)   Estimate whether a decision would change if estimated costs were x% higher than estimated, or estimated revenues y% lower than estimated.

The essence of the approach is therefore to **carry out the calculations with one set of values for the variables** and then **substitute other possible values** for the variables to see **how this affects the overall outcome**.

Example: sensitivity analysis

SS has estimated the following sales and profits for a new product which it may launch on to the market.

	$	$
Sales (2,000 units)		4,000
Variable costs: materials	2,000	
labour	1,000	
		3,000
Contribution		1,000
Less incremental fixed costs		800
Profit		200

Required

Analyse the sensitivity of the project.

Solution

The **margin of safety**	= ((budgeted sales – breakeven sales)/budgeted sales) × 100%
The breakeven point	= fixed costs/contribution per unit
	= $800/($1,000/2,000 units) = 1,600 units
∴ Margin of safety	= ((2,000 – 1,600)/2,000) × 100% = 20%

If any of the **costs increase by more than $200**, the profit will disappear and there will be a **loss**.

Changes in variables that would result in a loss

- More than ((200/800) × 100%) 25% increase in incremental **fixed costs**
- More than ((200/2,000) × 100%) 10% increase in unit cost of **materials**
- More than ((200/1,000) × 100%) 20% increase in **unit labour costs**
- More than ((200/4,000) × 100%) 5% drop in **unit selling price**

Management would now be able to judge more clearly whether the product is likely to be profitable. The **items to which profitability is most sensitive** in this example are the **selling price** (5%) and **material costs** (10%). Sensitivity analysis can help to **concentrate management attention on the most important forecasts**.

8.1 'What if' analysis

KEY TERM

'WHAT IF' ANALYSIS looks at the results of varying a model's key variables, parameters or estimates.

Sensitivity analysis is a 'what if' technique that examines how a result will change if the original predicted values are not achieved or if an underlying assumption changes.

Once a model has been constructed, the consequences of changes or amendments to budget/plan assumptions may be tested by asking **'what if?' questions, a form of sensitivity analysis**. For example, a spreadsheet may be used to develop a cash flow model, such as that shown below.

	A	*B*	*C*	*D*
1		*Month 1*	*Month 2*	*Month 3*
2	Sales	1,000	1,200	1,440
3	Cost of sales	(650)	(780)	(936)
4	Gross profit	350	420	504
5				
6	Receipts:			
7	Current month	600	720	864
8	Previous month	–	400	480
9			–	–
10		600	1,120	1,344
11	Payments	(650)	(780)	(936)
12		(50)	340	408
13	Balance b/f	–	(50)	290
14	Balance c/f	(50)	290	698

Typical 'what if?' questions for sensitivity analysis

(a) What if the cost of sales is 68% of sales revenue, not 65%?

(b) What if payment from receivables is received 40% in the month of sale, 50% one month in arrears and 10% two months in arrears, instead of 60% in the month of sale and 40% one month in arrears?

(c) What if sales growth is only 15% per month, instead of 20% per month?

Using the spreadsheet model, the answers to such questions can be obtained simply and quickly, using the editing facility in the program. The information obtained should **provide management with a better understanding of what the cash flow position in the future might be**, and **what factors are critical to ensuring that the cash position remains reasonable**. For example, it might be found that the cost of sales must remain less than 67% of sales value to achieve a satisfactory cash position.

Section summary

Two useful approaches to sensitivity analysis

(a)   Estimate by how much costs and revenues would need to differ from their estimated values before the decision would change.

(b)   Estimate whether a decision would change if estimated costs were x% higher than estimated, or estimated revenues y% lower than estimated.

9   Simulation models

Introduction

One of the chief problems encountered in decision making is the uncertainty of the future. Where only a few factors are involved, probability analysis and expected value calculations can be used to find the most likely outcome of a decision. Often, however, in real life, there are so **many uncertain variables** that this approach does not give a true impression of possible variations in outcome.

To get an idea of what will happen in real life, one possibility is to use a **simulation model** in which the **values and the variables are selected at random**. Obviously, this is a situation **ideally suited to a computer** (large volume of data, random number generation).

9.1 The Monte Carlo method

The term 'simulation' model is often used to refer to modelling that **makes use of random numbers**. This is the 'Monte Carlo' method of simulation. In the business environment it can, for example, be used to examine inventory, queuing, scheduling and forecasting problems.

Random numbers are allocated to each possible value of the uncertain variable in proportion to the probabilities, so that a probability of 0.1 gets 10% of the total numbers to be assigned. These random numbers are used to assign values to the variables.

Example: simulation and spreadsheets

A supermarket sells a product for which the daily demand varies. An analysis of daily demand over a period of about a year shows the following probability distribution.

Demand per day Units	Probability
35	0.10
36	0.20
37	0.25
38	0.30
39	0.08
40	0.07
	1.00

To develop a simulation model in which one of the variables is daily demand, we would **assign a group of numbers to each value for daily demand**. The **probabilities are stated** to 2 decimal places, and so there must be **100 random numbers in total**, 00–99 (we use 00–99 rather than 1–100 so that we can use **two-digit random numbers**).

Note that **random numbers are assigned in proportion to the probabilities**, so that a probability of 0.1 gets 10% of the total numbers to be assigned, that is 10 numbers: 0, 1, 2, 3, 4, 5, 6, 7, 8 and 9.

The assignments would therefore be as follows:

Demand per day Units	Probability	Numbers assigned
35	0.10	00–09
36	0.20	10–29
37	0.25	30–54
38	0.30	55–84
39	0.08	85–92
40	0.07	93–99

When the simulation model is run, random numbers will be generated to derive values for daily demand. For example, if the model is used to simulate demand over a ten-day period, the **random numbers generated** might be as follows:

19007174604721296802

The model would then **assign values to the demand per** day as follows:

Day	Random number	Demand Units
1	19	36
2	00	35
3	71	38
4	74	38
5	60	38
6	47	37
7	21	36
8	29	36
9	68	38
10	02	35

You might notice that on none of the 10 days is the demand 39 or 40 units, because the random numbers generated did not include any value in the range 85–99. When a simulation model is used, there must be a long enough run to give a good representation of the system and all its potential variations.

9.2 Uses of simulation

In the supermarket example above, the supermarket would use the information to minimise inventory holding without risking running out of the product. This will reduce costs but avoid lost sales and profit.

A supermarket can also use this technique to estimate queues with predicted length of waiting time determining the number of staff required.

Question 14.7	Simulation

Learning outcome D1(b)

Gleamy Windows is a company that provides a window cleaning service to offices and shops in a local area. The workforce consists of ten workers, but there is a problem with absenteeism and the probability distribution of daily attendance is as follows:

Number at work	Probability
10	0.6
9	0.3
8	0.1

An analysis of past performance has shown that the number of windows that each worker can do in a day is as follows:

Number of windows per worker per day	Probability
120	0.15
125	0.24
130	0.27
135	0.19
140	0.15

The price charged for each window is 50c.

There are two variables, numbers at work and windows cleaned per worker per day.

Required

Complete the table below to show the allocation of groups of numbers to each value for each variable.

Number at work	Probability	Numbers allocated	Windows per worker per day	Probability	Numbers allocated
10	0.6		120	0.15	
9	0.3		125	0.24	
8	0.1		130	0.27	
			135	0.19	
			140	0.15	

Note how the numbers are allocated in the above exercise.

(a)   The **probabilities** for the numbers at work each day are **given to just one decimal place**, and so we can use **numbers in the range 0–9** rather than 00–99.

(b)   You might find it easiest to allocate number ranges by dealing with the lowest numbers in each range first. In the case of windows per worker per day, the lowest number range starts with 00. We can then add 15, 24, 27 and 19 respectively to get the lowest numbers in the higher ranges.

If we were to run the simulation model in the above exercise over a six-day period to estimate the daily revenue over this period, the **random numbers generated** might be as follows:

• For the number at work, 971088
• For the windows per worker per day, 230998429964

The **results** from the model would then be as follows:

Day	Random number	Number at work	Random number	Windows per worker per day	Total windows cleaned	Total revenue, at $0.50 per window
						$
1	9	8	23	125	1,000	500
2	7	9	09	120	1,080	540
3	1	10	98	140	1,400	700
4	0	10	42	130	1,300	650
5	8	9	99	140	1,260	630
6	8	9	64	130	1,170	585

If you have not already done so, **check to see how the figures in the number at work column and windows per worker per day column are derived** and perform the calculations for yourself.

The technique is often used to estimate **queues in shops**, banks, post offices and building societies. The length of waiting time predicted will enable estimates of staff requirements to be made. There are **two uncertainties** in such a scenario, however, as customers do not arrive at a constant rate and some customers require more or less time than the average service time. Two probability distributions and two allocations of random numbers would therefore be required.

Section summary

The **Monte Carlo method of simulation** uses random numbers to recognise that all variables are subject to change.

Chapter Summary

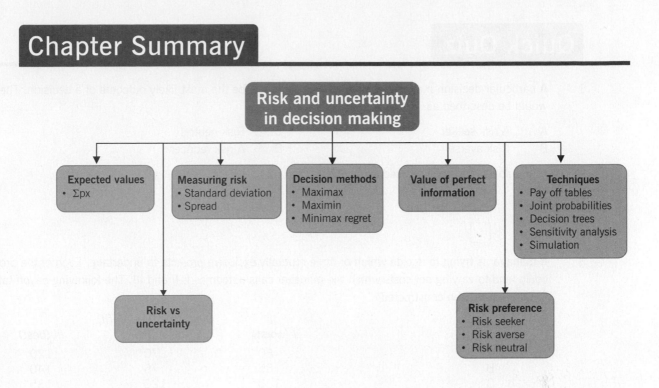

Risk and uncertainty in decision making

Expected values
- Σpx

Measuring risk
- Standard deviation
- Spread

Decision methods
- Maximax
- Maximin
- Minimax regret

Value of perfect information

Techniques
- Pay off tables
- Joint probabilities
- Decision trees
- Sensitivity analysis
- Simulation

Risk vs uncertainty

Risk preference
- Risk seeker
- Risk averse
- Risk neutral

Quick Quiz

1   A particular decision maker is concerned with what will be the most likely outcome of a decision. They would be described as:

    A   A risk seeker   • C   Risk neutral
    B   Risk averse   D   A risk reducer

2   A probability can be expressed as any value from −1 to +1.

    True   ☐

    False   ☑

3   A manager is trying to decide which of three mutually exclusive projects to undertake. Each of the projects could lead to varying net costs which the manager calls outcomes I, II and III. The following payoff table or matrix has been constructed.

| | | Outcomes (net profit) | |
Project	I (worst)	II (most likely)	III (best)
A	60	70	120
B	85	75	140
C	100	120	135

Using the minimax regret decision rule, which project should be undertaken?   **C**

4   If the decision maker is trying to maximise the figure, what figure would the decision maker choose at point B in the diagram below?

    A   40,000   C   13,900
    B   11,800   D   22,000

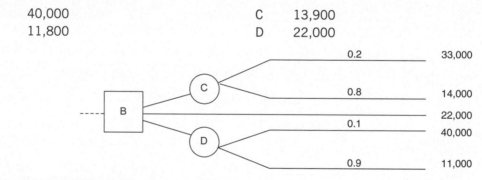

5   Given the probability distribution shown below, assign ranges of numbers in order to run a simulation model.

Probability	Numbers assigned	Probability	Numbers assigned
0.132	0.0 - 0.131	0.083	0.858 - 0.94
0.410	0.132 - 0.542	0.060	0.95 - 0.0
0.315	0.543 - 0.857		

6   Fill in the blanks.

Standard deviation, $s = \sqrt{}$

Where $\bar{x}$ is ...., x represents ...., p represents ....

7   AB can choose from five mutually exclusive projects. The projects will each last for one year only and their net cash inflows will be determined by the prevailing market conditions. The forecast net cash inflows and their associated probabilities are shown below.

Market conditions	Poor	Good	Excellent
Probability	0.20	0.40	0.40
	$'000	$'000	$'000
Project L	550	480	580
Project M	450	500	570
Project N	420	450	480
Project O	370	410	430
Project P	590	580	430

(a)   Based on the expected value of the net cash inflows, which project should be undertaken?

(b)   Calculate the value of perfect information about the state of the market.

Answers to Quick Quiz

1   C   Risk reducer is not a term we have covered!

2   False. Should be 0 to 1.

3   A table of regrets can be compiled, as follows, showing the amount of profit that might be forgone for each project, depending on whether the outcome is I, II or III.

	Outcome			Maximum
	I	*II*	*III*	
Project A	40*	50	20	50
Project B	15**	45	0	45
Project C	0	0	5	5

*100 – 60   **100 – 85 etc

The **maximum regret** is 50 with project A, 45 with B and 5 with C. The lowest of these three maximum regrets is 5 with C, and so project C would be selected if the minimax regret rule is used.

4   D   Choice between $((0.2 \times 33{,}000) + (0.8 \times 14{,}000)) = 17{,}800$ at C, 22,000, and $((0.1 \times 40{,}000) + (0.9 \times 11{,}000)) = 13{,}900$ at D.

5

Probability	Numbers assigned	Probability	Numbers assigned
0.132	000-131	0.083	857-939
0.410	132-541	0.060	940-999
0.315	542-856		

6   Standard deviation, $s = \sqrt{\Sigma p(x - \bar{x})^2}$

Where $\bar{x}$ is the EV of profit, x represents each possible profit, p represents the probability of each possible profit.

7   (a)

		EV $'000
Project L	$(550 \times 0.20 + 480 \times 0.40 + 580 \times 0.40)$	534
Project M	$(450 \times 0.20 + 500 \times 0.40 + 570 \times 0.40)$	518
Project N	$(420 \times 0.20 + 450 \times 0.40 + 480 \times 0.40)$	456
Project O	$(370 \times 0.20 + 410 \times 0.40 + 430 \times 0.40)$	410
Project P	$(590 \times 0.20 + 580 \times 0.40 + 430 \times 0.40)$	522

Project L has the highest EV of expected cash inflows and should therefore be undertaken.

(b)

Market condition	Probability	Project chosen	Net cash inflow	EV of net cash inflow $'000
Poor	0.20	P	590	118
Good	0.40	P	580	232
Excellent	0.40	L	580	232
EV of net cash inflows with perfect information				582
EV of net cash inflows without perfect information				534
Value of perfect information				48

Answers to Questions

14.1 EV calculations

The correct answer is C.

A	EV of cost = $20,850		C	EV of cost = $20,250
	EV of profit = $9,150			EV of profit = $9,750
B	EV of cost = $20,500		D	EV of cost = $20,550
	EV of profit = $9,500			EV of profit = $9,450

C has the highest EV of profit.

14.2 Using the standard deviation to measure risk

The correct answer is project A.

The projects have the same EV of net cash flow ($3,000); therefore a risk averse manager would choose the project with the smaller standard deviation of expected profit.

Project A

Cash flow	Probability	EV of cash flow	Cash flow minus EV of cash flow $(x - \bar{x})$	$p(x - \bar{x})^2$
$		$	$	$
2,000	0.3	600	−1,000	300,000
3,000	0.4	1,200	0	0
4,000	0.3	1,200	+1,000	300,000
		EV = 3,000		Variance = 600,000

Standard deviation = $\sqrt{600,000}$ = $775

Project B

Cash flow	Probability	EV of cash flow	Cash flow minus EV of cash flow $(x - \bar{x})$	$p(x - \bar{x})^2$
$		$	$	$
1,000	0.2	200	−2,000	800,000
2,000	0.2	400	−1,000	200,000
3,000	0.2	600	0	0
4,000	0.2	800	+1,000	200,000
5,000	0.2	1,000	+2,000	800,000
		EV = 3,000		Variance = 2,000,000

Standard deviation = $\sqrt{2,000,000}$ = $1,414

14.3 Standard deviation of the net present value

The correct answer is project B.

We can begin by calculating the EV of the NPV for each project.

| | Project A | | | Project B | |
NPV $'000	Prob	EV $'000	NPV $'000	Prob	EV $'000
−20	0.15	(3.0)	5	0.2	1.0
10	0.20	2.0	15	0.3	4.5
20	0.35	7.0	20	0.4	8.0
40	0.30	12.0	25	0.1	2.5
		18.0			16.0

Project A has a higher EV of NPV, but what about the risk of variation in the NPV above or below the EV? This can be measured by the standard deviation of the NPV.

The standard deviation of a project's NPV can be calculated as $\sqrt{\Sigma p(x - \bar{x})^2}$, where $\bar{x}$ is the EV of the NPV.

| | Project A, $\bar{x} = 18$ | | | | Project B, $\bar{x} = 16$ | | |
x $'000	p	x − $\bar{x}$ $'000	$p(x-\bar{x})^2$	x $'000	p	x − $\bar{x}$ $'000	$p(x-\bar{x})^2$
−20	0.15	−38	216.6	5	0.2	−11	24.2
10	0.20	−8	12.8	15	0.3	−1	0.3
20	0.35	+2	1.4	20	0.4	+4	6.4
40	0.30	+22	145.2	25	0.1	+9	8.1
			376.0				39.0

	Project A			Project B	
Standard deviation	=	√376	Standard deviation	=	√39.0
	=	19.391		=	6.245
	=	$19,391		=	$6,245

Although **Project A has a higher EV of NPV**, it also has a **higher standard deviation of NPV**, and so has **greater risk** associated with it.

Which project should be selected? Clearly, it depends on the attitude of the company's management to risk. If management are **risk averse**, they will opt for the **less risky project B**.

(If management were prepared **to take the risk of a low NPV in the hope of a high NPV** they will opt for **project A**.)

14.4 Simple decision tree

The correct answer is A.

The various outcomes must be evaluated using expected values.

EV at point B: (0.75 × 10,000) + (0.25 × 8,000) = 9,500
EV at point D: (0.6 × 20,000) + (0.4 × (4,000)) = 10,400
EV at point C: Choice between 10,400 and 11,000
EV at point A: Choice between B (9,500), C (10,400 or 11,000) and choice 3 (9,000)

If we are trying to maximise the figure, option 2 and then option 7 are chosen to give 11,000.

14.5 Decision based on EV of profit

The correct answer is option B and so the statement is true.

Without perfect information, the option with the highest EV of profit will be chosen.

Probability	Option A (national) Profit $	EV $	Option B (regional) Profit $	EV $	Option C (area) Profit $	EV $
0.3	(4,000)	(1,200)	0	0	1,000	300
0.5	2,000	1,000	3,500	1,750	1,500	750
0.2	10,000	2,000	4,000	800	2,000	400
		1,800		2,550		1,450

Marketing regionally (option B) has the highest EV of profit, and would be selected.

14.6 Perfect information

The correct answer is $1,500.

If perfect information about the state of consumer demand were available, option A would be preferred if the forecast demand is strong and option C would be preferred if the forecast demand is weak.

Demand	Probability	Choice	Profit $	EV of profit $
Weak	0.3	C	1,000	300
Moderate	0.5	B	3,500	1,750
Strong	0.2	A	10,000	2,000
EV of profit with perfect information				4,050
EV of profit, selecting option B				2,550
Value of perfect information				1,500

14.7 Simulation

Number at work	Probability	Numbers allocated	Windows per worker per day	Probability	Numbers allocated
10	0.6	0 – 5	120	0.15	00 – 14
9	0.3	6 – 8	125	0.24	15 – 38
8	0.1	9	130	0.27	39 – 65
			135	0.19	66 – 84
			140	0.15	85 – 99

Now try the questions from the Practice Question Bank

Number	Level
Q14.1 – Q14.6	Practice

PRACTICE QUESTION AND ANSWER BANK

What the examiner means

The very important table below has been prepared by CIMA to help you interpret exam questions.

Learning objectives	Verbs used	Definition
1 Knowledge		
What are you expected to know	• List	• Make a list of
	• State	• Express, fully or clearly, the details of/facts of
	• Define	• Give the exact meaning of
2 Comprehension		
What you are expected to understand	• Describe	• Communicate the key features of
	• Distinguish	• Highlight the differences between
	• Explain	• Make clear or intelligible/state the meaning of
	• Identify	• Recognise, establish or select after consideration
	• Illustrate	• Use an example to describe or explain something
3 Application		
How you are expected to apply your knowledge	• Apply	• Put to practical use
	• Calculate/ compute	• Ascertain or reckon mathematically
	• Demonstrate	• Prove with certainty or to exhibit by practical means
	• Prepare	• Make or get ready for use
	• Reconcile	• Make or prove consistent/compatible
	• Solve	• Find an answer to
	• Tabulate	• Arrange in a table
4 Analysis		
How you are expected to analyse the detail of what you have learned	• Analyse	• Examine in detail the structure of
	• Categorise	• Place into a defined class or division
	• Compare and contrast	• Show the similarities and/or differences between
	• Construct	• Build up or compile
	• Discuss	• Examine in detail by argument
	• Interpret	• Translate into intelligible or familiar terms
	• Prioritise	• Place in order of priority or sequence for action
	• Produce	• Create or bring into existence
5 Evaluation		
How you are expected to use your learning to evaluate, make decisions or recommendations	• Advise	• Counsel, inform or notify
	• Evaluate	• Appraise or assess the value of
	• Recommend	• Propose a course of action

BPP
LEARNING MEDIA

Chapter 1 Modern business concepts

1.1 Which of the following definitions are correct?

I Just-in-time (JIT) systems are designed to produce or procure products or components as they are required for a customer or for use, rather than for inventory.

II Flexible manufacturing systems (FMS) are integrated, computer-controlled production systems, capable of producing any of a range of parts, and of switching quickly and economically between them.

III Material requirements planning (MRP) systems are computer based systems that integrate all aspects of a business so that the planning and scheduling of production ensures components are available when needed.

A I only
B I and II only
C I and III only
D II and III only

1.2 Indicate which of the following is an aspect of JIT.

I The use of small frequent deliveries against bulk contracts

II The grouping of machines or workers by product or component instead of by type of work performed

III A reduction in machine set-up time

IV Production driven by demand

1.3 Which of the following are characteristics of work-in-progress under a JIT system of production?

I Zero defects
II Higher inventory to minimise interruptions in production
III Low set-up times
IV Production often made to customer specifications

A I, III and IV
B I, II and III
C III only
D All of the above

1.4 In a total quality management (TQM) environment, which of the following would be classified as an external failure cost?

I Cost of repairing products returned from customers
II Cost of customer service section
III Product liability costs
IV Cost of providing replacement items due to marketing errors

A None of the above
B All of the above
C I only
D III only

1.5 Which of the following is/are correct?

☑ Cost of non-conformance = cost of internal failure + cost of external failure
☑ Cost of conformance = cost of appraisal + cost of prevention
☐ Cost of non-conformance = cost of prevention + cost of appraisal
☐ Cost of conformance = cost of prevention + cost of internal failure

Chapter 2 Environmental costing

2.1 What type of framework can be used to classify environmental costs?

- A Environmental costing
- B Quality costing
- C Appraisal costing
- D Failure costing

2.2 Costs of developing performance measures and testing and inspecting are classified as which type of cost?

- A Environmental external failure costs
- B Environmental prevention costs
- C Environmental appraisal costs
- D Environmental internal failure costs

2.3 The following statements relate to environmental costing.

I Environmental costs are often hidden in general overheads and are therefore difficult to measure.

II Environmental costs can be clearly identified by using absorption costing.

Are the statements true or false?

- A Both statements are true.
- B Both statements are false.
- C Statement I is true and statement II is false.
- D Statement I is false and statement II is true.

2.4 Which of the following are reasons why management accountants should identify environmental costs?

- ☑ Identification can help to ensure correct pricing.
- ☑ Identification can help to avoid fines.
- ☑ Identification can help to ensure the business reputation is not damaged.
- ☑ Identification can lead to cost reduction.

Chapter 3 Absorption costing and activity based costing

The following information relates to Questions 3.1 and 3.2.

A firm of financial consultants offers short revision courses on taxation and auditing for professional exams. The firm has budgeted annual overheads totalling £152,625. Until recently, the firm had applied overheads on a volume basis, based on the number of course days offered. The firm has no variable costs and the only direct costs are the consultants' own time which they divide equally between the two courses. The firm is considering the possibility of adopting an activity based costing (ABC) system and has identified the overhead costs as shown below.

	£
Centre hire	62,500
Enquiries administration	27,125
Brochures	63,000

The following information relates to the past year and is expected to remain the same for the coming year.

Course	No of courses sold	Duration of course	No of enquiries per course	No of brochures printed per course
Auditing	50	2 days	175	300
Taxation	30	3 days	70	200

All courses run with a maximum number of students (30), as it is deemed that beyond this number the learning experience is severely diminished, and the same centre is used for all courses at a standard daily rate. The firm has the human resources to run only one course at any one time.

3.1 Calculate the overhead cost per course for both auditing and taxation using traditional volume based absorption costing.

3.2 Calculate the overhead cost per course for both auditing and taxation using activity based costing.

3.3 Using activity based costing, what is the overhead cost per unit of product Y?

	Product X	Product Y
Production (units)	500	2,000
Machine hours per unit	10	10
Production runs	5	2
Inspections during production	6	6
Production set-up costs	£168,000	
Quality control costs	£96,000	

A £48.00
B £37.71
C £66.00
D £105.60

3.4 Over-absorbed overheads occur when:

A Absorbed overheads exceed actual overheads
B Absorbed overheads exceed budgeted overheads
C Actual overheads exceed absorbed overheads
D Actual overheads exceed budgeted overheads

3.5 J Co uses absorption costing and had no opening inventory at the start of the 20X3. The following information is available for the year ended 31 December 20X3.

Sales	130,000 units
Production	150,000 units
Selling price per unit	£24
Manufacturing variable cost per unit	$15.00
Selling and distribution variable cost per unit	$0.50
Manufacturing fixed cost	$225,000
Selling and distribution fixed cost	$56,200

What was the net profit for the year ended 31 December 20X3?

Chapter 4 Marginal costing and throughput accounting

4.1 At the beginning of May 20X3, LB held an inventory of 1,680 units of product C. On 30 April 20X4 the inventory level was 1,120 units. The standard cost of product C is as follows:

	£
Material (15 kg × £6)	90
Labour (4 hours × £11)	44
Variable overhead (4 hours × £20)	80
Fixed overhead (4 hours × £32)	128
	342

The profit reported in the management accounts for the 12 months ended 30 April 20X4 was £1,219,712. If LB used marginal costing, what profit would have been reported for the period?

A   £1,148,032
B   £1,219,712
C   £1,291,392
D   It cannot be determined from the information provided

4.2   Which of the following statements about throughput accounting and the theory of constraints (TOC) is/are true?

I   In TOC, a binding constraint is an activity that has a higher capacity than preceding or subsequent activities, thereby limiting throughput.

II   A buffer inventory is permissible within TOC.

III   In TOC, throughput contribution = sales revenue – labour cost.

IV   In throughput accounting, profitability is determined by the rate at which money is earned.

A   All of the above
B   II and III
C   III only
D   II and IV

4.3   S Ltd manufactures three products, A, B and C. The products use a series of different machines but there is a common machine, P, that is a bottleneck.

The selling price and standard cost for each product for the forthcoming year is as follows:

	A	B	C
	$	$	$
Selling price	200	150	150
Direct materials	41	20	30
Conversion costs	55	40	66
Machine P – minutes	12	10	7

Calculate the return per hour for each of the products.

4.4   JJ Ltd manufactures three products: W, X and Y. The products use a series of different machines but there is a common machine that is a bottleneck.

The standard selling price and standard cost per unit for each product for the forthcoming period are as follows:

	W	X	Y
	£	£	£
Selling price	200	150	150
Cost			
Direct materials	41	20	30
Labour	30	20	36
Overheads	60	40	50
Profit	69	70	34
Bottleneck machine – minutes per unit	9	10	7

40% of the overhead cost is classified as variable.

Using a throughput accounting approach, what would be the ranking of the products for best use of the bottleneck?

4.5 A company manufactures four products: J, K, L and M. The products use a series of different machines but there is a common machine, X, which causes a bottleneck.

The standard selling price and standard cost per unit for each product for the forthcoming year are as follows:

	J	K	L	M
	£	£	£	£
Selling price	2,000	1,500	1,500	1,750
Cost				
Direct materials	410	200	300	400
Labour	300	200	360	275
Variable overheads	250	200	300	175
Fixed overheads	360	300	210	330
Profit	680	600	330	570
Machine X – minutes per unit	120	100	70	110

Direct materials is the only unit-level manufacturing cost.

Using a throughput accounting approach, the ranking of the products would be:

	J	K	L	M
A	1st	2nd	3rd	4th
B	1st	2nd	4th	3rd
C	2nd	1st	4th	3rd
D	2nd	3rd	1st	4th

4.6 A company operates a throughput accounting system. The details of product A per unit are as follows:

Selling price	£24.99
Material cost	£8.87
Conversion costs	£12.27
Time on bottleneck resource	6.5 minutes

Required £ 148.8

Calculate the return per hour for product A.

4.7 Fill in the blanks in the sentences below.

(a) The aim of TOC is to maximise .... while

keeping... and .... to a minimum.

(b) An assumption in TOC is that all operational expenses except direct material cost are

....

(c) An activity within an organisation which has a lower capacity than preceding or subsequent activities, thereby limiting throughput, is a .... or

....

(d) Under TOC, the only inventory that a business should hold, with the exception of possibly a very small amount of finished goods inventory and raw materials that are consistent with the JIT approach, is a buffer inventory held ....

4.8 When comparing the profits reported under absorption costing and marginal costing during a period when the level of inventory increased:

A Absorption costing profits will be higher and closing inventory valuations lower than those under marginal costing

B Absorption costing profits will be higher and closing inventory valuations higher than those under marginal costing

C Marginal costing profits will be higher and closing inventory valuations lower than those under absorption costing

D Marginal costing profits will be higher and closing inventory valuations higher than those under absorption costing

4.9 Summary results for Y Limited for March are shown below.

	£'000	Units
Sales revenue	820	
Variable production costs	300	
Variable selling costs	105	
Fixed production costs	180	
Fixed selling costs	110	
Production in March		1,000
Opening inventory		0
Closing inventory		150

Using marginal costing, the profit for March was:

A £170,000
B £185,750
C £197,000
D £229,250

Chapter 5 Limiting factor analysis

5.1 Z plc manufactures three products which have the following selling prices and costs per unit.

	Z1	Z2	Z3
	£	£	£
Selling price	15.00	18.00	17.00
Costs per unit: direct materials	4.00	5.00	10.00
direct labour	2.00	4.00	1.80
Overhead: variable	1.00	2.00	0.90
fixed	4.50	3.00	1.35
	11.50	14.00	14.05
Profit per unit	3.50	4.00	2.95

All three products use the same type of labour.

In a period in which labour is in short supply, the rank order of production is:

	Z1	Z2	Z3
A	First	Second	Third
B	Third	Second	First
C	Second	First	Third
• D	First	Third	Second

5.2   Z Ltd manufactures three products, the selling price and cost details of which are given below.

	Product X £	Product Y £	Product Z £
Selling price per unit	75	95	96
Costs per unit			
Direct materials (£5/kg)	10	5	15
Direct labour (£4/hour)	16	24	20
Variable overhead	8	12	10
Fixed overhead	24	36	30

In a period when direct materials are restricted in supply, the most and the least profitable uses of direct materials are:

	Most profitable	Least profitable
A	Y	X
B	Y	Z
C	Z	X
D	Z	Y

5.3   SW Ltd produces four products, A, B, C and D, and production capacity is limited. Product A has a C/S ratio of 27%, product B a C/S ratio of 22%, product C a C/S ratio of 19% and product D one of 11%.

Given unlimited demand for the four products, SW Ltd should concentrate on producing product A.

True

False   ☐

5.4   MNP plc produces three products from a single raw material that is limited in supply. Product details for period 6 are as follows.

	Product M	Product N	Product P
Maximum demand (units)	1,000	2,400	2,800
Optimum planned production	720	Nil	2,800
Unit contribution	£4.50	£4.80	£2.95
Raw material cost per unit (£0.50 per kg)	£1.25	£1.50	£0.75

The planned production optimises the use of the 6,000 kg of raw material that is available from MNP plc's normal supplier at the price of £0.50 per kg. However, a new supplier has been found that is prepared to supply a further 1,000 kg of the material.

Required

Calculate the maximum price that MNP plc should be prepared to pay for the additional 1,000 kg of the material.

5.5   The following details relate to three services provided by JHN plc.

	Service J £	Service H £	Service N £
Fee charged to customers	84	122	145
Unit service costs:			
Direct materials	12	23	22
Direct labour	15	20	25
Variable overhead	12	16	20
Fixed overhead	20	42	40

All three services use the same type of direct labour, which is paid £30 per hour.

The fixed overheads are general fixed overheads that have been absorbed on the basis of machine hours.

If direct labour is a scarce resource, the most and least profitable uses of it are:

	Most profitable	Least profitable
A	H	J
B	H	N
C	N	J
D	N	H

5.6 M Limited manufactures four products from different quantities of the same material which is in short supply. The following budgeted data relates to the products.

	Product M1 £/unit	Product M2 £/unit	Product M3 £/unit	Product M4 £/unit
Selling price	70	92	113	83
Materials (£4 per kg)	16	22	34	20
Conversion costs	39	52	57	43
	55	74	91	63
Profit	15	18	22	20
Machine time per unit in **minutes**	40	40	37.5	45

The conversion costs include general fixed costs that have been absorbed using a rate of £24 per machine hour.

The most profitable use of the raw materials is to make:

A   Product M1
B   Product M2
C   Product M3
D   Product M4

5.7 The following details relate to the four products made by EB Ltd.

	M £ per unit	V £ per unit	I £ per unit	F £ per unit
Selling price	17	22	10	38
Direct materials	3	12	1	20
Direct labour	4	1	2	2
Variable overhead	1	1	3	2
Fixed overhead	8	4	1	2
	16	18	7	26
Profit	1	4	3	12

All four products use the same labour and materials but in different quantities.

Complete the following:

In a period when the material used on these products is in short supply, the most profitable use of material is to make product ....I.................., the least profitable is to make product ....V.......... .

5.8 J Ltd manufactures three products, the selling prices, maximum demand and cost details of which are as follows:

	X £	Y £	Z £
Unit selling price	150	190	190
Unit costs			
Direct materials (£10/kg)	20	10	30
Direct labour (£8/hr)	32	48	40
Variable overhead	16	24	20
Fixed overheads	48	72	60
Maximum demand	590	840	660

In the forthcoming period, direct materials are restricted to 1,400 kg and the company has contracted to supply 100 units of Z and 130 units of Y to a customer (included in the maximum demand figures above). What is the profit-maximising production plan?

A	X 130 units;	Y 840 units;	Z 100 units
B	X 280 units;	Y 840 units;	Z 0 units
C	X 0 units;	Y 2 units;	Z 466 units
D	X 1 unit;	Y 840 units;	Z 186 units

5.9 Choose the correct words from those highlighted in the statement below.

The total costs of a company that has to subcontract work to make up a shortfall in its own in-house capabilities will be minimised if those units **made/bought** have the **lowest/highest** extra variable cost of **making/buying** per unit of scarce resource **used/saved**.

Chapter 6 Relevant costs

6.1 What is the relevant cost of the product units in a decision about the disposal of existing product units no longer required?

- A Net realisable value
- B Replacement cost
- C Variable cost
- D Full cost

6.2 BS plc has been asked to carry out a systems amendment for L Ltd. The amendment will require 400 programmer hours, and BS plc has only one programmer who is capable of doing the job.

The programmer is paid £40 per hour. Employers' NIC and pension contributions are 20% of salary. Other overheads are absorbed by adding 200% to direct salaries.

The programmer is scheduled to start work on a project for another customer, M Inc, the revenue from which is £60,000 and non-salary direct costs are £1,500. This job will also take 400 hours. If the programmer is assigned to the L Ltd job, BS plc will have to hire another programmer to carry out the M Inc job at a cost of £22,000.

The relevant cost of the programmer's time if BS plc carries out the systems amendment for L Ltd is £19,200.

True ☐

False ☒

6.3 Which of the following are non-relevant costs?

I Avoidable costs
II Opportunity costs
III Notional costs
IV Sunk costs

A All of them
B IV only
C None of them
D III and IV

6.4 A Ltd has three options for machine B. One of these options involves modifying the machine now at a cost of £7,200, which will mean that the company does not have to hire an alternative machine at a cost of £19,800. This modification would mean that machine B would have to be disposed of in one year's time at a cost of £4,000. Ignoring the time value of money, calculate the relevant cost of this option.

6.5 C Ltd is in the process of preparing a quotation for a special job for a customer. The job will require 700 units of material N. 400 units are already in stock at a book value of £50 per unit. The net realisable value per unit is £20. The replacement price per unit is £60. The material is in stock as the result of previous overbuying. No other use can be found for material N.

Required

Calculate the relevant cost of material N for this special job.

Chapter 7 Multi-product breakeven analysis

7.1 Z plc currently sells products Aye, Bee and Cee in equal quantities and at the same selling price per unit. The contribution to sales ratio for product Aye is 40%, for product Bee it is 50% and the total is 48%. If fixed costs are unaffected by mix and are currently 20% of sales, the effect of changing the product mix to **Aye 40%**, **Bee 25%** and **Cee 35%** is that the total contribution/total sales ratio changes to:

A   40%
B   54%
C   47.4%
D   32%

7.2 J Ltd produces and sells two products. The O sells for £12 per unit and has a total variable cost of £7.90, while the H sells for £17 per unit and has a total variable cost of £11.20. For every four units of O sold, three of H are sold. J Ltd's fixed costs are £131,820 per period. Budgeted sales revenue for the next period is £398,500.

Required

Calculate the margin of safety.

7.3 A company makes and sells three products, A, B and C. The products are sold in the proportions A:B:C = 1:1:4.

Monthly fixed costs are £55,100 and product details are as follows:

Product	Selling price £ per unit	Variable cost £ per unit
A	47	25
B	39	20
C	28	11

The company wishes to earn a profit of £43,000 next month. What is the required sales value of product A in order to achieve this target profit?

The following data relates to Questions 7.4 and 7.5

HG plc manufactures four products. The unit cost, selling price and bottleneck resource details per unit are as follows:

	Product W £	Product X £	Product Y £	Product Z £
Selling price	56	67	89	96
Material	22	31	38	46
Labour	15	20	18	24
Variable overhead	12	15	18	15
Fixed overhead	4	2	8	7
	Minutes	*Minutes*	*Minutes*	*Minutes*
Bottleneck resource time	10	10	15	15

7.4 Assuming that labour is a unit variable cost, if the products are ranked according to their contribution to sales ratios, the most profitable product is:

- A   W
- B   X
- • C   Y
- D   Z

7.5 Assuming that labour is a unit variable cost, if budgeted unit sales are in the ratio W:2, X:3, Y:3, Z:4 and monthly fixed costs are budgeted to be £15,000, the number of units of W that would be sold at the budgeted breakeven point is nearest to:

- A   106 units
- B   142 units
- C   212 units
- D   283 units

7.6 KEM Ltd produces and sells two products, the L and the E. The company expects to sell two L for every five E and have monthly sales revenue of £320,000. The L has a C/S ratio of 25%, whereas the E has a C/S ratio of 35%. Budgeted monthly fixed costs are £90,000.

Required

Calculate the budgeted breakeven sales revenue.

7.7 PER plc sells three products. The budgeted fixed cost for the period is £648,000. The budgeted contribution to sales ratio (C/S ratio) and sales mix are as follows:

Product	C/S ratio	Mix
P	27%	30%
E	56%	20%
R	38%	50%

The breakeven sales revenue is nearest to:

- A   £248,000
- B   £1,606,700
- • C   £1,692,000
- D   £1,522,700

Chapter 8 Short-term decision making

8.1 S Ltd is considering adapting its assembly process so that products can also be moulded at the same time. The existing assembly process machinery would have to be removed, either now at a dismantling cost of £100,000 and with the sale of the machinery for £800,000, or in 1 year's time at a dismantling cost of £110,000 and with sale proceeds of £600,000. Alternative machinery would have to be leased. This would cost £80,000 per annum. The existing assembly process machinery originally cost £2,000,000 when purchased 7 years ago. It is being depreciated at 5% per annum on a straight line basis. Analysing on an incremental opportunity cost basis and ignoring the time value of money, which of the following is correct?

- • A   Adapting now will produce savings of £130,000 more than adapting in one year.
- B   Adapting now will cost £130,000 more than adapting in one year.
- C   Adapting now will produce savings of £110,000 more than adapting in one year.
- D   Adapting now will cost £110,000 more than adapting in one year.

8.2 D Ltd's entire machine capacity is used to produce essential components. The variable costs of using the machines are £150,000 and the fixed costs are £400,000. If all the components were purchased from an outside supplier, the machines could be used to produce other items which would earn a total contribution of £250,000.

Required

Calculate the maximum price that D Ltd should be willing to pay to the outside supplier for the components, assuming there is no change in fixed costs.

Chapter 9 Linear programming

9.1 A company produces two types of orange juice, ordinary (X cartons per year) and premium (Y cartons per year).

Required

Determine the inequality that represents the fact that the amount of ordinary orange juice produced must be no more than twice the amount of premium orange juice produced.

9.2 In a linear programming problem, the constraints are $X \leq 41$ and $Y \geq 19$. Describe the feasible region, assuming where appropriate that the axes also constitute boundaries.

A   A rectangle to the left of $X = 41$ and below $Y = 19$
B   An infinite rectangle to the right of $X = 41$ and below $Y = 19$
C   An infinite region above $Y = 19$ and to the right of $X = 41$
• D   An infinite rectangle to the left of $X = 41$ and above $Y = 19$

9.3 In a linear programming problem, the objective function is to maximise contribution given by $50X + 250Y$.

The feasible region has vertices (0, 160), (40, 140), (80, 120) and (140, 0).

Insert the answer below.

The vertex representing the optimal solution is .... *(40, 140)* .

9.4 In a linear programming problem, contribution is $4X + 2Y$ and the vertices of the feasible region are P (0, 250), Q (50, 200) and R (100, 100). Which of the following statements is the full, correct statement about maximising contribution?

A   Contribution is maximised at point P.
B   Contribution is maximised at point Q.
C   Contribution is maximised at point R.
• D   Contribution is maximised at point Q and R, and all points on the straight line joining them.

9.5 Let X be the number of supervisors and Y be the number of other staff.

Required

Find the inequality to express the constraint that the number of supervisors must be no more than 20% of the total number of staff.

Chapter 10 Forecasting techniques

10.1 Sales of product D during 20X0 (control periods 1 to 13) were noted and the following totals calculated.

$\Sigma X = 91$ $\qquad\qquad$ $\Sigma Y = 1,120$ $\qquad\qquad$ $\Sigma XY = 9,247$ $\qquad\qquad$ $\Sigma X^2 = 819$

There is a high correlation between time and volume of sales. Using a suitable regression line, what is the predicted sales level of product D in control period 4 of 20X1, when a seasonal variation of −13 is relevant?

- A   552
- B   158
- • C   150
- D   176

10.2 A regression equation $Y = a + bX$ is used to forecast the value of Y for a given value of X. Which of the following increase the reliability of the forecast?

I   A correlation coefficient numerically close to 1
II   Working to a higher number of decimal places of accuracy
III   Forecasting for values of X outside the range of those used in the sample
IV   A large sample is used to calculate the regression equation

- A   I only
- B   I and II only
- C   I and III only
- • D   I and IV only

10.3 If $\Sigma x = 12$, $\Sigma y = 42$, $\Sigma x^2 = 46$, $\Sigma y^2 = 542$, $\Sigma xy = 157$ and $n = 4$, what is the correlation coefficient?

- • A   0.98
- B   −0.98
- C   0.26
- D   0.008

10.4 Monthly sales have been found to follow a linear trend of $y = 9.82 + 4.372x$, where y is the number of items sold and x is the number of the month. Monthly deviations from the trend have been calculated and follow an additive model. In month 24, the seasonal variation is estimated to be plus 8.5.

What is the forecast number of items to be sold in month 24 (to the nearest whole number)?

- A   106
- B   115
- • C   123
- D   152

10.5 Which of the following are necessary if forecasts obtained from a time series analysis are to be reliable?

I   There must be no unforeseen events.
II   The model used must fit the past data.
III   The trend must be increasing.
IV   There must be no seasonal variation.

- A   I only
- • B   I and II only
- C   I, II and III only
- D   I, II, III and IV

10.6 What is the purpose of seasonally adjusting the values in a time series?

    A   To obtain an instant estimate of the degree of seasonal variation

    B   To obtain an instant estimate of the trend

    C   To ensure that seasonal components total zero

    D   To take the first step in a time series analysis of the data

Chapters 11a and 11b Budgeting

11.1 What is budgetary slack?

    A   The difference between the costs built into the budget and the costs actually incurred

    B   The difference between the minimum necessary costs and the costs actually incurred

    C   The sum of the minimum necessary costs and the costs built into the budget

    D   The difference between the flexible budget and the costs actually incurred

11.2 Which of the following may be considered to be objectives of budgeting?

    I   Co-ordination

    II   Communication

    III   Expansion

    IV   Resource allocation

    A   All of them

    B   I, II and IV

    C   II, III and IV

    D   II and IV

11.3 What does the statement 'sales is the principal budget factor' mean?

    A   The level of sales will determine the level of cash at the end of the period.

    B   The level of sales will determine the level of profit at the end of the period.

    C   The company's activities are limited by the level of sales it can achieve.

    D   Sales is the largest item in the budget.

11.4 QT Co manufactures a single product, and an extract from their flexed budget for production costs is as follows:

	Activity level	
	80%	90%
	$	$
Direct material	2,400	2,700
Labour	2,120	2,160
Production overhead	4,060	4,080
	8,580	8,940

What would the total production cost allowance be in a budget flexed at the 83% level of activity (to the nearest $)?

    A $6,266

    B $6,888

    C $8,586

    D $8,688

11.5 An extract from a company's sales budget is as follows:

	$
October	224,000
November	390,000
December	402,000

Ten per cent of sales are paid for immediately in cash. Of the credit customers, 30 per cent pay in the month following the sale and are entitled to a 1 per cent discount. The remaining customers pay two months after the sale is made.

What is the value of sales receipts shown in the company's cash budget for December?

- A $285,567
- B $286,620
- C $290,430
- D $312,830

11.6 Extracts from a company's budget are as follows:

	August	September
Production units	12,600	5,500
Fixed production overhead cost incurred	$9,440	$7,000

The standard variable production overhead cost per unit is $5. Variable production overhead is paid 70 per cent in the month incurred and 30 per cent in the following month.

Fixed production overhead cost is paid in the month following that in which it is incurred and includes depreciation of $2,280 per month.

What is the payment for total production overhead cost shown in the cash budget for September?

- A $32,220
- B $42,870
- C $45,310
- D $47,590

11.7 The following extract is taken from the production cost budget of S Co.

Production (units)	2,000	3,000
Production cost ($)	11,100	12,900

What is the budget cost allowance for an activity level of 4,000 units?

- A $7,200
- B $7,500
- C $13,460
- D $14,700

11.8 The following details have been extracted from the payables' records of X Co.

Invoices paid in the month of purchase	25%
Invoices paid in the first month after purchase	70%
Invoices paid in the second month after purchase	5%

Purchases for July to September are budgeted as follows:

July	$250,000
August	$300,000
September	$280,000

For suppliers paid in the month of purchase, a settlement discount of 5% is received. What is the amount budgeted to be paid to suppliers in September?

- A $278,500
- B $280,000
- C $289,000
- D $292,500

Chapters 12 and 13 Standard costing and variance analysis

13.1 Which of the following statements about standards is/are true?

I   Can be prepared for all functions, even where output cannot be measured
II   Must be expressed in money terms
III   Aids control by setting financial targets or limits for a forthcoming period
IV   Should be revised every time prices or levels of efficiency change

A   None of the above
B   All of the above
C   III and IV
D   I, II and IV

13.2 JPM has recorded the following data in budget working papers.

Activity	Overhead cost
Labour hours	£
22,000	108,740
24,000	115,080
28,000	127,760
36,000	153,120

In control period 11, 30,600 labour hours were actually worked and the actual overhead cost was £154,952.

What is the total overhead expenditure variance?

A   £18,950 (A)
B   £57,950 (A)
C   £24,800 (A)
D   £136,002 (A)

The following information relates to Questions 13.3 and 13.4.

The standard cost and selling price structure for the single product that is made by CD is as follows:

	£ per unit
Selling price	82
Variable cost	(47)
Fixed production overhead	(29)
	6

The budgeted level of production and sales is 3,200 units per month.

Extract from the actual results for March

Fixed production overhead volume variance	£8,700 favourable
Fixed production overhead expenditure variance	£2,200 adverse

Inventory levels reduced by 200 units during the period.

13.3 What was the actual expenditure on fixed production overhead during March?

A   £86,300
B   £90,600
C   £92,800
D   £95,000

13.4 What was the actual sales volume during March?

A   2,900 units
B   3,300 units
C   3,500 units
D   3,700 units

The following information relates to Questions 13.5 and 13.6.

Product B requires 4.5 kg of material per unit. The standard price of the material is €6 per kg. The budgeted production for last month was 750 units. Actual results were as follows:

Material used	2,250 kg
Production	780 units
Material cost	€14,175

Due to worldwide increases in the price of the material used it was realised, after the month had ended, that a more realistic material standard price would have been €6.50 per kg.

13.5   (a)   Explain what is meant by a planning variance.   8Ro $1755

      (b)   Calculate planning and operational variances for material costs for the month.

13.6   State three possible causes of the operational usage variance you have calculated.

13.7   PQR Ltd operates a standard absorption costing system. Details of budgeted and actual figures are as follows:

	Budget	Actual
Sales volume (units)	100,000	110,000
Selling price per unit	£10	£9.50
Variable cost per unit	£5	£5.25
Total cost per unit	£8	£8.30

   (a)   Calculate the sales price variance.   55,000

   (b)   Calculate the sales volume profit variance.   20,000

13.8   SS Ltd operates a standard marginal costing system. An extract from the standard cost card for the labour costs of one of its products is as follows:

Labour cost

5 hours × £12	£60

Actual results for the period were as follows:

Production	11,500 units
Labour rate variance	£45,000 adverse
Labour efficiency variance	£30,000 adverse

Calculate the actual rate paid per direct labour hour.

The following data are given for Questions 13.9 to 13.11 below.

A company uses standard absorption costing. The following information was recorded by the company for October.

	Budget	Actual
Output and sales (units)	8,700	8,200
Selling price per unit	£26	£31
Variable cost per unit	£10	£10
Total fixed overheads	£34,800	£37,000

13.9   The sales price variance for October was:

     A   £38,500 favourable

     B   £41,000 favourable

   • (C)   £41,000 adverse

     D   £65,600 adverse

13.10 The sales volume profit variance for October was:

    (A)   £6,000 adverse
    B   £6,000 favourable
    C   £8,000 adverse
    • D   £8,000 favourable

13.11 The fixed overhead volume variance for October was:

    A   £2,000 adverse
    • B   £2,200 adverse
    C   £2,200 favourable
    D   £4,200 adverse

13.12 PP Ltd operates a standard absorption costing system. The following information has been extracted from the standard cost card for one of its products.

Budgeted production	1,500 units
Direct material cost: 7 kg × £4.10	£28.70 per unit

Actual results for the period were as follows:

Production	1,600 units
Direct material (purchased and used): 12,000 kg	£52,200

It has subsequently been noted that due to a change in economic conditions the best price that the material could have been purchased for was £4.50 per kg during the period.

(a)   Calculate the material price planning variance.
(b)   Calculate the operational material usage variance.

Chapter 14 Risk and uncertainty in decision making

Data for Questions 14.1 and 14.2

Mart is launching a new product next year. Forecasts of sales are as follows:

Annual sales $'000	Probability
4,000	0.10
4,400	0.15
4,800	0.35
5,200	?
5,600	?

These are predicted to be the only possible outcomes, and the probability of sales of $5.2m is exactly equal to the probability of sales of $5.6m. The contribution to sales ratio of the product will be 35%. Fixed costs will be $196,000 per quarter.

14.1   The expected value of annual profit is ....4900........

14.2   The probability of the product at least breaking even next year is ...., while the probability of the product earning a profit of at least $900,000 is ....

The following data are to be used when answering Questions 14.3 and 14.4.

A company expects to sell 1,000 units per month of a new product but there is uncertainty as to both the unit selling price and the unit variable cost of the product. The following estimates of selling price, variable costs and their related probabilities have been made.

		Unit variable cost		
Selling price £ per unit	probability %		£ per unit	Probability %
20	25		8	20
25	40		10	50
30	35		12	30

There are specific fixed costs of £5,000 per month expected for the new product.

14.3   The expected value of monthly contribution is:

  A   £5,890
  B   £10,300
  C   £10,890
  D   £15,300

14.4   The probability of monthly contribution from this new product exceeding £13,500 is:

  A   24.5%
  B   30.5%
  C   63.0%
  D   92.5%

The following data relates to both Questions 14.5 and 14.6.

TX Ltd can choose from five mutually exclusive projects. The projects will each last for one year only and their net cash inflows will be determined by the prevailing market conditions. The forecast net cash inflows and their associated probabilities are shown below.

	Market conditions		
	Poor	Good	Excellent
Probability	0.20	0.50	0.30
	$'000	$'000	$'000
Project L	500	470	550
Project M	400	550	570
Project N	450	400	475
Project O	360	400	420
Project P	600	500	425

14.5   Based on the expected value of the net cash inflows, which project should be undertaken?   M

14.6   What is the value of perfect information about the state of the market?

Chapter 1 Modern business concepts

1.1   B   Definitions I and II are correct.

1.2   I   The use of small frequent deliveries against bulk contracts – **yes**

II   The grouping of machines or workers by product or component instead of by type of work performed – **yes**

III   A reduction in machine set-up time – **yes**

IV   Production driven by demand – **yes**

Aspect I: JIT requires close integration of suppliers with the company's manufacturing process.

Aspect II: JIT requires the use of machine cells.

Aspect III: JIT recognises machinery set-ups as a non value added activity.

Aspect IV: Each component on a production line is produced only when needed for the next stage.

1.3   A

1.4   B   External failure costs are costs arising outside the manufacturing organisation of failure to achieve a specified quality (after transfer of ownership to the customer).

1.5   The following are correct.
Cost of non-conformance = cost of internal failure + cost of external failure
Cost of conformance = cost of appraisal + cost of prevention

Chapter 2 Environmental costing

2.1   B   Hansen and Mendoza (1999) suggest that many **environmental costs arise because of poor-quality controls**. They suggest that an **environmental cost report** should be **produced regularly** in the **format** of a **cost of quality report**.

2.2   C   Environmental **appraisal costs** are the costs involved with establishing whether activities are complying with environmental standards and policies. For example, developing performance measures, monitoring, testing and inspection costs, site survey costs.

2.3   C   Statement I is true. The problem with traditional management accounting systems is that they fail to analyse environmental costs. Costs such as water, energy and waste become hidden within production overheads. Statement II is false. Activity based costing, not absorption costing, is usually considered to be a useful way of identifying environmental costs.

2.4   All of them. Management accountants should be aware of the ethical reasons why environmental costs are important but there are many financial benefits that can be gained by identifying environmental costs.

Chapter 3 Absorption costing and activity based costing

3.1 **The correct answer is: auditing £1,606.58 per course; taxation £2,409.87 per course.**

	Auditing	Taxation	Total
Number of courses sold	50	30	
Duration of course (days)	2	3	
Number of course days	100	90	190

$$\text{Overhead cost per course day} = \frac{£152,625}{190} = £803.29$$

Overhead cost per course

Auditing   £803.29 × 2 days = £1,606.58

Taxation   £803.29 × 3 days = £2,409.87

3.2 **The correct answer is: auditing £1,995.40 per course; taxation £1,761.85 per course.**

$$\text{Centre hire cost per course day} = \frac{£62,500}{190\,*} = £328.95$$

*See working in Answer 3.1.

$$\text{Enquiries administration cost per enquiry} = \frac{£27,125}{(50 \times 175) + (30 \times 70)} = £2.50$$

$$\text{Brochure cost per brochure printed} = \frac{£63,000}{(50 \times 300) + (30 \times 200)} = £3$$

Overhead costs per course using ABC

		Auditing £ per course		Taxation £ per course
Centre hire at £328.95 per day	(× 2)	657.90	(× 3)	986.85
Enquiries admin at £2.50 per enquiry	(× 175)	437.50	(× 70)	175.00
Brochures at £3 per brochure printed	(× 300)	900.00	(× 200)	600.00
		1,995.40		1,761.85

3.3 A   Set-up cost per production run

$$= \frac{£16,000}{(5+2)}$$

$$= £24,000$$

Cost per inspection

$$= \frac{£96,000}{(6+6)}$$

$$= £8,000$$

Overheads to product Y:

	£
Set-up costs	
(£24,000 × 2)	48,000
Quality control costs	
(£8,000 × 6)	48,000
	96,000

$$= \frac{£96,000}{2,000}$$

$$= \underline{£48}$$

3.4 A **Description B** could lead to under-absorbed overheads if actual overheads far exceeded both budgeted overheads and the overhead absorbed. **Description C** could lead to under-absorbed overheads if overhead absorbed does not increase in line with actual overhead incurred.

3.5 $853,750

Net profit = sales revenue – cost of sales – selling and distribution costs

Sales revenue = 130,000 units × $24 = $3,120,000

Manufacturing cost per unit = $15.00 + ($225,000/150,000 units) = $16.50

∴ Cost of sales = 130,000 units × $16.50 = $2,145,000

Selling and distribution costs = (130,000 units × $0.50) + $56,250 = $121,250

∴ Net profit = $3,120,000 – $2,145,000 – $121,250 = $853,750

Chapter 4 Marginal costing and throughput accounting

4.1 **The correct answer is C.**

Inventory levels have fallen so marginal costing reports the higher profit.

	£
Absorption costing profit	1,219,712
+ fixed overhead included in inventory level change	
((1,680 – 1,120) × £128)	71,680
Marginal costing profit	1,291,392

If you chose option A, you deducted the fixed overhead included in the inventory level change. If inventory levels decrease, absorption costing will report the lower profit because, as well as the fixed overhead absorbed during the period, fixed overhead which had been carried forward in opening inventory is released and included in cost of sales.

Option B is the absorption costing profit. The marginal costing profit must be different, however, because there has been a change in inventory levels.

4.2 **The correct answer is D.**

Statement I is incorrect because a binding constraint is an activity that has a lower capacity than preceding or subsequent activities.

Statement III is incorrect because throughput contribution = sales revenue – material cost.

4.3 Return per hour = (sales revenue-material costs)/hour

	Sales revenue $	Material cost $	Sales less materials	Return per hour
A	200	41	159	(× (60/12)) $795
B	150	20	130	(× (60/10)) $780
C	150	30	120	(× (60/7)) $1,029

4.4 The ranking of the products for best use of the bottleneck is W, Y, X.

Throughput accounting approach

	W £	X £	Y £
Selling price	200	150	150
Direct material	(41)	(20)	(30)
Throughput	159	(130)	(120)
Throughput per minute on bottleneck	159/9 = 17.67	130/10 = 13	120/7 = 17.14
	1	3	2

4.5 D We need to rank in terms of the throughput contribution per time on the bottleneck resource.
(Because direct materials cost is the only unit-level manufacturing cost, conversion costs cannot be directly allocated to products and hence we do not use the TA ratio.)

	J	K	L	M
Hours per product	2	$1^2/_3$	$1^1/_6$	$1^5/_6$
	£	£	£	£
Selling price	2,000	1,500	1,500	1,750
Direct material cost	410	200	300	400
Throughput contribution	1,590	1,300	1,200	1,350
Throughput contribution per hour	£795	£780	£1,029	£736
Ranking	2	3	1	4

4.6 Return per hour = (sales – material cost) per hour on bottleneck resource
∴ Return per 6.5 mins = £(24.99 – 8.87)

$$\therefore \text{ Return per hour} = £(24.99 - 8.87) \times \frac{60}{6.5} = £148.80$$

4.7 (a) The aim of TOC is to maximise **throughput contribution** while keeping **inventory** and **operational expenses** to a minimum.

(b) An assumption in TOC is that all operational expenses except direct material cost are **fixed**.

(c) An activity within an organisation which has a lower capacity than preceding or subsequent actions, thereby limiting throughput, is a **bottleneck** or **binding constraint**.

(d) Under TOC, the only inventory that a business should hold, with the exception of possibly a very small amount of finished goods inventory and raw materials that are consistent with the JIT approach, is a buffer inventory held **immediately prior to the bottleneck/binding constraint**.

4.8 B Closing inventory valuation under absorption costing will always be higher than under marginal costing because of the absorption of fixed overheads into closing inventory values. The profit under absorption costing will be greater because the fixed overhead being carried forward in closing inventory is greater than the fixed overhead being written off in opening inventory.

4.9   A   Using marginal costing, the profit in March was:

	£'000	£'000
Sales revenue		820,000
Less variable production costs [£300,000 − $\frac{150}{1,000}$ × £300,000]		(255,000)
		565,000
Less: fixed production costs	180,000	
variable selling costs	105,000	
fixed selling costs	110,000	
		(395,000)
		170,000

Chapter 5 Limiting factor analysis

5.1   D

	Z1	Z2	Z3
	£	£	£
Selling price per unit	15	18	17.00
Variable costs per unit	7	11	12.70
Contribution per unit	8	7	4.30
Labour cost per unit	£2	£4	£1.80
Contribution per £1 of labour	£4	£1.75	£2.39
Rank order of production	1	3	2

If you chose **option A**, you ranked according to contribution per unit.

If you chose **option B**, you ranked according to variable cost per unit.

If you chose **option C**, you ranked according to labour cost per unit.

5.2   B   The products must be ranked in order of their contribution per kg of direct material.

	X	Y	Z
	£ per unit	£ per unit	£ per unit
Selling price	75	95	96
Variable cost	34	41	45
Contribution	41	54	51
Kg of material used per unit	2	1	3
Contribution per kg	£20.50	£54	£17
Ranking	2	1	3

If you chose **option A**, you ranked according to unit contribution.

If you chose **option C**, you ranked according to selling price.

If you chose **option D**, you ranked according to usage of material.

5.3   **True**. The company should concentrate on the product with the highest C/S ratio.

5.4   Limiting factor is raw material.

	M	N	P
Contribution per kg of limiting factor			
£4.50/(£1.25 ÷ £0.50)	£1.80		
£4.80/(£1.50 ÷ £0.50)		£1.60	
£2.95/(£0.75 ÷ £0.50)			£1.97
Ranking	2	3	1

Usage of the 6,000 kg

	Kg
2,800 units of P (× (£0.75/£0.50))	4,200
720 units of M (× (£1.25/£0.50))	1,800
	6,000

Optimum production with additional 1,000 kg

	Kg
(1,000 – 720) units of M (× (£1.25/£0.50))	700
100 units of N (× (£1.50/£0.50))	300
	1,000

Contribution obtainable

	£
280 units of M (× £4.50)	1,260
100 units of N (× £4.80)	480
	1,740

This contribution is after charging £0.50 per kg.

∴ Contribution before material cost = £1,740 + (1,000 × £0.50) = £2,240 = maximum amount that should be paid.

5.5 A

	Service J	Service H	Service N
Contribution per unit	£45	£63	£78
Labour hours required per unit	$1/2$	$2/3$	$5/6$
Contribution per labour hour	£90	£94.50	£93.60
Ranking	3	1	2

5.6 A

	M1	M2	M3	M4
	£	£	£	£
Selling price	70	92	113	83
Less: materials	(16)	(22)	(34)	(20)
conversion costs	(39)	(52)	(57)	(43)
Plus general fixed costs (W)	16	16	15	18
Contribution	31	34	37	38
Kg of material	4	5.5	8.5	5
Contribution per kg	£7.75	£6.18	£4.35	£7.60
Ranking	1	3	4	2

Working

M1   £24 × 40/60 = £16

M2   £24 × 40/60 = £16

M3   £24 × 37.5/60 = £15

M4   £24 × 45/60 = £18

5.7 In a period when the material used on these products is in short supply, the most profitable use of material is to make product **I**; the least profitable is to make product **V**.

	M	V	I	F
Contribution per unit	£9	£8	£4	£14
Material cost per unit	£3	£12	£1	£20
Contribution per £ of material	£3	£0.67	£4	£0.70
Ranking	2	4	1	3

5.8 A

	X	Y	Z
Unit contribution	£82	£108	£100
Kg required per unit	2 kg	1 kg	3 kg
Contribution per kg	£41	£108	£33.33
Ranking	2	1	3

	Kg used
Produce 100 units of Z (× 3 kg)	300
Produce 130 units of Y (× 1 kg)	130
	430
Produce remaining (840 – 130) units of Y (× 1 kg)	710
Use balance to produce 130 units of X (× 2 kg)	260
	1,400

Option B takes no account of the requirement to produce 100 units of Z.

Option C has ranked on the basis of unit profit and has taken no account of the contract requirements.

Option D has ranked on the basis of contribution per unit and has taken no account of contract requirements.

5.9   The total costs of a company that has to subcontract work to make up a shortfall in its own in-house capabilities will be minimised if those units **bought** have the **lowest** extra variable cost of **buying** per unit of scarce resource **saved**.

Chapter 6 Relevant costs

6.1 A   Their net realisable value will, of course, depend on the manner in which they are to be disposed. It might be scrap value less any disposal costs or, if they are sold for an alternative use once work has been carried out on them, the net realisable value will be selling price less the costs of the further work.

Option B is incorrect because replacement cost is not an appropriate relevant cost, as the units are no longer required.

Option C is incorrect because variable cost is only relevant in certain circumstances (if net realisable value is the same as variable cost).

Option D is incorrect because full cost includes absorbed fixed overheads, which are not relevant.

6.2 **False**. The hire of a programmer is the incremental cost that would be incurred if the programmer works on the L job. It is therefore £22,000.

6.3 D   **I** is incorrect because this term is used to describe a cost that will differ under some or all of the decision options.

II is incorrect because relevant costs can be expressed as opportunity costs.

Notional cost (**III**) is a hypothetical accounting cost used to reflect the benefit from the use of something for which no actual cash expense is incurred.

Sunk cost (**IV**) is a term used to describe a cost that has already been incurred or committed and which is therefore not relevant to subsequent decisions.

6.4   Modification = £7,200, hire costs avoided = £(19,800) and disposal costs = £4,000 and so the relevant cost is a saving of £8,600.

6.5   400 of the units required are already in stock. They have no other use and if not used for this job, they could be sold. The opportunity cost of using these 400 units is therefore the sales revenue forgone. The remaining 300 units would have to be purchased. The relevant cost is therefore (400 × £20) + (300 × £60) = £26,000.

Chapter 7 Multi-product breakeven analysis

7.1 C

	Aye	Bee	Cee	Total
C/S ratio	0.4	0.5	*0.54	
Market share	× $^1/_3$	× $^1/_3$	× $^1/_3$	
	0.133	0.167	0.18	0.48

*balancing figure

With revised proportions:

	Aye	Bee	Cee	Total
C/S ratio	0.40	0.500	0.540	
Market share	0.40	0.250	0.350	
	0.16	0.125	0.189	0.474

If you chose **option A**, you have selected the C/S ratio of the Aye.

If you chose **option B**, you have selected the C/S ratio of the Cee.

If you chose **option D**, you incorrectly calculated Cee's C/S ratio as 0.1 (possibly because you thought the sum of the C/S ratios should be 1.0).

7.2 **Contribution per unit**

O   £(12 – 7.90)   = £4.10

H   £(17 – 11.20)   = £5.80

Contribution per mix

(£4.10 × 4) + (£5.80 × 3) = £33.80

Breakeven point in terms of mixes

Fixed costs/contribution per mix = £131,820/£33.80 = 3,900 mixes

Breakeven point in units

O   3,900 × 4   = 15,600

H   3,900 × 3   = 11,700

Breakeven point in revenue

		£
O	15,600 × £12 =	187,200
H	11,700 × £17 =	198,900
		386,100

Margin of safety

Budgeted sales – breakeven sales = £(398,500 – 386,100) = £12,400

7.3 **Contribution per unit**

A   £22

B   £19

C   £17

Contribution per mix

(£22 × 1) + (£19 × 1) + (£17 × 4) = £109

Required number of mixes

(Fixed costs + required profit)/contribution per mix

= £(55,100 + 43,000)/£109

= 900 mixes

Required sales of A

$900 \times 1 = 900$ units

$900 \times £47 = £42,300$ revenue

7.4	C		W	X	Y	Z
			£ per unit	£ per unit	£ per unit	£ per unit
		Selling price	56	67	89	96
		Variable costs	49	66	74	85
		Contribution	7	1	15	11
		C/S ratios	$^7/_{56} = 0.125$	$^1/_{67} = 0.015$	$^{15}/_{89} = 0.169$	$^{11}/_{96} = 0.115$
		Ranking	2	4	1	3

7.5 D   Contribution per mix

$= (2 \times £7) + (3 \times £1) + (3 \times £15) + (4 \times £11) = £106$

$\therefore$ Breakeven point in number of mixes $= £15,000/£106 = 141.5$

$\therefore$ Number of W sold at breakeven point $= 2 \times 141.5 = 283$ units

7.6   Average C/S ratio $= \dfrac{(2 \times 25\%) + (5 \times 35\%)}{7}$

$= 32\%$

Sales revenue at breakeven point $= \dfrac{\text{fixed costs}}{\text{C/S ratio}}$

$= £90,000/0.32$

$= £281,250$

7.7 C   Average C/S ratio $= \dfrac{(3 \times 27\%) + (2 \times 56\%) + (5 \times 38\%)}{(3 + 2 + 5)} = 38.3\%$

At breakeven point, contribution = fixed costs

$\therefore \dfrac{£648,000}{\text{Breakeven sales revenue}} = 0.383$

$\therefore$ Breakeven sales revenue $= £1,691,906$

Chapter 8 Short-term decision making

8.1 A   **By adapting now instead of in one year's time**
Sale of machinery would produce additional income of £800,000 – £600,000 = £200,000.

Removal of machinery would save £100,000 – £110,000 = £10,000.

Leasing machinery would cost an additional £80,000 – £0 = £80,000.

There will therefore be additional savings of £200,000 + £10,000 – £80,000 = £130,000.

If you chose **option B**, you calculated the correct amount but you got your costs and savings muddled up.

If you chose **option C**, you probably deducted the savings on the removal of machinery instead of adding it.

If you chose **option D**, you probably deducted the savings on the removal of machinery instead of adding it and got the direction of the cash flow the wrong way round.

8.2   Price = variable costs saved of £150,000 + contribution earned on other products of £250,000 = £400,000

Chapter 9 Linear programming

9.1   This inequality should be that X must be at most 2Y, ie X ≤ 2Y.

9.2   D   The region to the left of X = 41 satisfies X ≤ 41, while that above Y = 19 satisfies Y ≥ 19.

Option A is incorrect because the region you have described is bounded by X ≤ 41, but Y ≤ 19 instead of Y ≥ 19.

Option B is incorrect because the region you have described is bounded by X ≥ 41 and Y ≤ 19 instead of by X ≤ 41 and Y ≥ 19.

Option C is incorrect because the region you have described is bounded by Y ≥ 19 but by X ≥ 41 instead of X ≤ 41.

9.3   The vertex representing the optimal solution is **(0,160)**.

Evaluating contribution at the vertices gives 40,000 at (0, 160), 37,000 at (40, 140), 34,000 at (80, 120) and 7,000 at (140, 0), and so (0, 160) represents the optimal solution.

9.4   D   Contribution is 500 at P, 600 at Q and 600 at R. This means that the outcomes represented by Q and R and all points on the straight line joining them will all lead to the optimal contribution of 600.

For **option A**, you have chosen the vertex that gives minimum contribution.

For **option B**, it is not sufficient to claim that Q is optimal, since this is not the full solution.

For **option C**, it is not sufficient to claim that R is optimal, since this is not the full solution.

9.5   The constraint requires that X ≤ (X+Y)/5 and so 5X ≤ X + Y. Hence 4X ≤ Y.

Chapter 10 Forecasting techniques

10.1   **The correct answer is C.**

During 20X0, there are 13 control periods and so n = 13. The regression line is Y = a + bX.

$$b = \frac{n\Sigma XY - \Sigma X \Sigma Y}{n\Sigma X^2 - (\Sigma X)^2}$$

$$= \frac{(13 \times 9,247) - (91 \times 1,120)}{(13 \times 819) - (91)^2}$$

$$= 7.731$$

$$a = \frac{\Sigma Y}{n} - \frac{b\Sigma X}{n}$$

$$= \frac{1,120}{13} - \frac{(7.731 \times 91)}{13}$$

$$= 32.037$$

Regression line is Y = 32.037 + 7.731X

Control period 4 of 20X1, X = 17

∴ Y = 32.037 + (7.731 × 17) = 163 units

Adjusting by the seasonal variation of –13, predicted sales = 163 – 13 = 150 units

If you chose option A, you mixed up your 'a' and 'b' values and forgot the seasonal adjustment.

If you chose option B, you used X = 18.

If you chose option D, you added the seasonal variation instead of deducting it.

10.2 D I A correlation coefficient close to +1 or –1 indicates a strong linear relationship between X and Y. The regression equation is therefore more reliable for forecasting.

II Working to a high number of decimal places gives spurious accuracy unless both the data itself is accurate to the same degree and the methods used lend themselves to such precision.

III Forecasting for values of X outside the range of the original data leads to unreliable estimates, because there is no evidence that the same regression relationships hold for such values.

IV The regression equation is worthless unless a sufficiently large sample was used to calculate it. In practice, samples of about ten or more are acceptable.

I and IV increase the reliability of forecasting.

10.3 A The formula for the correlation coefficient is provided in your exam. There are no excuses for getting this question wrong.

Correlation coefficient, $r = \dfrac{n\Sigma XY - \Sigma X\Sigma Y}{\sqrt{[n\Sigma X^2 - (\Sigma X)^2][n\Sigma Y^2 - (\Sigma Y)^2]}}$

$= \dfrac{(4 \times 157) - (12 \times 42)}{\sqrt{[4 \times 46 - 12^2][4 \times 542 - 42^2]}}$

$= \dfrac{628 - 504}{\sqrt{(184 - 144) \times (2{,}168 - 1{,}764)}}$

$= \dfrac{124}{\sqrt{40 \times 404}}$

$= \dfrac{124}{127.12}$

= 0.98 (to 2 decimal places)

10.4 C y = 9.82 + (4.372 × 24)
y = 114.748

∴ Forecast = 114.748 + 8.5
= 123.248
= 123

10.5 B I Forecasts are made on the assumption that everything continues as in the past.

II If the model being used is inappropriate, for example if an additive model is used when the trend is changing sharply, forecasts will not be very reliable.

III Provided a multiplicative model is used, the fact that the trend is increasing need not have any adverse effect on the reliability of forecasts.

IV Provided the seasonal variation remains the same in the future as in the past, it will not make forecasts unreliable.

I and II are therefore necessary and hence the correct answer is B.

10.6 B   Seasonally adjusting the values in a time series removes the seasonal element from the data, thereby giving an instant estimate of the trend.

Chapters 11a and 11b Budgeting

11.1 **The correct answer is B.**

11.2 B   **Co-ordination** (I) is an objective of budgeting. Budgets help to ensure that the **activities of all parts of the organisation are co-ordinated towards a single plan**.

Communication (II) is an objective of budgeting. The budgetary planning process **communicates targets** to the managers responsible for achieving them, and it should also provide a **mechanism for junior managers to communicate to more senior staff** their estimates of what may be achievable in their part of the business.

Expansion (III) is not in itself an objective of budgeting. Although a budget may be set **within a framework of expansion plans**, it is perfectly possible for an organisation to **plan for a reduction in activity**.

Resource allocation (IV) is an objective of budgeting. Most organisations face a situation of **limited resources** and an objective of the budgeting process is to ensure that these resources are allocated among budget centres in the most efficient way.

11.3 C   The **principal budget factor** is the factor that limits the activities of an organisation. Although cash and profit are affected by the level of sales (options A and B), sales is not the only factor that determines the level of cash and profit.

11.4 D   The total production cost allowance in a budget flexed at the 83% level of activity would be $8,688 (to the nearest $).
Direct material cost per 1% = $30.

Labour and production overhead:

			$
At	90%	Activity	6,240
At	80%	Activity	6,180
Change	10%		60

Variable cost per 1% activity = $60/10% = $6.

Substituting in 80% activity:

Fixed cost of labour and production overhead = $6,180 – (80 × $6)
 = $5,700

Flexed budget cost allowance:

	$
Direct material $30 × 83	2,490

Labour and production overhead:

	$
Variable $6 × 83	498
Fixed	5,700
	8,688

11.5 A

	$
Cash sales in December ($402,000 × 10%)	40,200
Receipts from November credit sales ($390,000 × 90% × 30% × 99%)	104,247
Receipts from October credit sales ($224,000 × 90% × 70%)	141,120
Total sales receipts in December	285,567

11.6 C

	$
Variable production overhead payment:	
For August production (12,600 × $5 × 30%)	18,900
For September production (5,500 × $5 × 70%)	19,250
Total variable production overhead payment	38,150
Fixed overhead cash payment ($9,440 – $2,280)	7,160
Total cash payment	45,310

11.7 D

	Units	$
High activity	3,000	12,900
Low activity	2,000	11,100
Increase	1,000	1,800

Variable cost per unit $= \dfrac{\$1,800}{1,000} = \$1.80$ per unit

$$\text{Fixed cost, substituting in high activity} = \$12,900 - (3,000 \times \$1.80)$$
$$= \$7,500$$

	$
Budget cost allowance for 4,000 units:	
Variable cost (4,000 × $1.80)	7,200
Fixed cost	7,500
	14,700

Option A is the variable cost allowance only and option B is the fixed cost allowance only. If you selected option C, your variable cost per unit calculation was upside down ($1,000/1,800 instead of $1,800/1,000).

11.8 C The amount budgeted to be paid to suppliers in September is $289,000.

Workings

	July $	August $	Paid in month September $	October $	November $
Purchases					
July $250,000	59,375[1]	175,000[2]	12,500[3]		
August $300,000		71,250[4]	210,000[5]	15,000[6]	
September $280,000			66,500[7]	196,000[8]	14,000[9]
			289,000		

1	$250,000 × 25% × 0.95	= $59,375
2	$250,000 × 70%	= $175,000
3	$250,000 × 5%	= $12,500
4	$300,000 × 25% × 0.95	= $71,250
5	$300,000 × 70%	= $210,000
6	$300,000 × 5%	= $15,000
7	$280,000 × 25% × 0.95	= $66,500
8	$280,000 × 70%	= $196,000
9	$280,000 × 5%	= $14,000

Chapters 12 and 13 Standard costing and variance analysis

13.1 **The correct answer is A.**

I   The use of standards is limited to situations where repetitive actions are performed and output can be measured.

II   Standards need not be expressed in monetary terms.

III   Standards achieve control by comparison of actual results against a predetermined target.

IV   The most suitable approach is probably to revise standards whenever changes of a permanent and reasonably long-term nature occur.

13.2 **The correct answer is A.**

Determine fixed cost using the high-low method.

	Hours	£
Highest activity level	36,000	153,120
Lowest activity level	22,000	108,740
Difference	14,000	44,380

$$\therefore \text{Variable cost per hour} = £44,380/14,000$$
$$= £3.17$$

∴ Fixed cost (substituting in lowest activity level)

$$= £(108,740 - (22,000 \times £3.17))$$
$$= £39,000$$

Expenditure should have been:	£	£
Fixed	39,000	
Variable (30,600 × £3.17)	97,002	
		136,002
But was		154,952
Variance		18,950 (A)

If you selected option B, you forgot to include the budgeted fixed overhead.

If you selected option C, you performed a pro-rata calculation on the budgeted cost for 36,000 hours to determine the budgeted cost at actual activity level.

Option D is what expenditure should have been.

13.3 **The correct answer is D.**

	£
Budgeted fixed overhead expenditure (3,200 units × £29)	92,800
Fixed production overhead expenditure variance	2,200 (A)
Actual fixed production overhead expenditure	95,000

If you selected option A, you adjusted the budgeted overhead unnecessarily for the fixed overhead volume variance.

If you selected option B, you had the right idea about adjusting the budgeted overhead for the expenditure variance, but you should have added the variance rather than subtracting it.

If you selected option C, you chose the budgeted fixed overhead expenditure for the month.

13.4 **The correct answer is D.**

	Units
Budgeted production	3,200
Volume variance in units (£8,700 ÷ £29)	300 (F)
Actual production for March	3,500
Reduction in inventory volume	200
Actual sales for March	3,700

If you selected option A, you subtracted the volume variance in units from the budgeted production. However, the volume variance is favourable and so the actual production must be higher than budgeted.

If you selected option B, you subtracted the inventory reduction from the actual production volume. However, if inventories reduce, sales volume must be higher than production volume.

Option C is the actual production for March. Since the inventory volume altered, sales must be different from the production volume.

13.5 (a) A planning variance calculates the difference in standard cost arising due to changes from the original standard that are not controllable by operational managers because they are caused by planning errors. In the scenario described, a planning variance has arisen because of the worldwide increase in material prices. This is outside the control of operational managers and should therefore be analysed separately from variance related to operational performance.

(b) **Planning variance**

	€
Revised standard cost (780 × 4.5 kg × €6.50)	22,815
Original standard cost (780 × 4.5 kg × €6.00)	21,060
	1,755 (A)

Operational price variance

	€
Actual cost of actual kg used	14,175
Revised standard cost of actual kg (2,250 × €6.50)	14,625
	450 (F)

Operational usage variance

780 units should have used (× 4.5 kg)	3,510 kg
but did use	2,250 kg
Operational usage variance in kg	1,260 kg (F)
× revised standard price per kg	× €6.50
Operational usage variance in €	€8,190 (F)

13.6 Three possible courses of a favourable operational usage variance are as follows:

(a) The material was of a higher quality than in the standard, therefore wastage was lower than standard.

(b) The original standard usage per unit was set too low.

(c) The direct labour were more highly skilled than standard, and therefore they used the material more efficiently than standard.

13.7 (a) £55,000 A

Sales price variance

	£'000
Sales revenue from 110,000 units should have been (× £10)	1,100
But was	1,045
	55 (A)

(b) £20,000 F

Sales volume variance = 100,000 units – 110,000 units
= 10,000 units (F)

Sales volume profit variance = 10,000 units × standard gross profit margin per unit
= 10,000 × (£10 – £8)
= £20,000 (F)

13.8 The labour rate variance is calculated as:

Actual hours worked at actual rate – actual hours worked at standard rate
Or actual hours worked × (actual rate – standard rate)
= actual hours worked × (actual rate – £12) = £45,000 (A)

> **Top tips.** As we have two unknowns in this relationship, we need to look at the efficiency variance to find the actual hours worked.

Labour efficiency variance:

(Actual hours worked – 11,500 units × 5 hours) × £12 = £30,000 (A)

(Actual hours worked – 57,500) × 12 = 30,000 (A)

$$\text{Actual hours worked} - 57,500 = \frac{30,000}{12} = 2,500$$

Actual hours worked = 60,000

60,000 × (actual rate – £12) = 45,000

Therefore (actual rate × 60,000) – 720,000 = 45,000

$$\text{Actual rate} = \frac{45,000 + 720,000}{60,000} = £12.75$$

13.9 B £41,000 favourable

Actual quantity sold × (actual price – standard price)

8,200 units × (£31 – £26) = £41,000 (F)

13.10 A £6,000 adverse

Sales volume profit variance = (8,700 – 8,200) × standard gross profit margin per unit (W)

Working

	£	£
Selling price per unit		26
Less: variable cost per unit	10	
fixed overhead per unit		
$\frac{34,800}{8,700} =$	4	
	14	
	12	

500 units × £12 = £6,000 adverse

13.11 A   £2,000 adverse

> **Note**. The fixed overhead volume variance is a measure of the over or under absorption of fixed overhead costs caused by actual production volume differing from that budgeted. It is calculated as the difference between actual and budgeted production/volume multiplied by the standard absorption rate per unit.

500 units × £4* = £2,000 adverse

The variance is adverse as fewer units have been produced.

*Calculated in question above.

13.12 (a)   Material price planning variance:

(Revised standard cost – original standard cost) × actual materials

(4.50 – 4.10) × 1,600 units × 7 kg = £4,480 (A)

(b)   Actual quantity should have been 11,200 but was 12,000

Operational material usage variance:

(Standard quantity – actual quantity) × revised standard

(11,200 – 12,000) × £4.50 = £3,600 (A)

Chapter 14 Risk and uncertainty in decision making

14.1   **The correct answer is $931,000.**

We need to know the probabilities of the two highest sales values. Since the sales levels given are predicted to be the only possible outcomes, the sum of the probabilities must be equal to 1. The probabilities of the two highest sales values are therefore (1 – 0.1 – 0.15 – 0.35)/2 = 0.2.

EV of sales = $m(4 × 0.1 + 4.4 × 0.15 + 4.8 × 0.35 + 5.2 × 0.2 + 5.6 × 0.2) = $4.9m

	$
EV of contribution = $4.9m × 35%	1,715,000
Fixed costs ($196,000 × 4)	784,000
EV of annual profit	931,000

14.2   **The correct answers are 100% and 40%.**

To break even the contribution must be equal to the fixed costs.

Annual contribution required = $784,000

Contribution/sales = 35%

$784,000/sales = 35%

Sales = $2,240,000

The probability of achieving sales of at least $2,240,000 is 100%.

To earn a profit of at least $900,000, contribution required = fixed costs + profit = $784,000 + $900,000 = $1,684,000.

Contribution/sales = 35%

$1,684,000/sales = 35%

Required sales = $4,811,429

The probability of achieving sales in excess of this amount is 0.2 + 0.2 = 0.4 = 40%.

14.3 D

Selling price £/unit	Probability	Unit var cost £	Probability	Combined probability	Monthly contribution* £	Expected value** £
20	0.25	8	0.20	0.050	12,000	600
	0.25	10	0.50	0.125	10,000	1,250
	0.25	12	0.30	0.075	8,000	600
25	0.40	8	0.20	0.080	17,000	1,360
	0.40	10	0.50	0.200	15,000	3,000
	0.40	12	0.30	0.120	13,000	1,560
30	0.35	8	0.20	0.070	22,000	1,540
	0.35	10	0.50	0.175	20,000	3,500
	0.35	12	0.30	0.105	18,000	1,890
				1.000		15,300

*(selling price – variable cost) × 1,000

**monthly contribution × combined probability

The **expected value** of contribution is £15,300. Note contribution excludes fixed costs.

14.4   C   The probability of monthly contribution > £13,500 = 0.08+0.2+0.07+0.175+0.105
= 0.63

14.5

		EV $'000
Project L	(500 × 0.2 + 470 × 0.5 + 550 × 0.3)	500.0
Project M	(400 × 0.2 + 550 × 0.5 + 570 × 0.3)	526.0
Project N	(450 × 0.2 + 400 × 0.5 + 475 × 0.3)	432.5
Project O	(360 × 0.2 + 400 × 0.5 + 420 × 0.3)	398.0
Project P	(600 × 0.2 + 500 × 0.5 + 425 × 0.3)	497.5

Project M has the highest EV of expected cash flows, and should therefore be undertaken.

14.6

Market condition	Probability	Project chosen	Net cash inflow $'000	EV of net cash inflow $'000
Poor	0.2	P	600	120
Good	0.5	M	550	275
Excellent	0.3	M	570	171
EV of net cash inflows with perfect information				566
EV of net cash inflows without perfect information (from Question 14.5 above)				526
Value of perfect information				40

APPENDIX
MATHEMATICAL TABLES

PRESENT VALUE TABLE

Present value of £1 ie $(1+r)^{-n}$ where r = interest rate, n = number of periods until payment or receipt.

Periods (n)	Interest rates (r)									
	1%	2%	3%	4%	5%	6%	7%	8%	9%	10%
1	0.990	0.980	0.971	0.962	0.952	0.943	0.935	0.926	0.917	0.909
2	0.980	0.961	0.943	0.925	0.907	0.890	0.873	0.857	0.842	0.826
3	0.971	0.942	0.915	0.889	0.864	0.840	0.816	0.794	0.772	0.751
4	0.961	0.924	0.888	0.855	0.823	0.792	0.763	0.735	0.708	0.683
5	0.951	0.906	0.863	0.822	0.784	0.747	0.713	0.681	0.650	0.621
6	0.942	0.888	0.837	0.790	0.746	0.705	0.666	0.630	0.596	0.564
7	0.933	0.871	0.813	0.760	0.711	0.665	0.623	0.583	0.547	0.513
8	0.923	0.853	0.789	0.731	0.677	0.627	0.582	0.540	0.502	0.467
9	0.914	0.837	0.766	0.703	0.645	0.592	0.544	0.500	0.460	0.424
10	0.905	0.820	0.744	0.676	0.614	0.558	0.508	0.463	0.422	0.386
11	0.896	0.804	0.722	0.650	0.585	0.527	0.475	0.429	0.388	0.350
12	0.887	0.788	0.701	0.625	0.557	0.497	0.444	0.397	0.356	0.319
13	0.879	0.773	0.681	0.601	0.530	0.469	0.415	0.368	0.326	0.290
14	0.870	0.758	0.661	0.577	0.505	0.442	0.388	0.340	0.299	0.263
15	0.861	0.743	0.642	0.555	0.481	0.417	0.362	0.315	0.275	0.239
16	0.853	0.728	0.623	0.534	0.458	0.394	0.339	0.292	0.252	0.218
17	0.844	0.714	0.605	0.513	0.436	0.371	0.317	0.270	0.231	0.198
18	0.836	0.700	0.587	0.494	0.416	0.350	0.296	0.250	0.212	0.180
19	0.828	0.686	0.570	0.475	0.396	0.331	0.277	0.232	0.194	0.164
20	0.820	0.673	0.554	0.456	0.377	0.312	0.258	0.215	0.178	0.149

Periods (n)	Interest rates (r)									
	11%	12%	13%	14%	15%	16%	17%	18%	19%	20%
1	0.901	0.893	0.885	0.877	0.870	0.862	0.855	0.847	0.840	0.833
2	0.812	0.797	0.783	0.769	0.756	0.743	0.731	0.718	0.706	0.694
3	0.731	0.712	0.693	0.675	0.658	0.641	0.624	0.609	0.593	0.579
4	0.659	0.636	0.613	0.592	0.572	0.552	0.534	0.516	0.499	0.482
5	0.593	0.567	0.543	0.519	0.497	0.476	0.456	0.437	0.419	0.402
6	0.535	0.507	0.480	0.456	0.432	0.410	0.390	0.370	0.352	0.335
7	0.482	0.452	0.425	0.400	0.376	0.354	0.333	0.314	0.296	0.279
8	0.434	0.404	0.376	0.351	0.327	0.305	0.285	0.266	0.249	0.233
9	0.391	0.361	0.333	0.308	0.284	0.263	0.243	0.225	0.209	0.194
10	0.352	0.322	0.295	0.270	0.247	0.227	0.208	0.191	0.176	0.162
11	0.317	0.287	0.261	0.237	0.215	0.195	0.178	0.162	0.148	0.135
12	0.286	0.257	0.231	0.208	0.187	0.168	0.152	0.137	0.124	0.112
13	0.258	0.229	0.204	0.182	0.163	0.145	0.130	0.116	0.104	0.093
14	0.232	0.205	0.181	0.160	0.141	0.125	0.111	0.099	0.088	0.078
15	0.209	0.183	0.160	0.140	0.123	0.108	0.095	0.084	0.074	0.065
16	0.188	0.163	0.141	0.123	0.107	0.093	0.081	0.071	0.062	0.054
17	0.170	0.146	0.125	0.108	0.093	0.080	0.069	0.060	0.052	0.045
18	0.153	0.130	0.111	0.095	0.081	0.069	0.059	0.051	0.044	0.038
19	0.138	0.116	0.098	0.083	0.070	0.060	0.051	0.043	0.037	0.031
20	0.124	0.104	0.087	0.073	0.061	0.051	0.043	0.037	0.031	0.026

CUMULATIVE PRESENT VALUE TABLE

This table shows the present value of £1 per annum, receivable or payable at the end of each year for

n years $\dfrac{1-(1+r)^{-n}}{r}$.

Periods (n)	Interest rates (r)									
	1%	2%	3%	4%	5%	6%	7%	8%	9%	10%
1	0.990	0.980	0.971	0.962	0.952	0.943	0.935	0.926	0.917	0.909
2	1.970	1.942	1.913	1.886	1.859	1.833	1.808	1.783	1.759	1.736
3	2.941	2.884	2.829	2.775	2.723	2.673	2.624	2.577	2.531	2.487
4	3.902	3.808	3.717	3.630	3.546	3.465	3.387	3.312	3.240	3.170
5	4.853	4.713	4.580	4.452	4.329	4.212	4.100	3.993	3.890	3.791
6	5.795	5.601	5.417	5.242	5.076	4.917	4.767	4.623	4.486	4.355
7	6.728	6.472	6.230	6.002	5.786	5.582	5.389	5.206	5.033	4.868
8	7.652	7.325	7.020	6.733	6.463	6.210	5.971	5.747	5.535	5.335
9	8.566	8.162	7.786	7.435	7.108	6.802	6.515	6.247	5.995	5.759
10	9.471	8.983	8.530	8.111	7.722	7.360	7.024	6.710	6.418	6.145
11	10.368	9.787	9.253	8.760	8.306	7.887	7.499	7.139	6.805	6.495
12	11.255	10.575	9.954	9.385	8.863	8.384	7.943	7.536	7.161	6.814
13	12.134	11.348	10.635	9.986	9.394	8.853	8.358	7.904	7.487	7.103
14	13.004	12.106	11.296	10.563	9.899	9.295	8.745	8.244	7.786	7.367
15	13.865	12.849	11.938	11.118	10.380	9.712	9.108	8.559	8.061	7.606
16	14.718	13.578	12.561	11.652	10.838	10.106	9.447	8.851	8.313	7.824
17	15.562	14.292	13.166	12.166	11.274	10.477	9.763	9.122	8.544	8.022
18	16.398	14.992	13.754	12.659	11.690	10.828	10.059	9.372	8.756	8.201
19	17.226	15.679	14.324	13.134	12.085	11.158	10.336	9.604	8.950	8.365
20	18.046	16.351	14.878	13.590	12.462	11.470	10.594	9.818	9.129	8.514

Periods (n)	Interest rates (r)									
	11%	12%	13%	14%	15%	16%	17%	18%	19%	20%
1	0.901	0.893	0.885	0.877	0.870	0.862	0.855	0.847	0.840	0.833
2	1.713	1.690	1.668	1.647	1.626	1.605	1.585	1.566	1.547	1.528
3	2.444	2.402	2.361	2.322	2.283	2.246	2.210	2.174	2.140	2.106
4	3.102	3.037	2.974	2.914	2.855	2.798	2.743	2.690	2.639	2.589
5	3.696	3.605	3.517	3.433	3.352	3.274	3.199	3.127	3.058	2.991
6	4.231	4.111	3.998	3.889	3.784	3.685	3.589	3.498	3.410	3.326
7	4.712	4.564	4.423	4.288	4.160	4.039	3.922	3.812	3.706	3.605
8	5.146	4.968	4.799	4.639	4.487	4.344	4.207	4.078	3.954	3.837
9	5.537	5.328	5.132	4.946	4.772	4.607	4.451	4.303	4.163	4.031
10	5.889	5.650	5.426	5.216	5.019	4.833	4.659	4.494	4.339	4.192
11	6.207	5.938	5.687	5.453	5.234	5.029	4.836	4.656	4.486	4.327
12	6.492	6.194	5.918	5.660	5.421	5.197	4.988	4.793	4.611	4.439
13	6.750	6.424	6.122	5.842	5.583	5.342	5.118	4.910	4.715	4.533
14	6.982	6.628	6.302	6.002	5.724	5.468	5.229	5.008	4.802	4.611
15	7.191	6.811	6.462	6.142	5.847	5.575	5.324	5.092	4.876	4.675
16	7.379	6.974	6.604	6.265	5.954	5.668	5.405	5.162	4.938	4.730
17	7.549	7.120	6.729	6.373	6.047	5.749	5.475	5.222	4.990	4.775
18	7.702	7.250	6.840	6.467	6.128	5.818	5.534	5.273	5.033	4.812
19	7.839	7.366	6.938	6.550	6.198	5.877	5.584	5.316	5.070	4.843
20	7.963	7.469	7.025	6.623	6.259	5.929	5.628	5.353	5.101	4.870

At the time of printing the final Mathematical Tables and Formulae sheet had not been confirmed by CIMA. Please check the CIMA website for the latest information on what information will be provided in the exams.

Probability

$A \cup B$ = A **or** B. $A \cap B$ = A **and** B (overlap). P(BIA) = probability of B, **given** A.

Rules of addition

If A and B are **mutually exclusive**: $P(A \cup B) = P(A) + P(B)$

If A and B are **not** mutually exclusive: $P(A \cup B) = P(A) + P(B) - P(A \cap B)$

Rules of multiplication

If A and B are **independent**: $P(A \cap B) = P(A) * P(B)$

If A and B are **not** independent: $P(A \cap B) = P(A) * P(BIA)$

$E(X) = \sum (\text{probability} * \text{payoff})$

Descriptive statistics

Arithmetic mean

$$\bar{x} = \frac{\sum x}{n} \text{ or } \bar{x} = \frac{\sum fx}{\sum f} \text{ (frequency distribution)}$$

Standard deviation

$$SD = \sqrt{\frac{\sum(x - \bar{x})^2}{n}}$$

$$SD = \sqrt{\frac{\sum fx^2}{\sum f} - \bar{x}^2} \text{ (frequency distribution)}$$

Index numbers

Price relative = $100 * P_1 / P_0$

Quantity relative = $100 * Q_1 / Q_0$

Price: $\dfrac{\sum W \times P_1 / P_0}{\sum W} \times 100$ where W denotes weights

Quantity: $\dfrac{\sum W \times Q_1 / Q_0}{\sum W} \times 100$ where W denotes weights

Time series

Additive model: series = trend + seasonal + random
Multiplicative model: series = trend * seasonal * random

Financial mathematics

Compound interest (values and sums)

Future value of S, of a sum X, invested for n periods, compounded at r% interest:

$$S = X[1+r]^n$$

Annuity

Present value of an annuity of £1 per annum receivable or payable, for n years, commencing in one year, discounted at r% per annum:

$$PV = \frac{1}{r}\left[1 - \frac{1}{[1+r]^n}\right]$$

Perpetuity

Present value of £1 per annum, payable or receivable in perpetuity, commencing in one year discounted at r% per annum:

$$PV = \frac{1}{r}$$

Learning curve

$$Y_x = aX^b$$

Where: Y_x = the cumulative average time per unit to produce X units

a = the time required to produce the first unit of output
X = the cumulative number of units
b = the index of learning

The exponent b is defined as the log of the learning curve improvement rate divided by log 2.

Inventory management

Economic order quantity

$$EOQ = \sqrt{\frac{2C_oD}{C_h}}$$

Where: C_o = cost of placing an order
C_h = cost of holding one unit in inventory for one year
D = annual demand

INDEX

Note. **Key terms** and their page references are given in **bold**.

Notes

Notes

Notes

Notes

Review Form – Paper P1 Management Accounting (11/16)

Please help us to ensure that the CIMA learning materials we produce remain as accurate and user-friendly as possible. We cannot promise to answer every submission we receive, but we do promise that it will be read and taken into account when we update this Study Text.

Name _____ Address _____

_____

_____

How have you used this Study Text?
(Tick one box only)

☐ Home study (book only)

☐ On a course: college _____

☐ With 'correspondence' package

☐ Other _____

Why did you decide to purchase this Study Text? *(Tick one box only)*

☐ Have used BPP Texts in the past

☐ Recommendation by friend/colleague

☐ Recommendation by a lecturer at college

☐ Saw information on BPP website

☐ Saw advertising

☐ Other _____

During the past six months do you recall seeing/receiving any of the following?
(Tick as many boxes as are relevant)

☐ Our advertisement in *Financial Management*

☐ Our advertisement in *Pass*

☐ Our advertisement in *PQ*

☐ Our brochure with a letter through the post

☐ Our website www.bpp.com

Which (if any) aspects of our advertising do you find useful?
(Tick as many boxes as are relevant)

☐ Prices and publication dates of new editions

☐ Information on Text content

☐ Facility to order books off-the-page

☐ None of the above

Which BPP products have you used?

Text	☑	Passcards	☐
Kit	☐	i-Pass	☐

Your ratings, comments and suggestions would be appreciated on the following areas.

	Very useful	Useful	Not useful
Introductory section	☐	☐	☐
Chapter introductions	☐	☐	☐
Key terms	☐	☐	☐
Quality of explanations	☐	☐	☐
Case studies and other examples	☐	☐	☐
Exam skills and alerts	☐	☐	☐
Questions and answers in each chapter	☐	☐	☐
Chapter overview and summary diagrams	☐	☐	☐
Quick quizzes	☐	☐	☐
Question Bank	☐	☐	☐
Answer Bank	☐	☐	☐
OT Bank	☐	☐	☐
Index	☐	☐	☐

	Excellent	Good	Adequate	Poor
Overall opinion of this Study Text	☐	☐	☐	☐

Do you intend to continue using BPP products?   Yes ☐   No ☐

On the reverse of this page there is space for you to write your comments about our Study Text. We would welcome your feedback.

The BPP Learning Media author team of this edition can be emailed at: cimaqueries@bpp.com

Please return this form to: CIMA Head of Programme, BPP Learning Media Ltd, FREEPOST, London, W12 8BR

Review Form (continued)

TELL US WHAT YOU THINK

Please note any further comments and suggestions/errors below. For example, was the text accurate, readable, concise, user-friendly and comprehensive?